ABAP Objects

Other titles in the series

Flying start with SAP R/3 by Gabriele Schicht and Andrea Schmieden

SAP R/3 Quality Management by Michael Hölzer and Michael Schramm

SAP R/3 Plant Maintenance by Britta Stengl and Reinhard Ematinger

SAP R/3 Financial Accounting by Sandra Brinkmann and Axel Zeilinger

Security and Data Protection with SAP Systems by Werner Hornberger and Jürgen Schneider

mySAP.com Industry Solutions by Prof Dr Henning Kagermann and Dr Gerhard Keller

SAP R/3 Performance Optimization by Thomas Schneider

SAP R/3 Change and Transport Management by Sue McFarlane Thetzger and Susanne Roehrs

SAP R/3 System Administration by Liane Will

ABAP Objects

Introduction to Programming SAP Applications

Dr Horst Keller and Sascha Krüger

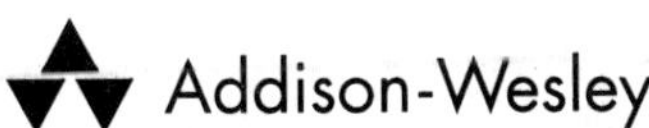

An imprint of PEARSON EDUCATION
London · Boston · Indianapolis · New York · Mexico City · Toronto · Sydney · Tokyo · Singapore · Hong Kong · Cape Town · New Delhi · Madrid · Paris · Amsterdam · Munich · Milan · Stockholm

PEARSON EDUCATION LIMITED

Edinburgh Gate
Harlow, Essex CM20 2JE
Tel: +44 (0)1279 623623
Fax: +44 (0)1279 431059
Website: www.pearsoned.co.uk

First published in Great Britain in 2002

First published in German in 2001 by Galileo Press, Gartenstr 24, 53229 Bonn.

ISBN: 0 201 75080 5

British Library Cataloguing in Publication Data
A CIP catalogue record for this book can be obtained from the British Library

Library of Congress Cataloguing in Publication Data
Keller, Horst, 1960–
ABAP objects : introduction to programming SAP applications / Horst Keller and Sascha, Krüger.
p. cm.
Includes bibliographical references and index.
ISBN 0-201-75080-5
1. ABAP/4 Computer program language) 2. SAP R/3. 3. Clients/server computing. I. Krüger, Sascha, II. Title.

QA.76.73.A12 K45 2002
005.13′3–dc21

2002019190

10 9 8 7 6

Translated by PI International.
Typeset by Pantek Arts Ltd, Maidstone, Kent.
Printed and bound in Great Britain by Biddles Ltd., King's Lynn, Norfolk

Contents

3 BASICS OF ABAP PROGRAMMING

4 BASIC ABAP LANGUAGE ELEMENTS

7 PROGRAMMING SCREENS

APPENDICES

Preface from SAP

ABAP, the programming language of SAP for business applications, is a language with a long-standing tradition. Having started off over 20 years ago as a reporting language in the mainframe world and having developed between 1985 and 1995 into a complete 4GL with SQL integration and language support for dialog and transaction programming, ABAP is now a modern object-oriented, statically typed yet flexible, portable and universally applicable programming language offering particular support for control- and web-based applications.

However, ABAP is more than just a language. It is embedded within a complete development environment with all the editors, tools and repositories needed for large and complex software development projects. A large number of services contained in SAP's application server middleware infrastructure can also be addressed readily and independently of a particular platform.

I am delighted that the two authors, Horst Keller and Sascha Krüger, have taken it upon themselves to portray the object-oriented basic structure of modern ABAP alongside the full scope of the programming concepts developed over time in ABAP. Within a single book they offer the reader the distinct advantage of being able to find descriptions of both the new concepts of object-oriented development with ABAP Objects and the older technologies of earlier releases – a knowledge of which remains essential due to the volume of ABAP code still in existence.

I hope that this book will bring all readers further joy and success in programming in ABAP.

Walldorf, August 2000
Andreas Blumenthal
Development Manager ABAP Language
SAP AG

Preface from SHS Informationssysteme AG

Dear Reader

As a member of the board of SHS Informationssysteme AG it is a particular pleasure for me that our employee Sascha Krüger has found time in his busy schedule to publish the present book on ABAP Objects together with Dr Horst Keller. Practical and customer-driven implementation based on a thorough theoretical grounding in technological developments as well as dedication is the sole basis for any successful project.

In the past SAP has played a significant part in the development of standard ERP software and will, in particular through mySAP.com, continue to do so in the future. From the position of our company, SAP's development in CRM (Customer Relationship Management) with new technological and strategic market orientation is of particular interest in this respect. Following the ERP boom of the past two decades, these customer-oriented systems are now in widespread use throughout companies – above all in the telecommunications industry with its enormous growth in new customers.

Anyone wishing to be successful in this kind of market must come to terms with the SAP Basis technology in order to integrate CRM systems in their existing IT landscape. As many leading companies implement the SAP System, this requires innovative concepts. Not least through the use of EAI (Enterprise Application Integration) tools, object-orientation is being increasingly established as the standard in integration. With ABAP Objects, SAP is intensifying its support of object-oriented (outbound) development and thereby allowing the seamless integration of different object models such as DCOM and CORBA.

The present book by Dr Horst Keller and Sascha Krüger is an introduction to the new world of ABAP Objects and will give you an understanding of how to start with or change to a new programming model. Our wish for both authors is that this book will soon become the standard for the new type of object-oriented development under SAP and will become an indispensable resource in practical applications.

Munich, August 2000
Dr Stefan Möller

SHS Informationssysteme AG

Member of the Board

Foreword

In recent years the ABAP programming language has undergone an enormous development, the latest stage of which has been the gradual introduction of ABAP Objects between Releases 4.0 and 4.6. Of the books concerned with ABAP currently available on the market, only a few really get to grips with the new language concept. Those that refer to ABAP Objects do so only in terms of a supplement to existing material. This situation therefore led us to write the present book on ABAP Objects. As, however, ABAP Objects cannot be considered in isolation from ABAP as a whole, it developed into a comprehensive description of the ABAP programming language based on the current Release 4.6.

If you compare the current scope of the language with that of Release 3.0, for which the last official ABAP book [KRE96] was written, you will find many other new additions apart from the introduction of ABAP Objects. These include the integration of the ABAP type concept into the ABAP Dictionary, the introduction of new internal tables, the possibility of using GUI controls and not least the redesigned ABAP Workbench, to name but a few. All these new concepts have finally transformed ABAP from a language focused on generating lists and processing transactions to a universally applicable programming language. This development required us to present ABAP from a universal standpoint, with less emphasis on the earlier programming paradigms of reporting and dialog programming. In this context, it has been helpful that the book has been written jointly by an SAP employee and an external consultant. The insider view from a member of the ABAP Language Group, with precise ideas as to how ABAP should be used, has blended well with the view of an external user with a knowledge of ABAP gained from training seminars, previous publications and daily experience. We have used the synergy effect resulting from these different viewpoints to provide you with a thorough and yet practical guide to ABAP Objects.

Certainly, we could not have successfully concluded this project without the direct and indirect contribution of many people in drawing up and checking the manuscript. We are grateful to the following colleagues from the "ABAP and GUI" department of SAP who despite their many duties found time to proof-read the sections on their specialized subjects: Thomas Bareiß, Adrian Görler, Mathias Hanbuch, Rolf Hammer, Peter Januschke, Ulrich Koch, Andreas Neubacher, Helmut Prestel,

Andreas Simon Schmitt, Werner Schuster, Christoph Stöck, and Ralf Wendelgass. In particular we thank Mrs Kerstin Gebhard from the ABAP Training Development department who read large parts of the manuscript and was always on hand to provide constructive criticism. We would like to thank the students Wolfgang Kiess and Torben Simon for creating the ABAP system field overview and proof-reading some of the chapters. Jürgen Heymann kindly provided us with the object-orientation literature references. We would also like to thank anyone else we have not mentioned but who has suggested improvements along the line.

We have Michael Demuth's initiative to thank for the fact that the accompanying CDs contain an SAP Basis system including the example programs from this book. Andrea Fritsch entered the examples into the system and created the template. Jürgen Krüger supported us with the downloadable files for the transport request for the example programs. For the program for generating training data we used an ABAP training template from Thilo Buchholz. Lastly, we would like to thank also Tomas Wehren and his team from Galileo Press, in particular Iris Warkus, for their cooperation.

For the English edition we would especially like to thank Gabriele Buchner, Michèle Coghlan, and Julie Plummer from Product Management (Development Platforms) for their indispensable commitment during our technical editing of the translated text.

Horst Keller would also like to thank the Development Manager of the ABAP Language Group, Andreas Blumenthal, for all his support with the project in providing all the necessary resources and many useful hints. Above all he is indebted to his wife Ute for her patience and encouragement over the many evenings and weekends he spent working on the book.

Sascha Krüger would like to thank Stefan Möller, board member of SHS Informationssysteme AG, and the manager of the Cologne office, Frank Pensel, for their support. He would also like to thank his SHS project team for their excellent cooperation which allowed him to spare the time for writing this book. Particular thanks go to his wife Katja who continued to support his authoring commitments throughout, despite the restrictions it placed on their private life.

Horst Keller
Walldorf, August 2000

Sascha Krüger
Cologne, August 2000

CHAPTER 1

Introduction

Before you get to grips with the material, here are a few tips on how to use this book.

1.1 WHAT IS ABAP OBJECTS?

You are probably reading this book to obtain a clear answer to this question. We shall provide you with the answer in its most succinct form from the outset.

ABAP Objects is the object-oriented extension of the ABAP programming language.

ABAP Objects and ABAP are inextricably linked and therefore any book concerning ABAP Objects by definition also concerns ABAP.

ABAP is the programming language of SAP. Since its first release it has undergone several evolutionary stages, the latest of which is ABAP Objects, issued with Release 4.6. Other stages will doubtless follow. Let us consider the developments to date:

- In the seventies ABAP stood for "Allgemeiner Berichts-Aufbereitungs Prozessor" (General Report Preparation Processor). Implemented as a macro assembler within R/2, ABAP was used solely to generate reports.
- By the mid-eighties ABAP had developed into an interpreter language which was a main component of the R/2 System and which could cope with the requirements of creating business application programs. In particular, dialog-controlled transactions could now be programmed using ABAP.
- The early nineties saw the release of the SAP R/3 System and ABAP was introduced as a 4th generation programming language under the name ABAP/4, "Advanced

Business Application Programming." This did not involve simply adding a programming language to R/3, actually it formed the software basis of the entire system. With the exception of the system core written in C, all SAP application modules, components of the R/3 Basis System, and even the development environment were created in ABAP/4.

- At the turn of the new century ABAP completed a new stage in its evolution with ABAP/4 being superseded by ABAP Objects. To be more precise, ABAP Objects is only the object-oriented language extension which implements all the major concepts of the object-oriented programming paradigm such as encapsulation, inheritance, and polymorphism. We shall therefore refer to ABAP when we mean the overall language of ABAP, and ABAP Objects when discussing the object-oriented aspects.

A frequently asked question is whether the introduction of ABAP Objects implies that the existing ABAP is now obsolete. This is of course not the case. There are more than 100 million lines of productive ABAP code which still have to function after the advent of ABAP Objects. Therefore great care was taken throughout all development stages to maintain maximum downward compatibility with former versions. This has led to the current situation where ABAP supports two programming models in parallel: a classic procedural and an object-oriented programming model. In addition the language allows you to use ABAP Objects language elements in existing programs, and conversely you can use almost all previous language elements in ABAP Objects.

Using the previous language elements in ABAP Objects has the immeasurable advantage that you can continue to use the strengths of a programming language which has focused on developing client–server business applications. This includes supporting multilingual applications, easy access to the SAP System database, and the option of performing business calculations. In addition you can use an integrated development environment which supports the creation of large application systems by different developers.

Of course, downward compatibility has its price: the language scope of ABAP includes many obsolete constructs which have since been replaced by improved concepts, but which have had to be left in order to support older ABAP programs. In this book we shall largely avoid outdated language elements and will mention them only where they are considered necessary for gaining an understanding of older programs. Within ABAP Objects, i.e. in classes, many of these obsolete language elements are syntactically forbidden. This does not constitute an incompatible change since older coding cannot exist within classes. In newer programs, however, only the syntax allowed in ABAP Objects should be used, both within and outside of classes.[1]

1. The ABAP keyword documentation contains a detailed listing of the language constructs prohibited in ABAP Objects.

1.2 TARGET READERSHIP

The readership we wish to address covers a broad spectrum. We are targeting beginners as well as "old hands" in SAP programming, as with ABAP Objects even the most experienced SAP developers will be encountering new territory. We do assume basic programming expertise. For example, we will not explain what a loop is, but how it is implemented in ABAP. To work with this book and to understand ABAP Objects, you do not have to be familiar with ABAP or with object-orientation; but, of course, knowledge of either subject will help you get started. We offer a thorough introduction to all the concepts and techniques necessary for creating and editing SAP applications in Release 4.6.

For anyone participating in ABAP training this is exactly the right book for supporting and expanding on the course. We offer a solid foundation for junior developers and an easy conversion to ABAP Objects for senior developers. Project members confronted with Release 4.6 can also benefit from reading this book. In addition we wish to provide all students and interested parties with a deeper understanding of SAP programming and on this basis encourage them to get more involved with the subject of ABAP Objects.

If you have been programming with ABAP for many years you will find that we present many language elements and concepts differently from those you will be used to. We are following the approach SAP has used since Release 4.0 for its documentation and training. We would therefore encourage you to take a fresh look at ABAP from this perspective. We hope this will provide you with a better understanding of many aspects which might have seemed obscure in the past, and that you will be able to frame your existing knowledge within the overall picture presented here.

If you are a beginner, you will be introduced directly to the basics of ABAP programming and be spared any unnecessary baggage from the onset. However, we shall still point you towards older concepts so that you will be able to analyze, understand, and maintain existing programs.

1.3 HOW TO READ THIS BOOK

If you are devoting yourself seriously to ABAP for the first time with this book, it will probably be of little help to start reading from the first page and finish at the end. As with a spoken language, it is impossible to learn a programming language by reading a book from start to finish. You will only progress by practicing, i.e. by analyzing existing programs and getting to grips with examples of specific problems. You can benefit from this process even if you already have some experience in SAP programming. This is why we have placed special emphasis on providing a wide range of examples covering all the concepts explored.

This book follows a new approach to the ABAP programming language in its structure, deviating from many familiar structures found in existing literature. The previous book by SAP authors on ABAP programming [KRE96] generally followed the classical division between reporting and dialog programming. In the present book, however, you will find no such chapters. We aim to present ABAP as a universal tool for all application programs. This new approach has been necessitated not least by the fact that ABAP has now become a hybrid language, supporting both the procedural and the object-oriented programming models. As we aim to provide a well-knit portrayal of ABAP, we find ourselves at a crossroads between the old and the new world. We will therefore now provide a brief overview of each chapter to show the topics covered and how you can best use them.

- ***Chapter 2, A practical introduction***

  This chapter is designed for anyone wanting to "get their hands dirty" straight away. You are given a guided tour of ABAP and ABAP Objects and join us in developing a fairly complicated program containing the key elements of all ABAP applications. At the same time you will learn how to handle the new ABAP development environment with Release 4.6. We shall not explain every detail in this chapter, and so you will probably not understand everything straight away. In fact, the chapter will raise more questions than it answers. However, the following chapters will provide detailed information and explanations for all aspects covered. We recommend that even experienced ABAP developers read this chapter because in it we start to work with object-oriented language elements and also use one of the new GUI controls.

- ***Chapter 3, Basics of ABAP programming***

  ABAP has certain characteristics which it is essential to understand in order to apply the language successfully. In Chapter 3 you will learn about where ABAP programs run, how they are structured in principle, and what happens in the background when you execute an ABAP program. We shall explain how the runtime environment and event control work. Although slightly theoretical, you should read this short chapter carefully. It introduces and describes many terms which form the basis for an understanding of the other chapters.

- ***Chapter 4, Basic ABAP language elements***

  This chapter has its equivalent in many programming language books. In it you will be introduced to the elementary modules with which you can implement the functionality of your programs. The type concept, operations, and expressions as well as control structures are just some of the topics treated in this chapter. We shall also cover in detail internal tables, character string processing, and error handling. This chapter adopts almost the character of a language reference and you will probably not read it through in one go. You can rather use it to gain introductory information on the various concepts and later look up the concrete syntax of various statements as well as find examples of how to use them.

- ***Chapter 5, The ABAP programming models***

  This chapter has two main functions. Firstly, it shows you the options you have for structuring your ABAP programs. Secondly, it builds the bridge between the classical (procedural) and the new (object-oriented) worlds of ABAP programming. In the first part of the chapter we will show you the options available in the procedural programming model for modularizing your programs with procedures, and the significance of local and global data. In the second part we will contrast these findings with the concepts of the object-oriented programming model and thereby provide the transition to the basics of object-oriented programming with ABAP Objects. What we cannot achieve in this chapter (nor in the book as a whole) is an introduction to object-oriented analysis or object-oriented design. These topics are largely independent of the programming language and are covered extensively in many other good books. However, you will cope with this chapter even if you have no experience in object-oriented programming. Each of the new language elements and its underlying concepts is explained in detail.

- ***Chapter 6, Advanced concepts of object-oriented programming with ABAP Objects***

  This chapter forms a seamless link to Chapter 5 and concentrates on all the elements which make the object-oriented approach really powerful. We focus on inheritance, polymorphism, interface, and the event concept, and with the aid of examples we show you how to handle these language elements. In short, this chapter provides the basis for advanced programming with ABAP Objects.

- ***Chapter 7, Programming screen layouts***

  Here you will find an extensive and systematic illustration of how to program screens with ABAP. At the beginning we explain the general concepts of screen programming and then discuss how to create selection screens and classical lists. You will also find how to create and handle dialog messages in this chapter. A large part of the chapter is a recapitulation of concepts which were already valid before ABAP Objects. Finally we examine the GUI controls of the Control Framework (CFW) which you can only use with the new language elements of ABAP Objects. While beginners cannot avoid this chapter, we recommend that people with experience in ABAP programming at least glance over the first sections as they will certainly gain some new insights into familiar concepts. The last part is completely new and should be read by everyone.

- ***Chapter 8, Working with external data***

  Virtually no ABAP program can manage without processing external data. At the forefront of this is accessing the central database of an SAP System. The chapter examines all the statements for read and write access to the database and provides extensive guidelines on how to use them efficiently. In addition we summarize the key aspects for accessing files and introduce you to working with data clusters. The end of the chapter provides a summary of the authorization checks for ABAP programs. Like Chapter 7, this chapter can be read independently of the object-oriented extension. As many examples in the entire book use database access, you will probably want to keep returning to Chapter 8.

We hope you will find in the course of this book that ABAP is not difficult to learn despite its power, and that on the contrary many language elements have been introduced to save you work and to create stable and powerful applications.

1.4 HOW TO USE THIS BOOK IN PRACTICE

To work effectively with this book you should have access to an SAP System. The enclosed CDs contain a complete SAP Basis System which you can install on your PC, containing all the example programs referred to. You can also download all examples from the it-minds website (**www.it-minds.com/goto/abapobjects**): the source code of the example programs in text format as well as the files for a transport request, in order to import all example objects into an existing SAP System.

We shall use the SAP flight data model for all exercises in this book which require access to the SAP System database. This is a simplified form of a flight booking system, concerning flights, flight connections, bookings, etc. The flight data model is essentially a set of relational database tables which are linked by foreign key relationships.

The flight data model is used in all SAP ABAP training classes and in ABAP documentation for demonstration and exercise purposes. The database tables are part of every SAP System delivered. In order to fill the database tables with sample data, you can use the S_FLIGHT_MODEL_DATA_GENERATOR program contained in the Basis System of the enclosed CDs. You will also find its source code on the it-minds website.

The most important flight data model database tables for our purposes are shown below. The primary key fields have a light gray background. Appendix A provides the exact structure of each individual database table.

TABLE 1.1 **This four-column table contains the ID, the full name, the currency code and the web address of some international airlines.**

SCARR – An Airline Table

CARRID	CARRNAME	CURRCODE	URL
...	...		
LH	LUFTHANSA	DEM	HTTP://WWW.LUFTHANSA.COM
...	...		

TABLE 1.2 This table consists of 15 columns and contains flight connections offered by the airlines from the SCARR table.

SPFLI – A Flight Connection Table

CARRID	CONNID	CITYFROM	AIRPFROM	CITYTO	AIRPTO	...
...	...	...	....	...	...	...
LH	0400	FRANKFURT	FRAU	NEW YORK	JFK	...
...	...	...	...	...	...	...

TABLE 1.3 This table consists of nine columns and contains the data of actual flights for flight connections from the SPFLI table.

SFLIGHT – A Flight Table

CARRID	CONNID	FLDATE	...
...	...	...	...
LH	0400	2000/06/27	...
...	...	...	...

TABLE 1.4 This table consists of 19 columns and contains the flight bookings for the flights from the SFLIGHT table.

SBOOK – A Flight Booking Table

CARRID	CONNID	FLDATE	BOOKID	...
...	...	...		...
LH	0400	....		...
...	...	...		...

In addition to the columns mentioned, each of these tables has a first column containing a client ID which is, however, only significant if the data of several commercially independent companies is kept within a single SAP System (see Section 8.1.5). In the examples in this book we will only work with these database tables. In the following practical introduction we shall, for example, read and display the flight connections of an airline selected by the user. Figure 1.1 shows the section of the flight data model used by us as a SERM (Structured Entity Relationship Model) diagram.

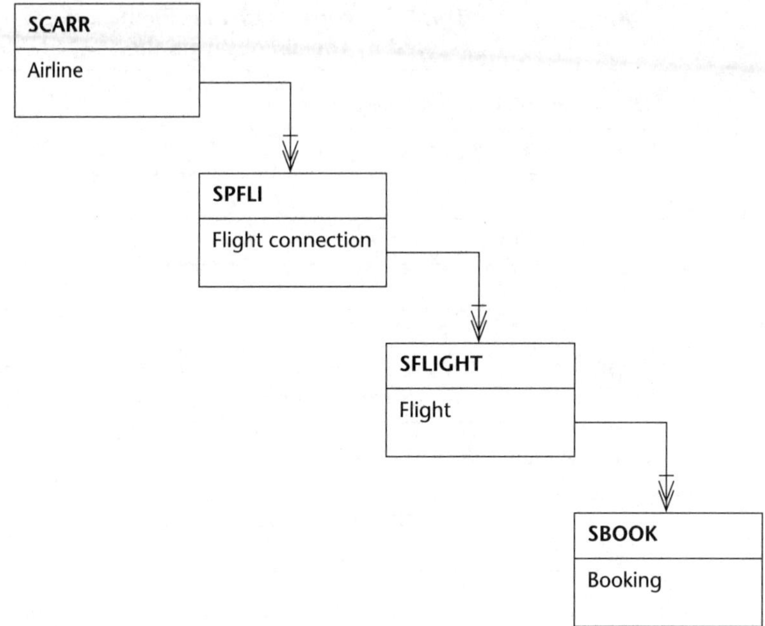

FIGURE 1.1 A section from the SAP Flight Data Model

1.5 SYNTAX CONVENTIONS

Alongside many source code examples, you will find in this book numerous syntax diagrams which illustrate the key areas of application for a statement. Table 1.5 describes the syntax conventions of the diagrams. We have placed special emphasis on keeping similar conventions to the ones used in the SAP System online help and the ABAP training documentation.

TABLE 1.5 Syntax conventions

Key	Definition
KEYWORD	All keywords and additions to statements which are part of the language scope are shown in upper case.
operand	Operands and similar expressions are shown in lower case.
[]	Square brackets mean that you can use the sections of the statement enclosed therein, although this is not obligatory. Do not include the square brackets.
|	A line between two options means that you can use only one of the two options.
{}	If when you use the line, |, the alternative options are not clearly identifiable, they will be indicated by pointed brackets. These brackets are not included either.
()	Round brackets must always be included as part of the statement.
,	A comma means that you can enter as many of the options separated by commas as you wish. The commas are part of the syntax.
f1 f2	Expressions with indexes mean that you can list as many expressions as you wish.
...	Dots mean that you can use here any elements you like that will fit into the respective context.

CHAPTER 2

A practical introduction

Join us on our first tour of the world of ABAP. In this chapter we will show you step by step how to create a program and how to handle the development environment. By the end of the chapter you will have written your first extensive program in ABAP.

2.1 INTRODUCTION

This chapter is a guided tour or tutorial of the ABAP language. Together we will create a program that reads data under certain conditions from the database and displays it in a list. The introduction will touch on many key concepts of the ABAP language that will be covered systematically in later chapters. We will also introduce the use of the **ABAP Workbench** with Release 4.6, which otherwise will not be covered specifically in this book.

Let's start with a few basics. You know that SAP supplies business application systems that generally maintain their data in a variety of tables within a central database. The application programs of the SAP System work with the data from these database tables. This means that data is read, analyzed, displayed, modified, reset, and passed to other programs. ABAP is a programming language that has been specifically designed for these requirements of business data processing, and all application programs of the SAP System that work with the database are written in ABAP. ABAP allows the developer to concentrate mainly on logical tasks, without having to bother about the details of the SAP System architecture. One of the main strengths of ABAP is that with little effort and in a comfortable development environment you can write relatively small programs that provide a complete dialog between user and database.

In this practical introduction we shall make full use of this particular aspect of ABAP. We will program a small application to perform user-driven database access, specifically accessing the database tables of a flight data model (see Appendix A). The program will allow the user to enter an airline and then access the SPFLI database table according to the user input. The data imported from the database table will then be displayed on screen.

2.2 FIRST STEPS WITH THE ABAP WORKBENCH

The development environment for ABAP programs and all their components is the **ABAP Workbench**. We must therefore access the ABAP Workbench in the SAP System to write an ABAP program. The ABAP Workbench is a component of the SAP Basis system and is part of every SAP System. However, you need authorization as an SAP developer within your SAP System to work with the Workbench. The ABAP Workbench is itself also written entirely in ABAP.

In addition to development authorization, you must have a developer key. This key is registered with SAP through SAPNet and allows a developer to be assigned to any modified original objects in the SAP System. Even though in the course of this book we shall make no modifications to originals, you must still be registered as a developer.

2.2.1 Getting started with the ABAP Workbench

To access the ABAP Workbench, open the **Tools** node in SAP Easy Access followed by the **ABAP Workbench** node (see Figure 2.1).

SAP Easy Access

The sub-nodes provide an overview of the various functions of the ABAP Workbench. At first sight it may be difficult to find your bearings. There is no specific node that allows you to write an ABAP application program directly. However, if you open the **Development** node (see Figure 2.2), you will find a list containing several key programming tools of the ABAP Workbench, including the *ABAP Editor*, which allows you to edit ABAP programs; the *Screen Painter* and the *Menu Painter*, which allow you to create screens; the *Function Builder* and *Class Builder*, which allow special ABAP programs such as functions and classes to be programmed; and the ABAP *Dictionary*, which can be used to perform global data declarations in the *ABAP Dictionary*. The abbreviations, such as SE38, SE51, etc., are the transaction codes of the individual tools (see Section 7.1.3).[1]

1. To ensure the transaction codes are visible, the **Display Technical Names** entry must be selected in the **Extras – Settings** menu.

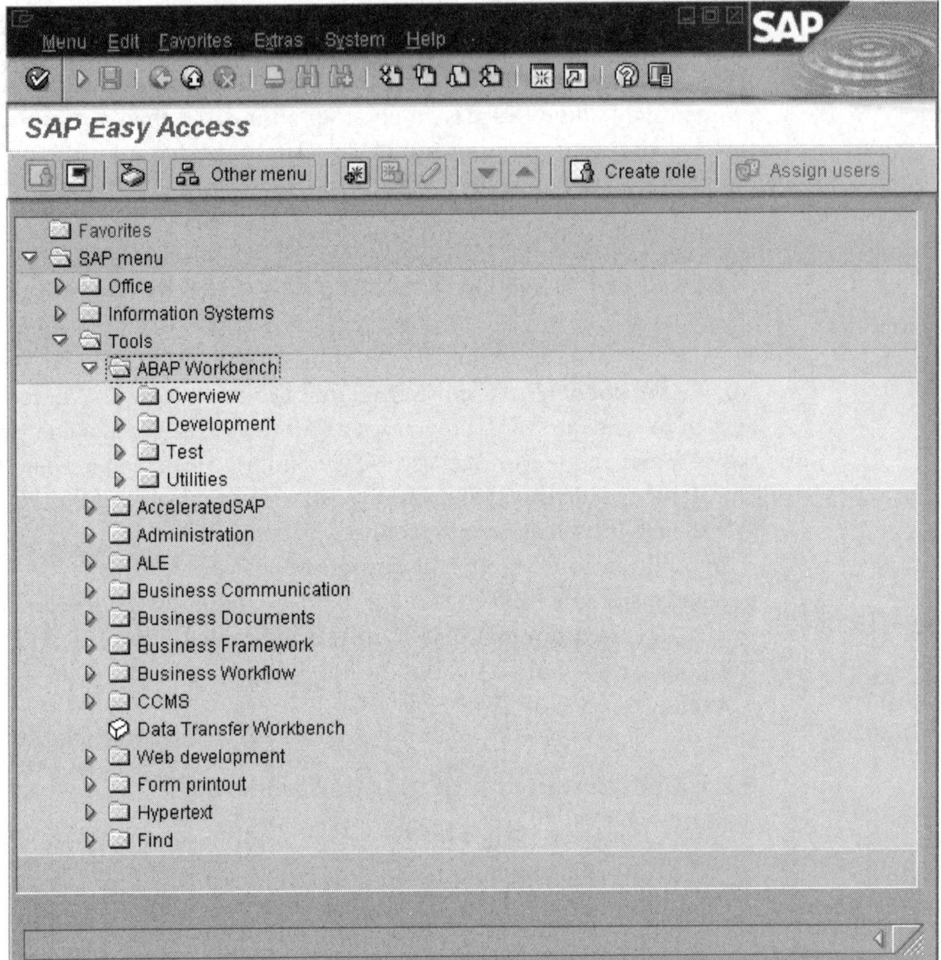

FIGURE 2.1 Accessing the ABAP Workbench via SAP Easy Access. Copyright © SAP AG

Tools

The number of tools indicates that an application program contains several components, such as source code and screens. We could start the **ABAP Editor** directly in this list to create an ABAP program or to edit an existing one. However, we would then be able to edit only one component of the program at a time, namely the source code, and would not have an overview of the other program components. Therefore it is only worthwhile choosing a specific component if you already know the program and components you wish to edit, and wish to access them quickly and directly.

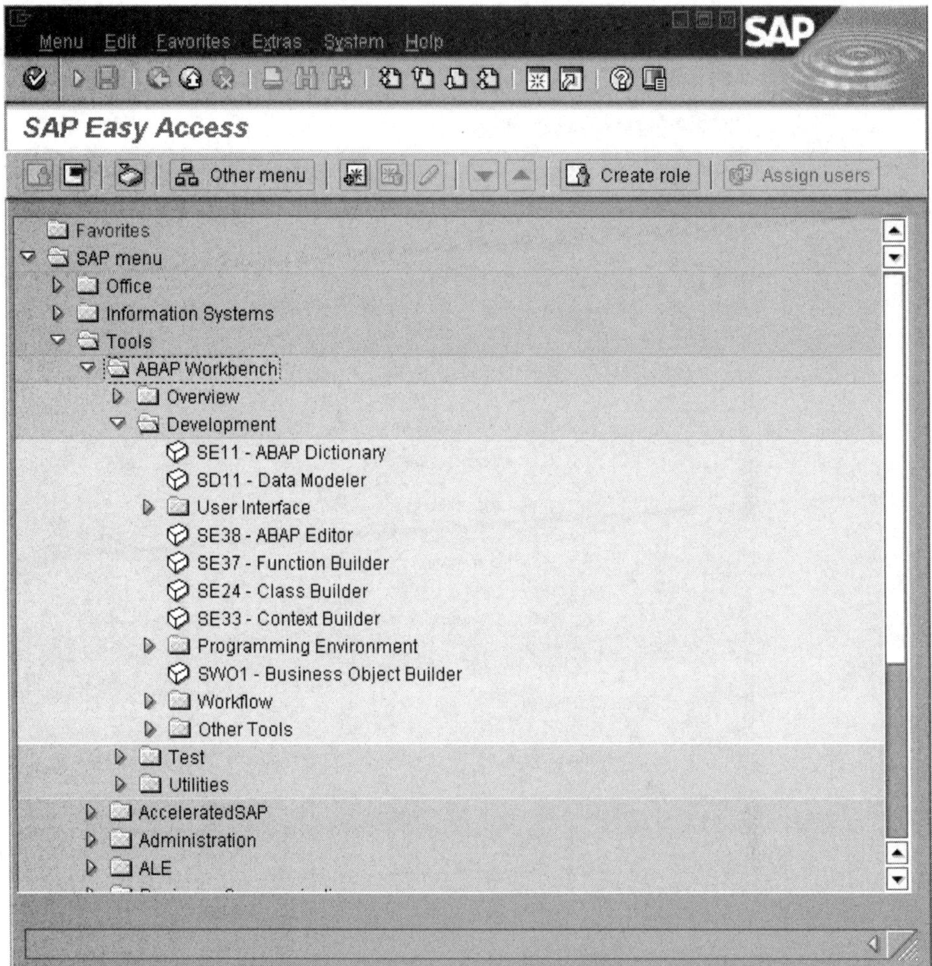

FIGURE 2.2 The various tools of the ABAP Workbench. Copyright © SAP AG

Overview

We will now propose another way of gaining entry to ABAP programming. Open the **Overview** node. Here you will find the **Object Navigator** listed (see Figure 2.3).

Favorites

The **Object Navigator** is the starting tool for the ABAP Workbench. If you find it too complicated to look for the starting node in SAP Easy Access each time, we recommend creating a favorite on the top level. To do this, select **Object Navigator** in SAP Easy Access and choose **Add to Favorites**, or choose **Favorites –**

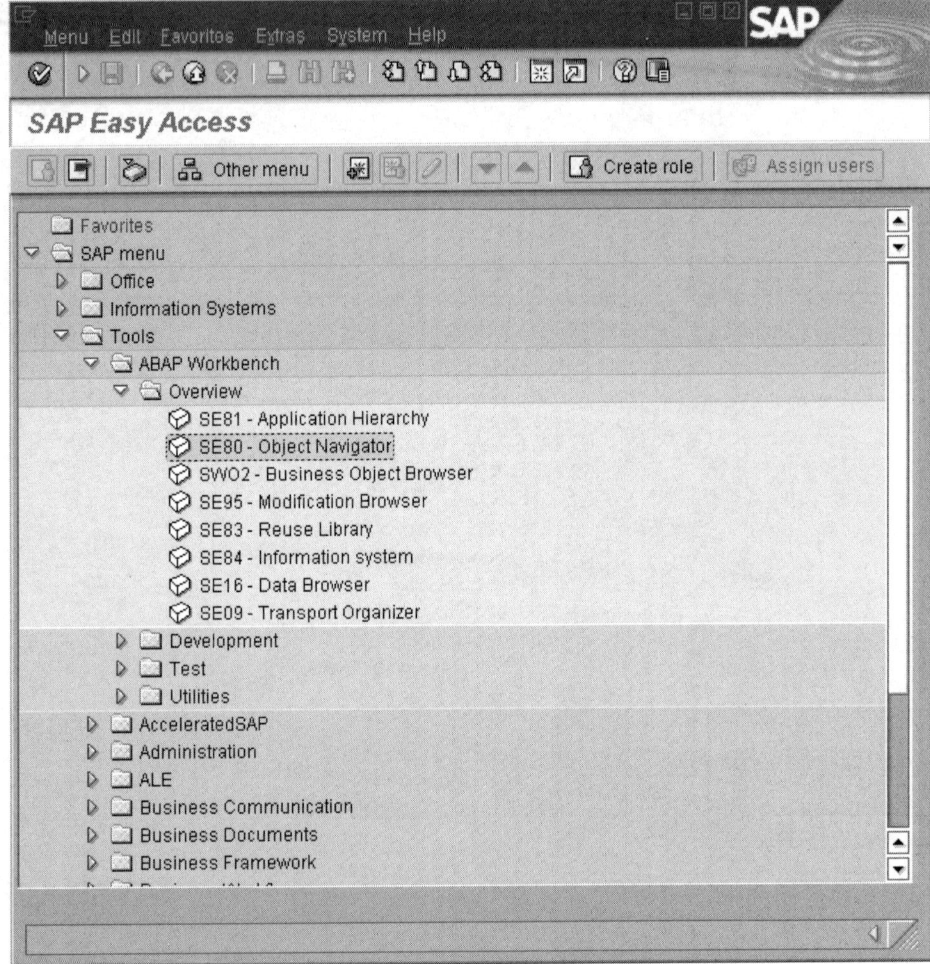

FIGURE 2.3 Calling the Object Navigator. Copyright © SAP AG

Add Transaction and then enter the transaction "SE80."[2] From now on you will always find the **Object Navigator** node on the top level under **Favorites** in your SAP initial screen (see Figure 2.4).

2. We shall be using the terms "selection" and "choose/select" quite often. Depending on their context, they can refer to double-clicking the mouse, pressing a pushbutton, selecting an icon or a menu entry, etc. The SAP System user interface usually offers a variety of selection options for a function which we cannot list in full. In general, the most important functions can be selected via icons at the top of the screen or via the keyboard function keys. All functions can be achieved through menu entries. We will show you through the course of this book how you can define this for your own programs.

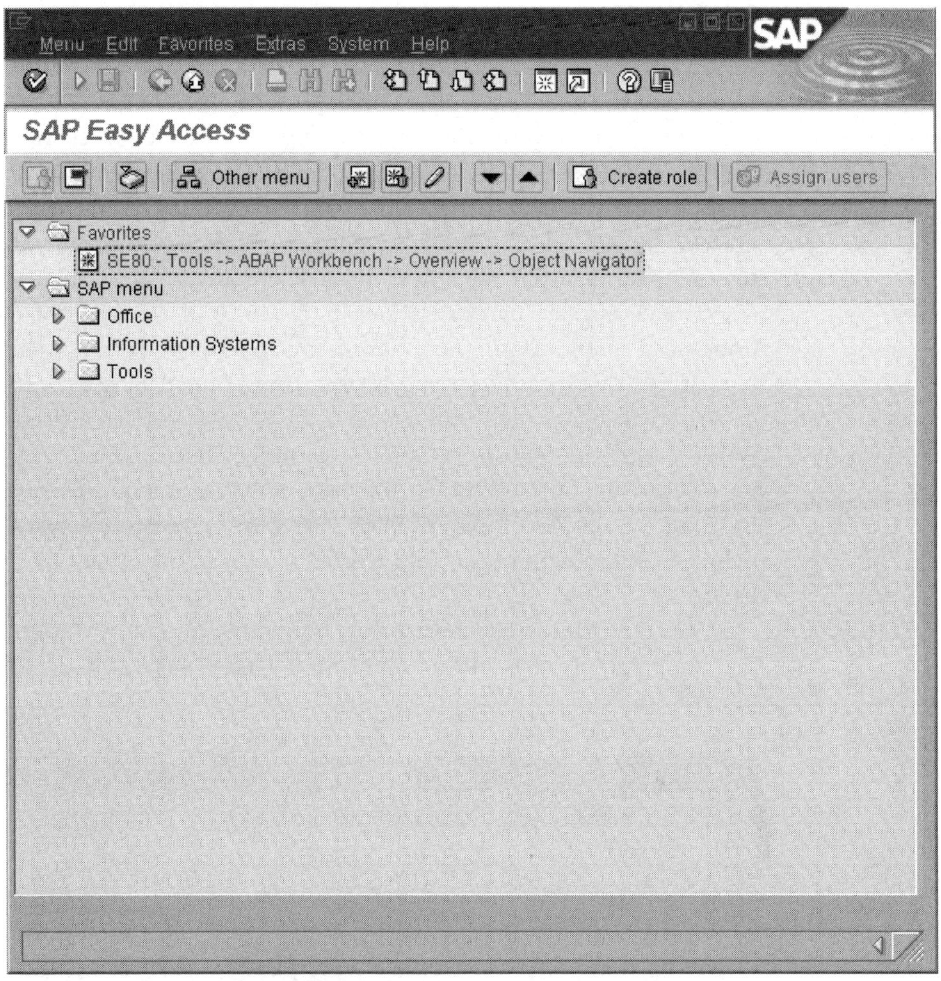

FIGURE 2.4 The Object Navigator as a favorite. Copyright © SAP AG

You can now always call the Object Navigator directly after logging onto the SAP System by choosing this node. As in previous releases, you can also call the Object Navigator by entering "/nse80" in the standard toolbar[3] input field from any SAP screen.

3. Although the input field of the standard toolbar is not visible as standard with Release 4.6A, it can be opened by clicking on the little triangle in the standard toolbar.

2.2.2 Working with the Object Navigator

As soon as it is called for the first time, the Object Navigator is displayed as shown in Figure 2.5.

Repository object

As the name suggests, the Object Navigator provides access to objects. Since the Object Navigator is part of the ABAP Workbench, the objects involved are those that can be edited with the tools of the ABAP Workbench. We refer to these objects as **repository objects**. These include all the ABAP programs of the SAP System with all their components such as source code and layouts. There are, however, many other repository objects such as global data definitions in the **ABAP Dictionary** or database table definitions (also in the ABAP Dictionary). Together these development objects form a **repository**. This repository is a special section of the database contents of the central database, which includes the programs of the SAP System itself instead of customer data.

Object list

You access the repository objects via **object lists** in the Object Navigator. You must select one of these lists in the drop-down list box in the top left-hand corner. In Figure 2.5 the **Development class** object list has been selected. Choose the input help key on the right of the field to obtain a list of the other object list options (see Figure 2.6).

Since you wish to write a program, choose the third entry, **Program**. Enter a name for your program and confirm using *Enter* ↵ (see Figure 2.7).

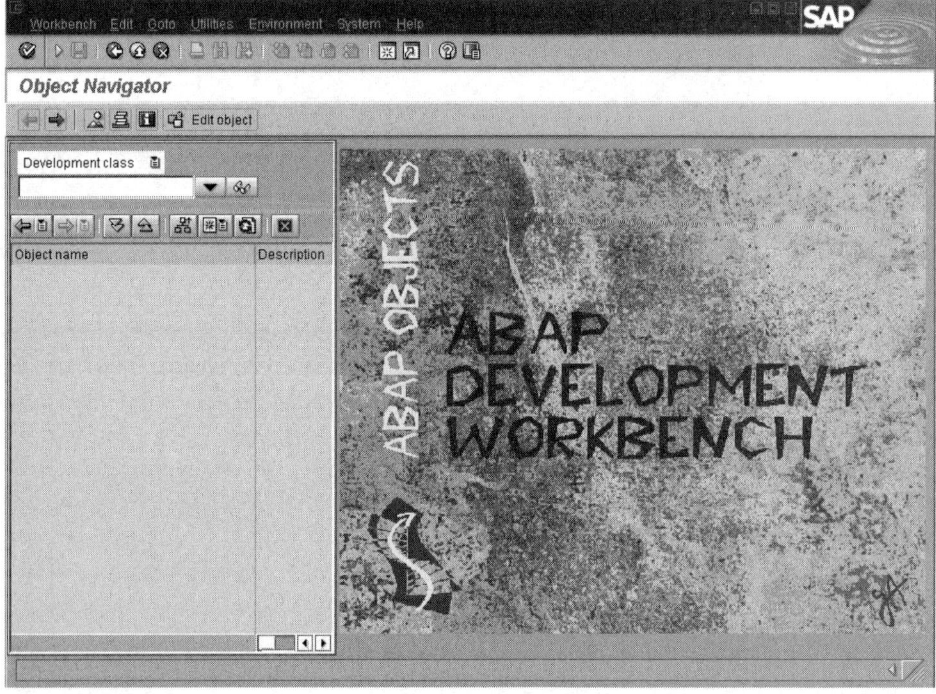

FIGURE 2.5 Object Navigator initial screen. Copyright © SAP AG

FIGURE 2.6 Object lists in the Object Navigator. Copyright © SAP AG

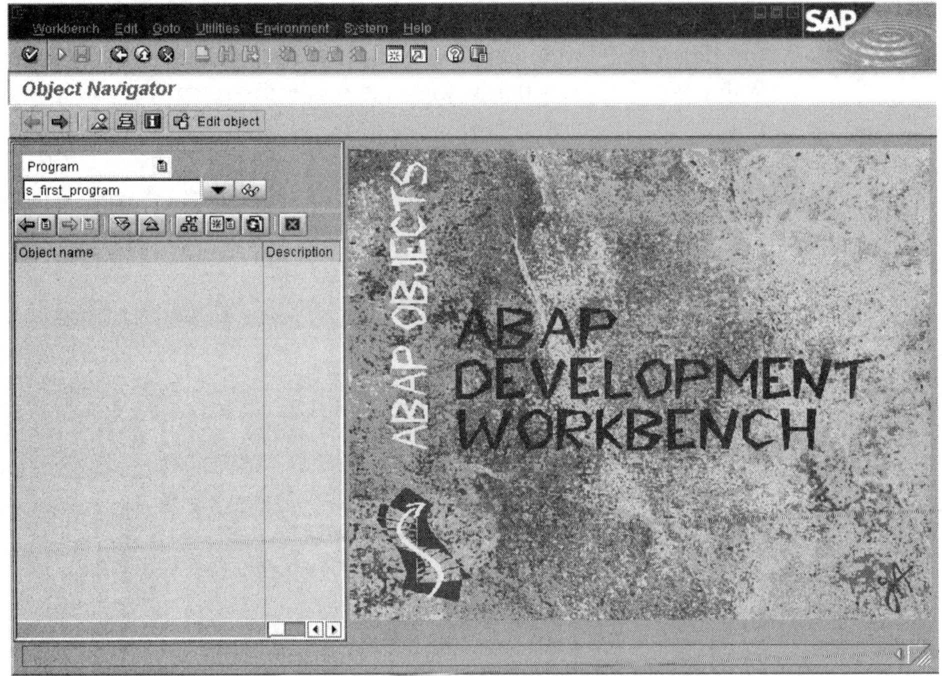

FIGURE 2.7 Entering a new program name. Copyright © SAP AG

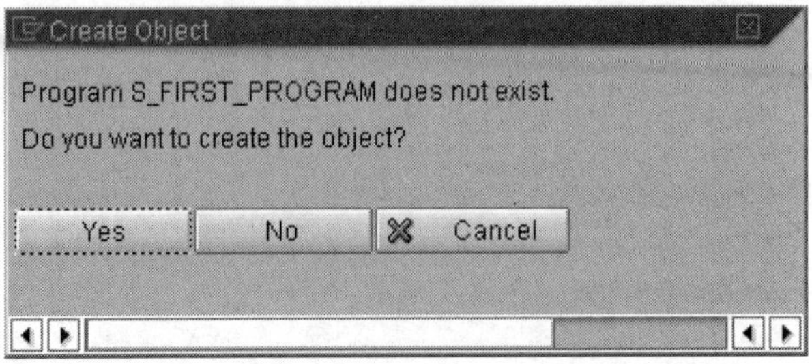

Create Object

Program S_FIRST_PROGRAM does not exist.

Do you want to create the object?

Yes | No | Cancel

FIGURE 2.8 Creating an ABAP program. Copyright © SAP AG

If there is no program with this name, the prompt in Figure 2.8 will appear. Otherwise try again with a different name.

Namespace

Bear in mind that customer programs have different naming conventions from SAP programs, and so as a customer, instead of the "S" used by SAP for the first letter, you will have to use a "Y" or a "Z" or the abbreviation reserved by SAP for your company. In this book we shall use "S" as a prefix for almost all repository objects. This means that our example programs will be in the SAP-specific namespace for you to use as templates.

Confirm the dialog box from Figure 2.8, and in the following dialog box in Figure 2.9 uncheck the check box for **Top Include**. Confirm here as well. We will expand on the role of Top Include at a later stage.

Program attributes

A dialog box now appears as shown in Figure 2.10. Here, you have to define specific program attributes.

Program type

One of the most important attributes of a program is its type. As we will see later in more detail, a program's type determines its entire way of operating. The default value of the Workbench is the **executable program** type. Since we wish to execute our program we leave it as it is and choose **Save**. A prompt then appears for a **development class** (see Figure 2.11).

This term has already appeared as a possible object list type. What does it signify? A development class[4] provides a structure for development objects. You organize your work

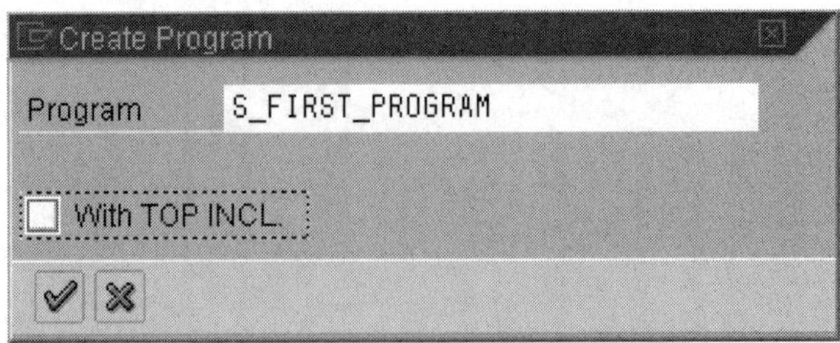

FIGURE 2.9 Prompt for a Top Include. Copyright © SAP AG

4. Please note that development classes and repository objects have got nothing to do with classes and objects in ABAP Objects.

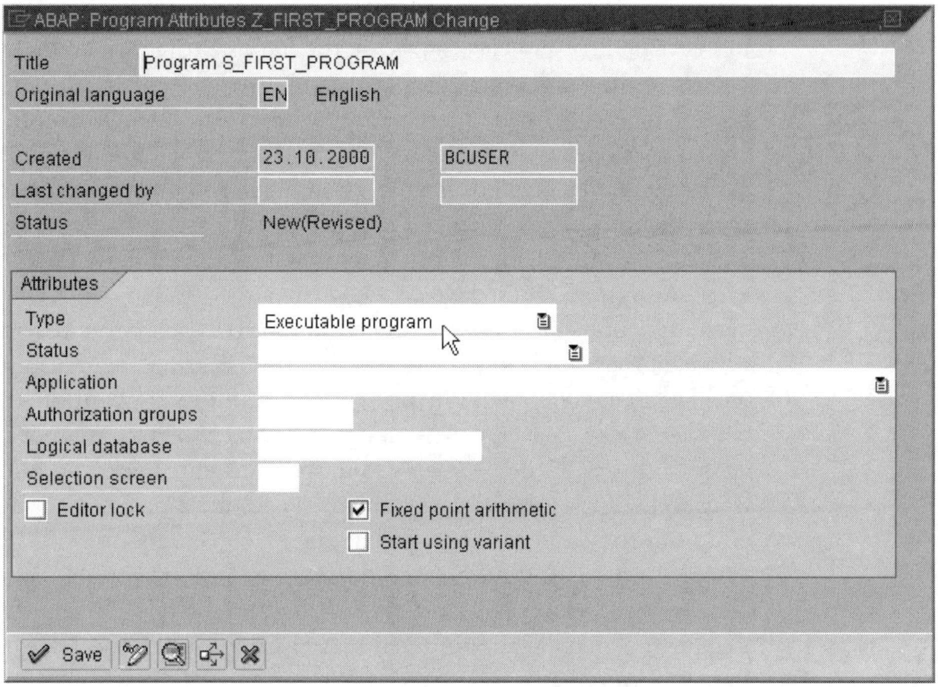

FIGURE 2.10 Defining program attributes. Copyright © SAP AG

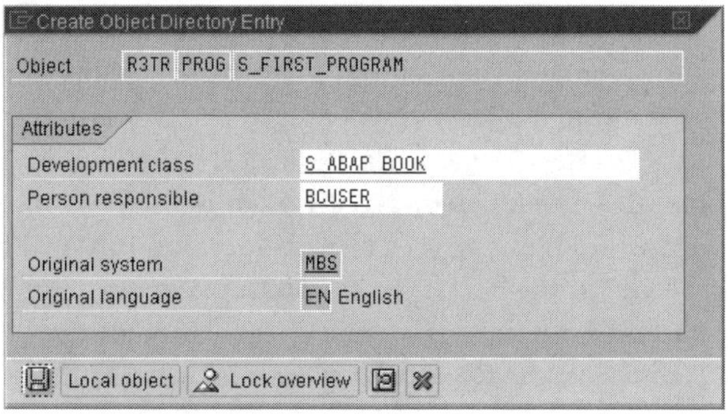

FIGURE 2.11 Assigning a development class. Copyright © SAP AG

by assigning various objects to a development class. All repository objects – i.e. not just programs but all objects that can be modified with the ABAP Workbench – must be assigned to a development class. If you specify a development class as an object list type in the Object Navigator, you can then access all the objects of this development class.[5]

5. As of Release 6.10 the term development class has been replaced by **Package**. A package includes all the attributes of a development class but in addition offers nesting, interfaces, and visibility definition.

Development class

Development classes are actually repository objects themselves. As well as organizing development projects they have the important task of connecting development objects to the SAP Change and Transport System. The latter is responsible for transporting objects between different SAP Systems. For obvious reasons, applications are always developed in a development system, never in a production system. The application programs created in this system have to be transported, mainly via other consolidation or test systems, to a production system where the business data is located. The SAP Change and Transport System is used to define **transport layers** for each SAP System. These layers specify the target systems into which objects from a given development system are to be transported. Each development class is assigned to one of these transport layers and therefore specifies the transport attributes of all its development objects. In principle, a naming convention is used to specify whether or not a development class and its objects are transportable. A development class starting with the "$" sign cannot be transported and you cannot assign it to a transport layer. All other development classes must be assigned to a transport layer and both the class and their development objects thereby are subject to the SAP Change and Transport System. Modifications in transportable development classes are organized into tasks and are carried out solely in **Transport** or **Correction Requests**, which are administered by transaction SE09, the **Transport Organizer** of the ABAP Workbench.

In our case we shall use a transportable development class S_ABAP_BOOK, which ultimately will contain all the repository objects required for this book. For example, for exercise purposes you can create your own non-transportable development class $_ABAP_BOOK. To do this, proceed in the Object Navigator exactly as if you were creating a program and simply enter the new name in the **Development class** object list type in the top left-hand corner in the Object Navigator. However, SAP also provides a special development class called $TMP, which is also designed for local, non-transportable development objects. Each developer can store his or her own exercise and demo programs in $TMP. In the dialog box in Figure 2.11 you can either enter "$TMP" as the development class and choose **Save**, or directly select the **Local object** button. Both have the same effect. Through the **Local Objects** object list type (see Figure 2.6), the Object Navigator provides each developer with direct access to his or her local exercise objects. Naturally, the assignment of a development object to a development class can be amended later.

Once you have specified the development class, the basis for creating a program is complete. In the object list of the Object Navigator you will now find the entry S_FIRST_PROGRAM. You can click this with the alternate mouse button and will then see a context menu with the editing options (see Figure 2.12).

If you choose **Change** in this context menu, the **ABAP Editor** appears in the right side of the Object Navigator screen (see Figure 2.13).

ABAP Editor

Figure 2.13 shows how the Object Navigator appears as you would normally see it when editing repository objects. The object list on the left-hand side shows your objects hierarchically in a tree structure. Throughout this introduction a large

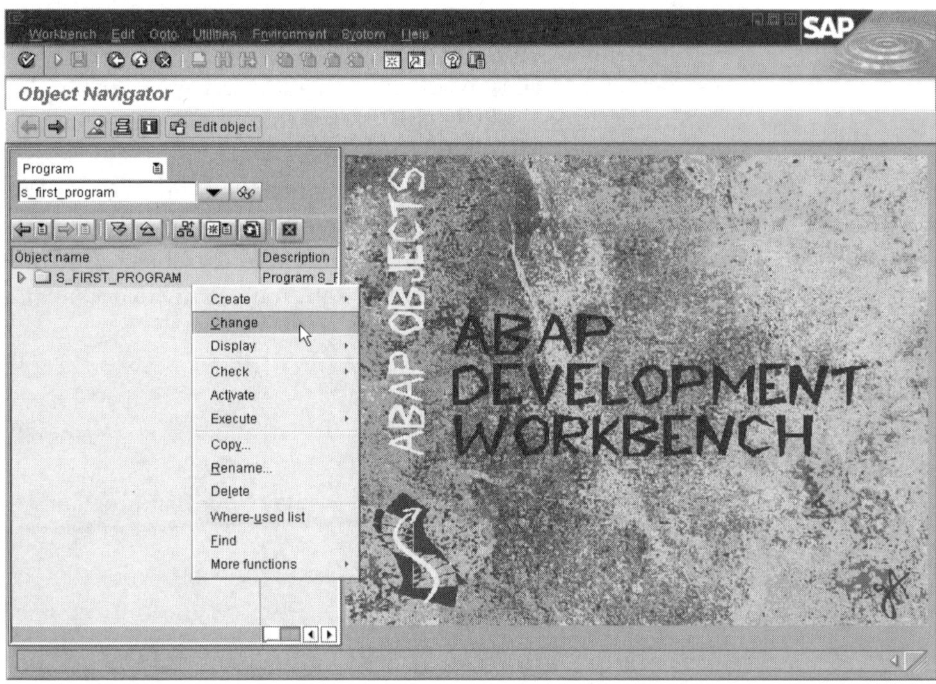

FIGURE 2.12 Object Navigator and program. Copyright © SAP AG

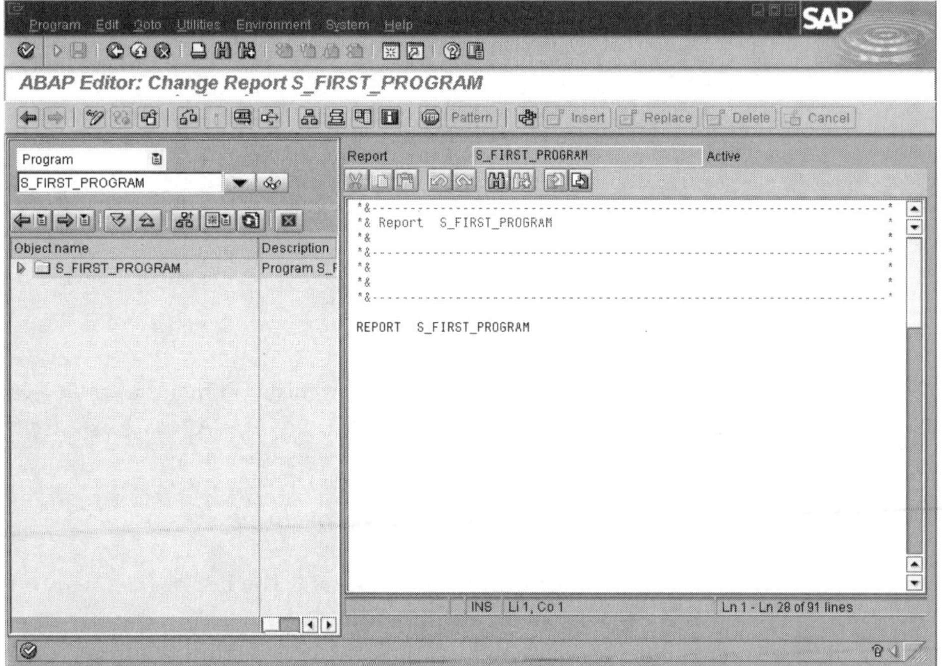

FIGURE 2.13 The Object Navigator and the ABAP Editor. Copyright © SAP AG

number of subnodes will be added to the S_FIRST_PROGRAM node. If you choose an object by double-clicking it, or select it using the alternate mouse button, the corresponding tool of the ABAP Workbench automatically opens on the right-hand side. In this case it is the ABAP Editor. We shall become equally familiar with the other tools we will require throughout this book.

Navigation

Thus, we do not need to consider beforehand which tool we will need to edit particular subobjects of a development project, as is the case with accessing in Figure 2.2. Instead, we shall always consider a development object in its overall context and allow ourselves to be guided to the right tools by the automatic navigation mechanisms of the ABAP Workbench.

2.3 THE FIRST PROGRAM

We are now ready to tackle the source code of our first program. We shall first take a brief look at the syntax.

2.3.1 ABAP syntax

To get to grips with ABAP syntax, let us look at the framework that the ABAP Workbench provides. This consists of a few comment lines along with a first statement called REPORT (see Listing 2.1).

LISTING 2.1 Program lines predefined by the Workbench

```
*&---------------------------------------------------------*
*& Report S_FIRST_PROGRAM                                  *
*&                                                         *
*&---------------------------------------------------------*
*&                                                         *
*&                                                         *
*&---------------------------------------------------------*
REPORT S_FIRST_PROGRAM.
```

As you can see, the first seven lines are just comment and the eighth line is a statement. This is in fact the basic syntax rule of ABAP: each ABAP program consists of comments and statements.

Comments

Comment lines begin with an asterisk (*). The rest of the line can follow any format and is shown by the Editor in a different color. You can use the double quotation mark (") if you want to mark just the rear section of a line as comment. It can be inserted in any column (including the first). All signs in a line with an asterisk (*) at the first point and all signs following a " are ignored by the Compiler.

Statements

Statements consist of individual ABAP words and end with a period. The first ABAP word is known as a **keyword**. The other words are then either operands, operators, or additions to keywords. In our case the keyword is REPORT and the operand S_FIRST_PROGRAM. ABAP words must be separated by at least one space. Since operators – such as plus and minus signs or brackets – are also valid ABAP words, they must also be separated from their operands by spaces. Other than this there are no restrictions concerning source code formatting. There can be more than one statement in a program line and a statement may extend over several program lines.

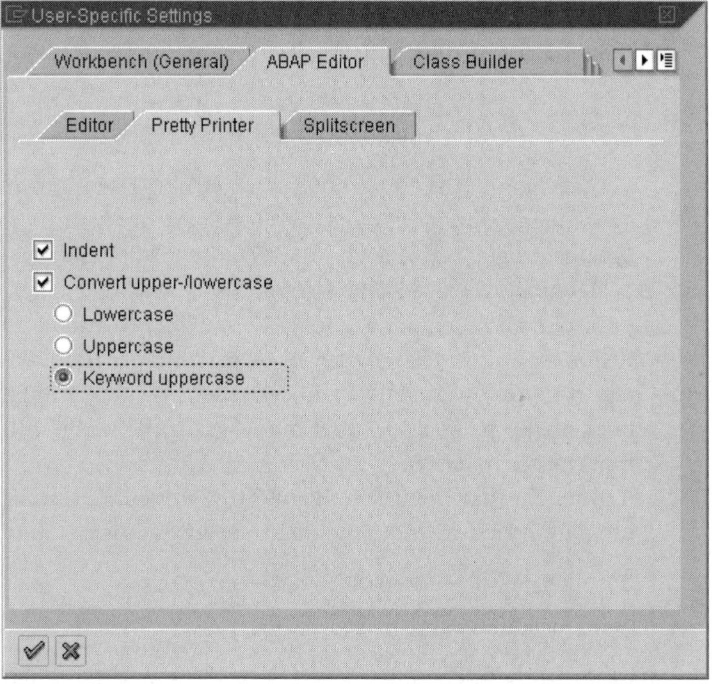

FIGURE 2.14 Pretty Printer settings. Copyright © SAP AG

Pretty Printer

The ABAP Compiler does not distinguish between upper and lower case; writing REPORT has the same meaning as report and RePort. However, for the sake of clarity, in this book all ABAP keywords and their additions are written in capitals, while all operands are always written in lower case. ABAP Editor supports the process with its **Pretty Printer** function. To set the Pretty Printer for your own particular requirements, choose **Tools – Settings** in ABAP Editor and then the **Pretty Printer** tab. You can now make your settings as illustrated in Figure 2.14.

If you then select the **Pretty Printer** button in the ABAP Editor, the ABAP statement in our program changes, as shown in Listing 2.2.

LISTING 2.2 Effect of the Pretty Printer

```
REPORT s_first_program.
```

With our chosen settings the Pretty Printer also improves the program layout through indenting according to the program structure. From now on we will show all example programs in the way that the Pretty Printer formats them, and recommend that you also perform this function frequently.

2.3.2 General program structure

All executable ABAP programs start with a statement introducing the program. All subsequent statements are therefore part of this program. With the exception of Include programs (see Section 5.2.2), the ABAP Editor will always show the full range of statements of an ABAP program.

In our first program the REPORT statement introduces the program. This name is historical and indicates that an executable program was previously used solely for reporting purposes. As we will see later, executable programs still support reporting but can also be used for other purposes. At the moment it is sufficient for us to know that the program s_first_program will be introduced with our first statement.

Two parts

After the statement introducing the program, each ABAP program follows a fixed program structure. ABAP programs are always divided into two parts:

- a global declaration part
- a procedural part.

In the **global declaration part**, which immediately follows the statement introducing the program, declarative statements can be used to make definitions and declarations that are visible and valid throughout the entire ABAP program.

The declaration part is followed by the **procedural part**, in which the actual processing logic of the ABAP program is defined. The procedural part is divided into

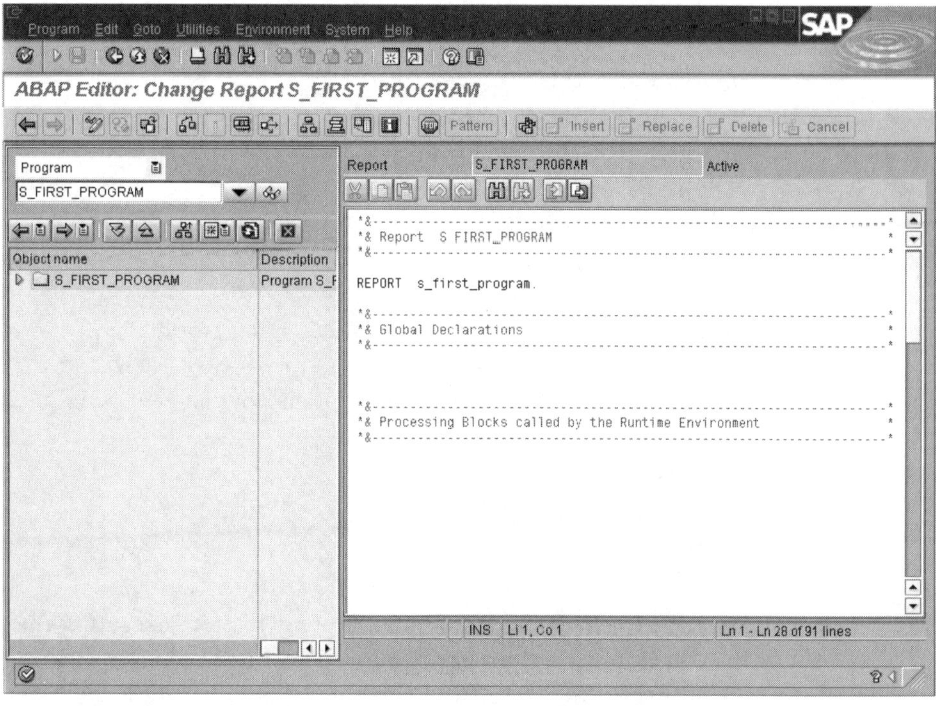

FIGURE 2.15 General program structure. Copyright © SAP AG

individual procedural units, which we call **processing blocks**. Each ABAP statement that is not part of the global declaration part always belongs to a specific processing block. The statements within a processing block are processed sequentially. The order of the processing blocks in the procedural part is of no significance for executing the program. The sequence in which the processing blocks are executed while the ABAP program is running is controlled in the SAP System by the ABAP runtime environment.

Comment lines

To maintain the clarity and legibility of an ABAP program, it is advisable to make this program structure transparent by using comment lines. We shall therefore structure our programs properly from the very beginning and so we change the comment lines, as shown in Figure 2.15.

2.3.3 Insert: a "Hello World!" program

In every book concerning programming languages, it is customary to start with a very basic program, which displays a "Hello World!" message. This book is no exception. We will insert this little typing exercise before starting with the program indicated in Section 2.1. Change the source code of the program as shown in Listing 2.3.

LISTING 2.3 The "Hello World!" program

```
*&---------------------------------------------------------------*
*& Report S_FIRST_PROGRAM                                        *
*&---------------------------------------------------------------*
REPORT s_first_program.
*&---------------------------------------------------------------*
*& Global Declarations                                           *
*&---------------------------------------------------------------*
PARAMETERS input(16) TYPE c DEFAULT 'Hello World!'.
*&---------------------------------------------------------------*
*& Processing Blocks called by the Runtime Environment          *
*&---------------------------------------------------------------*
START-OF-SELECTION.
  WRITE 'The input was:'.
  WRITE input.
```

Syntax check

We want to check that the syntax is correct before executing the program. Choose the **Check** function, for example in the context menu of the program name in the object list. In the status line you should obtain a message stating that no syntax errors were found. Put this to the test and insert an error. For example, write `WRTE` instead of `WRITE` in the last statement and check the syntax again. The error will be immediately reported at the bottom right in Object Navigator (see Figure 2.16). Use the **Correct** function to correct the program immediately.

Activation

Once your program has been tested for errors it must be activated for execution. To do this, choose the **Activate** function in the Object Navigator. Once the program has been activated, a message will appear in the status line. Your program can now be executed by all users in the current SAP System, for example via **System – Services – Reporting**.[6]

Execution

We wish to start running the program directly from Object Navigator and therefore choose the **Execute – Direct processing** function in the context menu of the program name. First, a screen layout appears with an input field (**INPUT**), which contains the "Hello World!" default value (see Figure 2.17). We call this type of screen layout a **selection screen**.

Now choose **Execute** or **F8**. The screen layout changes to the display shown in Figure 2.18. We call this type of screen layout a **classical list**.

6. Activating a program ensures that it is compiled and that this version is identified in the system as being executable. In this way you can modify and save the source code without affecting the active version. The new version is run only when the program has been activated again. This applies to all repository objects.

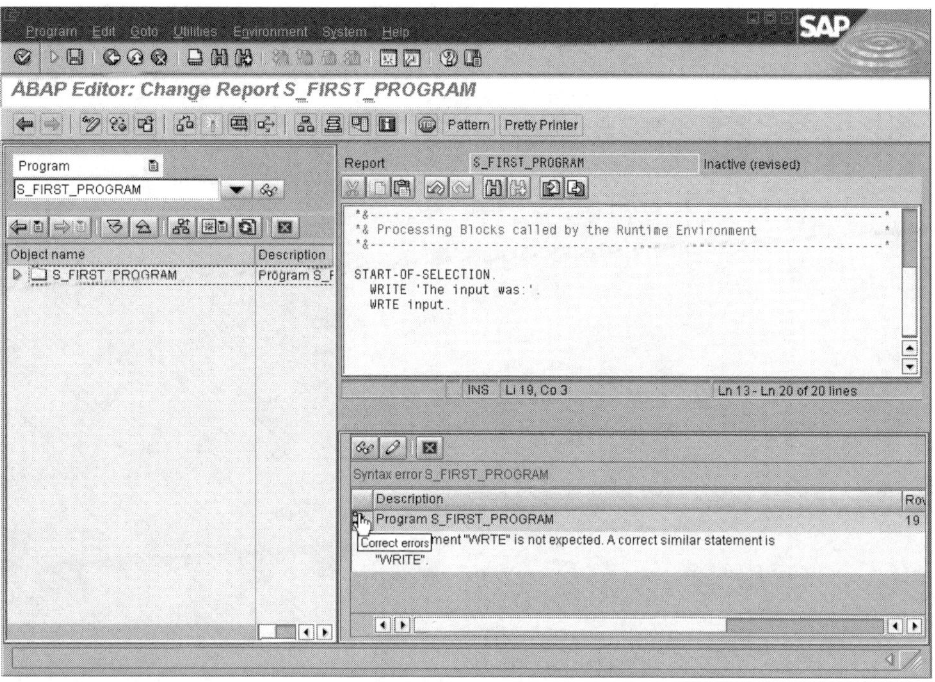

FIGURE 2.16 Syntax check. Copyright © SAP AG

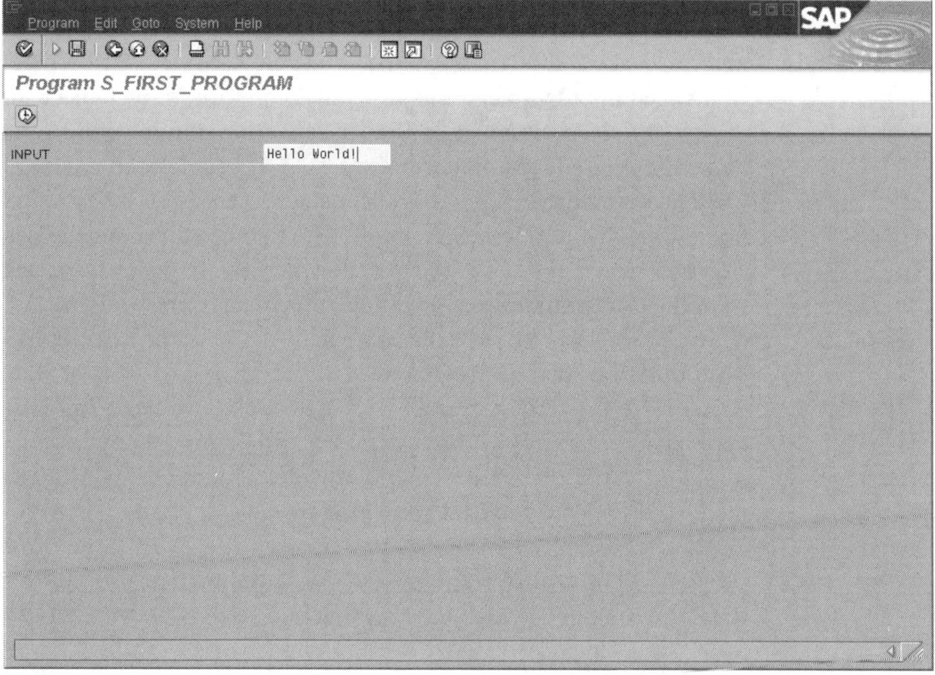

FIGURE 2.17 Selection screen. Copyright © SAP AG

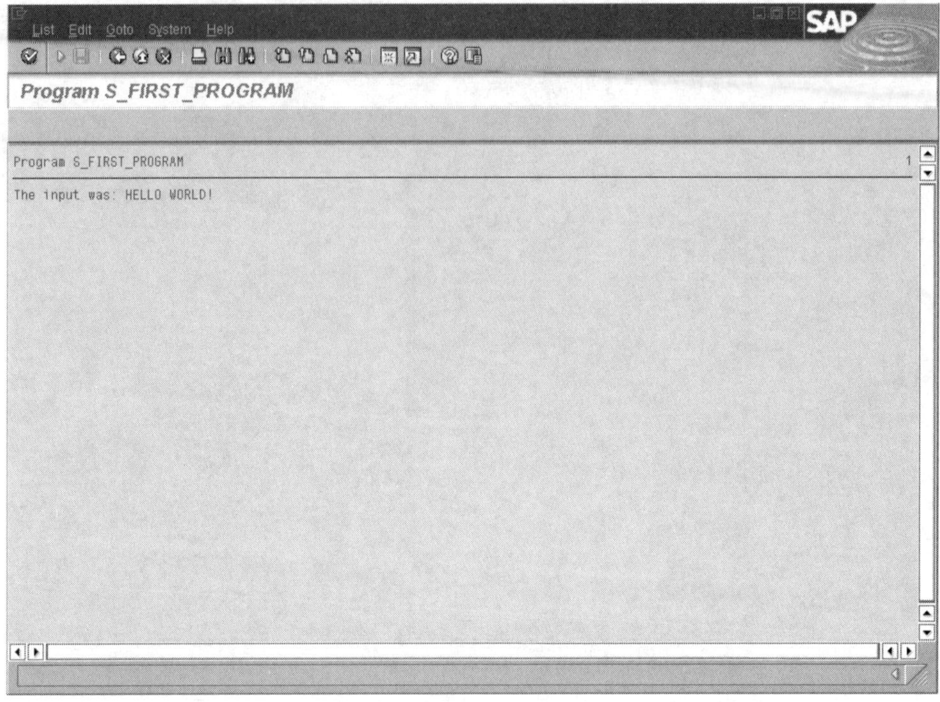

FIGURE 2.18 Classical list. Copyright © SAP AG

If you now choose **Back**, **Exit**, or **Cancel** you will return to the selection screen and can make a different entry. You must choose **Back**, **Exit**, or **Cancel** on the selection screen in order to end the program and return to the **Object Navigator**.

Layout

Our simple program is therefore already demonstrating remarkably complex behavior. A single statement, `PARAMETERS`, has defined a complete screen layout including a menu list and active icons in a standard toolbar. It has also declared an internal field, `input`, which is supplied by the user input on the selection screen. The selection screen appears automatically when the program starts and when we return from the list, without us having programmed anything to do this.

Processing block

The `START-OF-SELECTION` statement defines a processing block, which in this case consists of two `WRITE` statements. The task of the `WRITE` statements is to write data to the list screen. The processing block is called automatically and the list appears automatically without us having programmed anything to do this. Like the selection screen, the list screen also provides a functional user interface in the form of menu and standard toolbars, for which we have not had to do anything.

All this is simply because we have chosen the **Executable program** type for our program. Behind this program type lies a predefined procedure in the ABAP runtime environment, which ensures that the screens and the `START-OF-SELECTION` processing block are called. We therefore see that while a simple "Hello World!"

program in ABAP may be easy to program, its operation in the client–server environment of the SAP System is anything but trivial. We shall explore this in more detail in Chapter 3.

Chained statement

We also want to use our very first program to describe a feature of ABAP syntax that will save writing and improve readability. ABAP provides the option of creating chained statements. This means that statements with an identical beginning can be grouped together. To create a chained statement a colon is inserted after the identical section of the statement. Thereafter the other sections of the statements are separated by commas. The fixed section of a statement is generally not just restricted to a keyword, which means that with skilled application you can achieve highly efficient writing methods. Listing 2.4 shows how the two `WRITE` statements in our "Hello World!" program can be written in a chained statement. Never forget, however, that in reality a chained statement represents several statements and that the Compiler always breaks down a chained statement into its component parts.

LISTING 2.4 Chained statement

```
START-OF-SELECTION.
  WRITE: 'The input was:', input.
```

2.3.4 View of the first application program

Now we have successfully completed our "Hello World!" program, we can turn our attention to more worthwhile tasks. Remember our aim is to provide user-driven access to the SPFLI database table and to show the results. Therefore, we need to program user prompts, database access, and a display. The final result should be that the prompt and the display, as illustrated in Figure 2.19, appear on a single screen.

SAP List Viewer

The automatically generated selection screens and lists from the "Hello World!" program are not sufficient to do this; we need to program our own screen. To display the data we will use the **SAP List Viewer** (ALV), which SAP provides as a global class in the class library.

2.3.5 Copying programs

We will carry on working with our `S_FIRST_PROGRAM` program. If you liked your "Hello World!" program so much that you want to keep it, you can copy it into another program in the Object Navigator. To do this, choose **Copy** in the context menu of the program name and enter the target program name – such as "`S_VERY_FIRST_PROGRAM`." In a customer system, of course, you must observe the namespace conventions. A dialog box appears, asking you which part objects of the program are to be copied (see Figure 2.20). Here you can see that a program consists of more than just the source code.

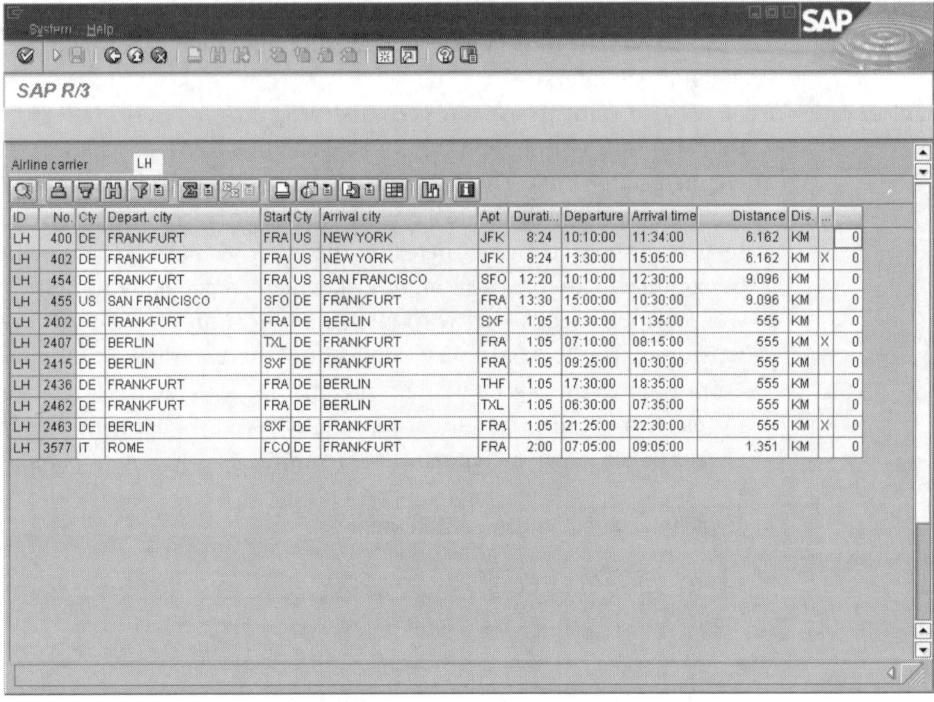

ID	No.	Cty	Depart. city	Start	Cty	Arrival city	Apt	Durati...	Departure	Arrival time	Distance	Dis.	...	
LH	400	DE	FRANKFURT	FRA	US	NEW YORK	JFK	8:24	10:10:00	11:34:00	6.162	KM		0
LH	402	DE	FRANKFURT	FRA	US	NEW YORK	JFK	8:24	13:30:00	15:05:00	6.162	KM	X	0
LH	454	DE	FRANKFURT	FRA	US	SAN FRANCISCO	SFO	12:20	10:10:00	12:30:00	9.096	KM		0
LH	455	US	SAN FRANCISCO	SFO	DE	FRANKFURT	FRA	13:30	15:00:00	10:30:00	9.096	KM		0
LH	2402	DE	FRANKFURT	FRA	DE	BERLIN	SXF	1:05	10:30:00	11:35:00	555	KM		0
LH	2407	DE	BERLIN	TXL	DE	FRANKFURT	FRA	1:05	07:10:00	08:15:00	555	KM	X	0
LH	2415	DE	BERLIN	SXF	DE	FRANKFURT	FRA	1:05	09:25:00	10:30:00	555	KM		0
LH	2436	DE	FRANKFURT	FRA	DE	BERLIN	THF	1:05	17:30:00	18:35:00	555	KM		0
LH	2462	DE	FRANKFURT	FRA	DE	BERLIN	TXL	1:05	06:30:00	07:35:00	555	KM		0
LH	2463	DE	BERLIN	SXF	DE	FRANKFURT	FRA	1:05	21:25:00	22:30:00	555	KM	X	0
LH	3577	IT	ROME	FCO	DE	FRANKFURT	FRA	2:00	07:05:00	09:05:00	1.351	KM		0

FIGURE 2.19 Screen output of first program. Copyright © SAP AG

The default entry is sufficient for our mini-program. If you choose **Copy** again, you will be asked for the development class for the target program. It is best to enter the same development class as before, "$TMP," or your own development class, such as "$_ABAP_BOOK." The program is then copied and you will find two entries in the respective development class object list in the Object Navigator.

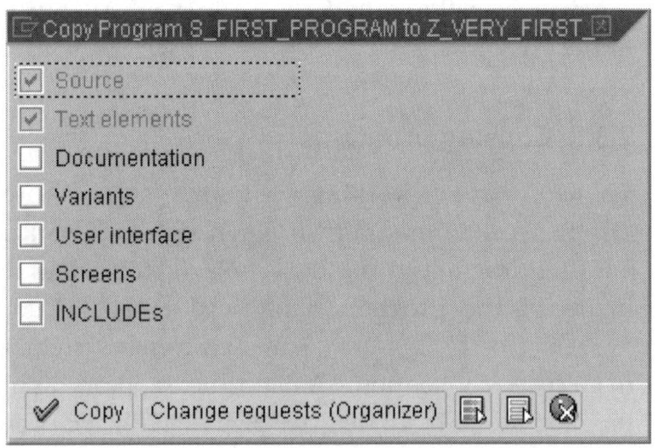

FIGURE 2.20 Copying the program. Copyright © SAP AG

Once the "Hello World!" program has been saved we can restore our source code from the first program to the condition of Figure 2.15 and start working on our first real application program.

2.3.6 Creating a screen

The key elements of any ABAP program that communicates with users are its screens. This is why screens in the SAP System do not simply have a layout; they also have a **process logic**. In the SAP System, the term **screen** therefore refers more to a dynamic program (the German expression for screen in an SAP system is **Dynpro**). We shall use the SAP term **screen** when we speak about the components of an ABAP program and refer to **screen layout** when describing the visible part of the screen on the physical screen.

Screen

Screens are edited with the **Screen Painter** tool in the ABAP Workbench. Only selection screens and lists do not require this work, as we have seen in our "Hello World!" program. For these special layouts, the corresponding screens are generated during the compilation of an ABAP program from the respective ABAP statements. To create a screen yourself, apply the forward navigation of the ABAP Workbench. Add the new processing block START-OF-SELECTION to the program S_FIRST_PROGRAM as shown in Listing 2.5.

LISTING 2.5 Calling a screen

```
*&-----------------------------------------------------------------*
*& Processing Blocks called by the Runtime Environment             *
*&-----------------------------------------------------------------*
* Event Block START-OF-SELECTION
START-OF-SELECTION.
  CALL SCREEN 100.
```

Screen number

A program's screens are identified by numbers between 1 and 9999. The CALL SCREEN **100** statement calls the screen with the number 100. However, currently there is no such screen. You therefore have to double-click 100 and confirm the dialog box that appears (see Figure 2.21).

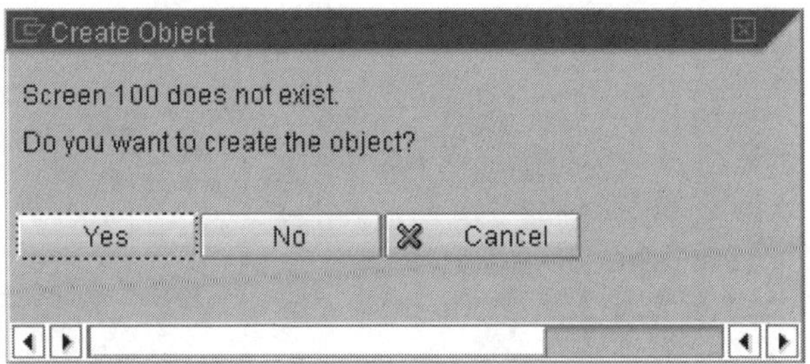

FIGURE 2.21 Creating a screen. Copyright © SAP AG

We are already familiar with this dialog box from Figure 2.8. If an object is selected that does not exist, the ABAP Workbench always offers to create it. However, if the object already exists, it is opened with the corresponding tool.

Attributes

As with ABAP programs, you must first customize the screen attributes. In this case we just want to enter a brief description and leave the other attributes to the default values. You specify the attributes on a tab of the Screen Painter, which now appears on the right-hand side of the Object Navigator (see Figure 2.22). Note that the number "100" is predefined as the next screen. This means that the screen will call itself when it is finished! In this case we have predefined a loop, which we will have to exit by appropriate means.

Screen flow logic

Save the attributes and now choose the **Flow logic** tab of the Screen Painter. Here you need to program the screen process logic (see Figure 2.23). The corresponding programming language is a small set of statements that are similar to, but not part of, ABAP. We are after all in the Screen Painter, not in the ABAP Editor. As with an ABAP program, the screen process logic is divided into processing blocks: to be precise, at least into the two blocks predefined by the Screen Painter: `PROCESS BEFORE OUTPUT` (`PBO`) and `PROCESS AFTER INPUT` (`PAI`). The first of these two is executed immediately after the screen is called, at the PBO event. After that the actual layout is

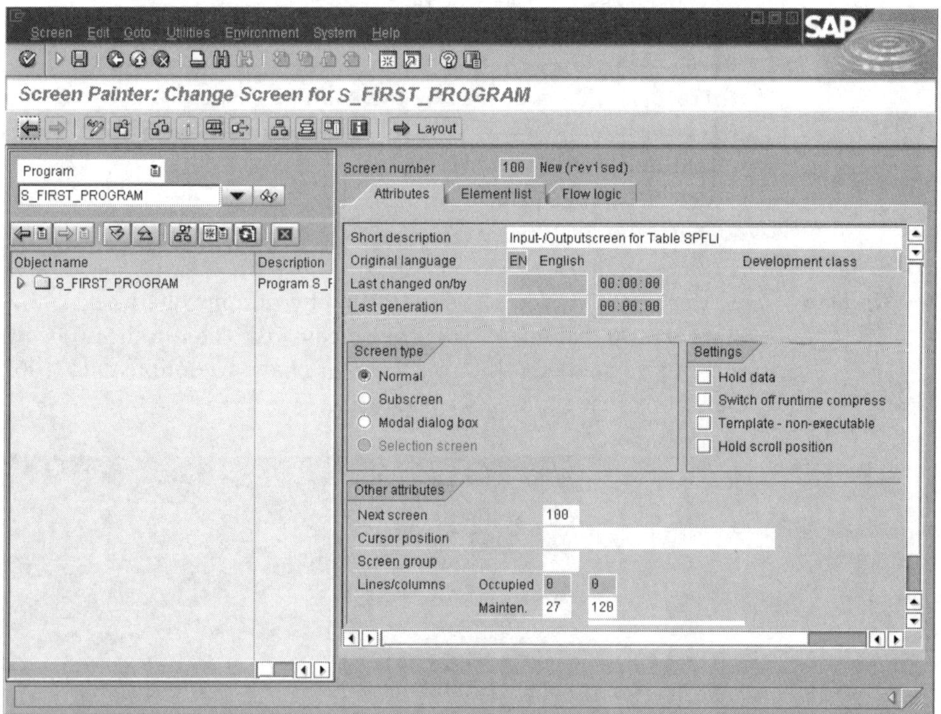

FIGURE 2.22 Defining screen attributes. Copyright © SAP AG

displayed. The second is executed at the PAI event, which is triggered by a user action on the screen. The main task of the statements in these processing blocks is to call up **dialog modules** in the ABAP program. The Workbench has already provided two corresponding `MODULE` statements as comments, from which we shall simply remove the comment asterisks, as illustrated in Figure 2.23.

Therefore we need to ensure that the corresponding dialog modules are created in our ABAP program. However, first we want to save the status of our screen and conclude the work in Screen Painter by defining its layout. To do this, choose **Layout**, which will open the **Graphical Screen Painter** (see Figure 2.24).

Layout

On the left-hand side, you will see a list of graphic elements that you can position on the screen surface, such as text fields, input/output fields, or checkboxes. We wish to create the input field for the airline you can see in Figure 2.19 with the same type attributes as the CARRID column of the SPFLI database table, so that the user can only enter suitable values at this point. This is very easy in the ABAP Workbench, since all the database tables are defined with one of its tools, the ABAP Dictionary (see Section 4.2.5). The Screen Painter therefore knows all the database tables in the SAP System and allows us to copy their column types directly for screen fields. Choose the respective symbol or the F6 key, as illustrated in Figure 2.24, and you will obtain another

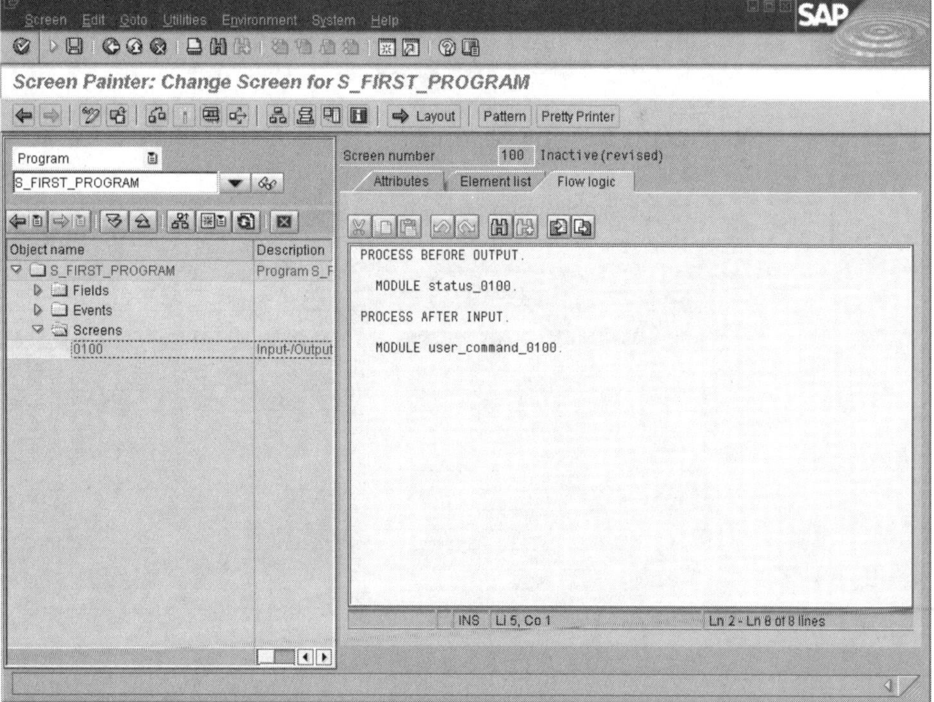

FIGURE 2.23 Screen flow logic. Copyright © SAP AG

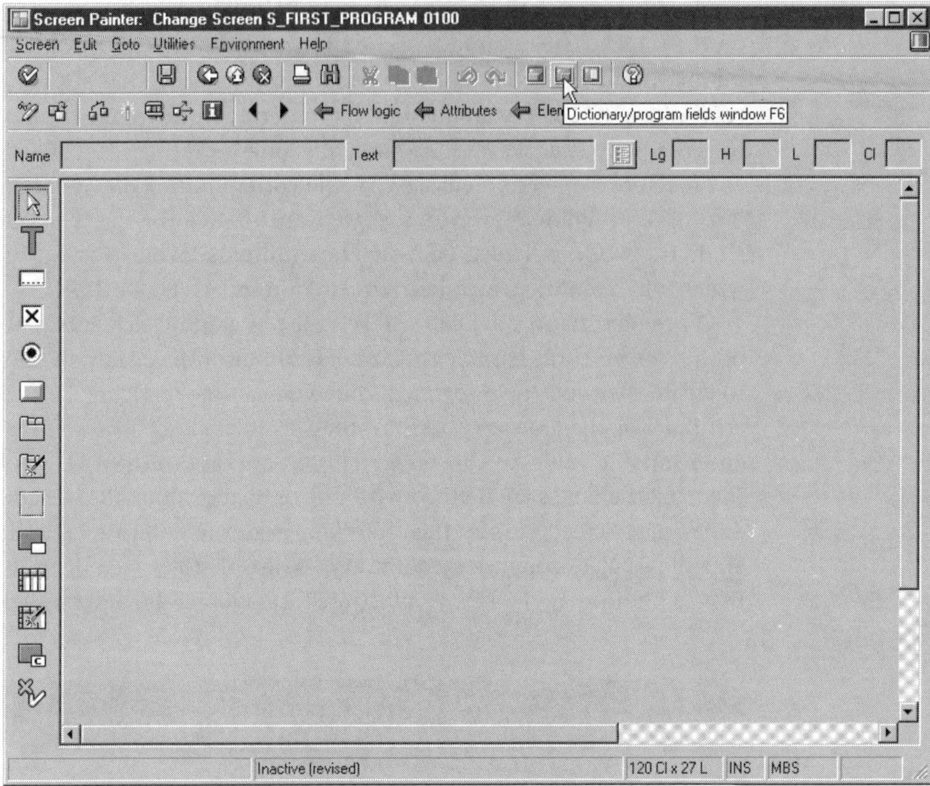

FIGURE 2.24 The Graphical Screen Painter. Copyright © SAP AG

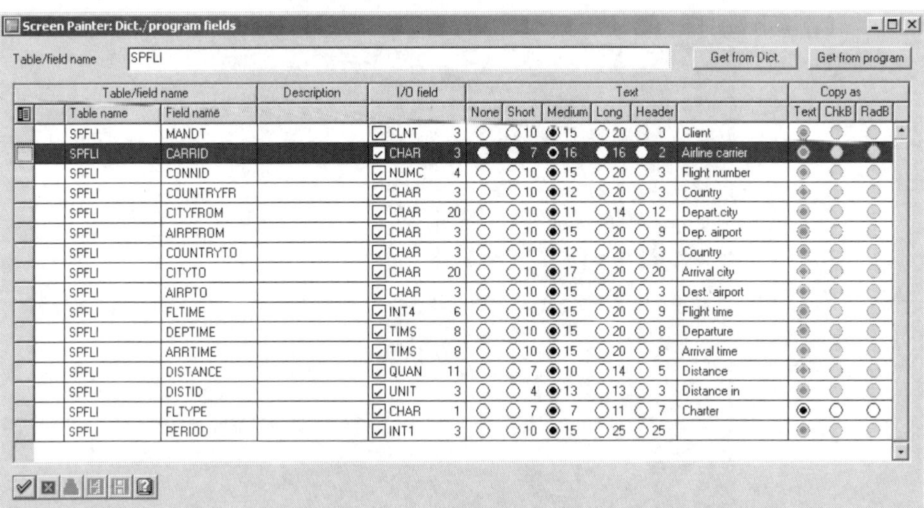

FIGURE 2.25 Copying a Type from the ABAP Dictionary. Copyright © SAP AG

window where you can enter a **Table/field name**. Since we wish to work with the SPFLI table in our example program, enter "SPFLI" in this input field and choose **Get From Dict**. Now all the columns from the database table are displayed, including some copying options (see Figure 2.25).

ABAP Dictionary

Select the row with the field name CARRID and choose the green tick at the bottom left. If you now move the cursor over the Graphical Screen Painter, you will see a template that you can position on the layout (see Figure 2.26).

Move the template to the top left-hand corner and click on the left mouse button. You will obtain the three-digit input field shown in Figure 2.27 called SPFLI-CARRID together with the text **Airline carrier**. The text is therefore already predefined in the Dictionary.

Save your work and now choose **Screen – Test** or the **F8** key. If you confirm the dialog box that appears, you can check the screen you have just created (see Figure 2.28).

Input help

Note that on the right of the input field an input help key automatically appears, which we have not specifically defined. If you select this or press the **F4** key in the

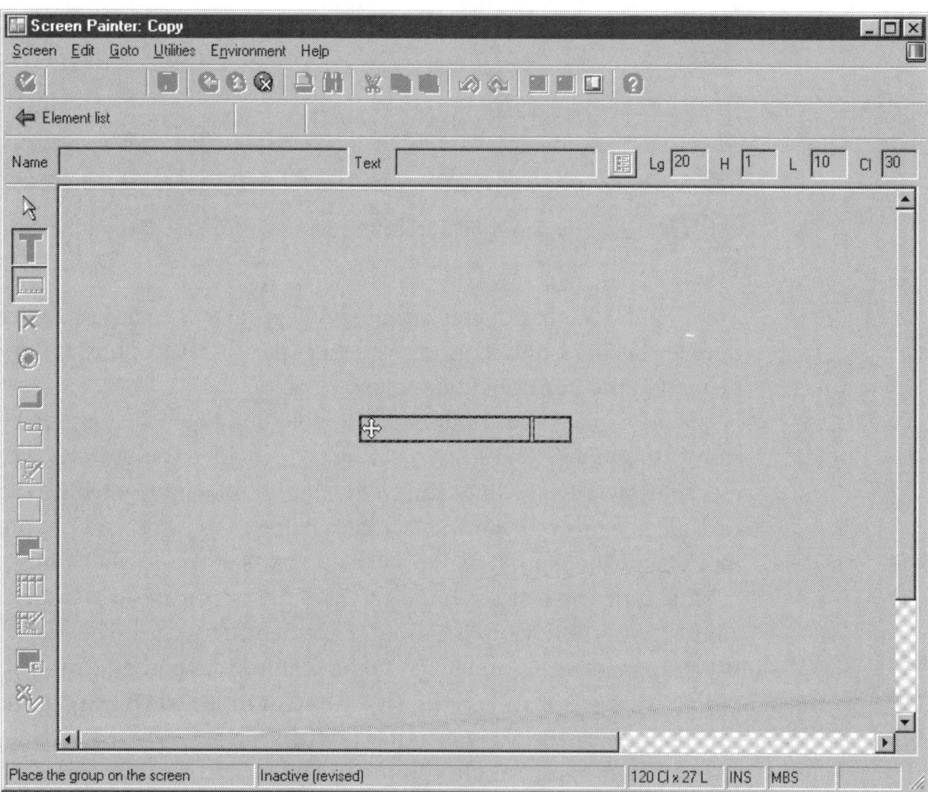

FIGURE 2.26 Positioning the template from the Dictionary. Copyright © SAP AG

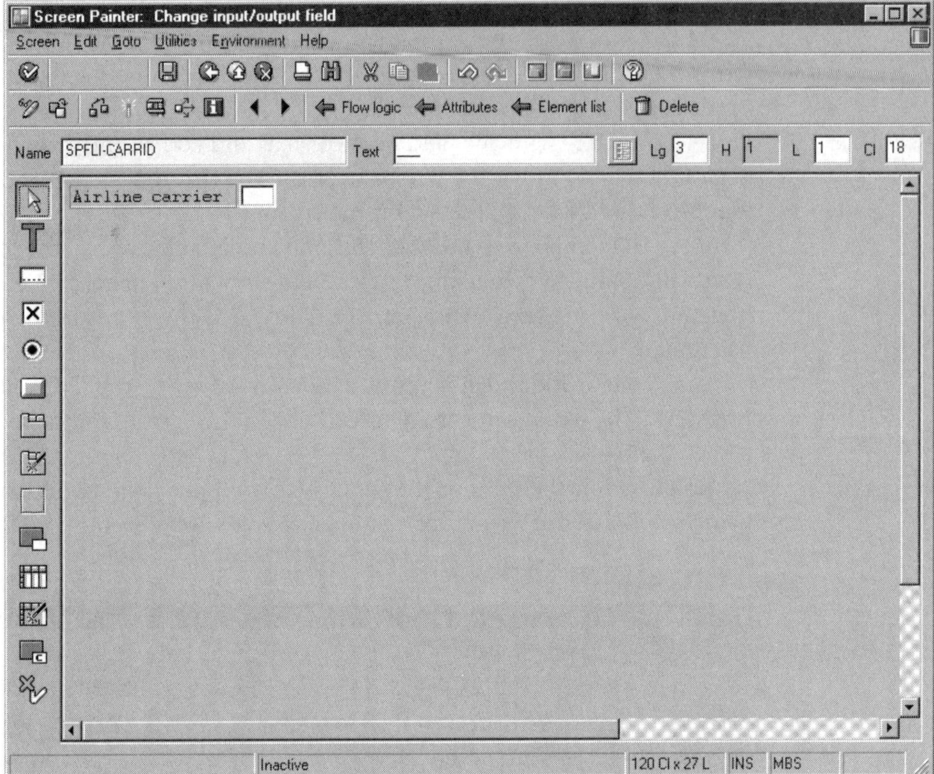

FIGURE 2.27 Input field from the ABAP Dictionary. Copyright © SAP AG

input field, a list of possible airlines will appear in which you can choose an entry by double-clicking on it. This input help is part of the flight data model and has been defined in the ABAP Dictionary.

You have made this input help available simply by copying the input field from the ABAP Dictionary. The ABAP Dictionary provides the option of various input help mechanisms, which can be linked to columns of database tables or other types. In our case all the entries from the SCARR database table are read out and displayed as an input help. The input help is provided to users of the finished program as in testing.

Now quit the test screen with the F3 key and return to the Graphical Screen Painter. We still have to prepare the elements shown in Figure 2.19 for data output. What appears to be somewhat complicated is actually quite easy, because for data output we will use an existing **GUI Control** for the **SAP List Viewer** (ALV). Here it is sufficient to use the Screen Painter to define an area where the data is to be displayed.

In the left-hand bar choose the **Custom Control** icon (see Figure 2.29). You can now expand a frame in the screen area as large as you wish, as illustrated in the

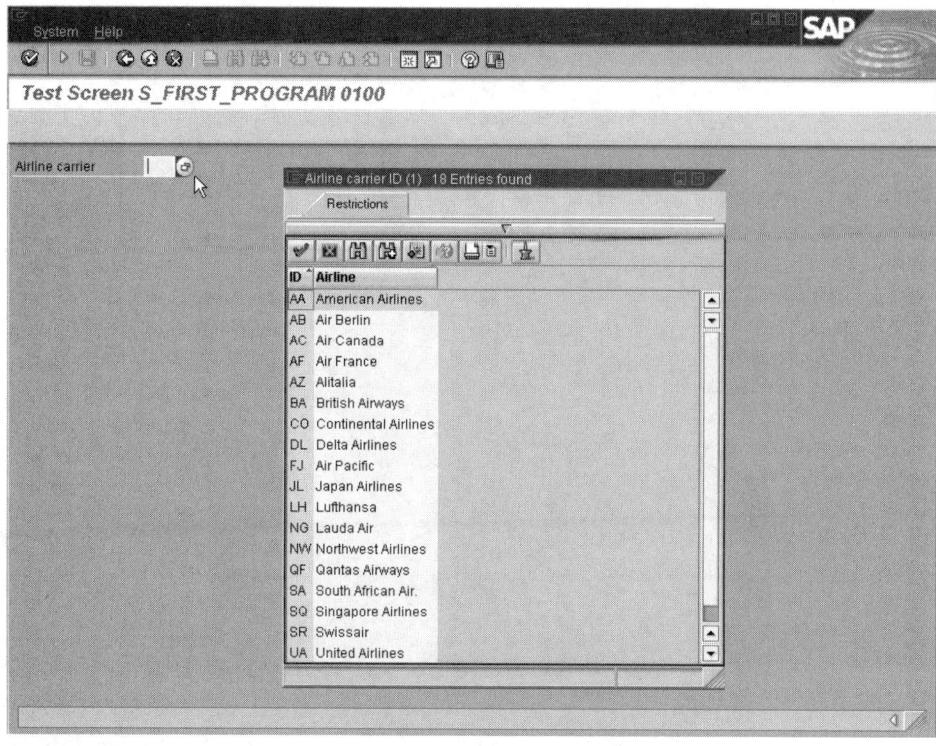

FIGURE 2.28 Testing the screen. Copyright © SAP AG

figure. A custom control is an empty area that can be filled by the ABAP program. Give the area the name "LIST_AREA" and save your work.

Object List

We have now fully defined our screen and can activate it for use in the ABAP program. To do this, choose the **Activate** symbol, confirm the dialog box that appears, and navigate back through the Screen Painter until you see the ABAP Editor again in the Object Navigator. Note that the **Screens** entry has now been added to the object list of our program. If this is not the case, choose **Refresh Object List** in the object list standard toolbar. If you select screen 100 in the object list, the Screen Painter will open again.

2.3.7 Dialog modules in the ABAP program

Before we can test our previous work we must first create the two dialog modules in the ABAP program that are called from the screen process logic. It would be equally possible to forward navigate by double-clicking on the module names in the Screen Painter process logic. However, we can also enter the dialog modules directly into our ABAP program and manually insert the statements for defining the two dialog modules below the processing block START-OF-SELECTION, as illustrated in Listing 2.6.

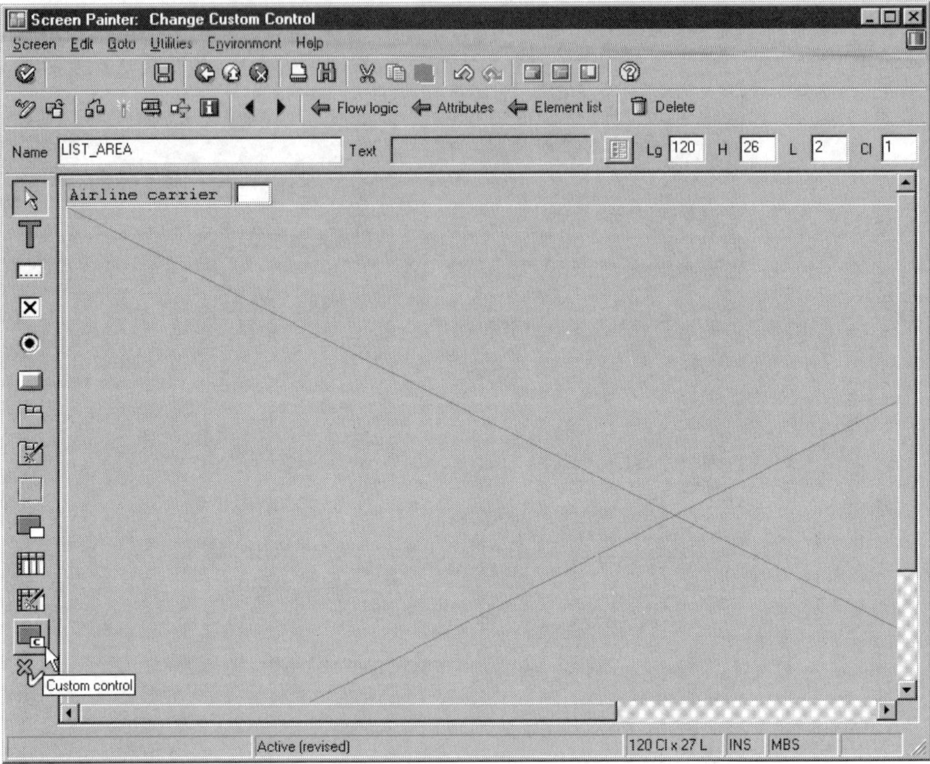

FIGURE 2.29 Custom Control. Copyright © SAP AG

LISTING 2.6 Creating dialog modules

```
* Event Block START-OF-SELECTION
START-OF-SELECTION.
  CALL SCREEN 100.

* Dialog Module PBO
MODULE status_0100 OUTPUT.
ENDMODULE.

* Dialog Module PAI
MODULE user_command_0100 INPUT.
ENDMODULE.
```

Our program is now syntactically perfect, ready to be activated and executed. However, if you do this (and this is a common beginner's error) the defined screen layout will be displayed, but you will not be able to exit it unless you close the entire window or enter a transaction code such as "/nse80" in the input box of the standard toolbar.

2.3.8 Working with the ABAP Debugger

To see what our program can do so far, we can run it in debugging mode. To do so, select **Execute – Debugging** in the program context menu. This starts the **ABAP Debugger** where we have the option of running the program line by line and stopping it if we find a semantic error (see Figure 2.30).

Single step

Initially, the program cursor is on the REPORT statement. If you select the single step icon or the F5 key it moves to the `CALL SCREEN` statement in the `START-OF-SELECTION` processing block. The next single step calls the screen, which takes us to the `status_0100` dialog module. Since no further statements are programmed there, our screen layout appears after the next single step (see Figure 2.31) and if you press *Enter* ↵ there, this takes us to the `user_statement_0100` dialog module.

The process now repeats itself. The next single step takes us back to the `status_0100` dialog module, and so on. We are in an endless loop. This is because we specified screen 100 itself as a follow-up screen in Figure 2.22. Once the screen has started, it continues calling itself up at the end of the PAI event.

However, in the ABAP Debugger we can interrupt the loop by choosing **Debugging – Off**. This returns us to the condition we were in before the Object Navigator was called, and we must start it again to continue working.

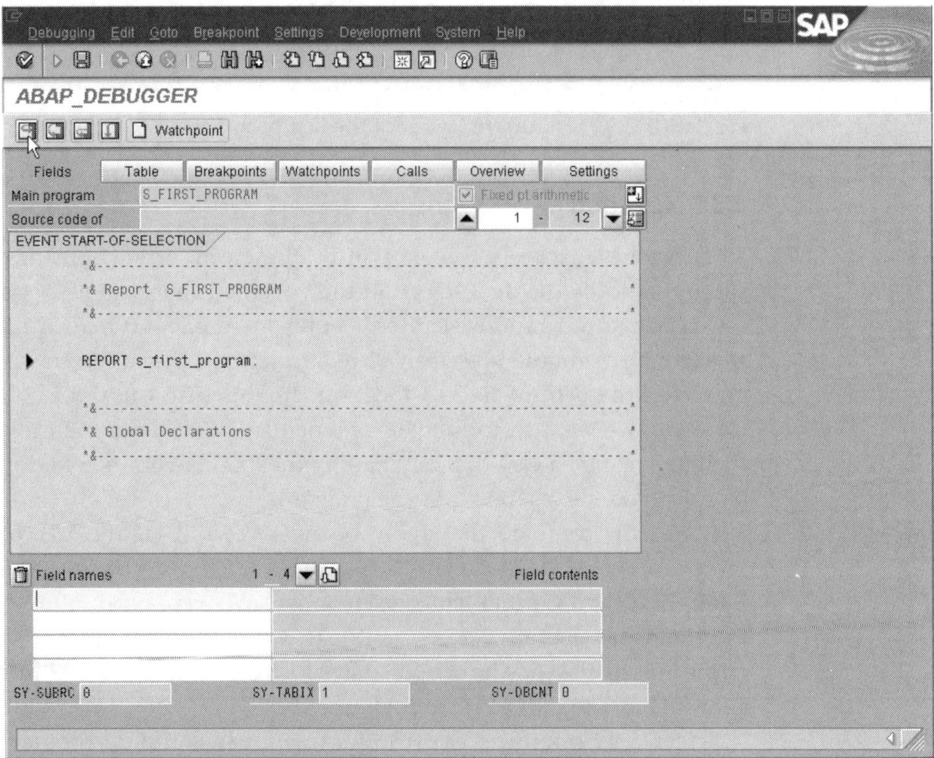

FIGURE 2.30 The ABAP Debugger. Copyright © SAP AG

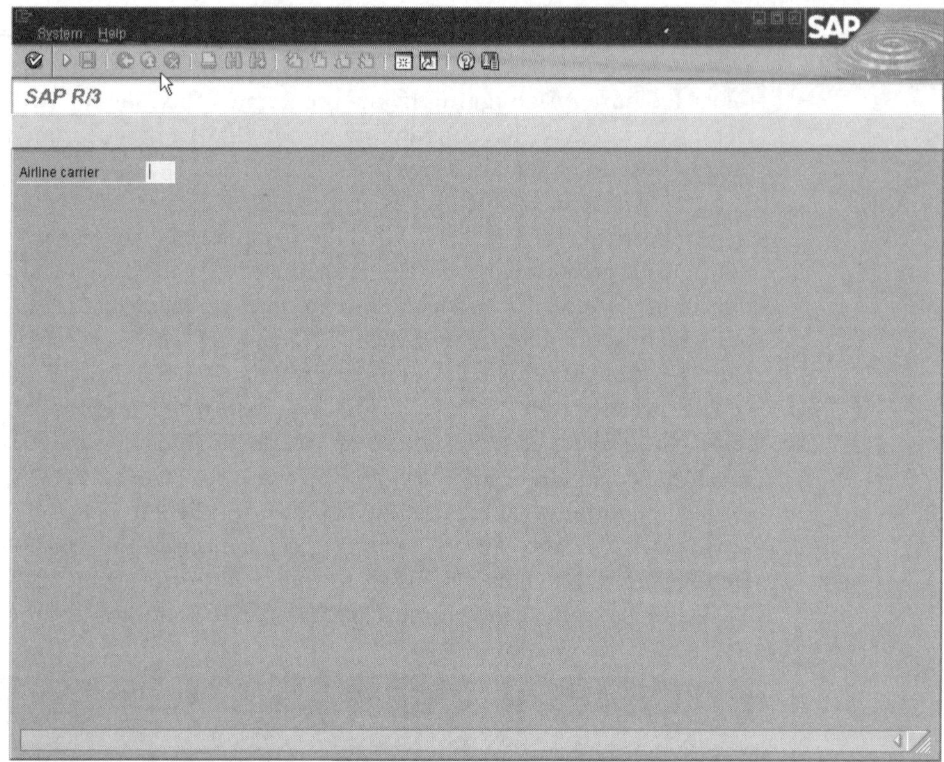

FIGURE 2.31 Current layout of the first program. Copyright © SAP AG

2.3.9 Creating a GUI status

So far we have lacked a way of exiting the screen. An obvious method would be to specify statically the next screen in the screen attributes. Since we only have a single screen in our program, we can only enter the number 0 here as the next screen. By specifying the follow-up screen 0 we ensure that after a screen's PAI event the program returns behind its call location, in this case the `CALL SCREEN` statement. However, we want to use the automatic display of our screen in the program and therefore require a way of programming the loop to end. In addition, the user should be able to decide when to quit the program.

User interface

If we now compare the layout of our screen in Figure 2.31 with the selection screen in Figure 2.17 and the list in Figure 2.18, we notice that in our screen the **Back**, **Exit**, and **Cancel** icons are inactive. We were given a pre-programmed user interface for selection screens and lists, which we do not have on the screens we create ourselves. We will therefore have to create a minimal user interface, which will allow the user to quit the screen.

PBO

Screen user interfaces consist of a menu bar, standard toolbar, and application toolbar. All these bars can exist as individual subobjects of an ABAP program and are grouped together in a **GUI status**. The GUI status of a screen is naturally set at the PBO event of the corresponding screen, and we will again use forward navigation to define a status for our screen. In dialog module status_0100 add the SET PF-STATUS statement, as shown in Listing 2.7.

LISTING 2.7 Setting a GUI status

```
* Dialog Module PBO
MODULE status_0100 OUTPUT.
  SET PF-STATUS 'SCREEN_100'.
ENDMODULE.
```

Double-click the SCREEN_100 literal and you will obtain the familiar dialog box for creating an object. Confirm this entry and maintain the attributes by entering a description under **Short text** and otherwise changing nothing (see Figure 2.32).

GUI status

After confirming your entry, the **Menu Painter** tool opens in the right-hand window of the Object Navigator. Open up the **Function key** bar here and write "BACK," "CANCEL," and "EXIT" over the appropriate icons in the standard toolbar (see Figure 2.33).

Function code

You have now defined **function codes** and linked them to three symbols on the standard toolbar. The symbols used here are incidentally linked to F3, ⇧ F3,

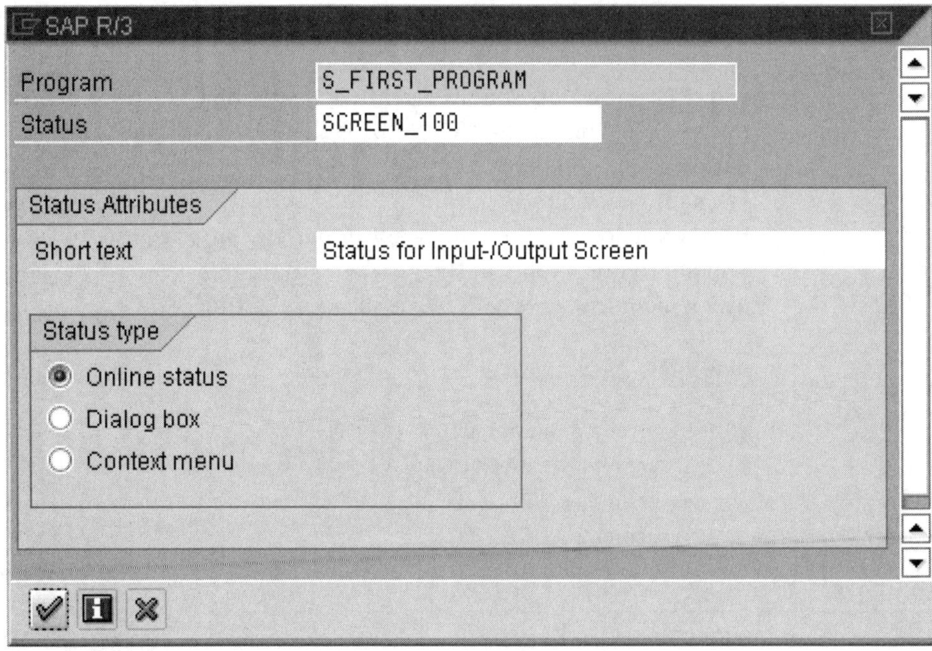

FIGURE 2.32 GUI status attributes. Copyright © SAP AG

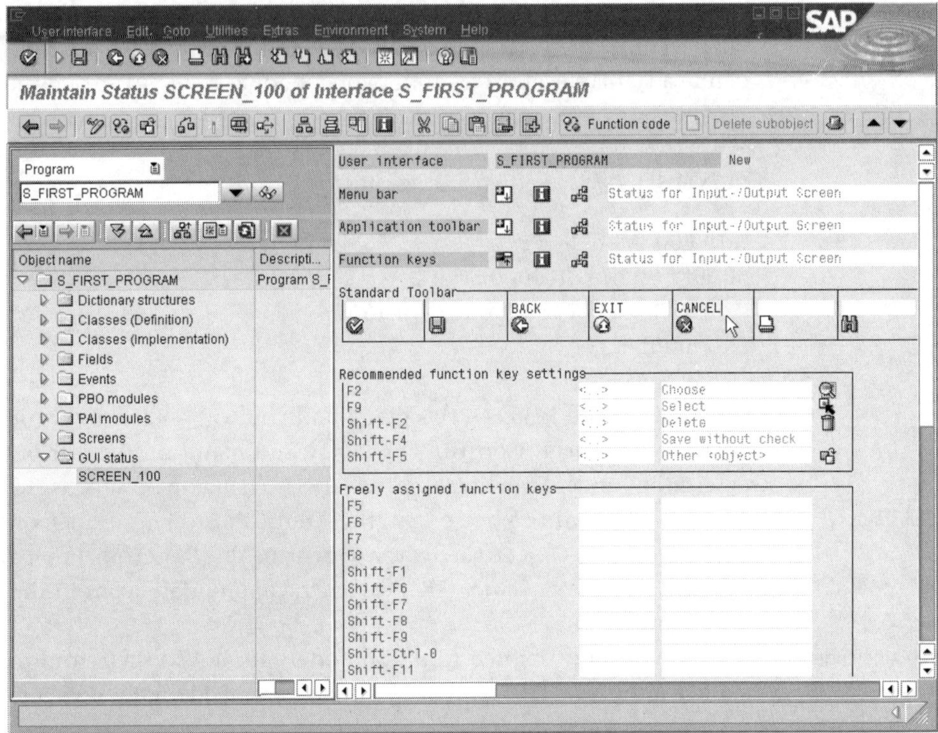

FIGURE 2.33 Defining function codes in the GUI status. Copyright © SAP AG

and **F12**. You now simply need to activate the GUI status and then navigate back to the ABAP Editor. The GUI status is then automatically copied to the object list of our program.

PAI

The three symbols will now be fully activated if you run or debug the program. However, choosing them does not terminate our screen loop because we do not yet respond to user inputs in the program. To do this we need the user_command_0100 dialog module that we will fill, as shown in Listing 2.8.

LISTING 2.8 Responding to user inputs

```
MODULE user_command_0100 INPUT.
  IF sy-ucomm = 'BACK' OR
     sy-ucomm = 'EXIT' OR
     sy-ucomm = 'CANCEL'.
     LEAVE PROGRAM.
  ENDIF.
ENDMODULE.
```

System field

Now test the program. If only *Enter* ↵ is entered on the layout, it will keep being called. However, if you select one of our three icons, the program will immediately stop running. The function code of the selected icons is provided in the sy-ucomm field for evaluation. In ABAP there is a whole range of these predefined **system fields** that start with sy-, are supplied with values from the ABAP runtime environment, and can be evaluated in the program.

Instead of the LEAVE PROGRAM statement you can also use the LEAVE TO SCREEN 0 statement. From what you have already learned about consecutive screens, it should be clear that this will also end the program. The program then returns behind CALL SCREEN and, since there are no more statements in the START-OF-SELECTION processing block, the program will end.

2.3.10 The data interface between the program and screen

Although we can now respond to user entries in the standard toolbar, our program still does not know which airline the user has entered in the layout input field. How does the ABAP program exchange data with its screens? An ABAP program communicates with its screens simply using global data, whereby the reference to individual screen fields is created by their having the same name. This is not particularly pretty, but unfortunately has developed this way historically. We therefore need to define a field in the global declaration part with the same name as our input field, SPFLI-CARRID. Furthermore, we have copied SPFLI-CARRID from the ABAP Dictionary. This means we also have to define the field of the same name in the ABAP program by copying it from the ABAP Dictionary. The relevant statement here is TABLES and we will add it to the global declaration part as shown in Listing 2.9.

LISTING 2.9 Global data as a screen interface

```
*&-----------------------------------------------------*
*& Global Declarations                                 *
*&-----------------------------------------------------*
* Screen Interfaces
TABLES spfli.
```

TABLES

The TABLES statement declares a local, structured field that has exactly the same structure as a line from the SPFLI database table. For our input field on the layout we need the spfli-carrid component of this structure.

Breakpoint

Now place the cursor in the ABAP Editor on the IF statement in the PAI module and choose **Utilities – Breakpoints – Set/Delete** or the stop sign. This will set a breakpoint for the ABAP Debugger. Execute the program from here, enter a value – e.g. "LH" – in the screen input field, and confirm using *Enter* ↵.

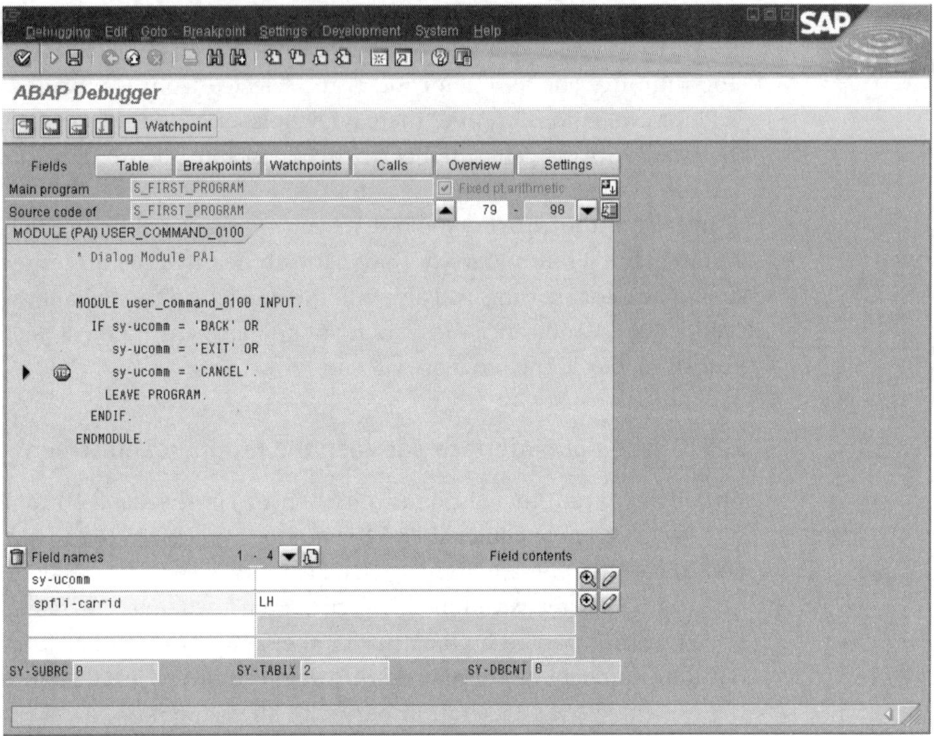

FIGURE 2.34 Breakpoint and field contents in the Debugger. Copyright © SAP AG

The program stops at the selected point in the Debugger. You can now enter fields of the ABAP program under **Field names** (you can also double-click a field name in the source code) and, after confirming using *Enter* ↵, view and even change its contents. In the situation shown in Figure 2.34 sy-ucomm is empty, and spfli-carrid contains the "LH" user input. If one of the active icons of our **GUI status** were selected in the corresponding function code, it could be viewed in sy-ucomm.

By selecting the **Continue** icon or the **F8** key, you can go from breakpoint to breakpoint in the Debugger, instead of in single steps. The Debugger has many other options for setting and deleting breakpoints. For example, double-clicking the IF statement in Figure 2.34 deletes the breakpoint again.

2.3.11 A classical main program

Our program has now reached a stage we can call a classical framework for our application. All the constructs we have so far introduced existed prior to ABAP Objects and will continue to exist alongside ABAP Objects. To distinguish these constructs from ABAP Objects constructs, we therefore use the attribute "classical." Our simple program can be considered a prototype for classical dialog programming. We have now prepared everything for programming the actual application, namely accessing the databases. At the START-OF-SELECTION we call up a classical screen, prepare it in a classical PBO dialog module, and can evaluate the user inputs in a classical PAI module.

Global data

Within a classical ABAP program, database access often takes place within the existing or an additional dialog module. This procedure has a serious disadvantage: although dialog modules are very useful for structuring the program, they do not have a local data area. **All** the fields we would need for data processing would have to be declared in the global data area of the ABAP program. You can imagine the difficulties this would create for large programs with a large number of screens and countless dialog modules. Every global field can be viewed and modified in any dialog module. If in addition the same fields are used repeatedly on different screens and in different dialog modules, the error margin increases dramatically.

2.3.12 Creating a class

In a classical ABAP program internal data encapsulation could only be achieved in subroutines. To avoid using global data we could therefore program our database access in a subroutine and call this from the PAI module. However, since the introduction of ABAP Objects with Release 4.5 we also have the option of defining local classes. We shall therefore use a class to encapsulate our application data and process it within the methods of the class. To do this, we shall create the application class, shown in Listing 2.10, in the global declaration part of our program behind the TABLES statement.

LISTING 2.10 Defining and implementing a class

```
* Class Definitions
CLASS application DEFINITION.
  PUBLIC SECTION.
    METHODS: read_data IMPORTING l_carrid TYPE spfli-carrid.
  PRIVATE SECTION.
    DATA spfli_tab TYPE TABLE OF spfli.
ENDCLASS.
* Class Implementations
CLASS application IMPLEMENTATION.
  METHOD read_data.
    SELECT *
    FROM   spfli
    INTO   TABLE spfli_tab
    WHERE  carrid = l_carrid.
  ENDMETHOD.
ENDCLASS.
```

A class is created in two sections, each between CLASS and ENDCLASS, whereby first its components are declared and then its methods are implemented. We define the encapsulation attributes of our class by defining visibility areas with the PUBLIC SECTION and PRIVATE SECTION statements. We start by declaring with METHODS a method called read_data, which can be viewed externally, and with DATA a data object called spfli_tab, which can only be viewed from within the class. The read_data method has an input parameter called l_carrid of the same type as spfli-carrid.

Data object

DATA is the most important statement for declaring fields in ABAP programs. Since DATA can be used to declare more than just elementary fields, we refer to the results of the DATA statement using the more general term **data objects**. In object-oriented programming it is common also to refer to data objects in classes as attributes of the class. Since we want to read several rows from the SPFLI database table, we use the addition TYPE TABLE OF to declare a table-like (that is, multi-row) data object or attribute, whose row type is taken from the definition of the SPFLI database table in the ABAP Dictionary. In ABAP, this kind of data object is called an internal table. Double-click spfli in the source code. The Object Navigator will open the definition of the SPFLI database table in the ABAP Dictionary (see Figure 2.35). Here we find the

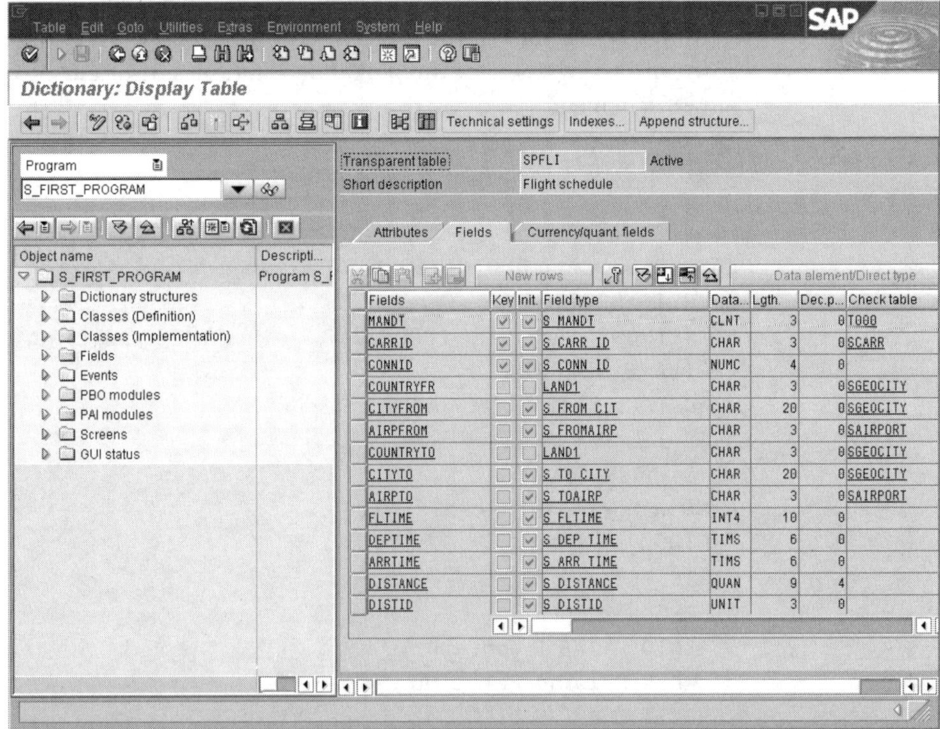

FIGURE 2.35 The SPFLI table in the ABAP Dictionary. Copyright © SAP AG

field names and data types of all the columns of this table. By using TYPE spfli in the DATA statement we ensure that the row types of the spfli_tab internal table and the SPFLI database table are identical.

Method

The functions of the read_data method are implemented between the METHOD and ENDMETHOD statements. In the method we access the database using a SELECT statement. SELECT is the ABAP statement that allows read access to all database tables defined in the ABAP Dictionary. With the statement shown in Listing 2.10 we import into our internal spfli_itab table all the columns (*) of the rows from the SPFLI database table in which the carrid field has the value of the l_carrid input parameter.

2.3.13 Working with objects

Before we can work with the application class we need to create an object of this class. In ABAP Objects, objects are addressed solely by **reference variables** (pointers). The object of our class should be available to both dialog modules in our program. For this reason we add the declaration of such a reference variable with the DATA statement behind the class in the global declaration part as shown in Listing 2.11.

LISTING 2.11 Declaring a reference variable

```
* Global Data
DATA object_ref TYPE REF TO application.
```

Reference

The object_ref variable is declared as a pointer for the application class. This means that it can point to objects of this class. We will now use the reference variable to create an instance of the application class and add the CREATE OBJECT statement, as shown in Listing 2.12, to the START-OF-SELECTION processing block.

LISTING 2.12 Creating an instance of a class

```
* Event Block START-OF-SELECTION
START-OF-SELECTION.
  CREATE OBJECT object_ref.
  CALL SCREEN 100.
```

Instantiation

The CREATE OBJECT statement creates an instance of the application class and the object_ref reference variable then points to this object. We can now use the reference variable to call the read_data method of the class and modify the PAI module, as shown in Listing 2.13.

LISTING 2.13 Calling a method

```
MODULE user_command_0100 INPUT.
  IF sy-ucomm = 'BACK' OR
     sy-ucomm = 'EXIT' OR
     sy-ucomm = 'CANCEL'.
    LEAVE PROGRAM.
  ELSE.
    CALL METHOD object_ref->read_data
         EXPORTING l_carrid = spfli-carrid.
  ENDIF.
ENDMODULE.
```

Unless the user selects one of the **Quit** symbols, the read_data method of the object pointing to object_ref will be called. We pass the input value of the user in the scarr-carrid field to the input parameter of l_carrid.

At this point it is time to check your work once more with the Debugger. Activate the program and start it in Debugging mode. Of interest here are the contents of the reference variable before and after the CREATE OBJECT statement is executed. Before the object is generated, the Debugger indicates the contents using "0<>" as a sign that the reference variable is pointing nowhere. However, when CREATE OBJECT is executed, it displays "5<APPLICATION>" to indicate that the reference variable is pointing to an object of the application class (the number 5 is an internal reference and may be different on your system).

Internal table

We are now interested in the contents of our spfli_tab internal table after the SELECT statement. Proceed in single steps (F5) until the instruction pointer is located after this statement, or choose **Breakpoint – Breakpoint at – Statement** in the Debugger and enter "SELECT." In the latter case you can use F8 to go directly to this statement. In either case, enter on screen an abbreviation for an airline. The internal table should be filled when the instruction pointer points to the ENDMETHOD statement behind the SELECT statement. Now choose the **Table** pushbutton in the Debugger, enter the name spfli_tab in the **Internal table** field, and confirm using *Enter* ↵. The Debugger now shows the contents of the internal table, which as expected contains a list of flights (see Figure 2.36).

2.3.14 Working with global classes

To complete the program we need to display the table contents on the layout of screen 100. As indicated, we will use global classes from the Class Library to do this. Unlike the local application class that we defined ourselves, global classes are independent repository objects that can be used in any ABAP program. To select their methods, you simply need to create a reference variable with a reference to this class and generate an instance of the class.

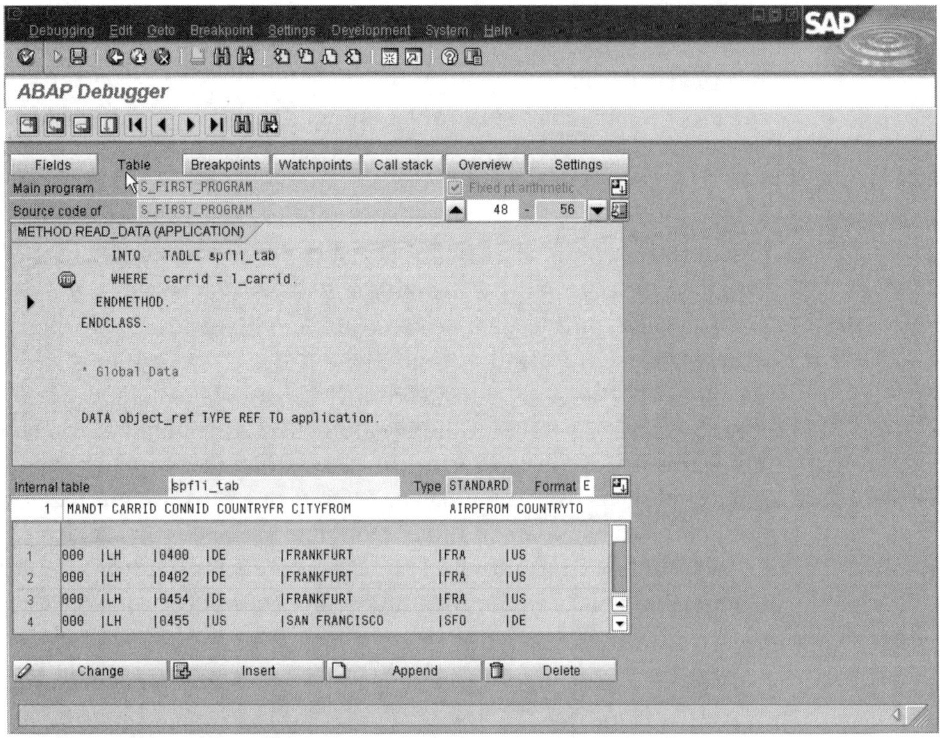

FIGURE 2.36 Internal table in the ABAP Debugger. Copyright © SAP AG

GUI control

To use the SAP List Viewer we need two global classes, CL_GUI_CUSTOM_CONTAINER and CL_GUI_ALV_GRID. The prefix CL_GUI_ indicates that both classes belong to the GUI component of the SAP Basis System. They are part of the **Control Framework**, which allows independent controls to be added to classical screens. Controls are software components of the SAP GUI, such as Text Editors or HTML Browsers. For each control provided by SAP GUI, the Control Framework contains a global class that can be used in an ABAP Program to address the GUI control.

We want to work with the SAP List Viewer control and therefore need the corresponding CL_GUI_ALV_GRID class. **Container Controls** are used to add controls to screens. We have already defined a custom control area with the Screen Painter on the layout of our screen (see Figure 2.29). The corresponding CL_GUI_CUSTOM_CONTAINER class acts as an interface to this control.

We want to work solely within our local class (application) with objects of both global classes. We therefore declare the respective reference variables as other private attributes of our local class (see Listing 2.14).

LISTING 2.14 Reference variables for global classes

```
PRIVATE SECTION.
  DATA: spfli_tab TYPE TABLE OF spfli,
        container TYPE REF TO cl_gui_custom_container,
        alv_list TYPE REF TO cl_gui_alv_grid.
```

Place the cursor on cl_gui_custom_container and double-click. The Object Navigator displays the class in the **Class Builder** tool (see Figure 2.37).

Class Builder

The **Class Builder** is used to create, modify, and display global classes. We can therefore use it to find out more about the classes we need. We can see that the CL_GUI_CUSTOM_CONTAINER class includes a public method called CONSTRUCTOR. If you are already familiar with object-oriented programming, you will rightly presume that this is the constructor of the class, which is automatically executed when an object of the class is instantiated. As users of a class, we must check whether its constructor has mandatory input parameters. To do this, place the cursor on the CONSTRUCTOR line and select the **Parameters** pushbutton. Double-clicking would automatically take you to the ABAP source code of the constructor. Figure 2.38 shows

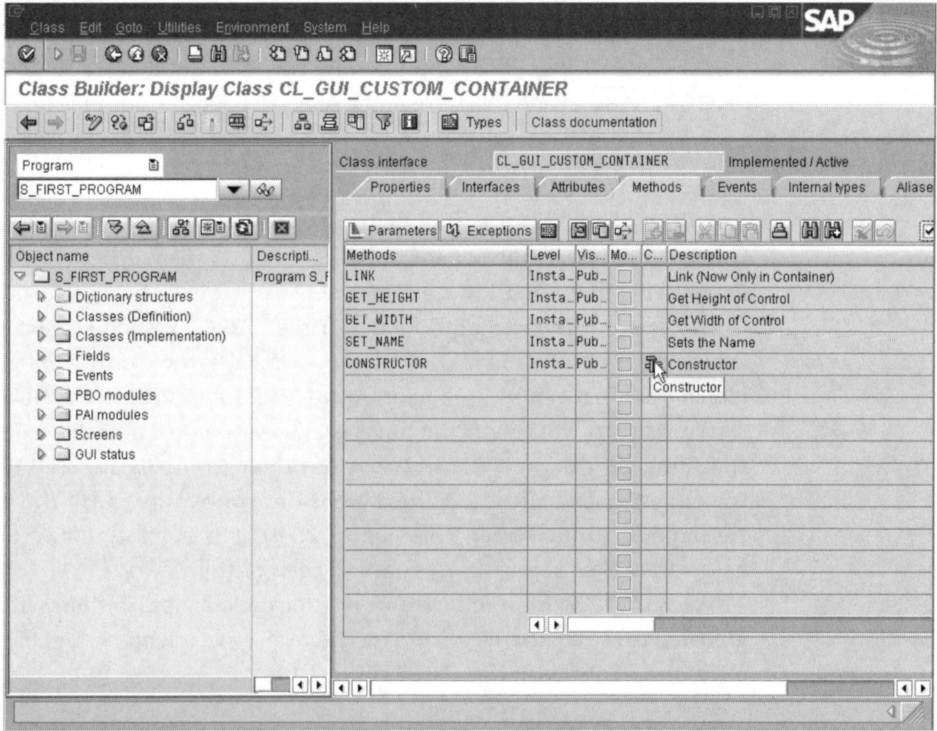

FIGURE 2.37 The Class Builder. Copyright © SAP AG

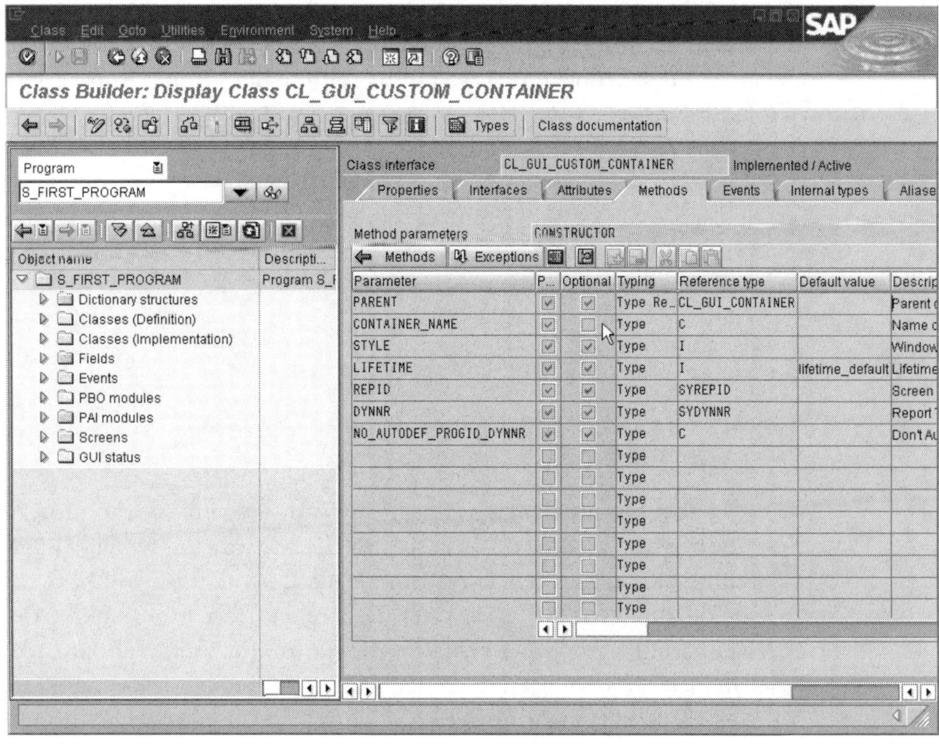

FIGURE 2.38 Constructor parameters. Copyright © SAP AG

that the constructor of the CL_GUI_CUSTOM_CONTAINER class has indeed a mandatory parameter called CONTAINER_NAME. We will have to assign this a value when we generate an instance.

We must now consider the point in our program at which we generate objects of both global classes. As we will require only a single object from each class, and this will need to be created only once, it would be expedient also to assign a constructor to our local application class. This constructor will then be run just once during `CREATE OBJECT object_ref`. As with the global class, the constructor in our local class must have the predefined name `constructor`. At the same time we shall provide another method, `fill_list`, which will write the data from the internal table to the ALV-Control. To do this, extend the `PUBLIC SECTION` of our class, as shown in Listing 2.15.

LISTING 2.15 Public methods of the local application class

```
PUBLIC SECTION.
  METHODS: constructor,
           read_data IMPORTING l_carrid TYPE scarr-carrid,
           fill_list.
```

As already mentioned, all methods have to be implemented. If you check the syntax in the current program status, you will find error messages. To free our program of syntax errors, you must add the lines from Listing 2.16 to the implementation section of our class.

LISTING 2.16 Implementing additional methods

```
METHOD constructor.
ENDMETHOD.

METHOD fill_list.
ENDMETHOD.
```

2.3.15 Final steps

Now that our program is syntactically correct again, we can program the implementation of the methods. We start with the constructor, which will generate objects of both global classes. We know from Figure 2.38 that we will have to enter a value for the CL_GUI_CUSTOM_CONTAINER class constructor. The simple CREATE OBJECT statement would produce a syntax error stating that the mandatory CONTAINER_NAME parameter has not been filled (try it out!). To find out how you fill this type of parameter, place the cursor in the ABAP Editor on the implementation of the constructor method, click the **Pattern** pushbutton and select **ABAP Objects patterns**. Fill the following dialog box as shown in Figure 2.39 and confirm it. In the **Instance** input field we have entered our local reference variable "CONTAINER" and "CL_GUI_CUSTOM_CONTAINER" for the class.

Statement pattern

The ABAP Workbench then generates the CREATE OBJECT statement, shown in Figure 2.40, for the CL_GUI_CUSTOM_CONTAINER class.

Constructor

The CREATE OBJECT statement has an addition called EXPORTING, which is used to fill the parameters of the constructor. All optional parameters are commented out. Only the non-optional CONTAINER_NAME parameter must be filled. Moreover, the EXCEPTIONS addition to the CREATE OBJECT statement allows exceptions to be handled – if an exception occurs, it passes the specified values to the system field, sy-subrc. However, in our first program we shall avoid this and modify the statement pattern as shown in Listing 2.17.

LISTING 2.17 Generating an object of a global class

```
METHOD constructor.
  CREATE OBJECT container
         EXPORTING container_name = 'LIST_AREA'.
ENDMETHOD.
```

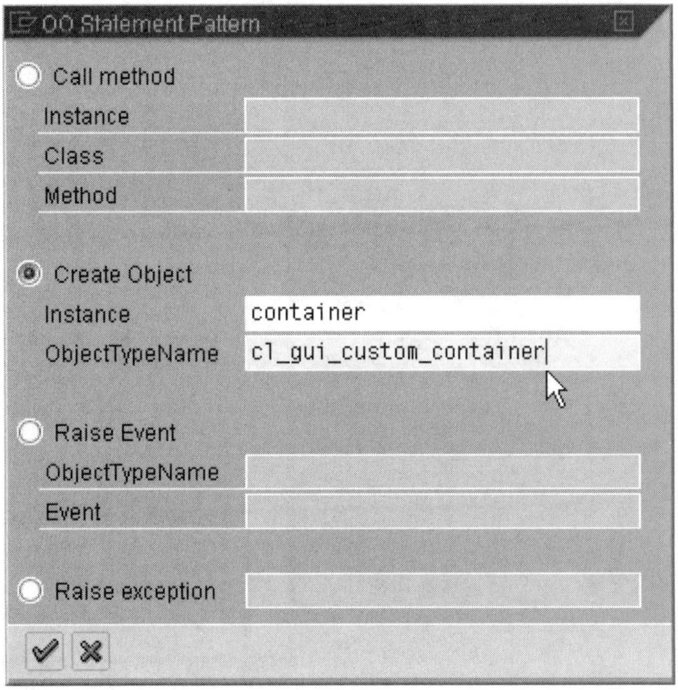

FIGURE 2.39 Generating a statement pattern. Copyright © SAP AG

We shall therefore pass the name of the Custom Control from our screen in Figure 2.29 to the CONTAINER_NAME parameter. This will link the Container Control to the screen area of our Custom Control. Next we have to create an object for the ALV Control. The latter also has a constructor, which requires an input parameter in order to link it with a Container Control. In addition, we must tell the ALV Control what line structure the displayed list should have and where its data is coming from. In the CL_GUI_ALV_GRID class this does not happen through the constructor; instead it provides a different method. To find out more about this, you can navigate to the **Class Builder** and view the documentation of this class. For the time being we will simply introduce the complete constructor of our local class in Listing 2.18.

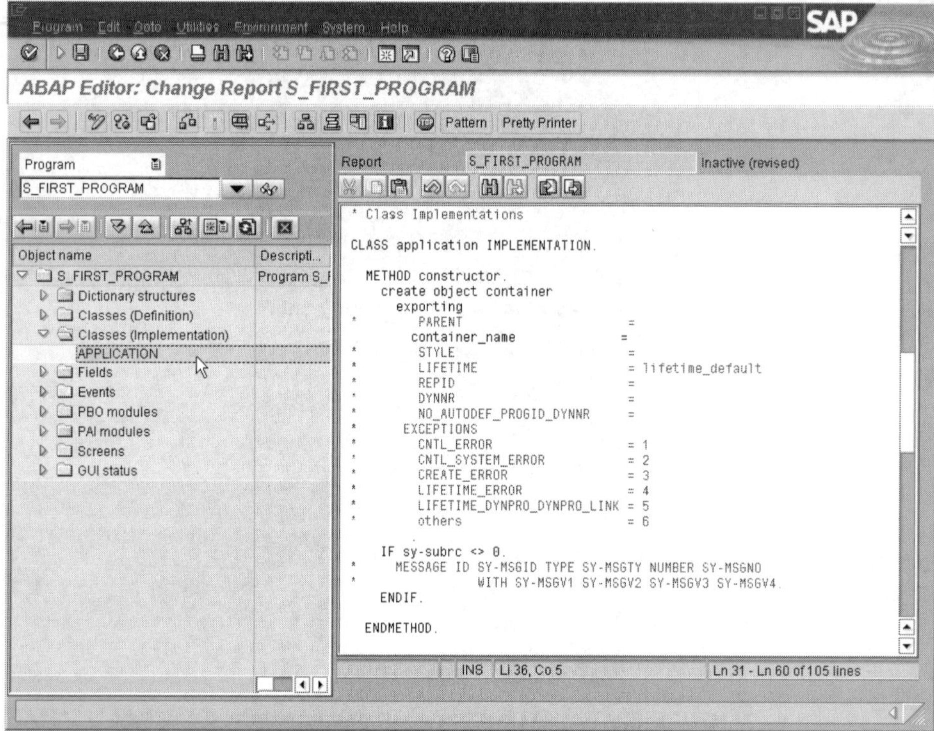

FIGURE 2.40 Statement pattern for CREATE OBJECT. Copyright © SAP AG

LISTING 2.18 Complete constructor of the local class

```
METHOD constructor.
  CREATE OBJECT container
         EXPORTING container_name = 'LIST_AREA'.
  CREATE OBJECT alv_list
         EXPORTING i_parent = container.
  CALL METHOD alv_list->set_table_for_first_display
        EXPORTING i_structure_name = 'SPFLI'
        CHANGING  it_outtab = spfli_tab.
ENDMETHOD.
```

With the second CREATE OBJECT statement, the object for the ALV Control is generated and supplied with the reference to the container object that is linked to the LIST_AREA section of the screen. Calling the set_table_for_first_display method structures the list in accordance with the SPFLI database table and links it with the internal spfli_tab table.

ALV Control

All we need to do now is transfer the data of the internal spfli_tab table to the ALV Control. The best time for this is at the PBO event, i.e. just before the screen is displayed. We call the fill_list method of our local class in the corresponding dialog module (see Listing 2.19).

LISTING 2.19 Calling the fill_list method

```
MODULE status_0100 OUTPUT.
  SET PF-STATUS 'SCREEN_100'.
  CALL METHOD object_ref->fill_list.
ENDMODULE.
```

So far the fill_list method has had no function. We add the method call shown in Listing 2.20.

LISTING 2.20 Implementing the fill_list method

```
METHOD fill_list.
  CALL METHOD alv_list->refresh_table_display.
ENDMETHOD.
```

And that's it! If you now activate and run the program, it will perform the functions indicated in Figure 2.19. Our screen loop allows the user to select new airlines and view the flights in the ALV Control until he or she quits the program. You can also test the functions in the application toolbar above the list. This provides you with all the SAP List Viewer functions.

Test the program extensively. Debug it step by step and look at the contents of the individual fields. Experiment with the Workbench functions. In creating the program many nodes have been added to our object list. Choose the object list nodes by double-clicking them or by using the right mouse key and see what happens. Accustom yourself to forward navigation by choosing source code items, and reverse navigation by using the corresponding arrow keys.

You should now have a sufficient basic understanding of the ABAP Workbench to draw on in the following chapters. The complete source code of the program and all the example programs are available in the Basis system on the enclosed CD and for download from the it-minds website (www.it-minds.com).

2.3.16 Resources

We have used many keywords in our first program without having explained them in detail. In most cases, the function of an ABAP keyword is implied by its name. You are probably already familiar with other constructs such as IF-ENDIF from other programming languages. Over the following chapters we will expand on the concepts that we have used in our first program and systematically explain the key ABAP statements.

ABAP keyword documentation

However, if you wish to gain a clearer picture of the function of individual keywords straightaway, you can call up the ABAP keyword documentation. This documentation is available throughout all phases of program development and you can best obtain it by placing the cursor on a keyword in ABAP Editor, for example `CLASS`, and then pressing the **F1** key.

The ABAP keyword documentation display window shown in Figure 2.41 shows a navigation tree[7] on the left-hand side. This contains all the ABAP keywords in order of subject. The right-hand side contains the corresponding help text. While navigating between the help texts the cursor automatically positions itself on the appropriate nodes. The display window not only provides various search options but also allows you to create an offline version of the ABAP keywords in HTML format.

Apart from the ABAP keyword documentation, which is primarily intended for immediate help during program development, the SAP System also offers an extended ABAP help that places more emphasis on an introduction to design. You can obtain this extended help by clicking, for example, on the Example Library picture in the display window of the ABAP keyword documentation.

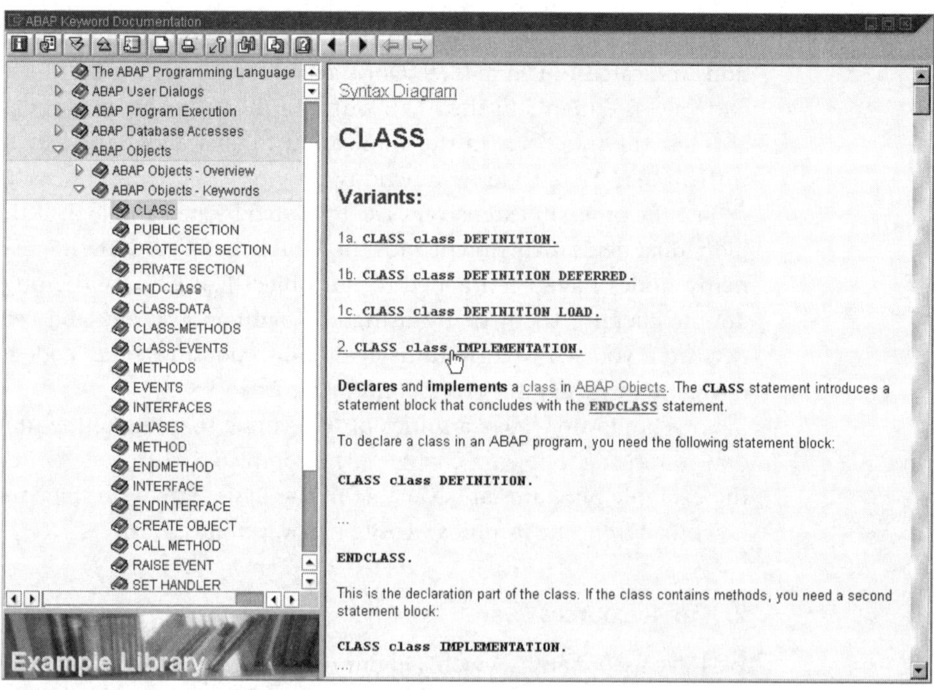

FIGURE 2.41 The ABAP keyword documentation. Copyright © SAP AG

7. As of Release 4.6C.

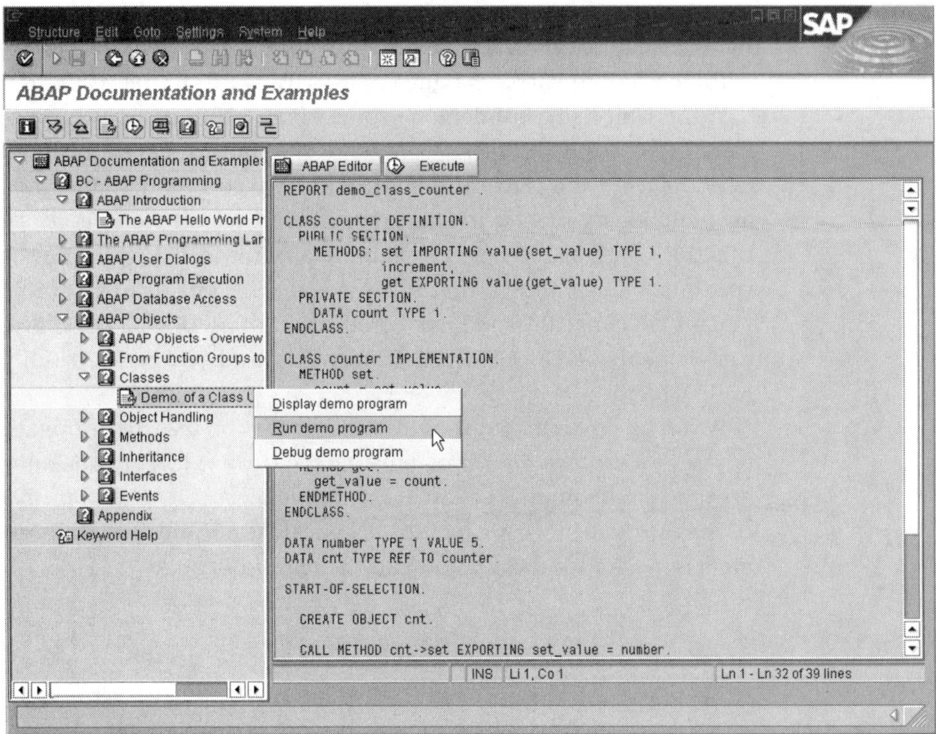

FIGURE 2.42 The ABAP documentation and Example Library. Copyright © SAP AG

ABAP Example Library

The book icons in the Example Library represent chapters of the extended help. The other icons represent a complete collection of the example programs from the extended help (see Figure 2.42). You can display, directly execute, or debug the example programs. As in our introduction, you can follow the path from "Hello World!" to ABAP Objects. As you read the book, we recommend making full use of this opportunity to put the theory into practice.

2.3.17 Final comments on the practical introduction

If you have followed us so far in our practical introduction you will already have learned much about ABAP. In addition to working with the ABAP Workbench and Debugger you will know:

- the syntax of ABAP
- that ABAP programs can be divided into modular units
- the various types of screens
- how to create local classes and generate objects.

In creating our first program we also took you through the history of ABAP. While items such as selection screens and lists were already used in the R/2 system, it is only with Release 4.6 that we can use controls using ABAP Objects on front ends.

ABAP Objects has undergone some major changes since the first release. As you can already see with our first program, the transformation is not yet complete. The development from classical ABAP to ABAP Objects is not a metamorphosis but rather an evolutionary process in which the old exists alongside the new, maintains its full functions and, as seen in the example of screens, is still in use today. This has the considerable advantage that hundreds of millions of lines of live ABAP code can remain unchanged despite the introduction of ABAP Objects. Classical programs can use elements of ABAP Objects if necessary and can partly or fully change over to ABAP Objects.

As far as possible, we should of course try to use the innovations of the latest releases for creating new programs. At the current level this is only possible in pure backend programming, i.e. excluding user dialogs. Therefore, in a book entitled *ABAP Objects* we still need to include classical ABAP and describe both programming models in parallel, the classical and the object-oriented.

CHAPTER 3

Basics of ABAP programming

As of Release 4.5 ABAP has become a hybrid programming language, which allows for both procedural and object-oriented programming. However, the runtime environment in which an ABAP program operates remains the same. Knowing how this runtime environment operates, how ABAP programs are structured, and what exactly happens when an ABAP program is run will help us ultimately to understand the procedural and object-oriented programming models. Join us as we take a look behind the scenes of the ABAP runtime environment.

3.1 THE ENVIRONMENT OF AN ABAP PROGRAM

The aim of this section is to provide you with an overview of the hardware and software landscape in which your ABAP programs operate. At first sight they appear to operate nowhere in particular within the SAP System and provide you with feedback on the screen layout. However, you will see that there is considerably more to it than meets the eye. When you have finished this section you will know where your ABAP programs operate and which components of the SAP System are involved. In the process, you will learn many new terms and concepts, which will help you gain a deeper understanding of an ABAP program within the SAP System.

3.1.1 The architecture of an SAP System

Every SAP System is based on a three-layer client–server architecture comprising a presentation, an application, and a database layer (see Figure 3.1). Because each of these layers is represented by its own software component, we often speak of a software-oriented client–server principle in this context. With this architectural configuration the overall system can be distributed among a range of computers or alternatively can operate on just one computer.[1] A number of scenarios are possible, both vertically (layers) and horizontally (components). A common configuration in practice is where the database system and one of the application servers, which provides special services for the database, run concurrently on a single computer. All the other application servers run on their own computers. The presentation layer components run mainly on the individual users' desktop computers.

Software layers

Each of the layers shown in Figure 3.1 plays a different role in the overall system, which we will now describe briefly.

Presentation layer

If you are sitting in front of a workstation and can see an SAP screen, it is the presentation layer that has generated this for you. The SAP GUI software components ensure that the SAP System user interface is shown and that the user's keyboard inputs and mouse clicks are recorded and passed to the application layer.

Application layer

The application layer is where an ABAP program carries out its work. The software components of the application layer consist of one or more application servers and a

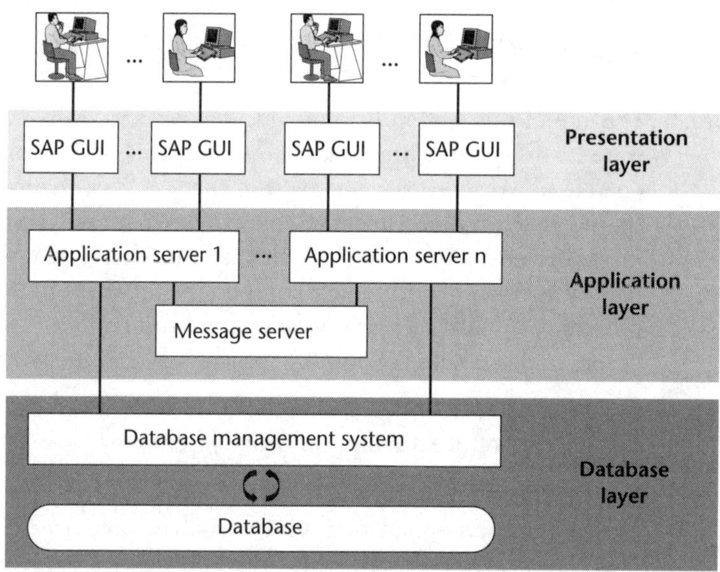

FIGURE 3.1 The client–server architecture of an SAP System

1. This should not happen often in a live SAP environment; however, from a technical viewpoint it is entirely feasible.

message server, responsible for communication between the application servers. Each application server provides a range of services for the operation of the SAP System. The application server's services are technically carried out by work processes, the number and type of which are predefined at the start of the SAP System. Work processes are components that are able to execute an application. An important point is that each work process is registered as a user in the database system for the entire runtime of an SAP System. During the system runtime, a database registration cannot be transferred from one work process to another.

In theory, you only need one application server to operate an SAP System. In practice, the services are usually divided among several application servers so that not all services are available to each application server. Each ABAP program is executed on an application server. It depends on the services of the application server as to where a program is actually executed. A program with user dialogs requires dialog services that a background-processing program does not.

Database layer

Each SAP System has a central database in which the **entire** dataset is stored. This means that not only the application data but also all the administration data, customizing settings, ABAP source code, etc. are stored here. The software component responsible for the database layer consists of the RDBMS (Relational Database Management System) and the actual database.

The most important aspect of Figure 3.1 for us as programmers is that the application layer lies between the presentation and database layers and that the individual application servers communicate with the SAP GUI and the database management system via network links. This clearly defines the role of ABAP programs in the SAP System client–server architecture: the fundamental task of ABAP programs is to process data from the database in a user-driven manner. They receive their inputs from the presentation layer and work with data in the database layer. There are of course many more interfaces and extensions to this picture, an exploration of which lies outside the remit of this book.

3.2 ABAP PROGRAMS IN THE CLIENT–SERVER ARCHITECTURE

The software layers shown in Figure 3.1 should be a matter of covering old ground for you. We now want to investigate more closely the effect this architecture has on the way ABAP programs are structured and executed. We shall first refine the picture by considering the SAP Basis System and then introduce a generalization with the concept of the ABAP runtime environment, which will be fully sufficient for an understanding of ABAP programming.

3.2.1 The SAP Basis System

This section provides a logical introduction to the execution of ABAP programs without concentrating on the technical details of the application servers and their work processes. To do this, we must first consider the SAP Basis System. As the BC component, the SAP Basis System is part of every SAP System. It is the central platform for all SAP applications written in ABAP. Figure 3.2 shows the logical components of the SAP Basis System in the client–server architecture of the SAP System.

Basis System Components

The SAP Basis System consists mainly of the following logical components:

- The **presentation components** are used for the interaction between ABAP programs and the user.
- The **ABAP Workbench** component is a fully fledged development environment for ABAP programs. It is fully integrated within the SAP Basis System and, like other SAP applications, is itself written in ABAP.
- The **kernel** component acts as a platform for all ABAP programs independently of hardware, operating system, and database. This runtime environment is mainly written in C/C++. All ABAP programs run on software processors (virtual machines (VMs)) within this component.

  Basis services administer user and processes, prepare a database interface, provide communication interfaces with other (SAP) systems, and assist in the administration of the SAP System.

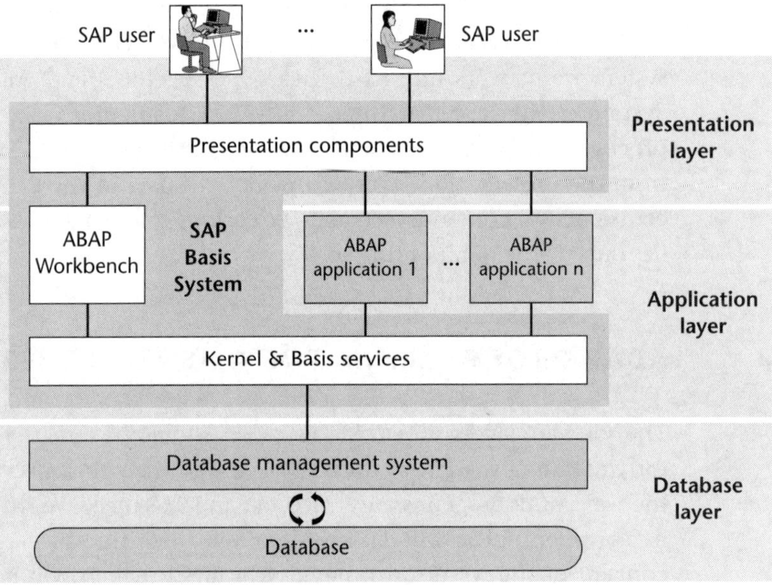

FIGURE 3.2 The SAP Basis System

All SAP application programs written in ABAP are embedded in the SAP Basis System. This makes them independent of whichever hardware and operating system you are using. However, it also means that you cannot run them outside the SAP Basis System. Figure 3.2 also shows that the SAP Basis System acts as an intermediary for the communication between the ABAP applications and the users on the one hand and the database system on the other.

3.2.2 The ABAP runtime environment

We can now simplify the picture by going from Figure 3.2 to Figure 3.3 and say that every ABAP program is encapsulated in a runtime environment provided by the SAP Basis System.

The runtime environment represents the highest controlling instance for an ABAP program. No ABAP program could run without it. It is responsible for the flow control of dialog sequences, takes care of the communication with the SAP System database, and is in particular responsible for the time sequence of an ABAP program.

Figure 3.3 is therefore of particular importance for ABAP programming as a whole. We have also indicated in Figure 3.3 that ABAP programs are comprised of processing blocks, which we will now discuss in further detail.

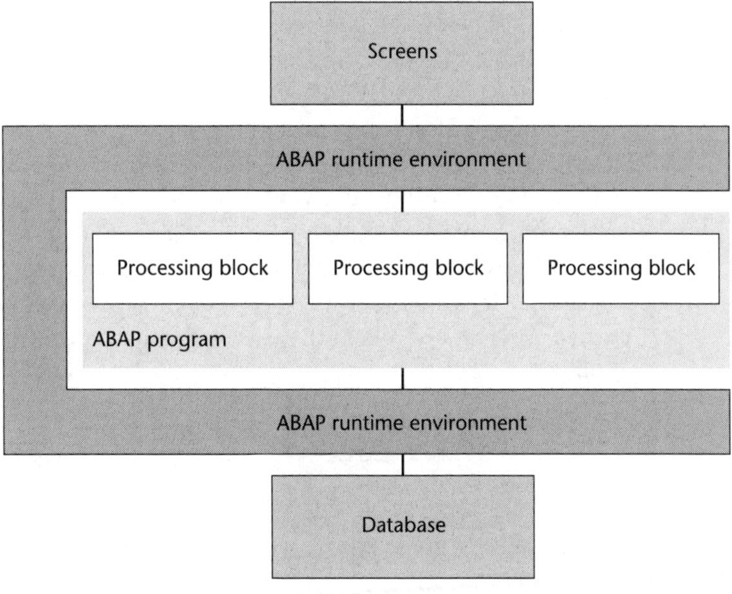

FIGURE 3.3 The ABAP runtime environment

3.3 ABAP PROGRAMS IN THE RUNTIME ENVIRONMENT

In this section we will consider how ABAP programs are structured and executed in the runtime environment. This section is essential for understanding existing programs and creating new ones.

3.3.1 ABAP program structure

To understand how an ABAP program runs and the role the runtime environment plays, we must start with the basic structure of an ABAP program, as indicated in Figure 3.4.

Declaration part

Each ABAP program consists of a global declaration part and a number of processing blocks that can play a variety of roles, depending on the application. The global objects are mainly data declarations that are visible in all processing blocks of the ABAP program. In some processing blocks local data can be declared that can then only be viewed locally, i.e. in the corresponding processing block.

Processing block

Processing blocks are indivisible syntax units. A processing block cannot include another processing block. They are called either by the runtime environment or by specific statements in other processing blocks, either internally or externally from another program. The first processing block of a program must therefore always be called by the runtime environment or from a processing block of another program. When the first processing block is called the entire program is loaded into the memory.

Call

Figure 3.5 shows how processing blocks are called. The runtime environment starts processing block 1 in ABAP program 1. This calls processing block 2 in the same program and processing block 3 in ABAP program 2. Processing block 3 calls processing block 4 in its own program. If you are already familiar with ABAP, you can interpret processing block 1 as the `START-OF-SELECTION` event block or as a dialog module. Processing block 3 is then typically a function module or, in ABAP Objects, a method of a global class. Processing blocks 2 and 4 can be local subroutines or methods of local classes.

Sequence

The order of the processing blocks in the programming code is totally irrelevant to the sequence in which they are executed. Only the code within a processing block is executed sequentially. When the execution of a processing block is finished, control is returned to its caller.

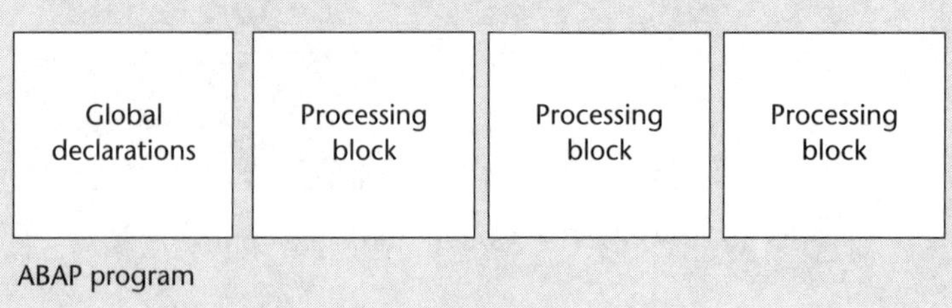

FIGURE 3.4 The structure of an ABAP program

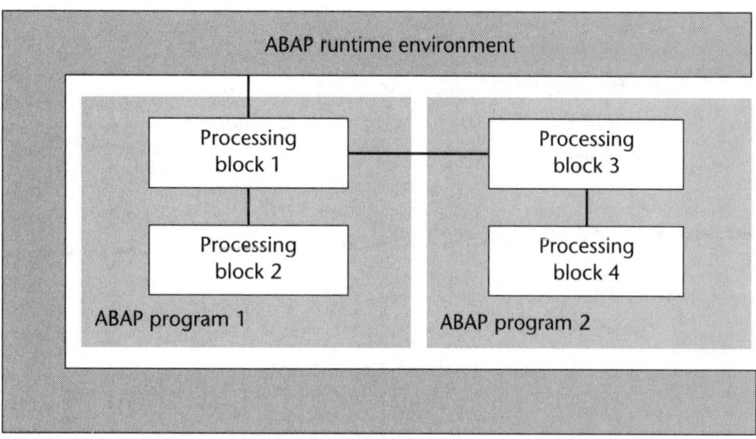

FIGURE 3.5 Calling processing blocks

Ending

The execution of a processing block can be ended in one of two ways. It can either end when the last statement of the processing block has been executed, or you can program the system to quit a processing block using the `CHECK` and `EXIT` statements with or without conditions. On each termination, control is returned to the caller of the processing block, i.e. either the runtime environment or the calling processing block. However, you should note that within loops (see Section 4.4.2), `CHECK` and `EXIT` affect only the current loop processing.[2]

Statements

All valid statements of an ABAP program that are not part of global data declarations belong definitively to a processing block. You can only read and understand an ABAP program if you are able to identify the various processing blocks and if you know at what point they will be executed. Before going into further details of individual processing blocks, let's consider the program in Listing 3.1.

LISTING 3.1 Which processing blocks are included in the ABAP program?

```
REPORT s_processing_blocks.
DATA: wa_spfli TYPE spfli,
      wa_sflight TYPE sflight.
SELECT SINGLE *
FROM   spfli
INTO   wa_spfli
WHERE  carrid = 'LH' AND
       connid = '0400'.
```

2. As of Release 6.10 there is a statement `RETURN` which always quits the processing block independent of the context.

```
PERFORM output USING wa_spfli.

FORM output USING l_spfli TYPE spfli.
  WRITE:  / l_spfli-cityfrom, l_spfli-cityto.
ENDFORM.

AT LINE-SELECTION.
  SELECT *
  FROM   sflight
  INTO   wa_sflight
  WHERE  carrid = 'LH' AND
         connid = '0400'.
    WRITE: / wa_sflight-fldate,
             wa_sflight-seatsmax,
             wa_sflight-seatsocc.
  ENDSELECT.
```

Do you recognize all the processing blocks? The FORM–ENDFORM block and the statements behind AT LINE-SELECTION are relatively easy to identify. However, where do the first SELECT statement and PERFORM belong? Set a breakpoint at the SELECT statement, start the program, and in the ABAP Debugger select *Overview* (see Figure 3.6).

In the lower part of the screen you will see a list of all the processing blocks of the ABAP program and a marker indicating the processing block to which the current statement belongs. The SELECT statement therefore belongs to the START-OF-SELECTION event block. The START-OF-SELECTION processing block is the standard processing block of an ABAP program to which all ABAP statements are assigned that are not part of the global declaration part and that precede the first specifically defined processing block. The SELECT–ENDSELECT statement block is actually a normal loop, which is processed iteratively, not a processing block.

Dead code

It should be noted, however, that statements between or after terminated processing blocks (in Listing 3.1 this would be between ENDFORM and AT LINE-SELECTION) are invalid and are never executed. This type of dead code is reported by the syntax check.

The two DATA statements in Listing 3.1 form the global data declaration part of the ABAP program. Their position in the program is not predefined syntactically. All declaration statements of a program that are not contained within processing blocks, that can store local data, are part of the global declaration part. However, a data declaration is not visible before the corresponding program line. We strongly recommend that you list all global data declarations at the start of the program before the first processing block.

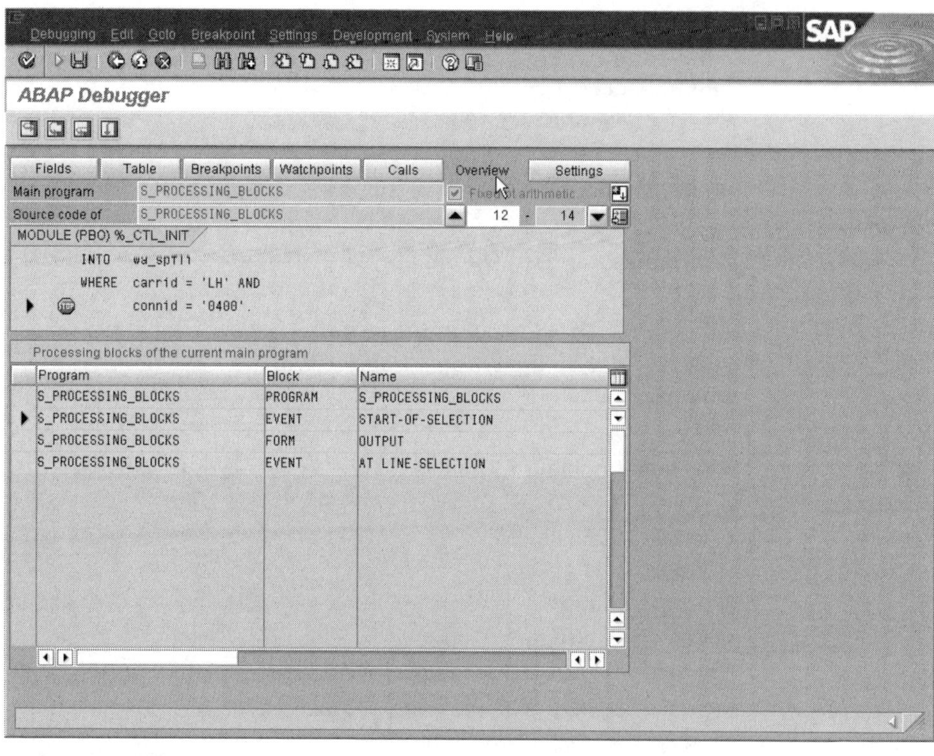

FIGURE 3.6 Processing blocks in the Debugger. Copyright © SAP AG

LISTING 3.2 Identifying processing blocks

```
*&---------------------------------------------------------------------*
*& Report  S_PROCESSING_BLOCKS_COMPLETE                                *
*&---------------------------------------------------------------------*

REPORT s_processing_blocks_complete.

* Global Data Declarations ----------------------------------------

DATA: wa_spfli TYPE spfli,
      wa_sflight TYPE sflight.

* Standard event ----------------------------------------------------

START-OF-SELECTION.
  SELECT SINGLE *
```

```
  FROM    spfli
  INTO    wa_spfli
  WHERE   carrid = 'LH' AND
          connid = '0400'.

  PERFORM output USING wa_spfli.

* Subroutine for List Output ---------------------------------------

FORM output USING l_spfli TYPE spfli.
  WRITE:  / l_spfli-cityfrom, l_spfli-cityto.
ENDFORM.

* Reaction on Mouse Double-click ---------------------------------

AT LINE-SELECTION.
  SELECT *
  FROM    sflight
  INTO    wa_sflight
  WHERE   carrid = 'LH' AND
          connid = '0400'.
    WRITE: / wa_sflight-fldate,
             wa_sflight-seatsmax,
             wa_sflight-seatsocc.
  ENDSELECT.

* End of Program ---------------------------------------------------
```

In Listing 3.2 we have completed the program from Listing 3.1 by adding the missing `START-OF-SELECTION` statement. We have also marked the boundaries of the individual processing blocks with comment lines. The program has exactly the same functionality and maintains this even if you change the order of the processing blocks in the program, for example by copying the `AT LINE-SELECTION` block before `START-OF-SELECTION` or before the `FORM` statement. Try this out.

Identification

If you are creating new programs you should not use the syntactical freedom of ABAP but identify all the processing blocks with comments and avoid standard mechanisms such as collecting non-assigned statements into the standard processing block. This enables the reader to compare the source code of the program and the structure from Figure 3.4 more easily.

3.3.2 Processing blocks

We will now introduce all the processing blocks that are possible in ABAP programs. We shall briefly explain the statements that define the processing blocks, how they are called, whether they can keep local data, and the ABAP programs in which they can be defined. As you will soon see, there is a wide variety of ABAP program types. The main differences between these types are in the way the program's processing blocks are called from the runtime environment and which processing blocks are possible within a program.

There are three types of processing block, which differ from each other in terms of their specific characteristics: event blocks, dialog modules, and procedures. In later chapters we will discuss in greater detail the exact use of the processing blocks in the context of their subject.

Event blocks

Event blocks are introduced by *event keywords*. They are ended implicitly by the next processing block or the end of the program as opposed to specifically by their own keyword. You should always mark the end of an event block in the program with a comment line. Event blocks have no local data area. A data declaration in an event block is added to the global data.

Runtime events

The execution of an event block is triggered by events in the ABAP runtime environment. If an appropriate event block is implemented in the ABAP program for an event of the runtime environment, the event block will be executed. Otherwise the event has no effect. Conversely, event blocks will not be executed in an ABAP program unless the associated event takes place while the program is being executed. A typical example is `AT LINE-SELECTION` in the above example program. As long as the user does not double-click on the list output, this event block will not be executed.

We will now introduce the various types of event blocks.

Program constructor event

Event keyword:

```
LOAD-OF-PROGRAM.
```

The corresponding event is triggered just once during the execution of the program: when the ABAP program is loaded into the memory. This applies to all program types except class pools. The statements in this block allow you to initialize the data of the program. The program constructor is therefore similar to the constructor of a class in object-oriented programming.

Reporting events

Event keywords:

```
INITIALIZATION.
START-OF-SELECTION.
GET table.
GET table LATE.
END-OF-SELECTION.
```

The corresponding events are triggered only when an executable program is running. Here, the START-OF-SELECTION event plays a leading role as the standard event. This means that all statements that have not been specifically assigned to another event block are automatically inserted at the beginning of the START-OF-SELECTION event block and executed with it. All other reporting events are designed for implementing special application logic, which occurs in executable programs if they are linked to logical databases. For more details see Section 3.3.5.

Selection screen events

Event keyword:

```
AT SELECTION-SCREEN ...
```

The corresponding events are triggered by the runtime environment when a selection screen is processed in executable programs, module pools, or function groups. Selection screens can be prepared and user actions evaluated in the event blocks. For more details see Section 7.2.5.

List events

Event keywords:

```
TOP-OF-PAGE.
END-OF-PAGE.
AT LINE-SELECTION.
AT USER-COMMAND.
```

The corresponding events are triggered by the runtime environment in executable programs, module pools, or function groups while a classical list is being generated or if the user performs an action on the displayed list. The statements in these blocks can format the list or process the user's requests. For more details see Section 7.3.7.

Screen events

These event blocks are defined in the screen flow logic as opposed to the ABAP program. The screen flow logic controls the processing of screens in SAP Systems. The event keywords of screen flow logic are:

```
PROCESS BEFORE OUTPUT.
PROCESS AFTER INPUT.
PROCESS ON HELP-REQUEST.
PROCESS ON VALUE-REQUEST.
```

The corresponding events, abbreviated to PBO, PAI, POH, and POV, are triggered by the runtime environment while the screen is being processed. The ABAP program's dialog modules are called in the event blocks of the screen flow logic, whereas the PBO event prepares the layout of a screen and PAI, POH, and POV events evaluate the user inputs. For more details see Section 7.1.

Dialog modules

Dialog modules are implemented in executable programs, module pools, or function groups between

```
MODULE.
```

and

```
ENDMODULE.
```

Like event blocks, dialog modules have no local data area and no parameter interface. A data declaration in a dialog module is also added to the global data.

During the above screen events dialog modules are called from the screen flow logic with `MODULE`. They contain the ABAP statements for the screen processing. For more details see Section 7.1.5.

Procedures

Procedures are the type of processing block you are most likely to recognize from other programming languages. Procedures have a local data area and can have a parameter interface. They can be called internally from within the same program or externally from another ABAP program (see Figure 3.5).

Local data

Procedures provide a means of modularizing ABAP programs directly and providing reusable software blocks. What we will cover in this section is by no means an exhaustive study of modularization techniques and reusing software components. Chapter 5 is reserved for a description of the following three types of procedure, where we shall focus on the new developments available through methods in ABAP Objects. For the time being we shall concentrate on the role procedures play as processing blocks.

Subroutines

Subroutines can be implemented between the

```
FORM ...
```

and

```
ENDFORM.
```

statements in any ABAP program except for class pools. They are called by the user using the PERFORM statement; the parameter interface is addressed using positional parameters, as in C or Pascal. For more details see Section 5.2.1.

Function modules

Function modules can only be defined in function pool type ABAP programs between the

```
FUNCTION ...
```

and

```
ENDFUNCTION.
```

statements. They are called with the CALL FUNCTION statement and the user fills the interface with keyword parameters and therefore must know their names. Many SAP functions are still encapsulated in function modules. For more details see Section 5.2.1.

Methods

Methods are part of the procedures repertoire since ABAP Objects was first introduced. They are defined in the implementation part of classes between the

```
METHOD ...
```

and

```
ENDMETHOD.
```

statements. They are called using CALL METHOD. The user fills the interface with keyword parameters. Functional methods that have exactly one resulting parameter can also be used as operands in expressions. When methods are declared as event handlers, they can also be triggered by events in ABAP Objects. We distinguish between instance methods and static methods that are either attached to objects or just to the class. For more details see Section 5.3.

The role of classes

Since the introduction of ABAP Objects, classes can now be defined in ABAP programs. How do classes behave in relation to a program structure consisting of processing blocks? Classes are defined between CLASS and ENDCLASS and each class has a separate declaration and implementation part. Like processing blocks, classes cannot be nested. Defining a class is like placing brackets around certain program components to create a new syntactical unit (see Figure 3.7).

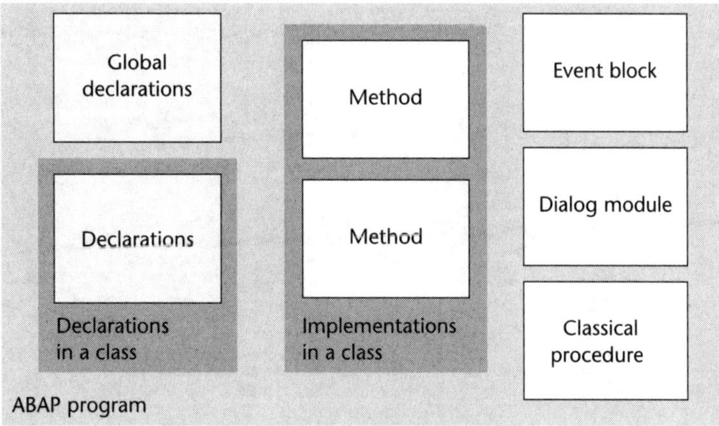

FIGURE 3.7 Classes in the program structure

Declaration

The declaration part of a class is introduced using `CLASS ... DEFINITION`. It includes declarations in a class and thereby changes their visibility. A declaration part with its data declarations is part of the other global declarations of a program and should also be included there.

Implementation

The implementation part of a class is introduced using `CLASS ... IMPLEMENTATION`. It includes the methods of a class and therefore belongs syntactically to the processing blocks of the program. The arrangement of the implementation part in relation to the other processing blocks is as arbitrary as the method sequence within the implementation part itself. However, for the sake of visibility, we recommend implementation close to the declaration.

Figure 3.7 shows that classes are fully integrated in the classical program structure and can be created alongside the classical components.

3.3.3 Program types

Each ABAP program has a type, which is defined in the program attributes (see Figure 3.8). Prior to Release 4.6, internal single-digit abbreviations were used for this. For example, an "executable program" was type 1. Now you can select the program type by entering its full name.

What is the purpose of all the different program types? The program type determines which processing blocks a program can contain, how the program is handled and executed by the runtime environment, and whether it can work with its own screens. The following ABAP program types are available.

Executable programs (Type 1)

Executable programs are introduced with the `REPORT` statement. They can contain their own screens and are executed via the `SUBMIT` statement or transaction codes.

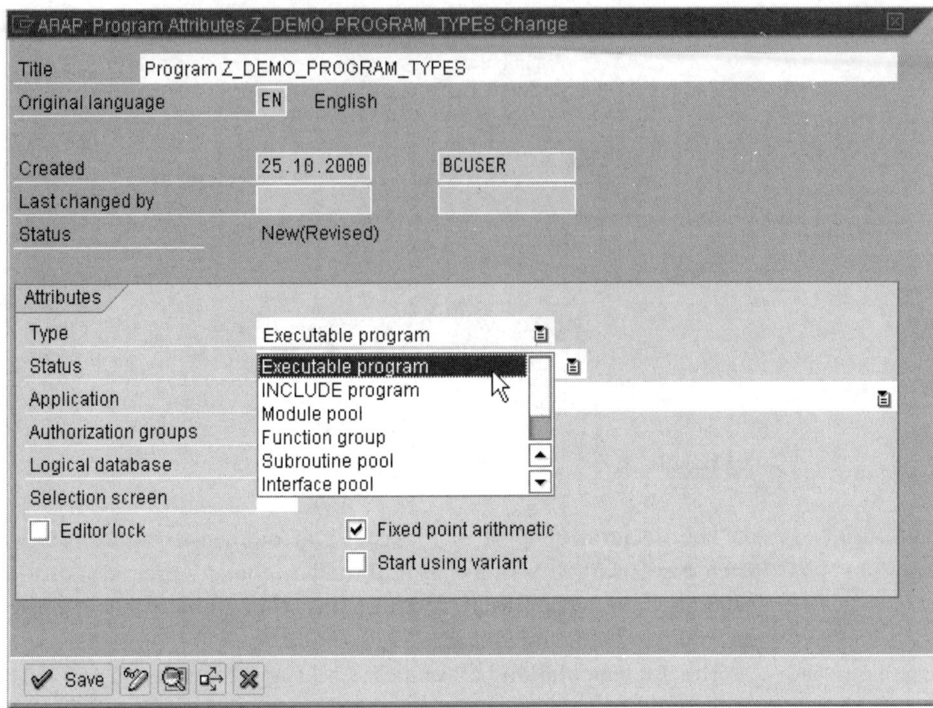

FIGURE 3.8 Program type in the program attributes. Copyright © SAP AG

Executable programs can contain all the various processing blocks in ABAP, except for function modules, and any number of local classes. They can be created directly with the ABAP Editor tool. While they are running, all the runtime environment events can occur.

Module pools (Type M)

Module pools are introduced with the `PROGRAM` statement. They can contain their own screens and can only be executed through transaction codes. Module pools can contain all the various processing blocks in ABAP, except for reporting event blocks and function modules, and any number of local classes. While they are running, all the runtime environment events can occur, except for reporting events. They can be created directly with the ABAP Editor tool.

Function groups (Type F)

Function groups or pools are introduced with the `FUNCTION-POOL` statement. They can contain their own screens. Normally, function groups are not executed directly. They are loaded by calling their function modules. They can contain all the various processing blocks in ABAP, except for reporting event blocks, and any number of local classes. They are the only programs that can contain function modules and are created with the Function Builder tool.

Class pools (Type K)

Class pools are introduced with the `CLASS-POOL` statement. They cannot contain their own screens and no other processing blocks than methods. Class pools can contain a single global class and any number of local classes. They cannot be executed directly. They are loaded by using their global classes.[3] They are created with the Class Builder tool.

Interface pools (Type J)

Interface pools are introduced with the `INTERFACE-POOL` statement. They cannot contain their own screens or processing blocks. They contain a single definition of a global interface, which can be implemented in any global or local class. They are created with the Class Builder tool.

Subroutine pools (Type S)

Subroutine pools are introduced with the `PROGRAM` statement. They cannot contain their own screens and apart from the `LOAD-OF-PROGRAM` event block can have only subroutines or methods of local classes as processing blocks. Subroutine pools are not executed directly. They are loaded by calling their procedures externally. They are created with the ABAP Editor.

Type groups

Type groups or pools are introduced with the `TYPE-POOL` statement. They cannot contain their own screens or processing blocks. They contain the definitions of global data types, which can be made visible in any ABAP program by the `TYPE-POOLS` statement. They are created with the ABAP Dictionary tool.

Include programs (Type I)

Include programs have no introductory program statement and, unlike all other program types, they do not represent independent compilation units with their own memory space. Include programs provide a library function for ABAP source code and can be embedded at any location in other ABAP programs using the `INCLUDE`

3. As of Basis Release 6.10 there will also be transaction codes which are linked with global classes and which implicitly generate an object of the class when used.

statement. Include programs have no technical relationship to processing blocks. However, it is preferable to separate logical program units, such as the declaration part for global data, and similar or individual processing blocks into independent include programs. The ABAP Workbench supports the automatic division of module pools, function groups, and class pools into include programs. You can create your own include programs directly with the ABAP Editor.

3.3.4 Screens

We have already mentioned the screens of ABAP programs on several occasions. As we have devoted a whole section of this book to the programming and processing of screens, we shall now provide a brief list of the various screen types. The following screens can belong to and be processed by executable programs, module pools, and function groups.

General screens

General screens or simply **screens** consist of the actual layout and a flow logic. The German term for a general screen is *Dynpro*, meaning dynamic program. The screen flow logic is a program layer that handles screen events and lies between the actual ABAP application program and the runtime environment. The layout and flow logic of a screen program are created with the Screen Painter tool.

Selection screens

Selection screens are special screens that are created through ABAP statements and not the Screen Painter. The flow logic of selection screens is embedded in the runtime environment; the screen events are converted to selection screen events.

Classical lists

Classical lists, previously known simply as lists, are screens with a special layout that has a single output area that can be filled with formatted contents using ABAP statements. As with selection screens, the screen flow logic is embedded in the runtime environment and its events are forwarded to the ABAP program as list events.

3.3.5 Program execution

From our description of program types we can see that almost all programs are loaded to ones that are already running. Only executable programs and module pools are executable from a user perspective. Starting a program by the user means starting it from a screen. This section on program execution therefore concerns only executable programs and module pools. The other program types will be treated in Chapter 5.

Control

If we now recall that ABAP programs consist of processing blocks and return to Figure 3.5, it is clear that in executing an ABAP program we are simply calling its processing blocks in a certain order. Consequently, an ABAP program is entirely controlled by the runtime environment.

Processor

To do this, the runtime environment contains **processors**. For example, there is a processor for handling screens and one for processing output lists. Here, the control processes are defined to call screen layouts and processing blocks in an order specific to the particular purpose. Control of the program is always assigned to a specific processor.

Figure 3.9 illustrates some of these processors. We have also included the above-mentioned screen flow logic. Whereas selection screen and list processors include the screen flow logic of their screens and send events directly to the ABAP program, you have to define the flow logic of general screens yourself. The screen processor sends its events to the PBO and PAI processing blocks where dialog modules of the ABAP program are called.

Starting an ABAP program involves quite simply executing one or more processes consecutively in the runtime environment. Which process is started first depends primarily on the program type and the kind of program call. The rest of the sequence depends on user actions on the screens, in particular with dialog-oriented applications.

When we refer in general to an ABAP program being executed, you should now be aware that the actual control is through the runtime environment or screen processes and that ABAP programs are nothing more than pools of processing blocks that can be externally executed as required. ABAP programs can also be programmed so that only

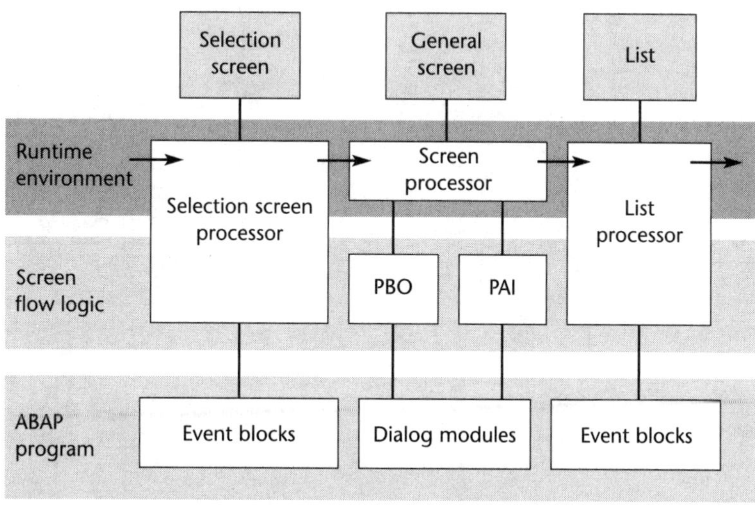

FIGURE 3.9 Runtime environment processors

the first processing block is externally activated and all other processing blocks are called internally. However, this kind of program offers the user hardly any interfaces.

We shall now explore in more detail the way in which executable programs and module pools are controlled by the runtime environment.

Executable program flow

SUBMIT

Executable programs can be started by entering their name in the "SA38" transaction (or by choosing **System – Services – Reporting**) or using the `SUBMIT` statement in ABAP. The "SA38" transaction is used simply to call the indicated program using `SUBMIT`. Technically, the ability to be called using `SUBMIT` is the primary characteristic of an executable program. From a user's viewpoint, executable programs are the only ABAP programs that can be started by entering their name.

When an executable program is called, a predefined sequence of processes is started in the runtime environment that triggers a predetermined sequence of events. Figure 3.10 shows the sequence of events in a flow chart. You will find here many of the events introduced in Section 3.3.1.

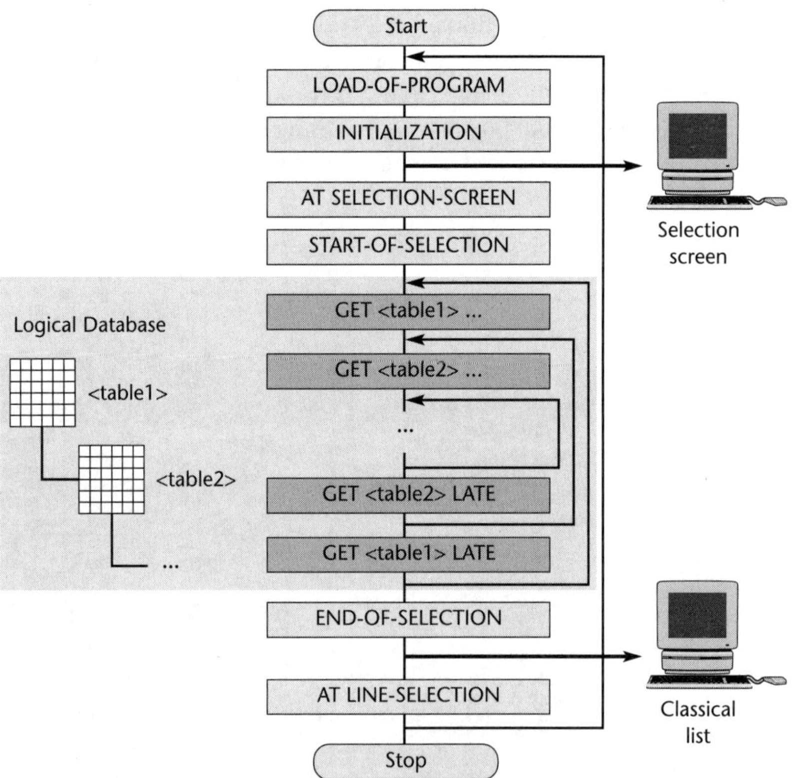

FIGURE 3.10 Runtime environment events in executable programs

Selection screen

As with all ABAP programs, the runtime environment first triggers the event for the `LOAD-OF-PROGRAM` program constructor.[4] However, the subsequent execution is specific to executable programs. If a selection screen is defined in the program, it can be prepared during the `INITIALIZATION` event and is then sent automatically from the runtime environment. User actions on the selection screen result in the `AT SELECTION-SCREEN` events. When selection screen processing is complete, the `START-OF-SELECTION` standard event is triggered.

Logical database

The following events are then triggered providing the executable program is linked to a logical database in its attributes. A logical database is a special ABAP program that contains the definition of a selection screen and a set of subroutines. The subroutines contain ABAP statements, which are generally used to read data from database tables. When an executable program with a logical database is run, the selection screen of the logical database is sent. The runtime environment then calls the subroutines of the logical database – in the sequence resulting from a hierarchical structure specified by the logical database. When a subroutine of the logical database has read a row of a database table, it triggers the `GET` table event of the runtime environment using the `PUT` table statement. This triggers the corresponding event block of the executable program where the data that has been read can be evaluated in a common data area. A logical database is therefore simply a reusable component that encapsulates details of the data selection.

LDB_PROCESS

The method that the logical database uses to prepare its data is not restricted to database access. It is possible to access any stored data or even generate your own data. As of Basis Release 4.0 logical databases can be called using the `LDB_PROCESS` function module in any program independently of an executable program. You maintain logical databases in the SE36 transaction. We will not examine this in greater depth at this point. For more details, refer to the documentation for this transaction.

When the logical database has finished its data selection, the runtime environment triggers the `END-OF-SELECTION` event. The data that has been read can be edited in the sum in the corresponding event block. Without attachment to a logical database `END-OF-SELECTION` is triggered immediately after `START-OF-SELECTION`. Then, it is not necessary to implement the corresponding event block since the entire code can be attached to the event block for `START-OF-SELECTION` just as well.

List

At the end of an executable program the runtime environment automatically displays the classical list defined during execution. User actions on the list produce list events. If the user leaves the list and no selection screen is defined in the program, the program will terminate. Otherwise, the runtime environment restarts the program. It can then only be terminated if the user interrupts his or her work on the selection screen.

The predefined flow of an executable program supports classical reporting tasks with the option of inputting selection parameters on a selection screen, subsequent

4. As from Release 4.6.

data processing, and data display in a list. For this reason, we also refer to the runtime environment processor that generates the flow shown in Figure 3.10 as the reporting processor.

The flow described here allows you now to understand our very first program, S_VERY_FIRST_PROGRAM from Section 2.3.3, and therefore all the programs that are based on it. In this program we defined a selection screen using PARAMETERS; implemented a single processing block START-OF-SELECTION; and in it defined a list with WRITE. For this program, Figure 3.10 is reduced to a single event, START-OF-SELECTION, and two screens. When the program is executed, first the selection screen is displayed and then START-OF-SELECTION is run. The list is then displayed and finally the program is re-started until the user exits the selection screen.

Module pool flow

Module pools are executed in a very different manner than executable programs. Executing a module pool does not start a process in the runtime environment that sends events to the ABAP program in a specified sequence. Neither can module pools be started by entering their name or using SUBMIT.

Transaction code

To start a module pool you need to create at least one screen and define a transaction code, which is linked to one of the module pool screens. This screen then becomes the initial screen of a transaction with the ability to call other screens of the module pool.

To start a transaction, enter the transaction code in the standard toolbar input field or select a menu item that is linked to the transaction. At the start of a trans-

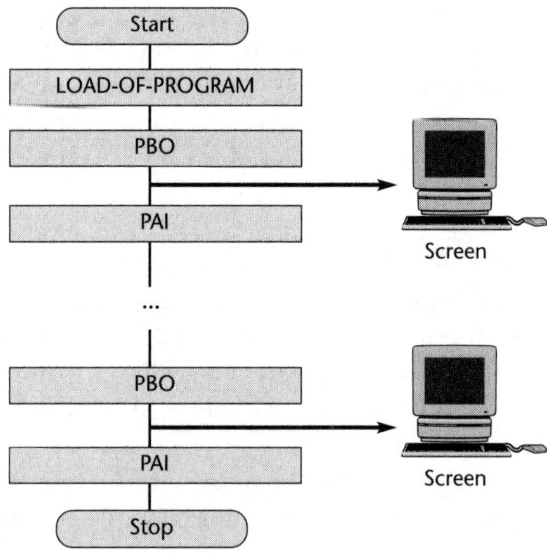

FIGURE 3.11 Runtime environment events in module pools

action the runtime environment loads the program into memory (which triggers LOAD-OF-PROGRAM) and triggers the PBO event of the initial screen. Once this event has been processed in the screen flow logic, the screen layout is sent. User actions on the screen layout trigger the PAI event in the runtime environment. Once this has been processed the runtime environment triggers the PBO event of the next screen and the process is repeated until the program is terminated through a statement such as LEAVE PROGRAM or when the last screen is reached.

Module pool

With this kind of program execution the role of the ABAP program is limited to making dialog modules that are called in the screen flow logic available – hence the name module pool. The call sequence is determined by consecutive screens whose order is normally largely influenced by the actions of the user.

Providing no selection screens are called with the CALL SELECTION-SCREEN statement or lists with the LEAVE TO LIST-PROCESSING statement, the execution of a module pool is controlled only by the screen processor, shown in Figure 3.9. In the chronological sequence of events this has the effect that PBO and PAI always alternate (see Figure 3.11).

Comparing the way in which programs are executed

Whereas event controlling in an executable program is governed predominantly by a predefined sequence of processes, when it comes to module pools developers have complete freedom to create the program flow themselves by programming the screen flow logic and the corresponding dialog modules.

However, this freedom is by no means restricted to module pools. You can also call screens in executable programs at any time using the CALL SCREEN statement and thereby leave the program controlling to the screen processor. If you do not respond to any of the reporting events except for START-OF-SELECTION and call an initial screen there, an executable program will behave just like a module pool except for the fact that it can be started by entering its name. We used this method in our first program, S_FIRST_PROGRAM in Section 2.3. If you really wish, you can even combine screens of executable programs with transaction codes. Executable programs will then run exactly like module pools, irrespective of their type, and no reporting events will occur.

In the same way that executable programs can contain screens and dialog modules, module pools can also contain selection screens and lists as well as the corresponding event blocks. However, their processes must then be called with the CALL SELECTION-SCREEN and LEAVE TO LIST-PROCESSING statements, since no automatic calls are triggered. Thus, the only restriction module pools have compared with reports is that there are no reporting events, nor can they be started using SUBMIT.

Reports versus transactions

Why do we distinguish between executable programs and module pools at all? The answer lies in the classical ABAP programming model, which made a clear distinction between report programming and transaction or dialog programming. If you already have some experience with ABAP programming from earlier Basis releases and are familiar with the literature, you will recall this distinction from the training courses and documentation.

In the past, we used to refer to reports and dialog programs. Reports provided read-only access to database data; dialog programs or transactions allowed you to modify it. A specialized program type was provided for each of these tasks. The reporting programmer created executable programs only and concentrated largely on their flow and screens. The dialog programmer created only module pools with general screens and corresponding transaction codes. The common technical basis that existed for all ABAP program types was simply not required for these programming models. Links between the two programming techniques, such as calling a screen in an executable program, were considered exceptions, and calling a selection screen outside an executable program was simply not possible prior to Release 4.0.

With the advent of ABAP Objects we have replaced this distinction with the overall perspective presented in this chapter. As an application developer, you have to decide which type of program execution matches your program's needs. There is no rule that limits read-only database access to executable programs or write access to module pools. There is equally no point in limiting the use of general screens to module pools. You must use general screens if you want to use the new programming techniques of ABAP Objects with GUI controls in executable programs.

It makes sense to use module pools if you do not require any of the mechanisms of an executable program and simply want to start your program with a transaction code. Executable programs have the advantage in that they can be started directly even if you do not require the other reporting events. Please note, however, that executing a transaction in the SAP System can be linked more easily with an authority check than running an executable program.

Function groups

In conclusion we should point out that all screen types can be equally used in the two programs mentioned here as well as in function groups. For example, you can call screens or selection screens in a function module using `CALL SCREEN` or `CALL SELECTION-SCREEN`, and handle their events in the function group. Screen programming is therefore not just confined to executable programs or module pools. You can encapsulate complete dialogs in function groups and call them from any ABAP program. Class pools, however, do not support any of the classical screens.

3.3.6 Calling programs internally

From a user perspective there are two ways of starting programs: direct execution using the program name for executable programs, or selecting a transaction code for module pools. These two ways of calling programs can also be performed in ABAP programs that are already running. We have mentioned the relevant `SUBMIT` statement for executable programs. The corresponding statements for transactions are `LEAVE TO TRANSACTION` and `CALL TRANSACTION`.

We can distinguish program calls from other ABAP programs by whether the calling program is being canceled completely or whether the called program is embedded in the calling program.

Canceling the calling program completely

You cancel the calling program completely by calling another program with

```
SUBMIT prog.
```

or

```
LEAVE TO TRANSACTION ta.
```

When the SUBMIT statement is executed, the calling program is deleted from memory along with all its data. When the called program is ended the program execution returns to the point at which the calling program was started. This point can be a previous program in the call sequence.

When the LEAVE TO TRANSACTION statement is executed, all previous programs in the call sequence are deleted from memory along with their data, besides the calling program. When the called program is ended the program execution returns to the point at which the first program of the call string was started.

LEAVE

We will also encounter the LEAVE statement in other contexts. A LEAVE statement is used to quit a program context completely and the execution does not return to the statement directly after this point. Although LEAVE can be used without additions, we recommend using LEAVE always with an addition, such as TO TRANSACTION seen here. Otherwise it is often difficult to predict where the program execution will actually branch to at runtime, since the behavior depends on the call mode of the current program.

Embedding the called program in the calling program

You can temporarily quit the calling program by calling another program with

```
SUBMIT prog AND RETURN.
```

or

```
CALL TRANSACTION ta.
```

In both cases, the calling program remains in memory with all its data. When the called program is terminated the program execution returns to the statement directly after the call location.

We will also see more of the CALL statement. CALL is the most important statement for temporarily quitting a program context in ABAP to execute another program unit. When the called unit is ended correctly the program returns behind the calling location.

3.3.7 Ending ABAP programs

The execution of an ABAP program is always ended when the corresponding process in the runtime environment ends. From an ABAP programmer's perspective, this is when the last of the processing blocks triggered by the runtime environment is ended.

You can, however, program ABAP programs to end at any time with the

```
LEAVE PROGRAM.
```

statement. As shown in the previous section, the `LEAVE TO TRANSACTION` statement and the `SUBMIT` statement without the `AND RETURN` addition also end an ABAP program.

3.4 MEMORY ORGANIZATION OF ABAP PROGRAMS

To conclude our introduction to the principles of ABAP programming we shall take a brief look at memory organization of ABAP programs. This section will introduce you to terms that will enhance your understanding of ABAP programs.

Figure 3.12 shows an overview of the memory organization, the structure of which we will explain as follows.

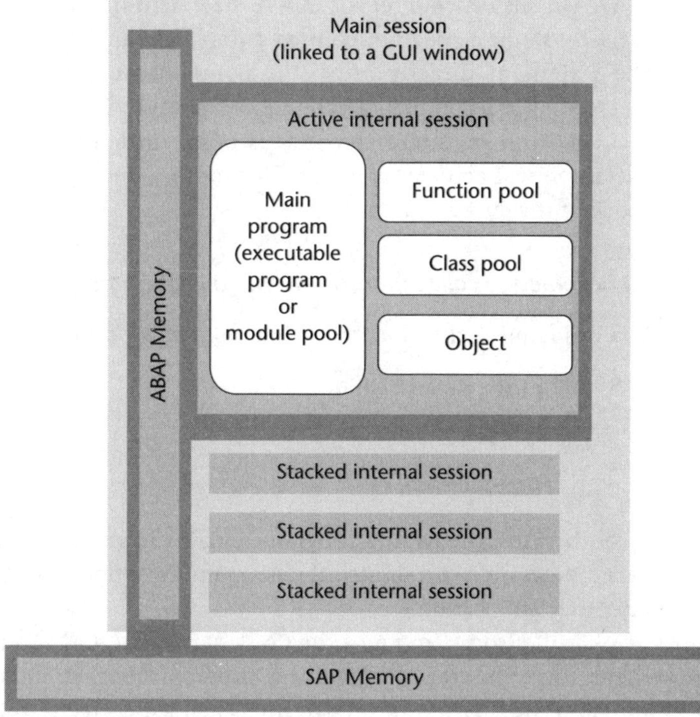

FIGURE 3.12 Memory organization of ABAP programs

Main session

When you log onto an SAP System, you open a main session on the application server, which is also known as an external session. You can open up to five more sessions at any one time by choosing **System – Create Session**. Each of these six sessions is linked to its own window in the SAP GUI and uses its own memory space on the application server. These sessions behave almost like independent SAP logons.

Internal session

Running an executable ABAP program or a module pool opens an internal session in the main session. The memory space of the ABAP program is part of the memory space of the main session. The data and objects of a program live in its internal session. However, in a main session only the internal session of the program that is currently running is always actively present. All the memory contents of the previous programs of a call sequence are stacked.

Call sequences

As we have seen before, ABAP programs can call other ABAP programs, whereby the caller is either completely quit or the system returns to the caller once the called program has terminated. If the system does not return to the previous program when the called program has been executed, the internal session of the called program replaces the internal session of the calling program and the contents of its memory are completely deleted. If, however, the system returns to the calling program, its session status is stacked while the called program is being executed. Together with its predecessors, a program forms a call sequence on the stack. Data can be transferred between the programs of a call sequence using the ABAP Memory.

ABAP Memory

The memory area of each main session has an area called ABAP Memory, which the programs in the internal session can access with `EXPORT TO MEMORY` and `IMPORT FROM MEMORY`. Data in the ABAP Memory is conserved through a sequence of program calls. To transfer data to a called program, it can be placed in the ABAP Memory with the `EXPORT` statement before the program is called. The internal session of the called program then replaces the internal session of the calling program and the data can be read from the ABAP Memory with the `IMPORT` statement. Data can be passed in exactly the same way when the system returns to the calling program (see also Section 8.3.1).

SAP Memory

The SAP Memory is a memory area to which all sessions of a SAP logon have common access. In ABAP programs, the `SET PARAMETER` and `GET PARAMETER` commands can be used to access the so-called SPA/GPA parameters stored in the SAP Memory. Input fields on screens can be linked to this type of parameter and default entries thereby established.

Loading programs

Running or calling an ABAP program loads an instance of the program into the internal session. The first program of an internal session is its main program. If in the main program of an internal session a procedure of another ABAP program is called or a public component of a global class of a class pool is addressed, an instance of the corresponding ABAP program is loaded into the internal session and remains there with its data and objects until the main program is ended. Added programs can also load extra programs. Every time an instance is loaded, the `LOAD-OF-PROGRAM` event is triggered in the loaded program except for class pools.

Generating objects

When objects are created through `CREATE OBJECT` in ABAP Objects, class instances are loaded into the internal session. All programs and objects of an internal session can access the instances of the same internal session. Thus, references to objects in the internal session can be passed to external procedures (subroutines, function modules, and methods).

Persistence

However, there are no memory spaces for cross-transaction objects on the application server. References cannot be stored in the ABAP Memory or SAP Memory. Persistent objects in the database must be handled by persistence services that are not part of ABAP's vocabulary.

CHAPTER 4

Basic ABAP language elements

Do you speak ABAP? If not, you will be doing so by the end of this chapter at the latest. In this chapter we will introduce you to the ABAP language elements required for working with program data. In the next chapter we will show you where to do it.

4.1 INTRODUCTION

The central task of any program, irrespective of its programming language, is to process data. Each programming language therefore requires basic language elements to define the program data, as well as language elements to run operations using this data. These language elements form the basis of any functionality a program can provide.

In the previous chapter we showed that the structure of an ABAP program consists of a global declaration part and processing blocks. In the present chapter we are not particularly concerned with where we are writing the language elements to. You must always bear in mind, therefore, that the example programs in this chapter serve only to illustrate the language elements and are not intended as instructions for production programs. In an actual application program you must always consider where you want to declare and process data. In principle, the statements in this chapter can be used in any processing block of an ABAP program. When you write production programs it depends on the programming model as to where you use the statements. This will form the subject of the next chapter.

4.2 DATA TYPES AND DATA OBJECTS

4.2.1 Introduction to the ABAP type concept

We will start with data you work with in ABAP programs. In principle, ABAP program statements work only with the data of the same program. External data such as user inputs on screens or data from the database must always be transported to data local to the program in order to be processed with ABAP statements.

Data object

Data local to the program lives in the program working memory. We refer to the section in the memory whose contents can be addressed and interpreted by the program as a data object.[1] ABAP statements therefore work with data objects. Each data object must be declared in the ABAP program and is only present during the execution of the program. If the contents of a data object are to be preserved beyond the program's runtime, they must be persistently saved before the program ends.

The most important statement for declaring a data object is `DATA`. Let's consider a simple `DATA` statement:

```
DATA  text(20) TYPE c VALUE 'Data Object'.
```

This statement creates a data object which the statements in a program can access via the name `text`. It is 20 characters long and has the initial contents "Data Object." `TYPE c` causes the contents to be stored in the memory in character-type form. The name, length, and storage type of the data in the memory are always uniquely defined for a data object at program runtime.

Data type

The specification after `TYPE` defines the **data type** of the data object. The data type determines how the data is stored in the memory. It reflects the fact that there are various kinds of data for different purposes. For example, we distinguish generally between character-type data, which is used to store and display values, and numeric data, which is used to perform calculations. Whereas with character-type data each character is individually stored according to a code table such as ASCII or Unicode and the data objects can have different lengths, with numeric data the overall value is coded platform-dependently and stored in an area with a predefined length. For example, data objects which represent integers always have a length of 4 bytes.

The data type of a data object shows an ABAP statement how to handle the data. Not all operations which a program can perform with data objects are suitable for all data types. For an arithmetic operation only numeric types would apply, while for a character output of a value only character types would be suitable. If you are using data objects in an ABAP statement which are not suitable for the operation, the runtime environment performs a type conversion into a suitable type, providing the contents of the data object allow this. For example, if a character data object contains a textual representation of a number, you can use it to calculate, because the representation is converted

1. Another term for data object would be simply **field**.

into a real numeric value before calculation takes place. The data type of a data object is therefore essential for handling a data object in operational statements.

Data processing

The basic task of ABAP programs is to process business data which is generally stored persistently in a database. To support this task, ABAP contains a comprehensive set of data types which supports specific operations for business data. This set ranges from elementary text fields as shown in the above example to a special numeric type for business calculations, as well as complex table-like types which provide structured internal storage of data from database tables.

All data types which can be used for data objects in ABAP are arranged in a systematic type hierarchy in which complex types can be constructed on the basis of elementary types. It is suitable to abstract the type description of a data object from its declaration completely, and ABAP allows you to construct independent data types and use them to declare data objects. For our previous example, this could look as follows:

```
TYPES  t_text(20)   TYPE c.
DATA   text         TYPE t_text VALUE 'Data Object'.
```

The TYPES statement defines a character data type t_text, 20 characters long. This data type can now be used in all the data declarations of the program. The initial value can of course only be specified when the data object is declared.

Independent data type

A data type defined with the TYPES statement is a complete construction rule for data objects in which all technical attributes are defined. This means that in complex programs you can first define the data types with which the program is to work and then use them in all the program modules to declare data objects. Independent types also play an important role in the type-specific passing of parameters to internal procedures. Subsequent modifications to the types can be carried out centrally and will affect all the data objects in the entire program and all internal interfaces.

ABAP Dictionary

The lifetime of a type defined by TYPE and its visibility are restricted to the program in which it is defined. However, you can declare data types not only within a program using the TYPES statement but also across programs in the **ABAP Dictionary**. The ABAP Dictionary is a system-wide visible repository for type descriptions which is maintained with the ABAP Workbench tool of the same name. This tool allows you to define in the ABAP Dictionary all the types you can create in an ABAP program with TYPES. Here, they are visible and usable for all ABAP programs and their components. You can therefore declare data objects of the same kind in different ABAP programs by referring to a type defined in the ABAP Dictionary. This allows you, on the one hand, to define types centrally so that they can be reused and, on the other, to pass data between programs: defining global types in the ABAP Dictionary is the basis of type-specific parameter passing during external procedure calls. Last but not least, the structures of all database tables in the SAP System are also stored as data types in the ABAP Dictionary. This means that you can create data objects with the structure of a database table in an ABAP program in order to process data from the database.

Following on from this introduction, we will now examine systematically the ABAP type concept and how it is applied. Because data types play an important role in ABAP programming as a whole, as we have seen, this section is somewhat more extensive than in other programming language books.

4.2.2 The ABAP type hierarchy

We can summarize the main points of our introduction:

- ABAP works with data types and data objects. Data types describe the attributes of data objects.
- Data types can be defined independently in ABAP programs or in the ABAP Dictionary. Data types do not occupy working memory. They are a template for creating a data object.
- A data object is an instance of a data type and uses as much memory as determined by its type. Data objects are the physical units with which ABAP statements work during runtime. The data type determines how the statements handle the object.
- Data objects can also be created without a fully predefined data type. The data type of this kind of data object is not independent, however, and appears in the program only as an attribute of the data object (for example, the data type "Twenty character length text" of our first `DATA` statement above). We refer to this kind of data type as an **anonymous** data type, whereas a data type defined with `TYPES` is a **named** data type.

These points characterize the ABAP type concept. All data types available in ABAP form the ABAP type hierarchy,[2] as illustrated in Figure 4.1.

Built-in data type

The nodes in Figure 4.1 show the various data types on the left and the classification of the corresponding data objects on the right. We have also indicated a series of labels (`c`, `d`, `f`...) for the elementary data types. These are the names of predefined data types which are always present in ABAP. In our very first example, we already used type `c` without having defined it. We call these types **built-in data types** to avoid any confusion with self-defined data types from the ABAP Dictionary.

Self-defined data type

Self-defined data types are based on built-in elementary data types. Our self-defined type `t_text` is based on data type `c`, for example, to which it has added a length specification. However, reference types are defined independently of the elementary data types. The complex data types are constructed from elementary types and reference types. We distinguish between a sequence of types in structures and a row-by-row repetition of types in tables. Therefore no data types have predefined names except for built-in data types.

2. We can generalize this hierarchy even more if we include the object types (classes and interfaces) of ABAP Objects. Data types and objects then become equal subnodes of a general root node for all types in ABAP.

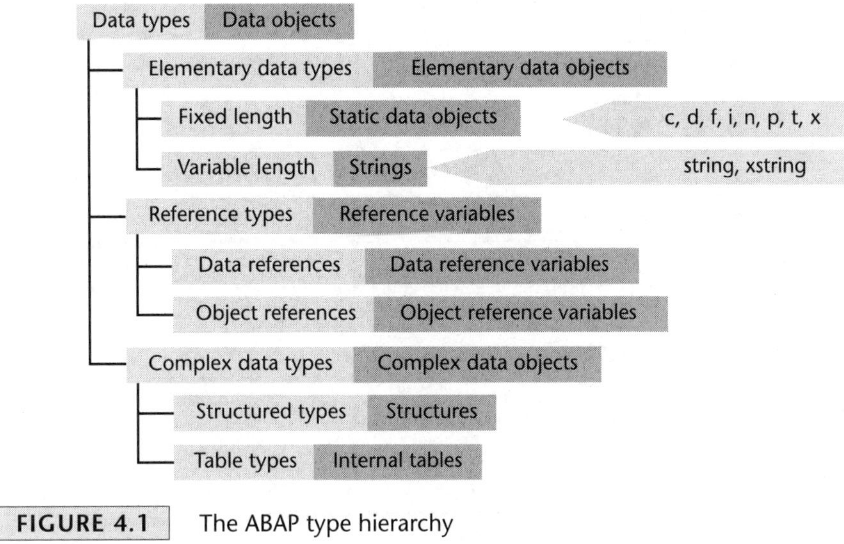

FIGURE 4.1 The ABAP type hierarchy

In the following sections we shall look first at the built-in elementary data types, and then describe how you can define all the data types and data objects of the type hierarchy.

4.2.3 Built-in elementary data types

By built-in data types we mean the types which the runtime system provides for an ABAP program. Currently, all built-in data types are also **elementary data types**, which means that none of them is composed of other types. We can distinguish between two kinds of built-in types: those whose length is statically determined when they are defined and those whose length can change dynamically at runtime.

Fixed length built-in data types

Let's consider first types with a static length. We call these fixed length built-in elementary data types. ABAP contains a total of eight of these data types. Table 4.1 lists them along with their most important technical attributes.

The meaning of the table columns is:

- **Type** is the name of the data type as used in a statement after `TYPE`.
- **Minimum – Maximum size** indicates how much memory space a data object of this type can occupy (as a minimum/maximum).
- **Standard size** indicates the value automatically added by the ABAP runtime environment if no specific length specification is provided in the `DATA` or `TYPES` statements.
- **Initial value** is the contents of a data object of this type when the program unit in which the data object is declared is first run, providing no `VALUE` addition is used in the `DATA` statement.

TABLE 4.1 The eight fixed length built-in ABAP data types

Type	Minimum–/ Maximum size [Bytes]	Standard size [Bytes]	Initial value	Description
i	4	4	0	Integer
p	1–16	8	0	Packed, packed number
f	8	8	0	Float, floating point number
c	1–65535	1	' '	Character, alphanumeric text
n	1–65535	1	'0...0'	Numeric text
d	8	8	'00000000'	Date
t	6	6	'000000'	Time
x	1–65535	1	'00 ... 00'	Hexadecimal

Incomplete data type

As you can see, type p, c, n, and x data objects do not always occupy the same amount of memory. These are **incomplete** or **generic data types**, which when used to declare data objects, require additional details concerning their length.[3] If no length is specified when declaring data objects of these types, the runtime environment implicitly uses the standard size. With the other types, i, f, d, and t, you need not and cannot specify a length when declaring the objects, as the standard size is always used. The length specified explicitly or implicitly when a data object is declared is the fixed length of the data object which is retained throughout the entire runtime of a program. The memory space required for this kind of data object is always the same.

We can divide the eight types into three numeric types (i, p, f), four character-type types (c, n, d, t) and one byte type (x). Numeric types are used to perform mathematical operations, character types to represent values, and the hexadecimal type to represent the uncoded contents of a byte.

Numeric type i

- Type i is a data type for integers with a value between -2^{31} and $+2^{31}-1$. It is often used as an index or counter variable. If a number with a decimal place is assigned to a type i data object as the result of a calculation or during an assignment, it is rounded either up or down.

  Example:

```
DATA index TYPE i.
index = 5.
DO index TIMES.
  ...
ENDDO.
```

3. However, when you use it for typing interface parameters and field symbols, no length is required.

Here we have a type i data object index which specifies the number of times a loop is executed.

Numeric type p

- Type p is a data type for packed numbers with a fixed number of decimal places (fixed point format). The number of decimal places is determined when a data object or a self-defined type is declared using the DECIMALS specification of the DATA or TYPES statements. If there is no specification, the number of decimal places is zero and type p data objects are treated as type i data objects. The value range of the numbers depends on the size of the data object as well as the number of decimal places. Two decimal digits are packed into each byte of a type p data object, and the sign is contained in the last half byte. A type p number can contain a maximum of 16 bytes or 31 decimal digits. Up to 14 decimal places are possible. Type p numbers are the best solution if you are calculating to exact decimal places. The results are rounded up or down to the last decimal place. On the other hand, calculations with type p data objects take up more computational time than with type i or f data objects. Type p is particularly suitable for amounts of money, dimensions, weights, etc. You should always mark the check box **Fixed Point Arithmetic** program attribute in the program attributes when using type p, as otherwise all the data objects of this type will be treated as integers.

  Example:

```
DATA number TYPE p DECIMALS 2.
number = 3 / 4.
```

  The type p data object number has a value of 0.75 after calculation.

Numeric type f

- Type f is a data type for floating point numbers. The term floating point number refers to the way these numbers are represented internally by bits. A floating point number consists of three components, the sign, the mantissa, and the exponent. The mantissa contains only the digits of the number while the exponent indicates the position of the decimal point. If you change the exponent, the decimal point is given a different position. The value range of a floating point number is between 1×10^{-307} and $1 \times 10^{+308}$ for positive and negative numbers including 0. The internal representation may result in rounding differences when computing with floating point numbers. Type f can therefore be used where large value ranges are required and accuracy is less important. Data type f cannot be used for input fields on screens, but is required for passing certain calculated values from the database (aggregate functions).

  Example:

```
DATA result TYPE f.
result   = sqrt( 2 ).
```

  After assignment, the type f data object result has the value 1.4142135623730951E+00.

Character type c

- Type c is a data type for any character strings of static length (character fields). It should be noted that trailing blanks in a type c data object are subject to special semantics: when type c data objects are processed, e.g. when different character strings are concatenated, trailing blanks are ignored. Type c also often replaces the missing Boolean data type. Unlike C/C++, where an integer is used, in ABAP a type c data object of length 1 is normally used. If a data object contains an "X," it is interpreted as "true." "False" on the other hand is represented by a space. For the latter there is also a predefined data object called space.

Example:

```
DATA text_line(72) TYPE c.
text_line = 'ABAP Programming is fun!'.
IF text_line <> space.
  WRITE / text_line.
ENDIF.
```

A character string in a literal is assigned to the type c data object text_line. You can compare with space to check whether the data object is filled.

Character type n

- Type n is a data type for numeric contents (numeric text field) but is not a numeric data type. It can contain numbers, but these are generally not used for calculations. If you are calculating with type n data objects, the system must first perform a conversion to a suitable numeric type. Typical applications are bank sorting code numbers, postal codes, PO box numbers, etc. This data type is also suitable for input fields on screens which accept only numbers, because the system then rejects all other input.

  Example:

  ```
  DATA postal_code(5) TYPE n.
  postal_code = '69189'.
  ```

  The type n data object postal_code only contains numbers.

Character type d

- Type d is a data type for dates. If there is a character string in a type d data object in the format YYYYMMDD (YYYY is the year, MM the month and DD the day), which contains a valid date such as "20001001," the field contents are interpreted in mathematical expressions as a date with which calculations can be performed (see Section 4.3.3). Other operations make use of the fact that type d is a character type. If input fields on screens have type d, the system checks whether a valid date is entered.

  Example:

  ```
  DATA date TYPE d.
  date = sy-datum.
  date = date + 2.
  ```

  The type d data object date is assigned the current date in the sy-datum system field. After calculation it contains the date of the day after tomorrow.

Character type t

- Type t is a data type for time. If there is a character string in a type t data object in the format HHMMSS (HH is the hour, MM the minute and SS the second), which contains a valid time such as "093000," the field contents are interpreted in mathematical expressions as a time with which calculations can be performed (see

Section 4.3.3). Other operations make use of the fact that type t is a character type. If input fields on screens have type t, the system checks whether a valid time is entered.

Example:

```
DATA time TYPE t.
time = sy-uzeit.
time = time + 3600.
time+2(4) = '0000'.
```

The type t data object time is assigned the current time in the sy-uzeit system field. Thereafter one hour is added, and then the last four positions are overwritten with zeros. It then contains the next complete hour.

Byte type x

- Type x is a data type for the hexadecimal representation of any byte strings (hexadecimal). Within a byte, a four-bit half byte can contain values between 0 and 15. These values are represented in hexadecimal form by the 16 characters 0,...,9, A,...,F. To represent a byte of a byte string in hexadecimal form you therefore need two characters, such as F7 for a byte with the contents 11110111 or the decimal value 247. Type x data objects can only contain the above 16 characters. Except in low-level programs, type x is used less often than other types since most ABAP applications are of a business nature.

  Example:

  ```
  DATA hex(3) TYPE x.
  hex = 'F72AB3'.
  ```

  The type x data object hex is assigned a literal which contains a hexadecimal character string. After assignment, the byte string in the memory contains three bytes with the decimal values 247, 42, 179.

Variable length built-in data types

With Release 4.6 ABAP offers two variable length built-in elementary data types in addition to fixed length built-in elementary data types. They differ from the fixed length type in that the length and therefore the memory requirement of data objects of this kind of data type can change dynamically at runtime and are not irrevocably defined when the data object is declared. We refer to these kinds of data object as *strings*.

Character type string

- The string type is the dynamic equivalent of static type c. It can contain character strings of any given length.

  Example:

  ```
  DATA text_string TYPE string.
  text_string = 'ABAP Programming is fun!'.
  ```

  The string type data object text_string is assigned the same character string as in the above example for type c. Whereas the type c data object had a fixed length of 72, the length of the string type data object is dynamically set to 24 and can be changed at any time by another assignment.

Byte type xstring

- The xstring type is the dynamic equivalent of static type x. It can contain byte strings of any given length.

  Example:

  ```
  DATA x_string TYPE xstring.
  x_string = 'FF'.
  ```

  The xstring type data object x_string is assigned the hexadecimal contents of a single byte. The length of the byte string is thereby dynamically set to one byte and can be changed at any time by another assignment.

Internally, strings are managed by references. The memory address of a string contains a fixed length reference which refers to the actual dynamic data object. This kind of data type is therefore called a *deep* data type, which has important consequences for the usage of these types in structures.

Using built-in data types

Like all data types, the ten built-in data types can be used in any statement containing TYPE. So far we have dealt with the DATA and TYPES statements with this addition. These are used to declare data objects and define independent data types.

TYPE

TYPE can also be used for typing field symbols (see Section 4.6.1) and interface parameters in procedures (see Section 5.2.1). The main difference between using TYPE in declarations and typings is that the generic data types p, c, n, and x are completed in declarations and type definitions, but remain incomplete in typings. For more details on generic types see Section 4.2.7.

4.2.4 Data types and data objects local to the program

The built-in data types are the basic elements you need to define additional data types local to the program and to create data objects. The statement for defining your own data types local to the program is TYPES, and the statement for declaring or creating data objects is DATA.[4] The syntax of both statements is basically identical.[5] This reflects the fact that each data type can be defined either independently or linked to a data object. Like built-in data types, independently defined data types can be used in all statements with TYPE, in particular when defining other complex data types or creating data objects of this type. Such data objects are instances of data types, in the same way that objects are instances of classes (object types) (see Section 5.3.3).

In the following sections we shall look at defining all the data types and data objects local to the program from the type hierarchy in Figure 4.1. As mentioned pre-

4. Apart from DATA there are other similar statements such as CONSTANTS, which we will refer to later.
5. The only difference is that with TYPES no initial value can be specified with VALUE.

viously, data objects can only be declared within a program, whereas data types can also be defined in the ABAP Dictionary across programs. We shall look at this in greater detail in Section 4.2.5.

Naming convention

The creation of data types and data objects is governed by certain naming conventions which also apply to other definitions local to the program, such as procedures.

- The name can be up to 30 characters long.
- All letters, numbers, and the underscore "_" are allowed.
- The name must start with a letter.
- The names of built-in data types or predefined data objects such as `space` or `sy-uname` must not be used.
- The names of ABAP keywords and their additions should not be used.

There are separate namespaces for data types and data objects local to the program. This means that a name can be the name of a data object as well as the name of a data type. However, types local to the program hide data types from the ABAP Dictionary of the same name. In this chapter we shall not go into further detail regarding the lifetime and visibility of data types and data objects local to the program. You will find more details on this subject in Section 5.2.3.

Self-defined elementary data types and elementary data objects

When defining your own elementary data types and declaring elementary data objects you can refer to built-in elementary data types.

The syntax for an elementary data type is:

```
TYPES  type(len) TYPE type [DECIMALS dec].
```

Accordingly, the syntax for an elementary data object is:

```
DATA  dobj[(len)] TYPE type [DECIMALS dec] [VALUE val].
```

TYPE

The statements define a type local to the program (type) or a `dobj` data object. Here, one of the ten built-in elementary data types is indicated after `TYPE`. For the incomplete `p`, `c`, `n`, and `x` types a length must be specified using `(len)` directly after the label. If no length is specified, which with `TYPES` is only possible outside classes, the runtime environment inserts the standard size from Table 4.1 in both statements.[6] `DECIMALS` is used to determine the number of decimal places with type p packed numbers. When declaring static data objects, you can use the `VALUE val` addition to determine a start value which then overrides the initial value from Table 4.1. `VALUE` is not permitted for declaring strings.

6. The runtime environment also sets the type to C if no type specification is made. However, this short form for `TYPES` is also only possible outside classes and should no longer be used there either.

The above statements refer to the built-in elementary data types. However, they can also refer to previously defined elementary data types in order to define new elementary data types or to create elementary data objects:

```
TYPES|DATA ... TYPE  type.
```

In this case TYPE is followed by a type local to the program previously defined with TYPES or an elementary data type from the ABAP Dictionary. The new data type or data object inherits all the attributes of the existing type.

However, you can also refer to existing data objects. To do this, you use LIKE.

```
TYPES|DATA ... LIKE  dobj.
```

LIKE

After LIKE you can specify an elementary data object of the same program which has already been declared with DATA.[7] The new data type or object inherits all the attributes of the existing data object. Generally, LIKE is used with the DATA statement rather than with the TYPES statement because there is little point in defining a type local to the program for which a data object already exists.

In Listing 4.1 we shall consider a basic example of elementary data types and objects.

LISTING 4.1 Elementary data types and objects

```
REPORT s_elementary_data.
TYPES t_result   TYPE p DECIMALS 2.
DATA: number_1 TYPE i          VALUE 3,
      number_2 LIKE number_1 VALUE 4,
      result   TYPE t_result.
result  = number_1 / number_2.
WRITE result.
```

The TYPES statement is used to define a t_result data type local to the program for packed numbers with two decimal places. Three DATA statements in a chained statement are used to declare three elementary data objects, of which the first is of built-in type i, the second inherits this type with LIKE, and the third refers to the t_result data type local to the program. You can now imagine that more data objects of the same program refer to t_result and that it is therefore possible to change the computing accuracy centrally in a single TYPES statement.

7. For compatibility reasons outside classes you can also refer to flat structures or database tables of the ABAP Dictionary with LIKE. In this case LIKE is used to refer to global data types instead of local data objects. Then data objects of the ABAP program hide data types of the ABAP Dictionary of the same name. This obsolete form of the LIKE reference violates the concept of separate namespaces and should no longer be used.

Reference types and reference variables

Reference types are data types for data objects which can contain a reference to other data objects or objects of classes in ABAP Objects. This kind of data object is called a reference variable or a pointer. Depending on the type of object being referenced, we speak of **data references** or **object references**.

Type constructor

To define a reference type in a program, you cannot refer to a built-in data type using TYPE. Instead you have to construct a new type. To do this, you use the REF TO **type constructor**. The syntax for data references is as follows.

```
TYPES|DATA ... TYPE REF TO  data.
```

And for object references:

```
TYPES|DATA ... TYPE REF TO {class|interface}.
```

The references in data objects of this type can point either to other data objects of any type or to objects of specific classes. Like strings, reference types are deep types because the data objects of these types only point to actual work data; they do not contain them. When you make assignments between reference variables, the common value semantics with which the actual work data is copied does not apply. Instead, a reference semantics is used with which pointers between objects are reassigned, so to speak. Section 4.6.2 will focus more on data references and Section 5.3.3 on object references.

If a required reference type local to the program or a corresponding reference variable is already present in the same program, you do not need to construct it again. Instead you can refer to it with TYPE or LIKE. In the same way you can use TYPE to refer to reference types in the ABAP Dictionary.

Complex data types

Complex data types are types whose data objects are not elementary in the memory. Instead, several data objects constitute composite logical units which can be addressed by a name. The advantage of these types is that their data objects can be treated as a single object during assignment or passing to procedures, but allow a detailed view of the individual components during processing. We distinguish between two kinds of complex types: **structured types** which consist of a sequence of any number of types, and **table-like types** which have a line type of which any number of instances can exist in the memory.

Structured types and data objects

A **structured type** is a data type for a data object which consists of components. We call this kind of data object a structure.[8] A program-local structured type or a structure is constructed as follows with the TYPES or DATA statements.

8. In earlier releases the term field string was used

```
TYPES|DATA: BEGIN OF  structure,
                  k1 {TYPE type|LIKE dobj} ...,
                  k2 {TYPE type|LIKE dobj} ...,
                  ...
                  kn {TYPE type|LIKE dobj} ...,
            END OF  structure.
```

Chained statement

Note that this statement with its use of the colon and commas represents a chained statement. We are therefore dealing with a whole series of individual TYPES or DATA statements, the results of which are grouped in a structure structure by BEGIN OF structure and END OF structure. The individual component definitions are arbitrary TYPES or DATA statements, and the components of structures can be any of the data types possible in ABAP. A component is therefore elementary, a reference type, itself a structure or a table-like type. For example, a nesting of structures can be created by referring to an existing structure from the same program or a structure from the ABAP Dictionary in the TYPE or LIKE addition of one of the components. It is also possible to nest the BEGIN OF and END OF statements. However, we only refer to a structure as deep if it contains at least one deep component such as an elementary field of the type *string*, a reference variable, or a table (see Section 4.2.6).

As we have already mentioned, instead of using a construction, a structure in a program can also be defined by a TYPE reference to an existing structured type of the same program or of the ABAP Dictionary, or by a LIKE reference to an already declared structure. The important thing is that it is possible to refer to the database tables of the SAP System.

```
TYPES|DATA structure TYPE dbtab.
```

A dbtab database in the ABAP Dictionary represents a structured type whose components correspond to the columns of the database table. You can therefore easily create structures from database tables to be used as work areas for data.

Structure components

To address an individual structure component in the program, you have to attach its name to the structure name with a hyphen (-):

```
structure-comp
```

The hyphen is therefore referred to as the **structure component selector** in ABAP. With nested structures this results in a chain of structure names.

Listing 4.2 shows an address as an example of structures. It consists of the following components: name, street, and city.

LISTING 4.2 Structured data types and data objects

```
REPORT s_structured_data.
TYPES: BEGIN OF t_street,
         name(40) TYPE c,
         no(4) TYPE c,
       END OF t_street.

DATA: BEGIN OF address,
        name(30) TYPE c,
        street TYPE t_street,
        BEGIN OF city,
          zipcode(5) TYPE n,
          name(40) TYPE c,
        END OF city,
        country(3) TYPE c VALUE 'SOL',
      END OF address.

address-name          = 'Luke Skywalker'.
address-street-name   = 'Milky Way'.
address-street-no     = '123d'.
address-city-zipcode  = '64283'.
address-city-name     = 'Tatooine'.
```

For the street we have created our own structured type `t_street` with the `name` and `no` components. For the address we declare an `address` structure as a data object. We declare the `street` component with the type `t_street`. The `city` component is also divided into two components, `zipcode` and `name`. The assignments show how the individual components are addressed. Although the term `name` occurs three times, each component can be uniquely addressed through its structure names.

Nested structure

Nested structures contain a hierarchy of structure components which is reflected in the chain of the names. If you wish to incorporate the components of a structure in another structure, in which the components of the resulting structure are to be on the same level, you can use the `INCLUDE` statement:

```
TYPES|DATA BEGIN OF struc1.
  ...
  INCLUDE TYPE|STRUCTURE struc2 AS name
          [RENAMING WITH SUFFIX suffix].
  ...
TYPES|DATA END OF struc1.
```

You use the TYPE variant for data types and the STRUCTURE variant for data objects. The INCLUDE statement is not an addition for the TYPES or the DATA statement. It interrupts the chained statement which then has to be restarted.

INCLUDE

The components of structure struc2 are incorporated into structure struc1 as components. They can be addressed either as a whole by the name with which they are included or individually by their component names. If there is a name conflict with existing components, RENAMING can be used to attach a suffix to the component name. This allows a structure to be included several times in another structure. Listing 4.3 shows an example:

LISTING 4.3 Including structure components

```
REPORT s_include_structure.
DATA: BEGIN OF street,
        name(40) TYPE c,
        no(4) TYPE c,
      END OF street.

DATA: BEGIN OF city,
        zipcode(5) TYPE n,
        name(40) TYPE c,
      END OF city.

DATA: BEGIN OF address,
        name(30) TYPE c.
      INCLUDE STRUCTURE street AS str
              RENAMING WITH SUFFIX _str.
      INCLUDE STRUCTURE city AS cty
              RENAMING WITH SUFFIX _cty.
DATA  END OF address.

address-name          = 'Han Solo'.
address-name_str      = 'Crab Nebula'.
address-no_str        = '18'.
address-zipcode_cty   = '69121'.
address-name_cty      = 'Dark Star'.

WRITE: / address-name,
       / address-str-name, address-str-no,
       / address-cty-zipcode, address-cty-name.
```

The components of the address structure are on the same level. Different suffixes avoid name conflicts between the name components. The assignments use the component names, and the WRITE statements the names by which the structures are included.

This kind of structure definition can be used, for example, to avoid complex nested structures with long name chains. Structures defined in this manner become particularly interesting when used in the ABAP Dictionary as templates for database tables. Database tables only allow structures to be used whose components are all on the same level. The ABAP Dictionary therefore contains a similar include technique which enables you to design structures with a single hierarchy level from other structures. If a data object is declared with reference to this kind of structure from the ABAP Dictionary as a work area for a database table, you can access the included structures in the ABAP program, exactly as shown in Listing 4.3.

Table types and internal tables

Table types describe dynamic data objects whose size, as with strings, is not determined during declaration. These data objects are called internal tables. Internal tables are specified by a table kind, a line type, and a table key. Local table types are defined using the TABLE OF type constructor. The syntax of the TYPES and DATA statements for table types or internal tables is:

```
TYPES|DATA ... {TYPE|LIKE} tabkind
               OF {linetype|lineobj}
               WITH key.
```

Table kind

The tabkind table kind determines the type of storage and access. We distinguish between standard tables (STANDARD TABLE), sorted tables (SORTED TABLE), and hashed tables (HASHED TABLE).

Line type

The line type is any local or global linetype data type addressed by TYPE, or the type of a lineobj data object addressed by LIKE. Internal tables can contain any number of lines of the specified line type in the memory. The line type is therefore known from the beginning, but not the number of lines. ABAP contains a special set of statements for filling and reading internal tables, which we will discuss in Section 4.7.

Like strings, internal tables are managed internally by references. Consequently they are deep data types. As the line type is arbitrary, internal tables can include elementary types, reference types, structures, and even internal tables. Particularly when dealing with structures whose components can be of any data type, this presents us with countless possibilities for creating highly complex data structures. Internal tables are also extremely well suited for managing object references in ABAP Objects.

Flat line type

The classical line type of an *internal table* which fits the common notion of a table with lines and columns is a structure with purely elementary components. Such an internal table is ideally suited for accepting several lines of a dbtab database table and can, for example, be defined as follows:

```
TYPES|DATA ... TYPE SORTED TABLE
               OF dbtab
               WITH UNIQUE KEY col1 col2 ...
```

This statement creates a table type or *internal table* as a sorted table whose line type has the same structure as the dbtab database table from the ABAP Dictionary. You can use WITH UNIQUE KEY to specify database table columns as a unique key to avoid duplicate lines. ABAP contains special SQL statements which retrieve data from database tables into these internal tables and vice versa (see Section 8.1.3).

4.2.5 Data types in the ABAP Dictionary

In the previous sections we introduced the syntax of the TYPES statement which you can use to define local data types. These data types are only visible within the ABAP program and are therefore not suitable for cross-program operations. If you wish to work with data which is available to all the programs in an SAP System, or if you wish to pass data between programs, you need type information which is independent of any individual ABAP program. The ABAP Dictionary serves this purpose. It is a cross-program storage system for type descriptions which all repository objects can access. Figure 4.2 shows the central role of the ABAP Dictionary to which ABAP programs, screens, and database tables, among others, refer.

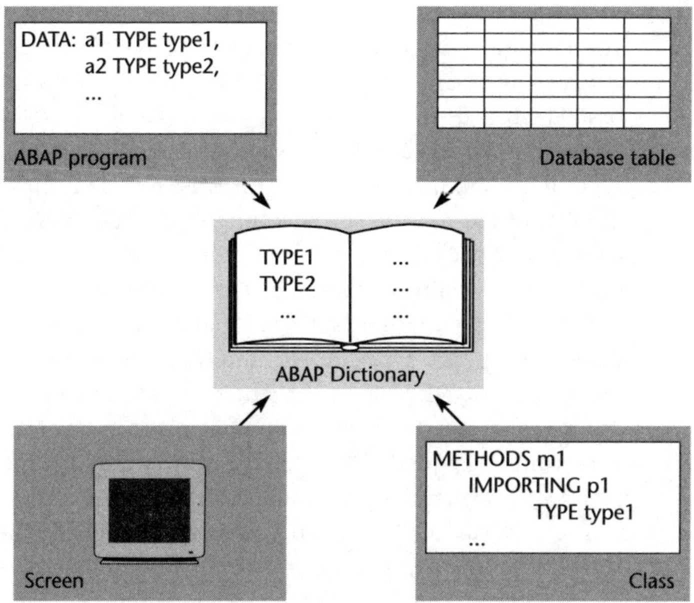

FIGURE 4.2 Data types in the ABAP Dictionary

All data types of the ABAP Dictionary can be used in ABAP programs in the same way as types local to the program. This means that they can be used in any statement containing `TYPE` to define types local to the program, to declare data objects, and to type interface parameters (see also the example for function modules in Section 5.2.1).

Screen

As you will see in Section 7.1, the data types of the ABAP Dictionary also play a large role in defining input and output fields on screens. They allow a type-specific passing of values between ABAP programs and screens and even provide input checks and input help for the latter. In this context, you can define **semantic information** for the data types in the ABAP Dictionary, such as descriptive texts, help texts or value tables, which are used in many areas of ABAP programming.

Database table

Finally, the relation between the ABAP Dictionary and database tables is of fundamental importance for business programs. The main application of an ABAP program is to access database tables of the SAP System. These database tables are also defined in the ABAP Dictionary. When a database table is defined, a structured type is first created in the ABAP Dictionary from which a physical database table is generated in the database system. In order to work with data from database tables, you can create data objects in an ABAP program which refer directly to the type of the database table in the ABAP Dictionary. Even if a database table is subsequently modified, all ABAP programs which refer to this type will be automatically updated.

We will now show you how to define all the data types of the type hierarchy shown in Figure 4.1 in the ABAP Dictionary.

Built-in elementary data types in the ABAP Dictionary

Like ABAP programs, the ABAP Dictionary contains a set of built-in data types which you can use as the basis for further types. The ABAP Dictionary contains considerably more built-in types than the ABAP programming language, and they are also named differently than in ABAP. The difference between the data types is due to the fact that the built-in data types of the Dictionary have to be compatible with the external data types of the database tables supported by SAP. If you refer to a data type from the ABAP Dictionary in an ABAP program, the elementary components of that type are converted to the built-in data types of the ABAP programming language. Table 4.2 shows a complete list of the built-in data types in the ABAP Dictionary and their equivalents in ABAP programs.

You cannot refer directly to all the built-in data types of the ABAP Dictionary in an ABAP program. However, you can use them to create self-defined types in the ABAP Dictionary which can then be used in the ABAP program. To do this, you call the ABAP Dictionary tool (transaction SE11) either directly or from within the Object Navigator (see Figure 4.3).

By choosing **Data Element**, **Structure**, **Table Type**, **Database Table**, or **View** in the context menu, you can define all the data types of the type hierarchy in Figure 4.1.

TABLE 4.2 **The built-in types of the ABAP Dictionary. The number of places does not imply the field length in bytes but the number of valid positions, excluding the formatting characters. The ABAP types b and s for INT1 and INT2 have internal significance only. For LCHR and LRAW, max is the value of a preceding INT2 field; for LANG, "internal" means in the Dictionary and "external" means representation on screens.**

Dictionary Type	Meaning	Allowed places m	ABAP Type
DEC	Calculation / amount field	1–31, in Tab.: 1–17	p((m+1)/2)
INT1	1-byte integer	3	b
INT2	2-byte integer	5	s
INT4	4-byte integer	10	i
CURR	Currency field	1–17	p((m+1)/2)
CUKY	Currency key	5	c(5)
QUAN	Quantity	1–17	p((m+1)/2)
UNIT	Unit	2–3	c(m)
PREC	Accuracy	16	s
FLTP	Floating point number	16	f(8)
NUMC	Numeric text	1–255	n(m)
CHAR	Character	1–255	c(m)
LCHR	Long character	256-max	c(m)
STRING	String	1 max	string
RAWSTRING	Variable byte string	1 max	xstring
DATS	Date	8	d
ACCP	Accounting period	6	n(6)
TIMS	Time	6	t
RAW	Byte sequence	1–255	x(m)
LRAW	Long byte sequence	256-max	x(m)
CLNT	Client	3	c(3)
LANG	Language	Internal 1, External 2	c(1)

Self-defined elementary data types in the ABAP Dictionary

The elementary data types of the Dictionary are defined as **data elements** (see Figure 4.4).

Domain

When you choose **Elementary Type** on the **Definition** tab page, you have two options. You can either specify a built-in type and its technical attributes such as

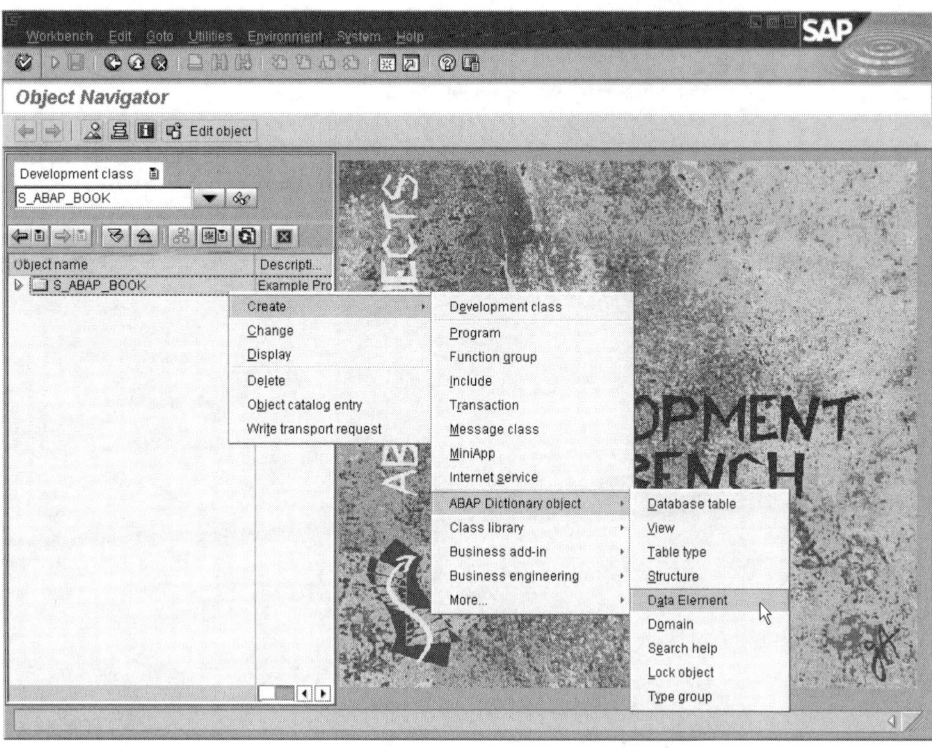

FIGURE 4.3 Calling the ABAP Dictionary. Copyright © SAP AG

length or decimal places directly (the equivalent of using the TYPES statement in ABAP), or you can specify a **domain**. Like the data element itself, a domain is an independent object in the ABAP Dictionary (see the context menu in Figure 4.3) which can be used by any number of data elements. A domain describes the technical attributes built-in type, length, and any decimal places. A data element with a domain inherits the domain's technical attributes.

Semantics

While the technical attributes of different data elements can be defined for reuse in a single domain, each data element has its own semantic attributes. For example, on the **Field label** tab page you must enter texts of various lengths which are automatically used on screens by tools such as the Screen Painter. By choosing the **Documentation** and **Supplementary documentation** pushbuttons, you can create texts which users see when they press F1 on a screen field of the type of the data element.[9] For further details on how the data elements of the ABAP Dictionary support field and input help, refer to Section 7.1.7.

9. All these texts are linked to the ABAP Workbench translation process. If your installation supports translation into other languages, these texts will automatically be sent to the worklist of your translators.

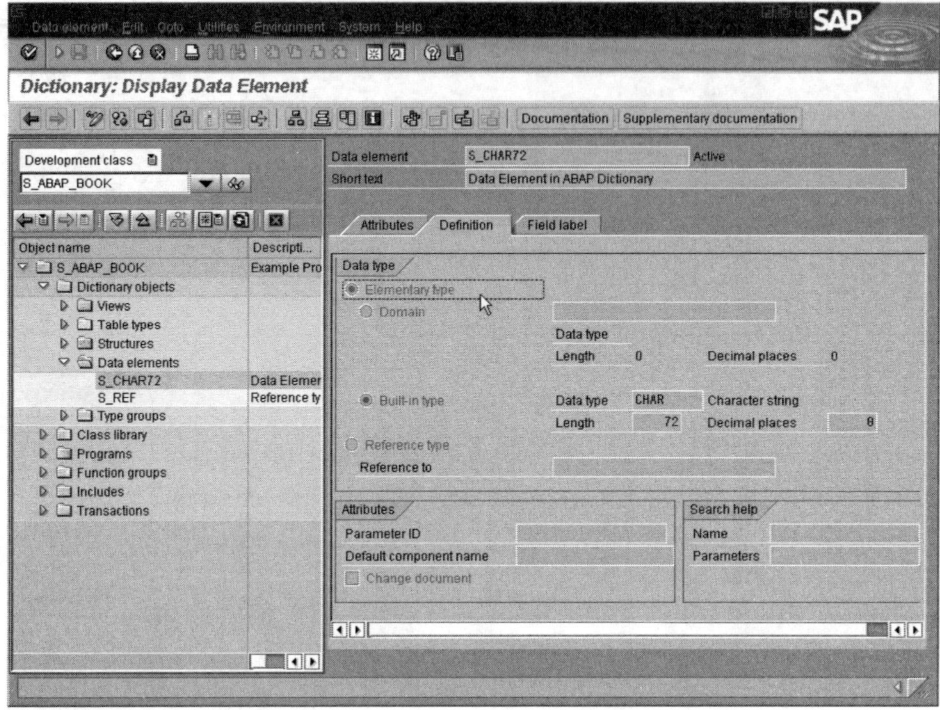

FIGURE 4.4 Creating a data element. Copyright © SAP AG

Each ABAP program can use the data elements of the ABAP Dictionary, once they have been activated, to declare data objects or for other typings:

```
DATA mychar TYPE s_char72.
```

Reference types in the ABAP Dictionary

The reference types of the ABAP Dictionary are also defined as data elements. In Figure 4.4 you simply need to select **Reference type** and specify in the field either "DATA" for data references or a global class or global interface from the class library for object references (see Figure 4.5).

With the ABAP Dictionary reference types you can declare reference variables in any ABAP program:

```
DATA myref TYPE s_ref.
CREATE OBJECT myref EXPORTING ...
```

For more details on object references and `CREATE OBJECT`, see Section 5.3.3.

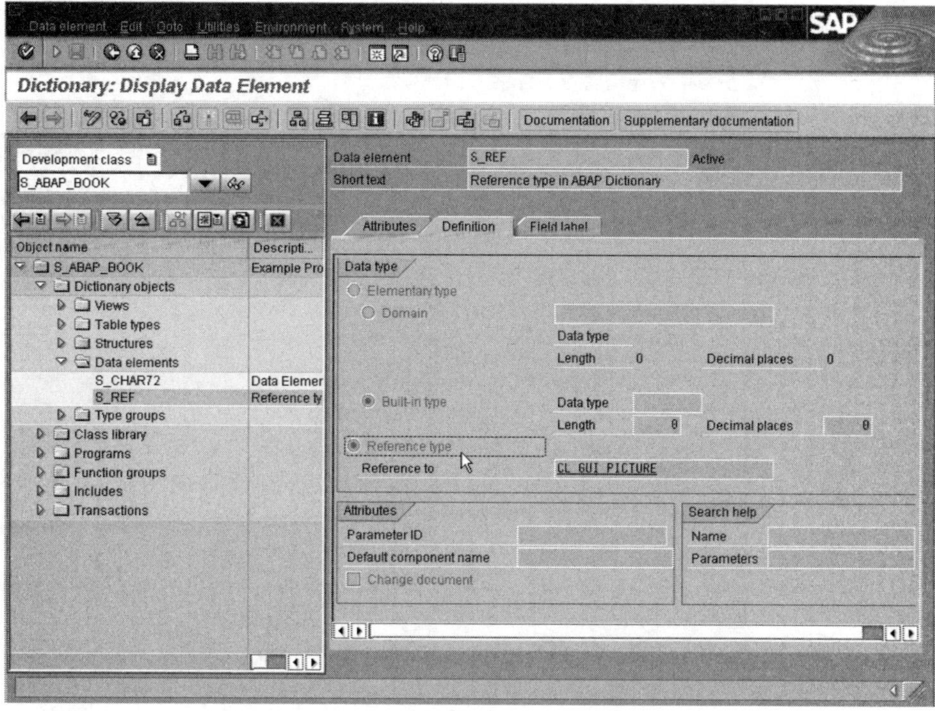

FIGURE 4.5 Reference type in the ABAP Dictionary. Copyright © SAP AG

Structured types in the ABAP Dictionary

Like structured types in the ABAP program, structured types in the ABAP Dictionary consist of any data types from the ABAP Dictionary. The components of structured types from the ABAP Dictionary can therefore be data elements, other structures, table types, database tables, or views. Figure 4.6 shows the maintenance dialog for structures in the ABAP Dictionary.

When you create a structure in the Dictionary, you must specify a name and a data type for each component. In this example, we have simply used the two previously defined data elements as component types.[10] Every ABAP program can now create local structures with this type:

```
DATA mystruc TYPE strucdemo.
mystruc-comp1 = 'Text'.
CALL METHOD mystruc-comp2->load_picture_from_url.
```

10. To include the components of existing structures in new ones, you can choose *Edit – Include – Insert* when you create a structure. This function provides the same options as the `INCLUDE` statement in ABAP programs.

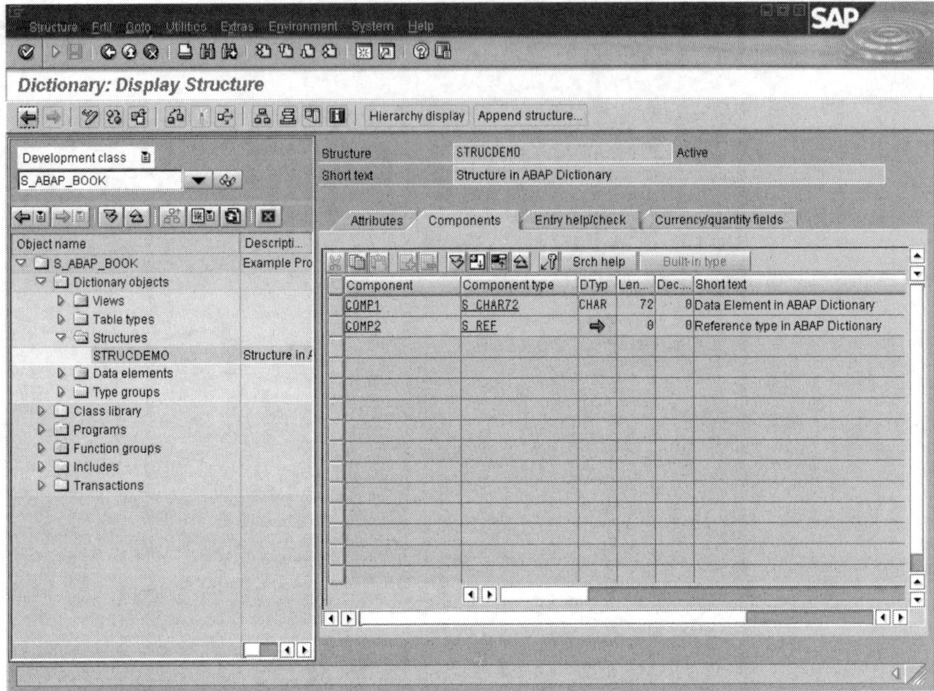

FIGURE 4.6 Structure in the ABAP Dictionary. Copyright © SAP AG

The first component of the structured data object is of type `c`, length 72, while the second component is an object reference variable of type `REF TO c1_gui_picture`.

You can also refer directly to the components of structured types of the ABAP Dictionary:

```
DATA mytext TYPE strucdemo-comp1.
```

This statement is equivalent to:

```
DATA mytext TYPE s_char72.
```

Table types in the ABAP Dictionary

Just like local table types, table types in the ABAP Dictionary describe the attributes of an internal table in the ABAP program. You should therefore never confuse table types with database tables. The maintenance dialog for a table type is shown in Figure 4.7.

Any other data type from the ABAP Dictionary can be specified as a line type. In our example, we determine the line type by our previously defined structure type. Similarly to the `TYPES` or `DATA` statement, the maintenance dialog allows you to

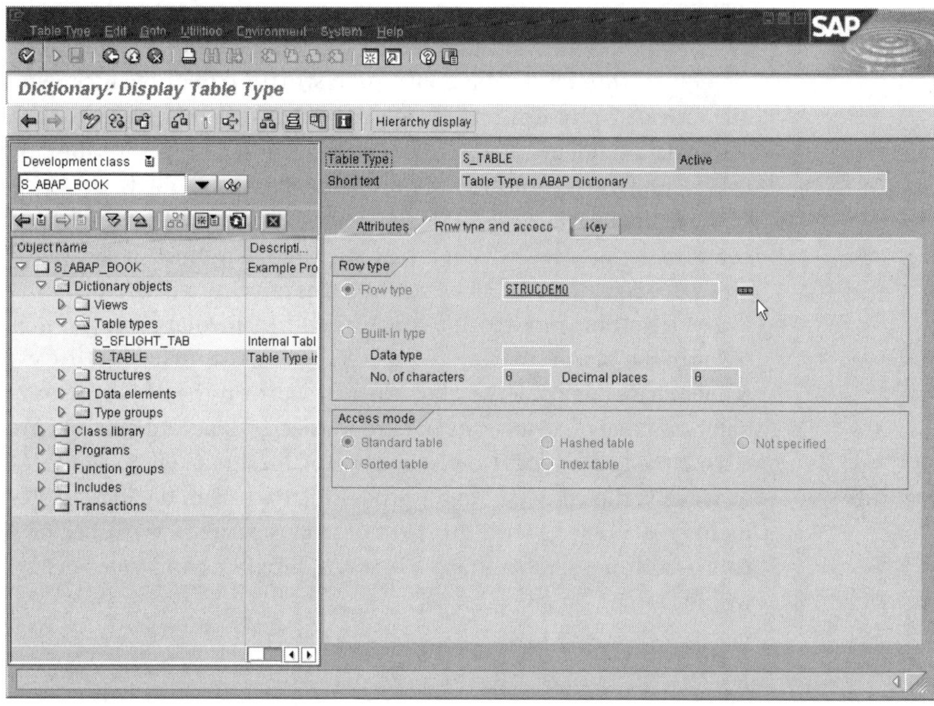

FIGURE 4.7 Table type in the ABAP Dictionary. Copyright © SAP AG

specify the table kind and the table key. You can then create internal tables in any ABAP program using this type:

```
DATA: mytable TYPE s_table,
      myline  TYPE LINE OF s_table.

LOOP AT mytable INTO myline.
  ...
ENDLOOP.
```

You see here that you can also create data objects which refer to the line type of an internal table. The `LINE OF` syntax can be used in all statements with the `TYPE` and `LIKE` additions. When declaring `myline` you can of course use `TYPE` directly to refer to the `strucdemo` line type, if it is statically known.

Database tables and views

Apart from storing type descriptions, the central task of the ABAP Dictionary is to manage the database tables of the SAP System. The display and maintenance dialog for a database table (see Figure 2.35 and Figure 8.2, for example) shows hardly any difference compared with Figure 4.6. In the ABAP Dictionary, database tables are described through structures which can only contain elementary components (data elements). Differently than with pure structure maintenance, when database tables are activated physical tables are generated with this structure in the database. The above data elements therefore not only act as data types in ABAP programs but moreover define the technical attributes of database table fields.

View

Views are logical views of one or more existing database tables in which the relevant columns are grouped within a new structure. For more details on the functionality of views, see Section 8.1.3. However, in terms of being a data type in the ABAP Dictionary, a view is nothing more than a structure with elementary components.

From the perspective of the ABAP program, it is first of all irrelevant whether there is a database table or a view behind a structure in the ABAP Dictionary. The name of a database table or a view can be used for declarations and typings just like the name of a structured data type. However, defining local data with reference to database tables or views is the cornerstone for processing data from database tables with ABAP statements. Data objects with this kind of data type act as type-specific work areas for any data read from database tables in ABAP programs and vice versa. A typical example would be:

```
DATA mytab TYPE SORTED TABLE
           OF spfli
           WITH UNIQUE KEY carrid connid.
SELECT *
FROM   spfli
INTO   TABLE mytab
WHERE  carrid = 'LH'.
```

These intuitively readable lines create an internal table with the same line type and table key as the `spfli` database table and retrieve data from the database table into the internal table. We will concentrate more on this topic in Section 8.1.3.

Type groups

To conclude our treatment of data types in the ABAP Dictionary, we need to discuss **type groups** briefly. The ABAP type hierarchy of the ABAP Dictionary which we have just introduced was implemented in Release 4.5. Previously, only database tables and flat structures could be defined as data types in the ABAP Dictionary. Nor was it possible to refer directly to individual data elements in ABAP programs other than through components of structures or database tables. Type groups were used in order to store all forms of data types on a cross-program basis. Type groups are special ABAP programs which are introduced with the `TYPE-POOL` statement and can only contain `TYPES` and `CONSTANTS` statements (for more information on constants, see Section 4.2.8).

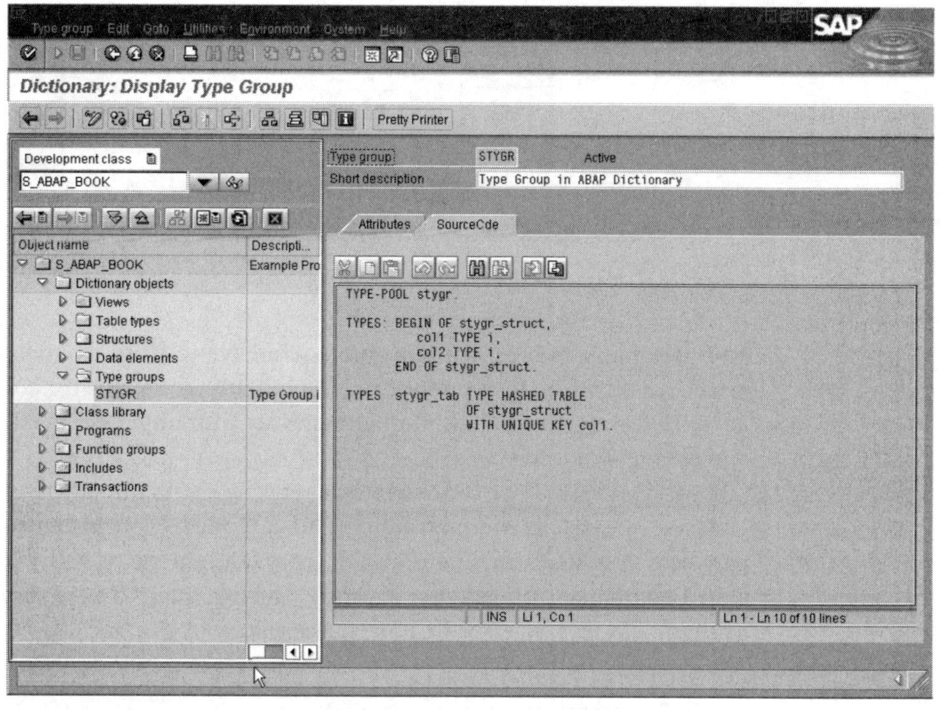

FIGURE 4.8 Type group in the ABAP Dictionary. Copyright © SAP AG

Type groups are also maintained with the ABAP Dictionary tool (see the context menu in Figure 4.3). The data types and constants of a type group must begin with the name of the type group as a prefix (see Figure 4.8).

Each ABAP program can work with these types providing it declares the type group in the program by using the TYPE-POOLS statement:

```
TYPE-POOLS  stygr.
DATA mytab TYPE stygr_tab.
```

Constant

If you now find a TYPE-POOLS statement in a program, you know its purpose and can go to the definition of the type group through forward navigation. However, you should no longer create new data types in type groups. Nonetheless, type groups remain the only way of creating cross-program constants in the ABAP Dictionary.

4.2.6 Flat and deep data types

Since the terms "flat" and "deep" in the context of data types are often misunderstood, we shall briefly summarize their meaning.

We describe all data types whose data object contents represent actual work data as **flat**. Fixed length elementary data types are therefore always flat. **Deep** data types are

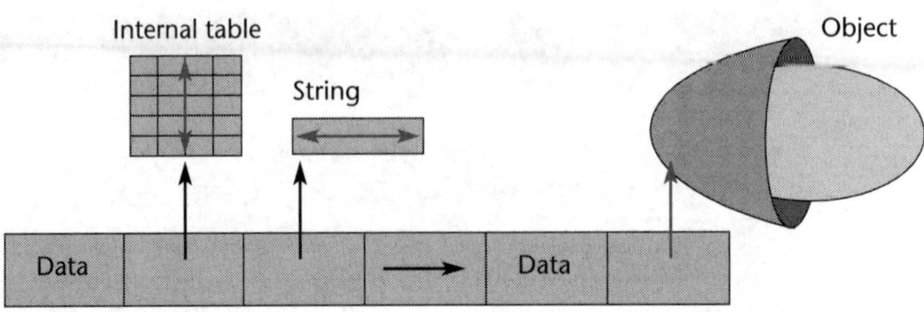

FIGURE 4.9 A deep structure

ones whose data object contents are a reference to work data in other parts of the memory. Accordingly, reference types explicitly designed to handle references are deep. However, strings and internal tables are also implicitly managed by references and are therefore also deep.

Structure

How does this affect structures? We refer to a structure as flat if it only contains flat types, i.e. fixed length elementary data types, as components. Nesting plays no part here. A nested structure is also flat, providing none of its substructures contains a deep component. However, a structure which contains a deep component in any of its nesting levels is referred to as deep (see Figure 4.9).

4.2.7 Generic data types for typings

So far we have dealt mainly with data types where all the technical attributes such as length and number of decimal places are known. The built-in elementary types `c`, `n`, `x`, and `p` are incomplete in that respect but are always supplemented by the corresponding values when they are used to define new data types or to declare data objects with the `TYPES` or `DATA` statements.

TYPE

However, data types are used not only to define data local to the program but also for typings. Typings are specifications of data types after a `TYPE` addition when defining interface parameters for procedures (see Section 5.2.1) or defining field symbols (see Section 4.6.1). The actual data type of interface parameters and field symbols is only transferred during program runtime when a data object is assigned. Typing means that only certain data objects can be assigned. If during a typing a fully known data type is specified which, for example, has been defined with `TYPES` or in the ABAP Dictionary, only data objects of this type can be used as transfer parameters for procedures or assigned to field symbols.[11]

However, interface parameters and field symbols often have to be generically typed. This means that the data type passed at runtime is checked only partly or not at all. This is the basis of dynamic programming in which procedures can work with

11. Typings are also possible with `LIKE`. In this case, the type is copied from an existing data object and is also fully known.

different types of transfer parameters, for example. On the other hand, partial typing is often necessary to ensure a certain degree of type safety. Section 5.2.1 contains a detailed example which shows how an interface parameter must be typed in order to be used as an internal table in a procedure.

For this kind of generic typing, a set of generic data types is available, some of which can only be used for typings (see Table 4.3).

TABLE 4.3 Generic data types in ABAP

Generic type	Meaning
`ANY`	Fully generic type
`ANY TABLE`	All table types
`INDEX TABLE`	Index tables
`TABLE`	Standard tables
`STANDARD TABLE`	Standard tables
`SORTED TABLE`	Sorted tables
`HASHED TABLE`	Hashed tables
`c, n, x, p`	Built-in types without length specification

Internal table

All other built-in and self-defined data types have fixed attributes, with one exception: if a table type is defined with `TYPES` or in the ABAP Dictionary without specifying a key, this is also a generic type which can only be used in typings.[12] The generic table types listed in Table 4.3 mean that the specified table type is used for typing, while the line type and table key are arbitrary. In Section 4.7.1 we shall focus more on generic table types.

4.2.8 Data objects in detail

In the previous sections we introduced the ABAP type concept in detail. You learned how to define local data types and data objects using the `TYPES` and `DATA` statements. The statement syntax is very similar, because when you declare data objects you can also create a new data type which then only exists as an attribute of the object. Whereas all data types can be defined across programs in the ABAP Dictionary, data objects are local to the program and exist only in the memory area of the program at runtime.

12. Remember that when you use a built-in generic type for the declaration of data objects, a standard value is supplemented for the length and the decimal places.

We will now provide you with some more essential information about data objects. In particular, we will introduce you to the various kinds of data objects that occur in ABAP. We will start with named data objects.

Named data objects

Variable

All the data objects we previously declared with the DATA statement have a name by which they can be addressed in the program. We refer to these data objects as **named**. You have also seen in the previous examples that we can assign values to data objects declared with DATA in the ABAP program. We therefore classify all data objects declared with DATA as **variables**. The contents of variables can be read and modified in a program. Variables are by far the most common data objects in ABAP programs, and consequently DATA is the most important declaration statement. The attributes of classes in ABAP Objects are also declared with DATA.

Constant

Constants are named data objects whose value is fixed for the duration of an ABAP program's runtime. Constants are declared with the CONSTANTS statement instead of DATA. The syntax of the CONSTANTS statement is that of the DATA statement with the exception that VALUE is mandatory with CONSTANTS. It is not possible to specify a VALUE when declaring strings, references, and internal tables. Therefore, only fixed length elementary data objects and flat structures can be declared as constants, and there are no constants with deep data types.

The corresponding syntax is:

```
CONSTANTS  const[(len)] {TYPE type|LIKE dobj}
           [DECIMALS dec]
           VALUE val.
```

The initial value val is determined by VALUE, and this cannot be changed at runtime. Any attempt to assign a different value to the const constant in the program will trigger syntax or runtime errors. Like variables, structured constants can be declared with the BEGIN OF and END OF additions.

By declaring constants with mnemonic names for recurring values, you make programs more readable. As with all data declarations, you should declare constants at a central point in the program in order to facilitate maintenance. A typical example for constants is:

```
CONSTANTS pi TYPE f VALUE '3.14159265359'.
DATA: radius TYPE p DECIMALS 2,
      area   TYPE p DECIMALS 2.
...
area = pi * radius ** 2.
```

If you wish to set a constant to its type-specific initial value, you can use VALUE as follows:

```
CONSTANTS ... VALUE IS INITIAL.
```

This form is of course also possible with DATA.

Selection screen parameter

In addition to DATA and CONSTANTS there is another statement which is very similar but has completely different semantics:

```
PARAMETERS   p[(len)] {TYPE type|LIKE dobj}
             [DECIMALS dec]
             [DEFAULT def] ...
```

As with DATA, a variable with the name p is declared, but at the same time an appropriate input field is created on a selection screen. Depending on where the declaration is made and the way the program is executed, the selection screen is either automatically displayed or must be called with CALL SELECTION-SCREEN. In Section 7.2 we will focus specifically on selection screens.

Table work area

The next kind of named data objects we need to cover are **table work areas**. Table work areas played an extremely large role in ABAP programming prior to Release 4.0, but have since lost much of their importance. Table work areas are declared with the TABLES statement. The syntax is:

```
TABLES  dbtab.
```

where dbtab is a database table, a view, or a flat structure from the ABAP Dictionary. The TABLES statement has basically the same effect as the following statement:

```
DATA dbtab TYPE dbtab.
```

A local data object with the same name and structure as the structured type dbtab from the ABAP Dictionary is declared. This is the table work area. Prior to Release 4.0 you had to declare table work areas with TABLES in order to access the relevant database tables in ABAP programs. As of Release 4.0 this constraint no longer applies. To avoid confusion through the multiple use of a name, only table work areas with a different name should be declared for accessing database tables:

```
DATA wa_dbtab TYPE dbtab.
```

As of Release 4.0, the TABLES statement is required in only two cases:

- If you are linking an executable program with a logical database, you need table work areas to receive the data from the logical database. In this context, you can also use the NODES statement instead of TABLES. Note that NODES can also be used for other data types from the ABAP Dictionary besides flat structures.
- If you are defining input fields on screens by getting data types from the ABAP Dictionary, you need table work areas to transport data between the screens and the ABAP program.

In all other cases the TABLES statement is now obsolete. In fact, it is even forbidden in ABAP Objects classes.

Text symbol

Before we move on to anonymous data objects (literals), we will introduce **text symbols**, which act as language-independent substitutes for text literals. Text symbols are a special kind of named data object which you create in a special maintenance screen of the ABAP Workbench and not with declaration statements. To display this screen, choose **Goto – Text elements – Text symbols** in the ABAP Editor (see Figure 4.10).

You can now enter any text for three-digit identifiers. These identifiers can consist of letters and numbers. The ABAP program provides these texts as data objects with the name `text-###`, where `###` is the three-digit identifier. In the program, you handle text symbols like type c fields of the length specified in column **mLen**. Their contents, however, are specified outside the program:

LISTING 4.4 Text symbols in an ABAP program

```
REPORT s_text_symbols.
DATA mytext(20) TYPE c.
mytext = text-010.
WRITE: / mytext, text-020.
```

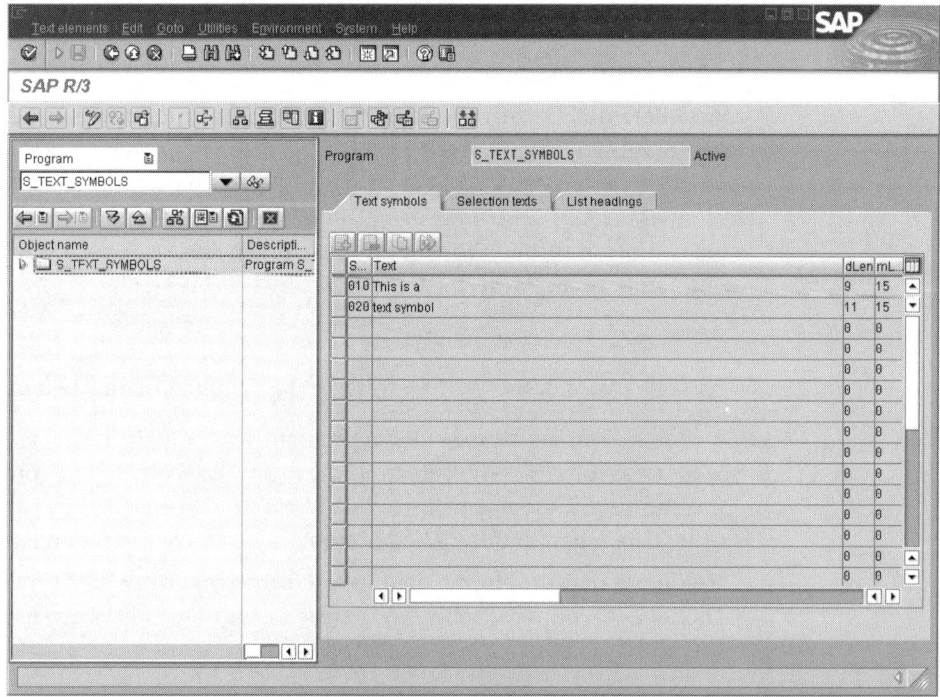

FIGURE 4.10 Creating text symbols. Copyright © SAP AG

This would be nothing special in itself, but like selection texts (see Section 7.2) and the titles of classical lists (see Section 7.3.4), text symbols are part of the text elements of an ABAP program. Like the texts of data elements in the ABAP Dictionary, these text elements are linked to the translation process.[13] You can therefore use text symbols whenever you want to use program texts as interface elements without having to take into account the language in which a user logs on. The runtime environment always uses the text in the logon language and thereby makes your program multilingual, without a translator having to change the source code. Text symbols are particularly suitable for use in classical lists (see Section 7.3.4) and in dialog messages (see Section 7.4).

If you are working in multilingual systems, you should never use text literals to represent texts. The ABAP Workbench supports you in replacing text literals with text symbols. If you double-click a text literal, the Workbench creates a text symbol with the contents of that literal. You can attach the text symbol identifier in brackets to the text literal, as follows:

```
... 'Text_literal'(###) ...
```

Here too, the text symbol is used instead of the text literal, depending on the logon language. The literal is only used in case no translation is available in the logon language.[14]

Literals

Literals are data objects which occupy program memory and are of a particular type, but which have no name. We therefore refer to literals as **anonymous** data objects. The content or value of literals is written directly in the source code and is used at the exact point in the program where it occurs. The value of a literal cannot be changed. We distinguish between two kinds of literals: text literals and numeric literals.

Text Literal

A text literal is an alphanumeric character string with a maximum length of 255 characters, enclosed in quotation marks. A text literal always has the built-in data type c, and its length is determined by the number of characters. Examples of text literals would be:

```
WRITE: / 'SAP AG',
       / 'Walldorf'.
```

Each text literal is at least one character long. Specifying `''` is the same as specifying `' '`. To create text literals which are longer than a line in the ABAP Editor, several text literals can be linked using the & character.

13. Allow sufficient space for the translation when specifying the maximum length **mLen** of a text symbol. For example, the German word "Feld" requires five letters for the English "field."
14. If you use `text-###` and the translation is missing, the text symbol is treated like a blank single-character text field.

```
WRITE / 'This ' &
        'is only ' &
        'one text literal'.
```

If instead a single text literal spans several editor lines, all the places between the quotation marks are interpreted as significant characters.

To show a quotation mark within a text literal, two quotation marks must be entered consecutively to avoid it being interpreted as the end of the text literal.

```
WRITE / 'Welcome to Bob''s Bar!'.
```

In these examples we have always placed the text literals after `WRITE`. Entering these lines into a program in the Editor and running it is the fastest way of seeing how the system handles text literals. Note, however, that text literals cannot be used in this way if your programs are to work independently of the user's logon language. Text literals written with `WRITE` on a classical list cannot be translated. In multilingual programs you should therefore replace all text literals with text symbols. To do this, simply double-click a text literal in the ABAP Editor (see above).

Numeric literal

A numeric literal is a sequence of numbers in the program code which can be preceded by a sign. Numeric literals are not enclosed in quotation marks. You can represent all numbers whose value lies within the value range of the built-in data type p with a field length of 16 without decimal places, i.e. numbers with a maximum of 31 digits plus sign. Numeric literals with a value between $-2^{31}+1$ and $2^{31}-1$ have the built-in data type i, all others are of type p. Examples of numeric literals include:

```
... 1234567890 ...
... -987654321 ...
```

However, you cannot represent numbers with decimal places using this kind of numeric literal, because outside of text literals a decimal point is always interpreted as the end of a statement. In order to represent non-integers or floating point numbers with their mantissa and exponent, you must use text literals as follows:[15]

```
... '+0.58498' ...
... '-8473.67' ...
... '12.34567-' ...
... '-765E-04' ...
... '1234E5' ...
... '+12E+23' ...
... '+12.3E-4' ...
... '1E160' ...
```

15. This also applies to numbers with more than 31 digits.

In the third text literal you see that it is possible to have a business notation with the sign following. As text literals are not numeric data types, a type conversion from type c into a suitable numeric type takes place when using this kind of text literal in assignments and arithmetic calculations (see Section 4.3.2).

```
DATA: float TYPE f,
      pack TYPE p DECIMALS 1.
float  = '-765E-04'.
pack   = '-8473.67'.
```

After the assignments the float and pack fields in the Debugger have the values 7.6499999999999999E–02 and –8473.7. The floating point number is therefore handled slightly less exactly internally, while the packed number is rounded up to its decimal places. It is not possible to assign a text literal with a mantissa and exponent to type i or p numeric fields. Such text literals may only contain numbers and a minus sign in the right format, whereby the minus sign can be before or after the number.

System fields

ABAP contains a set of predefined data objects called **system fields**. These are always present in ABAP programs and are filled by the runtime environment depending on the context. You can use system fields in the program to check the system status. Although system fields are variables, you should only access them in read-only mode as otherwise key information for the rest of the program execution could be lost. Only in a very few exceptions can system fields be overwritten in ABAP programs to control system behavior.[16]

The names and data types of the system fields are defined in the ABAP Dictionary as components of the structured data type SYST. There you find all system fields and their respective documentation. In each ABAP program, the runtime environment creates a structure called sy from this data type and fills the individual components while the program is executed. In ABAP programs you therefore address the individual system fields through sy-field. Listing 4.5 shows a simple example.

LISTING 4.5 Using system fields

```
REPORT s_system_fields.
WRITE: / 'Hello user', sy-uname,
       / 'the current date is', sy-datum,
       / 'the time is', sy-uzeit, 'o''clock.'.
```

sy-subrc

One of the most important system fields is sy-subrc, the return code. Many ABAP statements set sy-subrc to zero if execution is successful, and otherwise not equal to

16. An example is SY-LSIND for navigating in classical detail lists.

zero. We recommend that you check the contents of sy-subrc after every statement which sets the return code before you continue processing. For each statement the keyword documentation describes which system fields are affected.

The sy structure also contains many components which are either designed for internal use only or are no longer supplied at all. A complete list of system fields which can be used in application programs is provided in the Appendix A.

Determining attributes of data objects

It can often be necessary to determine the technical attributes of a data object at runtime. For example, you may want to know the data type, length, and number of decimal places of a generically typed parameter in a procedure before you use it to calculate. Prior to Release 4.6 ABAP only provided the DESCRIBE FIELD statement for this purpose. An example of DESCRIBE FIELD is given in Listing 4.6.

LISTING 4.6 The DESCRIBE FIELD statement

```
REPORT S_DESCRIBE_FIELD.
DATA: f1(20) TYPE c,
      f2 TYPE p DECIMALS 2.

PERFORM: test USING f1,
         test USING f2.

FORM test USING u_input TYPE ANY.
  DATA: t(1)  TYPE c,
        l     TYPE i,
        d     TYPE i.
  DESCRIBE FIELD u_input TYPE t LENGTH l DECIMALS d.
  WRITE: / 'type:',   t,  'length',    l,  'decimal  places', d.
ENDFORM.
```

Here, the PERFORM statement is used twice to call a subroutine test, whereby each time another data object is passed to the interface parameter u_input which is completely generic. The data type, length, and decimal place attributes are written by the additions of the DESCRIBE FIELD statement into local work fields of the subroutine and output to a list. The parameter u_input has a different type for each of the two calls. This basic program already gives you an insight into defining and calling subroutines, which we will discuss in more detail in Section 5.2.1.

The DESCRIBE FIELD statement originates from a time when the ABAP type hierarchy shown in Figure 4.1 consisted only of elementary types, flat structures, and internal standard tables without a table key, whose line type could only be a flat

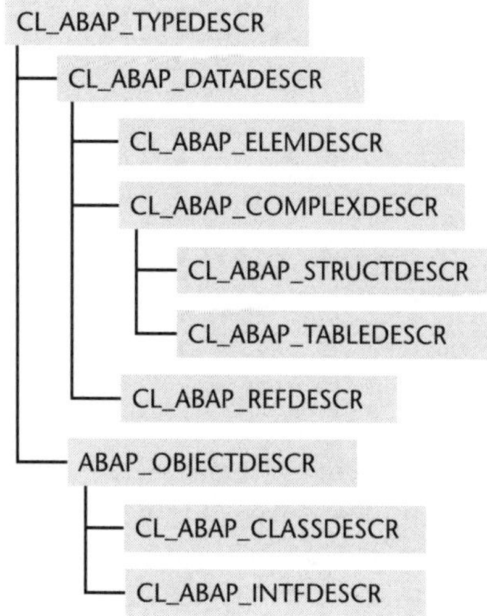

FIGURE 4.11 Global classes for RTTI

structure. The functionality of the `DESCRIBE FIELD` statement and its additions is therefore limited and can only be used for these basic cases.

There are now data objects with types of any complexity, and reference variables which can contain references to data objects and any kind of object in ABAP Objects. The type information that needs to be determined for a data object is much more extensive than with earlier data types. With reference variables we can even distinguish two kinds of type: the actual data type of the variable and the type of the object to which the reference variable is pointing. For more details on static and dynamic types, refer to Section 6.2.9.

RTTI

To handle these requirements for determining the type of a data object, the concept of **run-time type identification** (RTTI) was implemented in ABAP Objects. Instead of expanding the language scope to do this, a set of global classes has been provided in the ABAP class library.[17] The classes form an inheritance hierarchy which reflects the entire ABAP type hierarchy (see Figure 4.11). The public methods and attributes of the classes allow RTTI for all data objects or data types in ABAP programs.

Listing 4.7 shows a basic example of using the `cl_abap_typedescr` class.

LISTING 4.7 RTTI with global classes

```
REPORT s_rtti.
TYPES my_type TYPE p DECIMALS 2.
```

17. In future, a large number of such functions will be provided in so-called **system classes**.

```
DATA: my_data TYPE my_type,
      descr_ref   TYPE  REF TO cl_abap_typedescr.

descr_ref =
   cl_abap_typedescr=>describe_by_data( my_data ).

WRITE: / 'Typename:', descr_ref->absolute_name,
       / 'Kind :',    descr_ref->type_kind,
       / 'Length :',  descr_ref->length,
       / 'Decimals:', descr_ref->decimals.
```

The describe_by_data method is called using a function call, and in the process a data object my_data is passed to it. The syntax of ABAP Objects is described in more detail in Chapters 5 and 6. The result is a reference to an object of the class which contains the attributes of my_data in its public attributes. The results are:

- absolute_name: \PROGRAM=S_RTTI\TYPE=MY_TYPE
- type_kind: P
- length: 8
- decimals: 2

The self-defined type my_type is determined. You can see that the name contains not only the description of the TYPES statement but also the context of the data declaration, in this case the ABAP program. If the data object were declared in a class or procedure, the context specification would be longer. The class library contains detailed documentation for the RTTI classes.

4.3 OPERATIONS AND EXPRESSIONS

In Section 4.2 we covered data types and data objects in ABAP programs in considerable detail. This section is now concerned with the operations you can apply to data objects, particular features to note, and how the various operations acting on a data object depend on its data type.

4.3.1 Assigning values

Values are always assigned when you want to change the contents of a variable. You commonly use the MOVE statement or the assignment operator "=" to do this. In addition, you can reset data objects to their type-specific initial value using the CLEAR statement.[18]

18. Another assignment statement is WRITE TO which formats the contents in the target field as for a list output. However, we shall not expand on this statement in this book.

Value assignments for any data objects

To assign the contents of a source field to a target variable, use the statements

```
MOVE  source TO destination.
```

or

```
destination = source.
```

MOVE

Both statements have exactly the same effect. In both cases the `destination` variable is assigned the contents of the `source` data object. `Source` can also be a constant or a text literal, as its value is not changed by the assignment. For combining the operands, we can distinguish between three basic cases which determine the result of the value assignment.

1 The source and target data objects are completely **compatible**, i.e. they are identical in all technical aspects (data type, field length, and number of decimal places). The contents of the source object are transferred byte for byte to the target field.

2 The source and target data objects are **convertible**, but not completely compatible. In this case ABAP performs a type conversion. The contents of the source object are converted according to fixed rules and only then transferred to the target variable. Due to this additional step, more computing time is required for assignments that trigger a type conversion. We will introduce the rules of type conversion in Section 4.3.2.

3 If the data objects are neither compatible nor convertible, no assignment can take place. If the system recognizes this during the syntax check, a syntax error is generated; otherwise a runtime error occurs.

Assigning structures by component

The above rules apply to structures as for all other data objects. Two similar structures can easily be assigned to each other.

```
DATA: struct1 TYPE structure,
      struct2 TYPE structure.
struct1 = struct2.
```

During the assignment the whole of the source structure is seen as a unit and copied to the target structure. There you can access the components individually again. However, often you only want to assign specific components of a structure to those of another structure. To do this, you can of course use many single `MOVE` statements. However, ABAP also supports you with the following special statement:

```
MOVE-CORRESPONDING  sourcestruct TO destinationstruct.
```

This statement identifies all the components with the same name in the two structures and assigns them one by one according to the above rules. Listing 4.8 shows an example in which the two components of a local structure are assigned to a target structure whose data type is declared in the ABAP Dictionary. During the assignment only the `carrid` and `connid` components of the `wa_spfli` structure are changed.

LISTING 4.8 The `MOVE-CORRESPONDING` statement

```
REPORT s_move_corresponding.
DATA: BEGIN OF wa_connection,
        carrid TYPE spfli-carrid     VALUE 'LH',
        connid TYPE spfli-connid     VALUE '400',
      END OF wa_connection.
DATA  wa_spfli  TYPE spfli.
MOVE-CORRESPONDING wa_connection TO wa_spfli.
```

Setting a variable to its initial value

To reset a variable to its type-specific initial value, use the statement:

```
CLEAR f.
```

Note that this does not refer to the start value which can be assigned to a variable using the `VALUE` addition of the `DATA` statement.

Clear

The `CLEAR` statement has the following effect on data objects of different data types:

- Elementary data objects

  The contents of elementary data objects are reset to the initial value shown in Table 4.1, depending on the data type.

- Structures

  Structures are broken down into individual components until these components themselves are no longer structures. These individual components are then initialized according to their data type.

- Reference variables

  A reference variable which has been reset to its initial value no longer points to an object. This is comparable with a NULL pointer.

- Internal tables

  All the lines of the internal table are deleted.

4.3.2 Type conversions

The above assignment rules state that assignments without type conversion are only possible between compatible data objects whose attributes are identical. In all other cases, either a type conversion takes place or the assignment is simply not possible. This means, for example, that a conversion will also take place during an assignment between two type c data objects if they differ in length.

Conversion rule

If an assignment[19] is made between incompatible data objects, ABAP searches for an appropriate conversion rule to execute the statement. Two data types which are governed by such a rule are **convertible**. The type conversion rules in ABAP are defined in a way that ensures that as many data types as possible can be converted into one another. Of course, the plausible basic rule applies that the contents of the source field must constitute a meaningful value for the data type of the target variable.

Contents dependency

If it is already statically clear that a type conversion is not possible, the data types are inconvertible. For example, it does not make sense to allow conversions between data types d and t or between elementary fields and internal tables. In cases where a conversion rule exists, a runtime error may nevertheless be triggered if the contents of the source field do not correspond to the data type of the target variable at the time the assignment is made. For example, when assigning a type c or string character field to a numeric variable, you cannot statically check whether the contents actually represent a valid number, or, when assigning numbers to a numeric value, whether the value range has been exceeded. Therefore, errors may well occur at runtime in programs that are syntactically correct. Incorrect assignments are either genuine programming errors or can arise during generic programming, if for example you are working in procedures with input parameters and do not know their contents. In these cases it is appropriate to catch the runtime error of the `conversion_errors` error class between the `CATCH` and `ENDCATCH` statements. Listing 4.9 shows an example:

LISTING 4.9 Runtime error when assigning convertible types

```
REPORT s_conversion_errors.

DATA: f1(10) TYPE c VALUE 'Text',
      f2(10) TYPE c VALUE '1234'.

PERFORM: times2 USING f1,
         times2 USING f2.

FORM times2 USING u_input TYPE c.
  DATA result TYPE i.
  CATCH SYSTEM-EXCEPTIONS conversion_errors = 4.
    result = u_input * 2.
  ENDCATCH.
```

19. We can expand the term assignment to all operations which modify the contents of data objects. This includes especially the passing of data interface parameters of procedures.

```
    IF sy-subrc = 0.
      WRITE: / u_input, '* 2 =', result.
    ELSE.
      WRITE: / u_input, 'is no number'.
    ENDIF.
  ENDFORM.
```

In subroutine times2 a calculation is made with a type c input parameter, u_input. This is theoretically possible because text fields can be converted into numbers. However, there is no guarantee that the contents are actually a number. Therefore the calculation is only executed for the call in which field f2 is passed.[20] For more details on catching runtime errors refer to Section 4.8.2.

We will now briefly discuss the key conversion rules.

Assignments between elementary data types

There are ten built-in elementary data types. ABAP contains rules for conversions between all of these types with the exception of types d and t, between which a conversion is unsuitable. We will now summarize the basic rules for each of the various target field types.

- Type c target field

  The contents of all character-type fields are placed left-justified in the target field. If the target field is too short, there is a right truncation, if it is too long, the right-hand side is padded with blanks.

  The contents of all numeric fields are represented according to type and contents with sign, decimal point, or mantissa/exponent and placed right-justified in the target field. If the target field is too short, the contents are rounded up or truncated at the left. The latter is indicated by the * character.

  The contents of byte fields are converted into a hexadecimal character string in which a byte is represented by two characters and placed in the target field.

- String type target field

  The same rules apply as for the type c target field, whereby the resulting string length is always based on the required number of characters. In this process there are never any trailing blanks, nor any right truncation.

- Type n target field

  Only the digits from the contents of character-type fields are considered and placed right-justified in the target field. If the target field is too short, there is a left truncation; if it is too long, the left-hand side is padded with zeros.

20. Of course, it would be better here to type the input parameter u_input with reference to a numeric data type.

The numeric contents of numeric fields are converted into a digit string without a sign or decimal point and placed right-justified in the target field.

The decimal numeric value is determined from the contents of byte fields and placed with digits in the target field. Only the last four bytes are taken into account.

- Type d target field

  When character-type fields are assigned, a type d target field is treated in the same way as an 8-character type c field. You must ensure that a valid date in the format YYYYMMDD is assigned (see also Section 4.3.3).

  The numeric contents of numeric fields and the decimal value of the last four bytes of byte fields are considered as the number of days since 01.01.0001 and converted into a date in the format YYYYMMDD.

- Type t target field

  When character-type fields are assigned, a type t target field is treated in the same way as a 6-character type c field. You must ensure that a valid time in the format HHMMSS is assigned (see also Section 4.3.3).

  The numeric contents of numeric fields and the decimal value of the last four bytes of byte fields are considered as the number of seconds since 00:00:00 and converted into a time in the format HHMMSS.

- Type i, p, or f target fields

  The contents of text fields and numeric texts must be interpretable as a number and are converted according to its value; with the exception of target type f, the number is rounded up to its decimal places. With type d or t source fields, the date and time are converted respectively into the number of days since 01.01.0001 and seconds since 00:00:00.

  Numeric fields are converted into each other according to their value, providing the value range of the target field is not exceeded.

  The decimal numeric value of the last four bytes is determined from the contents of byte fields and placed in the target field.

- Type x target fields

  Text fields can only contain the 16 hexadecimal characters. These are packed into bytes, transferred left-justified, and padded with zeros or truncated on the right. If the text field contains something other than a hexadecimal character, conversion is terminated at this point and the rest of the target field padded with zeros.

  With type d or t source fields the date and time are converted respectively into the number of days since 01.01.0001 and seconds since 00:00:00, and the numeric value is converted into its binary representation.

  The numeric value of numeric fields is converted to type i, and the resulting four bytes are placed right-justified in the target field. Negative numbers are displayed in two's complement form (bit-by-bit complement plus one).

Byte fields are transferred left-justified and truncated or padded with zeros on the right.

- *xstring* type target fields

  The same rules apply as for the type x target field, whereby the resulting string length is always based on the required number of bytes.

Assignments between reference variables

Only type-specific assignments are possible between reference variables, i.e. you can assign object references to object references and data references to data references. References are not converted. Instead, the reference, i.e. the address of an object in the memory, is transferred unchanged. When you make an assignment between object references, the type of the reference variable and the type of the object to which the source variable is pointing play an important role. We will cover this in more detail in Chapter 6.

Assignments with structures

When making assignments which involve structures, we need to distinguish between flat and deep structures (see Section 4.2.6). If you make an assignment between deep structures, the structures must be compatible. There are no conversion rules for deep structures.

Flat structures, on the other hand, are governed by a conversion rule which allows assignments between incompatible flat structures and even between elementary fields and structures. In this case, the structures concerned are treated as a single type c field whose length matches the sum of its component lengths plus the length of any alignment gaps (see below). If a short structure is converted into a longer one, the components at the end are therefore not initialized according to type, but filled with blanks. It is therefore preferable to assign longer structures to shorter ones and not vice versa.

Alignment

This kind of conversion is generally feasible only if the structures have purely character-type or byte-type components, to ensure that the individual components are correctly interpreted after being assigned. Assigning structures with numeric components in this manner could result in meaningless or illegal values. What makes things more complicated is that type i and f fields are aligned, i.e. they occupy special platform-specific addresses in the memory. For example, the address of a type i field must be divisible by 4, the address of a type f field normally by 8. If structures contain components of these types, they will also be aligned and may contain filler fields before these components (alignment gaps). The filler fields are added to the length of the character field during conversion. Therefore at least the parts of structures which contain numeric components should be placed at the very beginning of the structure and have the same design.

Unicode

Finally, we should point out that ABAP will support Unicode as of the next release. In a Unicode system, text characters no longer occupy a single byte as before. Instead, their length depends on the platform, and they can also be aligned. Therefore in future, Unicode-enabled ABAP programs will only allow you to make assignments between structures in which the **Unicode fragment view** of the source and target fields is identical. In the Unicode fragment view, flat structures are broken down into their character-type, byte-type, and other areas.[21] It is important to consider this fragment view also in the present release when working with structures, to avoid having to make comprehensive changes when you eventually switch to a Unicode system. The best solution would be to assign flat structures to each other only if they are compatible. Such assignments are never critical.

Assignments between internal tables

Internal tables can only be assigned to other internal tables. Whether internal tables can be assigned depends not on the table type or the table key, but only on the line type: internal tables can be assigned to each other if their line types are compatible or can be converted into each other. The individual lines from the source table are assigned to lines of the target table using the same semantics as between individual data objects of the corresponding line types. Of course, the contents of the source table are also important in this kind of assignment. Although the success of the assignment does not depend on the number of lines, runtime errors may be triggered even with compatible line types if, for example, duplicate entries are created in a target table with a unique key.

4.3.3 Numeric operations

A numeric operation is the calculation of a mathematical expression, the result of which is assigned to a target variable. The syntax of a numeric operation is:

```
[COMPUTE] result = mathematical expression.
```

The `COMPUTE` statement is optional. The `result` target variable can be any field which is able to represent numeric values. Of course, it is advisable to use one of the three numeric data types `i`, `p`, and `f`. On the right side of the assignment operator (=) there can be a mathematical expression which represents an arithmetic calculation or an individual mathematical function.

Calculation type

The result of the calculation on the right side has a data type which is determined by the data type of its operands and the data type of `result` (see below). If this calculation type is not the same as the data type of the `result` target variable, the result is converted into its type.

21. Such a fragment does not have alignment gaps.

Arithmetic calculations

Arithmetic calculations usually occur as a mathematical expression of a numeric operation. However, some arithmetic calculations can also be performed via special keywords. Table 4.4 shows all the operators and their corresponding keywords, if any. For all operations the result of the operation is assigned to field f1.

TABLE 4.4 **Arithmetic operators in ABAP**

Operation	Calculation with mathematical expression	Calculation with special keyword
Addition	f1 = f2 + f3.	ADD f2 TO f1
Subtraction	f1 = f2 – f3.	SUBTRACT f2 FROM f1
Multiplication	f1 = f2 * f3.	MULTIPLY f1 BY f2
Division	f1 = f2 / f3.	DIVIDE f1 BY f2
Integer Division	f1 = f2 DIV f3.	–
Remainder of Integer Division	f1 = f2 MOD f3.	–
Exponentiation	f1 = f2 ** f3.	–

The following rules apply when using operators:

- The entire arithmetic operation is performed with a **calculation type**. The calculation type with which ABAP evaluates the arithmetic expression can be one of the three numeric data types i, p, or f. The operands f1, f2, and f3 can be any field whose contents can be converted into one of the numeric types. The mathematical functions of the next section are also possible as operands.
- The calculation type is determined from the respective data type with the largest value range, whereby the data type of the result field is also taken into account. The value range of data type f is greater than that of p, which in turn is greater than that of i. If functions occur as operands, either the function arguments or the functions themselves determine the data type (see below). Before performing the calculation, all operands are converted into the calculation type and the result is converted back into the data type of the result field if necessary. Note, however, that too many conversions will adversely affect the computing speed, and so, if possible, you should declare all operands and the result field with the same numeric data type.
- With divisions the divisor must not be zero if the dividend itself is not zero. Dividing by zero will trigger a catchable runtime error (see example in Section 4.8.2).

- It is possible to form parenthetical expressions. In all other cases, the precedence rules apply, which state that multiplication and division have a higher precedence than addition and subtraction. Calculations for operators of the same precedence are carried out from left to right with one exception: exponentiation is carried out from right to left. Therefore, `f1 ** f2 ** f3` is the same as `f1 ** ( f2 ** f3 )` and not the same as `( f1 ** f2 ) ** f3`.
- With arithmetic calculations, you must note that the operators +, -, *, **, and / as well as opening and closing brackets are separate words in ABAP, which require a space before and after them.[22]

Mathematical functions

ABAP provides several built-in mathematical functions which either represent a complete mathematical expression or can be used as operands in arithmetic calculations. As with arithmetic calculations, the arguments of the functions can be any field whose contents can be converted to a numeric value. We can distinguish between functions which do and do not affect the calculation type of a mathematical expression (Tables 4.5 and 4.6 respectively).

TABLE 4.5 Functions not affecting the calculation type

Function	Meaning
abs	Absolute value of the argument
sign	Sign of the argument. Return values: x < 0: sign(x) = –1 x = 0: sign(x) = 0 x > 0: sign(x) = 1
ceil	Smallest integer value which is not less than the argument
floor	Largest integer value which is not greater than the argument
trunc	Integer part of the argument
frac	Decimal part of the argument

The result type of the functions from Table 4.5 is the argument type.[23] With this kind of function it is not the function but rather the data type of the argument which affects the calculation type of the mathematical expression. An example:

22. Only for mathematical functions the syntax is `func(argument)`.
23. We also say the functions are overloaded.

TABLE 4.6 **Type f floating point functions**

Function	Meaning
acos, asin, atan, cos, sin, tan	Trigonometric functions
cosh, sinh, tanh	Hyperbolic functions
exp	Exponential function with basis e (e=2.7182818285)
log	Natural logarithm with basis e
log10	Logarithm with basis 10
sqrt	Square root

```
DATA: result(20) TYPE c,
      float TYPE f VALUE '2.5E00'.
result = trunc( float ).
```

Here we are using a type c target field exceptionally, so that its data type does not affect the calculation type and the data type of the function can be determined. After the statement is executed, it contains the character string 2.0000000000000E+00, and the calculation type is f, as expected.

Floating point function

The functions in Table 4.6 always have the result type f. They are called floating point functions. If necessary, they convert their argument to this type before the calculation is performed. If a floating point function is used in a mathematical expression, the calculation type of the overall expression is type f. An example:

```
DATA: result(20) TYPE c,
      int TYPE i VALUE 2.
result = sqrt( int ).
```

Here we calculate the square root of a type i number. The calculation result is 1.4142135623731E+00, i.e. type f.

Business calculations

As it is primarily business applications which are created in the SAP System, business calculations with exact results must be supported. As already mentioned in Section 4.2.3, data type p fields are provided for business calculations, i.e. packed numbers with decimal places. To ensure that the runtime environment takes the decimal places of a packed number into account, the checkbox **Fixed Point Arithmetic** must be selected in the program attributes (see Figure 2.10).[24] Otherwise ABAP calculates

24. There are historical reasons for the fact that it is even possible to create programs without fixed point arithmetic at all: when ABAP was originally developed, packed numbers did not have any decimal points. Setting a specific program attribute allowed developers to change existing programs step by step. The procedure will be the same for converting ABAP programs into Unicode-enabled ABAP programs in Release 6.10.

using integer arithmetic, and the decimal places, which are determined by the DECIMALS parameter of the TYPES or DATA statements, will only affect the formatting on screens. An example:

```
DATA pack TYPE p DECIMALS 0.
pack = 1 / 3 * 3.
```

Without the **Fixed Point Arithmetic** program attribute the result will be 0, because the system computes with integer arithmetic. However, with the **Fixed Point Arithmetic** the result will be 1. The calculation type is p with an accuracy of 31 digits.

Date and time calculations

In some cases you may need to perform calculations with a type d date or a type t time. It is true that these data types are of character type,[25] but if you use a type d or t field in a mathematical expression, the field contents will be converted into the numeric calculation type of that expression. In Section 4.3.2 you learned that in this kind of conversion the contents are changed to the number of days since 01.01.0001 or the number of seconds since 00:00:00. When you assign a number to a type d or t field, the reverse conversion takes place. Listing 4.10 shows an example of date and time calculations.

LISTING 4.10 Date and time calculations

```
REPORT s_date_time.
PARAMETERS t_start TYPE t DEFAULT '080000'.
DATA: d_start TYPE d,
      year_days TYPE i,
      working_hours TYPE i.
d_start = sy-datum.
d_start+4(4) = '0101'.
year_days = sy-datum - d_start + 1.
working_hours = ( sy-uzeit - t_start ) / 3600.
WRITE: / 'Day', year_days, 'in year', sy-datum(4),
       / 'Accumulated working hours:', working_hours.
```

The PARAMETERS statement creates an input field on a selection screen in which the user can enter a start time in the t_start field. A start date d_start is set to 1 January of the current year by assigning the system field sy-datum and accessing a subfield (see Section 4.5.3). From this we can calculate the current day of the year. Using the current

25. The character-type format is used to represent a date or a time in the database or on the screen. Screen display is additionally formatted by the general logon data of the end-user.

time and the time entered we can calculate the number of hours worked to date. With the `WRITE` statement we make a subfield access to `sy-datum` to show the current year.

Validity

Correct computing with date and time presupposes of course that there is a date or time in the valid format in a source field. You can check the validity of the contents of date or time fields as follows: if a date or time field has invalid contents, the runtime environment sets the result of the conversion to a numeric value to zero. As conversion also takes place in logical expressions with different operand types (see Section 4.3.4), the validity can often be checked in a single expression.

```
DATA: date TYPE d,

date = '20000231'.
IF date = 0.
  ...              "Error
ELSE.
  ...              "OK
ENDIF.
```

The logical expression is true because `date` contains an invalid value and is set to zero for the comparison. Strictly speaking, the logical expression is of course also true for the valid date 01.01.0001. Although this date should hardly ever occur in application programs, checking the time can create a problem in that the valid time 00:00:00 certainly can occur. In this case, work fields must come to our assistance:

```
DATA time TYPE t.

DATA: test1 TYPE i,
      test2 TYPE t.

time = 'ABCXYZ'.

test1 = time.
test2 = test1.

IF time <> test2.
  ...                  "Error
ELSE.
  ...                  "OK
ENDIF.
```

The contents of `test2` do not match the contents of `time`, as the latter is set to zero during the assignment to `test1`.

Time stamp

If you want to mark dates uniquely, you often require more exact values for date and time than the `sy-datum` and `sy-uzeit` system fields can provide. In this case you can use **time stamps**. A current time stamp can be placed in the field f of an ABAP program using

```
GET TIME STAMP FIELD  f.
```

Time stamps are always globally unique as they are stored independently of the local time zone in UTC (Universal Time Coordination) time. Time stamps can be requested in short or long format. The short format contains the current date including the time, while the long format contains in addition seven decimal places for fractions of seconds which provide accuracy of up to 100 nanoseconds. The format requested depends on the data type of the target field f which can be declared with reference to the TIMESTAMP and TIMESTAMPL data elements of the ABAP Dictionary. There are other statements such as CONVERT TIME STAMP, which convert the time stamp into a date and time of a given time zone.

4.3.4 Logical expressions

A logical expression will return either a "true" or "false" result. Since ABAP does not have a Boolean data type to express these values, you cannot use logical expressions on the right side of assignments. Instead you can use logical expressions to formulate conditions in control structures (see Section 4.4).

Relational operators

In most logical expressions two data objects are compared via an operator. The basic relational operators for logical expressions available in ABAP are shown in Table 4.7. Note that letter abbreviations can be used instead of mathematical symbols.[26]

TABLE 4.7 Relational operators

Operator	Meaning
=, EQ	Equal to
<>, NE	Not equal to
<, LT	Less than
<=, LE	Less than or equal to
>, GT	Greater than
>=, GE	Greater than or equal to

Operators are used to compare two data objects, as for example in:

```
... f1 <= f2 ...
```

26. For the sake of clarity it is best to follow our example in this book and use only mathematical symbols.

The expression is true if the contents of f1 are less than or equal to the contents of f2. As with assignments, the data types of the two operands must be either compatible or convertible. We shall explore type conversions in logical expressions in more detail below.

Linking and reversing logical expressions

AND, OR, NOT

To link several logical expressions into a single logical expression, use the AND or OR logical linking operators.

To link several logical expressions into a single expression which is only true if all the expressions grouped within it are true, you link the expressions with AND. To link several logical expressions into a single expression which is true if at least one of the expressions grouped within it is true, you link the expressions with OR. You can reverse the result of a logical expression by placing the NOT operator at the beginning.

The expression: 0 < 1 AND 1 < 2 is true, but the expression NOT 0 < 1 AND 1 < 2 is false.

NOT takes precedence over AND, and AND takes precedence over OR. However, you can use any combination of parenthetical expressions to determine the processing order. As in mathematical expressions, ABAP interprets each parenthesis as a single word. You therefore need at least one space before and after each parenthesis.

ABAP processes logical expressions from left to right. If it detects that one of the subexpressions is true or false, no further comparisons or checks are made for this subexpression. The execution speed can therefore be improved by arranging logical expressions in such a way that comparisons which often turn out false are at the beginning of a series of ANDs, and complicated comparisons, such as searching for character strings, are at the end of the chain.

Comparing compatible elementary data objects

No conversion is performed when you compare compatible elementary operands. Numeric fields (types i, f, p) and numeric text fields (type n) are compared according to their numeric value. Character-type fields are always compared from left to right. The first different character from the left determines which operand is the greater. Specific rules govern the various data types:

- Text fields (type c) are compared according to the underlying character code, so for example 'a' < 'b'.
- In date fields (type d) the later date is greater than the earlier one, hence '20000101' > '19991231'.
- In time fields (type t) the later time is greater than the earlier one, hence '200000' > '140000'.
- Hexadecimal fields (type x) are compared in terms of their byte value.

Comparing incompatible elementary data objects

In logical expressions data objects can have different technical attributes. However, as for assignments, they must be convertible. The conversion rules for logical expressions supplement the rules for type conversions in Section 4.3.2.

Conversion

We will first consider data objects with the same data types but different lengths. Here, the shorter operand is converted to the length of the longer operand prior to the comparison. The following rules apply:

- Type p packed numbers with different lengths are compared with reference to their numeric value, and hence no padding is required.
- Type c text fields are padded with blanks on the right. Hence, for example the following expression is "true"

  ```
  'abc ' = 'abc'
  ```

  Actually, 'abc ' and 'abc ' are compared.[27]
- Type n numeric texts are padded with zeros on the left.
- Type x hexadecimal fields are padded with hexadecimal zero on the right.

If the operands have different data types, type conversions are performed according to the following hierarchy:

1. If one of the operands is a type i, p, or f numeric field, the system also converts the other operands into a numeric type. The same hierarchy as in arithmetic calculations applies: type f is higher than p, which in turn is higher than type i.
2. If one of the operands is a type d date field or a type t time field and the other operand is a numeric field, the system converts the date or time field into the numeric type. If the other operand is byte-type, the date or time field will also be interpreted as byte-type.
3. If one of the operands is a type c text field and the other operand a type x hexadecimal field, the system converts the operand from type x to type c.
4. If one of the operands is a type c text field and the other a type n numeric field, the system converts both operands to type p.

Comparing reference variables

Two reference variables are only equal if they point to the same object; otherwise they are not equal. A comparison of size for reference variables is defined internally and always provides the same results in the same context. It is suitable for sorted arrays of references, for example for finding specific references in internal tables.

27. Be careful with strings! If there is a string on the right with contents "abc" the comparison will not be true as a string has no trailing blanks.

Comparisons between structures

In the same way that you can make assignments involving structures in the ABAP type concept, structures can also be compared with other structures or even elementary fields.

Compatible structures are split into their components, which are then compared. Two compatible structures are the same if all their components are the same. If structures are unequal, the first unequal component determines which of the structures is greater or smaller.

Incompatible structures can be compared if they are convertible, i.e. flat. If you compare incompatible flat structures or flat structures with elementary fields, the respective structures are converted into type c fields before the comparison, and then treated as elementary fields.[28]

Comparing internal tables

Internal tables can also be compared with each other. The first criterion for comparing internal tables is the number of lines. The more lines an internal table contains, the greater it is. If two internal tables have the same number of lines, they are compared line by line and component by component. If the table line components are nested internal tables, they are compared recursively. With operators other than the equal operator the comparison stops after the first unequal pair of components and returns the corresponding result.

Other comparisons and checks

Besides the relational operators used in other programming languages, ABAP contains some additional operators for logical expressions:

IS operator

You use the IS operator to check:

- Whether a data object contains its type-specific initial value:

  ```
  ... f IS INITIAL ...
  ```

  This expression is true for every data object after a CLEAR statement.

- Whether a field symbol has been assigned to a data object:

  ```
  ... <fs> IS ASSIGNED ...
  ```

  For more information see Section 4.6.1.

28. Note, however, that the constraints we have shown for the conversion rule for structures also apply to comparisons.

- Or whether a formal parameter of a procedure has been filled or checked during a procedure call:

  ```
  ... f IS {SUPPLIED|REQUESTED} ...
  ```

  For more information see Section 5.2.1.

BETWEEN operator

You use the BETWEEN operator to check whether the contents of a data object lie within a certain interval.

```
... f1 BETWEEN  f2 AND f3 ...
```

The f2 and f3 interval limits are also taken into account.

IN operator

You use the IN operator to check whether the contents of a data object comply with the logical conditions of a selection table.

```
... f IN  seltab ...
```

A selection table is an internal table in which every line contains an individual logical condition. A selection table for field f is created either with the RANGE OF type constructor:

```
DATA seltab LIKE RANGE OF f.
```

or the statement:

```
SELECT-OPTIONS seltab FOR f.
```

Selection screen

The SELECT-OPTIONS statement also defines input fields on a selection screen where the user can enter the logical conditions of the selection table. We shall cover selection tables in more detail when dealing with selection screens in Section 7.2.3.

Logical operators for character-type fields

Finally, ABAP contains another set of logical operators which are especially designed for comparisons between character-type fields. For example, if you want to find out if a certain character string is contained in another character string, you can use the CS operator to do this. For example, the logical expression 'ABAP Objects' CS 'ABAP' is true. In Section 4.5.2 we will study comparisons between character strings.

4.4 CONTROL STRUCTURES

The basic building blocks of structured programming are:

- **Sequences**, i.e. the execution of statements without a condition
- **Selections**, i.e. the execution of alternative statements on the basis of a condition (conditional branch)
- **Iterations**, i.e. cyclical repetition of statements (loops)

In this section we will concentrate on selection and iteration (sequences are trivial), with the aim of giving a brief overview of the syntax for the relevant control structures. In this respect the ABAP concepts differ little from those of other programming languages. However, we want to emphasize once again that these control structures in ABAP can only be programmed within processing blocks. A processing block is therefore a syntactical unit which contains sequential coding and its control structures. A control structure must always end within its processing block. The control of the program flow through control structures represents the inner control of a processing block, while the control of an ABAP program through the processes of the runtime environment (see Section 3.3.5) is the external control.

In addition to the control structures dealt with in this section there are other control structures such as loops over internal tables (see Section 4.7.2), reading database tables in a loop (see Section 8.1.3), or control structures for handling errors (see Section 4.8.2).

4.4.1 Conditional branches

To execute statements only under a certain condition, i.e. to make a distinction on a case basis, you can use the `IF / ENDIF` and `CASE / ENDCASE` control structures in ABAP.

Selection using `IF / ENDIF`

Let's first take a glance at the syntax:

```
IF  logical expression_1.
  ... "Statement_block 1
[ELSEIF  logical expression_2.]
  ... "Statement_block 2
[ELSEIF logical expression_3.]
  ... "Statement_block 3
...
[ELSE.]
  ... "Statement_block n
ENDIF.
```

The conditions are formulated with logical expressions which you learned in the previous Section 4.3.4. If logical expression 1 is true, statement block 1 is performed and program processing is continued after ENDIF.[29] If logical expression 1 is false, logical expression 2 is checked and the same procedure is used. If none of the logical expressions is true, the statement block after ELSE is executed. You can use any number of ELSEIF statements and a maximum of one ELSE statement, but only one of the statement blocks will be executed. Listing 4.11 shows that it is possible to nest several control structures.

LISTING 4.11 Program branches with the IF statement

```
REPORT s_if_endif.
IF sy-saprl < '45A'.
  WRITE: / 'ABAP Release', sy-saprl,
           'is not objectoriented'.
ELSE.
  IF sy-saprl < '46A'.
    WRITE: / 'ABAP Release', sy-saprl,
             'is partly objectoriented'.
  ELSE.
    WRITE: / 'ABAP Release', sy-saprl,
             'is fully objectoriented'.
  ENDIF.
ENDIF.
```

Selection using CASE / ENDCASE

The syntax for a CASE control structure is as follows:

```
CASE f.
  WHEN f1 [OR ...].
    ... "Statement_block 1
  [WHEN f2 [OR ...]]
    ... "Statement_block 2
  ...
  [WHEN OTHERS.]
    ... "Statement_block n
ENDCASE.
```

In this control structure, data object f is compared with other data objects. For the first comparison, which is true, the corresponding statement block after WHEN is executed

29. Please do not confuse the term "statement block" with "processing block." A statement block is a sequence of operational statements which can be programmed within processing blocks.

and program processing is continued after ENDCASE. If none of the comparisons is true, the statement block after WHEN OTHERS is executed. You can use any number of WHEN statements but you can only have one WHEN OTHERS statement. As with IF, CASE control structures can be nested. Listing 4.12 gives an example for CASE.

LISTING 4.12 Program branches with the CASE statement

```
REPORT s_case_endcase.
CASE sy-datum+4(2).
  WHEN '12' OR '01' OR '02'.
    WRITE / 'Winter'.
  WHEN '03' OR '04' OR '05'.
    WRITE / 'Spring'.
  WHEN '06' OR '07' OR '08'.
    WRITE / 'Summer'.
  WHEN '09' OR '10' OR '11'.
    WRITE / 'Autumn'.
  WHEN OTHERS.
    WRITE 'Illegal Date'.
ENDCASE.
```

After this brief introduction to program branching we shall now focus on loops.

4.4.2 Loops

Loops allow you to execute a statement block repeatedly. We distinguish between conditional and unconditional loops.

Conditional loops

With the WHILE statement you can execute a statement block until a certain condition is no longer satisfied. The syntax of a WHILE loop is:

```
WHILE  logical expression.
  ... "Statement_block
ENDWHILE.
```

The processing of the statement block within the WHILE and ENDWHILE statements is repeated as long as the logical expression is satisfied or until a termination statement such as EXIT is reached. For the duration of the loop pass, the sy-index system field contains the number of previous loop passes including the current one. Any change to sy-index will not affect the number of loop passes performed and should never be made.

The example in Listing 4.13 uses two nested WHILE loops.

LISTING 4.13 Nested WHILE loops

```
REPORT s_while_endwhile.
DATA: inner_limit TYPE i VALUE 5,
      outer_limit TYPE i VALUE 5,
      inner_index TYPE i,
      outer_index TYPE i.

WHILE outer_limit > 0.
  outer_index = sy-index.
  WRITE: / 'Outer loop:', sy-index,
           'Limit:', outer_limit.
  inner_limit = 5.
  WHILE inner_limit > 0.
    inner_index = sy-index.
    WRITE: / '    Inner loop:', sy-index,
             '    Limit:', inner_limit.
    inner_limit = inner_limit - 1.
  ENDWHILE.
  outer_limit = outer_limit - 1.
ENDWHILE.
```

The program shows that `sy-index` always contains the index of the current loop. If from within a nested loop you want to access the index of an outer loop from an inner loop, you must use an auxiliary variable.

Unconditional loops

While the execution of a conditional loop depends on a logical expression, you can use the `DO` statement to program an unconditional loop whose statement block will be repeated until the loop is exited with a statement such as `EXIT`, or until the number of predefined loop passes is reached. The syntax of a `DO` loop is:

```
DO  [n TIMES].
  ... "Statement block
ENDDO.
```

`TIMES` limits the number of loop passes to `n`. If the value of `n` is zero or negative, the loop will not be executed. Here too, `sy-index` is set to the current loop index for each loop.

Loop control

A loop can be exited at any time. ABAP offers you a range of termination statements to do this.

- You can terminate a loop pass with the `CONTINUE` statement. After this statement the other statements of the current statement block are skipped and the next loop pass is executed.
- To terminate a loop under a certain condition, you use the `CHECK logical_expression` statement in the loop's statement block. If the condition is not true, the other statements in the current statement block are skipped and the next loop pass is executed.
- To terminate a loop completely and unconditionally, you can use the `EXIT` statement in the loop's statement block. After this statement the loop is completely exited and the program flow continued after the closing statement (`ENDDO` or `ENDWHILE`). With nested loops only the current loop is terminated.

Figure 4.12 summarizes the effects of each termination statement.[30]

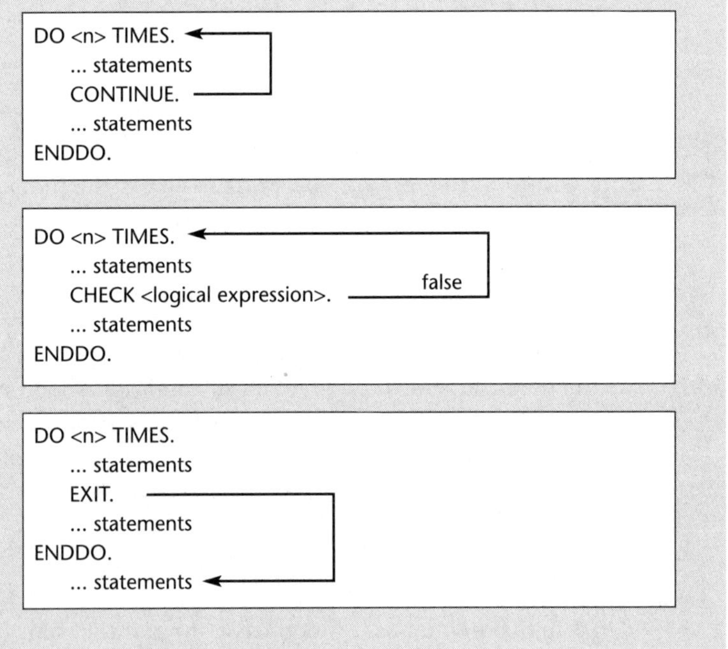

FIGURE 4.12 Termination statements for loops

30. The `CHECK` and `EXIT` statements can also be used outside of loops. In this case you terminate the current processing block.

To conclude, here is a brief example in which the CHECK statement is used in a DO loop to output the even values of the loop index.

LISTING 4.14 Using the CHECK statement

```
PROGRAM s_do_enddo.
DATA: is_zero TYPE i.
DO 20 TIMES.
  is_zero = sy-index MOD 2.
  CHECK is_zero = 0.
  WRITE:/ sy-index, 'is even.'.
ENDDO.
```

4.5 PROCESSING CHARACTER STRINGS

The term character string refers to the contents of all character-type data objects of types c, d, n, t, and string. ABAP contains a range of operations and comparisons which are especially designed to process character strings. In these operations the contents of the operands are interpreted as character-type, irrespective of the actual data type, and no conversion takes place. To ensure meaningful results, only character-type operands can be used in character string processing.[31] If a structure only has character-type components, the contents of the entire structure can be processed as a single character string.

4.5.1 Operations with character strings

Like many other programming languages, ABAP provides statements for executing special operations with character strings. We will now demonstrate the most important operations with a few examples.

Concatenating character strings

To join two character strings to form a single string, use the CONCATENATE statement. The syntax is:

```
CONCATENATE  s1 ... sn
             INTO s_dest [SEPARATED BY sep].
```

This statement concatenates the character strings s1 to sn and assigns the result to the variable s_dest. If you wish you can use the SEPARATED addition to set a separa-

31. In non-Unicode systems, byte-type fields can also be processed as character strings. This will no longer be possible in Unicode systems as of Release 6.10. Instead there will be special byte operations.

tor between the individual parts. If the target field is shorter than the overall length of the source fields, the character string is truncated to the length of the target field. It is therefore advisable to use the string data type in this kind of operation, as it can always accommodate the required length of the target character string. The example in Listing 4.15 demonstrates the use of the statement.

LISTING 4.15 Using the CONCATENATE statement

```
REPORT s_concatenate.
DATA: s1(72) TYPE c,
      s2(72) TYPE c,
      s3 TYPE string.

s1 = 'ABAP'
s2 = 'Objects'
CONCATENATE s1 s2 INTO s3 SEPARATED BY SPACE.
WRITE / s3.
```

Note that trailing blanks, as mentioned in Section 4.2.3, are ignored in data type c text fields.

Splitting character strings

Character strings can not only be concatenated but also split down into individual parts. To do this, ABAP provides the SPLIT statement with the following syntax:

```
SPLIT  s_source AT sep INTO s1 ... sn.
```

The s_source character string is split into individual parts before and after the sep separator and distributed among the individual target fields s1 to sn, whereby sep is not copied. If there are not enough target fields available, the last target field is filled with the remaining part of the source character string, including the separators.

If you do not know the number of the resulting target fields, you can also split a character string into the lines of an internal table using

```
SPLIT c AT del INTO TABLE itab.
```

The statement adds a new table line to itab for each part of the character string. Listing 4.16 shows an example.

LISTING 4.16 Splitting a character string with SPLIT

```
REPORT s_split.
DATA: text TYPE string,
      itab TYPE TABLE OF string.
```

```
text = 'ABAP Objects is the key ' &
       'for OOP in the SAP system'.
SPLIT text AT space INTO TABLE itab.
LOOP AT itab INTO text.
  WRITE / text.
ENDLOOP.
```

Searching for characters

To find a specific search pattern in a character string, use the `SEARCH` statement. The syntax is:

```
SEARCH  s1 FOR s2.
```

The `s1` character string is searched for the `s2` character string. If the search is successful, `sy-subrc` is set to zero and `sy-fdpos` to the position of the character string in `s1`. Otherwise `sy-subrc` is set to four.

`SEARCH` enables you to perform a wildcard search which allows a variety of search forms. Let's consider Listing 4.17 and the resulting screen output in Figure 4.13.

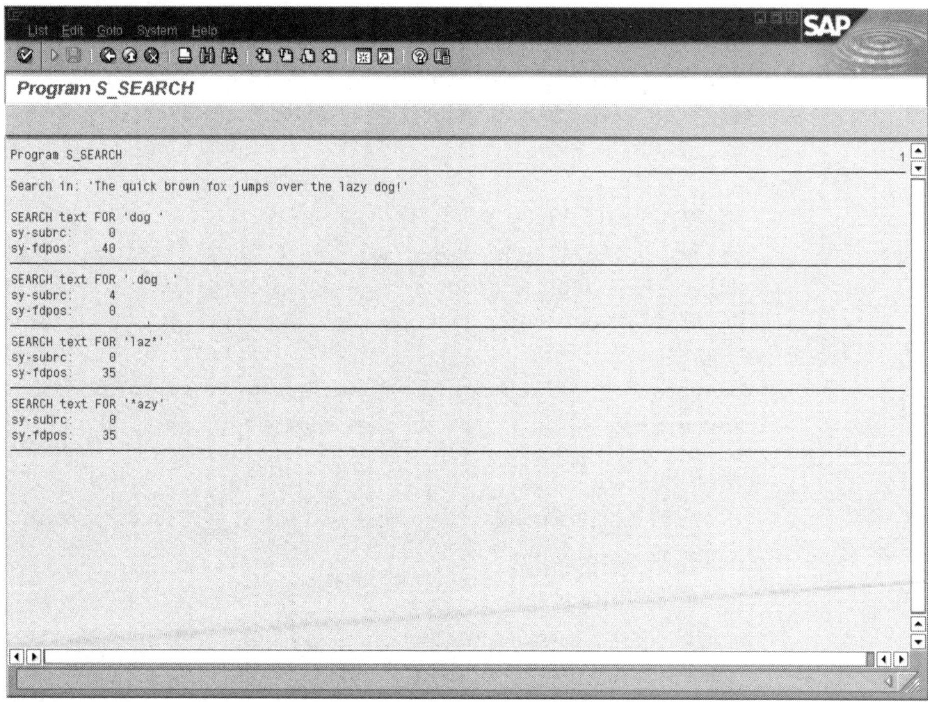

FIGURE 4.13 The screen output of Listing 4.17. Copyright © SAP AG

LISTING 4.17 Finding a search pattern in a character string

```
REPORT s_search.

DATA: text TYPE string.
text = 'The quick brown fox jumps over the lazy dog!'.

WRITE: / 'Search in:',
         '''The quick brown fox jumps over the lazy dog!'''.
SKIP.

SEARCH text FOR 'dog '.
WRITE: / 'SEARCH text FOR ''dog '''.
WRITE: / 'sy-subrc:', sy-subrc, / 'sy-fdpos:', sy-fdpos.
ULINE.

SEARCH text FOR '.dog .'.
WRITE: / 'SEARCH text FOR ''.dog .'''.
WRITE: / 'sy-subrc:', sy-subrc, / 'sy-fdpos:', sy-fdpos.
ULINE.

SEARCH text FOR 'laz*'.
WRITE: / 'SEARCH text FOR ''laz*'''.
WRITE: / 'sy-subrc:', sy-subrc, / 'sy-fdpos:', sy-fdpos.
ULINE.

SEARCH text FOR '*azy'.
WRITE: / 'SEARCH text FOR ''*azy'''.
WRITE: / 'sy-subrc:', sy-subrc, / 'sy-fdpos:', sy-fdpos.
ULINE.
```

We have used four different search methods to find a specific search pattern. The following forms for the s2 pattern are possible during the search:

- s2

  The character string in s2 is searched for in s1. Blank spaces at the end of s2 are ignored during the search.

- .s2.

  The character string in s2 is searched for in s1. Blank spaces at the end of s2 are taken into account during the search.

- s2*

  A word[32] starting with the character string in s2 is searched for in s1.
- *s2

  A word ending with the character string in s2 is searched for in s1.

There are other additions to the SEARCH statement which can be found in the ABAP keyword documentation.[33]

Searching and replacing characters

To replace certain characters of a character string with other characters, use the REPLACE statement:

```
REPLACE  s1 WITH s2 INTO s_dest.
```

The first occurrence of s1 is searched for in the s_dest character string. If the s1 character string is found, it is replaced by s2, whereby s1 and s2 can have different lengths. If the search character string is not found, the sy-subrc field has the value of 4. You can evaluate the value in sy-subrc to completely replace all occurrences of s2 with s1. Listing 4.18 shows how to do this.[34]

LISTING 4.18 Complete "search and replace"

```
REPORT s_replace.
DATA text TYPE string.
text = 'Token 1, Token 2, Token 3, Token 4'.
WHILE sy-subrc = 0.
  REPLACE ', ' WITH ' - ' INTO text.
ENDWHILE.
WRITE / text.
```

You must ensure that the replacement character string does not contain the character string you are searching for, as otherwise you will generate an endless loop.

Determining the length of a character string

You can use the strlen(s) function to determine the length of a character string in a data object. strlen is a function which can be used in a numeric operation (see Section 4.3.3).

32. Here, a word is defined as part of a character string which is either enclosed in separators or is at the beginning or end of a character string. Separators include spaces, commas, full stops, semi-colons, colons, question marks, exclamation marks, brackets, slashes, plus and equal signs.
33. As of Release 6.10 there is an improved statement FIND which replaces SEARCH.
34. As of Release 6.10 there is an improved statement REPLACE which automatically performs this.

It does not take trailing blanks into account. Listing 4.19 shows an example in which the result is 12 although the length of the overall text field is 72.[35]

LISTING 4.19 The strlen function

```
REPORT s_strlen.
DATA: text(72) TYPE c VALUE 'ABAP Objects',
      len TYPE i.
len = strlen( text ).
WRITE: / 'Length of', text, 'is', len.
```

Other character string statements

In addition to the character string processing statements already mentioned, ABAP contains a few others such as:

- SHIFT to shift character strings in data objects
- CONDENSE to delete blanks
- TRANSLATE to transform characters
- CONVERT TEXT to create a format capable of sorting
- OVERLAY to overlay two character strings.

At this point we shall not discuss these in detail. If you wish to know more about these statements, please refer to the ABAP keyword documentation.

4.5.2 Comparing character strings

In Section 4.3.4 we mentioned that there are special operators used solely for comparisons between character strings. ABAP contains a total of eight operators which can be used to perform character string comparisons.

- CO (contains only)

  s1 CO s2 is true if s1 only contains characters which also occur in s2. The comparison takes lower and upper case characters into account. If the comparison is false, sy-fdpos contains the offset of the first character of s1 that is not contained in s2.

- CN (contains not only)

  s1 CN s2 is true if s1 contains not only characters which also occur in s2. The comparison takes lower and upper case characters into account. If the comparison is false, sy-fdpos contains the offset of the first character of s1 that is not contained in s2.

35. You determine the length of the text field with the DESCRIBE FIELD statement.

- CA (contains any)

  s1 CA s2 is true if at least one character from s2 is contained in s1. The comparison takes lower and upper case into account. If the comparison is true, sy-fdpos contains the offset of the first character of s1 that is also contained in s2.

- NA (contains not any)

  s1 NA s2 is true if s1 does not contain any characters from s2. The comparison takes lower and upper case characters into account. If the comparison is false, sy-fdpos contains the offset of the first character of s1 that is contained in s2.

- CS (contains string)

  s1 CS s2 is true if s2 occurs in s1. The comparison does not take lower and upper case characters into account. If the comparison is true, sy-fdpos contains the offset of s2 in s1.

- NS (contains no string)

  s1 NS s2 is true if s2 does not occur in s1. The comparison does not take lower and upper case characters into account. If the comparison is false, sy-fdpos contains the offset of s2 in s1.

- CP (covers pattern)

  s1 CP s2 is true if s1 fits the pattern in s2. Wildcards can be used to create the pattern. The "*" stands for any character string, the "+" character for any character. The comparison does not take lower and upper case characters into account. If the comparison is true, sy-fdpos contains the offset of s2 in s1.

- NP (no pattern)

  s1 NP s2 is true if s1 does not fit the pattern in s2. Again, wildcards can be used. The comparison does not take lower and upper case into account. If the comparison is false, sy-fdpos contains the offset of s2 in s1.

Let's consider an example in Listing 4.20.

LISTING 4.20 Comparing character strings

```
PROGRAM string_comparison.

DATA: s1 TYPE string,
      s2 TYPE string.

s1 = 'ABAP Objects'.
s2 = 'Objects'.

IF s1 CS s2.
  WRITE: / s2, 'is contained from position', sy-fdpos,
           'in', s1.
ENDIF.
```

Here you see the two key aspects which are important for all character string comparisons. On the one hand a logical expression is evaluated for which a special operator is used (in this case CS, contains string). On the other the sy-fdpos system field contains the offset for the position of the s2 character string in the s1 character string.

4.5.3 Addressing subfields

As you have seen in previous examples in this chapter, the ABAP syntax allows you to address subfields of a data object by specifying the offset/length. This kind of addressing is suitable not only for character-type fields but also for byte-type fields. If a structure or at least an initial part of a structure is purely character-type or byte-type, it may also be suitable to address subfields of a structure, although it is always better to access structures through their components. You should never address subfields in numeric data objects or structures in which character components, byte components, and numeric components are mixed. The contents of the resulting subfields often cannot be interpreted meaningfully.[36] In particular, the alignment gaps mentioned in Section 4.3.2 create problems.

The syntax for addressing a subfield is as follows:

```
f[+off][(len)]
```

Offset/Length

If f is a data object which contains a character string, the subsection of this character string which has an offset of off characters and a length of len characters is addressed. If you specify the offset without the length the rest of the field is addressed, and if you specify the length without the offset the first len characters are addressed. Offset and length specifications can be data objects whose contents can be interpreted as a positive number. If you attempt to address an area outside the field, a syntax error or a runtime error occurs.

A simple example of subfield addressing is shown in Listing 4.21.

LISTING 4.21 Specifying offset and length

```
REPORT s_offset_length.

SELECTION-SCREEN BEGIN OF SCREEN 500.
PARAMETERS: day(2)   TYPE c,
            month(2) TYPE c,
            year(4)  TYPE c.
SELECTION-SCREEN END OF SCREEN 500.

DATA new_date TYPE d.
```

36. As of Release 6.10 a stricter syntax check will be carried out in Unicode systems. In particular, the mixing of character-type and byte-type subfields, which is currently allowed, will be prohibited.

```
year    = sy-datum(4).
month = sy-datum+4(2).
day     = sy-datum+6(2).

CALL SELECTION-SCREEN 500 STARTING AT 10 10.

new_date(4) =    year.
new_date+4(2) = month.
new_date+6(2) = day.

IF new_date <> 0.
  WRITE new_date DD/MM/YY.
ELSE.
  WRITE 'Wrong Date!'.
ENDIF.
```

First, the subfields for year, month, and day from the sy-datum system field are read into individual fields. The user can then change these parameters on a selection screen (see Section 7.2). A field new_date is then composed as a new date. The validity of the date is checked as described in Section 4.3.3.

4.6 FIELD SYMBOLS AND DATA REFERENCES

So far in all our examples we have accessed our data objects statically, i.e. we have always addressed them by the name given to them when they were declared. It is now time to introduce a more advanced concept of addressing data objects.

Field symbols and data references are used to access data objects dynamically in ABAP programs. Whereas a data object can always be accessed statically through the name of the data object, field symbols and data references allow data objects to be accessed whose name and attributes are only known at runtime.

When you declare a data object during programming you are already determining its name and technical attributes statically. These details are valid for the entire duration of an ABAP program and cannot be changed. But what happens if your program can only decide at runtime what kind of data object it wants to work with? In this case you can address data objects with field symbols dynamically or even create them dynamically using data references.

Value semantics

Field symbols are symbolic names for data objects. When working with field symbols value semantics apply. When you access field symbols you address the contents of the assigned data object. Field symbols in expressions are treated exclusively as dereferenced pointers.

Reference semantics

Data references are the addresses of data objects. When working with data references reference semantics apply. Data references are the contents of data reference variables, and when you access reference variables you address the data reference itself. To access the contents of the data object to which a data reference is pointing, the data reference must be dereferenced.

4.6.1 Field symbols

Field symbols are placeholders or symbolic names for existing data objects. A field symbol does not reserve a physical space for a field, instead it points to a data object. Field symbols can point to any data objects. The data object to which a field symbol is pointing is assigned to it dynamically at program runtime. A field symbol is similar to a dereferenced pointer in the C programming language, i.e. a pointer to which the contents operator "*" is applied. Data reference variables are the true equivalent of pointers, as these are variables which contain a memory address (reference) and can be used without the contents operator. We will look at data reference variables in Section 4.6.2.

Field symbols are used to work generically with data objects. This means that you can program operations without knowing the data objects that are actually being used at runtime. You can also use field symbols for casting data objects. This means that you treat the contents of a data object according to a type other than the data object type.

By way of introduction we shall implement a brief example program which uses a field symbol.

LISTING 4.22 Basic example of field symbols

```
REPORT simple_field_symbol.

FIELD-SYMBOLS <fs> TYPE ANY.
DATA: city(30) TYPE c,
      zipcode(5) TYPE n.

ASSIGN city TO <fs>.
<fs> = 'Cologne'.

ASSIGN zipcode TO <fs>.
<fs> = '50931'.

WRITE:/ zipcode, city.
```

In Listing 4.22 we declare two data objects of different types and a field symbol using the `FIELD-SYMBOLS` statement. With the `ASSIGN` statement we assign the city data object to the field symbol. After this assignment it makes no difference whether we execute an operation with the field symbol or directly with city. Assigning the "Cologne" character string to the <fs> field symbol therefore writes in the city field. We proceed in the same way with the zipcode field, using the same field symbol. The WRITE output shows that the city and zipcode have been correctly assigned to the two data objects.

This brief example has already highlighted two key elements for working with field symbols:

- Declaring a field symbol
- Assigning a data object to a field symbol

In the following sections we will devote more attention to these topics.

Declaring a field symbol

To declare field symbols you use the FIELD-SYMBOLS statement. Its basic form is as follows:

```
FIELD-SYMBOLS  <fs> {TYPE type|LIKE dobj}.
```

The pointed brackets form part of the field symbol name and must therefore be specified in the program. You use the TYPE or LIKE addition to type the field symbol. Typing determines which data objects can be assigned to the field symbol. Both generic and fully qualified type specifications are possible. Generic types can be found in Table 4.3. All other types are complete.

Generic typing of a field symbol

All data objects whose subattributes match the typing can be assigned to a generically typed field symbol. Since it is not known statically which kinds of the missing attributes are passed to the field symbol due to the assignment of a data object, you cannot access these attributes, or at best only dynamically. For example, a field symbol typed with ANY can never be handled as an internal table, but it can be handled as a table if it is typed with ANY TABLE. Listing 4.23 shows another example.

LISTING 4.23 Generically typed field symbol

```
REPORT s_generic_field_symbol.

TYPES: BEGIN OF t_address,
          street(30) TYPE c,
          no(5) TYPE n,
        END OF t_address.
```

```
DATA: wa_address TYPE t_address,
      address_tab TYPE HASHED TABLE
                  OF t_address
                  WITH UNIQUE KEY no,
      key(4) TYPE c VALUE 'NO'.

FIELD-SYMBOLS <fs> TYPE ANY TABLE.

ASSIGN address_tab TO <fs>.

* Syntax error
READ TABLE <fs> WITH TABLE KEY no = '1' INTO wa_address.

* this is the way to do it
READ TABLE <fs> WITH TABLE KEY (key) = '1' INTO wa_address.
```

The first `READ TABLE` statement results in a syntax error, as there is no static access to the `no` component. However, if you dynamically specify the name of the key column (in upper case) as the contents of the `key` field, no syntax error occurs. The system only evaluates `key` at runtime. If the field contains the name of an existing column, the table can be read, otherwise a runtime error is triggered.

Fully qualified typing of a field symbol

A fully typed field symbol can only be assigned data objects which are of exactly its type. Unlike with generically typed field symbols, all the technical attributes of the field symbol are already statically known in this case. Accessing the field symbol is the same as accessing the data object itself, and all operations which can be executed with the data object can also be executed with the field symbol.

Assigning a data object to a field symbol

In the previous field symbol examples you have seen that we can assign a data object to a field symbol using `ASSIGN f TO <fs>`. The assignment can be either static or dynamic.

Static `ASSIGN` *and subfield addressing*

We always talk of static `ASSIGN` if the name of the data object to be assigned to the field symbol is already known when the program is created. A field symbol can be assigned not only entire data objects but also subfields which you address by specifying the offset and length. The syntax is the same as for the subfield addressing we saw in Section 4.5.3:

```
ASSIGN  f[+off][(len)] TO <fs>.
```

Assigning subfields to field symbols therefore allows us to operate on parts of data objects with symbolic names. Of course, the same constraints as described in Section 4.5.3 apply.[37] Consider the example in Listing 4.24.

LISTING 4.24 Static ASSIGN with addressing of subfield

```
REPORT s_field_symbols_for_sections.
DATA: BEGIN OF address,
          street(20) TYPE c VALUE 'Woodway',
          no(4)      TYPE c VALUE '1234',
          zip(5)     TYPE c VALUE '98765',
          city(20)   TYPE c VALUE 'Horse Village',
        END OF address.

FIELD-SYMBOLS: <street_no> TYPE c,
               <zip_city>  TYPE c.

ASSIGN: address(24)     TO <street_no>,
        address+24(25) TO <zip_city>.

WRITE: / <street_no>,
       / <zip_city>.
```

Here we assign two subfields of a character structure to two field symbols. The first two components are referenced using <street_no> and the last two with <zip_city>. In the next section but one we will show you a more elegant variant of the ASSIGN statement for assigning components of structures to field symbols.

Dynamic ASSIGN

If the name of the data object which you wish to assign to a field symbol is only known at runtime, you can use the following variant of the ASSIGN statement:

```
ASSIGN (f) TO <fs>.
```

This assigns the data object whose name is in the f field to the <fs> field symbol. After successful assignment, sy-subrc has a value of zero. If no data object with a suitable name is found, there is no assignment to the field symbol and the sy-subrc field is set to a value of four. After a dynamic assignment you should always check sy-subrc before accessing the field symbol to ensure a runtime error is not triggered. Subfields cannot be addressed during a dynamic ASSIGN.

37. Up to and including Release 4.6, the runtime environment does not check for field symbols whether the subfield is actually within the field f, so that memory areas outside the boundaries of f can be addressed. In Unicode systems as of Release 6.10, this will be disallowed.

Checking the assignment

You can use the logical expression

```
... <fs> IS ASSIGNED ...
```

to check whether a data object has been assigned to a field symbol. The expression is "true" if the <fs> field symbol is pointing to a data object.

Initializing field symbols

You can use the statement

```
UNASSIGN <fs>.
```

to ensure that no data objects are assigned any longer to a field symbol. After UNASSIGN the field symbol has the same status as it had directly after its declaration[38] and the above logical expression is "false."

Assigning structures by component

You can use a special form of the ASSIGN statement to address the components of structures dynamically. This could be considered, for example, if in a procedure you want to access the components of a structured formal parameter which is generically typed. In this case you cannot access the data object statically or dynamically via the name of the structure components. The following syntax of the ASSIGN statement, however, allows the components to be addressed dynamically.

```
ASSIGN COMPONENT comp OF STRUCTURE struc TO <fs>.
```

This assigns the comp component of the struc structure to the <fs> field symbol. If comp is a type c data object, its contents are interpreted as the name of the component. If comp has a different type and the contents can be interpreted as a number, the latter indicates the position of the component. Listing 4.25 shows an example.

LISTING 4.25 Assigning structures by component

```
REPORT s_dynamic_access_to_components.

DATA: wa_spfli TYPE SPFLI.

SELECT SINGLE *
```

38. Strictly speaking, this applies only to typed field symbols where the FIELD-SYMBOLS statement contains the TYPE addition. By default, an untyped field symbol is assigned the built-in data object space during definition. Untyped field symbols are therefore prohibited in ABAP Objects classes and the ANY type must be specified for fully generic field symbols.

```
  FROM SPFLI
  INTO wa_spfli.

PERFORM write_any_line USING wa_spfli.

FORM write_any_line USING u_line TYPE ANY.
  FIELD-SYMBOLS: <fs_component> TYPE ANY.
  DO.
    ASSIGN COMPONENT sy-index
      OF STRUCTURE u_line TO <fs_component>.
    IF sy-subrc <> 0.
      EXIT.
    ENDIF.
    WRITE / <fs_component>.
  ENDDO.
ENDFORM.
```

Here, in a subroutine write_any_line the individual components of a formal parameter u_line are addressed successively via their number (position) in the structure and are assigned to the local field symbol <fs_component>. If you attempt to assign a component that is not present, sy-subrc has a value of four and the loop is exited. The procedure is not bound to the structure passed. Within this procedure no other access to the components of passed structures is possible unless you use the option of casting data objects.

Casting data objects

When you assign data objects to field symbols, a cast can be performed on any data type. This means that any memory area can be considered assuming a specific type. It is therefore possible to access subfields or components of structures symbolically and without the need to specify offset or length.

Cast

A cast is created by the CASTING addition to the ASSIGN statement. The CASTING addition also allows you to assign to field symbols data objects whose type is not compatible with the typing of the field symbol. We distinguish between casts with implicit and casts with explicit type specifications.

Cast with implicit type specification

If the field symbol is typed either fully or with one of the generically built-in ABAP types c, n, p, or x, the following form of the ASSIGN statement can be used:

```
ASSIGN f TO <fs> CASTING.
```

When the field symbol is accessed, the contents of the assigned data object are interpreted as if they were of the type of the field symbol. The length and alignment of the data object must, however, be compatible with the type of the field symbol. If deep data types are included in the data type of the assigned data object or of the field symbol, the type and position of these components must correspond exactly. Listing 4.26 shows an example with a fully typed field symbol.

LISTING 4.26 Casting with implicit type specification

```
REPORT s_field_symbols_casting.
TYPES: BEGIN OF t_date,
         year(4)   TYPE n,
         month(2)  TYPE n,
         day(2)    TYPE n,
       END OF t_date.

FIELD-SYMBOLS <fs> TYPE t_date.

ASSIGN sy-datum TO <fs> CASTING.

WRITE: / sy-datum,
       / <fs>-year , / <fs>-month, / <fs>-day.
```

In this case a field symbol <fs> is fully typed with the local type t_date. Using the CASTING addition to the ASSIGN statement the field symbol can be addressed according to the structure of t_date. Without the CASTING addition the assignment would be impossible, since sy-datum is not compatible with the type of the field symbol.

Cast with explicit type statement

If the field symbol is typed generically as opposed to fully, the following form of the ASSIGN statement can be used:

```
ASSIGN f TO <fs>
       CASTING  {TYPE type|LIKE dobj} [DECIMALS dec].
```

When the field symbol is accessed, the contents of the assigned data object are interpreted as if they were of the type specified. A data object name can also be entered in round brackets after TYPE. The contents of the data object will then denote the data type at runtime.

You must not enter types which are unsuitable for explicit casting of data objects, e.g. a cast of a standard table to a sorted table or a cast of an object reference to a data reference. You cannot therefore specify table types such as SORTED TABLE or reference types with REF TO after TYPE. If implicitly deep data types are included in the data type specified, these components must also occur in exactly the same way in the assigned data object with respect to type and position.

TYPE/LIKE

The data type specified with TYPE or LIKE must be compatible with the generic typing of the field symbol. It can leave or specialize the generic typing, but cannot undo a technical attribute of the field symbol which is already known. For example, any permitted and even generic type can be specified with a field symbol of the fully generic type ANY. For a field symbol of the generic types c, n, p, or x, you can only determine the length or the number of decimal places. For a fully typed field symbol, no further specialization is possible anyway, and you are therefore not allowed to specify a type explicitly. If possible, this is checked statically; if not, this is checked at runtime.

DECIMALS

The DECIMALS addition is suitable if the contents of the assigned data object can be interpreted as a packed number. The field symbol then contains dec decimal places. DECIMALS can only be used if no type is specified or if type p is specified after TYPE. Type p is implicitly used if no type is specified. LIKE and DECIMALS must not be used together.

In the example of Listing 4.27 the <fs> field symbol is fully generic. With the CASTING addition to the ASSIGN statement a cast is performed to the local type t_date for the sy-datum field. Although the <fs> field symbol can now be treated like a structure, it does not recognize any components. It must therefore be assigned to another field symbol <f> by component.

LISTING 4.27 Casting with explicit type specification

```
REPORT s_field_symbols_casting_type.
TYPES: BEGIN OF t_date,
         year(4)   TYPE n,
         month(2)  TYPE n,
         day(2)    TYPE n,
       END OF t_date.

FIELD-SYMBOLS: <fs> TYPE ANY,
               <f>  TYPE n.

ASSIGN sy-datum TO <fs> CASTING TYPE t_date.

WRITE / sy-datum.
DO.
  ASSIGN COMPONENT sy-index OF STRUCTURE <fs> TO <f>.
  IF sy-subrc <> 0.
```

```
    EXIT.
  ENDIF.
  WRITE / <f>.
ENDDO.
```

4.6.2 Data references

The data objects a program works with are stored and managed in the memory. Each of these data objects begins at a certain place (address) in the memory. The address is determined by the compiler or the runtime system and cannot be influenced by the developer. We also call the address of a data object in the memory its **reference**. When you declare a data object you generally access the data object through the name you have given it. References are an alternative access option besides field symbols but can also be used to create data objects dynamically.

References are stored in reference variables. In ABAP, references occur either as data references or as object references. Accordingly, we distinguish between data reference variables and object reference variables. In this section we will focus on data references and in Section 5.3.3 we will explain object references.

Data reference variables

Data reference variables are **pointers** to any kind of data object and can be used to create data objects dynamically. Conversely, references to existing data objects can be retrieved and stored in data reference variables. So that you can work with a data object using its reference, the address of the data object must be evaluated or dereferenced. Dereferencing is achieved via a special assignment to a field symbol.

A data reference variable is created with:

```
DATA dref TYPE REF TO  data.
```

Pointer

After its declaration, a reference variable is initial, i.e. it does not point to any object. It is not possible to dereference an initial reference variable. There are various ways of providing a reference variable with a reference.

- A reference to a data object is obtained for the reference variable.
- An existing data reference from another reference variable is assigned to the reference variable.
- A data object is dynamically created with the reference variable.

Obtaining references for data objects

The following statement can be used to place data references to existing data objects in a reference variable:

```
GET REFERENCE  OF dobj INTO dref.
```

dobj is either a statically declared data object or a field symbol which is pointing to any data object. If a field symbol is specified to which no data object has been assigned yet, a runtime error occurs. Listing 4.28 shows an example for obtaining a reference.

Assigning data references

References between data reference variables are assigned with the MOVE statement or the assignment operator (=), but they can also be assigned when internal tables are filled or during passing to interface parameters of procedures. During such an assignment both operands must be of the data reference type. Assignments to object reference variables or other variables are not possible. After the assignment the reference in the target variable points to the same data object as the reference in the source variable. Listing 4.28 also shows an example of assigning data references.

Dereferencing data references

In order to access the contents of a data object to which a data reference is pointing, the data reference must first be dereferenced. Dereferencing is performed with the dereferencing operator (->*):

```
ASSIGN  dref->* TO <fs> [CASTING  [type|(name)]].
```

The data object to which the data reference in the reference variable dref is pointing is assigned to the field symbol <fs> with this statement. If the assignment is successful, sy-subrc is set to zero.

If the field symbol is fully generic, it inherits the data type of the data object. If the typing of the field symbol is partial or full, the compatibility of the data types is checked. A cast of the assigned data object is also possible.

If the data reference in dref is initial or invalid, dereferencing is not possible. The field symbol is not changed and sy-subrc is set to four.

LISTING 4.28 Example of data references

```
REPORT s_data_reference.
DATA: dref TYPE REF TO data,
      dref_int   TYPE REF TO data,
      dref_pack  TYPE REF TO data,
      int   TYPE i VALUE 5,
      pack TYPE p DECIMALS 2 VALUE '123.45'.
FIELD-SYMBOLS <fs> TYPE ANY.
```

```
GET REFERENCE OF int INTO dref.
dref_int = dref.
ASSIGN dref_int->* TO <fs>.
WRITE / <fs>.

GET REFERENCE OF pack INTO dref.
dref_pack = dref.
ASSIGN dref_pack->* TO <fs>.
WRITE / <fs>.
```

In the example of Listing 4.28 there are three data reference variables with which any data objects can be referenced at runtime. Figure 4.14 shows the situation at the end of the program. Three reference variables are pointing to two data objects. Before the second `GET REFERENCE` statement `dref` was also pointing to `int`. With the second `GET REFERENCE` the pointer was set to `pack`.

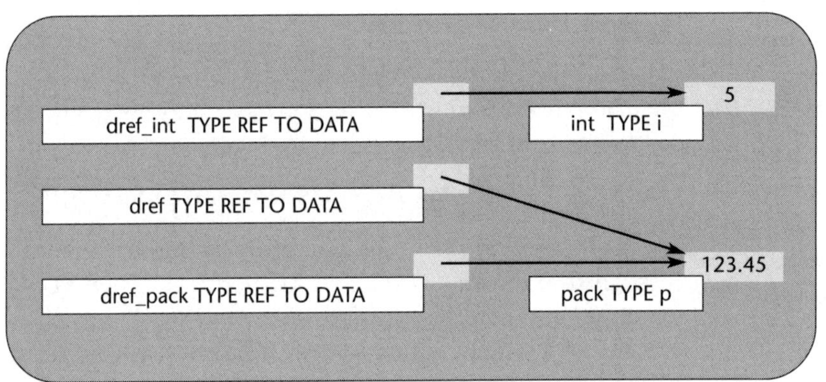

FIGURE 4.14 Data reference variables pointing to data objects

Creating data objects dynamically

All data objects which are declared in the declaration part of a program are created statically and are present when the program starts. To create a data object dynamically during the execution of the program, you need a data reference variable and the statement:

```
CREATE DATA  dref {TYPE {type|(name)}|LIKE dobj}.
```

This statement creates a data object in the internal session of the current ABAP program, and the data reference in the data reference variable `dref` points to this object once the statement has been executed. The dynamically created data object does not have its own name and can only be addressed via the data reference variable. The only way to access the contents of dynamically created data objects is to dereference the data reference. A dynamic data object is present in the memory as long as it is referenced by a reference variable. If there are no longer any reference variables pointing to a dynamic data object, the data object is transferred to automatic **garbage collection** and deleted.

The data type of the data object must be specified with TYPE or LIKE.[39] In CREATE DATA you can use TYPE to specify the data type dynamically as the contents of a field, which is not possible in other ABAP statements. In this case name is the name of a field which contains the name of the required data type.

Linked list

By using data reference variables it is possible to manage complex data structures such as linked lists or trees. We will therefore conclude this topic with an example in Listing 4.29 in which we construct and output a basic linked list dynamically. The example uses all the operations with reference variables which we have previously discussed.

LISTING 4.29 Example of dynamic data objects

```
REPORT s_dynamic_data_objects.

* Data declarations

TYPES: BEGIN OF t_item,
          content TYPE i,
          next TYPE REF TO data,
        END OF t_item.

DATA: dref_start TYPE REF TO data,
      dref_new TYPE REF TO data.

FIELD-SYMBOLS <fs_new> TYPE t_item.

* Create dynamic list

DO 10 TIMES.
  CREATE DATA dref_new TYPE t_item.
  ASSIGN dref_new->* TO <fs_new>.
  <fs_new>-content = sy-index ** 2.
  IF sy-index = 1.
    dref_start = dref_new.
  ENDIF.
  PERFORM append_item USING dref_start
                             dref_new.
ENDDO.
```

39. As of Release 6.10 even internal tables can be dynamically constructed via CREATE DATA using the type constructor TABLE OF. Currently, you can only refer to existing table types.

```
PERFORM show_list_content USING dref_start.

* Subroutines

FORM append_item USING dref_start TYPE REF TO data
                       dref_new TYPE REF TO data.
  FIELD-SYMBOLS <fs_curitem> TYPE t_item.
  DATA dref_cur TYPE REF TO data.
  IF dref_start = dref_new.
    EXIT.
  ENDIF.
  dref_cur = dref_start.
  ASSIGN dref_cur->* TO <fs_curitem>.
  WHILE NOT <fs_curitem>-next IS INITIAL.
    dref_cur = <fs_curitem>-next.
    ASSIGN dref_cur->* TO <fs_curitem>.
  ENDWHILE.
  <fs_curitem>-next = dref_new.
ENDFORM.

FORM show_list_content USING dref_start TYPE REF TO data.
  FIELD-SYMBOLS <fs_curitem> TYPE t_item.
  DATA dref_cur TYPE REF TO data.
  dref_cur = dref_start.
  WHILE NOT dref_cur IS INITIAL.
    ASSIGN dref_cur->* TO <fs_curitem>.
    WRITE: / <fs_curitem>-content.
    dref_cur = <fs_curitem>-next.
  ENDWHILE.
ENDFORM.
```

The list is to contain type t_item elements. Each element contains a value (current number) and a pointer to the next list element in the chain. The pointer of the last element is always initial. In addition, we always include a reference to the first element and the element which is to be newly attached to a list. The reference to the start of the list keeps the whole list alive.

In a loop we create ten elements. At the beginning of each loop pass we create a type t_item element to which the dref_cur reference variable points. After dereferencing this reference variable we use the field symbol <fs_new> to assign the squared value of the current loop index to the content component. To the append_item subroutine we pass a reference to the first and the newly created list element.

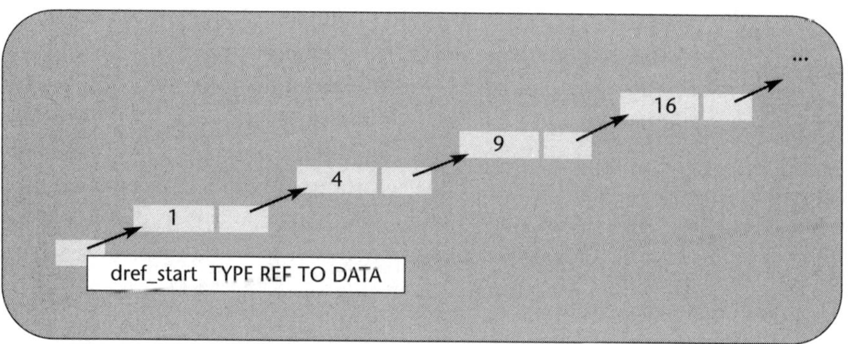

FIGURE 4.15 Linked list with dynamic data objects

The append_item subroutine attaches the data object to which dref_new is pointing to the list. If the reference variables for the start element and new element are pointing to the same data object, this will be the first list element and the subroutine is exited immediately. Otherwise the entire list is processed as we move from one element to the next with <fs_curitem>-next. If the field is initial we have come to the end of the list. This is the place to attach a new element, so we assign the reference to the new list element to <fs_curitem>-next. Figure 4.15 shows how the linked list is implemented in the memory. The reference variable dref_start points to the first dynamic data object on the list, which points to the next, etc.

The show_list_content subroutine runs through the entire list. In each loop pass, the reference to the current list element is assigned to the pointer dref_cur. The pointer is dereferenced and the value of the content component is output.

If this all appears too complicated for storing and outputting a dynamic list of square numbers, you are absolutely right. For this kind of task ABAP contains internal tables. The following section will deal with how to process them.

4.7 INTERNAL TABLES

In the previous section we showed that it is theoretically possible to use data references to create complex data structures in the memory dynamically. However, as we saw in Listing 4.29, handling these structures is very complicated and therefore error-prone. ABAP offers instead a special data type which allows you to store complex dynamic data objects independently of an explicit pointer administration. These data objects are the internal tables we first encountered in Section 4.2.4.

The name originates from a time when the line type of an internal table was limited to flat structures only. Prior to Release 3.0 internal tables represented database tables internally in the memory. As of Release 3.0 the line type is arbitrary. The spectrum of internal tables ranges from arrays of elementary fields to classical database-type tables to highly complex dynamic data objects where the lines or line components can be internal tables themselves.

Lines

The main characteristic of internal tables is that for any given line type any number of lines can be stored in the memory. The number of these lines is only determined at program runtime.[40] Internal tables are managed implicitly by the runtime environment. ABAP contains a set of special statements for working with internal tables which spare you from having to do the actual work with complex dynamic data objects. The above example of a linked list in Listing 4.29 is simplified considerably by the use of an internal table, as Listing 4.30 shows:

LISTING 4.30 Number list in an internal table

```
REPORT s_itab_array.
DATA: number TYPE i,
      array  TYPE STANDARD TABLE
               OF i
               WITH KEY table_line.
DO 10 TIMES.
  number = sy-index.
  APPEND number TO array.
ENDDO.
LOOP AT array INTO number.
  WRITE / number.
ENDLOOP.
```

Listing 4.30 shows the declaration of the internal standard table array, which has the elementary data type i as its line type and whose key consists of the entire line. You can already see two typical statements for filling and processing an internal table: APPEND and LOOP AT.

This method of handling complex dynamic data objects with a few simple statements makes internal tables one of the most powerful language tools in ABAP. Hardly any application programs can run without internal tables.[41] In the following sections we shall introduce the main statements for internal tables.

4.7.1 Defining internal tables

In Section 4.2.4 we introduced the definition of internal tables as data types or data objects:

40. Of course, the number of lines of an internal table is restricted by the capacity of the system installation used. Theoretically, an internal table could occupy a memory space of two gigabytes, including internal management. However, the memory is generally not available for a single internal table alone. On a 32-bit platform you will therefore not be able to have internal tables which occupy more than 500 megabytes. With hashed tables the maximum number of lines is fixed at two million.

41. On the other hand, ABAP does not contain any arrays as is common in other programming languages and whose memory requirements are fixed when the program is executed.

```
TYPES|DATA itab {TYPE|LIKE} tabkind
                 OF {linetype|lineobj}
                 WITH key
                [INITIAL SIZE n].
```

We now want to concentrate in more detail on the following three characteristics: table kind tabkind, line type linetype or lineobj, and table key key. We shall also explain the addition INITIAL SIZE.

Table kind

The table kind determines how an internal table is managed internally and how it is accessed in the ABAP program. Deciding which table kind to use depends on the operations you want to carry out and on how often you want to access the table in your program.

Standard table

To define standard tables you use the STANDARD TABLE expression for tabkind. The individual lines of a standard table are internally managed by a logical index. When you fill a standard table new lines are either appended to the table or inserted at certain positions. You can obtain read-access either by specifying a key or via the index. If you access via the index, the program logic must know which lines belong to a specific index. When you insert lines in, or delete lines from, standard tables the remaining table lines in the memory are not affected. Only the index is reorganized.

Sorted table

For sorted tables you use the SORTED TABLE expression for tabkind. Like standard tables, sorted tables are managed through a logical index. However, sorted tables differ from standard tables in that their entries are always arranged in ascending order according to the table key. Access to sorted tables is the same as for standard tables.

Hashed table

For hashed tables you use the HASHED TABLE expression for tabkind. With hashed tables, the order of the entries is not managed internally through an index. Instead, the entries are unordered in the memory and managed by a hash algorithm. The position of an entry is calculated directly through a hash function from the key value. With hashed tables, index-based access is not possible.

Hierarchy

The three table kinds form the branches of a hierarchy which is shown in Figure 4.16.

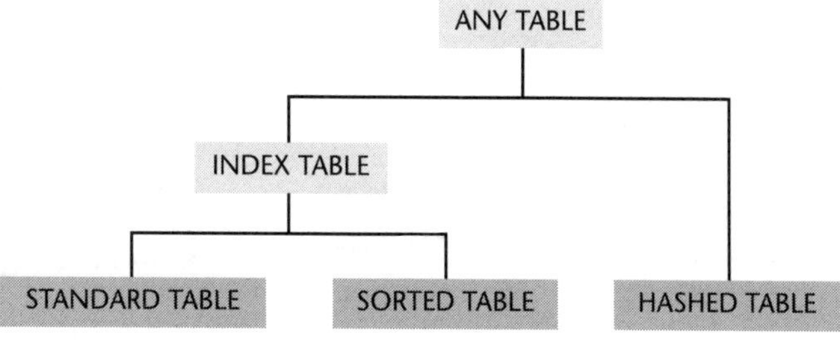

FIGURE 4.16 Hierarchy of table kinds in ABAP

Generic table

The table kinds ANY TABLE and INDEX TABLE listed here cannot be used to declare internal tables as they do not uniquely define the table kind. They are generic types, which we have already listed in Table 4.3, to be used for typing. The generic type ANY TABLE means that a field symbol or an interface parameter of a procedure can be an internal table of any kind. Therefore the only types of access which can be programmed are those which are permitted for all table kinds. In particular, no index access is allowed as this is not possible with hashed tables. However, index access can be programmed for field symbols and interface parameters of the generic type INDEX TABLE, because the actual type can only be a table with index administration, i.e. a standard table or a sorted table. An example of this can be found in Section 5.2.1.

You also can use ANY TABLE and INDEX TABLE in the TYPES statement to create self-defined generic table types such as:

```
TYPES itab TYPE INDEX TABLE
           OF type.
```

or

```
TYPES itab TYPE ANY TABLE
           OF type
           WITH KEY key.
```

In the first case a generic table type is defined whose line type is determined whereas the table kind is an index table and the table key is arbitrary. In the second case the table kind is arbitrary while the line type and the components of the table key are determined. With generic table types, the uniqueness of the key (UNIQUE or NON-UNIQUE, see below) cannot be defined.

Line type

As mentioned previously, the line type linetype is any local or global data type of the ABAP type hierarchy which is determined by the TYPE or LIKE addition. The line type of a classical table is a flat structure, and a common application for this is a reference to the structure of a database table in the ABAP Dictionary (see example in Section 4.2.4). However, a key role is also played by arrays of elementary types or reference variables. Listing 5.16 shows, for example, how an internal table manages pointers to objects in ABAP Objects. Finally, line types which themselves contain internal tables are ideally suited to managing complex objects. An example of this is the structure cxtab_control, which you need to manage table controls on the screen (see Section 7.5.3).

Table key

The table key plays a major role in accessing and sorting internal tables. The following applies to the table key key:

- If the line type is structured, each comp component of the line type which is not a table and does not contain any tables can be included in the key.

  ```
  [UNIQUE|NON-UNIQUE] KEY  comp1 ... compn.
  ```

  The order in which the components are specified is taken into account when the key is evaluated.

- If the line type is not structured, the pseudo component table_line can be entered as the key:

  ```
  [UNIQUE|NON-UNIQUE] KEY table_line.
  ```

  In this case the entire line contents are regarded as the key value. However, it is also possible to specify table_line for a structured line type. In this case all the components of the line are included in the key.

- You can also specify a standard key:

  ```
  [UNIQUE|NON-UNIQUE] DEFAULT KEY.
  ```

  The standard key consists of all the components of a structured table which do not have a numeric data type (i, f, p) and which are not tables themselves. Prior to Release 4.0 this was the only possible key for internal tables. For a table with an elementary line type, the standard key has the same meaning as table_line.

Uniqueness

By using the UNIQUE or NON-UNIQUE additions you can determine whether the key is unique or non-unique. If the key is unique, a line with specific key field contents can occur only once in the internal table. Whereas standard tables can have only non-unique keys and hashed tables only unique keys, sorted tables can be defined with either kind of key.

Initial memory requirements

Internal tables are stored block-wise in the memory. Using the addition

```
... INITIAL SIZE  n.
```

you can influence the size of the first block by specifying the number of table lines n required at the beginning. If you do not specify a value, the runtime environment automatically allocates a suitable memory area. In either case additional memory is allocated if the current block is insufficient. It only makes sense to specify the initial memory requirements if the number of table entries is fixed from the start and you want to adjust the initial memory requirements accordingly. This can be important, in particular, for tables which are themselves components of tables and contain only a few lines.

Abbreviations for standard tables

Prior to Release 4.0 standard tables with a standard key were the only available internal tables.[42] To simplify the definition of this most commonly used table kind, additions in the DATA statement can be omitted:

```
DATA itab TYPE [STANDARD] TABLE
          OF linetype
          [WITH [NON-UNIQUE] DEFAULT KEY].
```

Additions in pointed brackets do not have to be specified, and so the shortest form of declaring a standard table with a standard key is the following statement:

```
DATA itab TYPE TABLE OF  linetype.
```

TYPE TABLE OF

The runtime environment supplements these short forms automatically to produce the complete statement:

```
DATA itab TYPE STANDARD TABLE
          OF linetype
          WITH NON-UNIQUE DEFAULT KEY.
```

In principle the same applies to the TYPES statement with the exception that a table type without a key specification is always a true generic type which is not supplemented with the standard key and therefore can only be used for typings (see Section 4.2.7).

Example of definition of internal tables

LISTING 4.31 Defining internal tables

```
REPORT s_itab_example.

TYPES: BEGIN t_OF address,
         street(20)  TYPE c,
         city(20)    TYPE c,
       END OF t_address.

TYPES t_address_tab TYPE STANDARD TABLE
                    OF t_address
                    WITH NON-UNIQUE KEY city.

DATA: BEGIN OF company,
```

42. Prior to Release 4.0 internal tables were also defined solely with an OCCURS addition to the TYPES and DATA statements. Although this addition is now obsolete, it still occurs in many older programs.

```
    name(20)    TYPE c,
    addresses   TYPE t_address_tab,
  END OF company.

DATA company_tab LIKE HASHED TABLE
                 OF    company
                 WITH UNIQUE KEY name.

DATA company_sorted_tab LIKE SORTED TABLE
                        OF    company
                        WITH UNIQUE KEY name.
```

Listing 4.31 shows the definition of two internal tables, t_address_tab and company_tab, whereby t_address_tab is contained in company_tab. For this purpose t_address_tab is defined as a table type. A data object of this type occurs in our example only as the component addresses of the structure company. The data type of company is used as the line type for the tables company_tab and company_sorted_tab.

4.7.2 Working with internal tables

When working with internal tables we can distinguish between accessing individual lines and accessing the entire table. We shall deal first with accessing individual lines. In this context, we can distinguish between key access and index access. We shall only introduce the most important forms of the respective statements.[43] You can find the many other options in the online documentation. At the end of the section we will show in an example how some of the statements introduced here can be used.

Index access and key access

Key access addresses lines via the table key and is possible for all table kinds. Index access addresses lines via the internal index and is therefore only possible for standard tables and sorted tables. After an index table has been accessed, the system field sy-tabix is always filled with the index of the addressed line. After successful access to lines of internal tables, the system field sy-subrc is filled with the value zero, otherwise with a value other than zero. Table 4.8 summarizes the options for accessing individual table kinds.

The last line of Table 4.8 also specifies a preferred access mode for the various table kinds. This recommendation is derived from the fact that working with internal

43. In particular, we shall not deal with the various possibilities of making dynamic specifications in these statements.

TABLE 4.8 Accessing the different table kinds

	Standard table	Sorted table	Hashed table
Index access	Yes	Yes	No
Key access	Yes	Yes	Yes
Key values	Non-unique	Unique or non-unique	Unique
Preferred access	Primarily index	Primarily key	Key only

tables usually involves working with large amounts of data. One standard application area for internal tables is to load large amounts of data from the database into the memory in order to process it faster and more efficiently. In such cases it is essential to consider the time involved in the various access modes.

Although index access is generally the quickest means of accessing a line of an internal table, since there is a direct internal reference, this is often not the most suitable means, especially when working with data from a database. When index access is used, the program must know the assignment between index and contents of the table line, whereas with key access the contents of the table line itself are evaluated. Key access is therefore more appropriate for many applications, albeit slower.

Access time

The time needed for a key access depends largely on the table kind.

- In a key access to standard tables, the system searches all lines linearly for the key value. The average search time is therefore directly proportional to the number of lines.
- In a key access to sorted tables, the runtime environment automatically performs a binary search (interval search) for the key value. The average search time is proportional to log_2 of the number of lines.
- In a key access to hashed tables, the runtime environment calculates the position of the line from the key value using a hash function. The search time is not affected by the number of lines and always constant.

Runtime measurement

Figure 4.17 shows an example for measuring[44] the average runtime required for a key access to the different table kinds as a function of the number of lines. For each of the three table kinds, we measured the times needed for key access to all lines and then calculated the average value. You can find the corresponding program in the Basis system of the attached CD under the name S_ITAB_ACCESS. After approximately 50 lines, the curves reflect the behaviour we predicted above. Note the logarithmic scale of the representation. With 10,000 lines, access to a hashed table is twice as fast as access to a sorted table, which in turn is 170 times faster than access to a standard table.

44. The runtime was measured in an SAP development system based on a kernel not optimized with respect to runtime. In an optimized production system, the absolute times are usually below the ones shown in Figure 4.17.

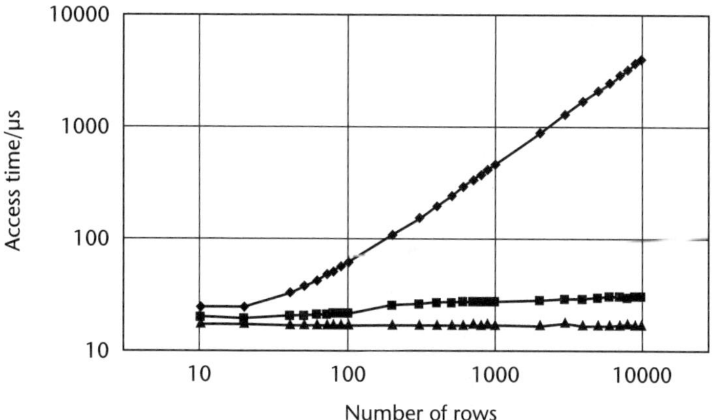

	10	100	1000	10000	
Standard table	20 µs	64 µs	530 µs	5300 µs	◆
Sorted table	18 µs	21 µs	28 µs	31 µs	■
Hashed table	17 µs	17 µs	17 µs	17 µs	▲

FIGURE 4.17 Runtime measurement for key access

Depending on the purpose of an internal table within a program (number of lines, frequency of access) you should therefore always use the appropriate table kinds. For small tables with up to around 100 lines, or for tables which you do not or only rarely access by key, you can use standard tables. Large tables without duplicate entries which you want to access only by key should always be created as hashed tables. Sorted tables are always preferable if a table must exist in sorted form during the entire runtime.[45]

Inserting table lines with `INSERT`

You use the `INSERT` statement to fill an internal table with lines. For index access the syntax is:

```
INSERT  line INTO itab INDEX idx.
```

This statement inserts the `line` data object into the `itab` internal table before the line with the `idx` index. The new line receives the `idx` index, and the index of the following lines is incremented by one.

45. If you sort a standard table with the `SORT` command and perform a binary search with the `BINARY SEARCH` addition to the `READ TABLE` statement, you will incidentally achieve the same runtimes as for sorted tables.

INDEX/TABLE

For key access the syntax is:[46]

```
INSERT line INTO TABLE itab.
```

This statement inserts the line data object into the itab internal table as follows:

- With standard tables line is simply attached as the last line of the internal table. With standard tables INSERT therefore actually operates not as a true key access but exactly like the APPEND statement below.
- With sorted tables the internal table is searched for the key values in line and the line is inserted accordingly.
- With hashed tables the line is inserted into the internal table by hash management based on its key values.

To ensure that line matches the line type of the internal table and that therefore the key value can be evaluated in line, line must be compatible with the line type of the internal table. The following statement can be used to declare this kind of data object:

```
TYPES|DATA line {TYPE|LIKE} LINE OF  {itabtype|itabobj}.
```

You can insert more than one line from other tables with compatible line types into an internal table by replacing the expression line in the above INSERT statement with the following expression:

```
... LINES OF jtab [FROM idx1] [TO idx2] ...
```

In this way the lines of the jtab table are inserted line by line into itab according to the same rules as for each individual line. If jtab is an index table, you can use the FROM and TO additions to insert sections of the table.

Inserting table lines in condensed form with COLLECT

If you use INSERT to add a line to an internal table with a unique key whose key values are already present, sy-subrc is set to four and the line is not added. This is the most common method of building internal tables without duplicating entries. In addition there is a special statement which you can use to build tables without duplicating entries.

```
COLLECT  line INTO itab.
```

If there is no line with an identical key in the table, COLLECT acts like a key access

46. In most statements for processing internal tables, index access and key access differ in that one contains the INDEX addition and the other the TABLE addition. Nevertheless, the statements for index access and key access are often so similar that you must program with great care to prevent your program from behaving completely differently to how it should. See also footnote 48.

with INSERT. If you attempt to use COLLECT to add a line whose key values are already present in the table, sy-subrc is not set to four, but instead the values of the numeric non-key fields of the data object line are added to the corresponding fields of the table line. You can therefore use COLLECT to specifically add numeric values with unique keys. In all other cases, you should use the INSERT statement.

Appending table lines with APPEND

For standard tables there is a special type of syntax for attaching one or more lines:

```
APPEND  line TO itab.
```

or

```
APPEND LINES OF jtab [FROM idx1] [TO idx2] TO itab.
```

The APPEND statement acts in exactly the same way for standard tables as the above key access with INSERT. It provides a very fast method of filling standard tables with lines. As the table key of standard tables is never unique, the table does not have to be searched for existing entries. The APPEND statement can also be used for sorted tables, but requires that the lines to be attached comply with the sorting.

Reading table lines with READ

To read the contents of individual lines from an internal table, use the READ statement. For index access the syntax is:

```
READ TABLE  itab INDEX idx {INTO wa|ASSIGNING <fs>}.
```

This statement copies the contents of the line with the index idx into a work area wa or assigns the line to the field symbol <fs>.

For key access the syntax is:

```
READ TABLE itab FROM key {INTO wa|ASSIGNING <fs>}.
```

or

```
READ TABLE itab
           WITH TABLE KEY comp1 = f1 ... compn = fn
           {INTO wa|ASSIGNING <fs>}.
```

In the first case key is a data object which is compatible with the line type of the internal table and whose key components must be filled with values before the READ statement. The first line found in the internal table, whose key values correspond to those in key, is then read. In the second case you specify the key values in the READ statement itself by specifying a value f_i for each component $comp_i$ of the table key.

There is also a variant of the READ statement which allows an arbitrary key to be specified.

```
READ TABLE itab
          WITH KEY comp1 = f1 ... compn = fn
          {INTO wa|ASSIGNING <fs>}.
```

If you do not have the TABLE addition before KEY, any number of components $comp_i$ of the internal table can be used as a search key.[47]

Output behavior

You have two options for controlling the output behaviour of the READ statement. If you specify INTO wa, the contents of the line found are assigned to the data object wa. The data type of the data object must therefore match the line type of the internal table and is best declared compatible. The READ statement also has a TRANSPORTING addition for this output variant, which you can use to determine which components are actually to be transported to the data object.

If you specify ASSIGNING <fs>, no values are assigned. Instead, the field symbol <fs> points to the table line in the memory after the statement, and the table line can be evaluated or modified using <fs>. The alternative use of work areas or field symbols is characteristic for read or write access to lines of internal tables. Figure 4.18 summarizes the two options.

Deleting table lines with DELETE

To delete a line of an internal table, use the DELETE statement. The syntax for index access is:

```
DELETE TABLE itab INDEX idx.
```

This statement deletes the table line with the index idx. For key access the syntax is

```
DELETE itab FROM key.
```

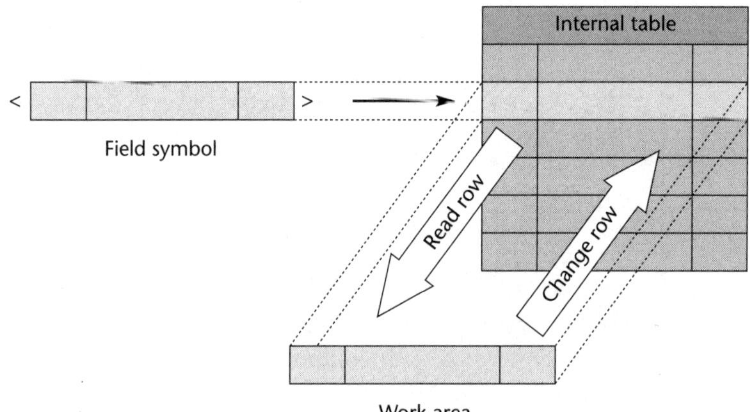

FIGURE 4.18 Read and write access to internal tables

47. For tables with non-structured line type, the pseudo component table_line can be specified in such cases.

or

```
DELETE TABLE itab
       WITH TABLE KEY comp1 = f1 ... compn = fn.
```

Both these variants operate exactly as in the READ statement. In the first case key is again a data object which is compatible with the line type of the internal table, and the first line found in the internal table whose key values correspond to those in key is deleted. In the second case you specify the key values in the DELETE statement itself, by specifying a value f_1 for each component $comp_i$ of the table key.

To delete several lines of an internal table in one statement, you can use the DELETE statement for index tables as follows:

```
DELETE itab [FROM idx1] [TO idx2].
```

All lines with indices between idx_1 and idx_2 are deleted.[48] The following variant is available for all table kinds:

```
DELETE itab WHERE logical expression.
```

After WHERE there can be a logical expression in which the first operand of each comparison must be a component of the internal table. The statement deletes all the lines for which the logical expression is "true."

Modifying table lines with MODIFY

To modify the contents of an existing line of an internal table, you can either assign the contents of a work area to the line or access the line directly via a field symbol.

Work area

To assign the contents of a work area to a line, use the MODIFY statement. The syntax for index access is:

```
MODIFY  itab FROM line INDEX idx.
```

This statement assigns the contents of the line data object to the table line with the index idx. The syntax for key access is:

```
MODIFY TABLE itab FROM line.
```

In this case the system searches in the internal table itab for the first line whose key values match the values of the corresponding line components, which is then overwritten with the contents of line. The data object line must therefore be declared type-specific, and filled with search values in its key fields and with the values to be modified in the other components before the statement.

48. However, this statement can also result in a typical error situation when working with internal tables. Without the TABLE addition after DELETE the system interprets the operand after FROM as an index specification, whereas with the TABLE addition it is seen as a work area for key access. Therefore be careful with the syntax.

Like the DELETE statement, the MODIFY statement has a WHERE addition, which allows a logical expression to be specified in order to modify several lines of an internal table simultaneously:

```
MODIFY itab FROM line
            TRANSPORTING comp1 ... compn
            WHERE logical expression.
```

Using the TRANSPORTING addition you must specify which components of the data object line are to be assigned to the corresponding components of the lines which satisfy the logical expression. With sorted and hashed tables no table key components must be specified. The TRANSPORTING addition can, if required, also be specified with the two previous variants of the MODIFY statement.

Field symbol

If you are pointing to a line with a field symbol after reading an internal table with READ or in a LOOP loop (see below), you can modify the line contents by simply assigning new contents to the field symbol.

Loop processing of internal tables with LOOP

As well as accessing individual lines directly you can process internal tables in a special loop.

```
LOOP  AT itab {INTO wa|ASSIGNING <fs>}.
  ... "Statement block
ENDLOOP.
```

This control structure makes each line of the internal table in turn available to the statement block between the LOOP and ENDLOOP statements. As with the READ statement, in the LOOP statement either the line contents are assigned to a work area wa or the line is assigned to a field symbol <fs>. The order in which the table lines are read depends on the kind of table:

- For standard tables, the lines are processed according to their logical index.
- For sorted tables, the lines are processed according to their sort sequences.
- For hashed tables the lines are read in the order in which they were added to the internal table. However, if a hashed table has been previously sorted with the SORT statement, the lines are read in the sorting order.
- For index tables, in the LOOP statement the sy-tabix system field is filled with the index of the current line. If the loop has been fully processed, sy-tabix will retain the value it had before it entered the loop.

For index tables you can use the additions

```
... FROM idx1 TO idx2.
```

to limit the number of lines to be processed, which can be beneficial for the runtime. To restrict the number of lines for any given table, you can use the addition

```
... WHERE logical expression.
```

which is known from the DELETE and MODIFY statements.

Control level processing

In the statement block between the LOOP and ENDLOOP statements you can perform **control level processing**. **Control levels** mean that consecutive lines can be divided into groups according to the contents of their leading components. You can group lines into control levels by sorting the internal table in exactly the order which corresponds to its structure, i.e. initially after the first component, then after the second component, and so on. This need not be the order in the table key; however, tables whose table key corresponds to the first fields are particularly suitable for control level processing. To evaluate the control levels, use the AT and ENDAT statements within the LOOP loop.

```
LOOP AT itab ...
  ...
  AT NEW  comp.
    ... "Statement block
  ENDAT.
...
  AT END OF  comp.
    .. "Statement block
  ENDAT.
  ...
ENDLOOP.
```

These control structures divide the LOOP statement block again into several statement blocks which are executed when the control levels change. Control level processing spares you from having to read line contents for logical expressions. You commonly use control levels to format data for a condensed representation in lists. An example of control level processing is shown in Listing 7.28.

Sorting internal tables

To sort an internal table according to the contents of its key fields, simply use the statement:

```
SORT  itab [ASCENDING|DESCENDING].
```

You can use the ASCENDING and DESCENDING additions to determine the order in which you wish to sort, whereby the default setting is ascending. The SORT statement is, of course, only useful for standard tables and hashed tables, as sorted tables are always sorted in ascending order according to the table key. Hashed tables are typically sorted before being processed in a loop (LOOP) as only in loops are their lines available in sorted order. Sorting a standard table, on the other hand, also affects index access, as it changes the assignment of the index to the table lines.

Own key

If you want to sort independently of the table key, use the BY addition:

```
SORT itab [ASCENDING|DESCENDING]
          ... BY comp_i [ASCENDING|DESCENDING] ...
```

Here you can specify all $comp_i$ components of the internal table in the desired sort order or the table_line pseudo component. For each component by which you wish to sort, you can determine individually whether you wish the sort order to be ascending or descending, whereby the default setting is determined by the entry directly after itab.

Operations with the overall table

Irrespective of their inner structure, within an ABAP program internal tables are data objects like any other field. For this reason other operations besides sorting with the SORT statement can be performed with the overall table, providing they are useful. We shall now itemize a few types of access to overall tables.

- Assigning internal tables

  As we saw in Section 4.3.2, you can assign an internal table to another internal table if their line types are convertible. The table kind and the key do not determine whether two tables can be assigned. However, as with all assignments, the contents must be suitable. For example, a runtime error is triggered if an assignment results in a hashed table with non-unique key values.

- Initializing internal tables

  Like other data objects, you initialize internal tables with the statement:

  ```
  CLEAR itab.
  ```

  Resetting an internal table to its initial value will cause all the lines to be deleted.

- Comparing internal tables

  As mentioned in Section 4.3.4, internal tables can even be compared with each other in logical expressions, whereby first the number of lines is used as a comparison criterion, followed by the lines themselves.

- Passing internal tables

  The entire contents of internal tables can be passed to interface parameters when procedures are called. In addition ABAP offers many more options for storing internal tables, such as storing in a data cluster (see Section 8.3) or in a file on the presentation or application server (see Section 8.2). Moreover, all Open-SQL statements contain variants which allow data from database tables to be exchanged directly with internal tables (see Section 8.1.3).

Example of working with internal tables

LISTING 4.32 Working with internal tables

```
REPORT s_itab_example.

...
DATA address TYPE t_address.

DATA idx TYPE sy-tabix.
FIELD-SYMBOLS <fs> LIKE company.

* Filling Internal Tables

company-name = 'Racing Bikes Inc.'.
address-street  = 'Fifth Avenue'.
address-city    = 'New York'.
APPEND address TO company-addresses.
address-street  = 'Second Street'.
address-city    = 'Boston'.
APPEND address TO company-addresses.
INSERT company INTO TABLE company_tab.

CLEAR company.
company-name = 'Chocolatiers Suisse'.
address-street  = 'Avenue des Forets'.
address-city    = 'Geneve'.
APPEND address TO company-addresses.
address-street  = 'Kleine Bachgasse'.
address-city    = 'Basel'.
APPEND address TO company-addresses.
address-street  = 'Piazza di Lago'.
address-city    = 'Como'.
APPEND address TO company-addresses.
INSERT company INTO TABLE company_tab.

* Reading Internal Tables

READ TABLE company_tab
     WITH TABLE KEY name = 'Racing Bikes Inc.'
     ASSIGNING <fs>.
```

```
WRITE: / <fs>-name.
LOOP AT <fs>-addresses INTO address.
  WRITE: / sy-tabix, address-street, address-city.
ENDLOOP.
ULINE.

* Modifying Internal Tables

address-street = 'Rue des Montagnes'.
address-city   = 'Geneve'.
READ TABLE company_tab
     WITH TABLE KEY name = 'Chocolatiers Suisse'
     INTO company.
READ TABLE company-addresses TRANSPORTING NO FIELDS
            WITH TABLE KEY city = address-city.
idx = sy-tabix.
MODIFY company-addresses FROM address INDEX idx.
MODIFY TABLE company_tab FROM company.

* Moving and sorting Internal Tables

company_sorted_tab = company_tab.
LOOP AT company_sorted_tab INTO company.
  WRITE / company-name.
  SORT company-addresses.
  LOOP AT company-addresses INTO address.
    WRITE: / sy-tabix, address-street, address-city.
  ENDLOOP.
ENDLOOP.
```

Listing 4.32 works with the internal tables from Listing 4.31. We fill the tables at the beginning with a few lines. As the company-addresses component is a standard table, we use APPEND to attach the address structure line by line. However, as company_tab is a hashed table we must insert company using INSERT.

We then use READ to assign a line from company_tab to the field symbol <fs> and process its table-like addresses component in a loop, whereby we assign the contents of the lines to the address structure. As addresses is an index table, sy-tabix can be evaluated.

To modify the contents of the street component of a line in the inner table addresses, we determine the index of the desired line with the READ statement and use it in MODIFY. To apply this modification also to the corresponding line of the external hashed table, we use the key access of the MODIFY statement.

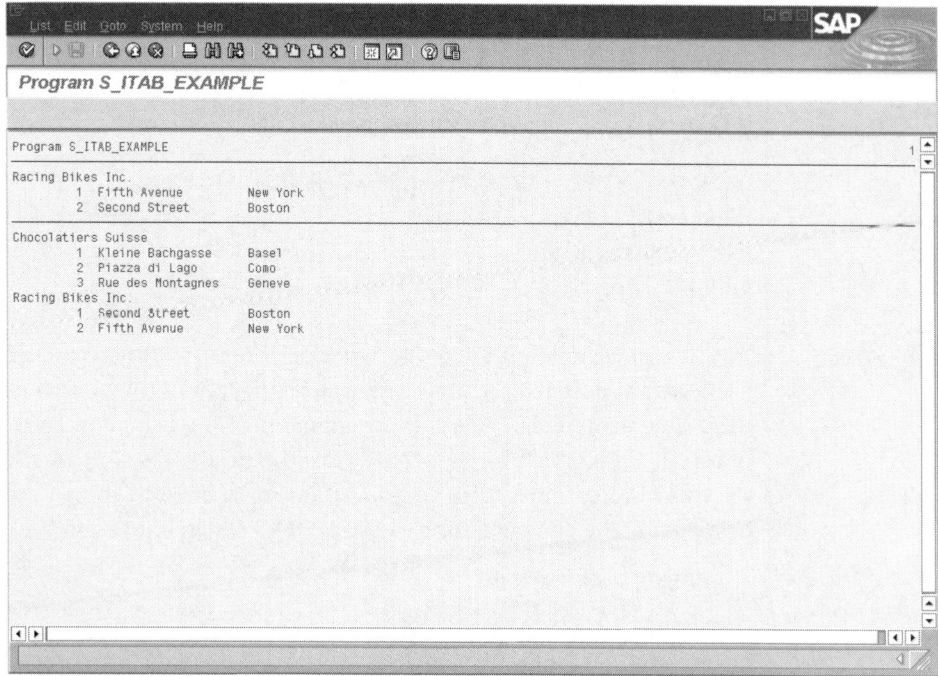

FIGURE 4.19 Example program of internal tables. Copyright © SAP AG

Finally we assign the hashed table to a sorted table of the same line type. This sorts the entries automatically according to the `name` table key. The entries of the inner standard table are, however, sorted using the `SORT` command. A nested loop (`LOOP`) outputs the contents of the tables. Figure 4.19 shows the list output of the program.

4.7.3 Internal tables with header lines

To conclude our discussion of internal tables we must briefly consider internal tables with **header lines**. Although they are obsolete and forbidden in ABAP Objects, unfortunately they still occur in many programs. Apart from the table itself, an internal table with a header line contains another data object which has exactly the same name as the internal table and the same data type as a line of the internal table. This header line can be used instead of the work areas which we have specified in the above statements for internal tables after the `FROM`, `TO`, and `INTO` additions. For internal tables with header lines these additions can even be left out completely because ABAP then implicitly uses the header line.

Before Release 3.0 internal tables with header lines were the only way of creating internal tables.[49] From Release 3.0 internal tables without header lines have become the

49. An internal table was declared solely by using the obsolete `OCCURS` addition after `BEGIN OF` when creating a structure. A header line and an internal table were then created in the program at the same time.

standard. If you still want to create an internal table with a header line outside of classes, you must specify the `WITH HEADER LINE` addition to the `DATA` statement. An example:

LISTING 4.33 Internal table with header line

```
DATA itab TYPE TABLE OF spfli WITH HEADER LINE.
itab-carrid = 'LH'.
itab-connid = '0400'.
APPEND itab.
```

Abbreviation

In this case a standard table `itab` with the structured line type `spfli` from the ABAP Dictionary is declared together with a structure `itab` of the same type. The second and third statements assign values to components of the structure. The `APPEND` statement is a short form which implicitly attaches the header line to the internal table. If you see this kind of short form in a program, it is an indication that header lines are being used. The complete form of the `APPEND` statement would be:

```
APPEND itab TO itab.
```

Namespace

Header lines therefore may save some writing, but have a major disadvantage in that they violate the unique namespace for data objects: two distinct data objects have the same name. When you use the name in an ABAP statement it depends on the statement and the position in the statement as to whether it is interpreted as an internal table or as its header line. Most statements such as assignments or parameter passing interpret the name as a header line specification and not as an internal table. In these kinds of statement, in order to address the internal table when a header line is present, you have to attach two square brackets (`[ ]`) to the name. An example:

```
DATA itab TYPE TABLE OF spfli WITH HEADER LINE,
     jtab TYPE TABLE OF spfli WITH HEADER LINE.
itab = jtab.
itab[] = jtab[].
```

The first assignment works with the header lines, while the second assignment works with the internal tables. Although ABAP has clear rules as to where the header line and table are used, overall this ambiguity tends to be confusing. For this reason you should only use tables without header lines where the name always refers to the table. The correct syntax in ABAP Objects for our example in Listing 4.33 is therefore:

```
DATA itab TYPE TABLE OF spfli,
     itab_line LIKE LINE OF itab.
itab_line-carrid = 'LH'.
itab_line-connid = '0400'.
APPEND itab_line TO itab.
```

In these statements you can identify the operands uniquely through their names without having to bother with the meaning of their respective positions.

4.7.4 Extract datasets

For the sake of completion, in conjunction with internal tables we want to introduce you to another construct of the ABAP language which allows you to dynamically store and sort structured data in the memory as well as to process it in loops. This construct is known as an extract dataset, or extract for short. Extracts are a rather old component of ABAP and not part of the ABAP type hierarchy. You can create exactly one single unnamed extract dataset for each ABAP program.

Field group

Like an internal table, an extract dataset consists of a dynamic set of lines. However, unlike internal tables, the line structures of the individual lines can vary. To each line structure which is to occur in the extract dataset, a name must be assigned with the statement

```
FIELD-GROUPS  fg.
```

in the global declaration part of the program. The structure of a field group `fg` is created during program runtime with the statement

```
INSERT  f1 f2 ... INTO fg.
```

whereby f_1, f_2, ... are data objects with a flat data type which are globally declared in the program. To fill an extract dataset you use the statement:

```
EXTRACT  fg.
```

Extract

This attaches the contents of the fields f_1, f_2 ... of the `fg` field group to the extract dataset of the program as a line. You can attach variously defined field groups to a single extract. If one of the field groups has the special name `header`, it acts as a standard sort key of the extract and its fields also automatically become the starting part of all the other field groups in the program.

Like internal tables, extracts can be sorted with the `SORT` statement. If no internal table is specified in `SORT`, the statement affects the extract dataset of the program. The extracts are read in a loop which is simply defined by

```
LOOP.
  ...
ENDLOOP.
```

Loop

Like `SORT`, a `LOOP` statement without any additions therefore affects the extract dataset of the program and not an internal table. This loop returns the extracted contents line by line to the fields of the field groups involved. As with internal tables, control level processing is possible. Listing 4.34 gives a simple example of an extract dataset which, like Listing 4.30, creates a list of square numbers.

LISTING 4.34 Filling and processing extract datasets

```
REPORT s_extract.
DATA: f1 TYPE i,
      f2 TYPE i.
FIELD-GROUPS header.
INSERT f1 f2 INTO header.
DO 10 TIMES.
  f1 = sy-index.
  f2 = sy-index ** 2.
  EXTRACT header.
ENDDO.
SORT DESCENDING.
LOOP.
  WRITE: / f1, f2.
ENDLOOP.
```

Our main reason for showing you the extract statements was to avoid confusion with statements for internal tables when you encounter them in a program. Today, extract datasets are still used for control level processing of data from different database tables which have the same fields at the beginning. Programming these tasks with internal tables can be more complicated and can affect runtime costs.

4.8 ERROR HANDLING IN ABAP PROGRAMS

In this chapter we have introduced you to the majority of the language elements you need to implement functionality in ABAP programs. In so doing we have shown you the most important concepts and statements. However, for almost all the language elements listed in this book ABAP contains other options and variants for special requirements. You will find the syntax and meaning of all statements in the online documentation for the ABAP language. Because of the variety of the language it is, however, unavoidable that you will make syntactical as well as semantic errors when programming. These will certainly decrease as you become more experienced with ABAP.

Whereas semantic errors can only be traced via intensive test running of your program under application conditions, syntax errors are much easier to detect. We distinguish between errors which can be identified statically when you write the program and those which occur only at runtime. As a rule, a program with statically identifiable errors cannot be compiled or executed. A syntactically correct program may be executable but, depending on its data, may encounter statements which cannot be executed. In this case the system will respond with a runtime error and terminate program processing. Depending on circumstances, however, it may be possible to catch this kind of runtime error.

We shall now briefly examine how to find and process statically identifiable errors and runtime errors.

4.8.1 Statically identifiable errors

To trace statically identifiable errors ABAP provides a **syntax check** and an **extended program check**.

Syntax check

You can call the syntax check at any time when creating the program in the ABAP Editor using **Check**. Syntax checking is automatic when a program is activated and before it is run for the first time. If the check finds an error, the check is immediately terminated and an error message generated. A program with syntax errors can be activated but not executed. In many cases, the ABAP Editor suggests a correction which you can use. A new syntax check is then performed. An example of this was shown in Section 2.3.3.

Syntax error

Besides syntax errors, the syntax check also displays warnings. In this case the check is not terminated and theoretically the program can be executed. However, you should always correct syntax warnings as they usually indicate errors which can be expected at runtime, and also because SAP might turn warnings into genuine syntax errors in later releases.

Extended program check

Many checks which are statically feasible are not carried out in every syntax check for reasons of efficiency. Instead you should call **Program – Check – Extended Program Check** at least once before the program is released. The extended program check performs a complete check of all statically identifiable errors, which for example also includes a check of the parameter passing to externally called procedures.[50]

Figure 4.20 shows the control panel for the extended program check. For reasons of efficiency and clarity, the extended program check is divided into subtests which can be switched on and off individually.

Errors which are only found by the extended program check allow you to execute a program but trigger runtime errors during the program flow, for example if a value is to be passed to a non-existing parameter of a function module.

Like the syntax check, the extended program check issues not only errors but also warnings which have the same meaning as warnings in the syntax check.

50. This affects mainly external subroutines and function modules. Parameter passing to methods from the class library is controlled via the syntax check.

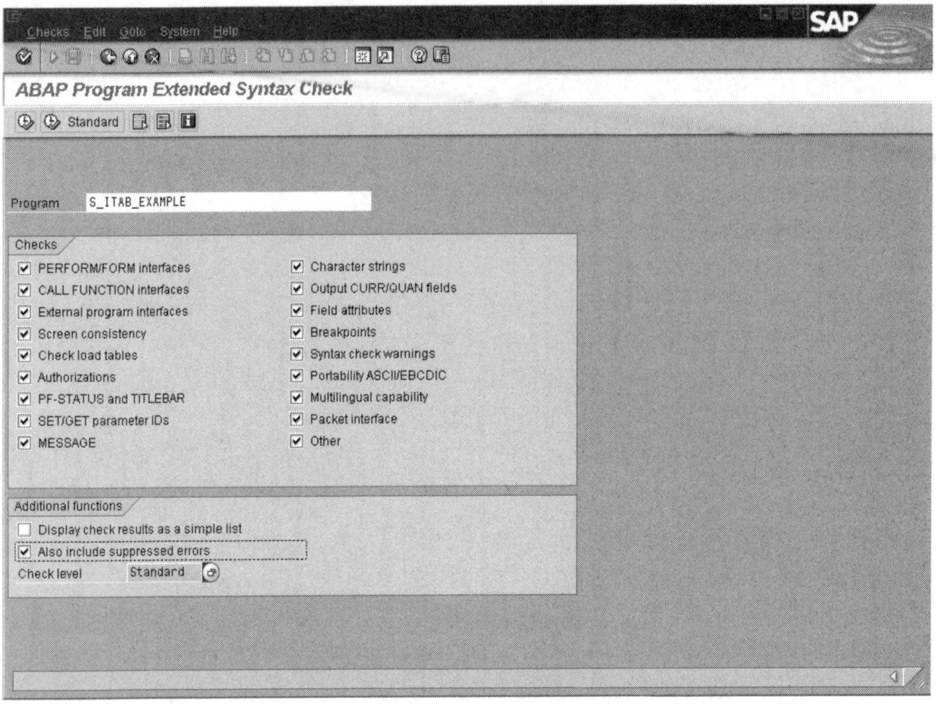

FIGURE 4.20 Extended program check. Copyright © SAP AG

4.8.2 Runtime errors

The static checks cannot completely rule out runtime errors. For example, you cannot statically check all the places where arguments of statements are dynamically specified as field contents. If the runtime environment encounters an error situation while the program is running, it triggers a runtime error. We distinguish between catchable and non-catchable runtime errors. The various runtime errors are listed in the keyword documentation for each ABAP statement along with an indication of whether they are catchable or not.

Catchable runtime errors

Runtime errors are catchable if they are caused by situations which can be handled meaningfully in the program. Catchable runtime errors are grouped together in **Error Classes** which allow similar errors to be handled together.

You can handle catchable runtime errors with the statement:

SYSTEM EXCEPTIONS

```
CATCH SYSTEM-EXCEPTIONS  exc_1 = rc_1 ... exc_n = rc_n.
  ...
ENDCATCH.
```

The exc_i expressions describe either a catchable runtime error or the name of an error class. The rc_i expressions are numeric literals. If one of the specified runtime errors occurs in the statement block between CATCH and ENDCATCH, the program is not terminated. Instead it goes directly to ENDCATCH. After ENDCATCH the rc_i number value assigned to the runtime error is contained in the sy-subrc system field as a return value. In the keyword documentation for CATCH you will find a list of all catchable runtime errors, and how they are assigned to error classes and keywords.

Like IF and ENDIF for example, the CATCH and ENDCATCH statements define control structures which can be nested to any depth. CATCH can only be used to catch the runtime errors of the current call level, not those of called procedures.[51]

LISTING 4.35 Catchable runtime error

```
REPORT s_runtime_error.

DATA: result TYPE p DECIMALS 3,
      number TYPE i VALUE 11.

CATCH SYSTEM-EXCEPTIONS arithmetic_errors = 4.
  DO.
    number = number - 1.
    result = 1 / number.
    WRITE: / number, result.
  ENDDO.
ENDCATCH.
IF sy-subrc = 4.
  WRITE / 'Arithmetic Error!'.
ENDIF.
```

Listing 4.35 shows how an arithmetic error is handled. The program calculates the quotient from 1 and number ten times until the catchable error bcd_zerodivide occurs. This runtime error is part of the arithmetic_errors error class and is caught by it.

Non-catchable runtime error

In addition to catchable runtime errors there are runtime errors which are caused by conditions which will not allow the ABAP program to continue. This kind of runtime error is not catchable. If a non-catchable error occurs, and also if a catchable error is not handled with CATCH, the ABAP runtime environment will immediately terminate the program, and create and display a **short dump**.

51. As of Release 6.10 SAP is introducing a new kind of exception handling which is based on system classes. Runtime errors and exceptions in procedures (see Section 5.2.1) will be handled consistently and can be passed on over various call levels.

Short dump

A short dump is divided into several blocks which document the error. The overview of the short dump shows you which information is contained, such as contents of data objects, active calls, control structures, etc. You can branch from the short dump display to the ABAP Debugger; here the cursor is positioned on the termination point. Figure 4.21 shows a section of the short dump when Listing 4.35 is run without the CATCH and ENDCATCH statements.

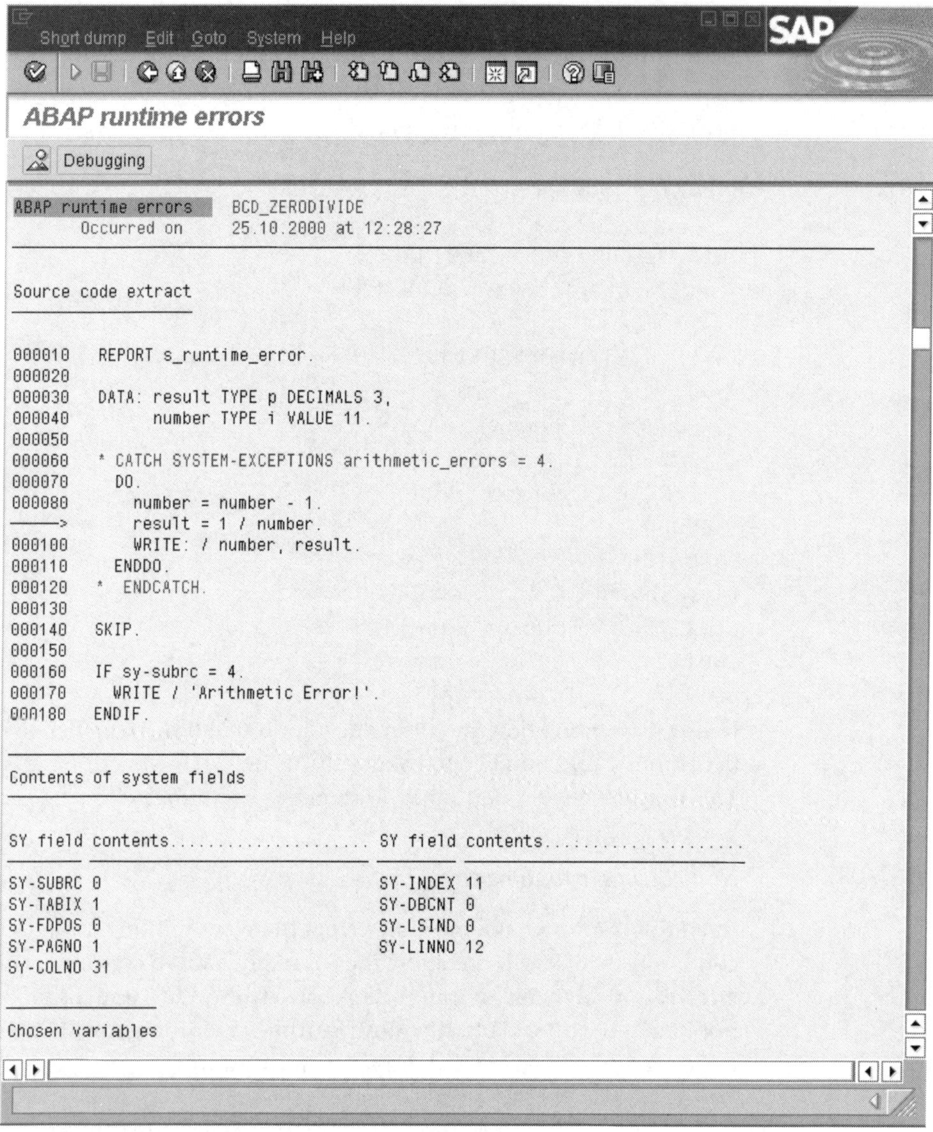
Short dump Edit Goto System Help
SAP
ABAP runtime errors
Debugging
ABAP runtime errors BCD_ZERODIVIDE
Occurred on 25.10.2000 at 12:28:27
Source code extract
REPORT s_runtime_error.
DATA: result TYPE p DECIMALS 3,
number TYPE i VALUE 11.
* CATCH SYSTEM-EXCEPTIONS arithmetic_errors = 4.
DO.
number = number - 1.
result = 1 / number.
WRITE: / number, result.
ENDDO.
* ENDCATCH.
SKIP.
IF sy-subrc = 4.
WRITE / 'Arithmetic Error!'.
ENDIF.
Contents of system fields
SY field contents.................... SY field contents....................
SY-SUBRC 0
SY-TABIX 1
SY-FDPOS 0
SY-PAGNO 1
SY-COLNO 31
SY-INDEX 11
SY-DBCNT 0
SY-LSIND 0
SY-LINNO 12
Chosen variables

FIGURE 4.21 Short dump of a runtime error. Copyright © SAP AG

By default, short dumps are saved in the system for 14 days. The transaction for managing short dumps is ST22. Short dumps can also be saved without a time restriction using the **Keep** function. If problems occur with an ABAP program which you cannot resolve, you can send the relevant excerpts from the short dump to SAP. A short dump forms the basis for problem solving both for the hotline and for the remote consulting service.

CHAPTER 5

The ABAP programming models

The previous chapter introduced you to the ABAP language elements for implementing functionality in ABAP. You now know how to declare types and data and how to work with this data. However, we have not yet discussed where to use these language elements. In our basic example programs we simply declared the data globally and executed the processing during the standard event of the runtime environment. Of course, this is by no means sufficient for complex applications, and therefore we shall now introduce the two ABAP programming models.

5.1 INTRODUCTION

In Chapter 3 we introduced the structure and execution of ABAP programs within the ABAP runtime environment and in Chapter 4 we showed you the language elements you can use in ABAP programs. You learned about language elements which declare data types and data objects and those which work with data. In this chapter we shall introduce the structuring options ABAP provides for writing application programs with these language elements.

We distinguish between a classical (procedural) programming model and an object-oriented programming model. Prior to the advent of ABAP Objects, ABAP mainly supported the procedural programming model. With the introduction of ABAP Objects language elements for object-oriented programming were added to ABAP. Within an SAP System you now find both procedural and object-oriented programs, as well as mixtures of the two.

Basically, both programming models are based on the question of where you declare data in an ABAP program and where you can work with this data, or in other words, in which of the program areas illustrated in Figure 3.7 you write the language elements introduced in Chapter 4.

The classical (procedural) programming model offers you procedures in which you can implement a functionality for reuse. When a procedure is called, you pass input data through an interface, from where you also collect the results. Within a procedure you declare auxiliary variables which are not required outside of the procedure.

The object-oriented programming model adds classes to the procedural concept. The procedures of the object-oriented programming model are called methods, and largely fulfill the same role as procedures in the procedural programming model, i.e. they implement functionality and encapsulate data which is required temporarily. Classes on the other hand open up a completely new level of programming. You can encapsulate data and corresponding methods in classes and create independent objects of these classes. This allows a program to work with units in which data and the corresponding functionality are combined and their lifetime is controlled by the program.

5.2 THE CLASSICAL (PROCEDURAL) PROGRAMMING MODEL

The procedural programming model is based on the modularization of programs into functional units with local data areas. In this section we shall consider the various modularization techniques and their effect on the visibility areas and lifetime of data objects.

5.2.1 Modularization

As you have seen in Section 3.3.1, ABAP programs are generally modularized through their processing block structure. Simply in order to be executed, each ABAP program requires as a minimum an event block such as `START-OF-SELECTION` with executable programs or a dialog module with module pools. These processing blocks are called by the runtime environment. There is no parameter interface nor a local data area. They can only access the global data of the ABAP program and are therefore not suitable for modularization which also needs to take into account aspects of data encapsulation.

Apart from the inherent modularization into event blocks and dialog modules which is based on the control of ABAP programs by the runtime environment, you can modularize ABAP programs, like the programs of most other programming languages, by using procedures with their own name and data area. Modularizing a program into procedures, i.e. dividing the program into several source code parts which goes beyond the main division into event blocks and dialog modules, has a variety of benefits:

- Program readability

  Imagine you have to handle an extensive source code whose event blocks and dialog modules are not divided into smaller units. In this case you need to understand the processing blocks as a whole. If, however, you move details which are not necessary for the overall picture to their own procedures which are called through a mnemonic name, you can concentrate on the more important sections of the program.

- Program maintenance

  The main advantage and also the main application area of procedures is the encapsulation of reusable software components behind precisely defined interfaces. If the same functionality is needed in more than one part of the program, it should be modularized in a procedure. This reduces the amount of source code and is also the main prerequisite for the maintainability of a program. If the functionality ever needs to be changed, it need only be changed in the procedure. If the interface remains unchanged in the process, the call points remain unaffected. If the interface is changed, the syntax check indicates the call points to be adjusted.

- Data encapsulation

  All the data required to execute a function can be encapsulated in a procedure and is only present while the procedure is being executed. By moving functionality to procedures you avoid creating unnecessary data in the global data area of a program where it exists for the entire program runtime and can be accessed by any program statement.

As you will see later, the reuse of software components and data encapsulation also play a large role in the object-oriented programming model.

In ABAP, the procedural programming model offers two forms of modularization, either internally through subroutines or externally through function modules.

Internal modularization with subroutines

In this case, the source code of an ABAP program is divided into subroutines according to its functionality using the `FORM` and `ENDFORM` statements. These subroutines can be called with the `PERFORM` statement. Subroutines can be stored either locally within the same program as the calling `PERFORM` statement or in another ABAP program from where they can be called with an external `PERFORM`. Figure 5.1 shows a processing block in ABAP program 1 which first calls a subroutine `sub1` in ABAP program 2 and then a subroutine `sub1` in the same ABAP program. The called subroutine `sub1` in ABAP program 2 itself calls a local subroutine `sub2`. We shall concentrate on calling local subroutines since classical ABAP contains function modules for external modularization.

It has become customary to place all subroutines at the end of the source code to enhance program clarity. This reduces the risk of creating statements not assigned to a processing block which cannot be reached. In particular, this applies to programs that work with event blocks as these are not explicitly ended by an `END` statement.

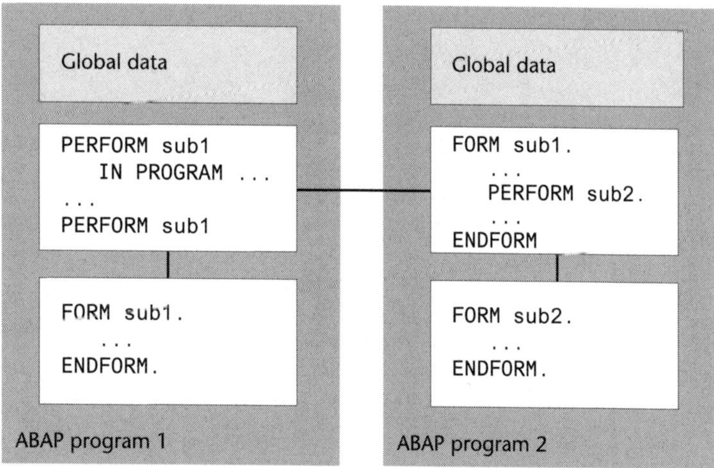

FIGURE 5.1 Defining and calling subroutines

The syntax of the FORM statement for defining a subroutine is as follows:

```
FORM  form
  USING   ...
          {VALUE(u_i)|u_i} [TYPE type|LIKE dobj]
          ...
  CHANGING ...
          {VALUE(c_i)|c_i} [TYPE type|LIKE dobj]
          ...
  ...
ENDFORM.
```

A subroutine introduced with FORM must always be exited with the ENDFORM statement. Like all processing blocks, subroutines cannot be nested. When you define a subroutine you can define a parameter interface with the USING and CHANGING additions.

Let's start with a simple subroutine without a parameter interface. Listing 5.1 shows an example for defining and using this kind of basic subroutines. As you can see, a subroutine can also be called from another subroutine.

LISTING 5.1 Basic subroutine

```
REPORT s_simple_forms.

* Processing Blocks

START-OF-SELECTION.
```

```
  PERFORM write_one.
  PERFORM write_two.
  PERFORM write_three.
  PERFORM write_one_two_three.

FORM write_one.
  WRITE / 'One'.
ENDFORM.

FORM write_two.
  WRITE 'Two'.
ENDFORM.

FORM write_three.
  WRITE 'Three'.
ENDFORM.

FORM write_one_two_three.
  PERFORM write_one.
  PERFORM write_two.
  PERFORM write_three.
ENDFORM.
```

In this case the screen output appears as shown in Figure 5.2.

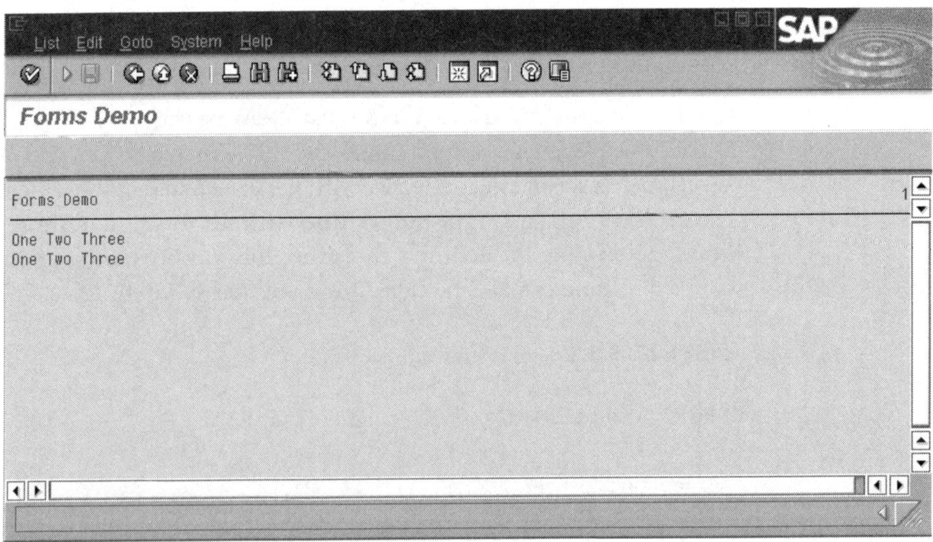

FIGURE 5.2 The screen output of Listing 5.1. Copyright © SAP AG

Parameter interface definition

The subroutines defined in Listing 5.1 did not have a parameter interface, and no transfer parameters needed to be passed to them during the call. However, the option of passing parameters to a subroutine is very important as this is the only way of using highly generalized algorithms in the subroutine which return a result depending on the transfer parameters. The `USING` and `CHANGING` additions to the `FORM` statement are used to define the parameter interface. A list of parameters u_i and c_i can be specified after `USING` and `CHANGING`, whereby for each parameter the type of parameter passing (by value or reference) and a typing with `TYPE` or `LIKE` can be specified. To pass values during the call there are additions of the same name in the `PERFORM` statement.

Formal parameters

Let's take a closer look at the various ways of defining parameters. We call the interface parameters of a procedure formal parameters, while the values passed with `PERFORM` during the call are called actual parameters. There are four ways of defining formal parameters.

- **Defining with ... `USING` u_i ...**

  When you define parameters with `USING`, no local data object is created in the subroutine for the formal parameter u_i. Instead, a reference to the actual parameter is passed during the call. Therefore, there is no actual data transport.[1] If the formal parameter is changed in the subroutine, this change has a direct impact on the actual parameter. Note that formal parameters defined with `USING` should only be used as input parameters which are not changed in the subroutine.

- **Defining with ... `USING VALUE(`u_i`)` ...**

  When you define parameters with `USING VALUE`, a local data object is created as a copy of the actual parameter in the subroutine for the formal parameter u_i. If the formal parameter is changed in the subroutine, this will not affect the actual parameter, which retains its value when the system returns from the subroutine. Formal parameters defined with `USING VALUE` therefore act as real input parameters.

- **Defining with ... `CHANGING` c_i ...**

  Defining parameters with `CHANGING` is exactly the same as defining them with `USING`. For documentation purposes `USING` should be used in formal parameters which are not changed in the subroutine, and `CHANGING` for formal parameters which are changed in the subroutine.

- **Defining with ... `CHANGING VALUE(`c_i`)` ...**

  Defining parameters with `CHANGING VALUE` works in a similar way to defining with `USING VALUE`, but the local copy of the actual parameter is copied back to the actual parameter if the subroutine is correctly exited with the `ENDFORM`, `CHECK`

1. By passing the reference you are in fact working on the same data object.

or EXIT statements. If the subroutine is canceled with an error message, the actual parameter remains unchanged.

As the various additions for parameter definition and their function tend to cause confusion, we have summarized the above in Table 5.1 to aid clarity.

TABLE 5.1 Additions for defining parameters in subroutines

Definition	USING	USING VALUE	CHANGING	CHANGING VALUE
Type of passing	Pass by reference	Pass by value	Pass by reference	Pass by value
Actual parameter change?	Yes	No	Yes	Yes, when exiting with ENDFORM, CHECK or EXIT

If you are already familiar with ABAP or if you look in the keyword documentation under FORM, you will see that we have not explained how to define formal parameters with the TABLES addition. Prior to the introduction of the type concept with Release 3.0, formal parameters defined with TABLES were the only way of passing internal tables to subroutines.[2] This addition is no longer necessary, as you can now type the formal parameters as internal tables.

Table 5.1 also shows the CHECK and EXIT statements for exiting a procedure on a program-controlled basis. The syntax of the statements is the same as for exiting loops (see Section 4.4.2), but affects the overall procedure.

Typing formal parameters

While a subroutine is being executed, a formal parameter basically takes on all the technical attributes of the actual parameter which has just been passed. A single formal parameter can therefore have completely different data types, depending on the actual parameter which has been passed. To ensure that a formal parameter has a specific data type when programming a subroutine, you must type the formal parameter.

TYPE/LIKE

To do this, you use the TYPE and LIKE additions. After TYPE you can specify all the data types of the ABAP type hierarchy which are visible at this point. These are all the predefined data types, all the types of the ABAP program which are defined with TYPES, and all the global types from the ABAP Dictionary. After LIKE you can specify all the data objects of the ABAP program which are visible at this point. When you type formal parameters, the data type of the actual parameter being passed is checked. Only if the passed data type is compatible with the typing can the parameter be passed, otherwise a syntax or runtime error occurs.

2. Especially, you must be aware of the fact that a header line (see Section 4.73) is automatically created in the subroutine for every table parameter specified after TABLES.

Formal parameters can either be fully or partially typed. For full typing you either use TYPE to specify a data type whose technical attributes are already specified, or you use LIKE to specify a data object. For partial typing you use one of the generic data types from Table 4.3, such as INDEX TABLE, or a generic table type defined with TYPES. For full typing the technical attributes of the passed actual parameter must fully match the typing of the formal parameter. For generic typing only the specified attributes are checked; the remaining attributes of the actual parameter are arbitrary.

If you do not carry out specific typing for a formal parameter, it is implicitly typed with TYPE ANY. All technical attributes of the passed actual parameters are then arbitrary. To maintain a program in a readable format, you should always explicitly type the formal parameters. In fact, this is syntactically prescribed for ABAP Objects methods.

Typing formal parameters has an immeasurable advantage in that when you program the subroutine you already know fully or partially the technical attributes the formal parameters will have during execution, and therefore can use appropriate processing statements. Let's consider the following subroutine by way of example:

```
FORM test USING u_par TYPE ANY.
  DATA wa ...
  READ TABLE u_par INTO wa INDEX 1.
ENDFORM.
```

This subroutine is syntactically incorrect because it attempts to access the u_par parameter as an internal table using the READ TABLE statement. However, as u_par is typed with ANY, it can have any data type at runtime, and therefore cannot be handled as an internal table. We therefore improve the subroutine as follows:

```
FORM test USING u_par TYPE ANY TABLE.
  DATA wa ...
  READ TABLE u_par INTO wa INDEX 1.
ENDFORM.
```

Internal table

We have typed u as an internal table. It is now possible to process it with READ TABLE. However, the program is still syntactically incorrect because it is trying to access it through an index. Since u_par is typed with ANY TABLE, its data type can also be a hashed table at runtime, and this is not possible for index accessing. We can therefore either replace the index access with a key access which is valid for all table forms:

```
FORM test USING u_par TYPE ANY TABLE.
  DATA wa ...
  wa = ...
  READ TABLE u_par INTO wa FROM wa.
ENDFORM.
```

or type u_par more strictly as an index table:

```
FORM test USING u_par TYPE INDEX TABLE.
  DATA wa ...
  READ TABLE u_par INTO wa INDEX 1.
ENDFORM.
```

The last two subroutines are syntactically correct and also show how you handle internal tables in subroutines.

Calling a subroutine

As already mentioned, you call a subroutine with the PERFORM statement. The basic form of the syntax is as follows:

```
PERFORM  form [USING   ... a_i ...]
              [CHANGING  ... a_j ...].
```

Other variants allow you, for example, to call a subroutine contained in another ABAP program, or even call a subroutine depending on certain conditions. However, for the purposes of local modularization we do not need to study these variants in any further detail.

Actual parameter

The use of the USING and CHANGING additions is based strictly on the definition of the parameter interface of the subroutine called. For each formal parameter you must specify a specific actual parameter whose data type is compatible with the typing of the formal parameter. When you assign actual parameters to formal parameters, it is solely the sequence of the parameters in the PERFORM statement which is decisive. The first actual parameter is passed to the first formal parameter of the subroutine, etc. The type of parameter passing, i.e. by reference or by value, is uniquely defined in the definition of the formal parameter in the FORM statement. The parameters of subroutines are therefore positional parameters and not keyword parameters. We will encounter the latter in function modules and methods.

Listing 5.2 shows an example of calling subroutines with parameter passing.

LISTING 5.2 Calling subroutines

```
REPORT s_perform.

* Global Declarations

PARAMETERS: p_carrid TYPE sflight-carrid,
            p_connid TYPE sflight-connid.

TYPES t_sflight_tab TYPE STANDARD TABLE OF sflight
                    WITH KEY carrid connid fldate.
```

```
DATA sflight_tab TYPE t_sflight_tab.

* Processing Blocks

START-OF-SELECTION.
  PERFORM select_data USING     p_carrid
                                p_connid
                      CHANGING  sflight_tab.
  PERFORM write_data  USING     sflight_tab.

FORM select_data USING     u_carrid LIKE p_carrid
                           u_connid LIKE p_connid
                 CHANGING  c_sflight_tab TYPE t_sflight_tab.
  SELECT *
  FROM   sflight
  INTO   TABLE c_sflight_tab
  WHERE  carrid = u_carrid AND
         connid = u_connid.
ENDFORM.

FORM write_data USING u_sflight_tab TYPE t_sflight_tab.
  FIELD-SYMBOLS <fs_sflight> LIKE LINE OF u_sflight_tab.
  LOOP AT u_sflight_tab ASSIGNING <fs_sflight>.
    WRITE: / <fs_sflight>-carrid,
             <fs_sflight>-connid,
             <fs_sflight>-fldate.
  ENDLOOP.
ENDFORM.
```

The program in Listing 5.2 summarizes local modularization through subroutines. At the START-OF-SELECTION event, two subroutines of the same program are called in order to read and display data from a database table. The formal parameters of the subroutines are fully typed, and suitable data objects of the program are passed to them as actual parameters during the call. Note the local definition of a field symbol in the write_data subroutine. This field symbol is used to read the internal table 1_sflight_tab and only exists while the subroutine is running. In Section 5.2.3 we shall explore local data declarations in more detail.

External modularization with function modules

Function modules play a major role in classical ABAP. They are by far the most commonly used method of mapping cross-application reusable software components for an SAP System. Function modules are procedures which are specially designed for external calling from other ABAP programs. For this reason function modules require a more generic management than subroutines. You can only create function modules with the **Function Builder** tool of the ABAP Workbench in special ABAP programs of the **Function Group** type. Figure 5.3 shows a processing block in an ABAP program which calls two function modules of a function group. Each function module is unique within an SAP System, and therefore the function group does not have to be specified during the call. Figure 5.3 also shows that function modules can be called locally from within their function group. However, the main purpose of function modules is their external calling. For the internal modularization of function groups you would use local subroutines or methods of local classes.

RFC

Function modules can not only be called within a single SAP System. By means of **Remote Function Call** (RFC), other SAP Systems, R/2 systems, and even non-SAP systems can use all function modules of an SAP System which have been released for RFC.

Function modules and function groups

When you call function modules in ABAP programs or maintain them with the Function Builder,[3] you may gain the impression that function modules are isolated objects in the SAP System. In fact, many function modules are designed to be used that way. However, from a technical viewpoint, a function module is a procedure of an ABAP program, just like a subroutine.

What distinguishes function modules from subroutines is how they are managed by the ABAP Workbench. Each function module is a unique repository object which

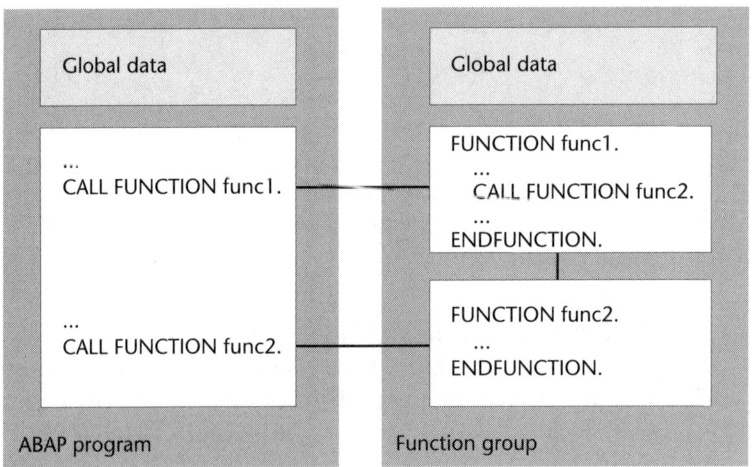

FIGURE 5.3 Defining and calling function modules

3. Especially when you start the Function Builder directly (transaction SE37) and not from within the Object Navigator.

is known to all other ABAP programs. Also, the parameter interface of a function module is completely public, so that any user can pass type-specific parameters. The only ABAP programs in which function modules can be created are function groups. The primary purpose of a function group is therefore to act as the main program for function modules. From a technical viewpoint, a function group plays the same role for a function module as, for example, an executable program for its subroutines.

As function groups are normal ABAP programs like executable programs and module pools, in addition to function modules they can contain a global declaration part as well as all the other standard processing blocks in ABAP (apart from processing blocks for reporting events, see Section 3.3.2). The role of a function group can therefore extend beyond simply acting as a container for function modules. For example, data types, data objects, selection screens, and local classes can be defined in the global declaration part. Function groups can even contain their own screens (see Section 7.1). The function modules of the function group can use the global declarations (see Section 5.2.3) and call the screens. The response to user actions on the screens must also be handled in the function group in the form of processing blocks. A function group is therefore an excellent way of encapsulating user dialogs in an ABAP program in a reusable manner.

Main program

You should never lose sight of the fact that a function module is a processing block of what can be a very complex function group. If a function module from another ABAP program is called externally, exactly the same thing happens as for any other external procedure call: the entire main program of the called procedure is loaded with all its components into the internal session of the calling program and remains there until the internal session is destroyed (see Section 3.4).

When you create function modules you must consider carefully how to organize them in function groups. A function group should only contain function modules that use the same function group components, to avoid these being loaded into the memory unnecessarily. For the same reason you should never mix frequently used function modules with less frequently used ones in a function group. Conversely, function modules which are frequently called in a program should not be distributed among various different function groups if it can be avoided, so that as few additional programs as necessary need to be loaded.

Global data

And finally a word on the global data of the function group (see also Section 5.2.3). If the function modules of a function group use the global data of the function group, you must always bear in mind that this data is retained in the loaded function group after a function module has been exited. Any function module of the same function group called at a later stage will find the data just as the previous function module left it. If you are already familiar with object-orientation, you can consider a loaded function group as an object in the internal session, whereby the global data represents the private attributes, and the function modules work with this data as public methods. You can exploit this aspect, for example, by loading large internal tables once into a function group and accessing them with various function modules. The `LOAD-OF-PROGRAM` event is suitable for this kind of initialization of global data. On the other hand, you must make sure that global data used in different function modules for different purposes is not set to the wrong values when a function module is called. In addition, you cannot load a function group into the internal session of a caller several times in order to work with different global data contents simultaneously. These function group restrictions are overcome in ABAP Objects by classes. In ABAP Objects several objects of the same class can be loaded into an internal session, and the caller can control the lifetime of these.

To illustrate more precisely how function groups and function modules work and how they are structured, in the next sections we will create a function group and function modules and supply them with the necessary attributes. The function group will contain two function modules which have the same functionality as the two subroutines in Listing 5.2.

Creating function groups

Like all repository objects, we shall create our function group and its function modules in the Object Navigator. Although you can also call the Function Builder directly (transaction SE37) in order to create a function group in a submenu, using the Object Navigator is far more transparent (see Section 2.2.2).

Object Navigator

In the Object Navigator, choose **Function Group** as the object list type, enter a name for your function group, and choose Enter [↵] to confirm. As usual, you will be asked if you want to create the object if it does not already exist, and can then enter a short text (see Figure 5.4).

Confirm the dialog box by choosing Save and assign a development class to the new function group (e.g. $TMP). If everything has worked, you will find the function group in the object list of the Object Navigator. You can now immediately start to create function modules for this group by right-clicking the function group and choosing **Create – Function Module** in the context menu (see Figure 5.5).

Figure 5.5 shows the other components you can create for the function group, such as subroutines, screens, etc. This illustrates again that function groups can have the same components as other ABAP programs. Note also that a subnode for include programs has appeared in the object list. The ABAP Workbench does not place the source code for the function group in a single ABAP program, but instead organizes it in include programs for the sake of clarity (see Section 5.2.2). However, source code modularization in include programs does not affect in any way what we have previously said about the structure of ABAP programs in Section 3.3.1.

Creating function modules

We shall start with the function module for reading data from the SFLIGHT table. After choosing **Function module** in Figure 5.5 you can enter a name or a short text

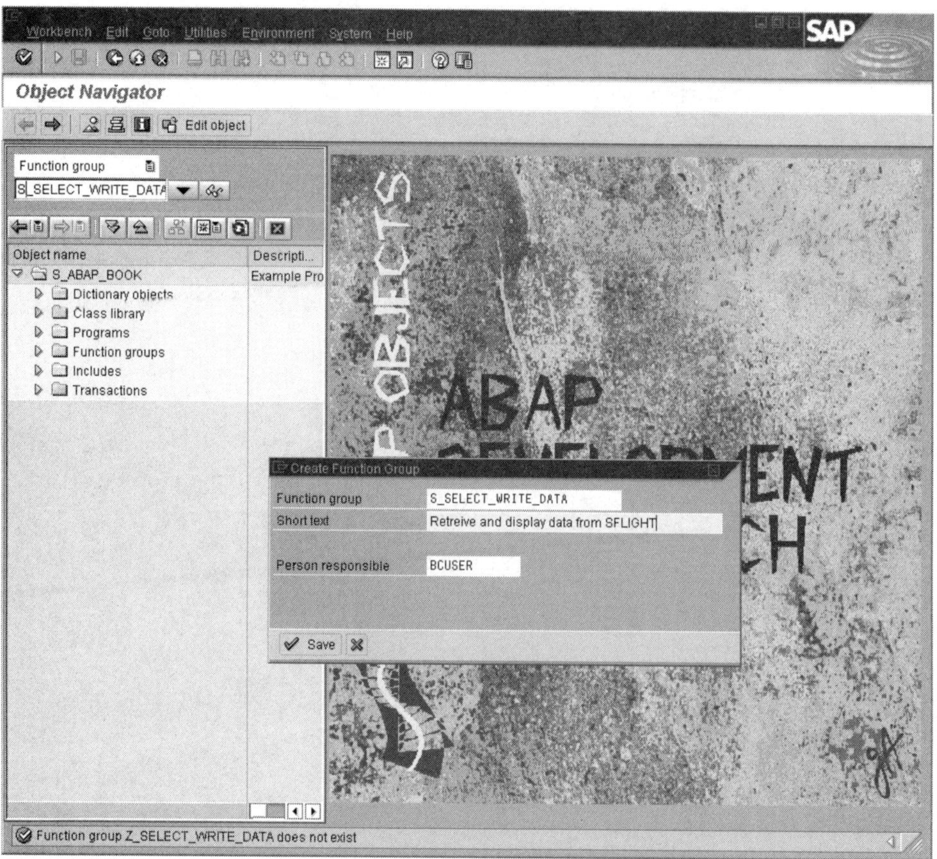

FIGURE 5.4 Creating a function group. Copyright © SAP AG

for the function module as usual. The Function Builder now appears on the right side of the Object Navigator (see Figure 5.6). Please note that the prefix for the customer namespace for function modules is "Y_" and "Z_" instead of simply "Y" and "Z" as for ABAP programs.

Function Builder

The Workbench has now created the new function module and you can maintain its elements on the tab pages of the Function Builder. Figure 5.6 shows all the elements we need for our function module: its **Attributes**, the interface parameters consisting of **Import**, **Export**, **Changing**, and **Tables** parameters, **Exceptions** for error handling, and the **Source code**, where the functionality is implemented.

The **Attributes** tab page contains general management information on the function module. Here you can determine some of the key attributes of the module. The processing type is particularly important. If, for example, you wish to access the function module from another system, you must mark it as a **Remote-enabled module**. However, for our example you do not need to make any changes to this tab page.

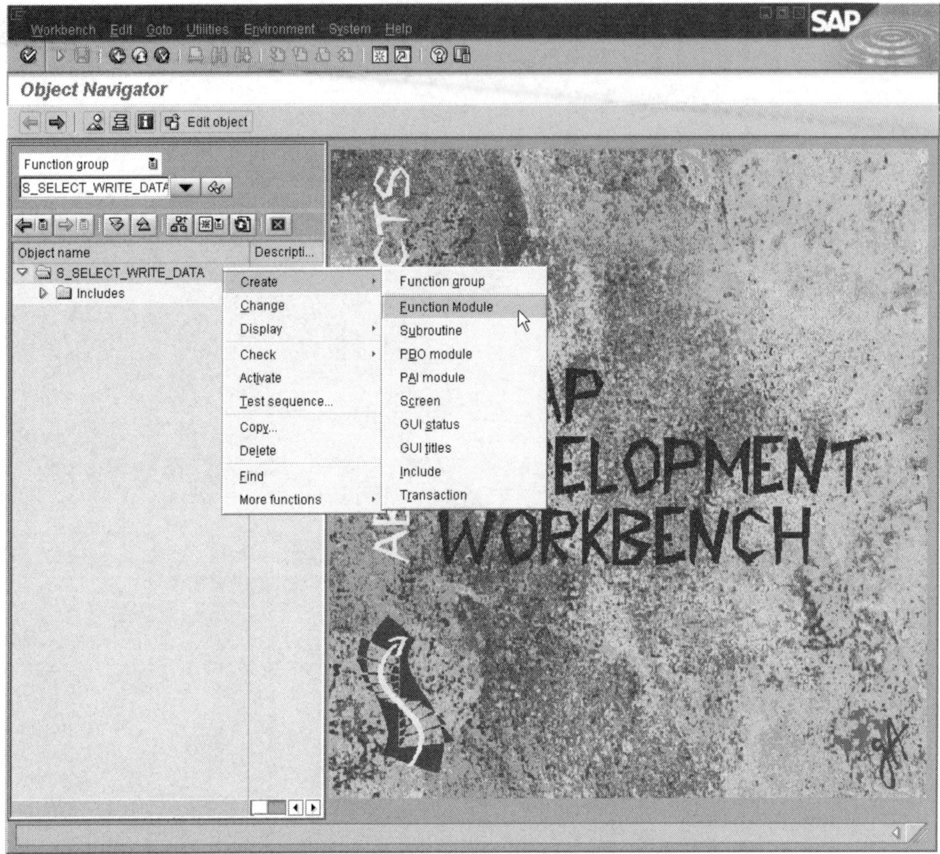

FIGURE 5.5 Creating a function module. Copyright © SAP AG

Defining the parameter interface

Function modules, like subroutines, have a parameter interface. Import, export, and changing parameters are available and in addition there is a special type of parameter for passing an internal table. In principle the same applies to these table parameters as we said previously concerning the `TABLES` parameters of subroutines: with appropriate typing, internal tables can also be passed via other parameter types. As you will soon see, the interface parameters of function modules can only be declared with reference to global data types of the ABAP Dictionary. Since with Release 4.5 any data type can be defined in the ABAP Dictionary, including internal tables, special table parameters are now no longer necessary and should not be used.[4]

The important parameter forms for us are:

4. Remote-enabled function modules are an exception to this rule, as no reference to the data types of the ABAP Dictionary can be made for calls outside the SAP System. Here you must work with the table parameter.

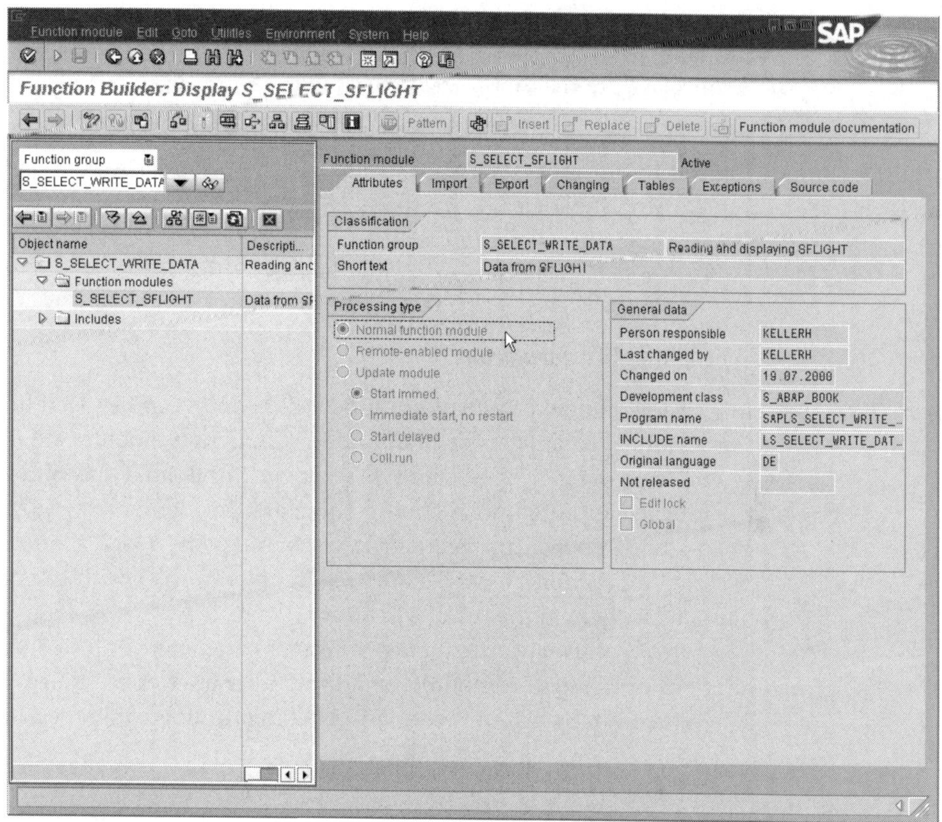

FIGURE 5.6 The Function Builder in the Object Navigator. Copyright © SAP AG

- Import parameters

  These are formal parameters through which a caller can pass input parameters to the function module. Differently than with subroutines, the input parameters of a function module can be identified as **Optional** so that they do not have to be supplied by the user. You can assign an initial value to an optional input parameter with which the parameter is filled if the caller does not specify a corresponding actual parameter.

- Export parameters

  These are formal parameters with which a caller can use the return values of a function module in actual parameters. Export parameters can, but do not have to, be received.

- Changing parameters

  These are formal parameters which act simultaneously as import and export parameters. The value of a changing parameter is passed by the user to the function module. The function module can change this value and then return it to the calling program. Like importing parameters, changing parameters can also be identified as optional, so that no actual parameter needs to be specified.

By default, parameters are passed to function modules by reference. However, you can specify for each parameter in the Function Builder that it should be passed by value. Using the logical expressions `IS SUPPLIED` and `IS REQUESTED` for optional formal parameters, you can check in the function module whether an actual parameter has been assigned to them during the call.

Typing interface parameters

Formal parameters

In principle, formal parameters of function modules can be typed in exactly the same way as formal parameters of subroutines. As function modules are used throughout a system, only references to data types known throughout the system can be used in the interface of function modules: these are the elementary ABAP data types, the generic types known throughout the system (e.g. `ANY TABLE`), and the types defined in the ABAP Dictionary (see Figure 5.7). In order to work with self-defined types, you must create them in the ABAP Dictionary.

Figure 5.7 illustrates the typing of formal parameters of function modules. In the interface of a function module `func` formal parameters are typed with reference to data types from the ABAP Dictionary. A calling ABAP program declares data objects of

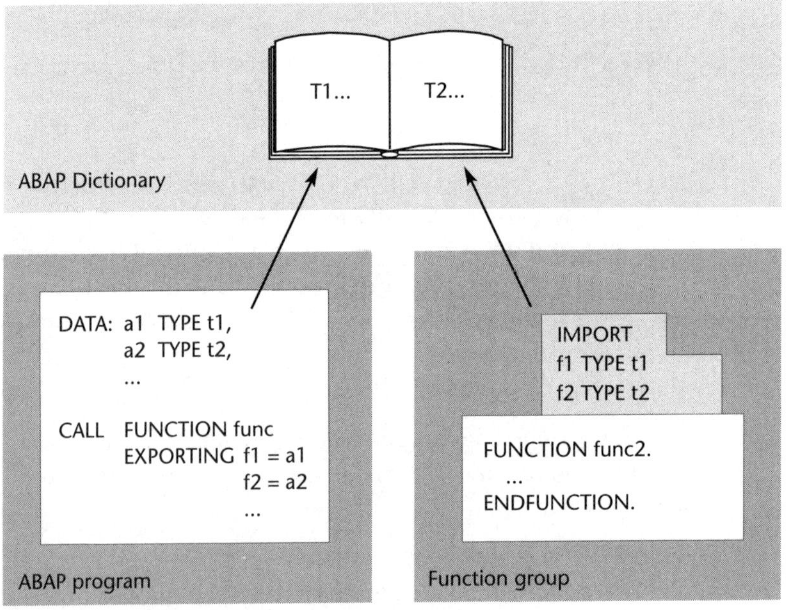

FIGURE 5.7 Typing interface parameters

the same data type and passes these as type-specific actual parameters when the function module is called.

Now take another look at Listing 5.2. Here we have used a table type t_sflight_tab defined with TYPES for typing. Neither subroutine of that program is therefore suitable for use by external programs, as the caller cannot use TYPE to refer to this type when declaring the actual parameters.

ABAP Dictionary

For our function modules we shall therefore create a corresponding data type in the ABAP Dictionary and use it for typing (see also Section 4.2.5). To do this, you call the ABAP Dictionary (transaction SE11), choose **Data type**, enter a name, and specify **Table type** in the subsequent dialog box. On the tab page of the maintenance dialog for the table type you can maintain the row type (in this case SFLIGHT), the access type, and the keys (see Figure 5.8). On activation this data type will be available to all ABAP programs.

After this preparatory work we can now define the interface of our function module. As with the select_data subroutine from Listing 5.2 we shall specify two

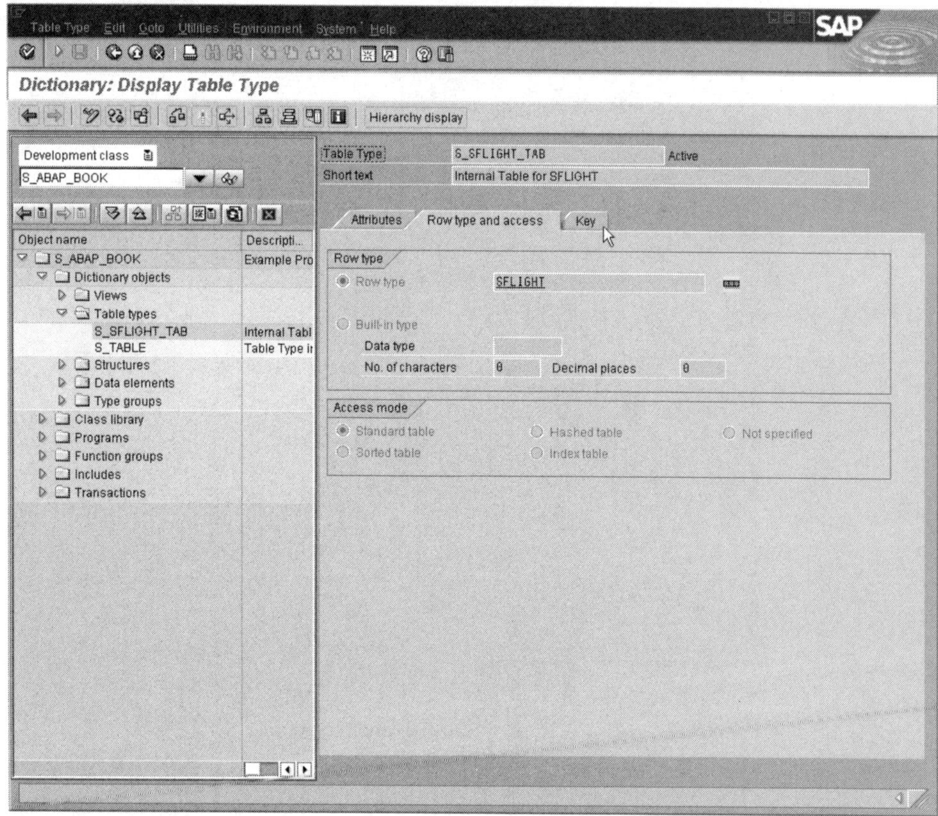

FIGURE 5.8 Self-defined table type for typing. Copyright © SAP AG

input parameters and one output parameter.[5] To do this, you choose the corresponding tab pages and fill them as indicated in Figures 5.9 and 5.10. The explanatory short texts are copied by the Workbench from the ABAP Dictionary but can be modified.

Preparing exceptions

Exceptions allow a caller to respond to errors which occur while a function module is being executed. You can define exceptions for potential error situations on the **Exceptions** tab page. If such a situation occurs while a function module is being executed, the exception can be triggered through the `RAISE except` or `MESSAGE RAISING` statements. These statements are only useful when function modules or methods (the latter can also trigger exceptions) are being executed.

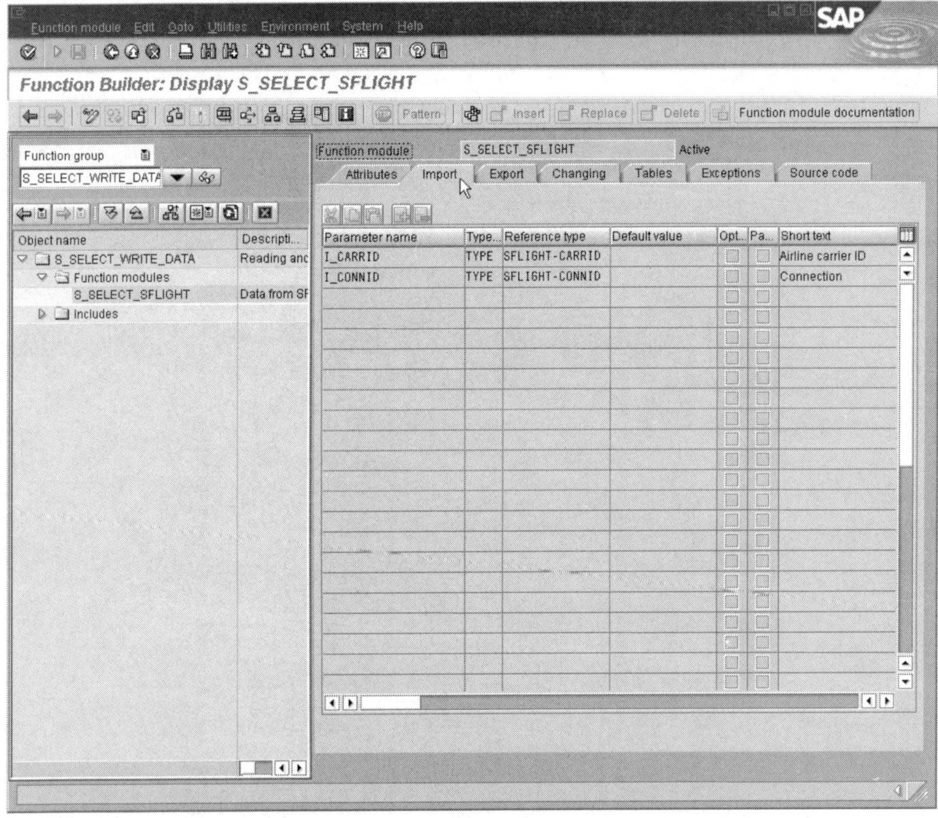

FIGURE 5.9 Import parameters. Copyright © SAP AG

5. We are using an export parameter here as an output parameter because its semantics are better suited to the `CHANGING` parameter of our previous subroutine.

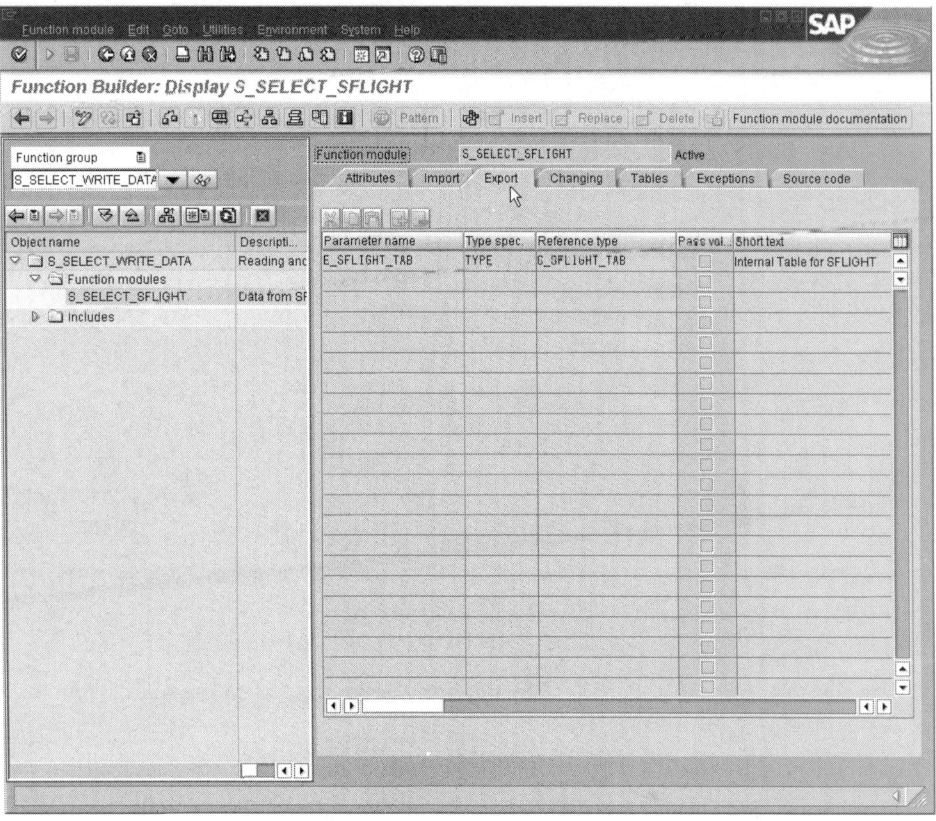

FIGURE 5.10 Export parameters. Copyright © SAP AG

Exception

In our example we shall define an exception which is always triggered if no data has been read from the SFLIGHT table. Choose the **Exceptions** tab page and enter the "NOTHING_FOUND" exception in the table. How you trigger the exception will follow in the next section. How the user can react to the exception is explained below in the "Calling Function Modules" section.

Source code

When you have defined the formal parameters and exceptions you must implement the functionality of the function module in its source code. When you change to the **Source code** tab page, you will see that the system has created a frame using the `FUNCTION` and `ENDFUNCTION` statements. You will also find the defined parameter interface as a comment. This is purely for your information and should not be changed. The only thing important for the actual signature of the function module is the definition on the various tab pages (**Import**, **Export**, **Changing**, **Tables**, **Exceptions**) of the Function Builder. Each time the parameters defined on these pages are changed, the comment is regenerated.

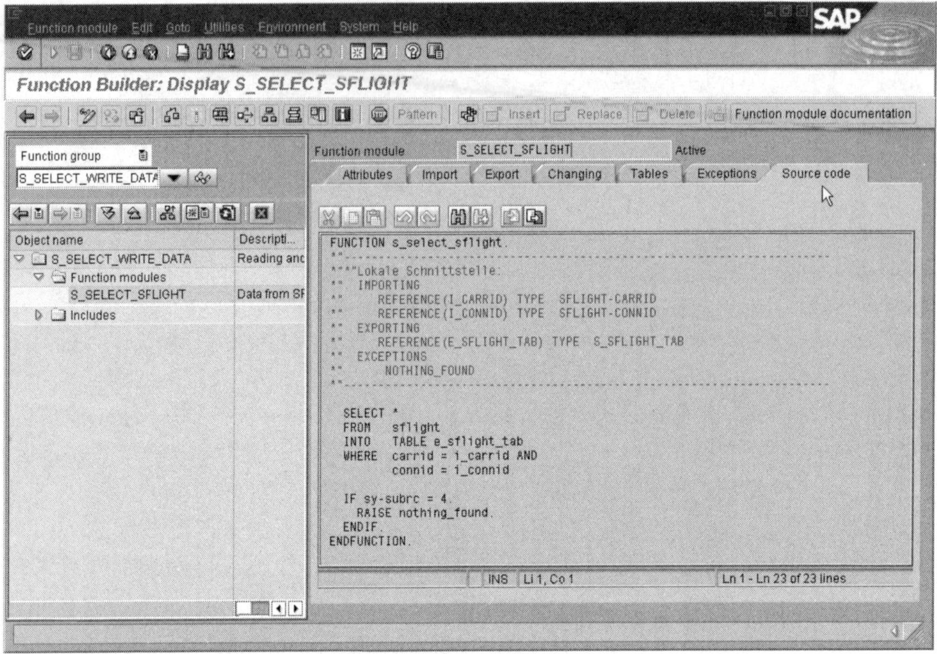

FIGURE 5.11 Function module source code. Copyright © SAP AG

In the frame provided, enter the source code for reading the data. You can copy the source code of the subroutine from Listing 5.2 almost unchanged. Additionally, if no data has been read, the NOTHING_FOUND exception should be triggered. To do this, use the RAISE statement. In Figure 5.11 you can check if you have done everything correctly.

Once all the elements of the function module are ready, you must activate it so that it can be later tested and used in a program. To do this, choose the **Activate** function. If this results in a syntax error, try to activate the function group first as a whole. You can then activate individual components.

Testing function modules

In order to test a function module, you do not have to call it from one of your own programs because the Function Builder provides you with a test environment which you can call with the **Test / Execute** function in the Function Builder.

Here you can supply the parameters of the function module and execute it with **F8**. In our example you can enter values for the import parameters and after the execution of the function module view the result in the e_sflight_tab table (see Figure 5.12). If you specify values for the input parameters that trigger the exception, the exception will also be displayed here.

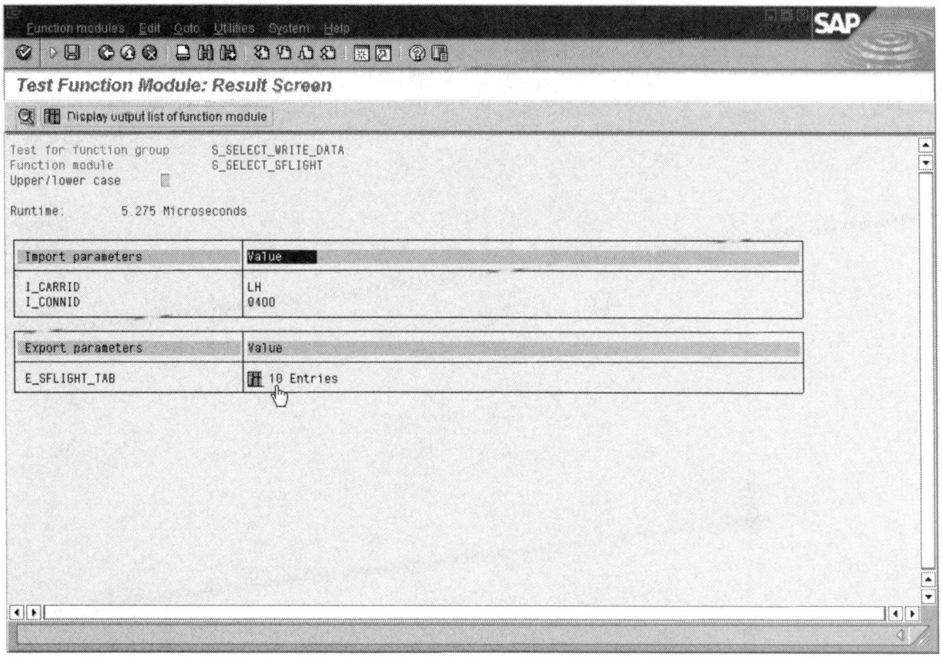

FIGURE 5.12 Testing a function module. Copyright © SAP AG

The test environment can serve you well, particularly with complex function modules. You have the option of creating test data directories and therefore performing specific retests when modifying the module. For more information on the test environment of the Function Builder refer to the ABAP Workbench documentation.

Documenting and releasing function modules

Once you have successfully created and tested a function module you can release it, if you wish, for general use in the **Function Module – Release** menu. However, first you must remember to document its interface and functionality sufficiently by choosing **Function Module Documentation**. This is the only way of ensuring it can be reused. Remember also that you can no longer change the interface of a released function module without first informing all the users.

Another function module

Now that we have shown how to create the S_SELECT_SFLIGHT function module, we can also create a second function module, S_WRITE_SFLIGHT, in the same function group which has the same function as the second subroutine from Listing 5.2 (see Figure 5.13).

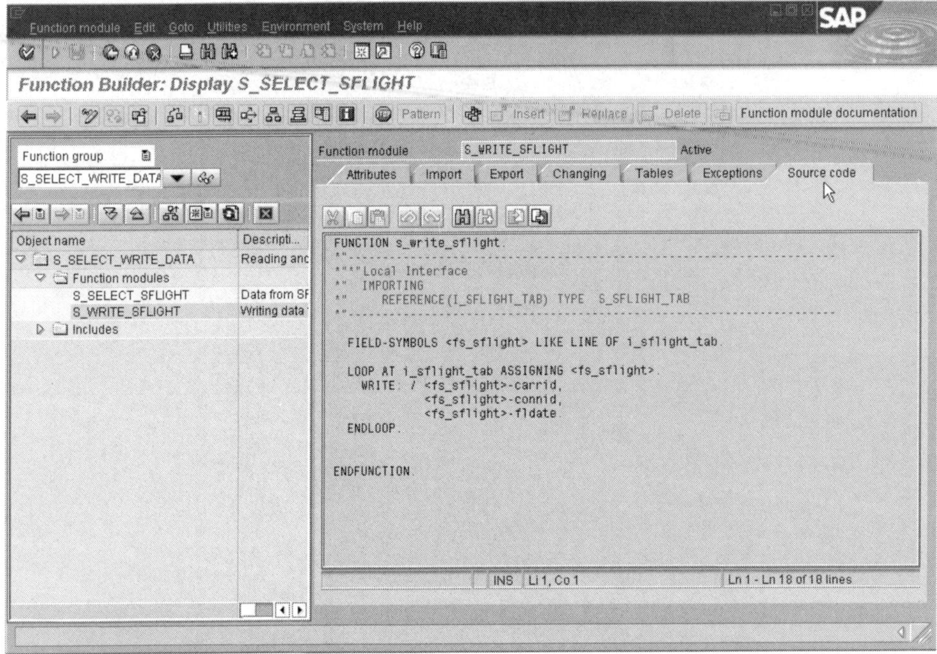

FIGURE 5.13 Another function module. Copyright © SAP AG

Calling function modules

Once both function modules have been activated, we can call them in any ABAP program within the same SAP System. To call a function module you use the `CALL FUNCTION` statement, whose syntax is as follows:

CALL FUNCTION functionmodule
  [EXPORTING $f_1 = a_1 \ldots f_n = a_n$]
  [IMPORTING $f_1 = a_1 \ldots f_n = a_n$]
  [CHANGING $f_1 = a_1 \ldots f_n = a_n$]
  [EXCEPTIONS $e_1 = r_1 \ldots e_n = r_n$
    [ERROR_MESSAGE $= r_E$]
    [OTHERS $= r_o$]].

Actual parameter

The name of the function module (`functionmodule`) is always specified as a data object, i.e. as a literal or variable. Actual parameters a_i are assigned to formal parameters f_i of the parameter interface explicitly with the equals sign (=). These assignments always have the form `Formal Parameter = Actual Parameter`. The equals sign (=) is not an assignment operator in this case. At first sight this might be slightly confusing because values returned from the function module also appear on the left-hand side of the equals sign.

All parameters are always addressed in the program from the viewpoint of the user. If you have identified a parameter as an importing parameter in the Function Builder, it will be filled through the EXPORTING addition to the CALL FUNCTION statement.

Handling exceptions

Function module exceptions can be handled with the EXCEPTIONS addition. Each exception e_i can be assigned a return value r_i, whereby r_i can be any number. If an exception is triggered during execution, the system interrupts the processing of the function module and does not return any values from the function module to the program except for those which have been passed by reference. If e_i is specified after EXCEPTIONS, sy-subrc is assigned the value r_i. If you specify OTHERS after EXCEPTIONS, all exceptions which are not explicitly listed are linked with a single return value. Exceptions which are triggered but not handled will result in a runtime error. The same return value r_i is permissible for more than one exception. The special exception ERROR_MESSAGE is described in Section 7.4.3 in the context of messages.

We shall now apply this syntax to calling our two function modules. Listing 5.3 shows a program which declares two parameters and an internal table sflight_tab which are compatible with the typing of the formal parameters of the function modules. It is best to add the call of the function modules using the **Pattern** function of the ABAP Editor. The ABAP Workbench then generates the correct statement with a listing of all the interface parameters.

LISTING 5.3 Calling function modules

```
REPORT s_call_function.

* Global Declarations

PARAMETERS: p_carrid TYPE sflight-carrid,
            p_connid TYPE sflight-connid.

DATA sflight_tab TYPE s_sflight_tab.

* Processing Blocks

START-OF-SELECTION.
  CALL FUNCTION 'S_SELECT_SFLIGHT'
       EXPORTING
             i_carrid       = p_carrid
             i_connid       = p_connid
       IMPORTING
             e_sflight_tab = sflight_tab
       EXCEPTIONS
             nothing_found  = 1
             OTHERS         = 2.

  IF sy-subrc = 0.
```

```
    CALL FUNCTION 'S_WRITE_SFLIGHT'
         EXPORTING
               i_sflight_tab = sflight_tab.
  ELSE.
    WRITE 'No data'.
  ENDIF.
```

S_WRITE_SFLIGHT is only called when the S_SELECT_SFLIGHT function module has been successfully processed, otherwise the exception is handled.

5.2.2 Excursion: source code modularization

At this point we shall make an excursion into a different kind of modularization which, despite having nothing to do with the procedural programming model, can be usefully explained by means of function groups. We have already mentioned that the ABAP Workbench generates include programs when a function group is created.

The ABAP Workbench performs an automatic source code modularization which provides an ABAP program with a better structure. This source code modularization allows a program which is split into procedures to be maintained more easily, by for example storing each function module in a single source code module or grouping all subroutines of a program within a source code module. The most common way of modularizing the source code is by means of include programs.

Include programs

Include programs (type I programs) move parts of the source code of large programs to separate units. These units can be maintained and transported independently of the actual program. Include programs are not necessarily related to the processing blocks of a program. It is, however, reasonable to divide ABAP programs into include programs according to their general structure. In general there is an include for the global data of the program, the *top include*, and as already mentioned, several includes for the various processing blocks. An include program cannot be run independently, but must be included in other programs. It is possible to incorporate an include program in another include program, but an include cannot be incorporated in itself, as this would result in an endless program.

To incorporate an include program in another program, use the statement:

```
INCLUDE  incl.
```

This has the same effect as copying the source code of the incl include program to where the statement is. The contents of the include program are also evaluated during the syntax check. Include programs are not dynamically loaded at runtime, instead they are incorporated during program generation. After generation the runtime object of a program statically contains all incorporated include programs.

The following example shows you how to create and incorporate include programs. Listing 5.4 is the include program, for which you must choose the *Include program* program type when creating it. Listing 5.5 is a program which includes it. You can also see that an include does not have to start with a statement introducing the program. The system identifies it only through its program type.

LISTING 5.4 Example of a short include program

```
* *
* Include Programm S_INCLUDE_DEMO
* *
WRITE sy-uname.
```

LISTING 5.5 Including an include program

```
REPORT s_including_an_include.

WRITE: / 'Your user name is:'.
INCLUDE s_include_demo.
```

Source code library

Include programs created in this way can function as a library for reusing source code in various programs. This can be useful, for example, with very long data declarations which are to be used repeatedly. If you use include programs repeatedly, however, the naming convention mentioned below cannot be observed.

We will now turn to include programs which are automatically created by the ABAP Workbench. The ABAP Workbench modularizes the source code not only of function groups but also of module pools when you create them. We shall first consider the source code of our function group itself. To do this, double-click the function group from the object list of the Object Navigator and then choose the **Main program** button.

Figure 5.14 shows the source code of our function group. You can see that the actual program name is SAPLS_SELECT_WRITE_DATA. The system attaches the "SAPL" prefix to the name we have chosen. In Figure 5.14 there is a series of INCLUDE statements instead of a statement introducing the program. The include programs incorporated all follow a specific naming convention.

The prefix "L" is added to the name of the function group and a specific ending is also attached. If you double-click the include program with the TOP ending, you will see its source code:

LISTING 5.6 Top include of a function group

```
FUNCTION-POOL  s_select_write_data.
```

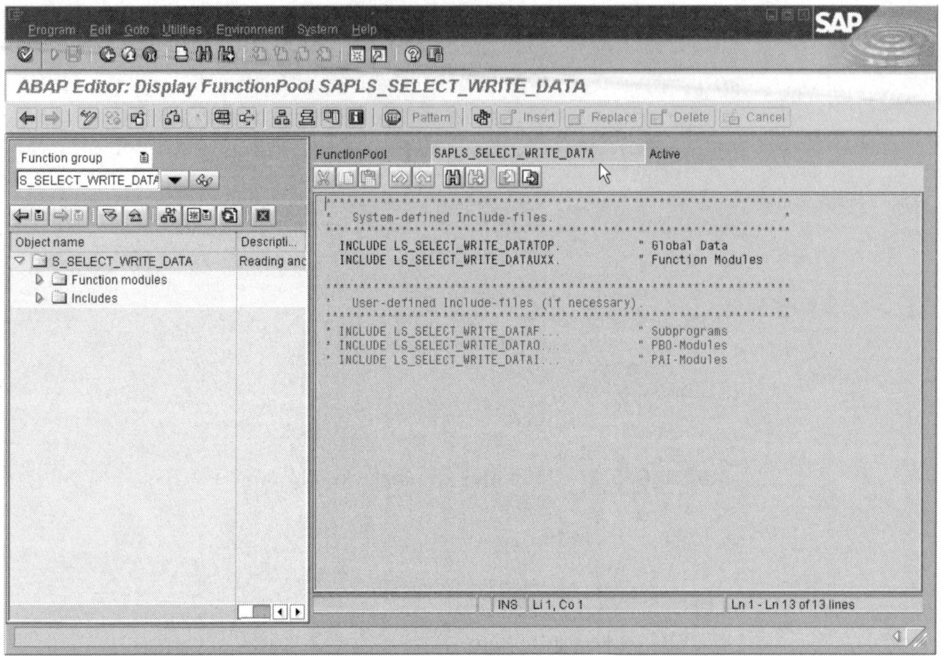

FIGURE 5.14 Function group source code. Copyright © SAP AG

Top include

Listing 5.6 only contains the `FUNCTION-POOL` statement introducing the program, which the system has created for you. Here you could now declare the global data of the function group. When the syntax of other include programs of the function group is checked, the corresponding top include is taken into account if you follow the naming convention. Otherwise include programs are always checked individually so that a useful syntax check is sometimes only possible on the entire ABAP program consisting of the include programs.

If you examine all the include programs of the function group you will find the structure shown in Figure 5.15.

The actual function modules are in separate include programs which themselves are incorporated in an include program. Seen as a whole, the include programs produce exactly the same function group structure as previously described, consisting of global declarations, if any, and processing blocks.

You can use the lines in comments in Figure 5.14 to generate and include other include programs. Include programs whose names end in "F..", "O..", and "I.." are designed for subroutines, PBO modules, and PAI modules of the function group. If you want to include event blocks, it is advisable to use the "E.." ending. Include programs which follow these naming conventions are generally incorporated by a single ABAP program and are not reused in other programs.

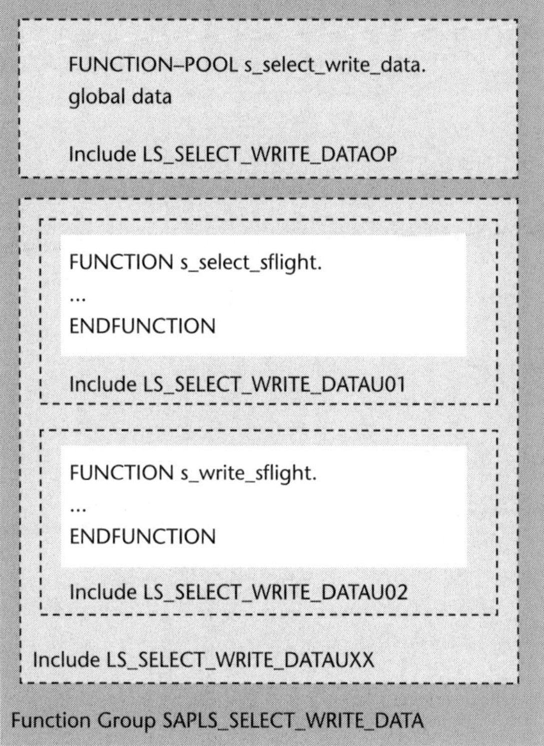
FUNCTION–POOL s_select_write_data.
global data
Include LS_SELECT_WRITE_DATAOP
FUNCTION s_select_sflight.
...
ENDFUNCTION
Include LS_SELECT_WRITE_DATAU01
FUNCTION s_write_sflight.
...
ENDFUNCTION
Include LS_SELECT_WRITE_DATAU02
Include LS_SELECT_WRITE_DATAUXX
Function Group SAPLS_SELECT_WRITE_DATA

FIGURE 5.15 Function group structure consisting of include programs

Macros

In addition to include programs, there is another form of source code modularization which we will mention at this point for completion's sake. If a statement sequence is to be reused several times in a program, this can be programmed once in a macro. The following syntax is used to define a macro:

```
DEFINE  macro.
  ... Statements
END-OF-DEFINITION.
```

The statements in the macro can contain up to nine placeholders &1 ... &9. Macros are only available locally in a program code. A macro must be defined in the program code before it is used. Thereafter, the macro can be used with the statement:

```
macro [p1 ... p9].
```

During program generation the macro is replaced by the corresponding statements, and in the statements the placeholders &i are literally replaced by the p_i parameters. You can use a macro in other macros. However, a macro cannot use itself. Listing

5.7 shows how a macro can be used to map the calculation of an area. The first placeholder is used to determine the geometric shape (square or circle) while the second placeholder is used to determine the basis for calculation of the area (side length or radius).

LISTING 5.7 Example of using macros

```
REPORT s_using_macros.

* Global Declarations

CONSTANTS: pi TYPE f VALUE '3.14159265'.
DATA: dimension TYPE f.

DEFINE shape_dimension.
  CASE &1.
    WHEN 'Square'.
      dimension = &2 * &2.
    WHEN 'Circle'.
      dimension = &2 * &2 * pi.
  ENDCASE.
END-OF-DEFINITION.

* Processing Blocks

START-OF-SELECTION.
  shape_dimension 'Square' 10.
  WRITE:/ 'Area square:', dimension.
  shape_dimension 'Circle' 10.
  WRITE:/ 'Area circle:', dimension.
```

Therefore, if you see a statement in an ABAP program which you cannot find in the keyword documentation, look through the entire preceding program part (including all incorporated include programs) to see if you find a `DEFINE` statement which defines the statement. This might be the case, for example, for longer calculations or complex list outputs with `WRITE`. However, you should avoid using macros yourself and concentrate solely on proper procedures.

5.2.3 Visibility and lifetime of data

Following our excursion into the realm of source code modularization, we shall now return to the procedural programming model and concentrate in more detail on the handling of data in this model. This section will also act as a transition stage to object-orientation, in which everything we have previously said remains valid but is supplemented by the advanced concept of classes.

So far we have dealt with the modularization of functionality and defining interfaces for procedures. We will now turn our attention to declaring data in the procedural model. We shall look at the role played by the global data in Figures 5.1 and 5.3 for the procedures and what happens when you declare local data in procedures.

When considering data in ABAP programs we must first ask ourselves where data can be declared. In simple terms: where can we use statements such as `DATA`?

Context

In the procedural programming model there are two contexts in which data can be declared: within procedures and outside procedures. We refer to all data declared within procedures as local. All other data is global data of the ABAP program. This applies also to data declared in event blocks and dialog modules. In ABAP Objects there is a third context, namely the class. Like programs, classes contain data and procedures (methods). Data declared in methods are local, while the remaining data of the class (the attributes) is global within the class.

We shall now examine the effect of context on the visibility and lifetime of the data. In other words: who can access the data and when is the data in fact present?

Visibility

In the procedural programming model visibility is defined inside out, so to speak (see Figure 5.16).

The statements of a procedure can access all local data objects of the procedure and all global data objects of the ABAP program.[6] If a local data object is declared with the same name as a global data object, it hides the global data object in the procedure.

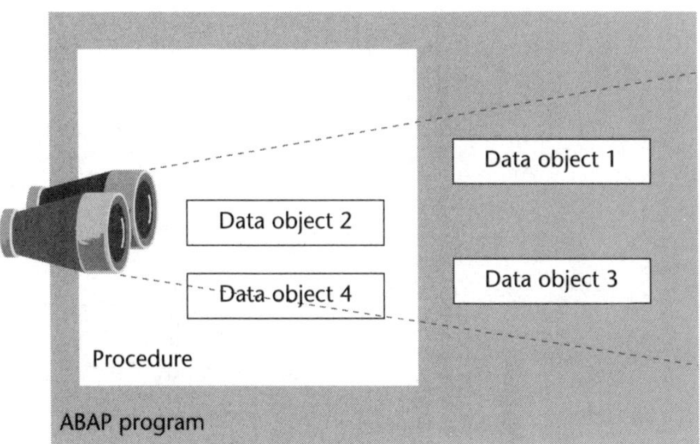

FIGURE 5.16 Visibility of data objects

6. There are restrictions to this, however: only that data is visible at a specific point in an ABAP program which is declared in the preceding source code.

The local data of a procedure is invisible from the outside. It cannot be addressed from within the ABAP main program or in other procedures. Procedures are the smallest encapsulation units for data in ABAP. The global data of an ABAP program is only visible in that particular ABAP program, i.e. within all procedures. However, no ABAP program has access to the global data of another ABAP program.

Class

ABAP Objects adds classes to the visibility levels in Figure 5.16. Figure 5.17 summarizes all contexts in which data objects can be declared in ABAP programs since ABAP Objects was introduced.

You can define the visibility of class attributes so that in specific cases you can also permit visibility from the outside in addition to visibility from the inside which exists by default. For more details, refer to Section 5.3.2.

Lifetime

In principle, data objects live as long as their context. For the local data of a procedure this means that it is only present in the memory while the procedure is being executed. Calling the procedure again creates a new context for local data objects. The old contents are not restored, but instead have the same initial value as for the first call.[7] For the lifetime of the formal parameters of a procedure's interface the same applies in principle as for the local data.

On the other hand, the global data of an ABAP program exists for as long as an ABAP program is being executed. In other words: the data of an ABAP program lives for as long as the program is loaded in an internal session (see Section 3.4).

Object

In the procedural programming model, the lifetime of data declared with `DATA` is therefore implicitly controlled by the lifetime of the corresponding contexts. You do not have an explicit option for removing data objects from the memory. You will see

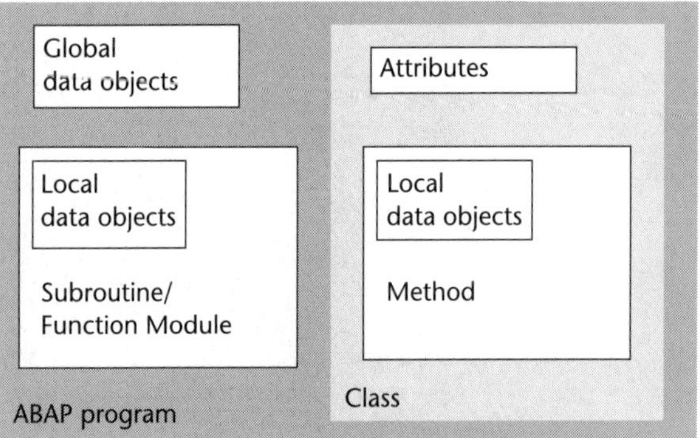

FIGURE 5.17 Global and local data objects in ABAP programs

7. To retain the value of local data between individual calls, you can use the `STATICS` statement instead of `DATA` in subroutines.

that in this respect there has been considerable progress in the change from classical ABAP to ABAP Objects. In ABAP Objects, the class is the context of data. The lifetime of its data is generally linked to the lifetime of the objects which are created from the class and which you control explicitly in the program.[8] Figure 5.18 summarizes the lifetime of data objects.

Consequences for the use of data

In the classical programming model we can therefore only work with data which is either temporarily present while a procedure is being executed or data which is present for the entire lifetime of the program. These conditions govern what kind of data you create and where.

Encapsulation

All data required temporarily to fulfill certain tasks should be encapsulated with the functions in procedures. Only data which is really required for as long as the program is being executed should be declared as global data. This could include, for example, internal tables for collecting data from the database (see Listing 5.1). ABAP also has some global data which you need to communicate with screens and logical databases. You must also declare this data globally in the ABAP program.

You should keep the amount of global data in programs to an absolute minimum and also keep an eye on this data so that it does not get changed by accident. In

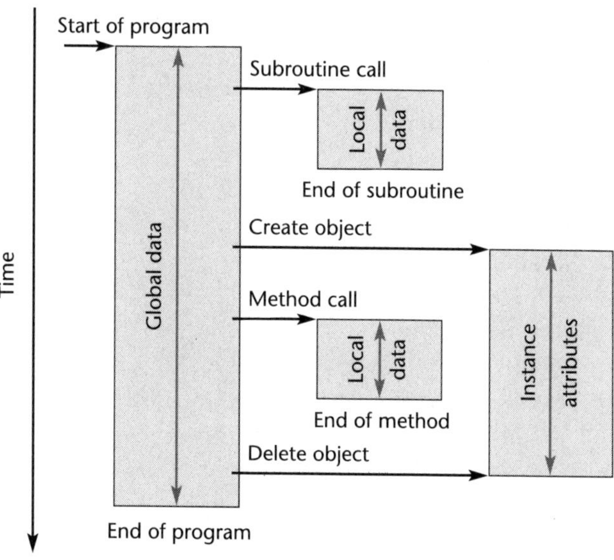

FIGURE 5.18 Lifetime of data objects

8. To be precise, this applies only to the **instance attributes**, not the **static attributes**. For further details see Section 5.3.2: Classes.

particular, you should avoid working directly with global data in procedures. Let's consider Listing 5.8.

LISTING 5.8 Subroutines and global data

```
REPORT s_perform_global.

* Global Declarations

PARAMETERS: p_carrid TYPE sflight-carrid,
            p_connid TYPE sflight-connid.

TYPES t_sflight_tab TYPE STANDARD TABLE OF sflight
                    WITH KEY carrid connid fldate.

DATA sflight_tab TYPE t_sflight_tab.

* Processing Blocks

START-OF-SELECTION.
  PERFORM select_data.
  PERFORM write_data.

FORM select_data.
  SELECT *
  FROM   sflight
  INTO   TABLE sflight_tab
  WHERE  carrid = p_carrid AND
         connid = p_connid.
ENDFORM.

FORM write_data.
  FIELD-SYMBOLS <fs_sflight> LIKE LINE OF sflight_tab.
  LOOP AT sflight_tab ASSIGNING <fs_sflight>.
    WRITE: / <fs_sflight>-carrid,
             <fs_sflight>-connid,
             <fs_sflight>-fldate.
  ENDLOOP.
ENDFORM.
```

The program in Listing 5.8 has the same function as the program in Listing 5.2. However, both subroutines are now working with the global data of the ABAP program instead of with formal parameters. Only the field symbol in write_data is local. Although the program in Listing 5.8 appears simpler than the program in Listing 5.2 at first sight, this kind of programming is more error-prone. In particular, this is true for large complex programs. If several procedures linked through call sequences are operating directly and "uncontrollably" on the same data, you can easily lose sight of the data status in the various stages of the program flow.

Interface

Only when you define parameter interfaces for procedures to which you pass global data (by reference for efficiency reasons) can you truly encapsulate functionality which is independent of the global data, and which at the same time forms the basis for the maintainability of the entire program.

Any modularization in the classical programming model performed according to these rules therefore clearly separates the functionality from the data. The procedures can be programmed relatively independently of the data passed to them.

In the following sections you will learn how ABAP Objects has eliminated this classical separation by introducing classes, and consequently created a new level of encapsulation which, when used correctly, makes programs easier to maintain than in the classical programming paradigm.

5.3 THE OBJECT-ORIENTED PROGRAMMING MODEL

Section 5.1 covered the main aspects of modularization and visibility of data objects in the classical programming model. In the following section we will introduce you to the basics of ABAP Objects. Later, in Chapter 6, you will become acquainted in detail with the advanced concepts of ABAP Objects.

5.3.1 How do we define object-orientation?

We have not written this book with the aim of providing a detailed introduction to object-oriented programming. There is plenty of literature available to cover this, a selection of which is contained in the Annex. We have focused on the concepts of object-orientation which are implemented in ABAP Objects. If you are already experienced in other object-oriented programming languages you will soon feel at home with this topic. If you are not experienced in object-oriented programming, you will find the basic concepts of this programming model provided here.

There is a wide variety of definitions for the concept of object-orientation. To ensure that you, the reader, and we, the authors, share the same view of this concept, we shall briefly illustrate how we define the concept.

In the real world we can identify a variety of objects which all have characteristics and specific functions. Take your car, for example: it has characteristics such as engaged gear, speed, etc. and functions such as starting, accelerating, and braking. In object-orientation we call the characteristics of an object **attributes** and the functions

methods. Of course, you also come into contact with objects when working with the SAP System. Examples of objects often used in business include customers, materials, invoices, etc.

Object-oriented programming tries to map the real-world objects with their attributes and methods as realistically as possible in program constructs. The aim is to create program flows in a similar way to how they would take place in the real world. This makes the dialog between the user and the developer easier. To put it in its most basic terms, the user can formulate requirements on a program in a language he or she is used to and the developer can convert these more directly than in the classical programming model.[9]

As you have seen in the previous section, in the classical programming paradigm, procedural programming, attributes (data), and methods (subroutines, function modules) are strictly separated. Modeling of the real world takes place on the basis of the data, for example in the relational data model in which objects from the real world are represented as tables which are linked with each other via foreign key relationships.

In the object-oriented programming model a different approach is used. Attributes and methods which belong to a specific object are grouped together (encapsulated) and made accessible to the user through a well-defined interface behind which the implementation details of the objects are hidden. Ideally, the attributes of an object are only changed by the methods of the object and not directly by the user of an object. This ensures that the status of the object is always consistent.

An object-oriented programming language supports this approach by means of suitable language elements. We call a programming language object-oriented if it has the following features:

- Abstraction

  This refers to the ability to reflect real-world processes as realistically in the programming language as possible. These processes can be of a business or a technical nature. An example of the latter is the handling of screen objects in application programs. In the object-oriented programming model, real-world problems are modeled in classes and mapped in objects while a program is being executed.

- Encapsulation

  Implementation details are hidden behind well-defined and documented interfaces. They ensure that the abstract representation of an object is used only in accordance with its specification.

- Inheritance

  New abstractions, i.e. classes, are derived from existing ones. They inherit all the attributes and methods of the higher-level class and can expand and specialize them. If we return to our car example, you can specialize the general class of vehi-

9. Between the requirements of the user and the implementation by the programmer lies the phase of object-oriented modeling. A description of object-oriented modeling lies far beyond the focus of this book.

cle into subclasses such as cars or trucks. These subclasses can be specialized further, by deriving semi-trailer or dumper trucks from trucks, for example.

- Polymorphism

  Different objects can present the same interface to the outside. A user only needs to know the interface and by using it he or she accesses various classes without knowing their details. In the real world you can regard the basic controls of a car as such an interface. If you know these controls you can drive off in almost any car in the world without worrying about the specific model.

Business object

When a programming language provides language elements which support these concepts, you can use it for object-oriented programming. However, not every program which has been developed with this kind of language is actually object-oriented.[10] Object-orientation is a programming paradigm or rather a design concept used to handle the inherent complexity of software. With reference to the SAP System there is little point in fully implementing a single report, which generally works independently of the rest of the system, in an object-oriented manner. Instead, what is required is a global view, as witnessed in some of the concepts already implemented in the SAP System. For example, access to existing business objects of the BOR (Business Object Repository) and the interaction of these objects can be simplified, while at the same time the implementation of self-defined objects can be supported by ABAP Objects. Likewise, access to the object models of front-end applications such as Microsoft Word or Excel is more comfortable.

Analysis and design

The object-oriented approach requires a very thorough planning stage, especially with large applications. Today there are several standard methods of object-oriented analysis (OOA) and object-oriented design (OOD), the use of which results in accurate and stable object models. In addition, there are even ready-to-use design templates for a variety of classic design problems. This ensures stability, maintainability, and, not least, protection of your investment in the software.

However, you will also see that using the language elements of ABAP Objects can bring advantages even if you are not remodeling your entire application in an object-oriented way. You can use the extended concepts of data and function encapsulation that classes offer to your advantage in small self-contained programs.

Wrapper

In addition, SAP now delivers elements which can be used on the screen such as GUI controls (see Section 7.5.4) and Desktop Office Integration, in an object-oriented wrapper. If you want to use these elements in your programs you must work with the language elements of ABAP Objects in the corresponding parts of your program. For example, you must define handler objects which respond to user input on the screen elements.

ABAP syntax

Finally, ABAP Objects also uses a purified ABAP syntax. If you implement functionality in classes you will realize that a lot of old and obsolete language constructs,

10. Conversely, object-oriented programming does not necessarily depend on an object-oriented language, although it does make it much easier.

which are permitted outside of classes purely for compatibility reasons, are syntactically forbidden. For example, you can no longer create internal tables with header rows. From our own experience we can say that using ABAP Objects results in a clean and secure programming style which makes programs easier and more maintenance-friendly than classical ABAP.

5.3.2 Classes

Classes form the basis of any object-oriented programming language. A class is the model or template for an object in the same way that a data type is the model for a data object. You can therefore say that a class is an object type. In order to work with objects in a program you must first define classes. Various objects can be created on the basis of a class, and their attributes can have the most diverse features (or values). If we return to our example of the car, the construction plans for the car represent a class. Cars can be produced on the basis of the plans, but their status can vary greatly. With one car the fourth gear might be engaged, whereas with another the reverse gear might be engaged. Although both are based on the same specification, they are completely independent of each other. The cars represent **instances** of the construction plan. In the same way we refer to **objects** as **instances** of **classes.**[11]

Instance

If the concept of an object as an instance of a class seems somewhat abstract from your previous experience as an ABAP programmer, just think what happens when you execute a program or call an external procedure from a program: every time, the whole of the respective program is loaded into the internal session (see Figure 3.12). Yet a program in an internal session is simply an instance or an object of the overall ABAP program. And just as the source code of a program is the model for its runtime instance in the internal session, a class is simply a piece of source code from which runtime instances can also be formed in the internal session. From a technical point of view, the only new thing about object-orientation is that you control the creation of objects in the program and can form multiple instances of a class in a single internal session.[12]

Local/global class

Starting with SAP Release 4.5, you can use ABAP Objects to define classes and create objects. We distinguish between local and global classes. Local classes can be defined within any given ABAP program and are only visible there. Global classes are created with the Class Builder tool of the ABAP Workbench in the **Class Library** and are visible in any ABAP program. Initially we will concentrate on local classes as we want to introduce you first to the new language elements of ABAP Objects and then the tool. Incidentally, it is unimportant whether you use local or global classes to create objects, except that these differ in their visibility. Objects of local classes can only be created in the same ABAP program, whereas objects of global classes can be created in any ABAP program.

11. In the general literature on object-oriented programming the terms *class* and *object* are unfortunately all too often mixed up and people refer to objects when they mean classes. Examples include *instances of objects* or *object instances*.
12. We hope we haven't shocked the object gurus among you too much, but inheritance and polymorphism also have their place later in the book!

Class definition

ABAP Objects provides the CLASS and ENDCLASS statements for defining classes. Syntactically, a class definition always consists of a declaration part and an implementation part. The declaration part contains a description of all the class components. Possible components include attributes, methods, and events. The individual methods are implemented in the implementation part of a class. Compared with an ABAP program, the declaration part corresponds to the global declaration part of the program, while the methods are the only possible processing blocks. The framework for a class therefore looks like this:

```
CLASS  class DEFINITION.
  ...
ENDCLASS.

CLASS  class IMPLEMENTATION.
  ...
ENDCLASS.
```

The first two statements define the declaration part while the last two define the implementation part.

Visibility sections

You have now learned that the various components of the class can be defined in the declaration part of a class. Each of these components must be assigned to a visibility section. The reason for this is as follows: a key feature of the object-oriented approach is encapsulation. The interface of an object should be straightforward and stable. Therefore only the most essential components should be visible to the class or object users. Most defined components are generally only required within a class. In this case there is no need to make them externally accessible because each accessible component must be documented and understandable for the user. A public component must not place the object in an inconsistent state. In particular, modifiable public attributes should be avoided because they can be changed by the user directly. It is always advisable to use non-modifiable attributes or methods which receive the value to be modified as a parameter and then modify the attribute within the object. If methods alone are used for this purpose, the object state will be fully encapsulated (and the OO designer a bit happier).

ABAP Objects supports three visibility sections in total. Figure 5.19 displays these sections graphically.

- PUBLIC

  All components which are assigned to this section are public and can be addressed by all users, methods of subclasses (heirs), and the methods of the class itself. They form the external interface of the class.

- `PROTECTED`

  The components of this section are protected and can be addressed by the methods of subclasses (heirs) and the methods of the class itself. They form the interface of the class to its subclasses.

- `PRIVATE`

  Components in this section are private and can only be used in the methods of the class itself.

The figure also shows the syntax for assigning various components to the three visibility sections:

```
CLASS class DEFINITION.
  PUBLIC SECTION.
  ...
  PROTECTED SECTION.
  ...
  PRIVATE SECTION.
  ...
ENDCLASS.
```

The option of defining visibility sections is one of the points that distinguish object-oriented programming from classical programming. In the procedural model, the

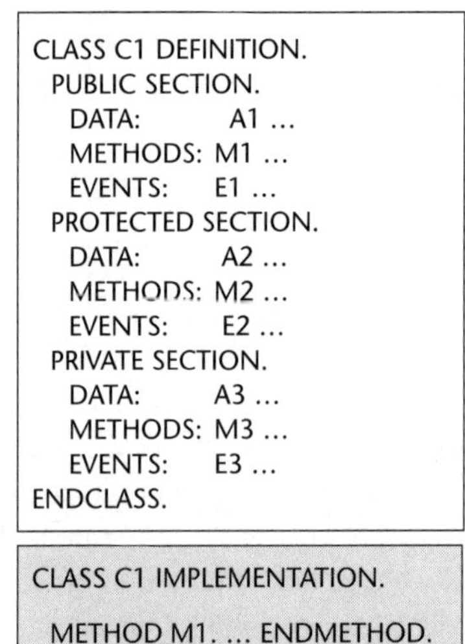

```
CLASS C1 DEFINITION.
  PUBLIC SECTION.
    DATA:      A1 ...
    METHODS:   M1 ...
    EVENTS:    E1 ...
  PROTECTED SECTION.
    DATA:      A2 ...
    METHODS:   M2 ...
    EVENTS:    E2 ...
  PRIVATE SECTION.
    DATA:      A3 ...
    METHODS:   M3 ...
    EVENTS:    E3 ...
ENDCLASS.
```

```
CLASS C1 IMPLEMENTATION.
  METHOD M1. ... ENDMETHOD.
  METHOD M2. ... ENDMETHOD.
  METHOD M3. ... ENDMETHOD.
ENDCLASS.
```

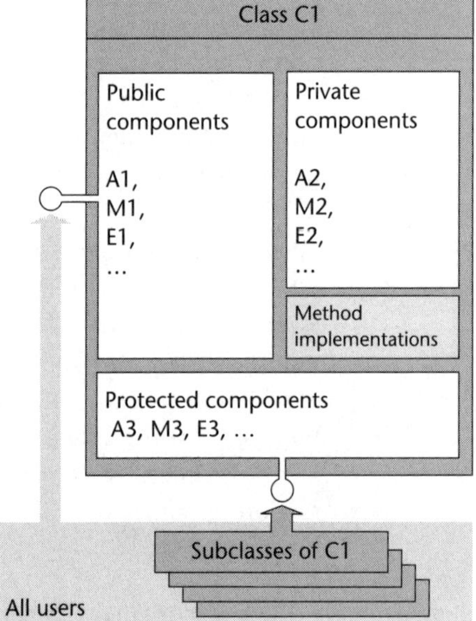

FIGURE 5.19 Visibility sections of a class

visibility of all the components is predetermined. For example, in a function group all the data objects are private and all the function modules or subroutines public, and you cannot change this. If you really wish, you can publish data in a class and, more importantly for object-oriented design, protect procedures from unauthorized use.

Components of a class

In the following section we will introduce you to the individual components of a class, i.e. attributes, methods, and events. As well as visibility, the lifetime of the individual components can also be determined. We distinguish between instance components and static components. Instance components exist in each object of a class (i.e. in every instance) independently of each other. Static components, on the other hand, only exist once per class, i.e. all objects within a class share the same static components. This means, for example, that a modification to a static attribute will be simultaneously visible in all objects. Another special feature is that the static components of a class can be used without creating an instance of the class. Let's now consider the individual components in more detail.

Attributes

Attributes are the data objects within a class. They reflect an object's state. As in classical ABAP, all data types of the ABAP type hierarchy can be used for attributes. The familiar `DATA` statement is used to declare instance attributes. To declare a static attribute you use the `CLASS-DATA` statement. Listing 5.9 shows an example of the declaration part of a class in which an instance attribute and a static attribute are declared.

LISTING 5.9 Declaring attributes of a class

```
REPORT s_class_attributes.

* Class Declarations

CLASS attributes DEFINITION.
  PRIVATE SECTION.
    DATA object_value TYPE i.
    CLASS-DATA object_count TYPE i.
ENDCLASS.
```

Variable

A `READ-ONLY` addition can be used with both `DATA` statements in the public section of a class. The effect of this addition is that an attribute declared with `DATA` can be externally read but only modified by methods of the class. Using this addition can avoid the need to provide a method each time an attribute of a class is accessed. Directly accessing an attribute is faster than calling a method.

Constant

Besides the data objects declared with DATA, you can also declare constants with the CONSTANTS statement. As constants must not be modified during compile time or at runtime, they are independent of instances and therefore comparable to static attributes.

Data type

Not least, self-defined types within a class can be declared with the TYPES statement. Like constants, data types of a class are independent of instances. In principle the same rules apply here as for ABAP programs developed according to the classical approach, only the visibility of the data types depends on the visibility section in which they are defined.

Methods

The way in which objects behave is implemented in the methods of a class. As we saw in Section 3.3.1, methods are nothing more than procedures which can only be used within a class. Like all procedures, methods are processing blocks with a parameter interface and in which you can declare local data. As with attributes, we distinguish between instance methods and static methods. Instance methods can access all attributes and events of their own class, while static methods can only access static attributes and static events. To use instance methods, you must first create an object of the class. Static methods can be used independently of objects. Methods are always listed at two points in a class definition. On the one hand, the method is declared in the declaration part of a class. With instance methods the METHODS statement is used for this, with static methods the CLASS-METHODS statement. This also defines the parameter interface of the method. On the other hand, the actual code to be executed is implemented between the METHOD and ENDMETHOD statements in the implementation part of the class. The latter applies for both instance methods and static methods. We will take a look first at the syntax of the METHODS statement. The CLASS-METHODS statement has the same syntax and is therefore not dealt with separately.

```
METHODS  meth
  IMPORTING  ... i_i TYPE type ...
  EXPORTING  ... e_i TYPE type ...
  CHANGING   ... c_i TYPE type ...
  EXCEPTIONS ... e_i ...
```

Parameter interface

This statement declares a method meth with its parameter interface. Differently than with subroutines, the definition of the parameter interface is separate from the actual implementation. The METHOD statement in the implementation part does not have any corresponding additions. Think back to the definition of the parameter interface of function modules (see for example Figure 5.9). You can relate the **Import**, **Export**, **Changing**, and **Exceptions** tab pages respectively to the IMPORTING, EXPORTING, CHANGING, and EXCEPTIONS additions above. The parameter interface of a method is therefore very similar to that of a function module. In Section 5.3.1 we shall go into more detail concerning the definition of the formal parameters.

For a simple example in Listing 5.10, we shall use just the IMPORTING and EXPORTING additions for the time being and add two methods to our previous example from Listing 5.9.

LISTING 5.10 Basic method declaration and implementation

```
REPORT s_class_methods.

* Class Declarations

CLASS attributes_and_methods DEFINITION.
  PUBLIC SECTION.
    METHODS:
      set_object_value
          IMPORTING VALUE(i_object_value) TYPE i,
      get_object_value
          EXPORTING VALUE(e_object_value) TYPE i.
  PRIVATE SECTION.
    DATA object_value TYPE i.
    CLASS-DATA object_count TYPE i.
ENDCLASS.

* Class Implementations

CLASS attributes_and_methods IMPLEMENTATION.
  METHOD set_object_value.
    object_value = i_object_value.
  ENDMETHOD.
  METHOD get_object_value.
    e_object_value = object_value.
  ENDMETHOD.
ENDCLASS.
```

In our example, the public method set_object_value can be used to set the private attribute object_value, and its value can be read with get_object_value.

Constructor

There are two special methods in addition to the methods we can create ourselves. One method called constructor is implicitly called for each instantiation of a new object. Another method called class_constructor is called the first time a class is accessed. We will describe this later in more detail.

Events

In the definition part of a class, events can be declared as components of a class. After declaration, all methods of the same class can trigger these events. Other methods of the same or a different class can be declared as special handler methods which react to these events.

In Section 6.4 of the following chapter we shall discuss events as class components, their exact function, and various applications in more detail. These concepts are already part of the advanced applications of ABAP Objects and we will not confuse you at this moment with code samples.

5.3.3 Objects and object references

In the last section we looked at classes and their structure, and you have already seen two example programs which contain ABAP Objects code. This code passes the syntax check in the ABAP Workbench without any problems but does not display any visible activity when the program is being run. A class definition is essentially merely a type definition. The only thing we are lacking now is objects, i.e. the instances of a class.

Creating and referencing objects

To create and access an object we require **object references** in **reference variables**. An object reference is nothing more than the address of an object in the memory. A reference variable is a data object which can contain object references and therefore point to objects. An object reference variable is either initial or points to a single object. It is possible for several reference variables to point to the same object.

We shall now take a look at our first object in practice and explain the necessary statements through Listing 5.11.

LISTING 5.11 The first object

```
REPORT s_first_object.

* Class Declarations

CLASS vehicle DEFINITION.
  PUBLIC SECTION.
    METHODS: accelerate,
             show_speed.
  PRIVATE SECTION.
    DATA speed TYPE i VALUE 0.
ENDCLASS.

* Class Definitions
```

```
CLASS vehicle IMPLEMENTATION.
  METHOD accelerate.
    speed = speed + 1.
  ENDMETHOD.
  METHOD show_speed.
    WRITE speed.
  ENDMETHOD.
ENDCLASS.

* Global Data

DATA ov1 TYPE REF TO vehicle.

* Classical Processing Blocks

START-OF-SELECTION.
  CREATE OBJECT ov1.
  CALL METHOD ov1->accelerate.
  CALL METHOD ov1->accelerate.
  CALL METHOD ov1->show_speed.
```

First we define a simple local class, vehicle. The class has a private attribute, speed, to represent the speed of a vehicle, and two public methods. The accelerate method accelerates the vehicle by one unit, while the show_speed method outputs the current speed on the screen.[13]

So far, nothing greatly new has happened. For the sake of clarity we have arranged the entire class definition here at the beginning of the program, physically separating the class from the code that uses it. There is no need for this with the implementation part. As you know, the methods of the implementation part are processing blocks which can be placed anywhere in the program. In complex programs all declarations, including the declaration parts of classes, should be at the beginning of the program (normally in the top include), and all processing blocks including the implementation parts of classes should then follow. This is the only way to ensure that all (public) declarations are visible in all implementations. What is new about this example is how objects are created and handled. The line

```
DATA ov1 TYPE REF TO  vehicle.
```

Pointer

is used to create a reference variable of the type "pointer to an object of the vehicle class." The TYPE REF TO addition can be used in any ABAP statement where a TYPE

13. We use the WRITE statement in the show_speed method. Note that in ABAP Objects the statements for classical list processing are no longer available in their full scope. However, the use of these statements is not critical for our basic examples.

addition is permitted. You can use this addition to refer to all classes which are visible at this point. These are either the local classes of the same program or all the global classes. The addition means that a reference variable can contain an object reference which points to objects of the specified class.

The line

```
CREATE OBJECT  ov1.
```

Instancing

is used to create an instance of the vehicle class and assign a reference to this instance to the variable ov1. The example shows the basic form of the CREATE OBJECT statement. This statement has other additions which are not relevant to us at the moment. Figure 5.20 shows a simplified representation of the situation in the internal session of the ABAP program after the CREATE OBJECT statement. An object of the vehicle class exists to which the reference variable is pointing.

After creating the object with the help of the reference variable you can access the visible components of the object using the reference variable. In our case only the methods are visible and we call them with the CALL METHOD statement. The syntax of the CALL METHOD statement is the same as that of CALL FUNCTION.

Assignment

As with other variables, assignments can be made between reference variables. In Listing 5.12 we have expanded the program in Listing 5.11 by declaring a second reference variable ov2 of the same type as ov1.

LISTING 5.12 Several reference variables

```
REPORT s_several_references.

...

* Global Data

DATA: ov1 TYPE REF TO vehicle,
      ov2 LIKE ov1.
```

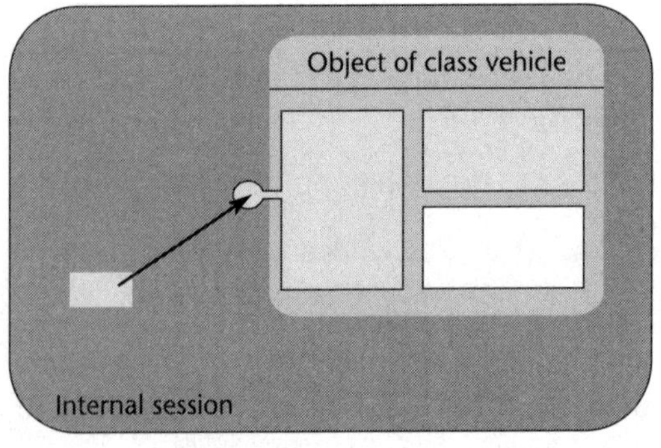

FIGURE 5.20 Reference variable, object reference, and object

```
* Classical Processing Blocks

START-OF-SELECTION.
  CREATE OBJECT ov1.
  ov2 = ov1.
  CALL METHOD ov2->accelerate.
  CALL METHOD ov2->accelerate.
  CALL METHOD ov2->show_speed.
```

As a result of the assignment `ov2 = ov1`, we have two object references to the same object (see Figure 5.21). However, the object only exists once in the memory, and only the additional reference occupies memory space for the size that the reference takes up.

You can equally use any reference variables which are pointing to an object to work with that object.[14]

Accessing object components

Working with objects is governed essentially by the following process:

1. Declare reference variables
2. Create objects
3. Use object components

Component selector

To access an object component, be it an attribute or a method, you always use the operator "->". The syntax of the access is as follows:

```
oref->comp
```

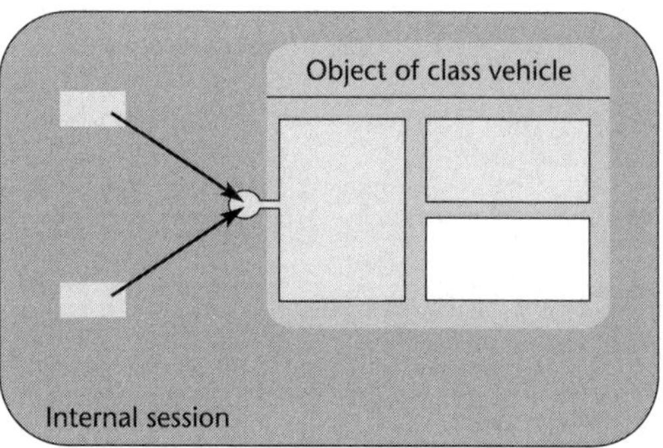

FIGURE 5.21 Several reference variables

14. This only applies, however, provided the reference variables have the same type. In the section on polymorphism you will learn more about this subject.

In this case oref represents a reference variable, and comp the name of the component to be addressed. The **object component selector** "->" allows access to the instance components and static components of an object. It is possible to access the static components of a class without creating an object, i.e. without an instance. In this case the **class component selector** "=>" is used. The syntax is

```
class=>comp
```

In this case the class name class is used, of course, instead of a reference variable.

Strings

As reference variables can also be declared as instance attributes or static attributes of classes, chains such as

```
oref1->oref2->comp
```

or

```
class=>oref->comp
```

or even longer forms are possible.

Self-reference

The above two selectors provide external access to the components of a class or object. Within the class a component can be addressed simply via its name, and it is not necessary to specify a reference variable. In some cases, however, it can be necessary for an object to know its own address, i.e. its own reference. If an object wishes to pass its own identity to another object, for example, it can use the local reference variable me which is predefined in any instance method and which always contains a reference to the address of its own object when the method is being executed. In addition, the self-reference allows attributes of its own class to be addressed in methods which have local data objects of the same name and thereby hide the attributes according to the principle of Figure 5.16. Listing 5.13 shows an example of the application of the self-reference.

LISTING 5.13 Example of self-reference

```
REPORT s_self_reference.

* Class Declarations

CLASS client DEFINITION.
  PUBLIC SECTION.
    DATA name(10) TYPE c VALUE 'Master' READ-ONLY.
    METHODS create_server.
ENDCLASS.

CLASS server DEFINITION.
  PUBLIC SECTION.
```

```
    METHODS acknowledge
      IMPORTING creator TYPE REF TO client.
  PRIVATE SECTION.
    DATA name(10) TYPE c VALUE 'Servant'.
ENDCLASS.

* Class Implementations

CLASS client IMPLEMENTATION.
  METHOD create_server.
    DATA server_ref TYPE REF TO server.
    CREATE OBJECT server_ref.
    CALL METHOD server_ref->acknowledge
         EXPORTING creator = me.
  ENDMETHOD.
ENDCLASS.

CLASS server IMPLEMENTATION.
  METHOD acknowledge.
    DATA name TYPE string.
    name = creator->name.
    WRITE: me->name, 'created by', name.
  ENDMETHOD.
ENDCLASS.

* Global Data

DATA client_ref TYPE REF TO client.

* Classical Processing Blocks

START-OF-SELECTION.
  CREATE OBJECT client_ref.
  CALL METHOD client_ref->create_server.
```

The program creates an object of the client class and calls its create_server method. The create_server method creates an object of the server class. This situation is represented in a simplified form in Figure 5.22.

The create_server method then calls the acknowledge method in the object created and passes its self-reference to the creator parameter. The acknowledge method accesses the public attribute name of the client class through the reference passed and transfers its contents to its local variable name. In the WRITE statement the method

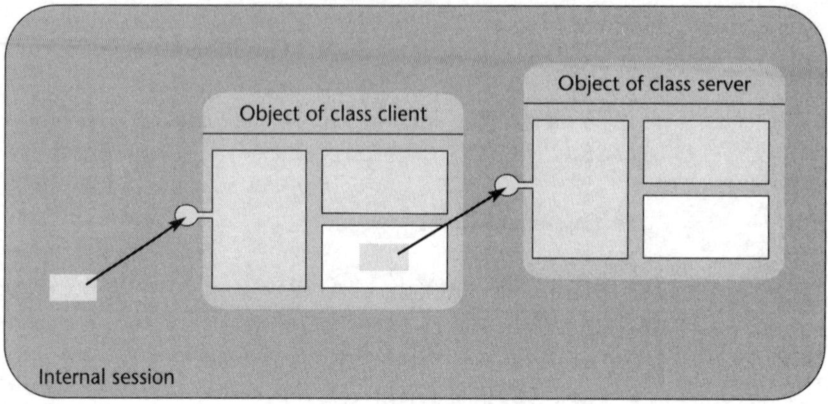

FIGURE 5.22 An object creating another object

then uses its self-reference to access the private attribute name of its own class which is hidden by the local variable. The output is: "Servant created by Master." To implement the acknowledge method you can also use the instance constructor of the server class which we will discuss later.

In Table 5.2 we have again listed all the accesses to class and object components which are important for us in this introductory chapter.

TABLE 5.2 Accessing class and object components

Access to	Syntax
... an instance attribute of an object ... a static attribute of an object	`oref->attr`
... a static attribute of a class	`class=>attr`
... its own instance attribute ... its own static attribute	`me->attr or` `attr`
... an instance method of an object ... a static method of an object	`CALL METHOD oref->meth`
... a static method of a class	`CALL METHOD class=>meth`
... its own instance method ... its own static method	`CALL METHOD me->meth or` `CALL METHOD meth`

Multiple instantiation

If, to date, you have had no experience of the concepts of object-oriented programming you might be asking yourself at this point, why did we have to make such an effort (in terms of writing) in ABAP Objects for our example in Listing 5.11 in order to map a very simple functionality? After all, the existing ABAP language elements have always been sufficient. To illustrate the major difference between ABAP Objects and previous ABAP, we shall write the same program again in the classical programming model with function modules. The code in Listing 5.14 implements the s_vehicle function group, analogous to the vehicle class. Of course, you can only create this group in the Function Builder, you cannot simply enter it in the Editor.

LISTING 5.14 The s_vehicle function group

```
FUNCTION-POOL s_vehicle.

DATA speed TYPE i VALUE 0.

FUNCTION accelerate.
  speed = speed + 1.
ENDFUNCTION.

FUNCTION show_speed.
  WRITE speed.
ENDFUNCTION.
```

Imagine we want to check the speed of vehicles in a program. Listing 5.15 shows a program which uses the function modules.

LISTING 5.15 Handling a vehicle in a function group

```
REPORT s_object_of_function_pool.

* Classical Processing Blocks

START-OF-SELECTION.
* Vehicle 1
  CALL FUNCTION 'ACCELERATE'.
  CALL FUNCTION 'ACCELERATE'.
  CALL FUNCTION 'SHOW_SPEED'.
* Vehicle 2
  ???
* Vehicle 3
  ???
```

Providing you are dealing with only one vehicle, everything is ok. If, however, you want to work with more than one vehicle, you cannot use the function group. There is no way of informing the program that we want to use the same set of functions for more vehicles. This is because there is only one instance of a specific function group available in the internal session (see Figure 5.23).

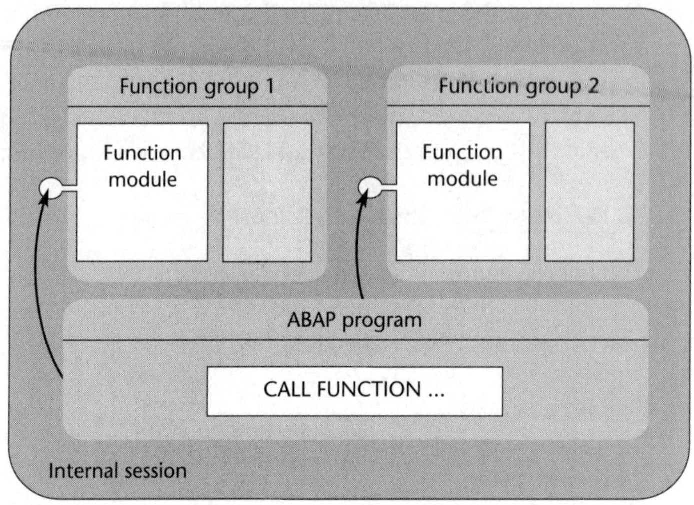

FIGURE 5.23 Creating instances with function groups

Function group as an object

To manage several vehicles we would therefore have to either create many copies of the function group[15] or incorporate a more complex management within the function group, whereby the interface would also have to contain a vehicle identification. As this is both complicated and error-prone, we would therefore prefer to show you in Listing 5.16 how the problem can be solved more elegantly in ABAP Objects.

LISTING 5.16 Several objects with different speeds

```
REPORT s_several_objects.

...

* Global Data

DATA: ov TYPE REF TO vehicle,
      ov_tab TYPE TABLE OF REF TO vehicle.

* Classical Processing Blocks

START-OF-SELECTION.
  DO 5 TIMES.
    CREATE OBJECT ov.
```

15. Whereby the unique namespace of function modules also gets in our way.

```
    APPEND ov TO ov_tab.
  ENDDO.
  LOOP AT ov_tab INTO ov.
    DO sy-tabix TIMES.
      CALL METHOD ov->accelerate.
    ENDDO.
    CALL METHOD ov->show_speed.
  ENDLOOP.
```

In this situation we refer to the same class as in Listing 5.11. As mentioned previously, in terms of executing the program it is irrelevant whether the class is defined locally in the same program or is global within the class library.

Pointer table

We create five different vehicle objects and store their object references in an internal table ov_tab immediately after they have been created. You can see that the ov reference variable can be used repeatedly for creating different objects and that it is no problem to use internal tables of the reference variable row type. Debug the program and look at the contents of ov and ov_tab. Figure 5.24 shows the situation at the end of the first DO loop. The rows of the internal table each reference an object and the single reference variable addresses the last object created. Once created, the various objects of a class exist independently of each other. They all contain a unique identity and all live in the same memory area.

Of course, we could have created more individual reference variables with reference to the vehicle class in order to create objects with them. However, internal tables are always the most appropriate tool for creating a list of the same kind of data object. We can also now create as many vehicles as we want in this program simply by varying the number of loop passes.

After creating the objects we read the internal table row by row again into ov and accelerate the vehicles to different speeds. When you start the program, the values one to five are output one after another on the screen.

Unlike working with a function group where we have only one instance, namely the program itself, in ABAP Objects we work with many independent instances which have their own local data area and which act as individual small programs. The effort to represent a program by means of classes and objects can therefore be fully justified even for minor problems.

Deleting objects

Objects occupy space in the memory, and if they are no longer required they can be deleted. In this context, objects depend on references. An object in ABAP Objects is deleted when there is no longer any reference pointing to it.[16] If this situation arises,

16. In fact, an additional condition applies. There must be no reference variable still pointing to the object and none of its methods must be registered as event handlers. We will look at events in Section 6.4, so we shall not explore this aspect any further at this point.

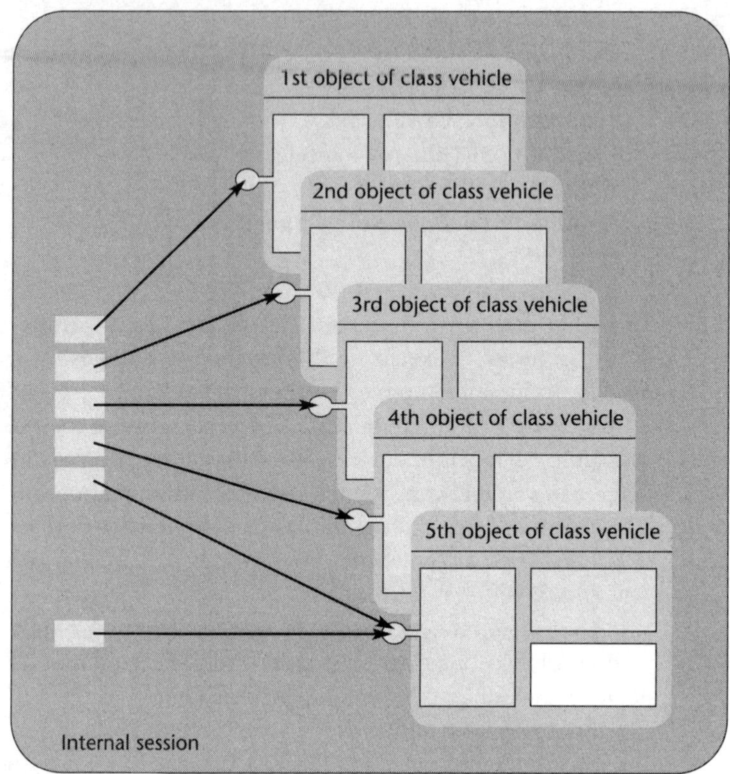

FIGURE 5.24 Several instances of a class

the **garbage collector** becomes active, deletes the object, and then releases the memory it occupied. You do not have to bother calling the garbage collector as this function is provided by the runtime environment.

The garbage collector is called periodically and searches for objects to which no reference is pointing. If an object to which no reference is pointing has attributes of the reference variable type, these references are tracked by the garbage collector. If no row reference variables are pointing to the objects found, these will also be deleted, as shown in Figure 5.25.

Garbage collection

In our examples from Listing 5.11 on, you can delete the objects by simply initializing the contents of the reference variables using the CLEAR statement. References to objects can also be lost through assignments between reference variables.

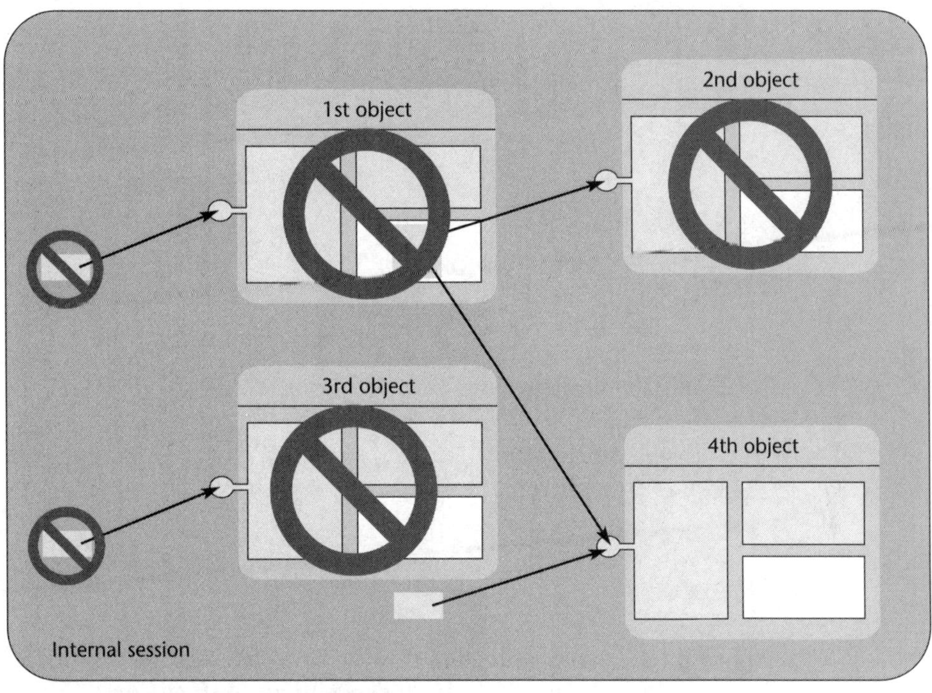

FIGURE 5.25 Garbage collector

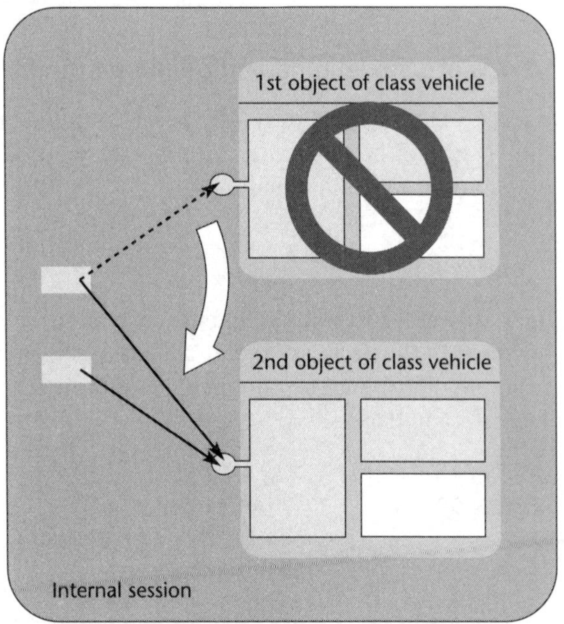

FIGURE 5.26 Activating the garbage collector through assignment

LISTING 5.17 Activating the garbage collector

```
REPORT s_garbage_collector.

...

* Global Data

DATA: ov1 TYPE REF TO vehicle,
      ov2 LIKE ov1.

* Classical Processing Blocks

START-OF-SELECTION.
  CREATE OBJECT: ov1,
                 ov2.
  ov1 = ov2.
  CLEAR ov2.
```

Listing 5.17 shows a program in which two reference variables ov1 and ov2 initially point to two different objects. By assigning ov2 to ov1, ov1 now points to the same object as ov2, and the other object is deleted (see Figure 5.26). After the CLEAR statement only ov1 keeps the remaining object alive.

5.3.4 More on defining and calling methods

In the previous examples we defined and called several methods. In this section we shall examine the parameter interface of methods in more detail and also explore other options for calling methods.

Parameter interface

The parameter interface of a method is defined by the additions to the METHODS statement in the declaration part of a class. The implementation part does not require any more details for the parameter interface. The complete syntax for defining the parameter interface is:

```
METHODS  meth
  IMPORTING  ... {VALUE(i_i)|i_i} {TYPE type|LIKE dobj}
                                 [OPTIONAL|DEFAULT def_i] ...
  EXPORTING  ... {VALUE(e_i)|e_i} {TYPE type|LIKE dobj } ...
  CHANGING   ... {VALUE(c_i)|c_i} {TYPE type|LIKE dobj } ...
                                 [OPTIONAL|DEFAULT def_i] ...
  EXCEPTIONS ...               x_i  ...
```

As mentioned before, the structure of the interface is similar to that of a function module. In the additions to the METHODS statement you see the syntactical equivalent of what the Function Builder tool only shows you as comment lines in the source code of a function module (see Figure 5.11).

You also find an equivalent for the TYPE, OPTIONAL, and DEFAULT additions on the tab pages in the Function Builder (see Figure 5.9). Compared with function modules, however, methods do not have a table parameter as this has become obsolete due to the current typing options.

Class Builder

If you are going to create global classes in the Class Builder later, you will not need the above syntax, just as it was not needed in the Function Builder, since the Class Builder also generates the statement in the background. However, one of the advantages of methods compared with function modules lies in the fact that you can use the syntax in the local classes of any program independently of a tool.

Formal parameter

You can create the following formal parameters with the additions to the METHODS statement:

- Use IMPORTING to specify one or more input parameters
- Use EXPORTING to specify one or more output parameters
- Use CHANGING to specify one or more parameters which are both input and output parameters.

You can use the other additions to determine the attributes of each formal parameter.

- Type of parameter passing

  The type of passing determines whether a parameter is passed by reference or by value. Pass by reference is the default. You can use the optional addition VALUE to specify pass by value. Another option which is not shown in the syntax diagram but can definitely be used is explicit pass by reference using the REFERENCE addition instead of VALUE.

- Typing

  You must[17] type each parameter of a method with the TYPE addition. You can make the same specifications after TYPE as with subroutines. Typing can therefore be either full or partial. Instead of TYPE you can use the LIKE addition with which you can refer to the data type of data objects visible at this point, such as class attributes already declared.

- Optional parameters/initial value

  Normally, an actual parameter must be passed to each input parameter of a method when the method is called. Only parameters marked with the OPTIONAL addition do not need to be filled when the method is called. An optional parame-

17. The emphasis here is on *must*. In subroutines and function modules you should type, but you are not compelled to.

ter which is not filled during the call contains either the type-specific initial value[18] when the method is executed, or you determine an initial value with the `DEFAULT` addition.

There is also a `RETURNING` parameter which can be used instead of `EXPORTING` or `CHANGING` parameters. This is described below in more detail.

Method calls

All methods can be called with the `CALL METHOD` statement. Each time the method is called, all the non-optional formal parameters of the method must be filled with type-specific actual parameters. The way parameters are filled during the method call with `CALL METHOD` is no different from when a function module is called with `CALL FUNCTION`, and the syntax is correspondingly:

```
CALL METHOD  oref->meth
             [EXPORTING  i1 = a1 ... in = an]
             [IMPORTING  e1 = a1 ... en = an]
             [CHANGING   c1 = a1 ... cn = an]
             [EXCEPTIONS x1 = r1 ... OTHERS = ro]
```

Actual parameter

Here too, the parameters characterized as `IMPORTING` in the declaration part of the class are filled when the method is called with the `EXPORTING` addition and vice versa. The assignment of formal and actual parameters always follows the paradigm:

```
Formal parameter = Actual parameter.
```

Again, the equals sign should not be seen as an assignment operator. It indicates the relationship between the formal and actual parameter. With the `IMPORTING` addition of the `CALL METHOD` statement a data object a_i is filled with the contents of e_i and not vice versa.

Handling exceptions

There is no difference in how exceptional situations in a method are handled with the `EXCEPTION` addition compared with function modules. Exceptions are triggered in the method by the `RAISE` exception and `MESSAGE RAISING` statements. If an exception occurs within a method, the sy-subrc system field is filled with a value r_i defined during the call and can be accessed by the user of the method.

Short form

If a method has no, one, or more input parameters but no output parameters, the following short forms of the `CALL METHOD` statement are possible.

```
CALL METHOD meth( ).
CALL METHOD meth( a ).
CALL METHOD meth(f1 = a1 ... fn = an ).
```

We shall now present a special form of method calling which does not require `CALL METHOD`, the functional method call.

18. If the parameter is typed with reference to `ANY`, the initial value is an empty character field of length 1.

Functional methods

In many other programming languages such as C, C++, or Java it is possible to perform function calls through expressions in operations instead of using special call statements. In the past, ABAP only allowed you to use predefined mathematical functions in this way, e.g. SQRT, in mathematical expressions of the COMPUTE statement. In ABAP Objects you can now use functional method calls in all the key statements. However, the requirement for this is functional methods. The syntax for declaring functional methods is:

```
METHODS  meth
  IMPORTING  ... {VALUE(i_i)|i_i} {TYPE type|LIKE dobj}
                                [OPTIONAL|DEFAULT def_i] ...
  RETURNING         VALUE(r)  {TYPE type|LIKE dobj}.
```

Return value

A functional method can have any number of IMPORTING parameters and just one RETURNING parameter. This **return value** must be passed by value and be fully typed. A functional method can be called as follows using CALL METHOD:

```
CALL METHOD oref->meth
            EXPORTING  i_1 = a_1 ... i_n = a_n
            RECEIVING   r =  a.
```

The RECEIVING addition assigns the RETURNING parameter to an actual parameter. However, the functional method call is much more interesting with the following expressions.

```
... oref->meth( ) ...
... oref->meth( a ) ...
... oref->meth( i_1 = a_1 ... i_n = a_n ) ...
```

These expressions can be used for functional methods with no IMPORTING parameters, or one or more at the following positions:

- As a source field for the MOVE statement
- As operands in arithmetic expressions of the COMPUTE statement
- As operands in logical expressions
- As an operand in the CASE statement in a CASE control structure
- As an operand in the WHEN statement in a CASE control structure
- As operands in the WHERE condition of the LOOP AT, DELETE, and MODIFY statements for internal tables.

When statements with functional methods are executed, first the methods are called and then the returned RETURNING parameters are used directly as operands.

In Listing 5.18 we have implemented a functional method, get_area, to calculate the area of a circle. We call the method once via CALL METHOD and once functionally.

LISTING 5.18 Functional method

```
REPORT s_functional_method.

* Class Declarations

CLASS circle DEFINITION.
  PUBLIC SECTION.
    METHODS get_area IMPORTING VALUE(i_radius) TYPE i
                     RETURNING VALUE(r_size)   TYPE f.
  PRIVATE SECTION.
    CONSTANTS pi TYPE f VALUE '3.14159265'.
ENDCLASS.

* Class Implementations

CLASS circle IMPLEMENTATION.
  METHOD get_area.
    r_size = i_radius ** 2 * pi.
  ENDMETHOD.
ENDCLASS.

* Global Data

PARAMETERS radius TYPE i.
DATA: o_circle TYPE REF TO circle,
      area TYPE f.

* Classical Processing Blocks

START-OF-SELECTION.
  CREATE OBJECT o_circle.

  CALL METHOD o_circle->get_area
              EXPORTING i_radius = radius
              RECEIVING r_size = area.
  WRITE: / area.

  area = o_circle->get_area( radius ).
  WRITE: / area.
```

Dynamic method call

So far we have called methods only statically. With the static method call, which should not be confused with calling static methods declared with CLASS-METHODS, the name and interface of the called method are determined during compile time. The developer writes the method name directly in the source code, which corresponds to the procedure used in all our examples.

But what happens if, when we create a program, we do not know the name of the method which we call at a specific point? Let's assume you have created a class which has two methods: one for outputting the contents of the SPFLI table and one for outputting the contents of the SFLIGHT table. The user must enter the name of the table on a selection screen, and the correct output is to appear as a list. Consider Listing 5.19.

LISTING 5.19 Dynamic method call

```
REPORT s_dynamic_method_call.

* Class Declarations

CLASS table_content DEFINITION.
  PUBLIC SECTION.
    METHODS: get_spfli,
             get_sflight.
  PRIVATE SECTION.
    DATA: wa_spfli TYPE spfli,
          wa_sflight TYPE sflight.
ENDCLASS.

* Class Implementations

CLASS table_content IMPLEMENTATION.
  METHOD get_spfli.
    SELECT * FROM spfli INTO wa_spfli.
      WRITE: / wa_spfli-carrid,
               wa_spfli-connid.
    ENDSELECT.
  ENDMETHOD.
  METHOD get_sflight.
    SELECT * FROM sflight INTO wa_sflight.
      WRITE: / wa_sflight-carrid,
               wa_sflight-connid,
               wa_sflight-fldate.
```

```
    ENDSELECT.
  ENDMETHOD.
ENDCLASS.

* Global Data

PARAMETERS table(20) TYPE c.
DATA o_table TYPE REF TO table_content.

* Classical Processing Blocks

START-OF-SELECTION.
  CREATE OBJECT o_table.
  CONCATENATE 'GET_' table INTO table.
  CATCH SYSTEM-EXCEPTIONS dyn_call_meth_not_found = 4.
    CALL METHOD o_table->(table).
  ENDCATCH.
  IF sy-subrc  = 4.
    WRITE 'Wrong Method Name!'.
  ENDIF.
```

Our method call follows the syntax

```
CALL METHOD oref->(f).
```

A dynamic method call can be achieved by inserting a field in brackets containing the name of a method, instead of the method name itself. This applies to instance methods, methods of its own class which are addressed with me->, and static methods. With static methods the class name can also be dynamically specified via (f)=>.

Similar dynamic calls are also possible with subroutines and function modules, and so this section has not yet provided you with anything particularly new if you are already well versed in classical ABAP. However, ABAP Objects does have an important new feature to offer: with method calls the actual parameters can be passed dynamically, which is not possible with subroutines or function modules. To allow this, the CALL METHOD statement provides the PARAMETER-TABLE and EXCEPTION-TABLE additions. The syntax is:

```
CALL METHOD  meth PARAMETER-TABLE  ptab
                  EXCEPTION-TABLE  etab.
```

Parameter table

The actual parameters and exceptions must first be placed in the ptab and etab internal tables and are passed to the method using the two additions. The internal tables must have specific row and table types for parameter passing to work. For this purpose, the type group ABAP in the ABAP Dictionary contains the line type

ABAP_PARMBIND and the table type ABAP_PARMBIND_TAB for the parameters. For the exception table there is the ABAP_EXCPBIND row type and the ABAP_EXCBIND_TAB table type. Look at the type definitions in the ABAP Dictionary to see which columns the tables have. You can find more detailed documentation on dynamic passing of actual parameters and exceptions in the ABAP keyword documentation.

Runtime error

If you try to dynamically call a non-existent method, a catchable runtime error is triggered which we catch in Listing 5.19 with CATCH - ENDCATCH.

Constructors

So far, we have created all the methods of a class and determined the call point in the program ourselves. Yet the classes of ABAP Objects, like the classes of many other object-oriented programming languages, have special methods known as **constructors**. A **constructor** is a special method which is automatically executed by the runtime environment. Constructors are used to set an object dynamically to a defined initial state. A constructor cannot be called with the CALL METHOD statement, nor can the developer influence the call point.[20] Like normal methods, constructors can be instance-dependent or instance-independent.

Instance constructors

Instance constructors are called once for each instance of a class after the complete creation of the instance with the CREATE OBJECT statement. Like conventional methods, the instance constructor must be declared in the declaration part of the class and implemented in the implementation part of the class. Two rules apply here. Firstly, the method must have the predefined name constructor and secondly it must be declared in the PUBLIC SECTION. The following syntax applies for the declaration:

```
METHODS constructor
  IMPORTING ... {VALUE(i_i)|i_i} {TYPE type|LIKE dobj}
                          [OPTIONAL|DEFAULT def_i] ...
  EXCEPTIONS ... x_i ....
```

Formal parameter

The fact that a constructor does not have output parameters shows that it is used solely to define an object's status and has no other purpose. Since a constructor is called implicitly during the CREATE OBJECT statement, the formal parameters must be filled during this statement. The CREATE OBJECT statement therefore has the same EXPORTING and EXCEPTIONS additions as the CALL METHOD statement. If an exception is triggered in a constructor, the object created is deleted during the CREATE OBJECT statement, and the corresponding reference variable is set to its initial value.

20. We will encounter an exception with inheritance.

Static constructors

The static constructor is called in a program once for each class before the class is accessed for the first time. Like the instance constructor, the static constructor must also be declared in the PUBLIC SECTION. The name of the static constructor with which it is declared and implemented is class_constructor. We shall glance at the syntax of the declaration:

```
CLASS-METHODS class_constructor.
```

No interface parameters can be defined for a static constructor. Like all static methods, static constructors can only access static attributes of their class.

Listing 5.20 illustrates how both kinds of constructor are used. At the same time, Listing 5.20 shows the ABAP Objects implementation of the task, which we have already solved in Listings 5.2 and 5.3 using subroutines and function modules.

LISTING 5.20 Use of constructors

```
REPORT s_select_display_sflight.

* Class Declarations

CLASS select_display_sflight DEFINITION.
  PUBLIC SECTION.
    CLASS-METHODS class_constructor.
    METHODS: constructor
               IMPORTING  i_carrid TYPE sflight-carrid
                          i_connid TYPE sflight-connid
               EXCEPTIONS nothing_found,
                          display_sflight.
  PRIVATE SECTION.
    CLASS-DATA list TYPE REF TO cl_gui_alv_grid.
    DATA sflight_tab TYPE s_sflight_tab.
ENDCLASS.

* Class Implementations.

CLASS select_display_sflight IMPLEMENTATION.
  METHOD class_constructor.
    CREATE OBJECT list
      EXPORTING i_parent = cl_gui_container=>screen0.
  ENDMETHOD.
  METHOD constructor.
```

```
    SELECT *
    FROM   sflight
    INTO   TABLE sflight_tab
    WHERE  carrid = i_carrid AND
           connid = i_connid.
    IF sy-subrc = 4.
      RAISE nothing_found.
    ENDIF.
  ENDMETHOD.
  METHOD display_sflight.
    CALL METHOD list->set_table_for_first_display
         EXPORTING i_structure_name = 'SFLIGHT'
         CHANGING  it_outtab = sflight_tab.
    CALL SCREEN 100.
  ENDMETHOD.
ENDCLASS.

* Global Data

SELECTION-SCREEN BEGIN OF SCREEN 500.
PARAMETERS: p_carrid TYPE sflight-carrid,
            p_connid TYPE sflight-connid.
SELECTION-SCREEN END OF SCREEN 500.

DATA: BEGIN OF ref_tab_line,
        carrid TYPE sflight-carrid,
        connid TYPE sflight-connid,
        oref   TYPE REF TO select_display_sflight,
      END OF ref_tab_line,
      ref_tab LIKE SORTED TABLE OF ref_tab_line
                   WITH UNIQUE KEY carrid connid.

* Classical Processing Blocks

START-OF-SELECTION.
  DO.
    CALL SELECTION-SCREEN 500 STARTING AT 10 10.
    IF sy-subrc <> 0.
      LEAVE PROGRAM.
    ENDIF.
    ref_tab_line-carrid = p_carrid.
    ref_tab_line-connid = p_connid.
```

```
    READ TABLE ref_tab INTO ref_tab_line
                       FROM ref_tab_line.
    IF sy-subrc <> 0.
      CREATE OBJECT ref_tab_line-oref
             EXPORTING  i_carrid = p_carrid
                        i_connid = p_connid
             EXCEPTIONS nothing_found = 4.
      IF sy-subrc = 4.
        MESSAGE i888(sabapdocu) WITH 'No data'.
        CONTINUE.
      ELSE.
        INSERT ref_tab_line INTO TABLE ref_tab.
      ENDIF.
    ENDIF.
    CALL METHOD ref_tab_line-oref->display_sflight.
  ENDDO
```

An internal table ref_tab is managed in the global data of the program, which contains key values for flights and a reference variable. The user can enter key values on a selection screen and, for any combination of key values, just one object of the select_display_sflight class is created. In the instance constructor of the class the private internal table sflight_tab is filled with data from the database table SFLIGHT. If no data is found, the nothing_found exception is triggered and the object is deleted. Otherwise the reference variable is stored in the internal table ref_tab which keeps the object alive.

For each input of key values for which there is data, the data is output to a list. To do this, the display_sflight method of the object is called which encapsulates the relevant data in its private internal table.

GUI control

While Listing 5.20 is being executed, the screen looks roughly as shown in Figure 5.27. As a classical list output is not possible for the functionality of this example, we have used screen elements such as a selection screen in a dialog box as well as GUI controls, about which you will learn more in Chapter 7.

In this context, the only important thing is that we have used the static constructor class_constructor to create a single object of the class cl_gui_alv_grid, to which the private static attribute list points in all objects of the class select_display_sflight, and which we use in all objects to display lists. The cl_gui_alv_grid class exists globally in the class library. You can see that we work with cl_gui_alv_grid in exactly the same way as with our local classes by declaring a reference variable for the class, creating an object, and calling a method via the object, component selector.

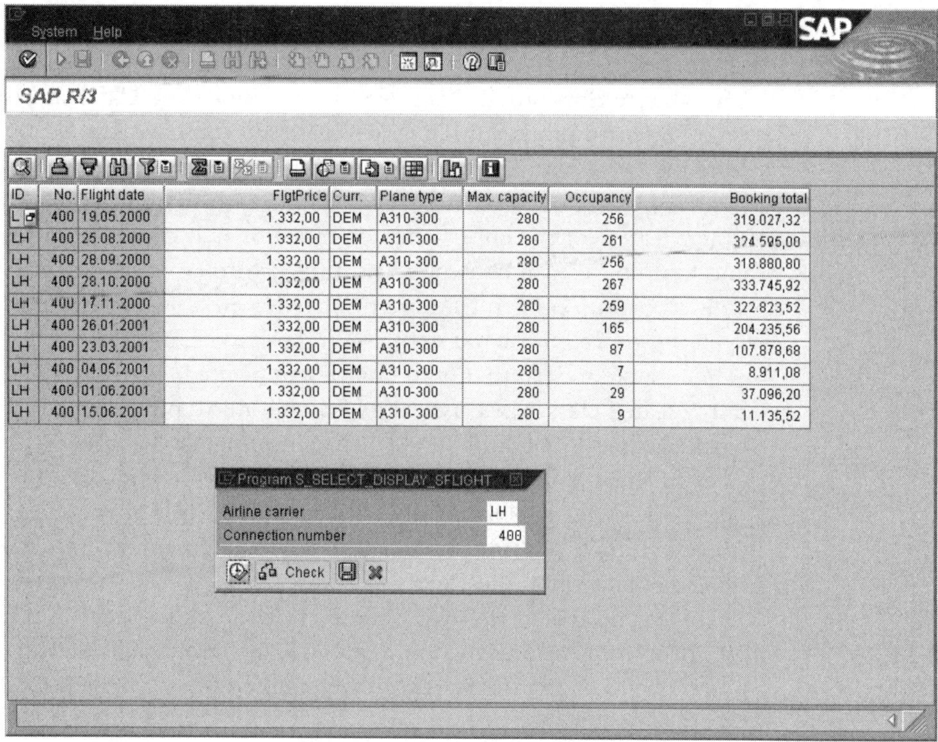

FIGURE 5.27 List output of SFLIGHT with ABAP Objects. Copyright © SAP AG

In practice you will often use constructors to provide newly created objects immediately with appropriate initial values. You could, of course, also call your own initialization method with corresponding parameters. Providing you do not forget this call after creating all new objects, this will work just as well. If other developers are also using your class you would have to document precisely how an object is to be initialized if constructors are not being used. Constructors make your life easier and protect users of your classes from making errors.

Destructors

If an object has a constructor method which is always called when the object has just been created, you could assume that there is also a method which is called when the object is deleted. Many programming languages have this kind of method, called **destructors**. For a variety of reasons (including performance, transaction design, etc.) ABAP Objects does not currently provide destructors.

5.4 SUMMARY AND OUTLOOK

This chapter has provided an overview of both the classical procedural and the object-oriented programming model in ABAP. You have learned that many elements from the two worlds are similar. In particular, methods are nothing other than procedures which are conceptually almost identical to subroutines and function modules. A new feature of the object-oriented model is that classes form the basis for objects and that objects can be explicitly handled through reference variables. These constructs open up numerous opportunities for an object-oriented implementation of applications which you did not have in the classical model.

You have also seen that both models can be used together in ABAP. So far, we have only created classes in classical executable ABAP programs containing processing blocks such as `START-OF-SELECTION`. In principle, we could have defined subroutines in these programs but we no longer recommend this. Instead, you should modularize your programs only with methods while at the same time using ABAP Objects. If methods only serve an instance-independent internal modularization, static methods will suffice.

There is no reason why you shouldn't define local classes in function groups and use them from within function modules. Conversely, you can call the existing function modules of the SAP System in any method of a class, be it local or global, to use existing functionality.

With your knowledge of classes, objects, and reference variables you now know the basics of ABAP Objects and how this programming model fits into the existing ABAP world. You should now be able to safely apply the elements of ABAP Objects you have encountered within your own example programs.

In this chapter we have mainly concentrated on the new features which distinguish ABAP Objects from classical ABAP from a technical viewpoint. What we have said should create a basis for understanding more advanced concepts of object-oriented programming. We have not yet reached the end of our introduction to object-oriented language elements. In the next chapter we will introduce you to key concepts such as inheritance, interfaces, and polymorphism, which for many are the real jewels in the crown of object-oriented programming. We have also saved the ABAP Objects concept of events and the description of the Class Builder for the next chapter.

CHAPTER 6

Advanced concepts of object-oriented programming with ABAP Objects

A physician, a civil engineer, and a computer scientist were arguing about what was the oldest profession in the world. The physician remarked: "Well, in the Bible, it says that God created Eve from a rib taken out of Adam. This clearly required surgery, and so I can rightly claim that mine is the oldest profession in the world." The civil engineer interrupted and said: "But even earlier, in the Book of Genesis, it states that God created the order of the heavens and the earth out of chaos. This was the first and certainly the most spectacular application of civil engineering. Therefore, fair doctor, you are wrong: mine is the oldest profession in the world." The computer scientist leaned back in her chair, smiled, and said confidently: "Ah, but who do you think created the chaos?"

Grady Booch [Boo 94]

6.1 INTRODUCTION

This quote comes from the book *Object-Oriented Analysis and Design with Applications* by Grady Booch where it introduces the chapter on "Complexity". An advantage of the object-oriented approach is the way it manages complexity. In the previous chapter you were introduced to the basic elements of ABAP Objects. Perhaps you also realized how powerful they can be for programming application programs. However, the elements we have introduced so far are by no means complete. In this chapter we shall introduce you to elements which are essential for object-oriented design. Applying them correctly represents the pinnacle of object-oriented programming and provides you with numerous opportunities for managing complexity.[1]

You can find all the concepts we have introduced so far, i.e. classes, objects, and object references, in almost any object-oriented programming language; they have been available in ABAP since Release 4.5. The concepts we will now introduce represent the selected advanced technologies which have been integrated into ABAP Objects following the examples of widely known object-oriented programming languages such as Java or C++. These are available in their full scope as of Release 4.6. In

1. We should not hide the fact, however, that an incorrect or misguided use of concepts such as inheritance can cause major problems. Careful object-oriented modeling is essential, especially when complex applications are to be handled by advanced concepts of object-orientation.

designing the language, we took great care not to lose sight of the area of application. ABAP has always been a language for creating business applications. Some concepts of object-oriented programming, such as multiple inheritance contained for example in C++, would have increased the complexity of the language without providing much additional benefit for SAP applications. ABAP Objects was implemented to be as understandable as possible (according to the ASAP principle, "As Simple As Possible"), whereby only long-standing object-oriented concepts were used. Following the example of Java, an interface concept was used to replace multiple inheritance.

Polymorphism

Another key term in this chapter is polymorphism. In ABAP Objects inheritance and interfaces are equal bases of polymorphism. We shall introduce you to the concept of polymorphism through inheritance and build on this when discussing interfaces.

In this chapter you will also learn the concept of events in ABAP Objects. Events allow an object to publish a change in status and also allow other objects to react to this. Events are fully integrated in the language environment of ABAP Objects as independent components of classes. You do not find this concept in all object-oriented programming languages.

At the end of this chapter we will introduce you briefly to the Class Builder of the ABAP Workbench to allow you to implement everything you have learned in global classes and interfaces.

6.2 INHERITANCE

6.2.1 Basic principles

Do you remember how we referred to classes in Section 5.3.2 as construction plans or specifications for objects? Imagine now you are writing "plane" and "ship" classes. For both classes you want to implement methods which control the objects or return information regarding their position and speed. Already you can see that you will have to write some parts of the classes twice. The inheritance mechanism of an object-oriented programming language provides you with options which will help you to reuse the same or similar parts of a class and build a hierarchy of classes.

If we consider our two classes "plane" and "ship" in more detail, we see that both are special cases of a vehicle. If we want to map a third class, "sailing ship," this again will be a special case of a ship. In order to create a hierarchical relationship between such classes, classes can be derived from each other by inheritance. In our example, "plane" and "ship" are derived from "vehicle", and "sailing ship" is derived from "ship." Derived or more specialized classes are called **subclasses**, and more general classes are called **superclasses**.

Single inheritance

ABAP Objects implements the mechanism of **single inheritance**, i.e. each class can have several subclasses but only one superclass.[2] In single inheritance, relation-

2. Other programming languages, such as C++, allow a class to inherit from several classes. This mechanism is called multiple inheritance and is not implemented in ABAP Objects.

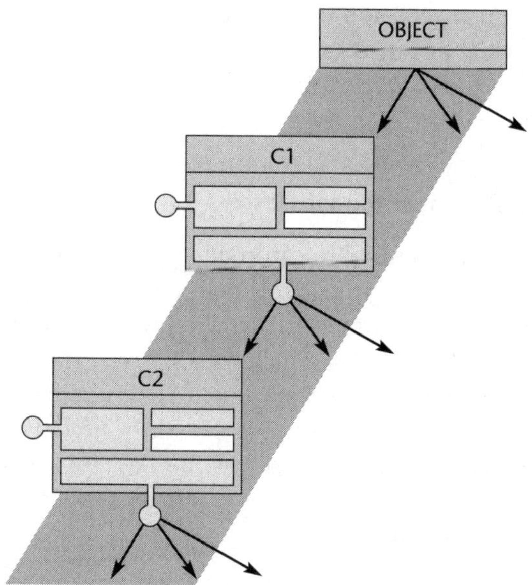

FIGURE 6.1 A path of the inheritance tree in ABAP Objects

ships can be represented in an **inheritance tree**. Each class of an object-oriented programming language in which single inheritance is used has a unique position as a node in such an inheritance tree. This also applies to our classes in Chapter 5, where we did not even mention inheritance. The superclasses of each class can be retraced along a unique path of the inheritance tree to a single root node of the tree. The root node is the superclass of all the classes of the inheritance tree.

Figure 6.1 shows this relationship graphically. The root node of the inheritance tree in ABAP Objects is the `object` class. The `object` class does not contain any components and is predefined in the SAP System.

Superclass/Subclass

In inheritance, a subclass adopts all the components, i.e. attributes, methods, and events, of its superclass, and can use them exactly like its own components. Through specialization, new elements, of which the superclass is unaware, can be added to each subclass. Elements can only be added in subclasses. It would contradict the whole concept of inheritance to remove anything.

Root class

Accordingly, the direct subclasses of the root class `object` cannot adopt components from their empty superclass; they can only add new components. This situation applies to our previous classes from Chapter 5: all classes in ABAP Objects which do not inherit specifically from another class are implicitly direct subclasses of `object`.

If we now form subclasses of our previous classes, they inherit the components of the classes and can add new components. Specialization therefore increases along a path of an inheritance tree the further you move away from the root. Conversely, as you move towards the root, the classes become more generalized.

If you look at a class which is further down in the inheritance tree you will see that the inherited components of the class originate from all classes which are higher up in the hierarchy. You can also imagine it in the sense that the definition of a subclass comprises all the definitions of all its superclasses up to `object`.

6.2.2 Syntax for subclasses

Following on from this introduction, we shall now deal with more specific issues and look more closely at implementing the inheritance concept in ABAP Objects. To do this we shall implement our "vehicle" example step by step. We therefore need a "vehicle" class, from which we will derive two classes: "plane" and "ship."

We have already mentioned that a superclass is not aware of any subclasses. Consequently, inheritance can only be determined when a subclass is defined because only this class knows the class from which it wishes to inherit. The syntax for deriving a subclass (subclass) from a superclass (superclass) is very straightforward and looks as follows:

```
CLASS subclass DEFINITION INHERITING FROM superclass.
  ...
ENDCLASS.
```

For each class which does not have a specific `INHERITING FROM` addition, the system implicitly supplements the `INHERITING FROM` object addition so that each class without an `INHERITING` addition automatically becomes a direct subclass of the `object` root class. Listing 6.1 shows how the class definitions for our example can look like.

LISTING 6.1 Basic example of inheritance

```
REPORT s_simple_inheritance.

* Class Declarations

CLASS vehicle DEFINITION INHERITING FROM object.
  PUBLIC SECTION.
    METHODS: accelerate,
             write_status.
  PROTECTED SECTION.
    DATA speed TYPE i.
ENDCLASS.

CLASS plane DEFINITION INHERITING FROM vehicle.
  PUBLIC SECTION.
    METHODS rise.
```

```
  PROTECTED SECTION.
    DATA altitude TYPE i.
ENDCLASS.

CLASS ship DEFINITION INHERITING FROM vehicle.
ENDCLASS.

* Class Implementations

CLASS vehicle IMPLEMENTATION.
  METHOD accelerate.
    speed = speed + 1.
  ENDMETHOD.
  METHOD write_status.
    WRITE: / 'Speed:', speed.
  ENDMETHOD.
ENDCLASS.

CLASS plane IMPLEMENTATION.
  METHOD rise.
    altitude = altitude + 1.
  ENDMETHOD.
ENDCLASS.

* Global Data

DATA: plane_ref TYPE REF TO plane,
      ship_ref TYPE REF TO ship.

* Classical Processing Blocks

START-OF-SELECTION.
  CREATE OBJECT: plane_ref,
                 ship_ref.
  CALL METHOD: plane_ref->accelerate,
               plane_ref->rise,
               plane_ref->write_status,
               ship_ref->accelerate,
               ship_ref->write_status.
```

The vehicle class contains a protected attribute speed and two public methods, accelerate and write_status. Note that we explicitly specify that vehicle inherits from object. Normally we leave the `INHERITING` addition out of such classes. We derive both the `plane` and `ship` classes from `vehicle`. In this way they inherit the attribute and the methods. As `speed` is declared in the `PROTECTED SECTION` it is also visible in the subclasses. We specialize the `plane` class with an additional attribute for the altitude and an additional method `rise` for rising. In this example the `ship` class does not contain any additional components which means that its objects do not differ from those of the `vehicle` class. As no methods are added, it does not require any implementation part.

We use the `plane_ref` and `ship_ref` reference variables to create an object of the two subclasses and to call their methods. You can see that the `accelerate` and `write_status` methods can be used in both subclasses. However, the `rise` method only exists in `plane`.

6.2.3 Visibility sections and namespaces in inheritance

In Section 5.3.2 we introduced the various visibility sections in classes. As mentioned before, a subclass adopts all the components of its superclasses. Of these, however, it can only see the public and the protected components. The private components of the superclasses are present but invisible.[3] During inheritance the visibility of a component never changes. This determines which components can be included in the visibility sections of a subclass.

- `PUBLIC`

  The public visibility section of a subclass contains all the public components of all superclasses as well as its own added public components. These components can be addressed externally through component selectors.

- `PROTECTED`

  The protected visibility section of a subclass contains all the protected components of all superclasses as well as its own added protected components. These components cannot be addressed externally through component selectors. From an external viewpoint, protected has the same meaning as private.

- `PRIVATE`

  The private visibility section of a subclass only contains its own private components. These components can only be addressed in the method implementations of the subclass.

Namespace

Consequently, all public and protected components of all classes on a path of the inheritance tree lie in a single namespace and therefore must have unique names. As private components are only visible within a class and cannot be used in subclasses, they need only have unique names within their class.

3. Note, however, that the methods inherited from the superclass do work with the private attributes of the superclass, as long as they are not redefined in a subclass.

This sounds very simple, but has far-reaching consequences. As you know, a superclass has no knowledge of its subclasses. If you therefore place any class in the class library and release it for application, you the developer cannot know which subclasses it will have after a certain time, apart from the ones you have defined. If you subsequently include new components in the private or protected area of your class and any subclass happens to contain its own component of the same name, you will make this class syntactically incorrect. The only safe way is therefore to add private components. In public classes not only the external interface but also the interface to any subclasses must therefore be kept stable.[4]

6.2.4 Method redefinition

In inheritance a subclass adopts all public and private methods of all its superclasses as its own components. When a method is called in the subclass, the method operates as it was implemented in the superclass and even works with the private attributes of the superclass. As the basic purpose of inheritance is specialization, it is possible that the method of a superclass will not behave as required in the subclass. In some cases something will need to be added to the previous implementation, in other cases the implementation will need to be changed completely. The behavior of the method for the external user should, however, remain the same as the user only sees the constant interface, not the implementation.

Instance Method

Instance methods can therefore be redefined in subclasses. To redefine a method, you must specify it again with the `METHODS` statement in its visiblity section in the declaration part of the subclass:

```
METHODS meth REDEFINITION.
```

The effect of the `REDEFINITION` addition is to reimplement the method in the implementation part of the subclass. The parameter interface of the method is not specified again and therefore always remains the same for all subclasses.[5] A redefined method in a subclass hides the corresponding method in the superclass. This applies to all object references which point to the subclass and all other subclasses which inherit from the subclass. When the method is accessed within the subclass, it is always the redefined method which is executed. Like the subclass' own methods, a redefined method accesses the private attributes of the subclass.

Pseudo reference

Through the `super` **pseudo reference** you can access the original method of the direct superclass within a redefined method of the subclass, thus getting round the fact that the superclass method is hidden by the redefined method. You always use

4. As of Release 6.10, a package concept will be introduced to the ABAP Workbench which provides a better overview of the number of subclasses.
5. Other object-oriented programming languages allow functions or methods to be overloaded. In this case you can specify your own modified parameter interface for an overridden or redefined method. ABAP Objects does not currently support this mechanism.

this reference if you want first to adopt the functionality of the superclass and then extend it. We shall now apply the method redefinition to our example in Listing 6.1. The write_status method of the vehicle class is not sufficiently specialized to be used in the subclasses, and we will therefore specialize it, as shown in Listing 6.2, by redefining it.

LISTING 6.2 Method redefinition example

```
REPORT s_method_redefinition.

...

CLASS plane DEFINITION INHERITING FROM vehicle.
  PUBLIC SECTION.
    METHODS: rise,
             write_status REDEFINITION.
  PROTECTED SECTION.
    DATA altitude TYPE i.
ENDCLASS.

CLASS ship DEFINITION INHERITING FROM vehicle.
  PUBLIC SECTION.
    METHODS write_status REDEFINITION.
ENDCLASS.

* Class Implementations

...

CLASS plane IMPLEMENTATION.
  METHOD rise.
    altitude = altitude + 1.
  ENDMETHOD.
  METHOD write_status.
    WRITE / 'Plane:'.
    CALL METHOD super->write_status.
    WRITE: / 'Altitude:', altitude.
  ENDMETHOD.
ENDCLASS.

CLASS ship IMPLEMENTATION.
  METHOD write_status.
```

```
    WRITE: / 'Ship speed:', speed.
  ENDMETHOD.
ENDCLASS.

...
```

We list the write_status method in both subclasses with the REDEFINITION addition and reimplement it in the respective implementation parts. This means that the ship class now also requires an implementation part. In the plane class we adopt the existing behavior using the super pseudo reference, but specialize the method through additional outputs. In the ship class we implement the method completely afresh without using the previous implementation, but retain its semantics.

6.2.5 Abstract classes and methods

If you simply wish to use a class as a model for subclasses and do not require any objects from this class, you can define it as an abstract class by using the ABSTRACT addition to the CLASS statement.

```
CLASS class DEFINITION ABSTRACT.
  ...
ENDCLASS.
```

ABSTRACT

You cannot create objects with CREATE OBJECT of a class defined in this way, and consequently you cannot access the instance components of the class.[6] The main purpose of abstract classes is to act as a model for subclasses. From abstract classes you can derive non-abstract classes, from which objects can be created.

Methods can also be defined as abstract. To do this, you use the ABSTRACT addition with METHODS when you declare the method. An abstract method cannot be implemented in its own class, but only in a non-abstract subclass. This is why a class which contains one or more abstract methods must also be defined overall as abstract. Otherwise, you could create an object with an addressable method but without any implementation. To implement an abstract method in a subclass, you use the normal mechanism of method redefinition and specify the REDEFINITION addition in the subclass. The only difference compared with a genuine redefinition is that the super pseudo reference cannot be used in the method.

Both non-abstract and abstract methods can be defined in an abstract class. Non-abstract methods are defined and implemented as usual. Non-abstract methods can even call abstract methods, as the names and interfaces are fully known. The behavior of the abstract method is only determined when the method is implemented in a subclass, and can therefore vary in different subclasses.

6. You can, however, use the static components of an abstract class, as these do not require an instance.

Let's consider again our example in Listing 6.1. The vehicle superclass is fairly rudimentary and so far we have not created an object from it. To prohibit this entirely, we shall define the class as abstract, as shown in Listing 6.3. In this class only the common elements of the subclasses are to be determined.

LISTING 6.3 Abstract class and method

```
REPORT s_class_abstract.

...

CLASS vehicle DEFINITION ABSTRACT.
  PUBLIC SECTION.
    METHODS: accelerate,
             write_status ABSTRACT.
  PROTECTED SECTION.
    DATA speed TYPE i.
ENDCLASS.

...

CLASS vehicle IMPLEMENTATION.
  METHOD accelerate.
    speed = speed + 1.
  ENDMETHOD.
ENDCLASS.

...

CLASS plane IMPLEMENTATION.
  METHOD rise.
    altitude = altitude + 1.
  ENDMETHOD.
  METHOD write_status.
    WRITE: / 'Plane speed:', speed.
    WRITE: / 'Altitude:', altitude.
  ENDMETHOD.
ENDCLASS.
```

Listing 6.3 shows only the differences compared with Listing 6.2. As we are redefining the write_status method in both subclasses of Listing 6.2 anyway, we have declared it as abstract in Listing 6.3 as well. Therefore it does not need to be implemented in the vehicle class. In the plane subclass from Listing 6.2 the super->write_status method therefore cannot be called any more. The subclasses as defined in Listing 6.1 can no longer inherit from vehicle since the implementation of the write_status method is completely missing here.

Design

The use of abstract classes and methods can play an important role in object-oriented design. Abstract classes provide their subclasses with a common interface and a functionality which is already implemented in part, but cannot, however, perform any suitable operations on their attributes. In a payroll system, for example, you can imagine a class which implements numerous tasks such as bank transfers, but contains the actual payroll transaction only in an abstract form. It is then the task of various subclasses to perform the correct payroll processing for the different jobs in the company.

As ABAP Objects does not support multiple inheritance, the use of abstraction through abstract classes is always restricted to the subclasses of a specific node within the inheritance tree. In Section 6.3 you will be introduced to interfaces which are another method for solving similar tasks irrespective of the position in the inheritance hierarchy.

6.2.6 Final classes and methods

As abstract classes and methods require subclasses to be defined in order to work with the classes at all, there can also be situations in which you want to protect a whole class or an individual method from uncontrolled specialization. This could be suitable, for example, if you later wish to make changes to a class without any subclasses becoming syntactically or semantically incorrect. In this context, remember our discussion about the namespace of components in inheritance in Section 6.2.3.

FINAL

For a final definition, use the FINAL addition instead of ABSTRACT in the CLASS or METHODS statements. No further subclasses can be derived from a final class. This means that a final class marks the definite end of a path in the inheritance hierarchy. A final method does not exclude subclasses, but cannot be redefined. As all methods of a final class are implicitly final, the FINAL addition must not be specified at this point. A final method cannot be abstract at the same time. A class can be final and abstract at the same time, but then only its static components can be used. Consequently, it would make no sense to declare instance components in this kind of class.

6.2.7 Static components in inheritance

So far you have only dealt with static components in the context of a single class. To use a static component you do not require instances. If instances are present, they share the same component. How does inheritance then affect static components?

Like all components, public and protected static components can only be declared once within a path of the inheritance tree. This means that a static component is not only shared by the objects of the declaring class but also by the objects of all its subclasses. It is possible to access public static components of an inheritance tree from the outside through the class component selector (=>) and all relevant class names (see Listing 6.4).

LISTING 6.4 Static attributes in inheritance

```
REPORT s_static_attributes.

* Class Declarations

CLASS c1 DEFINITION.
  PUBLIC SECTION.
    CLASS-DATA a1 TYPE string.
ENDCLASS.

CLASS c2 DEFINITION INHERITING FROM c1.
  ...
ENDCLASS.

* Classical Processing Blocks

START-OF-SELECTION.
  c2=>a1 = 'ABAP Objects'.
  WRITE c1=>a1.
```

In their methods, all objects of subclasses can access the public and protected static components of their superclasses equally. Modifications to static attributes are visible to all relevant classes or objects of the respective path in the inheritance tree. When a static attribute is addressed which belongs to a path of an inheritance tree, irrespective of the class name used in the class component selector, the class in which the attribute is declared is the one which is addressed. This affects the execution sequence of the static constructors of the respective classes.

As static components should appear just once in a path in order to be used jointly by all subclasses, static methods must not be redefined in ABAP Objects.

6.2.8 Constructors in inheritance

In Section 5.3.4 we introduced constructors as a means of initializing attributes of a class. While instance constructors can set the instance attributes of each individual object during `CREATE OBJECT`, the static constructors are responsible for the static attributes of the class before the class is accessed for the first time. As in inheritance a subclass inherits all the attributes of its superclass, the question automatically arises as to how the constructors ensure that the inherited attributes are also initialized when the subclass is used.

Instance constructors

As you know, you can declare a method with the predefined name `constructor` in the public visibility section of a class in order to use it as an instance constructor. How do instance constructors behave then in inheritance? The constructor method, like every instance method, is present in the inheritance tree, starting from the class in which it has been declared. All subclasses therefore inherit the instance constructor of their superclass.

The task of the instance `constructor` is to give an object a defined initial status. If an object of a subclass is created, the inherited instance attributes of the corresponding superclasses must also be initialized. Although an instance constructor of a subclass has access to the public and protected instance attributes of its superclasses, it does not know their private attributes. However, the private attributes of the superclasses must also be initialized, as all the non-redefined methods of the superclasses work with these attributes and expect correct values. The private attributes of the superclasses can therefore only be initialized in the respective class itself, as only here are they visible.

Redefinition

The instance constructor of a subclass therefore cannot fully initialize its superclasses, but can instruct its direct superclass to initialize itself. To ensure complete initialization of the subclass and its superclasses, the redefinition of instance constructors differs from other instance methods in the following ways:

- When an instance constructor is redefined, the `REDEFINITION` addition is not specified in the `METHODS` statement.
- The parameter interface of an instance constructor is defined in a completely new way during redefinition. The signature of the parameter interface of an instance constructor can therefore look different for each class of an inheritance tree.
- During implementation of a redefined instance constructor the instance constructor of the superclass must be called with the

  ```
  CALL METHOD super->constructor EXPORTING ...
  ```

  statement. This is the only exception to the rule that constructors cannot be called with `CALL METHOD`. Only the instance constructor which is declared in a path of the inheritance tree closest to the `object` root class does not have to make this call, as it does not inherit an instance constructor.

The redefinition of an instance constructor therefore represents a genuine redefinition which is valid for all subclasses until the next redefinition. This mechanism ensures that the instance constructor of each subclass can request individual input parameters and that initialization requests are passed up to the top of a path of the inheritance tree.

Execution

If an object of a subclass is created with CREATE OBJECT, the instance constructor of this subclass is implicitly executed. We can distinguish between the following cases:

1 If neither the subclass nor one of its superclasses has declared an instance constructor, no parameters need to be filled and of course nothing is executed.

2 If the subclass adopts the instance constructor of the superclass without redefining it, its non-optional input parameters must be filled and the instance constructor is executed.

3 If the subclass defines a completely new instance constructor or redefines it, the non-optional input parameters of the new interface must be filled, and the newly defined instance constructor is executed. If the direct superclass has an instance constructor, the latter is called with CALL METHOD super->constructor, and its non-optional input parameters have to be filled. The instance constructor of the superclass can itself have been defined completely anew or redefined or adopted unchanged by other superclasses.

When an instance constructor is called, be it implicitly with CREATE OBJECT or explicitly with METHOD super->constructor, the constructor can be defined either in the respective class itself or in a superclass. The latter is an important general feature when working with inheritance. When using a subclass you must always take the definition of the superclasses into account. When you create a class which at first sight does not contain an instance constructor, a syntax error may be triggered if an instance constructor is inherited from the superclass which requires an actual parameter. If you use the **pattern** function of the ABAP Editor, the correct statement CREATE OBJECT will always be generated (see Figure 2.40).

Three phase model

The execution of a redefined instance constructor of a subclass can be split into three phases which we have illustrated in Listing 6.5 with comment lines.

LISTING 6.5 Three-phase model of an instance constructor

```
METHOD constructor.
  " Phase 1:
  " Access to static attributes only
  ...
  " Phase 2: Call of superclass constructor
  CALL METHOD super->constructor EXPORTING ...
  " Phase 3:
  " Access to instance attributes also
  ...
ENDMETHOD.
```

In the individual phases the instance constructor performs the following tasks:

- Phase 1

  At this stage the preparations for calling the instance constructor of the superclass are made, and actual parameters are determined for its interface. Only local data or static attributes can be addressed at this stage, not instance attributes of the class. The constructor therefore behaves initially like a static method.

- Phase 2

  At this stage the instance constructor of the superclass is called with `CALL METHOD super->constructor`.

- Phase 3

  Executes the statements after the instance constructor of the superclass has been called. Now you can access the instance attributes of the class since the inherited public and protected attributes of the superclasses are now correctly initialized. These values can be used to make the necessary initializations for the class's own instance attributes.

So when a subclass is instantiated, a nested call of all the differently defined instance constructors takes place from the subclass to the superclasses, where the instance attributes of the highest superclass can only be addressed at the deepest nesting level, i.e. the highest superclass. When processing returns to the constructors of the lower-level subclasses, their instance attributes can then be addressed successively.

If you have not had any experience with concepts similar to instance constructors, this may all appear somewhat confusing. We have therefore shown how instance constructors can be applied by means of a simple example in Listing 6.6.

LISTING 6.6 Instance constructors in inheritance

```
REPORT s_inheritance_constructors.

* Class Declarations

CLASS vessel DEFINITION.
  PUBLIC SECTION.
    METHODS constructor IMPORTING i_name TYPE string.
  PROTECTED SECTION.
    DATA name TYPE string.
ENDCLASS.

CLASS ship DEFINITION INHERITING FROM vessel.
  ...
ENDCLASS.
```

```
CLASS motorship DEFINITION INHERITING FROM ship.
  PUBLIC SECTION.
    METHODS constructor IMPORTING i_name TYPE string
                                  i_fuelamount TYPE i.
  PRIVATE SECTION.
    DATA fuelamount TYPE i.
ENDCLASS.

* Class Implementations

CLASS vessel IMPLEMENTATION.
  METHOD constructor.
    name = i_name.
  ENDMETHOD.
ENDCLASS.

CLASS motorship IMPLEMENTATION.
  METHOD constructor.
    CALL METHOD super->constructor
         EXPORTING i_name = i_name.
    fuelamount = i_fuelamount.
  ENDMETHOD.
ENDCLASS.

* Global Data

DATA: o_vessel     TYPE REF TO vessel,
      o_ship       TYPE REF TO ship,
      o_motorship  TYPE REF TO motorship.

* Classical Processing Blocks

START-OF-SELECTION.
  CREATE OBJECT: o_vessel    EXPORTING i_name = 'Vincent',
                 o_ship      EXPORTING i_name = 'Mia',
                 o_motorship EXPORTING i_name = 'Jules'
                                       i_fuelamount = 12000.
```

This example shows three successive classes of the inheritance hierarchy. The vessel class has an instance constructor with an input parameter. From vessel we derive the class ship, which adopts the instance constructor unchanged. From ship we derive motorship. This class redefines the instance constructor with two input parameters.

We create an object from each of the classes and thereby fill the parameter interface of the constructors with actual parameters. The constructors are called in the following manner:

- The instance constructor of the object o_vessel is called during CREATE OBJECT and initializes an attribute using the passed actual parameter.
- The object o_ship is initialized during CREATE OBJECT via the same instance constructor as o_vessel, as its class does not redefine the instance constructor.
- The object o_motorship is initialized through its own instance constructor. In it the instance constructor of the direct superclass must be called via super->constructor. This is again the one inherited from vessel, and its parameter interface is filled.

You can follow the behavior of the program directly if you run it line by line in the ABAP Debugger.

Static constructors

In each class a static constructor with the predefined name class_constructor can be declared. The same applies in principle for redefining static constructors as well as for instance constructors. Declaring a static constructor in a subclass redefines, so to speak, the static constructor of its superclass for the requirements of the subclass. The REDEFINITION addition is not specified here either. In contrast to instance constructors, a static constructor does not have to call the static constructor of its superclass explicitly. Instead the runtime environment automatically ensures that the static constructors are called in the right order.

The first time a subclass is addressed in a program, its static constructor is executed. However, the previous static constructors of the entire inheritance tree must have been executed beforehand. As a static constructor should only be called once during program execution, the first time the subclass is addressed the system searches for the next highest superclass whose static constructor has not yet been executed. Then this static constructor is executed first, followed by the constructors of all subclasses until the addressed subclass is reached. In a subclass you can therefore always assume that the static attributes of the superclasses have been correctly initialized.

6.2.9 Object references in inheritance

As you learned in Section 5.3.3, object references are stored in reference variables and are used for accessing objects. The user of an object addresses it through a reference variable pointing to the object and chooses the visible object components using the object component selector. So far, the procedure has been quite plausible and is summarized again in the following lines:

```
DATA oref TYPE REF TO class.
...
CREATE OBJECT oref.
...
... oref->...
```

You declare a reference variable with reference to the class from which you want to create an object, create the object, and access the public components. The public components of the class are therefore its interface to the outside.

Interface

Let's consider this now from an inheritance perspective. As each subclass inherits all components of its superclass in the same visiblity section, the public visibility section of a subclass is always made up of the public visibility sections of its superclasses. Conversely, from a superclass perspective its public visibility section remains unaffected in each of its subclasses, no matter how far you go down the inheritance tree.

Consequently there is no reason for a user who can work with a superclass from the outside not to access one of its subclasses in the same way. The corresponding part of the interface is completely identical. This aspect opens up a whole new dimension of programming which, although it requires a certain amount of explanation, is one of the premises of polymorphism without whose possibilities no object-oriented language would be complete.

From a technical viewpoint, everything we have said boils down to the simple fact that you can use reference variables which have been declared with reference to a superclass to point to the objects of all the subclasses of this superclass. Expressed in code lines, this can be represented as follows:

```
DATA: o_super TYPE REF TO superclass,
      o_sub   TYPE REF TO subclass.
...
CREATE OBJECT o_sub.
o_super = o_sub.
```

If subclass is a subclass of superclass, the reference to the object of the subclass in o_sub can be assigned to the reference variable o_super. ABAP Objects even spares you from having to make the assignment. The CREATE OBJECT statement has a TYPE addition with which you can directly specify the class from which the object is to be created:

```
DATA o_super TYPE REF TO superclass.
...
CREATE OBJECT o_super TYPE subclass.
```

The statement creates an object of the subclass class to which the reference variable o_super is pointing.[7] This way you can create objects of all subclasses of a superclass

7. The superclass class can even be abstract in these situations. Reference variables which refer to abstract classes can therefore be useful even if there are no objects of the class.

(superclass) without having to create reference variables for the subclasses. In the previously mentioned standard form of the CREATE OBJECT statement, the reference variable type is implicitly used to determine the object class.

We now need to ask what can be done with objects to which reference variables of the type of their superclass are pointing. From what we have said before, it should be clear that you can only ever access those components of the object which are already known to the superclass. To describe this in more detail, we shall now introduce the concepts of **static** and **dynamic types**.

Static and dynamic type of reference variables

In Section 5.3.3 we described the type of a reference variable which is created with the

```
DATA oref TYPE REF TO class.
```

statement as a "pointer to an object of the class (class)." To be more precise, we should now call the type a "pointer to an object of the class (class) or one of its subclasses." At any rate this type, which we define with the DATA statement during variable declaration, is fixed throughout the entire program runtime and cannot be changed. We refer to it as the **static type** of the reference variable.

The static type expresses the class to which the object must belong, in order for the reference variable to point to it. However, we have just learned that these classes can vary. To express this, we use the **dynamic type**. The dynamic type of a reference variable is the class of the object to which the reference variable is pointing at any given moment. The dynamic type can therefore change during program runtime.[8] While we were working without inheritance, the static and dynamic types were always the same. After the statement:

```
CREATE OBJECT oref.
```

both the dynamic type and the static type of oref are the class (class) with which oref was declared. In inheritance the dynamic and static types can vary. After the statement:

```
CREATE OBJECT o_super TYPE subclass.
```

the dynamic type of o_super is the subclass class or "actual pointer to an object of the subclass class." The static type remains the superclass class or "can point to an object of the superclass class or one of its subclasses." A dynamic type which differs from the static type can also be created by assignments between reference variables, as already demonstrated. We illustrate this again in Figure 6.2.

We have also shown in Figure 6.2 which components the individual reference variables can access. The reference variables of the superclass static type can only be used

8. You can check the dynamic type of a reference variable at any time in the ABAP Debugger by viewing its value. The name of the class of the current object appears here.

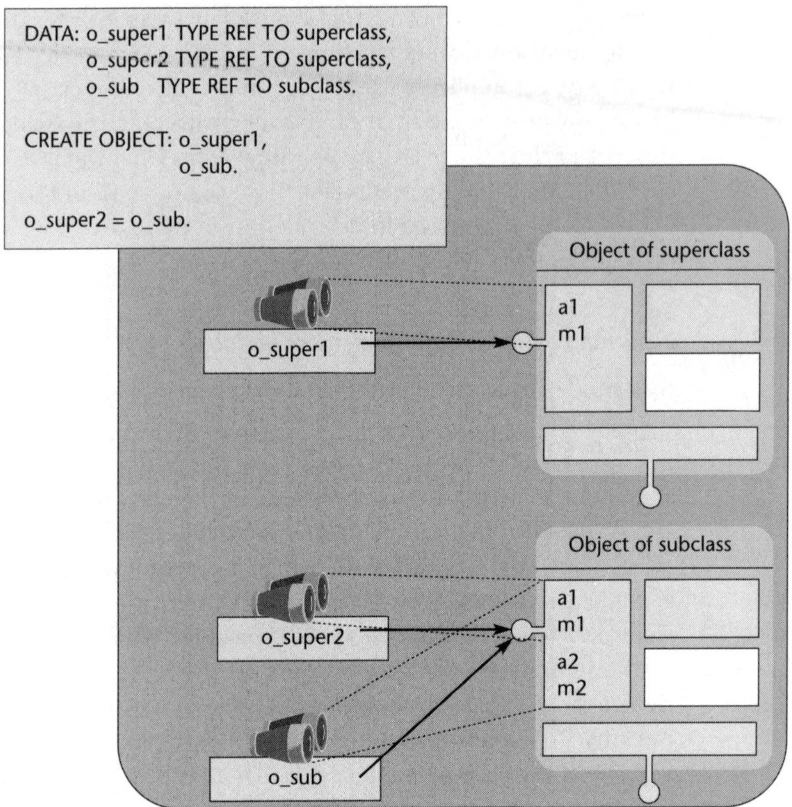
DATA: o_super1 TYPE REF TO superclass,
o_super2 TYPE REF TO superclass,
o_sub TYPE REF TO subclass.
CREATE OBJECT: o_super1,
o_sub.
o_super2 = o_sub.
Object of superclass
a1
m1
o_super1
Object of subclass
a1
m1
a2
m2
o_super2
o_sub

FIGURE 6.2 Static and dynamic types of reference variables

to access components which are defined on the level of the static type, i.e. in the superclass class. A reference with the static type of a superclass can therefore contain the address of an object of a subclass. However, it can only address components which already exist in the class determining their static type.

User's view

The static type therefore expresses the user's view of an object. The user, i.e. an ABAP program or a procedure, works with a reference variable and knows the static type of this variable. By knowing the static variable the user (and also the syntax check) knows which components are guaranteed to be in the objects and whether it can access them. However, the user does not know the dynamic type of the reference variable as this is only created at runtime and often depends on the context. The user therefore does not know which components might additionally be present (apart from the statically known components) and cannot statically address them.

Basic rule

It follows from what we have said that the dynamic type of a reference variable in the inheritance tree is either the same as the static type or one of its subclasses. The general rule is as follows:

If the static and dynamic types of a reference variable are different, the static type is always more general than the dynamic type.

The position of the static type in the inheritance tree defines the user's view of an object in the sense that the number of visible components of an object is more limited, the nearer the static type is to the node. The extreme case is a reference variable which you declare with the object static type using the statement:

```
DATA oref TYPE REF TO object.
```

The static type is the root class of the inheritance tree and does not know any components. This kind of reference variable can point to objects of **all** classes in ABAP Objects but cannot address any components.[9]

Redefinition

The fact that the dynamic and static types can be different becomes particularly interesting when methods are redefined in subclasses. The user calls the method of an object via a reference variable, whereby the dynamic type determines the form of method implementation to be actually carried out. This is the technical basis of polymorphism which we will explore in more detail in Section 6.2.10. First we will look at the consequences of what we have said above for assignments between reference variables.

Assigning reference variables

In our previous examples we often assigned reference variables to each other. An assignment between reference variables implies the passing of the object reference in the source variable to a target variable. In this context, nothing more than the address of an object in the memory is passed. After the assignment, both reference variables point to the same object. According to our previous definition of dynamic types, this simply means that the target variable takes on the dynamic type of the source variable.

As according to our above rule, the static type of a reference variable must always be the same or more general than the dynamic type; not all kinds of assignment are possible. Instead the basic rule applies that the static type of the target variable must be the same or more general than the dynamic type of the source variable.[10] In inheritance this means that the dynamic type of the source variable must be the same class or subclass of the static type of the target variable.

Prior to an assignment the system must check that this rule has been adhered to. We can distinguish between two cases here:

- Assignments in which it is possible to check that rule during the syntax check.
- Assignments in which the check can only be performed during runtime.

9. What we say about component access actually only applies to static access. Using a dynamic method call you can access existing components even via object type reference variables.
10. This applies, of course, to all kinds if assignment between reference variables which are possible within ABAP. This includes passing actual parameters to procedures and inserting into internal tables.

Narrowing cast

Our rule for assignments between reference variables is, of course, always satisfied when the static type of the target variable is more general than the static type of the source variable, as the dynamic type of the source variable at runtime can only be more specialized than its static type. The validity of such an assignment can be determined during the syntax check, as only static types are involved here. All assignments we have so far performed in this and in previous chapters satisfy this rule.

We describe such assignments as a **narrowing cast** or **up cast**. The term narrowing cast expresses that you are changing from a more specialized view to a more general view. The target variable knows only the same or fewer components than the source variable. The term up cast expresses that the static type of the target variable can only change to higher nodes from the static type of the source variable in the inheritance tree, but not vice versa. The following lines show the most general narrowing cast which is possible in ABAP Objects:

```
DATA: o_ref1 TYPE REF TO object.
      o_ref2 TYPE REF TO class.
...
o_ref1 = o_ref2.
```

You can assign any reference variable to one whose static type is the object root class. Such reference variables can therefore act as containers for references to any object, but do not permit static access to its components.

Widening cast

In most cases the narrowing cast is fully sufficient and the user commonly accesses the objects of subclasses through the interface of a superclass. We shall shortly develop this further when discussing polymorphism. However, there can be situations in which you want to change from a less detailed view to a more detailed one. For assignments this means that the static type of the target variable is more specialized than the static type of the source variable. We term such assignments, in contrast to narrowing cast, as **widening cast** or also as **down cast**.

Of course, for widening cast the basic rule applies that irrespective of the static type of the source variable, the static type of the target variable must be more general or the same as the dynamic type of the source variable. Or to put it differently: the object to which the source variable is referring must also contain all the components which the target variable wishes to see. However, as the actual dynamic type of a source variable is statically unknown, a static check is impossible. To express this, ABAP outputs an error message during the syntax check of the following assignment, for example:

```
DATA: o_ref1 TYPE REF TO object.
      o_ref2 TYPE REF TO class.
...
o_ref2 = o_ref1.
```

The o_ref1 reference variable can contain references to the objects of all the classes at runtime and it cannot be statically determined whether o_ref1 is actually pointing to an object of the class (class) or one of its subclasses. This check can only take place at runtime immediately before the assignment is executed. You must specifically instruct ABAP to bypass the static check by using the special casting operator "?=" instead of the normal assignment operator (=).[11] The following lines therefore will not result in a syntax error.

```
DATA: o_ref1 TYPE REF TO object.
      o_ref2 TYPE REF TO class.
...
o_ref2 ?= o_ref1.
```

If at runtime the dynamic type o_ref1 is more specialized than the static type of o_ref2, the assignment will take place. Otherwise a catchable runtime error move_cast_error occurs, which you can catch between CATCH and ENDCATCH. To help us understand that, we shall consider Listing 6.7 as a typical example of using a widening cast: a method can import general object references and tries to handle them in a specialized manner.

LISTING 6.7 Widening cast

```
REPORT s_widening_cast.

* Class declarations

CLASS vehicle DEFINITION.
  ...
ENDCLASS.
CLASS plane DEFINITION INHERITING FROM vehicle.
  ...
ENDCLASS.

CLASS ship DEFINITION INHERITING FROM vehicle.
  ...
ENDCLASS.

CLASS vehicle_handler DEFINITION.
  PUBLIC SECTION.
    METHODS handle_vehicle
            IMPORTING i_ref TYPE REF TO object.
ENDCLASS.

* Class implementations
```

11. If you are working with the MOVE ... TO statement instead of the assignment operator (=) you must replace TO with ?TO accordingly.

```
CLASS vehicle_handler IMPLEMENTATION.
  METHOD handle_vehicle.
    DATA: vehicle_ref TYPE REF TO vehicle,
          plane_ref   TYPE REF TO plane,
          ship_ref    TYPE REF TO ship.
    CATCH SYSTEM-EXCEPTIONS move_cast_error = 4.
      vehicle_ref ?= i_ref.
    ENDCATCH.
    IF sy-subrc = 0.
      WRITE / 'Working with vehicle'.
    ELSE.
      WRITE / 'This is not a vehicle!'.
      EXIT.
    ENDIF.
    CATCH SYSTEM-EXCEPTIONS move_cast_error = 4.
      plane_ref ?= i_ref.
    ENDCATCH.
    IF sy-subrc = 0.
      WRITE / 'Working with plane'.
    ENDIF.
    CATCH SYSTEM-EXCEPTIONS move_cast_error = 4.
      ship_ref ?= i_ref.
    ENDCATCH.
    IF sy-subrc = 0.
      WRITE / 'Working with ship'.
    ENDIF.
  ENDMETHOD.
ENDCLASS.

* Global Data

DATA: handler   TYPE REF TO vehicle_handler,
      vehicle_1 TYPE REF TO vehicle,
      vehicle_2 LIKE vehicle_1.

* Classical Processing Blocks

START-OF-SELECTION
  CREATE OBJECT: handler,
                 vehicle_1 TYPE plane,
                 vehicle_2 TYPE ship.
```

```
CALL METHOD: handler->handle_vehicle
               EXPORTING i_ref = handler,
             handler->handle_vehicle
               EXPORTING i_ref = vehicle_1,
             handler->handle_vehicle
               EXPORTING i_ref = vehicle_2.
```

In this example, we have again defined a class vehicle with two subclasses, plane and ship. In addition we have created a class, vehicle_handler, which is to work with individual vehicles in its handle_vehicle method. To do this, the method has an input parameter of the type "pointer to object." The formal parameter is therefore statically typed with the object class and accepts all object references. In the method, however, we shall access vehicles on an individual basis. To do this, we create specialized reference variables vehicle_ref, plane_ref, and ship_ref. Using combinations from widening casts and the CATCH statement we check the dynamic type of the passed actual parameter and, depending on the result, work with the special reference variables in a targeted manner. We have abbreviated the latter in this case solely through various WRITE outputs. If no reference to a vehicle has been passed, the method is exited with EXIT.

When the handle_vehicle method is called, a type-specific actual parameter must be passed. The type check during parameter passing corresponds to a narrowing cast. This means that in our case reference variables of any static type can be passed. Of course, it would also have been possible to type the formal parameter straight away with TYPE REF TO vehicle, so that only actual parameters of the vehicle static type or one of the subclasses could be passed. You can try it out.

In Listing 6.7 we implicitly perform narrowing casts in the CREATE OBJECT statement by creating objects of the plane and ship classes with object reference variables of the static type of the vehicle superclass. We then call the handle_vehicle method with various actual parameters. The first actual parameter is not recognized as a vehicle, but the other two are handled according to their dynamic type.

6.2.10 Polymorphism through inheritance

We have now largely concluded our introduction to the technical basis of the concept of inheritance in ABAP Objects. We can now finally turn our attention to the subject of polymorphism. Polymorphism (from the Greek for "many forms") is regarded by many as one of the most important concepts of object-orientation. However, polymorphism is often defined in quite vague terms in object-orientation literature. A typical definition is [RUM93]:

> **Polymorphism means that the same operation can behave differently in different classes.**

If you now consider everything you have learned so far about object-orientation, you might rightly ask what the word "operation" has to do here. If we merely replaced it with "method," polymorphism would be nothing of particular importance. You can declare a method with the same name in several independent classes and implement it there in different ways. For a user, however, calling methods of the same name entails completely different operations, because the user executes the methods through different calls (see Listing 6.8).

LISTING 6.8 This is not polymorphism

```
CLASS c1 DEFINITION.
  PUBLIC SECTION.
    METHODS meth.
ENDCLASS.
...

CLASS c2 DEFINITION.
  PUBLIC SECTION.
    METHODS meth.
ENDCLASS.
...
DATA: o1 TYPE REF TO c1,
      o2 TYPE REF TO c2.
...
CREATE OBJECT: o1, o2.
...
CALL METHOD: o1->meth,
             o2->meth.
```

True polymorphism only occurs when a user executes the same operations and the objects addressed behave differently. But how can objects which are addressed in the same way behave differently? After all, each object behaves exactly as defined in its class. Consider our extensive discussions on reference variables in Section 6.2.9: If you address an object via a reference variable, its behavior is uniquely determined by the dynamic type of the reference variables, but the static type of the reference variables does not have to be the same as the dynamic type. The user can therefore address objects of different classes through a single reference variable.

Redefinition

If in inheritance the static and dynamic types are different, the dynamic type is one of the subclasses of the static type. So how do you create different behavior in subclasses than superclasses? The answer can be found in Section 6.2.4: by redefining methods.

LISTING 6.9 Polymorphism through inheritance

```
CLASS c1 DEFINITION.
  PUBLIC SECTION.
    METHODS meth.
ENDCLASS.
...
CLASS c2 DEFINITION INHERITING FROM c1.
  PUBLIC SECTION.
    METHODS meth REDEFINITION.
ENDCLASS.
...
DATA o1 TYPE REF TO c1.
...
CREATE OBJECT o1 TYPE c1.
CALL METHOD o1->meth.
...
CREATE OBJECT o1 TYPE c2.
CALL METHOD o1->meth.
```

Listing 6.9 shows an identical method call which results in different behavior depending on the method implementation. If an object is instructed by a reference variable to execute a certain method, the dynamic type determines which implementation will be executed. The runtime environment always searches the inheritance tree, starting from the dynamic type of the reference variable, from bottom to top, looking for the most specialized method implementation.

We have therefore determined that polymorphism describes different behavior of objects from a user's perspective, and we can now offer a more precise definition:

Definition

Polymorphism means being able to address differently implemented methods, which belong to different objects of different classes, with the same name via the same interface.

Therefore it is never the objects themselves which behave polymorphically, but rather the reference variables which can take different dynamic types. In inheritance, polymorphic behavior can only be achieved by redefining methods in subclasses, as we have shown. In Section 6.3 you will encounter interfaces as the second basis of polymorphism in ABAP Objects.

However, at this point we must ask what is the point of having different implementations for a single method? You have seen that in a redefined method, although you have to adopt the entire interface of the inherited method unchanged, no syntactical restrictions apply to the implementation of the source code. You could program whatever you want in the method. But what about the user accessing an object via a reference variable? In the most general case the user knows the static type of the reference variable but not the dynamic type. If, for example, the user is a procedure and is working with an object reference which has been passed to it as an actual parameter, it can point to all the subclasses of the static type of the formal parameter without the procedure knowing that, and the methods can be implemented differently in the different subclasses. If a method were now to behave in a completely unpredictable manner for each call, it would be completely unusable. Polymorphism would then do more harm than good.

Semantics

A user should therefore always be able to expect from a method the behavior which is documented when the method is declared. Or in other words:

> **It must be possible to use subclasses via the interfaces inherited from the superclasses in such a way that the user cannot tell the difference.**[12]

From a technical viewpoint, a user must be able to use a static type independently of the dynamic type. This results in strict semantic rules on how a redefined method can be implemented in a subclass:

- The redefinition must contain the semantics of the previous implementation. It is useful to call it via the super pseudo reference.
- The redefinition must only be used for specialization.
- The other inherited components (attributes and events) must only be used in the sense intended in the superclass.

Only by following these rules does polymorphism become one of the main strengths of inheritance: users can handle different classes consistently, irrespective of their implementation. We shall now consider this using our vehicle example.

Example of polymorphism through inheritance

We shall define a general class for ships which contains a method for calculating the range. The range of different ships depends on various parameters, so we have to implement different methods in the corresponding subclasses. The program we will now develop also acts as the final example of inheritance, as it contains almost all of the previously discussed elements.

We shall start our example by defining a base class. In Listing 6.10 we define an abstract class ship which has a non-abstract method for determining the name of a ship.

LISTING 6.10 An abstract superclass ship

```
REPORT s_polymorphism_via_inheritance.

* Class Declarations

CLASS ship DEFINITION ABSTRACT.
```

12. This rule is known in object-orientation as the Liskov Substitution Principle (LSP) [LIS88]

```
  PUBLIC SECTION.
    METHODS: get_max_range ABSTRACT
                RETURNING VALUE(r_range) TYPE f,
             get_name
                RETURNING VALUE(r_name) TYPE string.
  PROTECTED SECTION.
    DATA name TYPE string.
ENDCLASS.

* Class Implementations

CLASS ship IMPLEMENTATION.
  METHOD get_name.
    r_name = name.
  ENDMETHOD.
ENDCLASS.
```

To begin with, we define the method get_max_range for calculating the range as an abstract method, as implementing it would not be suitable at this stage. This is why the entire ship class had to be abstract. It is important, however, to specify the parameter interface and the semantics of the method at this stage. Each class that wishes to inherit from ship has to fill the return value for the range, r_range, with a suitable value.

Next, we want to form two different subclasses of ship. We shall start in Listing 6.11 with the class motorship.

LISTING 6.11 A subclass motorship

```
CLASS motorship DEFINITION INHERITING FROM ship.
  PUBLIC SECTION.
    METHODS: constructor IMPORTING
                VALUE(i_name) TYPE string
                VALUE(i_fuel_consumption) TYPE f
                VALUE(i_fuel_amount) TYPE f,
             get_max_range REDEFINITION.
  PROTECTED SECTION.
    DATA: fuel_consumption TYPE f,
          fuel_amount TYPE f.
ENDCLASS.

CLASS motorship IMPLEMENTATION.
  METHOD constructor.
    name = i_name.
    fuel_consumption = i_fuel_consumption.
    fuel_amount = i_fuel_amount.
```

```
  ENDMETHOD.
  METHOD get_max_range.
    r_range = fuel_amount / fuel_consumption.
  ENDMETHOD.
ENDCLASS.
```

In this class we define an explicit instance constructor so that we can supply the objects of this class with the necessary initial values. We also redefine or implement the method get_max_range to determine the range of the motor ship. The range depends on the average fuel consumption and supply.

Finally, on the same hierarchy level as motorship we define another class, sailingship, in Listing 6.12.

LISTING 6.12 A subclass sailingship

```
CLASS sailingship DEFINITION INHERITING FROM ship.
  PUBLIC SECTION.
    METHODS: constructor IMPORTING
                VALUE(i_name) TYPE string
                VALUE(i_range_per_wind_speed) TYPE f
                VALUE(i_wind_speed) TYPE f
                VALUE(i_wind_duration) TYPE f,
             get_max_range REDEFINITION.
  PROTECTED SECTION.
    DATA: range_per_wind_speed TYPE f,
          wind_speed TYPE f,
          wind_duration TYPE f.
ENDCLASS.

CLASS sailingship IMPLEMENTATION.
  METHOD constructor.
    name = i_name.
    range_per_wind_speed = i_range_per_wind_speed.
    wind_speed = i_wind_speed.
    wind_duration = i_wind_duration.
  ENDMETHOD.
  METHOD get_max_range.
    r_range = wind_speed /
             range_per_wind_speed * wind_duration.
  ENDMETHOD.
ENDCLASS.
```

This class also has an instance constructor and also redefines the method for determining the maximum range. For calculating with a sailing ship we require, of course, completely different parameters than with a motorship. In this case the range depends on the wind speed, the distance covered during a specific wind speed, and the likely duration of the wind speed.

We have now finished defining the classes of our example and shall turn to a user of these classes in Listing 6.13. With our previous local classes, possible applications can only be defined in the same ABAP program. Remember, though, that we could also define the above classes globally. In this case, the source code of class definitions and users will not be in the same program.

LISTING 6.13 Applying polymorphic methods

```
* Global Data

DATA: o_ship TYPE REF TO ship,
      ship_tab TYPE TABLE OF REF TO ship.
      name TYPE string,
      range TYPE f.

* Classical Processing Blocks

START-OF-SELECTION.
  CREATE OBJECT o_ship TYPE motorship
         EXPORTING i_name = 'Motor Ship Wanda'
                   i_fuel_consumption = '0.2'
                   i_fuel_amount = 80.
  APPEND o_ship TO ship_tab.

  CREATE OBJECT o_ship TYPE sailingship
         EXPORTING i_name = 'Sailing Ship Black Magic'
                   i_range_per_wind_speed = 25
                   i_wind_speed = 60
                   i_wind_duration = 5.
  APPEND o_ship TO ship_tab.

  LOOP AT ship_tab INTO o_ship.
    name = o_ship->get_name( ).
    range = o_ship->get_max_range( ).
    WRITE: / 'Range of', name, 'is',
             range EXPONENT 0 DECIMALS 2, 'Miles'.
  ENDLOOP.
```

We declare an individual reference variable with the static type ship. We also declare an internal table with the very same row type. In this table we will store the object references of different objects. Remember though that the ship class is abstract. Our object references therefore can never point to objects of the ship class itself, only to objects of the subclasses. In this kind of situation, static and dynamic types are always different. We will shortly encounter this again with interfaces.

We create two objects, one of the motorship class and one of the sailingship class, and attach the corresponding references to the internal table shiptab. Remember that we are using a reference variable with the static type of the superclass. A narrowing cast takes place in the CREATE OBJECT statement. Nevertheless, we naturally have to fill the input parameters of the instance constructor to fit the created objects of the subclasses.

After this preliminary work we fully exploit the polymorphic behavior of the references in our internal table. We read the shiptab table in a loop into the reference variable o_ship and use it to call the method get_max_range in every loop pass. Although the static type is the ship class, the dynamic type ensures that the correct method is executed. In the loop we do not need to know the reference we are working with, but we can be sure that the correct implementation is always addressed, and this is the strength of polymorphic behavior.

Calling the get_name method is, however, not polymorphic. This method has already been implemented in the superclass and has not been redefined by a subclass. In this case the same method implementation is always carried out.

Benefit

Imagine now you could not access different method implementations with the same reference variable in our example. In this case it would not be possible to treat different ship types in the same way with a single-column internal table. You would have to create a separate column for each ship type and determine in the loop which ship type should be addressed. If you now also consider that we generally want to work with more than two subclasses and that these in turn can have subclasses, you realize the enormous maintenance effort that would be involved with your code. The above solution would at least remain syntactically correct even if more ship classes occurred. To obtain useful results, however, each new subclass must implement the method of the superclass correctly not only from a syntactical but also a semantic viewpoint.

The major benefit of polymorphism is therefore that you can write extremely generic programs which will remain stable when faced with new requirements. The ability to dispense with control structures such as CASE / ENDCASE or IF / ELSE / ENDIF, in order to control the dynamic types of the reference variables separately, can dramatically improve the maintainability of your programs (**case-less programming**). At the very least, from the user's perspective the source codes are structured more simply and are easier to read.

6.3 INTERFACES

6.3.1 Basic principles

So far in our consideration of ABAP Objects, classes have been the sole basis for defining and using objects. Classes form, on the one hand, the only model for creating objects and, on the other, define how a user can work with objects. The former is achieved by specifying a class after the TYPE addition to the CREATE OBJECT statement and the latter by specifying a class when declaring a reference variable. As we saw in the last section, this dual role of a class is reflected in the dynamic and static reference types.

The only relevant part of a class for users is its public interface which is built up of the components of its public visibility section. All other components are irrelevant to the users. As we saw in the last section, it can even be irrelevant to the users which class they are actually working with, because if the method redefinition is correctly used they can rely only on the interface statically known to them. This aspect becomes especially clear when using abstract methods in abstract classes. Such classes serve mainly to define interfaces which can only be used with objects of subclasses.

As ABAP Objects does not support multiple inheritance, the use of abstract classes for defining interfaces is restricted to its subclasses. After everything we have learned about the benefits of polymorphism, it would be thoroughly desirable to be able to define universally valid interfaces which can be used with equal validity in all classes.

Interface

In order to permit the same access to different classes irrespective of inheritance, ABAP Objects provides **interfaces**. An interface describes the public visibility section of a given class without itself implementing functionality. Like classes, interfaces are defined either locally in an ABAP program or globally in the class library as independent constructs. Along with classes they therefore represent the second cornerstone for implementing object-oriented language elements in ABAP Objects.

As interfaces do not implement their own functionality, no objects can be created from them, in a similar way to abstract classes. Instead, interfaces are added to or implemented in classes. If a class implements an interface, it can be addressed via the interface. Interface reference variables are used for this. These can point to objects of any class which implements the corresponding interface. As many classes can implement the same interface and its objects therefore can be addressed through a single interface reference variable, interfaces form the second basis of polymorphism in ABAP Objects, alongside inheritance.

Protocol

Interfaces form a looser connection between a class and a user than we have seen to date, since they provide an additional access level (protocol). This access level might even be specified by the user by defining an interface with all the functions required. Every class wishing to provide these functions then implements the interface and makes the functionality available. Conversely, a class can, of course, make its public visibility section available to the user as an interface either in full or in part and thereby decouple it from the actual class definition. This can have a positive effect on the maintenance of a class.

6.3.2 Definition of interfaces

Interfaces are independent constructs which expand the public visibility sections of classes. As with classes, we shall first discuss only the definition of local interfaces. The tool for defining global classes and interfaces will be introduced in Section 6.5. The syntax for defining a local interface is very straightforward:

```
INTERFACE  intf.
  DATA ...
  CLASS-DATA ...
  METHODS ...
  CLASS-METHODS ...
  EVENTS ...
  CLASS-EVENTS ...
ENDINTERFACE.
```

Defining an interface corresponds in principle to the declaration part of a class; instead of CLASS–ENDCLASS we simply use INTERFACE–ENDINTERFACE. Interfaces can contain exactly the same kind of components as classes. Unlike classes, however, interfaces do not need to be divided into various visibility sections, as interface components are always public.

Abstraction

Interfaces do not have an implementation part and the DEFINITION addition is not required. Defining an interface is similar to defining an abstract class which only contains abstract methods. In interfaces, methods are also defined along with their parameter interface; however, they are not implemented. In the same way that subclasses of abstract classes implement their abstract methods, all classes that wish to use an interface must implement its methods.[13]

6.3.3 Implementing interfaces in classes

Each class can implement one or more interfaces. The only requirement for implementing an interface is that the interface is known to the implementing class. It must therefore be defined locally in the same program or globally in the class library. The syntax for implementing interfaces is:

```
CLASS class DEFINITION.
  PUBLIC SECTION.
    ...
```

13. The similarity does not extend beyond instance methods, however. Static methods can also be defined in interfaces without implementation. This is not possible in abstract classes, as static methods cannot be redefined.

```
    INTERFACES: intf1, intf2 ...
  ...
ENDCLASS.
```

Interface component

Interfaces are incorporated solely in the public visibility section of a class through the INTERFACES statement. This means that the public visibility section of the class is expanded by the interface components. Each comp component of an implemented interface (intf) becomes a full component of the class and is identified within the class by the name intf~comp. A class can therefore have a component of the same name, or various implemented interfaces can contain components of the same name. They all lie within one namespace and are differentiated within the class by various intf~ prefixes. We therefore call the "~" sign the **interface component selector**.

The class must implement all the methods of all incorporated interfaces in its implementation part:[14]

```
CLASS class IMPLEMENTATION.
  ...
  METHOD intf1~...
    ...
  ENDMETHOD.
  ...
  METHOD intf2~...
    ...
  ENDMETHOD.
  ...
ENDCLASS.
```

Figure 6.3 provides an overview of an interface implementation.

The left-hand area of Figure 6.3 shows the definition of a local interface i1 as well as the declaration and implementation part of a local class c1, which implements interface i1 in its public section. Implementation in the other visibility sections is not possible. The interface method i1~m1 is implemented in the implementation part of the class.

The right-hand area illustrates the class structure, consisting of components of the corresponding visibility section and the implementation of the methods. The interface components expand the public visibility section of the class. All users have access to the class-specific public components and the interface components. You can also see that there is no naming conflict between the class component a1 and the interface component of the same name, as the latter is addressed via i1~a1.

If a class solely incorporates interfaces instead of declaring its own components in its public visibility sections, the entire public visibility section of the class is defined

14. This applies without exception. Interface methods cannot be marked as abstract in ABAP Objects because interfaces with abstract methods could only be implemented in abstract classes. Although this is possible in Java, ABAP Objects currently only supports universal interfaces.

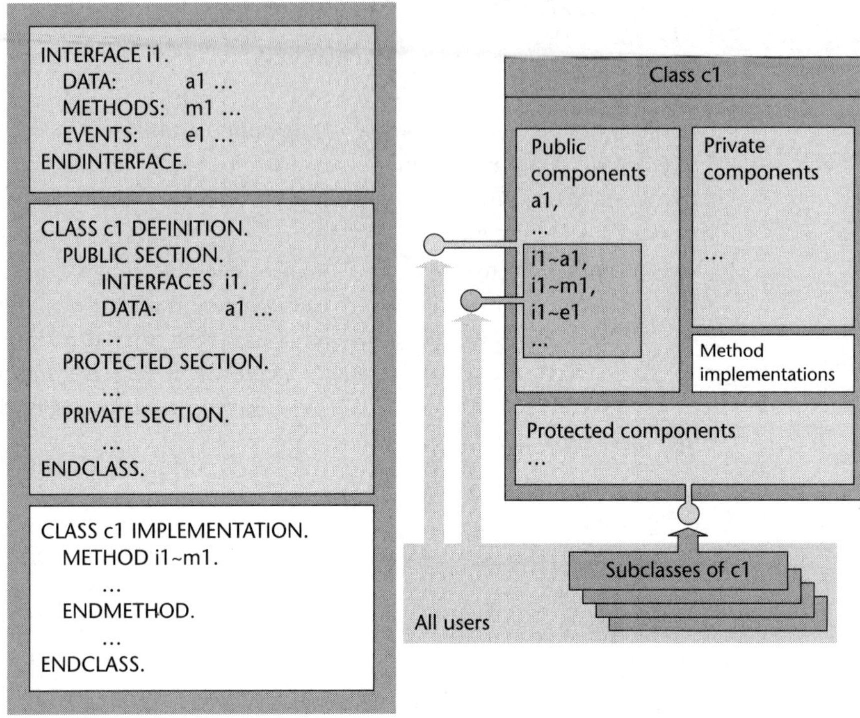

FIGURE 6.3 Overview of interfaces in classes

by interfaces and the terms "interface" and "public visibility section" actually mean the same for this class.

In Listing 6.14 we have provided an example of defining and implementing a single interface. We have used the same vehicle class as in Listing 6.1, but have moved the declaration of method write_status to an interface.

LISTING 6.14 Defining and implementing an interface

```
REPORT s_interface_definition.

* Interfaces

INTERFACE object_status.
  METHODS write_status.
ENDINTERFACE.

* Class Declarations
```

```
CLASS vehicle DEFINITION.
  PUBLIC SECTION.
    INTERFACES object_status.
    METHODS accelerate.
  PROTECTED SECTION.
    DATA speed TYPE i.
ENDCLASS.

* Class Implementations

CLASS vehicle IMPLEMENTATION.
  METHOD accelerate.
    speed = speed + 1.
  ENDMETHOD.
  METHOD object_status~write_status.
    WRITE: / 'Speed:', speed.
  ENDMETHOD.
ENDCLASS.

* Global Data

DATA vehicle_ref TYPE REF TO vehicle.

* Classical Processing Blocks

START-OF-SELECTION.
  CREATE OBJECT vehicle_ref.
  CALL METHOD: vehicle_ref->accelerate,
               vehicle_ref->object_status~write_status.
```

Listing 6.14 also shows a possible external access to the interface components. As the interface components become fully fledged class components, they can be addressed, as before, via reference variables of the static type of the class. You can see, however, that this type of access involves a lot of writing and is not particularly pretty, as the user has to know the technical details of the class. Here we access interface components via the normal class interface and do not use the interface itself at all. In Section 6.3.6 we will show you a much better way of accessing classes with interfaces, which eliminates the need to use the interface component selector outside the implementing class.

6.3.4 Composing interfaces

ABAP Objects allows you to compose a new interface from several existing ones. To do this, you use the INTERFACES statement in an interface definition instead of in a class.

```
INTERFACE intf1.
  comp
  INTERFACES: intf2, intf3, ...
ENDINTERFACE.
```

Component interface

Here, an interface intf1 is composed of its own components as well as other interfaces intf2, intf3, ... An interface which contains at least one other interface is called a **compound interface**. An interface which is contained in another interface is called a **component interface**. A component interface can itself be a compound interface. An interface which does not contain any compound interfaces is called an **elementary interface**.

Multiple composition

Let's consider the following multiple nested interfaces:

```
INTERFACE intf2.
  INTERFACES: intf1 ...
  ...
ENDINTERFACE.

INTERFACE intf3.
  INTERFACES: intf1, intf2 ...
  ...
ENDINTERFACE.
```

The compound interface intf3 has a component intf2 which is itself compound. Although it looks here as if the composition of several interfaces has resulted in a component hierarchy, this is in fact not the case. All component interfaces of a compound interface are on the same level. It is not possible to compose names such as intf3~intf2~intf1.

In the above example the component interface intf1 of the compound interface intf2 becomes a component interface of intf3. A compound interface contains each component interface precisely once. Although intf1 is included in intf3 both directly as a component interface of intf3 as well as via intf2, it only occurs once as intf3~intf1.

Implementing compound interfaces

When a compound interface is implemented in a class, all the interface components involved behave as if their interface has been implemented individually and only once. The interface components of the individual component interfaces expand the public visibility section of the class with their original names. As each interface occurs just once, this cannot result in a naming conflict. The way an implemented interface is composed is of no consequence when it comes to implementation in a class.[15] Let's consider an example:

```
INTERFACE intf1.
  METHODS meth.
ENDINTERFACE.

INTERFACE intf2.
  INTERFACES intf1.
  METHODS meth.
ENDINTERFACE.

INTERFACE intf3.
  INTERFACES intf1.
  METHODS meth.
ENDINTERFACE.

INTERFACE intf4.
  INTERFACES: intf2, intf3.
ENDINTERFACE.

CLASS class DEFINITION.
  PUBLIC SECTION.
    INTERFACES intf4.
ENDCLASS.

CLASS class IMPLEMENTATION.
  METHOD intf1~meth. ... ENDMETHOD.
  METHOD intf2~meth. ... ENDMETHOD.
  METHOD intf3~meth. ... ENDMETHOD.
ENDCLASS.
```

In this case a method meth of the same name is declared in three individual interfaces and with the help of the interface component selector is therefore also implemented differently three times. The composition of the interface is of no importance in this respect: The method intf1~meth is implemented only once although it is present in two interfaces intf2 and intf3, and the name intf4 does not occur at all in the implementation part of the class.

If you implement one or more of the other interfaces intf1, intf2 or intf3 in addition to intf4 in the above class, nothing changes in respect to the components or the

15. You will later see that the interface hierarchy does play a role in assigning interface references.

implementation part of the class, since the compiler ensures that for a class, as for compound interfaces, each component is present only once.

6.3.5 Alias names for interface components

The full name of a component which an interface adds to a class or another interface is intf~comp. An alias name can be defined for this name on the level on which the interface is added with the INTERFACES statement:

```
ALIASES  name FOR intf~comp.
```

Alias names can therefore be assigned when implementing interfaces in the declaration part of a class or when interfaces are composed during interface definition.

Alias names in classes

Alias names belong to the namespace of the components of a class and, like the other components, must be assigned to a visibility section. The visibility of an alias name outside the class is governed by its own visibility section and not the visibility section of the interface component assigned.

For example, in our source code from Listing 6.14 we can include an alias name for the interface method write_status (see Listing 6.15).

LISTING 6.15 Alias names in classes

```
REPORT s_interface_alias.
...
CLASS vehicle DEFINITION.
  PUBLIC SECTION.
    INTERFACES object_status.
    ALIASES write_status FOR object_status~write_status.
  ...
ENDCLASS.
...
CLASS vehicle IMPLEMENTATION.
  ...
  METHOD object_status~write_status.
    WRITE: / 'Speed:', speed.
  ENDMETHOD.
ENDCLASS.
...
CALL METHOD: vehicle_ref->accelerate,
             vehicle_ref->write_status.
```

You can see in Listing 6.15 that the method still has to be implemented with its full name, despite the alias name. The advantage of the alias name lies with the user. It is not so much the effort saved in writing when accessing the interface component. The alias name counts as a component of the class and is therefore suitable for accessing via a reference variable of the static type of the class. The class can use alias names to publish its interface components to the user as class-specific components. Alias names can also be used in classes to continue addressing class-specific components, which in the course of a development cycle are replaced by components from interfaces, under their old name. This means that the users of the class do not have to be adapted to the new name.

In our example in Listing 6.14 we changed the method write_status from Listing 6.1 to the method object_status~write_status, and thereby made all users syntactically incorrect. Through the alias name in Listing 6.15 the user can still use the original method call. This is, of course, much more important for global classes than for local ones, where users can only occur in the same ABAP program anyway.

Alias names in compound interfaces

As it is not possible to chain names in compound interfaces, alias names in component interfaces are the only way of addressing such components which otherwise would not be available in the compound interface. Let's consider an example:

```
INTERFACE intf1.
  METHODS m1.
ENDINTERFACE.

INTERFACE intf2.
  INTERFACES intf1.
  ALIASES m1 FOR intf1~m1.
ENDINTERFACE.

INTERFACE intf3.
  INTERFACES intf2.
  ALIASES m1 FOR intf2~m1.
ENDINTERFACE.
```

Via the alias name m1 in intf2 the intf3 interface can address component m1 of interface intf1 in its own ALIAS statement. Without alias names in intf2 this would not be possible, as the description intf2~intf1~m1 is not permitted. A user can now access the component m1 in intf1 from intf3 without needing to know anything about the composition of the interface.

```
DATA i_ref TYPE REF TO intf3.
...
CALL METHOD i_ref->m1.
```

Without alias names in intf3 the last line would have to look as follows:

```
CALL METHOD i_ref->intf1~m1.
```

The user should therefore know that intf3 is composed of intf2 which in turn is composed of intf1. In particular, with global interfaces you cannot expect the user to look at the composition of an interface in the Class Builder before being able to use a method of the interface. Incidentally, it is not necessary for the alias names always to have the original names.

If you have studied the above DATA statement closely, you should have noticed something new. We have declared a reference variable with reference to an interface. Previously we only dealt with reference variables which refer to classes. In the next section you will learn more about **interface references**.

6.3.6 Interface references

Reference variables allow us to access objects. Previously, all reference variables we worked with were created with reference to a class via

```
DATA classref TYPE REF TO class.
```

Class reference

These reference variables allowed us to address components of the public visibility section of objects of the class (class) or their subclasses. To distinguish this kind of reference variable from the following kind, we shall now call them **class reference variables** or **class references** for short.

The statement

```
DATA intfref TYPE REF TO  intf.
```

however, declares a reference variable with reference to an interface. We call this kind of reference variable an **interface reference variable** or an **interface reference** for short.

Interface reference

Interface reference variables, like class reference variables, can contain object references.[16] Although there are no instances of interfaces to which interface references can point, an interface reference can point to the objects of all classes which implement the corresponding interface. In this case it is unimportant whether the interface is implemented directly or as a component interface of a compound interface. Moreover, it is irrelevant whether the interface is implemented in the class itself or in one of its superclasses. In all these cases the system ensures that the interface components are available in the public visibility section of the object being referenced.

The static type of an interface reference variable is now an interface and not a class. As before, the dynamic type is the class of the object to which the interface reference is pointing at that moment. As in inheritance, it is the static type of the reference variable

16. Never confuse object references with class references or interface references. An object reference is always the contents of a references variable and thereby determines its dynamic type. We use class and interface references, on the other hand, to describe the static type of the reference variables.

that determines which object components the user can access statically. An interface reference therefore allows exactly those components of an object to be addressed which have been added to its class through the implementation of the interface.

Figure 6.4 shows how class and interface references point to the same object, but all components can only be addressed via the class reference while the interface reference only recognizes the interface components.

After this general introduction to interface references, two specific questions need to be addressed:

1. How do you get interface references to point to objects?
2. How does the user work with interface references?

The answer to the first question can be found in Figure 6.4: reference variables which point to objects can be assigned to interface reference variables. As in inheritance, certain rules apply here and we will discuss these further on. For now, we will concentrate on the second question.

Accessing interface components

In Listing 6.14 we accessed interface components of an object via a class reference, by using the full name of the component in the class:

```
... classref->intf~comp ...
```

If you point to an object with an interface reference, access is much easier: as the interface reference only recognizes components of its own interface, i.e. its static type, it can uniquely address these components without the intf~ prefix:

```
... intfref->comp ...
```

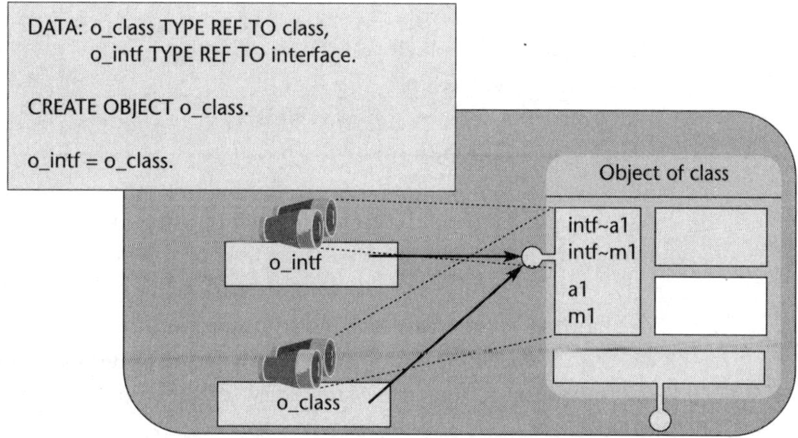
DATA: o_class TYPE REF TO class,
o_intf TYPE REF TO interface.
CREATE OBJECT o_class.
o_intf = o_class.
Object of class
intf~a1
intf~m1
a1
m1
o_intf
o_class

FIGURE 6.4 Access via class and interface references

This is the recommended method for accessing interface components in objects. It serves the actual purpose of interfaces.

User's View

Users work with interface references whose static type they know, and do not have to bother with the details of implementation. In principle, the users of an interface do not even have to know the class of the object they are working with. Refer also to Section 6.3.7 concerning polymorphism through interfaces.

If an intf~ prefix is nevertheless specified after an interface reference, intf can only be a component interface contained in its own interface. But here too access is better made directly through an interface reference variable of the type of the component interface. The interface component selector should generally not be used outside classes and interfaces. You can always avoid this by using appropriate assignments to interface reference variables (narrowing casts, see Listing 6.17).

Let's consider again our source code in Listing 6.14 in which we accessed the interface object_status of the vehicle class via a class reference. In Listing 6.16 we modify the part of the program which works with the object, to allow access to the write_status interface method via an interface reference.

LISTING 6.16 Interface reference

```
REPORT s_interface_reference.
...
* Global Data

DATA: vehicle_ref TYPE REF TO vehicle,
      status_ref  TYPE REF TO object_status.

* Classical Processing Blocks

START-OF-SELECTION.
  CREATE OBJECT vehicle_ref.
  status_ref = vehicle_ref.
  CALL METHOD: vehicle_ref->accelerate,
               status_ref->write_status.
```

The accelerate method cannot be called via the interface reference. An interface's view of an object is less detailed than that of the class reference. The assignment of vehicle_ref after status_ref is therefore a narrowing cast (see below).

Static interface component

You cannot access the static components of an interface declared with CLASS-DATA, CLASS-METHODS, or CLASS-EVENTS using the name of the interface and the class component selector. The only exception are constants declared with CONSTANTS.

```
... intf=>const ...
```

The static components belong to the static components of each implementing class. This means that static attributes have different values depending on the class and static methods can be implemented differently in each class. To access the static components of interfaces independently of instance, you would have to use a class name:

```
... class=>intf~comp ...
```

This should, however, remain the exception for the above-mentioned reasons. Instead, implementing classes can declare alias names for the static components of interfaces and thereby make the components addressable via the class name, like their own static components. However, you can access static components with interface reference variables after you have created objects from the implementing classes.

Assignments with interface reference variables

In Section 6.2.9 we dealt extensively with assignments between reference variables. All the rules we presented were based on the premise that the static type of a reference variable is always either more general than or the same as the dynamic type.

For an interface reference variable the static type is an interface and therefore never the same as the dynamic type which is always a class. The static type of an interface reference can therefore only be more general, and never the same as the dynamic type. As already mentioned, this means that the interface of the static type must be implemented in the class of the dynamic type. The type of implementation is completely irrelevant. The interface can be implemented directly or via a compound interface in the class or in one of its superclasses.

An assignment between reference variables is only possible if the above basic rule is satisfied for the target field. As with inheritance, we can now also investigate assignments with interface reference variables. In doing so we can again distinguish references where this is statically possible from those where the check can only take place at runtime. Only cases in which the target variable is more general than the source variable – and therefore allows a more restricted view of objects (narrowing cast) – can be statically checked. All other cases can only be checked dynamically (widening cast).

Narrowing cast

The assignment operator (=) is used for assignments with narrowing cast. For assignments with interface reference variables we can distinguish three cases:

- **Only the target variable is an interface reference**

  ```
  intfref = classref.
  ```

  The class of the class reference or one of its superclasses must implement the interface of the interface reference.

  This category includes the creation of an object via an interface reference.

  ```
  CREATE OBJECT intfref TYPE class.
  ```

The class (class) or one of its superclasses must implement the interface of the interface reference. We are familiar with this kind of object creation from inheritance. It saves you having to declare a class reference with a subsequent assignment to the interface reference.

- **Both reference variables are interface references**

  ```
  intfref2 = intfref1.
  ```

  This assignment is only possible if the static type of the target variable is the same interface as the static type of the source variable or if the static type of the source variable is a compound interface which contains the interface of the target variable as a component.

- **Only the source variable is an interface reference**

  ```
  classref = intfref.
  ```

  In this case the static type of the target variable must be the general class object. The dynamic type of the source variable can be any class which implements the interface, and except for object it is impossible to check statically whether it is actually the same as or more special than the class of the target variable.

In Figure 6.4 and Listing 6.16 we showed you narrowing casts in which the source variable is a class reference and the target variable an interface reference. This form of assignment to an interface reference probably is most common.

Assignments between interface references are of interest in connection with compound interfaces. Listing 6.17 shows an abstract example.

LISTING 6.17 Narrowing cast for interface references

```
REPORT s_interface_narrowing_cast.

* Interfaces

INTERFACE i1.
  METHODS meth.
ENDINTERFACE.

INTERFACE i2.
  INTERFACES i1.
  METHODS meth.
ENDINTERFACE.

* Class Declarations

CLASS c1 DEFINITION.
  PUBLIC SECTION.
```

```
    INTERFACES i2.
ENDCLASS.

* Class Implementations

CLASS c1 IMPLEMENTATION.
  METHOD i1~meth.
    WRITE / 'Method of interface i1'.
  ENDMETHOD.
  METHOD i2~meth.
    WRITE / 'Method of interface i2'.
  ENDMETHOD.
ENDCLASS.

* Global Declarations

DATA: iref1 TYPE REF TO i1,
      iref2 TYPE REF TO i2.

* Classical Processing Blocks

START-OF-SELECTION.
  CREATE OBJECT iref2 TYPE c1.
  iref1 = iref2.
  CALL METHOD iref1->meth.
  CALL METHOD iref2->meth.
```

An interface i2, which comprises an interface i1 and its own method meth, is implemented in the class c1. The class implements the methods of both interfaces. We create an object of class c1, to which the interface reference variable iref2 points initially. In the CREATE OBJECT statement a narrowing cast from c1 to i2 takes place. The assignment of iref2 to iref1 is another narrowing cast from i2 to i1. A reverse assignment would not be possible, as i1 is contained in i2 and not vice versa. Both interface references address exactly the methods of their interface. Instead of

```
CALL METHOD iref1->meth.
```

we could also have called the same method via

```
CALL METHOD iref2->i1~meth.
```

However, since we do not want to use the interface component selector (~) outside of classes or interfaces, we have performed the narrowing cast.

Assignments from interface references to class references of the object type are actually only of interest if reference variables are to be passed to procedures fully generically. For all other assignments of interface references to class references you must work with the widening cast.

Widening cast

All assignments with interface reference variables which are not described with the narrowing cast must be listed with the casting operator (?=) as a widening cast. The static type of the target variable is then more specialized than the static type of the source variable and can address more components in principle. You can only check at runtime if the dynamic type of the source variable is more specialized than or the same as the static type of the target variable, i.e. whether it also contains all the components.

Class reference cast

Let's consider two examples. First we shall assign an interface reference variable to a class reference which is not of the object type. To do this, we simply modify slightly the part of Listing 6.16 which works with the object.

LISTING 6.18 Widening cast for class reference

```
REPORT s_interface_widening_1.
...
* Global Data

DATA: vehicle_ref TYPE REF TO vehicle,
      status_ref  TYPE REF TO object_status.

* Classical Processing Blocks

START-OF-SELECTION.
  CREATE OBJECT status_ref TYPE vehicle.
  ...
  CATCH SYSTEM-EXCEPTIONS move_cast_error = 4.
    vehicle_ref ?= status_ref.
  ENDCATCH.
  IF sy-subrc = 0.
    CALL METHOD: vehicle_ref->accelerate,
                 status_ref->write_status.
  ENDIF.
```

We first create an object to which only the interface reference status_ref is pointing and expand the view of the object through the widening cast to the class reference vehicle_ref. The catchable runtime error is of course not triggered in this basic example, as we have ensured in the CREATE OBJECT statement that the dynamic type of the source variable is the vehicle class, which is also the static type of the target variable. This kind of programming always becomes interesting when the dynamic type is actually unknown, for example within a procedure whose importing parameters are statically typed as interface references (see also Listing 6.7).

Interface reference cast

For our second example, we assign one interface reference to another interface reference in Listing 6.19, whereby the static type of the target variable is not a component interface of the source variable. We shall start from our original example in Listing 6.14. We shall now also move the accelerate method to its own interface. "Accelerate" is a method which is not only required by vehicles but which can be implemented in almost any class for moving objects.

LISTING 6.19 Interface reference widening cast

```
REPORT s_interface_widening_2.

INTERFACE object_status.
  METHODS write_status.
ENDINTERFACE.

INTERFACE object_movement.
  METHODS accelerate.
ENDINTERFACE.

* Class Declarations

CLASS vehicle DEFINITION.
  PUBLIC SECTION.
    INTERFACES: object_status,
                object_movement.
  PROTECTED SECTION.
    DATA speed TYPE i.
ENDCLASS.

* Class Implementations

CLASS vehicle IMPLEMENTATION.
  METHOD object_movement~accelerate.
    speed = speed + 1.
```

```
  ENDMETHOD.
  METHOD object_status~write_status.
    WRITE: / 'Speed:', speed.
  ENDMETHOD.
ENDCLASS.

* Global Data

DATA: movement_ref TYPE REF TO object_movement,
      status_ref   TYPE REF TO object_status.

* Classical Processing Blocks

START-OF-SELECTION.
  CREATE OBJECT movement_ref TYPE vehicle.
  CALL METHOD movement_ref->accelerate.
  status_ref ?= movement_ref.
  CALL METHOD status_ref->write_status.
```

The two interfaces object_status and object_movement are completely independent of each other and can be included in any classes. The interface object_status represents an interface for outputting object attributes, while object_movement allows objects to be moved. Of course, a class such as vehicle can include both interfaces if it wants to offer both.

We create an instance of the vehicle class and point initially with the interface reference movement_ref to this instance. Only the interface components of object_movement are visible with this reference. We then assign the interface reference movement_ref to the interface reference status_ref. The static types vary and you cannot check statically whether the class of the object to which the source variable is pointing also implements the interface of the target variable. This is why the casting operator must be used. As we are sure that the dynamic type is vehicle and both interfaces are implemented, we do not catch the runtime error move_cast_error.

We change the view of the object with our assignment between independent interface references. Only the interface components of object_status are visible via the target variable. Figure 6.5 shows the situation after the widening cast. Both interface references point to the same object but do not know the same components.

6.3.7 Polymorphism through interfaces

As we saw when discussing polymorphism through inheritance in Section 6.2.10, polymorphic behavior is based on the fact that a user can use a single reference variable to point to objects of different classes in which different method implementations have been used.

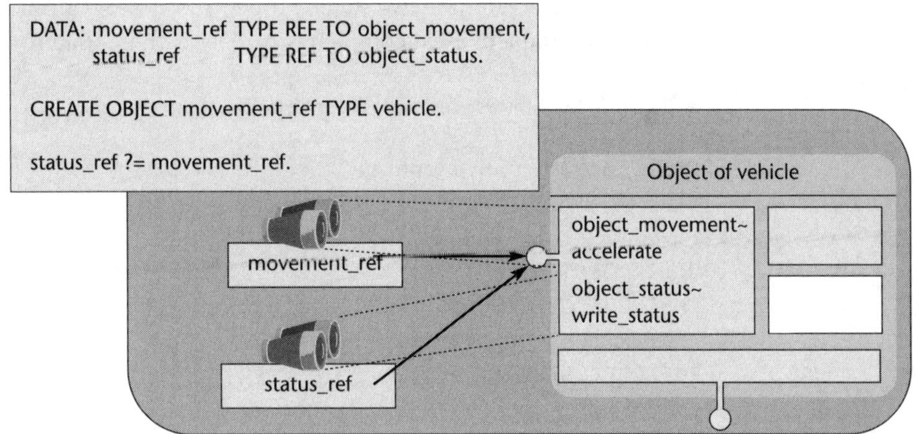
DATA: movement_ref TYPE REF TO object_movement,
status_ref TYPE REF TO object_status.
CREATE OBJECT movement_ref TYPE vehicle.
status_ref ?= movement_ref.
Object of vehicle
object_movement~
accelerate
object_status~
write_status
movement_ref
status_ref

FIGURE 6.5 Widening cast with independent interface references

Compare this statement with everything you have previously learned about interfaces: You know that each class which implements an interface must implement the methods of the interface. If different classes implement the same interface, the methods are generally also implemented differently. You also know that you can point with a single interface reference to objects of all classes which implement the interface. The behavior of methods which you call via interface references is therefore basically polymorphic.

The main purpose of interfaces is to provide users with uniform interfaces through which they can call methods without having to bother about the implementation details. The main difference between polymorphism through interfaces and polymorphism through inheritance is that with interfaces all classes which have implemented the interface can be used, not just classes which share an inheritance relationship. For the user of an interface the implementing class can be ultimately irrelevant, providing the result is correct.

Semantics

This presupposes of course that every class which implements an interface follows the semantics of the method in its method implementation exactly as it is declared in the interface. The implementation of an interface represents something like a contract between class and user. An interface is like a description (protocol layer) from which the user can expect a certain behavior. The implementing class is obliged to implement the methods in such a way that they meet with expectations. The implementation details differ, of course, from class to class. The result, however, must always correspond to the documentation of the interface. Ultimately these are the same rules that a subclass must follow when redefining a superclass method.

Listing 6.20 illustrates polymorphism through interfaces with an example. In addition to our vehicle class from Listing 6.14 we define another class, window, which also implements the object_status interface. The window class is implemented here in such a way that a window can have two statuses, open and closed. Of course, the write_status method must be implemented completely differently here than in vehicle.

LISTING 6.20 Polymorphism through interfaces

```
REPORT s_interface_polymorphism.
...
CLASS window DEFINITION.
  PUBLIC SECTION.
    METHODS open_close.
    INTERFACES object_status.
  PROTECTED SECTION.
    DATA status_flag(1) TYPE c.
ENDCLASS.
...
CLASS window IMPLEMENTATION.
  METHOD open_close.
    IF status_flag = ' '.
      status_flag = 'X'.
    ELSE.
      status_flag = ' '.
    ENDIF.
  ENDMETHOD.
  METHOD object_status~write_status.
    IF status_flag = ' '.
      WRITE / 'Window is closed'.
    ELSE.
      WRITE / 'Window is open'.
    ENDIF.
  ENDMETHOD.
ENDCLASS.

* Global Data

DATA: vehicle_ref TYPE REF TO vehicle,
      window_ref  TYPE REF TO window,
      status_tab TYPE TABLE OF REF TO object_status.

FIELD-SYMBOLS <status> TYPE REF TO object_status.

* Classical Processing Blocks
```

```
START-OF-SELECTION.
  CREATE OBJECT vehicle_ref.
  CALL METHOD   vehicle_ref->accelerate.
  APPEND vehicle_ref TO status_tab.
  CREATE OBJECT window_ref.
  CALL METHOD   window_ref->open_close.
  APPEND window_ref TO status_tab.

  LOOP AT status_tab ASSIGNING <status>.
    CALL METHOD <status>->write_status.
  ENDLOOP.
```

From each class we create an object to which a class reference is pointing, change the object status with a class-specific method, and attach the class reference to a table for interface references. The latter is a narrowing cast, as the table type is the common interface of the two classes.

Finally we run a loop through the table and access both objects through the interface references. We obtain different outputs through an identical method call. Although vehicles and windows are completely independent classes, the polymorphism of the interfaces allows us to access them in exactly the same way, and thanks to the correct implementation of the interface method, obtain useful results.

6.3.8 Interfaces and inheritance

To conclude our description of interfaces we shall briefly discuss the relationship between interfaces and inheritance and make a summary comparison between the two concepts.

The concepts of interfaces and inheritance are independent of each other and completely compatible. Any number of interfaces can be implemented in the classes of an inheritance tree, whereby each interface can only be implemented once for each path of the inheritance tree. This means that each interface component has a unique name `intf~comp` throughout the entire inheritance tree and is included in all subclasses of the class implementing the interface. Interface methods are fully fledged components of a class once they have been implemented and can be redefined in subclasses. Interface methods, however, cannot be declared as abstract or final in the definition of the interface.

Polymorphism

Both inheritance and interfaces allow for polymorphism independently of each other. In both cases polymorphism is based on the fact that you can access objects of different classes and differently implemented methods in the same way. When interfaces and inheritance are used at the same time, combinations of the two forms of polymorphism are possible. If a class implements an interface, this also applies for all the subclasses, and you can point to the objects of all the subclasses using the corresponding interface reference. The rule remains that the most special method implementation is searched for, starting from the dynamic type.

Coupling

It is always appropriate to use inheritance if different classes are in a generalization/specialization relationship. If, for example, we consider two classes, "freight plane" and "passenger plane," both classes contain components which can be declared in a common superclass, "plane." The major advantage of inheritance is that all subclasses adopt all the attributes programmed in the superclass and reuse them. At the same time this tightly couples superclasses and subclasses. A subclass depends heavily on its superclasses because it generally consists of the components of its superclasses. A subclass must know its superclass exactly. This became clear in our discussion of instance constructors in inheritance in Section 6.2.8. Any modification to non-private components of a superclass affects all the subclasses. Conversely, subclasses can also affect the design of superclasses with specific requirements. If you use inheritance to design classes, ideally you should have access to all the classes involved, as only the total number of classes of a path in the inheritance tree provide a meaningful whole. On the other hand, it is dangerous to attach yourself to any superclass by defining a subclass, if that superclass was not created by members of the same development team.

Decoupling

It is always appropriate to use interfaces if interfaces or protocols are to be described without involving a specific kind of implementation. An additional layer is introduced between user and class which decouples the users from a specific class and therefore makes them much more independent. Interfaces allow users to handle a variety of classes uniformly without the classes having to be coupled to each other at the same time. In object-oriented modeling, interfaces provide an abstraction which is independent of class: the services which users require can be described irrespective of the actual implementation. In addition, interfaces also achieve an aspect of multiple inheritance, as several interfaces can be implemented in a single class. If a programming language allows genuine multiple inheritance, it is generally used only in this sense. This means that only abstract classes with purely abstract methods can be considered for the various superclasses of a single subclass. Otherwise you would immediately have to ask which method implementation is being used in a subclass if it is already meant to be implemented in several superclasses. However, like superclasses in inheritance, with interfaces you must note that any subsequent modifications to interfaces can render all the classes implementing the interface syntactically incorrect.

6.4 EVENTS

So far in our portrayal of ABAP Objects we have concerned ourselves solely with attributes and methods of classes. Attributes describe the status of an object, methods access attributes and modify the status. Both are components of classes. So far we have not commented on the third possible component of classes, **events.**[17] Events allow the objects of a class to publish modifications to its status. Other objects can then respond to the change in status.

We shall describe all of this by means of an example: on board a plane are passengers, the cabin crew, and the pilots. The pilots and the passengers can press a button to call the stewardess. As soon as the "button pressed" event occurs, she determines who has pressed the button and performs a corresponding action. We are therefore dealing with three classes (passenger, pilot, and cabin crew). The instances of the passenger and pilot classes are able to trigger events which the instances of the cabin crew class are interested in and can respond to. Why do we introduce events here and not simply let pilots and passengers call a method in the instances of the cabin crew directly? There are two clear reasons for this:

1. When we press the button we do not know which stewardess, i.e. which instance of the cabin crew, will respond. Or in other words: the event trigger does not know the event handler.
2. The cabin crew can decide itself if the event should be registered. For example, the call button is ignored during take-off or landing. The event trigger therefore does not initially know if the event will even have an effect.

Both of these cannot be achieved with normal method calls. To call a method, the addressee must be known and a called method must always respond.

Publish and subscribe

The advantage of the event concept therefore lies in the fact that you can achieve a loose association between objects. We refer to this also as the **publish and subscribe mechanism**. One class or object can publish an event while another can be interested in it. Classes or objects which trigger events do not know who is interested in the event or what the recipients do with it. You will see that in ABAP Objects the **publish and subscribe** mechanism takes place on two levels, statically on a class level and dynamically on an object level. You also find typical applications of the event concept when programming screens. In Section 7.5.4 you will see how to react in ABAP Objects to events in GUI controls, such as mouse clicks.

Before going into detail we shall briefly summarize how the event concept is implemented in ABAP Objects and define some terms:

- **Events**

  A class can contain events as components. Each method can trigger the events of its class.

- **Handler methods**

  Methods of other classes or the same class can be declared as handler methods for the event.

17. The events we are discussing here have nothing to do with the events of the runtime environment such as `START-OF-SELECTION` etc.

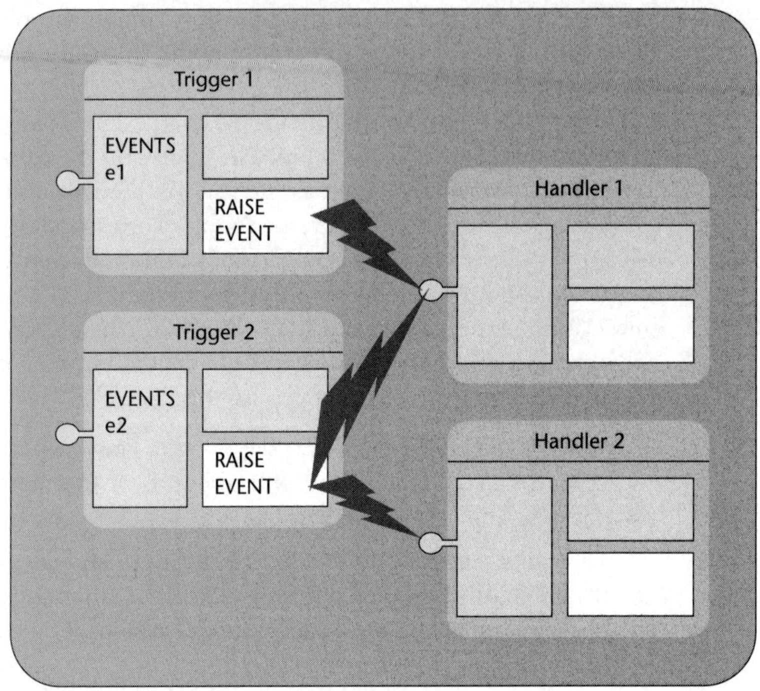

FIGURE 6.6 Event triggers and handlers

- **Registering handlers**

  Objects which contain handler methods for an event can be registered at runtime as handlers for the objects of the classes which can trigger the event.

In a class different events can be declared, in which the objects of many different classes may be interested. Conversely, a class can implement handler methods for the events of different classes (see Figure 6.6).

6.4.1 Defining and triggering events

To couple objects through events, we must program accordingly both the classes of the triggers as well as the classes of the handlers. Let's consider first a triggering class. You must declare each event which is to be triggered with the methods of a class in its declaration part.[18] Like all components of a class, events must be assigned to one of the three visibility sections of a class. This determines which users can handle an event. An event which is defined, for example, in the protected section of a class can only be handled by objects of the subclasses or of its own class. There are both

18. Like all other components, events can also be defined in interfaces.

instance-dependent events (**instance events**) and instance-independent events (**static events**). You can use the following syntax to declare an instance event:

```
EVENTS evt
       EXPORTING ...
                 VALUE(e_i) {TYPE type|LIKE dobj}
                            [OPTIONAL|DEFAULT def_i]
                 ...
```

Static events are defined with the CLASS-EVENTS statement, otherwise the syntax is the same. For events, a parameter interface can be defined which only contains exporting parameters which are passed by value. The handler methods for the event can import the parameters.

Triggering

To trigger an event defined in this way you use the RAISE EVENT statement in the methods of the same class. The syntax is:

```
RAISE EVENT evt EXPORTING ... e_i = a_i ...
```

In instance methods, all instance events and static events of the class can be triggered with this statement. In static methods only static events can be triggered, even if no object of the class exists. The RAISE EVENT statement interrupts the execution of the method at exactly this point and the runtime environment executes all the registered handler methods for this event. The triggering method is then continued after the RAISE EVENT statement.[19] All non-optional exporting parameters of the event must be filled with actual parameters using the EXPORTING addition, in order to fill the importing parameters of the handler methods.

Let's consider, by means of an example, how events are defined and triggered. In Listing 6.21 we define two classes, pilot and passenger, which can trigger the above event call_button_pressed.

LISTING 6.21 Definition and triggering of events

```
REPORT s_abap_objects_events.

* Class Declarations

CLASS pilot DEFINITION.
  PUBLIC SECTION.
    METHODS call_flight_attendant.
    EVENTS call_button_pressed.
ENDCLASS.
```

19. Handler method calls are processed in a cascading form. If another RAISE EVENT is executed in the handler method, this method will also be interrupted and the handler of the new event will be executed first.

```
CLASS passenger DEFINITION.
  PUBLIC SECTION.
    METHODS: constructor IMPORTING
                       VALUE(i_seatnumber) TYPE i,
             call_for_help.
    EVENTS call_button_pressed EXPORTING
                              VALUE(e_seatnumber) TYPE i.
  PROTECTED SECTION.
    DATA seatnumber TYPE i.
ENDCLASS.

* Class Implementations

CLASS pilot IMPLEMENTATION.
  METHOD call_flight_attendant.
    RAISE EVENT call_button_pressed.
  ENDMETHOD.
ENDCLASS.

CLASS passenger IMPLEMENTATION.
  METHOD constructor.
    seatnumber = i_seatnumber.
  ENDMETHOD.
  METHOD call_for_help.
    RAISE EVENT call_button_pressed
                EXPORTING e_seatnumber = seatnumber.
  ENDMETHOD.
ENDCLASS.

* Global Data

DATA: pilot TYPE REF TO pilot,
      passenger_1 TYPE REF TO passenger,
      passenger_2 TYPE REF TO passenger.

* Classical Processing Blocks

START-OF-SELECTION.
  CREATE OBJECT: pilot,
                 passenger_1 EXPORTING i_seatnumber = 11,
                 passenger_2 EXPORTING i_seatnumber = 17.
  CALL METHOD: pilot->call_flight_attendant,
               passenger_1->call_for_help,
               passenger_2->call_for_help.
```

In the pilot class we declare an event call_button_pressed for when the call button has been pressed. The class also has a method which triggers the event. Here we implement the RAISE EVENT statement. The class for passengers is structured in a similar way. Here too an event call_button_pressed is defined. Note, however, that although we have defined this event with the same name as the event in the pilot class, it has nothing in common apart from similar semantics. In the passenger class we define an exporting parameter for the event which is used to indicate the seat number from where the call was made when the event is triggered. We set the seat numbers for each passenger instance using the instance constructor. For passengers we also define a method for calling the cabin crew. We have to export a type-specific seat number using the RAISE EVENT statement.

Finally we create a pilot and two passengers and call the methods. Although the event is now triggered, we have not yet defined handlers to respond to it. We will describe this in the next section.

6.4.2 Handling events

In any class you can define event handler methods for the events of other classes or the class itself. Event handler methods, like any other methods, are declared with the METHODS or CLASS-METHODS statements, whereby the FOR EVENT addition determines their role as event handler. The syntax is:

```
METHODS  handler FOR EVENT  evt
                 OF {class|intf}
                 IMPORTING  ... e_i ... [sender].
```

Handler method

This declaration statically assigns the handler method to a single event of a class (class) or an interface (intf). The parameter interface of an event handler method is restricted solely to importing parameters which have been defined with the same name as exporting parameters when the corresponding event was declared. A handler method is not obliged, however, to import all the parameters. The importing parameters are not typed here, but instead adopt the typing of the exporting parameters of the event. The interface is therefore fully defined during the declaration of the event. The handler must adhere strictly to its definition. This allows the desired loose coupling between trigger and handler: the trigger is completely independent of any handlers. The syntax ensures that handler methods do not expect any parameters other than those that can be sent during the event.

Besides the parameters declared specifically during the event, handler methods for instance events can also import a sender parameter. This parameter is always implicitly present when an instance event is declared. It is typed as a reference variable of the type of the class in which the event is declared.[20] When the event is triggered

20. As of Release 6.10, the class or the interface after the FOR EVENT OF expression in the handler method declaration determines the type of sender.

with RAISE EVENT in an instance method, this parameter is implicitly filled with a reference to the triggering object. If a handler method imports sender, it can access the public visibility section of the triggering object via this parameter.

We shall now expand our example with event handlers and add the classes and the other coding from Listing 6.22 to the appropriate parts of Listing 6.21.

LISTING 6.22 Declaring event handlers

```
...
CLASS flight_attendant DEFINITION.
  PUBLIC SECTION.
    METHODS: constructor
                IMPORTING i_id TYPE string,
             help_the_pilot FOR EVENT
                call_button_pressed OF pilot,
             help_a_passenger FOR EVENT
                call_button_pressed OF passenger
                   IMPORTING e_seatnumber.
  PROTECTED SECTION.
    DATA id TYPE string.
ENDCLASS.

CLASS flight_attendant IMPLEMENTATION.
  METHOD constructor.
    id = i_id.
  ENDMETHOD.
  METHOD help_the_pilot.
    WRITE: / id, 'helps pilot'.
  ENDMETHOD.
  METHOD help_a_passenger.
    WRITE: / id, 'helps passenger on seat',
             e_seatnumber.
  ENDMETHOD.
ENDCLASS.
...
DATA: purser     TYPE REF TO flight_attendant,
      stewardess TYPE REF TO flight_attendant.
...
CREATE OBJECT: purser
                 EXPORTING i_id = 'Purser',
               stewardess
                 EXPORTING i_id = 'Stewardess'.
```

In Listing 6.22 we declared two handler methods for the events of the pilot and passenger classes in a flight_attendant class. The handler method help_a_passenger imports the seat number with the exact name as defined for the event in the passenger class.

We create two objects of the flight_attendant class, a purser and a stewardess. When you start the program, there is, however, no response to the events. The presence of event handler methods only means that an object is essentially capable of handling the respective events. The interaction of the triggering class and the handling class is only the static level of the publish and subscribe mechanism. We still need to program the dynamic part by registering the handler methods of the objects which are actually going to respond to the events.

Registration

In order for an event handler method to respond to a triggered event, the trigger to which it is to respond must be determined at runtime. Through this dynamic part of the publish and subscribe mechanism you couple methods in handler objects to triggering objects. The coupling can be undone at any time. In the above example the coupling would be made just after the plane's starting phase and undone before landing.

You create this coupling by registering handler methods with the SET HANDLER statement. The syntax for instance methods and instance events is as follows:[21]

```
SET HANDLER  ... ref_handler_i->handler_i ...
             FOR ref_sender
             [ACTIVATION  act].
```

This statement registers a list of instance methods in various objects for the events of just one object. In this case ref_handler and ref_sender are reference variables which point to objects with handler methods or events. Each listed instance method responds exactly to the event for which it is statically declared. A registration can be undone by specifying a blank character field act after the optional ACTIVATION addition. The optional default value of act for registration is "X".

You can also perform mass registration by using instead of

```
... FOR ref_sender ...
```

the expression

```
... FOR ALL INSTANCES  ...
```

This registers the listed handler methods for all objects which can trigger the event. This registration even applies in advance to triggering instances which had not been created at the time of registration.

21. We shall limit ourselves here to coupling objects. The mechanism is of course also defined for all possible combinations with static events and static handler methods, whereby it is also important whether events are declared in classes or interfaces. At this stage it is sufficient to say that FOR additions are forbidden with static events as only classes and not instances can trigger the events.

We can now complete our example in Listing 6.23 by registering handlers declared and instantiated in Listing 6.22 for the events of the objects of pilot and passenger.

LISTING 6.23 Registering handler methods

```
START-OF-SELECTION.
  CREATE OBJECT: pilot,
                 passenger_1 EXPORTING i_seatnumber = 11,
                 passenger_2 EXPORTING i_seatnumber = 17.

  CREATE OBJECT: purser
                   EXPORTING i_id = 'Purser',
                 stewardess
                   EXPORTING i_id = 'Stewardess'.

  SET HANDLER: purser->help_the_pilot
                 FOR pilot,
               stewardess->help_a_passenger
                 FOR ALL INSTANCES.

  CALL METHOD: pilot->call_flight_attendant,
               passenger_1->call_for_help,
               passenger_2->call_for_help.
```

With the method help_the_pilot our purser now responds to events of the pilot instance and the stewardess responds to all instances of the passenger class with help_a_passenger. Although purser and stewardess are instances of the same class, we have coupled them to different triggers. Look at the program by executing it line by line in the Debugger.

Runtime environment

To aid understanding, we shall conclude our description of events by briefly exploring how the runtime environment registers and executes event handler methods. Although the activity of the runtime environment is invisible to the developer, it has important consequences for the lifetime of objects.

For each object which can trigger events, there is an invisible handler table. For static events an instance-independent handler table is created for the corresponding class. In this table the runtime environment registers which methods are registered for which events. The table entries are dynamically managed solely by the SET HANDLER statement. For each event the handler table contains the names of the registered handler methods and references to the corresponding handler objects (see Figure 6.7). When an event is triggered the runtime environment runs through the corresponding event table and executes the methods listed there in their instances (or for static handler methods, in their classes).

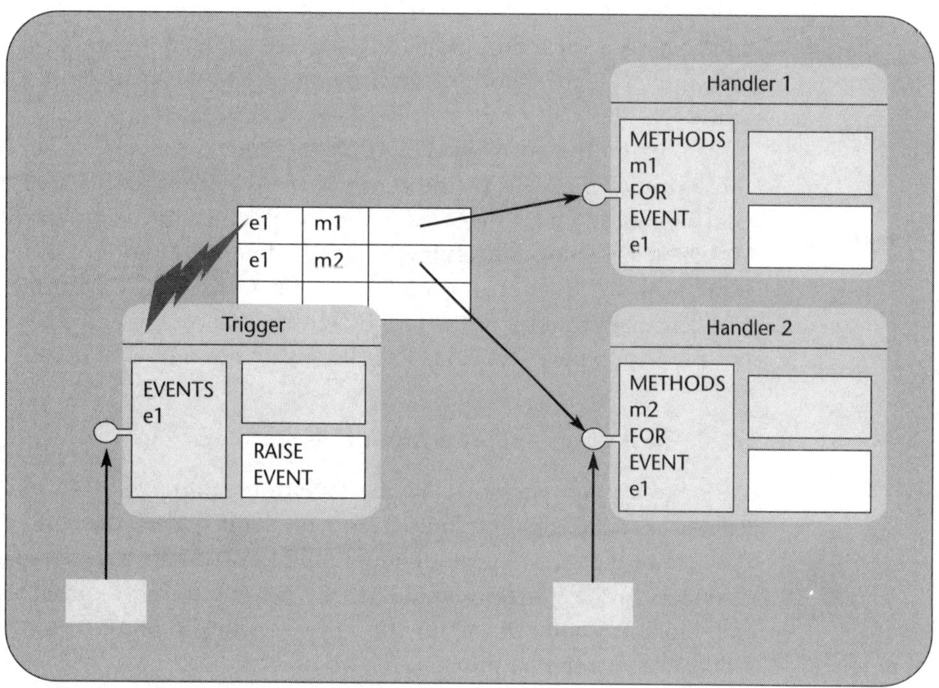

FIGURE 6.7 Event handler table

Like a reference in a reference variable, a reference to a handler object in a handler table counts as using the instance and therefore has a direct effect on its lifetime. In Figure 6.7 no specific reference variable of the ABAP program is pointing to the upper handler. Nevertheless, it is not deleted by the garbage collection as long as its registration is not reset in the handler table. If the triggering instance is deleted by the garbage collection, the entire handler table is deleted along with all its references.

6.5 GLOBAL CLASSES AND INTERFACES

All the classes and interfaces we have encountered in the previous chapters were local. This means that they can only be viewed in the program in which they have been defined. Global classes and interfaces on the other hand are repository objects and are therefore managed centrally.

Class library

This means that it is possible to provide class and interface libraries which can be used in any ABAP program. In one of the future SAP releases, for example, all the **BAPIs** (**Business Application Programming Interface**) will be available in the SAP System as methods of global classes of the **BOR** (**Business Object Repository**). Up to now, all BAPIs have been implemented as function groups, and the individual methods are mapped as function modules.

In terms of their components and their usage within a program there is no difference between local and global classes. We shall therefore keep this section to a minimum as there is nothing particularly new to say apart from a brief introduction to the Class Builder.

The main difference between the components of local classes or interfaces and those of global classes or interfaces is the way they are created and maintained. Global classes and interfaces are created with the **Class Builder** tool of the Workbench. A book concerning the language of ABAP cannot provide a full description of all the functions of the Class Builder. Instead, you can familiarize yourself with the main features of the tool by means of an example. First we shall look at the two program types in which global classes and interfaces are stored.

6.5.1 Class pools and interface pools

We have already encountered the Function Builder in Section 5.2.1. There you learned that the Function Builder is used to edit special ABAP programs of the function group type in which individual function modules are included. You define all interfaces in the Function Builder itself. The only thing you need to do then is enter the implementation of the function modules in the ABAP Editor. The Class Builder works to a very similar principle.

Main program

Like function modules or local classes, global classes or interfaces also need a complete ABAP main program in which they can be stored. While local classes and interfaces are directly entered by the developer in the source code of normal ABAP programs like executable programs, module pools, or function groups, the Class Builder creates a specific class pool or interface pool for each new global class or interface. A class pool of the program type K or an interface pool of the program type J acts as a container for precisely one global class or interface.

Unlike in other ABAP programs, classical event blocks, dialog modules, subroutines, and screens (see Chapter 7) cannot be defined in class pools. Screens are not permitted because the classical screens work solely with the global data objects of their ABAP program. However, in class pools only attributes of classes can be declared, not global data. Therefore, unlike almost all other ABAP programs, compiled class pools and interface pools cannot be executed through transaction codes. Currently, class pools can only be loaded in the internal mode of other ABAP programs if they are used in these programs.[22]

The executable statements of a class pool can only be programmed in methods as a class pool cannot contain other procedures. An interface pool does not contain any executable statements, and is only used for storing the definition of an interface. If you wish to modularize a class pool locally beyond the methods of the global class,

22. The next Basis Release will contain a new type of object-oriented transaction code which can be linked to classes and which creates an object of the class implicitly when called.

the Class Builder provides you with the option of creating local classes in the class pool. These local classes play the same part as our previous local classes in other ABAP programs and are not visible from the outside. You can use the methods of local classes similarly to subroutines in function modules, in order to remove reusable functionality from the actual class.

Just as when you work with function modules in the Function Builder, you rarely come into direct contact with ABAP main programs when you work with classes and interfaces in the Class Builder. You declare the components of their classes and interfaces and the interfaces thereof via the tool user interface and then only have to implement the methods in the ABAP Editor.

In the following sections we shall create a small global class which implements a counter with the following components:

- A type i attribute which contains the current counter status. It can be created in the private section since access should only be provided to an external user through corresponding methods.
- A method in the public section to increase the counter.
- A method in the public section to decrease the counter.

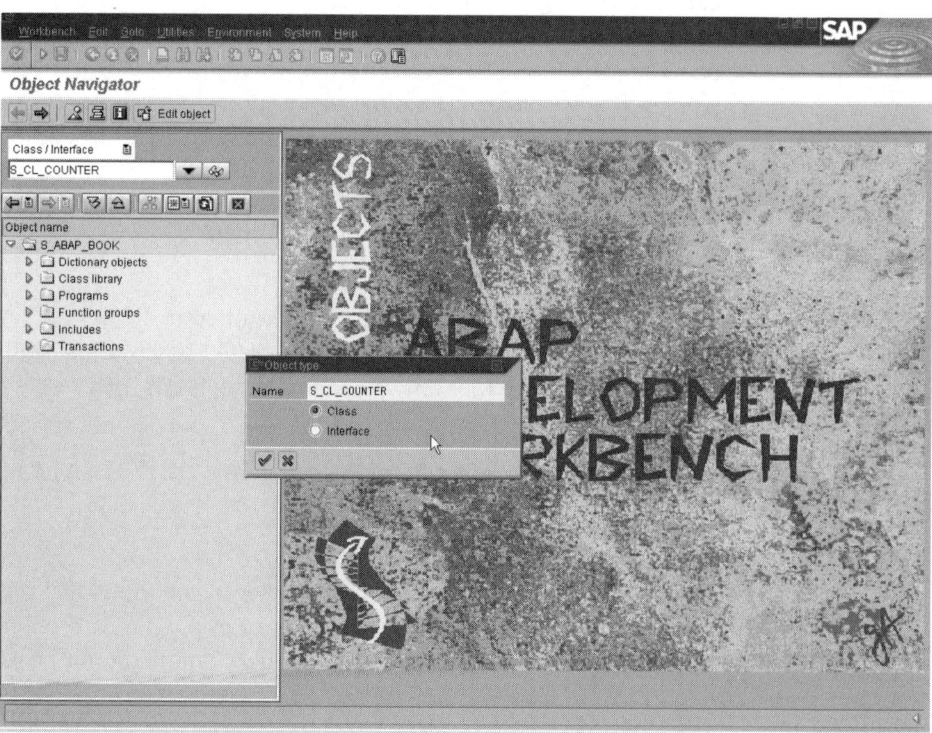

FIGURE 6.8 Choosing the object type. Copyright © SAP AG

- A method in the public section to return the current counter status.
- An instance constructor to initialize the counter with a specific value.

We shall not concentrate here on creating global interfaces, because the treatment in the Class Builder is essentially the same as declaring components in global classes.

6.5.2 Creating global classes

In order to develop our global example class, we work in the Object Navigator, as with all our repository objects. Like all tools, you can also call the Class Builder directly (transaction SE24), although here too we prefer the clear representation.

In the Object Navigator choose **Class/Interface** as the object list type, enter a name for your class and confirm with *enter* [↵]. You will be asked, as usual, if you want to create the object if it does not already exist. You can then decide whether you want to create a class or an interface (see Figure 6.8).

Note that the global classes provided by SAP all start with the "CL_" prefix. In the client namespace you must prefix here "Y_," "Z_" or your company's code. As for all programs in this book we shall use the prefix "S_."

Choose the **class** object type and confirm with *enter* [↵]. This will take you to the **Create Class** dialog box (see Figure 6.9).

On the right of the **Class** name field there is a **Create inheritance** button with which you can choose a superclass from which the class will inherit. As we are only creating a single isolated class here, this option is not applicable to our example. In addition, you can use this dialog to determine various features of the class:

- Description

  As usual, you enter a short descriptive text here.

- Instantiation

  The kind of instance generation is determined in this field. You determine here whether instances of this class can be created by all users (**public**), just by their subclasses (**protected**) or only by your own methods (**private**).[23]

- Final

  In this field you can identify the class as a final class so that no more classes can be derived from it.

- Only modeled

  This feature, which you will also encounter in the individual class components in the Class Builder, has no significance for Release 4.6. If the field is checked, the class will not be included in the class library and it cannot be used. In future this

23. The `CLASS ... DEFINITION` statement has corresponding additions for local classes: `PUBLIC`, `PROTECTED`, and `PRIVATE` which we have not used so far.

FIGURE 6.9 Creating the S_CL_COUNTER class. Copyright © SAP AG

indicator should enable classes to be designed from a graphic model without implementation.

Class Builder

Confirm the dialog box with *Save* and assign the new class to a development class, like all other repository objects. The Class Builder now appears on the right-hand side of the Object Navigator (see Figure 6.10).

You can now see that all the class components which we encountered when defining local classes are divided among the various tab pages of the Class Builder.

Attribute

We shall start with the private instance attribute of our class. If you click the **Attributes** tab page, you will see a table in which you can enter all the necessary details, in order to declare the attributes of a global class. From the individual column headers you can see that essentially the same information is required as for creating the attributes of a local class (see Figure 6.11). The best way to choose the kind and visibility of the attribute is through the corresponding value help (**F4**)

Constructor

We then turn to the methods, creating first of all our instance constructor. To do this, click the **Constructor** button in the application toolbar. This automatically brings the **Methods** tab page to the front and the first line is filled with the respective information (see Figure 6.12). Two steps are still missing to complete our constructor.

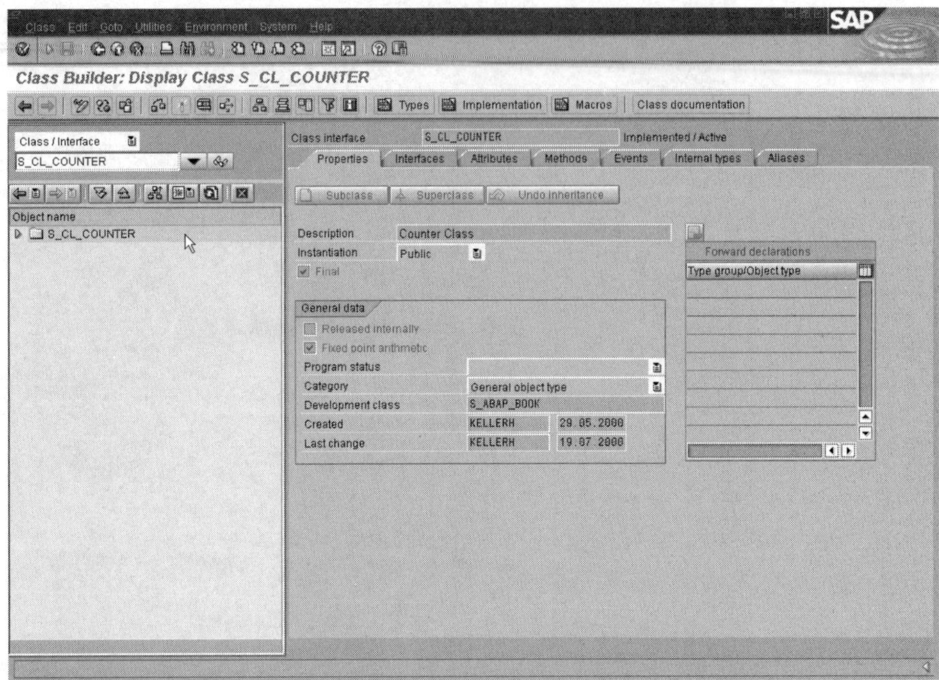

FIGURE 6.10 Class Builder in the Object Navigator. Copyright © SAP AG

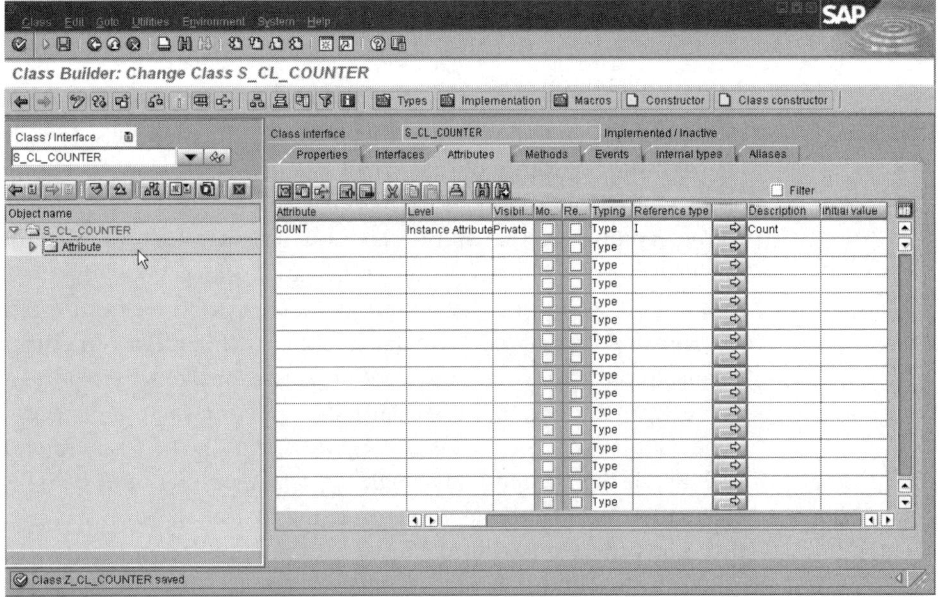

FIGURE 6.11 Creating an attribute of a global class. Copyright © SAP AG

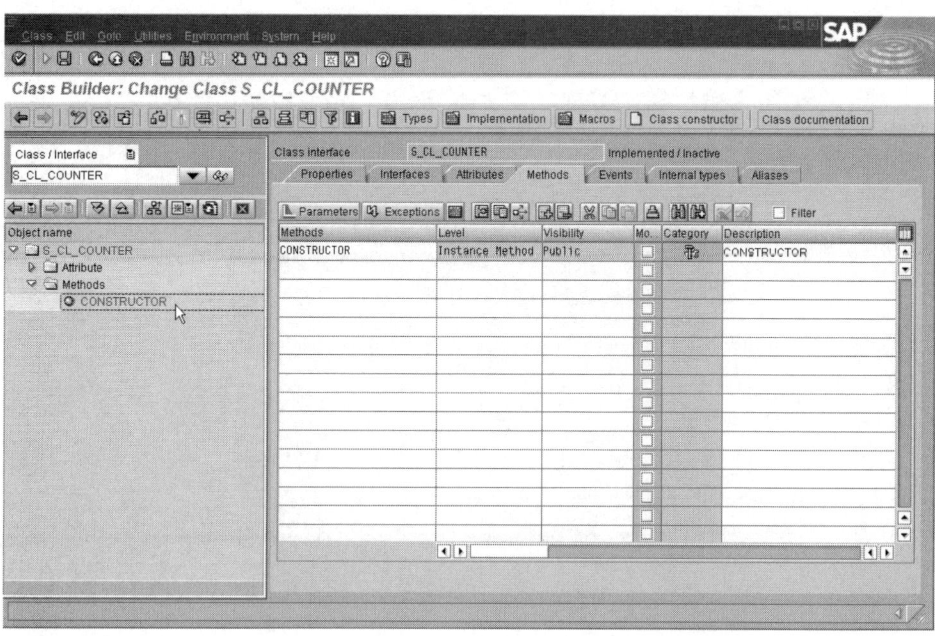

FIGURE 6.12 Creating an instance constructor. Copyright © SAP AG

Firstly, we must define the parameter interface with which we can set the counter to an initial value, and secondly, we must implement the source code of the constructor.

To define the parameter interface, you select the line with the method and choose the Parameters button at the top of the tab page. The system changes to the parameter input screen for the method (see Figure 6.13). Here we create a type i optional parameter I_START which is passed by reference and has the default value zero.

Implementation

To implement the method, you can either use the **Methods** button at the top of the tab page to return to the previous view, in order to enter the ABAP Editor by double-clicking the method name, or you can choose the **Source code** icon directly. In the ABAP Editor we implement the assignment of the passed parameter to the private attribute. The METHOD and ENDMETHOD statements are already specified. You only need to enter the functionality (see Figure 6.14).

We can now define the other methods in the same way. Navigate back to the **Methods** tab page and enter the corresponding names (see Figure 6.15).

Method

For the GET_COUNT method you define a type i returning parameter R_COUNT and implement the individual methods, as shown in Listing 6.24:

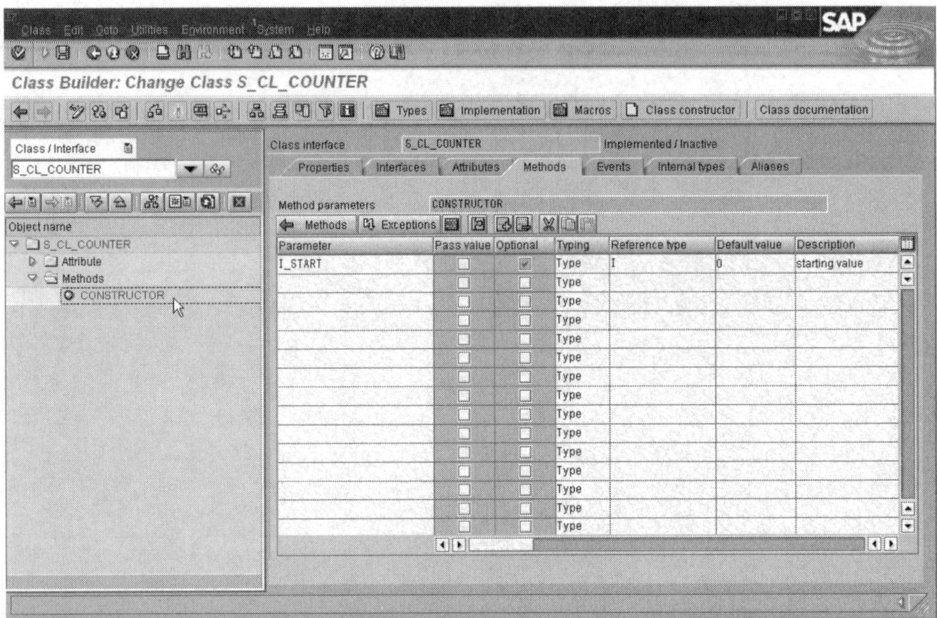

FIGURE 6.13 Parameter interface of methods. Copyright © SAP AG

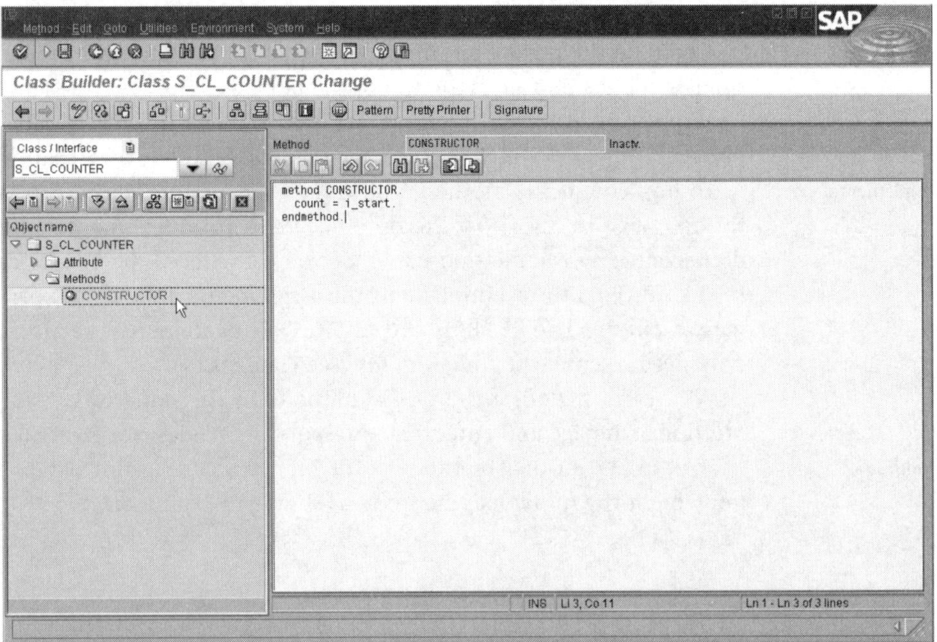

FIGURE 6.14 Implementing methods. Copyright © SAP AG

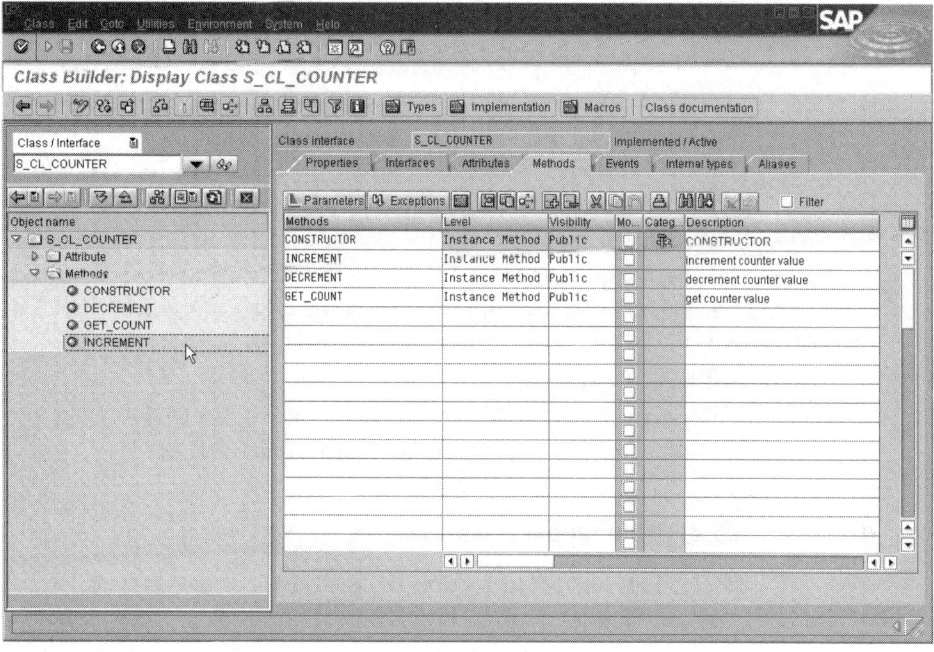

FIGURE 6.15 Method list in the class builder. Copyright © SAP AG

LISTING 6.24 Implementing the remaining three instance methods

```
METHOD increment.
  count = count + 1.
ENDMETHOD.

METHOD decrement.
  count = count - 1.
ENDMETHOD.

METHOD get_count.
  r_count = count.
ENDMETHOD.
```

Like all repository objects, global classes must be activated so that they can be tested or used. To do this, in the Object Navigator choose **Activate** and activate all the objects presented. From the list of objects to be activated you can see that a class pool is arranged in include programs like a function group.

6.5.3 Testing global classes

Now that we have created and activated our global class we can test it independently of an ABAP program, in a similar way to function modules. If you call the **Test** function in the Object Navigator, this will take you first to a screen on which you can create a test object of the class. To do this, you must fill the input parameters of the instance constructor.

The system then displays a screen on which you can test the class (see Figure 6.16). Here the public components of the class are listed and can be chosen.

In our case we can only execute methods because the COUNT attribute is not visible. However, to view COUNT during the execution of the methods, you can choose **Utilities – Debugging**.

Execute the INCREMENT method several times followed by the GET_COUNT method. The system displays the return value R_COUNT.

6.5.4 Using global classes

To conclude this short section we shall use our new class in an ABAP program. The class can be used in any ABAP program. There is nothing different in using a global

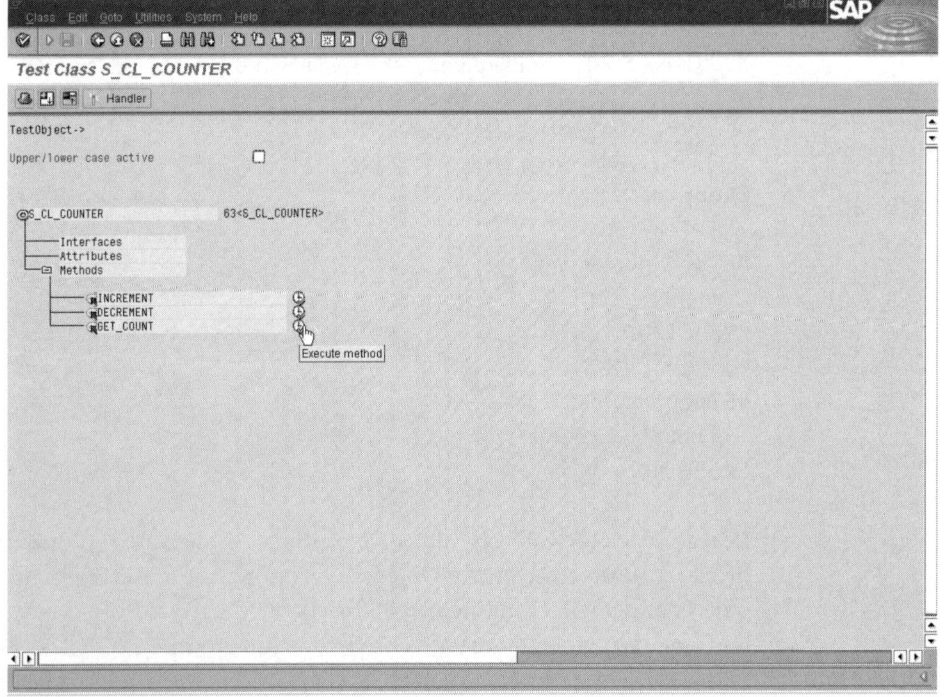

FIGURE 6.16 Testing the S_CL_COUNTER class in the Class Builder. Copyright © SAP AG

class compared with using a local class, with the exception that the class is not defined in the same ABAP program. Listing 6.25 shows an example of the application of our class S_CL_COUNTER:

LISTING 6.25 Using a global class

```
REPORT s_global_class_usage.

* Global Declarations

DATA: o_counter TYPE REF TO s_cl_counter,
      count TYPE i.

* Classical Processing Blocks

START-OF-SELECTION.
  CREATE OBJECT o_counter EXPORTING i_start = 5.
  DO 10 TIMES.
    CALL METHOD o_counter->increment.
  ENDDO.
  count = o_counter->get_count( ).
  WRITE / count.
```

As in previous applications of local classes, we create an object, fill the input parameters of the instance constructor, and call methods.

All global classes form the class library of the SAP System. You can access the contents of the class library with the Class Browser which you can start from the initial screen of the Class Builder (transaction SE24). Take a look at the classes provided. In particular, you will find here all the classes of the new Control Framework which provides you with powerful components for GUI programming. For more information on the new controls as well as some examples, see Section 7.5.4.

CHAPTER 7

Programming screens

Every programming language needs ways of letting users and programs communicate. In ABAP's client–server environment, these are the screens of the SAP System. This chapter will teach you all the essentials of screens and how you can use them in your ABAP programs.

7.1 GENERAL SCREENS

In the following sections we will cover how to define and process screens. Because of the depth of the material we will first deal with the basic issues of this topic in detail before tackling a practical example in Section 7.1.8 containing the most important aspects of screen programming. If the sections before then seem too theoretical, you can skip to the example program before returning to the basic principles.

7.1.1 What are screens?

Screens are originally (i.e. in German) called *dynpros*, which is the abbreviation for **dynamic program**. Consequently, a screen is more than just a layout. A screen consists mainly of the actual layout with its screen elements and a screen flow logic. The screen flow logic is divided into a minimum of two processing blocks: PBO (Process Before Output), which is processed before the layout is sent, and PAI (Process After Input), which is processed after a user action on the front end. Screens form the basis of the most general layouts within an SAP System.

In a classical SAP System in which user dialogs occur solely through the SAP GUI components, screens are in fact the driving components of the entire system. As soon as you log on to the SAP System you start working with screens. Each layout you see belongs to a screen. You enter your data on screens, and screens display the output data of the ABAP programs on the front end. Selection screens, lists, messages in dialog boxes, etc. are ultimately nothing more than instances of special screens. Even the GUI controls introduced with Release 4.6 (see Section 7.5.4) must be coupled to screens.

In future releases the development of SAP towards e-business will entail many new presentational methods such as ITS (Internet Transaction Server) or the WebDynpro as well as classical screens. These will form the subject of future publications.

ABAP program

Each screen belongs to just one ABAP program, both statically and at runtime. The layouts of screens present the user with the visible side of an application program, whereas the ABAP program defines the processing logic, which runs invisibly. While it is being processed a screen calls the dialog module of its ABAP program in which the user inputs are evaluated and the output data is prepared (see Figure 7.1). In addition, a GUI status can be set for each screen, which provides the user with interaction options using the menu, standard toolbar, application toolbar, and the keyboard function keys.

An ABAP program can have several screens as components or subobjects. From a screen perspective, several screens share the data declarations and dialog modules of their ABAP program. Historically, screens are older than ABAP programs. Before the language of ABAP was developed, screens accessed application logic programmed in machine code.

Screen sequence

When a screen has been processed the **next screen** appears. This screen is either taken from the screen definition or can be defined in the ABAP program. In this way the screens of an ABAP program form **screen sequences**. These screen sequences are

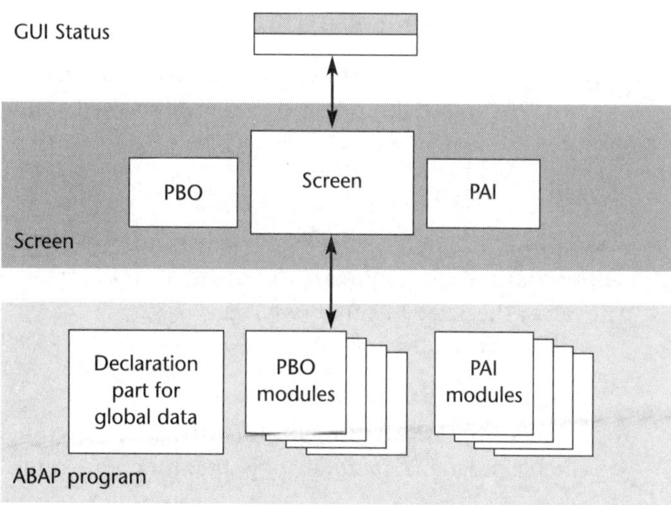

FIGURE 7.1 Screen and corresponding ABAP program

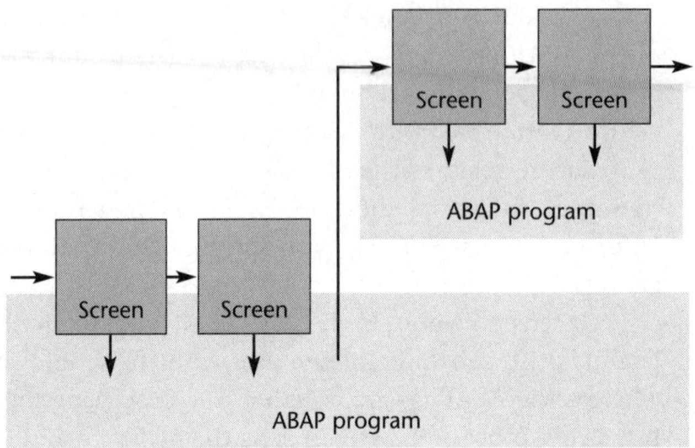

FIGURE 7.2 Screens, screen sequences, and ABAP programs

the basis of any dialog-oriented application in the SAP System where different screen processes result depending on the user actions.

Different screen sequences can be nested in each other by calling one screen sequence from another screen sequence of the same program or another ABAP program (see Figure 7.2).

If you log on to an SAP System, start one or more application programs, and then quit the SAP System, you have worked your way through several screen sequences, where the dialog modules of each screen sequence always belong to a common ABAP program. By choosing **System – Status** you can find the ABAP program to which the screen belongs from the **Program (Screen)** field.

7.1.2 Defining screens

Defining a screen involves editing several components in the Screen Painter tool of the ABAP Workbench. In Section 2.3.6 we showed you how you create a screen.

Screen attributes

Like ABAP programs, screens have attributes, which govern their behavior in the ABAP runtime environment. You maintain the attributes of a screen in the appropriate tab of the Screen Painter (see Figure 7.3).

The key attributes are:

- **Program**
  Name of the ABAP program to which the screen belongs. This can include executable programs, module pools, and function groups.
- **Screen number**
  Unique, maximum four-digit identification of the screen within the program.

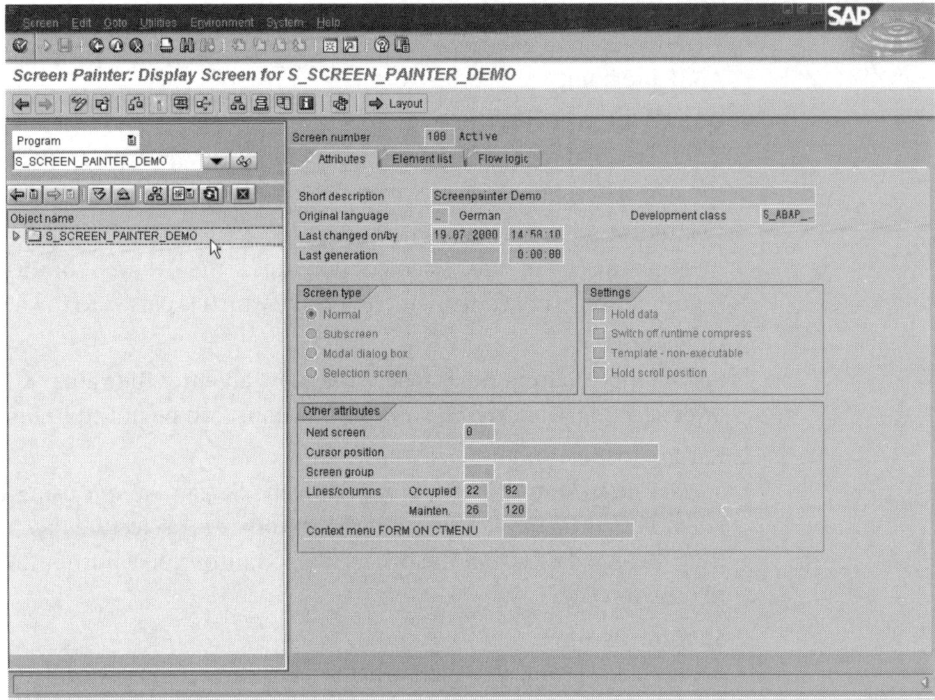

FIGURE 7.3 Maintaining attributes of a screen. Copyright © SAP AG

- **Screen type**
  The screen type determines whether the screen fills an entire GUI window or if it is to be shown as a modal dialog box that partially covers the previous screen. A **subscreen**-type screen can be displayed in a correspondingly defined screen area of another **screen** of the same program.
- **Next screen**
  Specifies the next screen of a screen sequence. A value of zero or no specification indicates that the current screen is the last in the screen sequence. Its own screen number means that the screen always calls itself. The screen number specified here can be dynamically overwritten in the ABAP program using the `SET SCREEN` statement.

Layout with screen elements

You maintain the actual layout of a screen with the **Graphical Screen Painter**, which you call using the *Layout* button from the **Screen Painter**. You can choose all the screen elements on the left-hand side of the Graphical Screen Painter and place them on the screen (see Figure 7.4). There are screen elements that only display contents and ones that permit user actions. The most important screen elements are:

- **Text fields and frames**
  Purely display elements whose contents cannot be changed by the user or the ABAP program.
- **Input/Output fields**
  Templates that are used to display data from the ABAP program or to input data by the user. They are linked to screen fields.
- **Pushbuttons**
  Areas on the layout that, when chosen, trigger the PAI event of the screen flow logic. A pushbutton is linked to a function code, which is passed to the ABAP program.
- **Checkboxes**
  Special input/output fields where the user can enter the value 'X' or ' ' by selecting or deselecting. Checkboxes, like pushbuttons, can be linked to function codes.
- **Radio buttons**
  Special input/output fields grouped in the Screen Painter using *Edit – Grouping – Radio Button Group – Define*. Users can only ever select a single field of a group; they thereby deselect all the others. Radio buttons, like pushbuttons, can be linked to function codes.
- **Subscreens**
  Areas on the layout in which other screens can be embedded.
- **Tabstrips**
  A tab on the layout that, when selected, allows you to switch between different subscreens.
- **Custom controls**
  Areas on the layout in which **GUI controls** can be displayed. GUI Controls are independent software components of the SAP GUI that communicate with the ABAP program by means of the Control Framework (CFW).
- **Table controls**
  Areas on classical layouts in which tabular input/output fields can be displayed. As of Release 4.6C, Table controls can be replaced by the ALV Grid Control (SAP List Viewer).

You can maintain attributes, such as appearance, for each screen element. You maintain the attributes of a screen element in the Graphical Screen Painter by double-clicking the element.

Screen Painter

Figure 7.4 shows the arrangement of some screen elements in the Graphical Screen Painter and the window where you can define the attributes of a screen element. Here, for example, we have specified a function code "PRESS" for the pushbutton of a layout.

Instead of maintaining each element individually, you can also select the *Element List* tab of the Screen Painter, which lists all the screen elements and their attributes (see Figure 7.5).

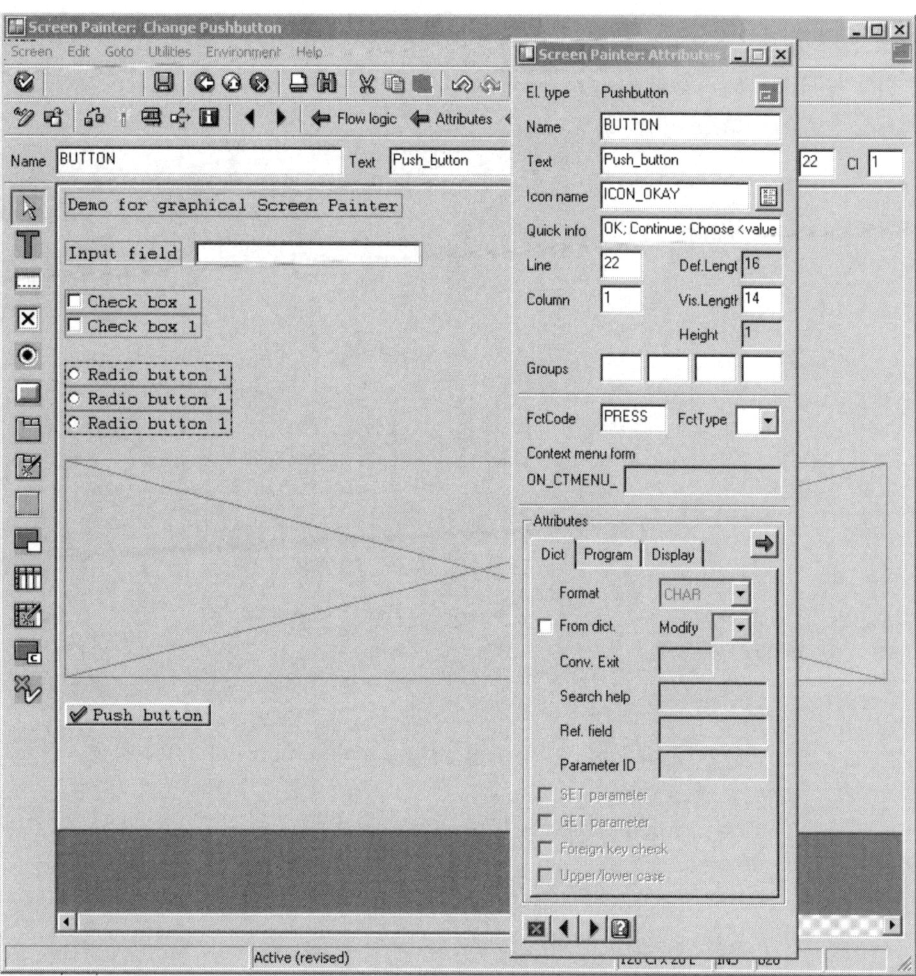

FIGURE 7.4 Screen elements in the Graphical Screen Painter. Copyright © SAP AG

The attributes defined in Screen Painter can be modified to an extent in the ABAP program. To do this you modify the predefined internal table `screen` at the PBO event. A common modification is to change the input-ready status of the field dynamically. For example, Figure 7.5 shows an element list containing a field called INPUT. To prevent this field from being input-ready, use the following code:

```
LOOP AT screen.
  IF screen-name = 'INPUT'.
    screen-input = '0'.
    MODIFY SCREEN.
  ENDIF
ENDLOOP.
```

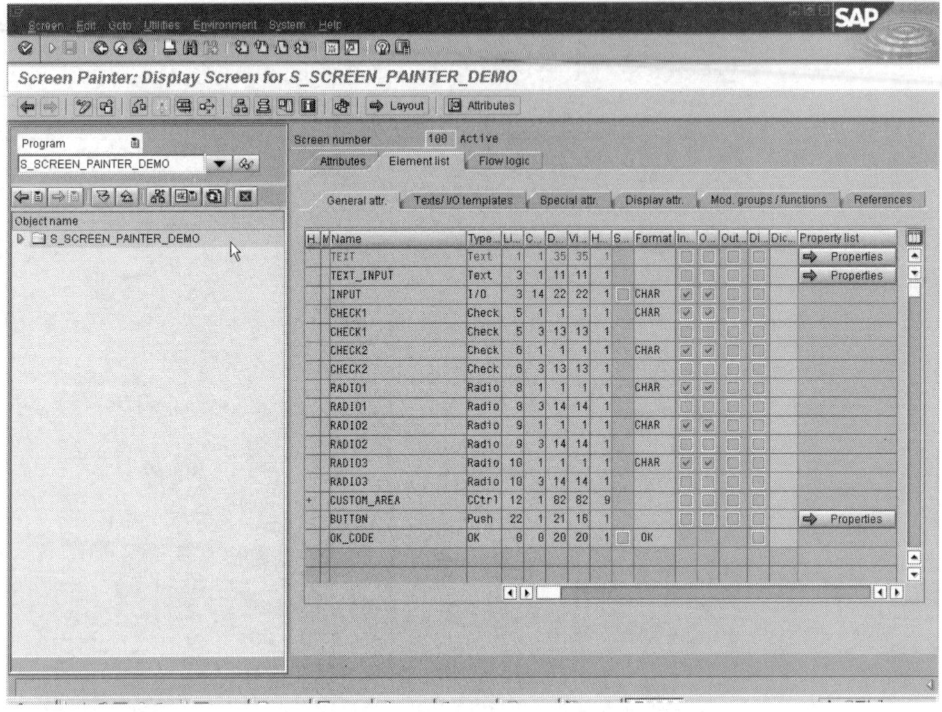

FIGURE 7.5 Element list of a screen. Copyright © SAP AG

The screen table can only be processed by its header row of the same name (see Section 7.7.3).

Screen fields

All screen elements that can receive user inputs are linked to screen fields. The data transport between the screen and the ABAP program takes place between these screen fields and global data objects of the same name in the ABAP program. Therefore, all modifiable screen elements must be provided with unique names. At the same time, the corresponding data objects must be declared in the ABAP program. The technical attributes of the screen fields such as length and data type are specified in the Screen Painter and should be selected accordingly for the data objects of the ABAP program (see Figure 7.6).

You can also proceed in the opposite manner: declare the required input and output fields only in the ABAP program, activate them, and then get the fields from the ABAP program into the screen in the Screen Painter.

Pure display elements such as text fields or frames are not linked to screen fields and do not necessarily require a unique field name. When screen elements are cre-

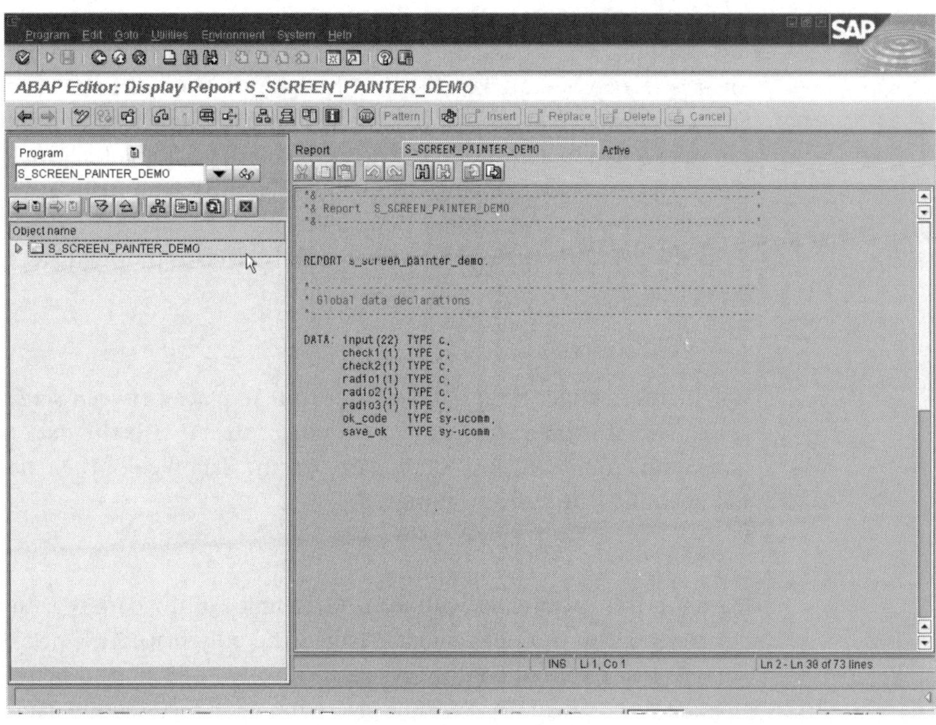

FIGURE 7.6 Global ABAP data objects for screen fields. Copyright © SAP AG

ated to which a text field is automatically assigned, such as checkboxes or selection buttons, text fields and screen elements have the same name (see Figure 7.5).

OK code field

In addition to the fields assigned to screen elements, each screen contains a 20-character OK code field (also called a function code field), which is not directly displayed on screen. The OK code field is always the last entry in the element list. It is used in user actions, such as selecting a pushbutton, to pass the corresponding function code to the ABAP program. In order to activate the OK code field you have to assign it a name in the element list. It has become customary to give the OK code field on every screen the same name, "**OK_CODE**". To evaluate it, you need a data object of the same name in the ABAP program. You specify the type of this field using the global type `sy-ucomm` (see Figure 7.6). When the pushbutton of our example screen from Figure 7.4 is chosen, the PRESS value is therefore passed to the `ok_code` field of the ABAP program.

Screen fields and the ABAP Dictionary

The ABAP Dictionary plays an even more important role in screen programming than in pure ABAP programming where it mainly acts as a global repository for type descriptions. In the ABAP Dictionary you can store semantic information in the form of descriptive texts, field and input helps for each data type. To use this information on a screen, you can get the required fields from the ABAP Dictionary in the Graphical Screen Painter, as we demonstrated in Section 2.3.6. When doing this you can refer to components of flat structures and database tables. This has the advantage that if the data type is changed subsequently, the screen fields as well as the fields in the ABAP program are automatically updated.

Tables

In the ABAP program you must specially declare the fields with the same name using the

```
TABLES struct.
```

statement, in order for a data transfer to take place between screen and ABAP program. This statement declares a data object `struct` with the data type `struct` of the same name from the ABAP Dictionary. For the data type of the data object `struct` the statement has the same meaning as:

```
DATA struct TYPE struct.
```

However, this declaration with a `TYPE` reference to the data type in the Dictionary is not sufficient to transfer the data. This is the only place in which the `TABLES` statement is still required.[1] Prior to Release 4.0, `TABLES` had to be specified before an Open-SQL statement, for example, every time you accessed the database.

To avoid naming conflicts between screen fields, program-internal work areas, and database tables, it is advisable to create special structures for the screens of your program in the ABAP Dictionary, containing all the required input and output fields of one or more screens of a program or development class. The work areas of the same name declared with `TABLES` in the ABAP program are then used only as an interface to screens (see the example program in Section 7.1.8).

Screen flow logic

The screen flow logic provides the procedural part of a screen and is defined in the *Flow Logic* tab of the Screen Painter. The programming language of the screen flow logic consists of a few keywords and has a similar syntax to ABAP, but should not be confused with ABAP.

Unlike in ABAP, there are no specific data declarations in the screen flow logic. The screen fields are defined either by the screen elements implicitly, or else are predefined like the OK field.

Processing block

In terms of structure, the screen flow logic consists of processing blocks, just like an ABAP program. There are exactly four event blocks, which are all introduced with the screen keyword `PROCESS`.

1. When using logical databases the `TABLES` statement can be replaced by the `NODES` statement.

```
PROCESS BEFORE OUTPUT.
  ...
PROCESS AFTER INPUT.
  ...
PROCESS ON HELP-REQUEST.
  ...
PROCESS ON VALUE-REQUEST.
```

The associated events are triggered by the ABAP runtime environment during screen processing.

- The processing block for the `PROCESS BEFORE OUTPUT` (PBO) event is processed immediately before the layout is sent. PBO is triggered at the moment when a screen is called (see Section 7.1.3). PBO processing therefore takes place after the PAI processing of the previous screen and is used to prepare the layout.
- The processing block for the `PROCESS AFTER INPUT` (PAI) event is triggered by every user action on the screen linked to a function code, and is used to process user inputs. After PAI processing the next screen is called and its PBO event is triggered.
- The POH and POV events cause the statements after `PROCESS ON HELP REQUEST` and `PROCESS ON VALUE REQUEST` to be processed. They are triggered when the user selects the field help (**F1**) or input help (**F4**) for a screen element. Your own help routines can be called here. After processing, the current screen processing continues.

In screen flow logic, the `PROCESS BEFORE OUTPUT` and `PROCESS AFTER INPUT` statements must be listed in the specified order. They are predefined when a screen in created in the Screen Painter (see Figure 7.7). The other two event blocks are optional and must only be specified if your program needs to respond to POH or POV in order to provide its own field or input help.

Behind each event keyword a small set of statements can be used whose main task is to call dialog modules in the corresponding ABAP program and to control the transport of data from the screen to the ABAP program.

Statement

The most important statements that can be used in event blocks of the screen flow logic are:

- `MODULE` for calling ABAP dialog modules
- `FIELD` for controlling the transport of screen fields
- `CHAIN` and `ENDCHAIN` for grouping together module calls in processing chains
- `CALL SUBSCREEN` for embedding a subscreen

For more details on individual statements refer to Section 7.1.5.

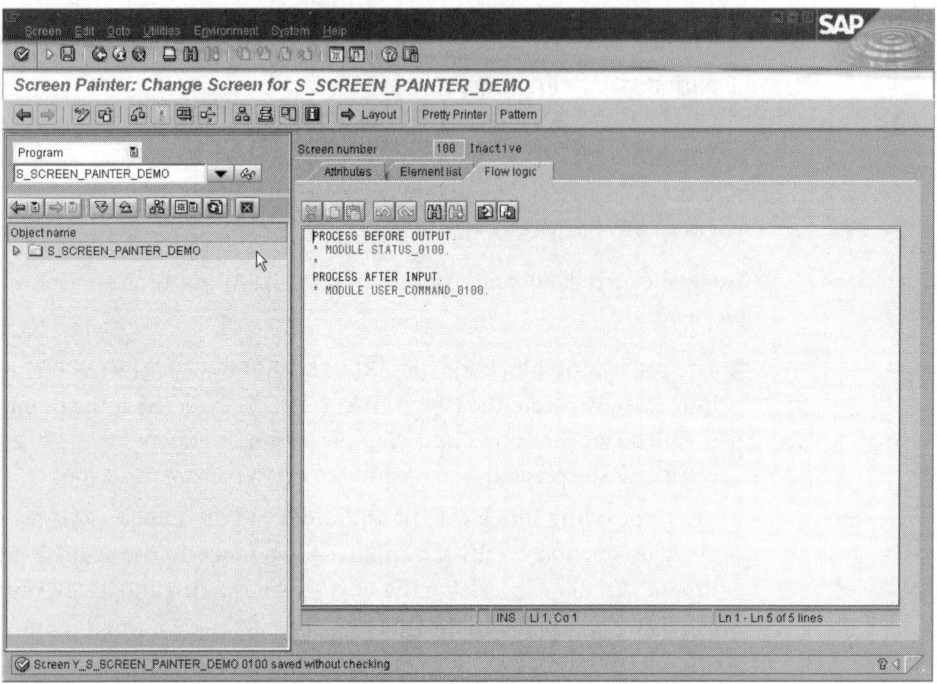

FIGURE 7.7 Predefined keywords used in the screen flow logic. Copyright © SAP AG

7.1.3 Calling screens and screen sequences

If you wish to work with screens or examine existing programs, you must know how screens are called. Figure 7.8 provides an overview of the various ways of calling screens.

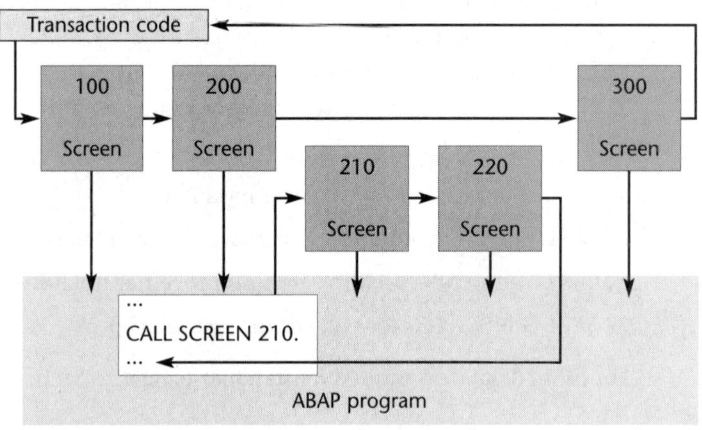

FIGURE 7.8 Possible screen calls

You can call screens outside an ABAP program using a transaction code or within an ABAP program using the `CALL SCREEN` statement. In addition, each screen can either call the next screen and thereby construct a screen sequence or terminate a screen sequence and return to where the call of the current screen sequence was made. The following sections will explain this in more detail.

Calling screens using a transaction code

In the Object Navigator, you can create a transaction code of up to 20 characters for any ABAP program that contains screens, by choosing **Create – Transaction – Dialog Transaction** in the context menu of the object list, in order to define the attributes of the transaction (see Figure 7.9).

Dialog transaction

Essentially you link the transaction code with any screen of the ABAP program. The selected screen thereby becomes the **initial screen** of a transaction.

What does the term transaction mean? In this context we use the term **transaction** to refer to the execution of an ABAP program started by a transaction code. Note, however, that the term transaction has several meanings. In OLTP (Online Transaction Processing), where several users work in dialog mode on a system, transaction is a general term for a user request [STA97]. The SAP definition of transaction as a program execution tends towards this general definition. In the context of

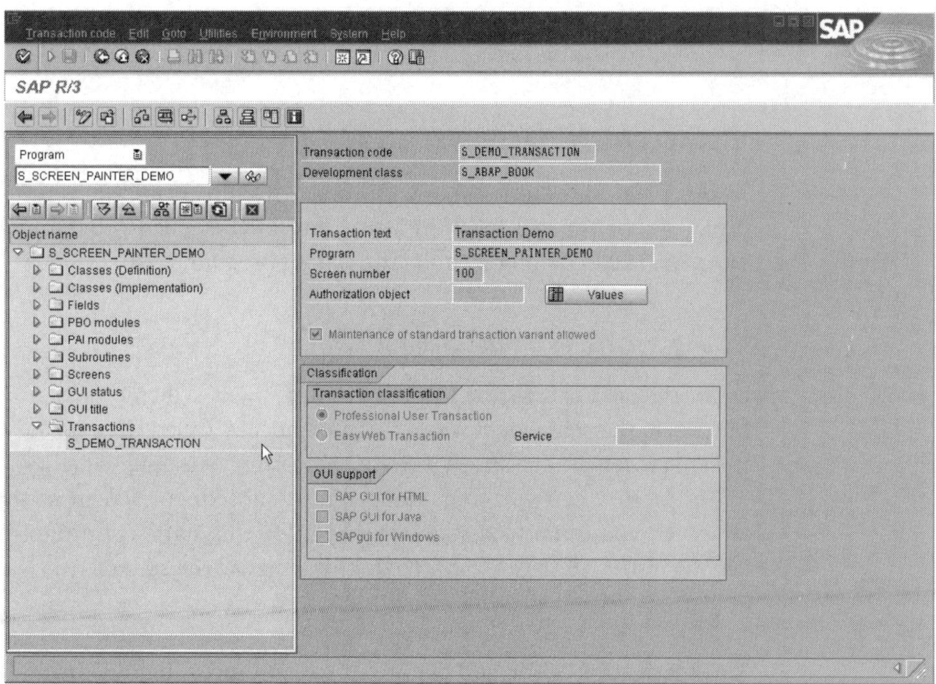

FIGURE 7.9 Creating a transaction code. Copyright © SAP AG

accessing database tables, however, the term transaction stands for modifications to the database state. As this is the very purpose of many screen-driven ABAP programs, in SAP the term transaction is often used synonymously for both.

Transaction call

How do I start a transaction? When a transaction code has been defined, you can start it immediately by directly entering the transaction code in the input field of the standard toolbar on any screen in the SAP System. The system then loads the ABAP program into memory and the PBO processing of the initial screen is triggered. The start of a transaction is therefore the same as calling a screen outside of its associated ABAP program.

Of course, end users should not have to start transactions by entering transaction codes, since this assumes they are aware of them. Instead, transaction codes are generally linked with elements of the user interface, such as menu entries. Choosing the graphic element then causes the transaction to be executed. A practical example of this was shown in the introduction in Figure 2.4, when we linked the transaction code of the Object Navigator, SE80, as a favorite with a node in SAP Easy Access. In our example from Figure 7.9 the new transaction can also be directly tested in the Object Navigator, by choosing **Execute – Direct** processing from the context menu of the object list.

Of course, you can also call transactions from ABAP programs. If you choose a node in SAP Easy Access that is linked to a transaction code, ultimately all that happens is that the corresponding ABAP program calls the selected transaction. The commands are:

```
CALL TRANSACTION  tcode ...
```

and

```
LEAVE TO TRANSACTION  tcode ...
```

As described in Section 3.3.6, with `CALL TRANSACTION` you return to the statement directly after the call location at the end of the called program whereas `LEAVE TO TRANSACTION` completely quits the calling program.

Calling a screen as a subsequent screen

Every screen has a subsequent screen (or "next screen"). When a screen has been processed, the subsequent screen is automatically called. This means that at the end of the PAI processing of a screen, the PBO processing of the subsequent screen always starts.

For each screen you must determine a subsequent screen in the Screen Painter. However, you can also dynamically override this static definition during screen processing in the ABAP program. To do this, you use the statement:

```
SET SCREEN  dynnr.
```

This means that at the end of current screen processing it is the screen `dynnr`, not the static subsequent screen, that is called. Both the static and a dynamically specified subsequent screen, with the exception of the special subsequent screen 0, must exist in the same ABAP program.

Screen sequence

Screens therefore form screen sequences that are defined by the subsequent screens. Since screens can be defined both statically and dynamically, you have complete freedom to group together any screen sequences from the screens of a program and to control their order according to current user actions. Remember our first application program S_FIRST_PROGRAM in Section 2.3. There we defined a loop-type screen sequence in which a screen repeatedly called itself. In the ABAP program, the sy-dynnr system field always provides access to the number of the current screen.

Screen number 0

All that remains is the question of how to terminate a screen sequence. This is where the screen number 0 we mentioned previously comes into play. Within a program there is no screen with the number 0. Instead you use this number to terminate a screen sequence. If you specify screen number 0 as a static subsequent screen or in the SET SCREEN statement, after the current screen processing the system returns to the statement immediately after the call location of the first screen in the screen sequence. If the first screen was the initial screen of a transaction, for example, the current ABAP program will be terminated and the system returns behind the call location of the transaction. The shortest screen sequence is a single screen, called using a transaction code or through the CALL SCREEN statement, which then goes directly to the subsequent screen 0.

Calling a screen with CALL SCREEN

In every processing block of an ABAP program that contains screens you can use the statement

```
CALL SCREEN dynnr.
```

to call any screen of the program. The called screen then becomes the first screen of a new screen sequence, just as the initial screen of a transaction is always the first screen of a screen sequence. When the subsequent screen 0 is reached in a screen sequence called using CALL SCREEN, the screen sequence is terminated and the program continues after the CALL SCREEN statement.

Nesting

If the CALL SCREEN statement is executed while a screen sequence is running – i.e. in a PBO or PAI module of any other screen – the called screen sequence is embedded in the currently running screen sequence. The current screen sequence is interrupted and a new one begins. Up to 50 screen sequences can be stacked on a screen sequence started by a transaction code. However, you should never stack more than 40 screen sequences, since the runtime environment can also embed additional screen sequences, e.g. for help and error dialogs.

An embedded screen sequence works with the global data of the ABAP program just like any other screen. When a screen sequence is called you should therefore take care not to overwrite any fields, such as the OK code field, which are required by the screens of the current sequence. This applies in particular to modal dialog boxes.

Dialog box

A modal dialog box is a special case of a screen embedded with CALL SCREEN. This kind of screen must be created in the Screen Painter with the **Modal Dialog Box**[2] screen type and can then be called with the ABAP statement:

```
CALL SCREEN dynnr
  STARTING AT  x1 y1
  ENDING AT    x2 y2.
```

While the dialog box is displayed the previous layout remains visible, but is inactive. Using the STARTING AT and ENDING AT options, you determine the initial and final position of the dialog box on the previous layout.

Leaving screens

If you do nothing else, a screen will quit when it reaches the end of its PAI processing. However, you can also program the screen processing to end by executing one of the two statements

```
LEAVE SCREEN.
```

or

```
LEAVE TO SCREEN  dynnr.
```

in the ABAP program. With the LEAVE SCREEN statement you can leave the current screen and go directly to its subsequent screen. The latter is either the static subsequent screen of the Screen Painter or is previously specified by SET SCREEN.

The LEAVE TO SCREEN statement is simply the short form of the two statements:

```
SET SCREEN dynnr.
LEAVE SCREEN.
```

Note that LEAVE SCREEN and LEAVE TO SCREEN do not terminate the overall screen sequence. The program simply goes to another screen in the same sequence, unless the subsequent screen has the number 0.

7.1.4 User actions on screens

The layouts of screens represent the classical interfaces between an ABAP program and its online users. In this section we shall look at the possible user actions on a screen.

Actions on screen elements

When a screen is called, its PBO logic is processed and the layout is then shown with its elements. The user can now work with the layout in various ways. There are two types of actions: those that trigger PAI processing and those that do not.

2. In general, screen 0 is recommended as next screen.

Function code

In general, the PAI event is caused by choosing screen elements that have been linked with a function code in Screen Painter. These include:

- Pushbuttons
- Checkboxes
- Radio buttons

Whereas pushbuttons without function codes are not particularly useful, linking checkboxes and radio buttons with function codes is not absolutely necessary and can be chosen on a case-by-case basis. Input fields are generally not linked to a function code and when filled they will not result in PAI processing, unless you are using drop-down list boxes (see Section 7.5.2).

Actions on the User Interface

As you know, an SAP front end generally offers a whole range of interaction options (apart from screen elements) with its menu, standard, and application toolbars (see Figure 7.10). As a developer of your own programs, you should also offer your users the functions of your program mainly through these resources. Often, so many functions are required that a screen with an equally large number of pushbuttons would be highly unergonomic. The linking of function codes with screen elements should therefore be restricted to the most important functions.

GUI status

How can you use menu, standard, and application toolbars? A GUI status is provided for this. A GUI status, like a screen, is an independent component of the ABAP program and is maintained with the Menu Painter tool from the ABAP Workbench.

A GUI status administers functions and makes them available to the screen user. Different types of GUI statuses have different purposes:

- Dialog status with menu bar, standard toolbar, and application toolbar for normal screens
- Special status for modal dialog boxes with an application toolbar
- Special status for context menus that can be activated with an alternate mouse click

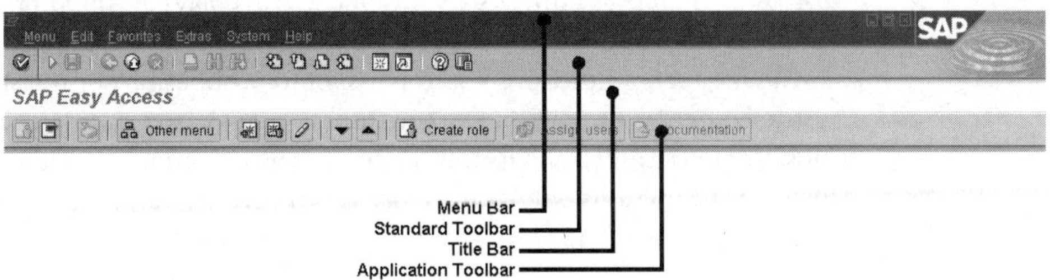

FIGURE 7.10 User interface of an SAP front end. Copyright © SAP AG

All these statuses can be defined alongside each other in the same ABAP program and work with the same functions of the program. We shall first concentrate on the dialog status.

Menu Painter

You define the functions of your program in the Menu Painter. To open the Menu Painter you choose, for example, in the Object Navigator the context menu of your program, followed by **Create – GUI Status**. There you define the functions by entering function codes and function texts and by linking them with the interactive elements of the GUI status. You can repeatedly use the same function, consisting of function code and function text, within a GUI status.

Function key

The interactive elements of a GUI status are the above-mentioned menu, standard, and application toolbars as well as the function key setting of the keyboard. You can also assign function codes to the function keys, such as ↵ or F5. In fact, a function code that you want to assign to the pushbutton or standard toolbar must first be linked to a function key. The icons of the standard toolbar are assigned to predefined function keys, such as F8 or ctrl + S, and a corresponding function text such as "Back" or "Save" is recommended. You can also assign icons to the functions on the application toolbar. No function code can be assigned to the function keys F1, F4, and F10. These functions are handled by the runtime environment.[3]

The Menu Painter supports you in your work by allowing you to use predefined functions as patterns. This means that you obtain functions with corresponding function texts, in the menu positions specified in the SAP Style Guide.

Figure 7.11 shows an example of working with the Menu Painter. Here we have assigned the function code PRESS, which was defined for the pushbutton of the demonstration screen from Figure 7.4, to the F5 key and a menu entry. By double-clicking PRESS we assigned an icon to this function. By opening up the application toolbar we also entered PRESS there. We defined three other new function codes, BACK, EXIT, and CANCEL, through entries in the standard toolbar and then assigned them to the menu entries that have been provided for them by previously selecting **Display standards**.

Double-clicking

The F2 function key is worth a special mention. This key is always linked with the double-click functions of the mouse. If you assign a function code to the F2 function key in the GUI status, this function can be triggered by the F2 key as well as by double-clicking a screen element. This plays an important part in classical list processing (see Section 7.3.7).

The number of functions you can assign to pushbuttons or the standard toolbar is restricted by the number of existing function keys. You should therefore assign the most common functions to the function keys and these bars, and contain the less important functions solely in the menus of the menu bar. Here you can create as many functions as you wish, as well as define sub-menus.

3. F1 and F4 call the field and input helps respectively, while F10 positions the cursor in the menu bar.

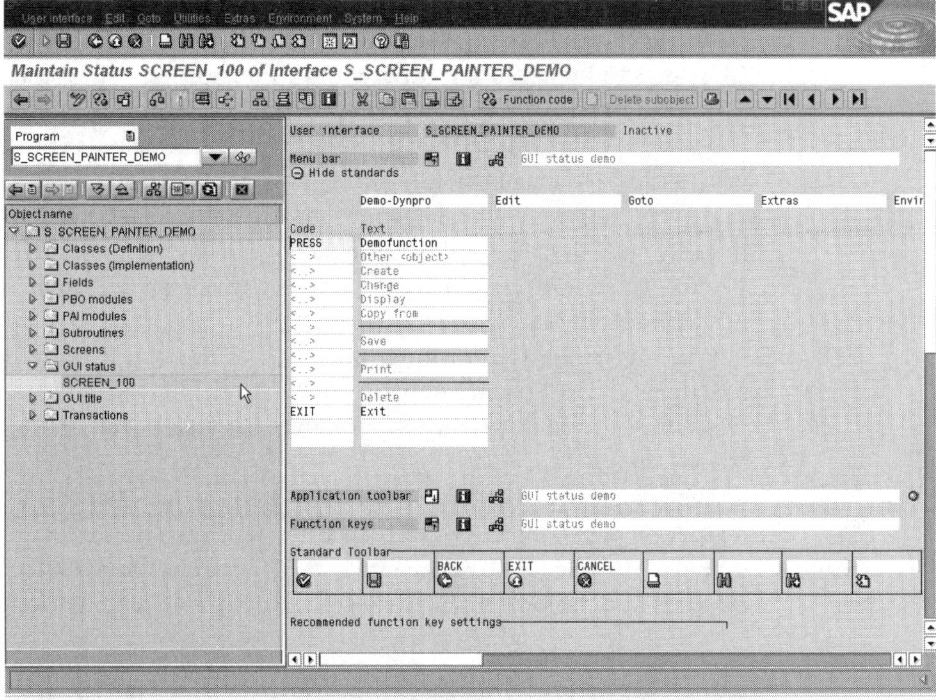

FIGURE 7.11 Working with the Menu Painter. Copyright © SAP AG

It should also be mentioned that the function key setting, application toolbar, and menu bar are independent components of the ABAP program, like the GUI status. In the Menu Painter you group these components into a GUI status. In Figure 7.11 each of these components initially bears the name of the GUI status, which, however, can be overridden at any time. You can therefore define sets of reusable settings that make the program functions available in different ways, and then combine these in different GUI statuses.

PBO

Depending on the functions you need, you then link your screens to the various GUI statuses of the program by executing the

```
SET PF-STATUS stat.
```

statement during PBO processing in a dialog module. This statement defines the user interface for all subsequent screens of a screen sequence until a new statement `SET PF-STATUS` sets another dialog status. It is also best to define the screen title of your screen at PBO with the statement:

```
SET TITLEBAR tit.
```

Titles are also GUI components of the program. To create a title you can, for example, activate forward navigation of the ABAP Workbench by double-clicking `tit`.

After setting a GUI status, its functions are available to the user on the same basis as the functions of screen elements with function codes. Choosing a function of the GUI status will result in the PAI event, with the exception of the above function keys F1, F4, and F10. Make sure you use the same function code for functions that you wish to offer both in the GUI status and on the layout. This lets the ABAP program evaluate it unambiguously in the ABAP program.

If everything we have said about the GUI status appears somewhat complicated, this is because the Menu Painter is in fact one of the more complex tools in the ABAP Workbench and we do not have the time to provide more than a fleeting insight into its full functions.

If you open the Menu Painter directly, not through forward navigation but by selecting it in SAP Easy Access or by calling transaction SE41, the Menu Painter initial screen is displayed (see Figure 7.12), with a list of all the objects administered by the Menu Painter.

The complexity of the Menu Painter lies in the fact that this tool is designed for highly complex transactions with a variety of screens. In such transactions the reuse of individual interface components is very important for usability – that is, the user can then find the same functions at the same place on different screens.

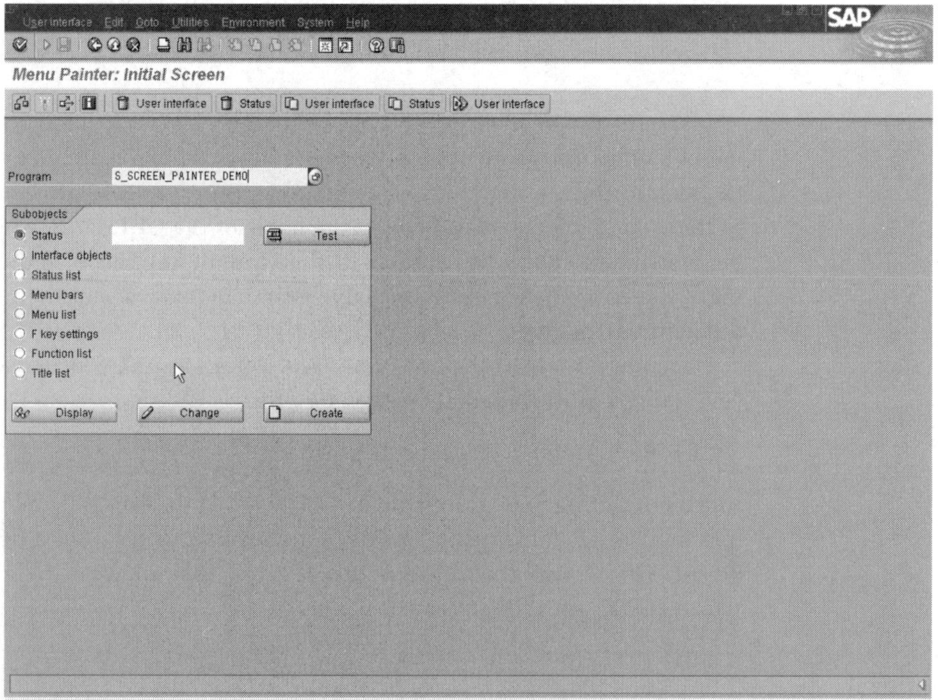

FIGURE 7.12 Entering the Menu Painter directly. Copyright © SAP AG

For simple applications or ones in which the complexity of many layouts is avoided by using tabs or GUI controls, the complexity of the Menu Painter boils down to the simple fact that the user is provided with a set of functions linked internally with function codes. By choosing **Goto – Object Lists – Function List** you find in the Menu Painter an overview of all the functions in the ABAP program. In a transaction with a single or just a few screens you will often get by with just one GUI status, as you can use the `EXCLUDING` addition to the `SET PF-STATUS` statement to specifically include or exclude the functions of the GUI status in the ABAP program.

Evaluating user actions

The OK code field mentioned in Section 7.1.2 is used to evaluate function codes. As soon as a user triggers the PAI event by selecting a function with a non-blank function code (the ↵ key in the Menu Painter is filled as standard with an empty function code for example), both the predefined sy-ucomm system field and the OK code field on the screen are filled with the corresponding function code. The value can be evaluated in the ABAP fields of the same name.

OK code field

In the ABAP program you should always work with the OK code field instead of the sy-ucomm system field, since sy-ucomm as a system field allows read access only. However, for the following reason it is advisable to initialize the OK code field before the current screen is terminated. At the PBO event, the contents of the OK code field in the ABAP program are assigned to the OK code field of the same name in the next screen (see Section 7.1.5). Thus this field may end up containing an undesired value during the processing of the next screen. To avoid this, you should save the function code at the start of PAI processing in an auxiliary variable and immediately clear the OK code field. You can then evaluate the contents of the help variable as shown in Listing 7.1.

LISTING 7.1 Evaluating function codes in a PAI module

```
MODULE user_command_0100 INPUT.
  save_ok = ok_code.
  CLEAR ok_code.
  CASE save_ok.
    WHEN 'BACK'.
      LEAVE TO SCREEN ...
    WHEN 'EXIT'.
      LEAVE PROGRAM.
    WHEN 'CANCEL'.
      LEAVE SCREEN.
    WHEN 'PRESS'.
      CALL METHOD screen_100=>handle_push_button.
  ENDCASE.
ENDMODULE.
```

7.1.5 Dialog module and data transport

Now that you know how to define a screen and provide the user with functions, we can concentrate on how a screen calls dialog modules in the ABAP program and how the input and output data is transported between the screen and the ABAP program.

Dialog modules are defined in the ABAP program with ABAP statements. However, dialog modules are called and the data transport is controlled through the statements of the screen flow logic.

Defining dialog modules

You define dialog modules in the ABAP program between the MODULE and ENDMODULE statements. Dialog modules that can be called at PBO have the addition OUTPUT, while those that can be called at PAI have the addition INPUT (see Listing 7.2).

LISTING 7.2 Defining dialog modules

```
* PBO Modules
MODULE  pbo_mod OUTPUT
   ...
ENDMODULE.
* PAI Modules
MODULE pai_mod INPUT
   ...
ENDMODULE.
```

At this point it is important to reiterate that dialog modules do not have a local data area. Data declarations in dialog modules are added to the global declarations of the ABAP program and should therefore not be used.

A dialog module is not linked to a specific screen of the ABAP program. You can call a dialog module in various ABAP program screens. By evaluating the sy-dynnr system field you always know which screen has just called the dialog module.

Module pool

The sole task of a classical ABAP program of the module pool type used to be to provide the program's screens with a collection of suitable dialog modules to process the screen data. The processing logic was generally defined directly in the dialog modules, which had the disadvantage that you could only work with global data. It is therefore advisable to use dialog modules now only for calling procedures, such as methods, which have their own data area (see the example in Section 7.1.8).

Calling dialog modules

The flow logic statement for calling a dialog module mod is:

```
MODULE  mod.
```

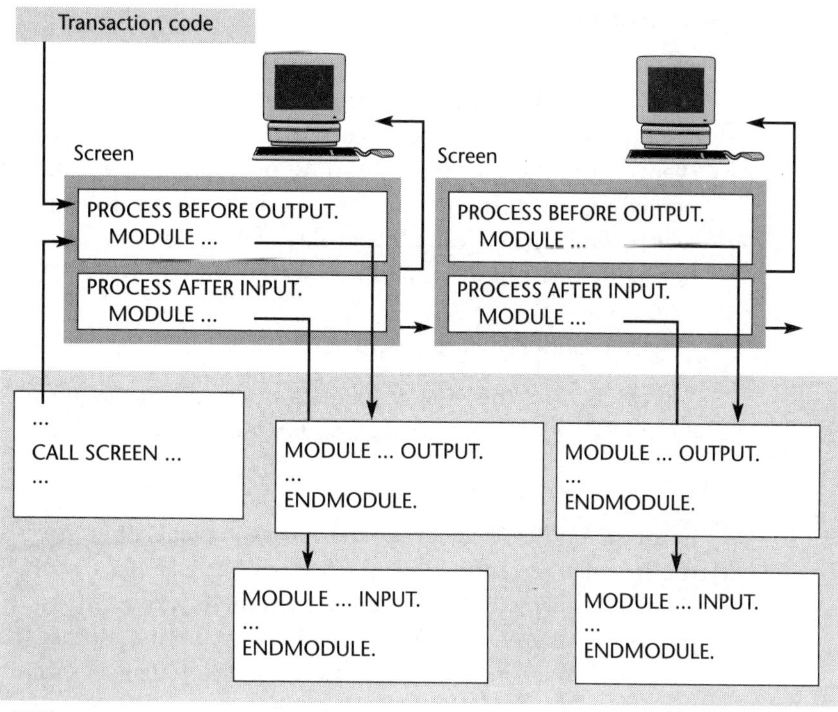

FIGURE 7.13 Calling dialog modules

This statement should not be confused with the ABAP statement for defining dialog modules. At the PBO event you can use `MODULE` to call all dialog modules that have been defined with the `OUTPUT` addition. At the PAI, POH, and POV events you can call dialog modules defined with the `INPUT` addition. Figure 7.13 summarizes how PBO and PAI modules are called.

You use the PBO event to prepare the screen layout display. The screen flow logic calls the corresponding ABAP dialog module. After PBO processing the screen layout is sent. The control changes from the application server to the presentation server. The screen layout is ready for input until the user triggers the PAI event with a corresponding action. The control then returns to the application server. You process the user inputs by calling suitably programmed dialog modules. After PAI processing, the PBO processing of the next screen starts.

Dialog step

The PAI processing of the current screen and the PBO processing of the next screen form a dialog step on the application server. The current screen layout remains displayed until PBO processing of the subsequent screen is concluded. However, it is not ready for input; instead it displays the hourglass to the user. This screen–dialog step–next screen sequence is SAP's own implementation of the general input–processing–output flow.

Automatic data transport

The transport of data between screen and ABAP program can be either automatic or programmed. Automatic data transport is shown in Figure 7.14.

Automatic data transport starts at the beginning of a dialog step (i.e. at the PAI event), from the screen to the ABAP program, and at the end of a dialog step, i.e. immediately before the new screen layout is sent, from the ABAP program to the screen. All data between global ABAP fields and screen fields of the same name are transported **within** the application server.

Program-controlled data transport

You can control the time of the data transfer from the screen to the ABAP program during PAI processing by using the statement

```
FIELD  dynpfield.
```

in the screen flow logic of the PAI processing block. In this case, the data transport of the specified screen field `dynpfield` does not take place at the beginning of PAI processing but when the `FIELD` statement is executed. At the beginning of PAI processing, therefore, the only fields transported are those that are not in a `FIELD` statement. You can therefore control the data transport specifically before individual dialog modules are called. Prior to the data transport the old values are available in the ABAP variables. Controlling the data transport becomes particularly significant in conjunction with conditioned module calls and input checks.

Conditioned module calls

By combining the `FIELD` statement with the `MODULE` statement you can make the calling of PAI modules dependent on certain conditions. To call a module `mod` when a screen field `dynpfield` contains a non-initial value, you use:

```
FIELD dynpfield MODULE mod ON INPUT.
```

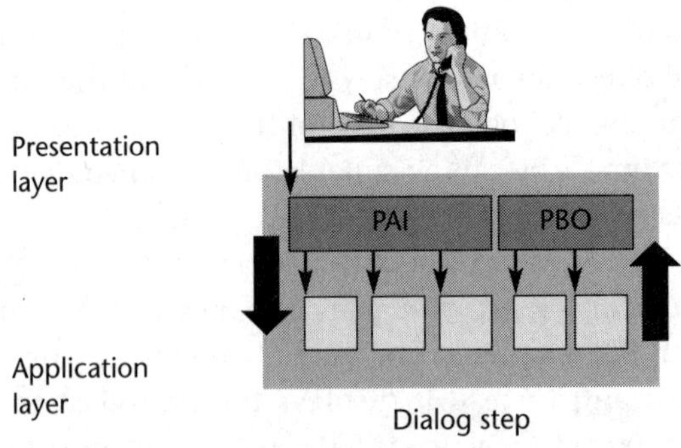

FIGURE 7.14 Automatic data transport

Single field

If you only want to call a module mod when the value of a screen field dynpfield has changed since the PBO event, in general by means of a user input, you use:

```
FIELD dynpfield MODULE mod ON REQUEST.
```

If you want to link conditions to several screen fields and also want to subject several module calls to the condition, you must group screen fields and module calls together in processing chains, which are defined between CHAIN and ENDCHAIN:

```
CHAIN.
  FIELD: dynpfield1, dynpfield2,...
  MODULE mod1 ON {CHAIN-INPUT|CHAIN-REQUEST}.
  FIELD: dynpfield3, dynpfield4,...
  MODULE mod2 ON {CHAIN-INPUT|CHAIN-REQUEST}.
  ...
ENDCHAIN.
```

Processing chain

The additions ON CHAIN-INPUT and ON CHAIN-REQUEST act in the same way as the ON INPUT and ON REQUEST additions for single fields. A dialog module is called as soon as at least one of the previously listed fields in the processing chain in a FIELD statement satisfies the condition. As you can see here, chained statements with a colon and commas are also possible in screen flow logic.

The function of the FIELD statement for controlling data transport remains the same in a processing chain.

7.1.6 Input checks

It is often necessary to check user inputs on screen layouts for errors and consistency before starting the actual data processing, such as database access. To do this, the runtime environment provides you with a range of automatic input checks. However, you can also program your own checks.

Automatic input checks

Automatic input checks are executed during the PAI event before the data is transferred to the ABAP program and before dialog modules are called. If the automatic input check finds an error, it is displayed in the status bar of the screen and the corresponding fields remain ready for input. The user must correct his or her inputs, which in turn triggers PAI again. The actual PAI processing starts when the automatic input check finds no more errors.

The system performs automatic input checks in the following sequence:

1 **Required entries**

Input fields can be identified in the Screen Painter as required entry fields. The user must fill each required entry field before PAI processing can begin.

2 Input format and value range

The user must enter type-specific values in input fields. A DATS-type date must, for example, be a character string with a length of ten characters in the format MM/DD/YYYY, where all characters must be digits and the characters for MM and DD must be less than or equal to 12 and 31 respectively.

3 ABAP Dictionary

If you have defined input fields by getting them from the ABAP Dictionary, and the field in the Dictionary is linked to a check table by means of a foreign key relationship, the user may only enter values that are present as foreign keys in the check table. In this case an automatic database access is performed, which you do not have to program.

If the copied field follows the two-stage domain concept and the corresponding domain has fixed values in the Dictionary, the user can only enter these values.

The runtime environment provides automatic input helps to help the user enter the correct values (see Section 7.1.7).

Avoiding automatic input checks

As described in the previous section, the automatically checked inputs must first be identified as being error-free before a module can be called. The user must fill all the required entry fields, and all the checks against the value lists and check tables must be satisfactorily concluded.

Function type

Users who simply want to interrupt processing, for whatever reason, may end up having to make extensive and (for them) unnecessary entries before they can quit the screen. To enable the user to quit a screen without these checks, you require type E function codes. You can enter this type in the attributes of screen elements on the screen layout (see Figure 7.4) or by double-clicking a function in the Menu Painter (see Figure 7.15).

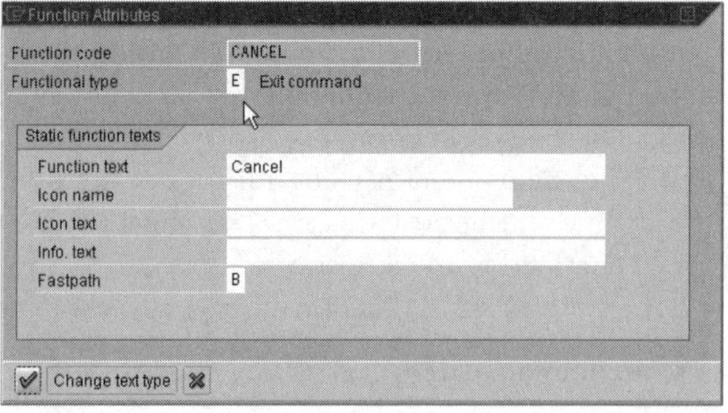

FIGURE 7.15 Maintaining the function type. Copyright © SAP AG

This function type is often assigned to all functions that are used to quit the front end. In Figure 7.11 these were BACK, EXIT, and CANCEL. In our example transaction in Section 7.1.8, however, we shall proceed in a slightly more sophisticated way.

Exit command

Functions with function type E do not start normal PAI processing. Instead they go immediately to the following module call in the screen flow logic:

```
MODULE mod AT EXIT-COMMAND.
```

When this statement is executed, only the OK code field is transported. The normal PAI event is processed only when no MODULE statement has the AT EXIT-COMMAND addition. Conversely, a normal un-typed function code will not cause this statement to be executed.

In the called PAI module you can use a suitable LEAVE statement to ensure that the system quits the entire program, a call chain, or just the current screen. If you do not leave the screen during the module, normal PAI processing will start after it has terminated, including automatic input checks and calling of the normal PAI modules.

Input checks you program yourself

To perform input checks to intercept errors that are not automatically detected, you must transport the fields to be checked to appropriate programmed dialog modules using the FIELD statement, where you display a suitable error dialog if an error occurs. To do this you use the FIELD and CHAIN statements we encountered in Section 7.1.5.

Single field

To check an individual field, you use:

```
FIELD  dynpfield MODULE mod.
```

If you output a warning or an error message in the mod dialog module – i.e. you use the MESSAGE statement with type W or E (see Section 7.4.3) – the appropriate input field on the current screen is made ready for input again and the user can repeat the input. PAI processing then starts again immediately at the FIELD statement after automatic checking and the previous modules are not called again.

Processing chain

To check several fields, you use a processing chain:

```
CHAIN.
  FIELD: dynpfield1, dynpfield2,...
  MODULE mod1.
  FIELD: dynpfield3, dynpfield4,...
  MODULE mod2.
  ...
ENDCHAIN.
```

If you display a warning or an error message in one of the dialog modules within a processing chain, the input fields of all the fields listed in the processing chain are made ready for input again. PAI processing then starts again immediately at the CHAIN statement after automatic checking.

This mechanism changes slightly if you specify the same field in several FIELD or CHAIN statements. When PAI processing continues with the corrected value, it starts again with the first FIELD or CHAIN statement that contains any one of the fields listed in the FIELD or CHAIN statement in which the error has occurred and that were changed by the user the last time the screen layout was displayed.

7.1.7 Field and input helps

As you know, you can place the cursor on any input field on any SAP screen layout and press the F1 or F4 keys to obtain a field help (direct help) or an input help (value list) for this screen element. In this section we will show you how to provide the user of your programs with such helps.

Field help

The range of possible field or F1 helps covers pre-defined display texts through calling complete ABAP programs, such as the ABAP keyword documentation in Figure 2.41. The predefined texts are generally created in the ABAP Dictionary but other documentation modules can also be called.

Texts from the ABAP Dictionary

If you have defined input fields by getting them from the ABAP Dictionary, the user automatically obtains a display of the data element documentation by pressing the F1 key. The **data element documentation** is a text that can be created for each data element (see Section 4.2.5) in the ABAP Dictionary. If the predefined documentation of a data element does not suit your application, in the data element maintenance in the ABAP Dictionary you can extend it with supplementary program and screen-specific documentation for the data element by choosing **Supplementary Documentation.**

Supplementary documentation

To display data element supplementary documentation, you must create the following event block for the POH event (Process On Help Request) in the screen flow logic:

```
PROCESS ON HELP-REQUEST.
  FIELD dynpfield WITH num.
```

Here, num is the number of the screen-specific data element supplementary documentation.

Other help texts

If the help texts from the ABAP Dictionary are not sufficient, you can call your own dialog modules at the POH event and program your help functions there.

```
PROCESS ON HELP-REQUEST.
  FIELD dynpfield MODULE mod.
```

POH

At the POH event, dialog modules can only be called in conjunction with the `FIELD` statement. The `mod` module is executed outside of the normal PAI processing at the moment when the user selects **F1**. Furthermore, the `FIELD` statement does not provide data transport for the `dynpfield` screen field at POH.

In the called dialog module you yourself must ensure that a suitable help is displayed. To do this you can use function modules such as HELP_OBJECT_SHOW to display any texts created in SAPScript or suitable function modules to access the SAP Knowledge Warehouse. Furthermore, you might even use GUI controls to display your own HTML documents.

Input help

One of the main strengths of classical SAP screens are the extensive input helps for input fields, which always correspond to the current dataset in the database. This is mainly achieved by defining search helps in the ABAP Dictionary, with which you can access the required database tables without having to program the database access yourself and receive predefined selection lists. In exceptional cases, however, you can also program your own input helps in dialog modules.

Input helps from the ABAP Dictionary

The ABAP Dictionary provides a complete hierarchy of input helps. If you have defined input fields by getting them from the ABAP Dictionary, the corresponding input help from the ABAP Dictionary will automatically be displayed to the user on pressing the **F4** key.

The following terms from the ABAP Dictionary play a part here:

- **Fixed values**
  When defining domains that often describe the technical features of data elements (see Section 4.2.5), you can limit the value range by specifying fixed values. The fixed values must not be confused with the specification of value tables. Unlike fixed values, as of Release 4.0 the latter are no longer used for input help.
- **Check tables**
  Relationships between relational databases are mapped in the ABAP Dictionary using foreign keys. A dependent table is called a foreign key table and a referred table is called a check table. The key fields of the check table or the search help linked to the check table can act as input helps for fields of the foreign key table.
- **Search helps**
  A search help is an independent repository object that you can create with the Dictionary tool (SE11) from the ABAP Workbench. A search help is the primary

tool for input help on screen fields. Search helps in the ABAP Dictionary can be linked with structure components, data elements, and check tables. You can also link search helps in the Screen Painter directly with screen fields.

Figure 7.16 shows how a search help is defined in the ABAP Dictionary. This search help defines the data from the hitlist from the SCARR table that is to be read (**Data collection**). It also specifies that the values found are displayed immediately without prior constraint in a selection list (**Dialog behavior**) and ensures that the CARRNAME field is displayed although CARRID is passed (**Parameter**).

To adapt a predefined search help to suit your requirements, you can also specify a function module you programmed yourself with a special interface in the **Search help exit** field. This is then called at predefined times when the search help is run.

Search help

The following list shows the input helps of the ABAP Dictionary in order of increasing priority. This means that an input help with a low number is only applied if it is not overridden by the definition of an input help with a higher number. By **Field** we mean a component of a structured data type from the ABAP Dictionary.

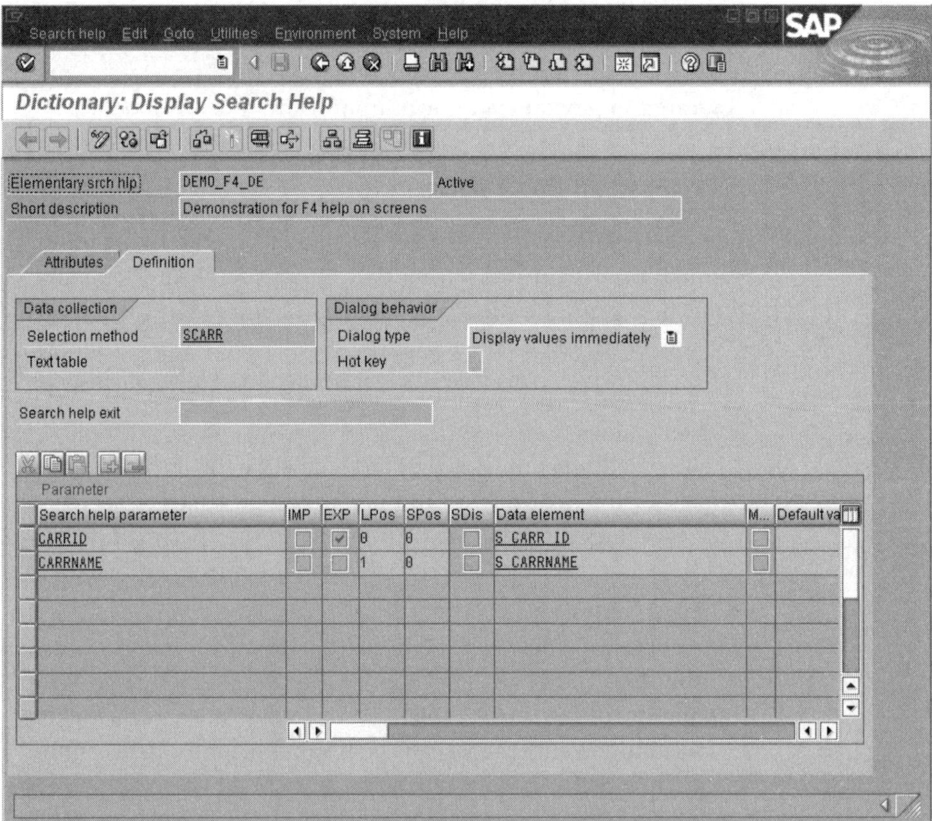

FIGURE 7.16 Defining a search help. Copyright © SAP AG

1 If no other input helps are defined for screen fields of data type DATS and TIMS, an interactive calendar or time help is displayed.

2 If neither a check table nor a search help is defined for a field, the data element of the field is not linked with a search help and if the domain of the input field has fixed values, these are displayed as an input help.

3 If no check table and no search help is specified for a field, but the data element itself is linked to a search help, this will be displayed.

4 If a check table without a text table and without its own search help is defined for a field, and if the field does not have its own search help, the contents of the key fields of the check table are displayed as an input help.

5 If a *text table* is defined for the check table of a field, the corresponding text from the text table will be displayed in the input help in the logon language of the user in addition to the key values.

6 If a custom search help is linked to the check table, the search help is displayed with the values from the check table, thereby enabling the value transport of several parameters.

7 If a search help is directly linked to the field in the ABAP Dictionary, the search help will be displayed as an input help.

8 You can also attach search helps directly to any given screen field in the Screen Painter. This attachment overrides the above mechanisms in the ABAP Dictionary.

When search helps are attached directly to fields in the ABAP Dictionary or screen fields, you should ensure that the search help only offers values that are also present in the check table, in order to avoid an error during the automatic input check.

Self-defined input help

Only if the options for input help in the ABAP Dictionary, including search help exits, really do not suffice for your requirements should you call your own dialog modules for the POV (Process On Value Request) event and create your fully independent input helps there:

```
PROCESS ON VALUE-REQUEST.
  FIELD dynpfield MODULE mod.
```

POV

As with the POH event, with POV you can also call dialog modules only in conjunction with the FIELD statement. The mod module is executed outside of normal PAI processing at the moment when the user chooses **F4** on the dynpfield field. There is no automatic data transport from the screen to the ABAP program with POV either, and the FIELD statement does not trigger the transport of dynpfield. Similarly, the PBO event is not triggered and no data is automatically transported from the ABAP program to the screen at the end of the called module(s).

In the mod dialog module you can create your own value list, generally through database access, and make this available to the user in any form, although preferably in dialog boxes. Prior to the introduction of controls technology, classical interactive lists were the best way of displaying the selection list, but now ALV Grid Controls are more suitable.

With selection lists you define yourself, however, you must take care of the data transport between the screen and the ABAP program. If your input help is to depend on values already entered, you must read them at the beginning of POV processing and you must transport the values selected by the user into the corresponding screen fields at the end. To do this, use the function modules DYNP_VALUES_READ and DYNP_VALUES_UPDATE.

Reuse Library

In the mod dialog module you can, however, also use part functions of the search help from the ABAP Dictionary. To gain an overview of the various functions, in SAP Easy Access under **ABAP Workbench** select the **Overview – Reuse Library** node (Transaction SE83, delivered with Basis Release 4.6C). If you open the **Standard – F4** node here, you will find all the function modules released for this purpose (see Figure 7.17) on the **Program objects** tab. As well as DYNP_VALUES_READ and DYNP_VALUES_UPDATE, F4IF_INT_TABLE_VALUE_REQUEST is of particular interest for input helps you program yourself. This function module displays your values created in the ABAP program as an internal table and returns the user's selection to the corresponding screen fields.

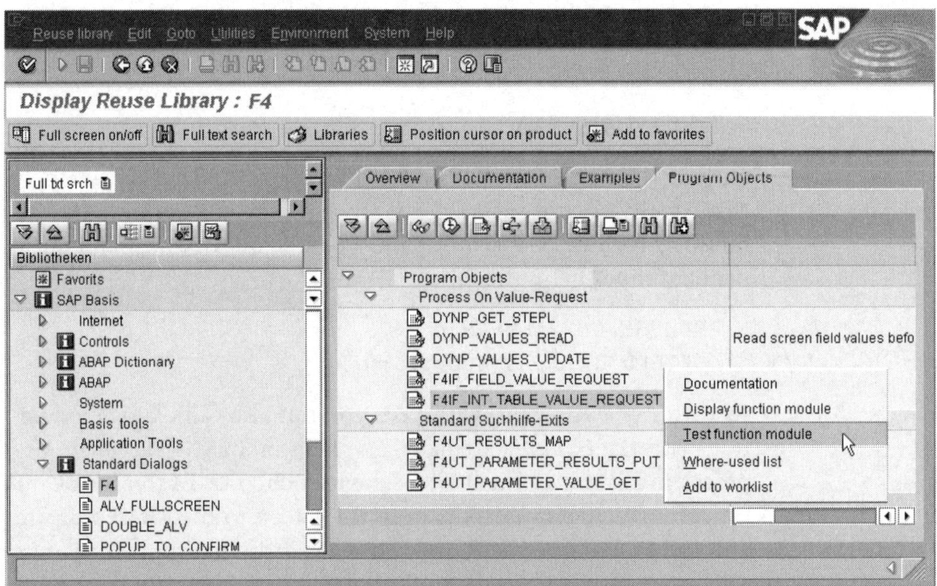

FIGURE 7.17 The Reuse Library. Copyright © SAP AG

7.1.8 An example transaction

In this section we will introduce you to the ABAP program S_CHANGE_PLANETYPE, which again incorporates the key aspects of screen programming in a practical example.

Introducing the example program

The program works with three screens, 100, 200, and 210. We have assigned the transaction code S_CHANGE_PLANETYPE to screen 100. When this transaction is called, the layout of screen 100 appears as shown in Figure 7.18.

All three input fields are required entry fields. The screen performs input checks and offers extensive input helps. A pushbutton allows the user to modify the plane type of the selected flight. If the user selects this function, the layout of screen 200 appears (see Figure 7.19).

Here we have displayed some information on the selected flight. The user can enter a different plane type and save it in the database. Here, too, an input help is offered and various input checks are performed. If the user wishes to save a plane type that does not have enough seats for the existing booking, an error message appears in the status bar and the new type is not saved (see Figure 7.20). The system then tells you whether or not your changes have been saved successfully.

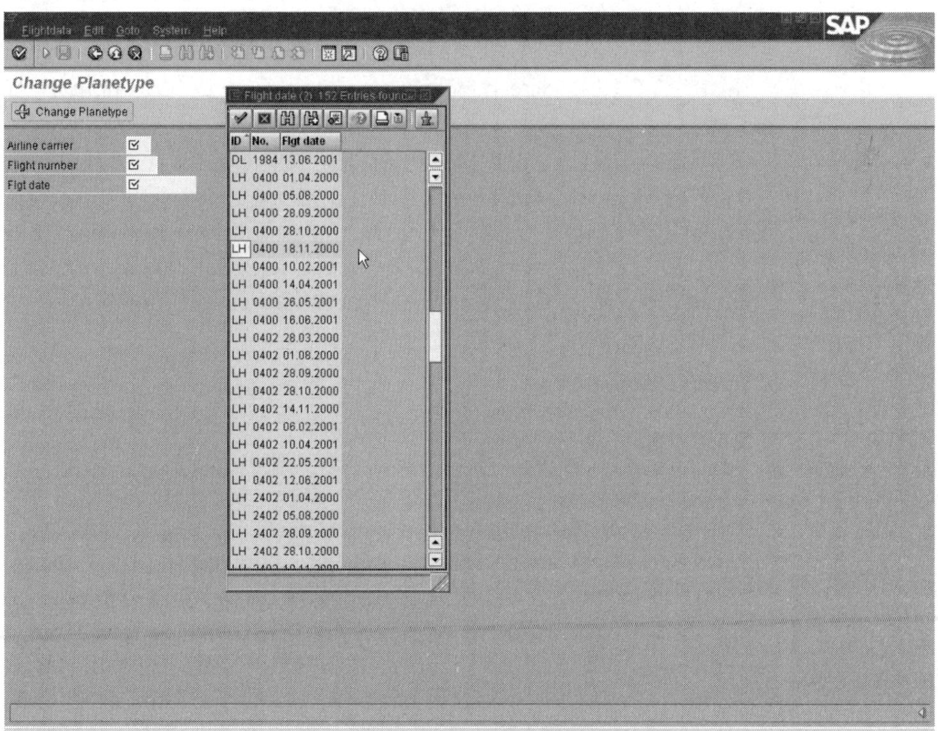

FIGURE 7.18 Initial screen of the example program. Copyright © SAP AG

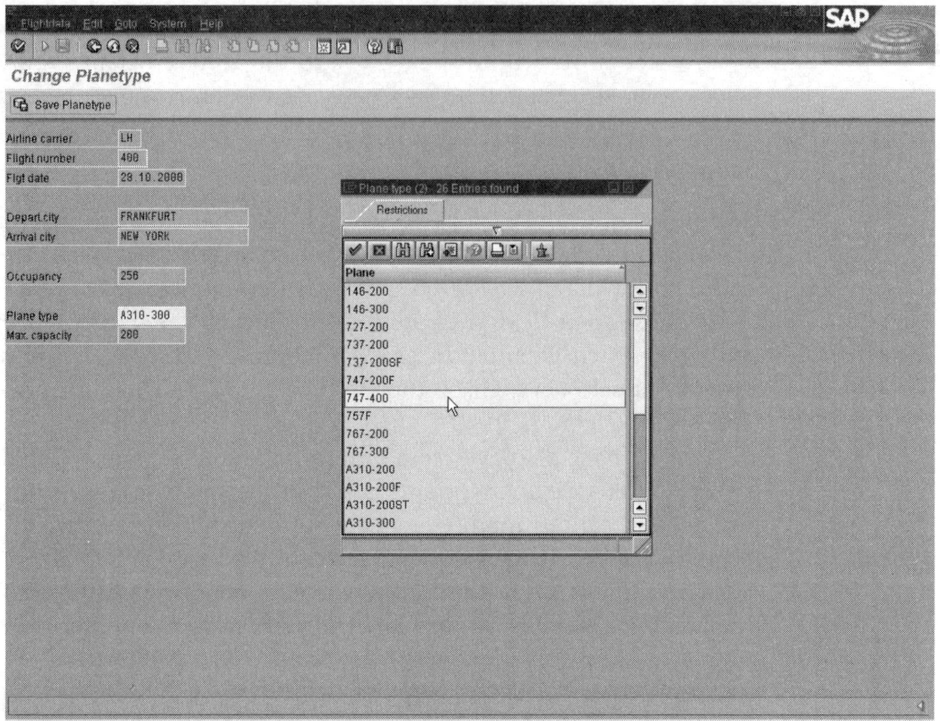

FIGURE 7.19 Screen for changing the plane type. Copyright © SAP AG

If after entering a new plane type the user wishes to quit the screen layout through **Back** or **Exit**, without having saved it, the screen layout of screen 210 appears as a modal dialog box in which he or she must confirm this (Figure 7.21).

Using the **Cancel** function, however, the user can terminate the processing of screens 100 and 200 at any time without further confirmation.

Screen Description

Screen 100

The static subsequent screen of screen 100 is screen 100 itself. If no other subsequent screen is set in the program, it will call itself. We have created the three input fields in the Graphical Screen Painter simply by copying the three fields CARRID, CONNID, FLDATE from the DEMO_CONN structure from the ABAP Dictionary, and in the attributes of all three input fields have checked the **Required Field** checkbox. In the element list of the screen we have given the OK field the name OK_CODE.

The DEMO_CONN structure has been specially created in the ABAP Dictionary for screens of the flight data model. It groups together fields of the individual database tables commonly used in screens and provides suitable input helps and input checks.

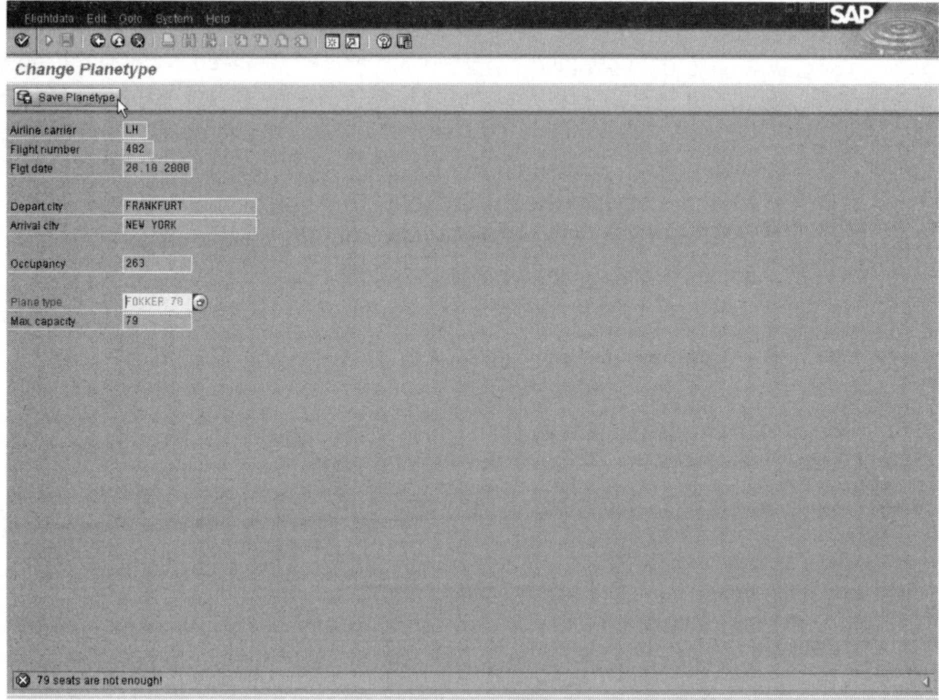

FIGURE 7.20 Error message in screen 200. Copyright © SAP AG

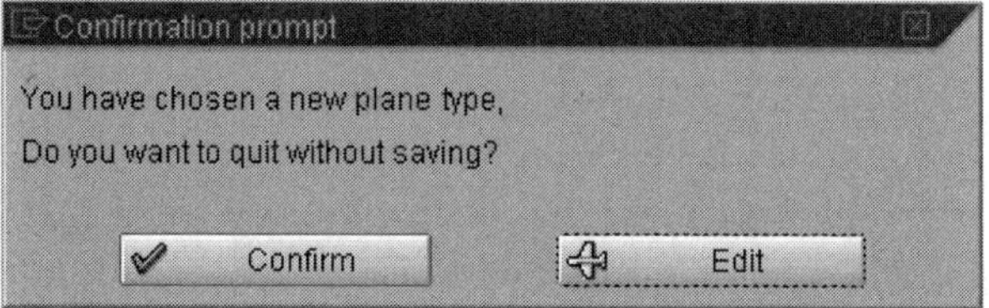

FIGURE 7.21 Screen 210 as a modal dialog box. Copyright © SAP AG

We have defined the screen flow logic of screen 100 as follows:

```
PROCESS BEFORE OUTPUT.
  MODULE set_status.
PROCESS AFTER INPUT.
  MODULE cancel AT EXIT-COMMAND.
  FIELD demo_conn-fldate MODULE handle_user_command.
```

At PAI we therefore call two dialog modules of which `cancel` can only be called with type E function codes and the other only with normal function codes. We have introduced the `FIELD` statement in order to be able to perform a custom input check for `demo_conn-fldate`.

Screen 200

The static subsequent screen of screen 200 is screen 200 itself. If no other subsequent screen is set in the program, it will call itself. We have copied the fields CARRID, CONNID, CITYFROM, CITYTO, SEATSOCC, PLANETYPE, and SEATSMAX from the DEMO_CONN structure from the ABAP Dictionary. For all fields besides PLANETYPE we have deactivated the **Input Field** checkbox in the attributes so that these fields are now only used for display purposes. In the element list of the screen we have again given the OK field the name OK_CODE.

For screen 200 the screen flow logic is:

```
PROCESS BEFORE OUTPUT.
  MODULE set_status.
PROCESS AFTER INPUT.
  MODULE cancel AT EXIT-COMMAND.
  FIELD demo_conn-planetype MODULE handle_user_command.
```

The only difference to the flow logic of screen 100 is that we have specified demo_conn-planetype behind the FIELD statement when the handle_user_command module is called. The custom input check should handle this field in this case. Screens 100 and 200 therefore call the same dialog modules of the ABAP program.

Screen 210

The static subsequent screen of screen 210 is screen 0. Unlike the other screens, we have defined screen 210 as a **modal dialog box** and reduced the size of the screen layout. We have created two pushbuttons on the screen layout to which we have assigned icons, texts, and the function codes CONFIRM and CHANGE_AGAIN. As with the other screens, we have named the OK code field OK_CODE.

The screen flow logic for screen 210 is:

```
PROCESS BEFORE OUTPUT.
  MODULE set_status.
PROCESS AFTER INPUT.
```

Screen 210 does not require a PAI module. As with the other screens, the PBO module set_status is called at PBO.

Description of GUI status

For our example program we have created the two GUI statuses SCREEN_100_200 and SCREEN_210. SCREEN_100_200 is designed to be used by both screens, 100 and 200.

GUI Status SCREEN_100_200

This GUI status is a dialog status with which we administer the functions listed in Table 7.1.

TABLE 7.1 Functions in the GUI Status SCREEN_100_200

Function Text	Function Code	Function Key	Application toolbar	Standard toolbar	Menu bar
Back	BACK	F3		X	Goto
Exit	EXIT	⇧ + F3		X	Flight data
Cancel	CANCEL	F12		X	Edit
Change plane type	CHANGE	F5	X		Flight data
Save plane type	UPDATE	F6	X		Flight data

Table 7.1 shows that in the Menu Painter, for example, we have assigned the CHANGE function code to the F5 function key, a key from the application toolbar, and a menu entry in the "Flight Data" menu. We have prepared the menu bar itself using **Display standards** and named the first menu "Flight Data."

For the **Cancel** function we have specified the function type E, while all other functions have a normal function code. For individual functions we have created additional attributes such as tool tips or icons, which we will not explain in detail now.

GUI status SCREEN_210

This status has been created as a status for modal dialog boxes and has been activated without changing anything in the Menu Painter. The status therefore does not administer any functions. We only need it to remove the status of previous screens when calling screen 210.

ABAP program description

We have chosen **Executable Program** as the program type for S_CHANGE_PLANETYPE so that we can also start it directly, i.e., without a transaction code. Since the source code contains many different processing blocks, for clarity's sake we have divided it into a range of include programs which follow the naming convention of the ABAP Workbench. Listing 7.3 shows the source code of S_CHANGE_PLANETYPE.

LISTING 7.3 Including includes in the example program

```
*&---------------------------------------------------------------------*
*& Report  S_CHANGE_PLANETYPE                                          *
*&---------------------------------------------------------------------*
REPORT s_change_planetype.

*&---------------------------------------------------------------------*
*& Global Declarations                                                 *
*&---------------------------------------------------------------------*
INCLUDE: s_change_planetypetop, "Global Data Declarations
         s_change_planetypef01. "Classes

*&---------------------------------------------------------------------*
*& Processing Blocks called by the Runtime Environment                 *
*&---------------------------------------------------------------------*
INCLUDE: s_change_planetypee01, "Runtime Events
         s_change_planetypeo01, "PBO Modules
         s_change_planetypei01. "PAI Modules
```

At runtime the program is composed from the include programs as they are listed in the program. We shall now consider the include programs in detail. We describe the program parts in their logical order and not as they are listed in the program.

Global data

Listing 7.4 shows the include for the global data declarations of the program.

LISTING 7.4 Include for global data declarations

```
*&---------------------------------------------------------------------*
*& INCLUDE S_CHANGE_PLANETYPETOP                                       *
*&---------------------------------------------------------------------*
* Screen Interfaces
TABLES demo_conn.
DATA: ok_code TYPE sy-ucomm,
      save_ok TYPE sy-ucomm.
```

We restrict our global data declarations to those data objects that are required for data exchange with the screens. Since we have created all the input and output fields of the screens by copying the DEMO_CONN structure from the ABAP Dictionary, we only need a single TABLES statement for these fields. We also need a data object for the OK field and a field of the same type for holding it in a temporary buffer.

Runtime environment events

Listing 7.5 shows the include for the only event block of the program.

LISTING 7.5 Include for START-OF-SELECTION event block

```
*&---------------------------------------------------------------------*
*& INCLUDE S_CHANGE_PLANETYPEE01                                        *
*&---------------------------------------------------------------------*
* Event Block START-OF-SELECTION
START-OF-SELECTION.
  CALL SCREEN 100.
```

Since we have chosen **Executable Program** as the program type, we can also start our program directly. So that it has exactly the same functions as if it had been launched using the transaction code, we immediately call screen 100 at the `START-OF-SELECTION` event, which is also the initial screen of the S_CHANGE_PLANETYPE transaction. Both executing the program directly and launching it using the transaction code start a sequence of screens, which are then executed in a sequence that results from the user's actions.

PBO Module

Listing 7.6 shows the include for the only PBO module in the program.

LISTING 7.6 Include for the PBO Module

```
*&---------------------------------------------------------------------*
*& INCLUDE S_CHANGE_PLANETYPEO01                                        *
*&---------------------------------------------------------------------*
* Dialog Module PBO
MODULE set_status OUTPUT.
  CASE sy-dynnr.
    WHEN 100.
      SET TITLEBAR  'TIT_100_200'.
      SET PF-STATUS 'SCREEN_100_200' EXCLUDING 'UPDATE'.
    WHEN 200.
      SET TITLEBAR  'TIT_100_200'.
      SET PF-STATUS 'SCREEN_100_200' EXCLUDING 'CHANGE'.
    WHEN 210.
      SET TITLEBAR 'TIT_210'.
      SET PF-STATUS 'SCREEN_210'.
  ENDCASE.
ENDMODULE.
```

FIGURE 7.22 Inactive functions on screens 100 and 200. Copyright © SAP AG

All three screens in our program share this PBO module in which their GUI status and title are set. We use the sy-dynnr system field to differentiate between the screens. We could equally have created a separate dialog module for each screen. In this case it would not have been necessary to differentiate between screens using sy-dynnr.

We have created the title of the screens using forward navigation. Note that although screens 100 and 200 use the same GUI status, other function codes are excluded by the EXCLUDING addition. You can see this clearly when the program is run if you open the **Flight Data** menu on screen 100 or 200. Both the **Change Plane Type** and **Save Plane Type** functions are visible but one or both are always inactive. In addition, no pushbutton appears for the function that has just been excluded (see Figure 7.22).

PAI module

Listing 7.7 shows the include for both PAI modules of the program.

LISTING 7.7 Include for PAI modules

```
*&---------------------------------------------------------------------*
*& INCLUDE S_CHANGE_PLANETYPEI01                                       *
*&---------------------------------------------------------------------*
* Dialog Modules PAI
MODULE cancel INPUT.
  CASE sy-dynnr.
    WHEN 100.
      LEAVE TO SCREEN 0.
    WHEN 200.
      LEAVE TO SCREEN 100.
```

```
  ENDCASE.
ENDMODULE.

MODULE handle_user_command INPUT.
  save_ok = ok_code.
  CLEAR ok_code.
  CASE save_ok.
    WHEN 'CHANGE'.
      CALL METHOD change_planetype=>get_data
           EXPORTING i_carrid    = demo_conn-carrid
                     i_connid    = demo_conn-connid
                     i_fldate    = demo_conn-fldate
           IMPORTING e_cityfrom  = demo_conn-cityfrom
                     e_cityto    = demo_conn-cityto
                     e_seatsmax  = demo_conn-seatsmax
                     e_seatsocc  = demo_conn-seatsocc
                     e_planetype = demo_conn-planetype.
      SET SCREEN 200.
    WHEN 'UPDATE'.
      CALL METHOD change_planetype=>check_planetype
           EXPORTING i_planetype = demo_conn-planetype
                     i_seatsocc  = demo_conn-seatsocc
           IMPORTING e_seatsmax  = demo_conn-seatsmax.
      CALL METHOD change_planetype=>update_planetype
           EXPORTING i_carrid    = demo_conn-carrid
                     i_connid    = demo_conn-connid
                     i_fldate    = demo_conn-fldate
                     i_planetype = demo_conn-planetype
                     i_seatsmax  = demo_conn-seatsmax.
      SET SCREEN 200.
    WHEN 'BACK' OR 'EXIT'.
      CASE sy-dynnr.
        WHEN 100.
          LEAVE TO SCREEN 0.
        WHEN 200.
          CALL METHOD change_planetype=>security_check
               EXPORTING i_planetype = demo_conn-planetype
                         i_ok_code   = save_ok.
      ENDCASE.
  ENDCASE.
ENDMODULE.
```

The cancel PAI module is only called when the user chooses the **Cancel** function on screen 100 or 200, since only this has the function type E. As with PBO we identify the current screen using sy-dynnr. For screen 100 we go to the dynamic subsequent screen 0 ending the screen sequence and thereby the entire program, since the system returns either to the call location of the transaction or after CALL SCREEN, depending on the type of execution. For screen 200 we go to the dynamic subsequent screen 100, and therefore from a user's perspective we return to the first screen layout.

The handle_user_command PAI module is called by all other functions on screens 100 and 200. In this dialog module we save the function code of the ok_code field in the save_ok field, initialize ok_code and identify the selected function in a CASE structure. Depending on the function we call static methods of the change_planetype class local to the program, in which we have defined the actual functions of the program. In the process we pass the user input data to the respective interface parameters.

For each function a dynamic subsequent screen to be displayed after the method has been executed is defined and thereby the screen sequence is also defined. With the BACK and EXIT function codes no method is called for screen 100; instead the screen sequence is directly terminated. With screen 200 a method is called, which if necessary displays the save prompt shown in Figure 7.21.

Local classes

Listing 7.8 shows the include for the local class of the program.

LISTING 7.8 Include for Local Class

```
*&---------------------------------------------------------------------*
*& INCLUDE S_CHANGE_PLANETYPEF01                                       *
*&---------------------------------------------------------------------*
* Class Definition
CLASS change_planetype DEFINITION.
  PUBLIC SECTION.
    CLASS-METHODS:
      get_data
        IMPORTING i_carrid     TYPE demo_conn-carrid
                  i_connid     TYPE demo_conn-connid
                  i_fldate     TYPE demo_conn-fldate
        EXPORTING e_cityfrom   TYPE demo_conn-cityfrom
                  e_cityto     TYPE demo_conn-cityto
                  e_seatsmax   TYPE demo_conn-seatsmax
                  e_seatsocc   TYPE demo_conn-seatsocc
                  e_planetype  TYPE demo_conn-planetype,
```

```
      check_planetype
        IMPORTING i_planetype  TYPE demo_conn-planetype
                  i_seatsocc   TYPE demo_conn-seatsocc
        EXPORTING e_seatsmax   TYPE demo_conn-seatsmax,
      update_planetype
        IMPORTING i_carrid     TYPE demo_conn-carrid
                  i_connid     TYPE demo_conn-connid
                  i_fldate     TYPE demo_conn-fldate
                  i_planetype  TYPE demo_conn-planetype
                  i_seatsmax   TYPE demo_conn-seatsmax,
      security_check
        IMPORTING i_planetype  TYPE demo_conn-planetype
                  i_ok_code    TYPE sy-ucomm.
  PRIVATE SECTION.
    CLASS-DATA c_planetype TYPE demo_conn-planetype.
ENDCLASS.

* Class Implementation
CLASS change_planetype IMPLEMENTATION.
  METHOD get_data.
    SELECT SINGLE p~cityfrom p~cityto
                  f~seatsmax f~seatsocc f~planetype
    FROM   ( spfli AS p
             INNER JOIN sflight AS f ON p~carrid = f~carrid
                                    AND p~connid = f~connid )
    INTO   (e_cityfrom,e_cityto,
            e_seatsmax,e_seatsocc,e_planetype)
    WHERE  p~carrid = i_carrid AND
           p~connid = i_connid AND
           f~fldate = i_fldate.
    c_planetype = e_planetype.
    IF sy-subrc <> 0.
      MESSAGE e888(sabapdocu) WITH text-010.
    ENDIF.
  ENDMETHOD.
  METHOD check_planetype.
    SELECT SINGLE seatsmax
    FROM   saplane
    INTO   e_seatsmax
    WHERE  planetype = i_planetype.
    IF e_seatsmax < i_seatsocc.
      MESSAGE e888(sabapdocu) WITH e_seatsmax text-020.
    ENDIF.
```

```
  ENDMETHOD.
  METHOD update_planetype.
    IF c_planetype <> i_planetype.
      UPDATE sflight
      SET    planetype = i_planetype
             seatsmax  = i_seatsmax
      WHERE  carrid = i_carrid AND
             connid = i_connid AND
             fldate = i_fldate.
      IF sy-subrc = 0.
        MESSAGE i888(sabapdocu) WITH sy-dbcnt text-030.
        c_planetype = i_planetype.
      ELSE.
        MESSAGE e888(sabapdocu) WITH text-040.
      ENDIF.
    ENDIF.
  ENDMETHOD.
  METHOD security_check.
    IF i_planetype <> c_planetype.
      CALL SCREEN 210 STARTING AT 32 8.
    ENDIF.
    IF ok_code = 'CHANGE_AGAIN'.
      SET SCREEN 200.
    ELSEIF ok_code = 'CONFIRM' OR
           ok_code = space.
      IF i_ok_code = 'BACK'.
        SET SCREEN 100.
      ELSEIF i_ok_code = 'EXIT'.
        SET SCREEN 0.
      ENDIF.
    ENDIF.
    CLEAR ok_code.
  ENDMETHOD.
ENDCLASS.
```

We have encapsulated all the functions of the transaction in three static methods of the local class change_planetype and defined another method for the save prompt from Figure 7.21. Prior to Release 4.5 we would have used local subroutines instead of methods. With methods we have the advantage of clearly defined interfaces, which we can declare in the declaration part of the local class.

The get_data method imports the user input data on screen 100; reads the corresponding output data for screen 200 using an INNER JOIN of the database tables

SPFLI and SFLIGHT and exports them again. In addition, the plane type that has been read is stored in a private static attribute of the class.

If no suitable values are found in the database table, the MESSAGE statement is used to display the message 888 of the message class SABAPDOCU as a type E error message (see Section 7.4.2). This interrupts the method and the entire PAI processing immediately and the layout of screen 100 is displayed again with the field DEMO_CONN-FLDATE ready for input. Message 888 does not contain any text at present. Instead it has four placeholders (&&&&) that can be dynamically filled in the program. We use the text symbol 010 that we have filled with "No flight found for this date!" using **Goto – Text Elements – Text Symbols**. The combination of the FIELD statement in the screen flow logic and the MESSAGE statement in the ABAP program therefore results in a custom input check.

The check_planetype method is also used for a custom input check. It imports the plane type entered on screen 200 and the number of seats booked to date. The maximum number of seats for the new plane type is read from the SAPLANE database table and compared with the previous bookings. If the new plane type does not have enough seats, the maximum number of seats and the text symbol 020 ("") are displayed as an error message through the MESSAGE statement. The system then displays the layout of screen 200 again with the DEMO_CONN-FLDATE field ready for input.

The update_planetype method is used to save a correct new plane type including the new maximum number of seats in the SFLIGHT database table. If the user has entered a new value, the Open-SQL statement UPDATE is executed for the appropriate database line. If the database has been accessed successfully, message 888 is displayed as a type I information message and in this case the number of the modified database lines is stored in sy-dbcnt and text symbol 030 is also displayed ("Table Entry Changed"). Otherwise another error message (text symbol 040, "Error during Database Access!") is displayed. This immediately terminates PAI processing.

UPDATE

The use of the UPDATE statement shown here is only suitable for this small example program with practice data. We have not concerned ourselves with adequate locks or other data consistency. What is just about acceptable for a single dialog step is not suitable for larger transactions for technical reasons. If consistent state of the database can only be created through several dialog steps, you must use the bundling techniques shown in Section 8.1.4.

The security_check method is called if the user wishes to quit screen 200 with *Back* or *Exit*. It checks whether the plane type has been changed. If this is the case, screen 210 is called using CALL SCREEN. This call embeds a new screen sequence in the previous sequence, which is based on screens 100 and 200. The new screen sequence consists of a single screen, which is displayed as a modal dialog box. Since this screen has the static subsequent screen 0 and does not call any PAI modules, any user action on its layout will continue the program directly after the CALL SCREEN statement where we can also evaluate the function codes in the OK field. In our example we have therefore incorporated the embedding of screen 210 in the primary screen sequence in a single method.

Automatic input checks and input helps

In our example we have only defined two input checks ourselves. Nevertheless, the screens also recognize other incorrect entries on the part of the user, such as invalid date format or no plane type specified. Furthermore, all valid values are offered in input helps, which we have not programmed either.

For these fields we therefore rely on the automatic checks and helps of the ABAP Dictionary, which are linked to the DEMO_CONN structure. If we inspect this structure with the ABAP Dictionary tool (SE11) we find the following relationships:

- The SCARR database table is specified as the check table for the CARRID component. The automatic input check compares the user input in the **Carrier** field against the contents of SCARR. Here the input help is also performed using the check table.
- The SPFLI database table is specified as the check table for the CONNID component. The automatic input check compares the user input in the **Carrier** and **Flight Number** fields against the contents of SPFLI.
  A search help called SDYN_CONN_CONNID is coupled to the CONNID component. This search help reads suitable values from the SPFLI table and offers them as an input help. If the user has entered a value for the **Carrier**, all the corresponding flight numbers are read and displayed as a single-column list. If the user has not entered a value for the **Carrier**, all existing carrier and flight number pairs are displayed in two columns.
- No check table is specified for the FLDATE components. Here, the automatic input check only checks the format of the user input in the **flight date** field. The user can enter a date for which there is no flight in the SFLIGHT table. We have therefore programmed our own input check with the FIELD and MESSAGE statements.

  However, a search help called SDYN_CONN_FLDATE is connected to the FLDATE components. This search help reads suitable values from the SFLIGHT table according to the existing user inputs and places them in single, double, or triple columns.
- The SAPLANE database table is specified as the check table for the PLANETYPE components. The automatic input check compares the user input in the **Planetype** field against the contents of SAPLANE. Here the input help is also performed using the check table.

7.2 SELECTION SCREENS

7.2.1 What are selection screens?

Selection screens are special screens, which you define in the ABAP program using ABAP statements without having to use the Screen Painter. When an ABAP program with selection screens is activated, the ABAP Workbench generates these screens with all their components, i.e. including the flow logic. You do not need to create dialog modules for selection screens in your ABAP program. Instead, user actions on selection screens result in a sequence of special events, which you can handle in event blocks.

Screen element

The screen elements of selection screens represent a subset of all the various elements on screens and include:

- Text fields and frames
- Input fields for individual values, including checkboxes and radio buttons
- Special input fields for complex selections
- Pushbuttons
- Subscreens
- Tabs.

Listing 7.9 shows an example of how to define and call a selection screen.

LISTING 7.9 Defining and calling a selection screen

```
*&---------------------------------------------------------------------*
*& Report  S_SELECTION_SCREEN_DEMO                                     *
*&---------------------------------------------------------------------*
REPORT s_selection_screen_demo.

*&---------------------------------------------------------------------*
*& Global Declarations                                                 *
*&---------------------------------------------------------------------*
* Selection Screen

SELECTION-SCREEN BEGIN OF SCREEN 500
                   AS WINDOW TITLE text-010.
PARAMETERS p_input(16) TYPE c.
SELECTION-SCREEN: SKIP,
                   BEGIN OF BLOCK b1
                     WITH FRAME TITLE text-020.
PARAMETERS: check1 AS CHECKBOX,
            check2 AS CHECKBOX,
            check3 AS CHECKBOX.
SELECTION-SCREEN: END OF BLOCK b1,
                   SKIP,
                   BEGIN OF BLOCK b2
                     WITH FRAME TITLE text-030.
PARAMETERS: radio1 RADIOBUTTON GROUP rad,
            radio2 RADIOBUTTON GROUP rad,
            radio3 RADIOBUTTON GROUP rad.
```

```
SELECTION-SCREEN: END OF BLOCK b2,
                  END OF SCREEN 500.

*&---------------------------------------------------------------------*
*& Processing Blocks called by the Runtime Environment     *
*&---------------------------------------------------------------------*
* Runtime Events
START-OF-SELECTION.
  CALL SELECTION-SCREEN 500 STARTING AT 10 10.
```

The selection screen is defined in the global declaration part with the SELECTION-SCREEN and PARAMETERS statements, and it is called at START-OF-SELECTION with the CALL SELECTION-SCREEN statement. It is displayed as a modal dialog box as shown in Figure 7.23.

Selection text

To display the text of the selection screen we have created text symbols and selection texts for the program (see Figure 7.24). To maintain the text elements choose **Goto – Text Elements** from the ABAP Editor or **Display – Text Elements** in the context menu of the program in the object list.

Figure 7.24 shows a **Dictionary Reference** column on the right-hand side in which you can select input fields whose data type is defined in the ABAP Dictionary. The selection texts are then copied from the corresponding data element in the ABAP Dictionary. You can also see on the left-hand side that the selection screen appears with the screen number 500 in the object list of the program. Here, you can call the Screen Painter and see how the selection screen has been generated. However, you must not modify the definition with the Screen Painter.

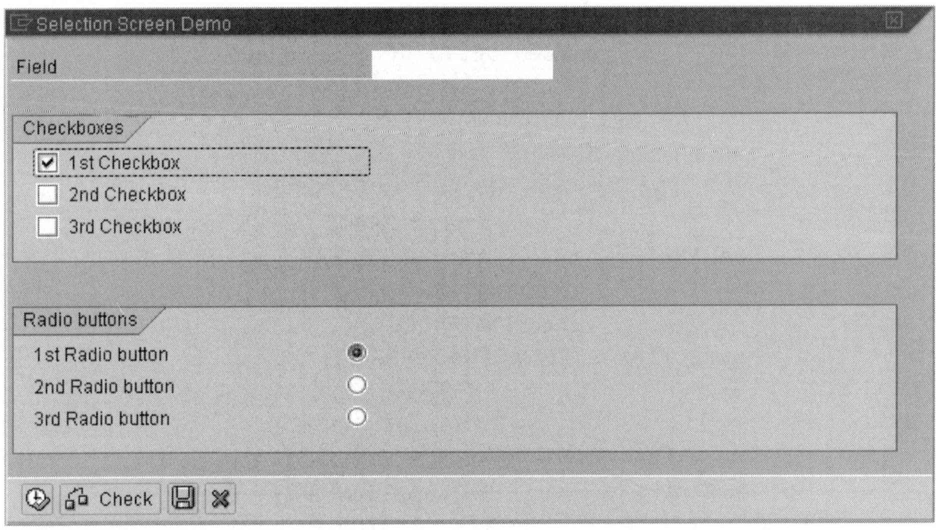

FIGURE 7.23 Selection screen display. Copyright © SAP AG

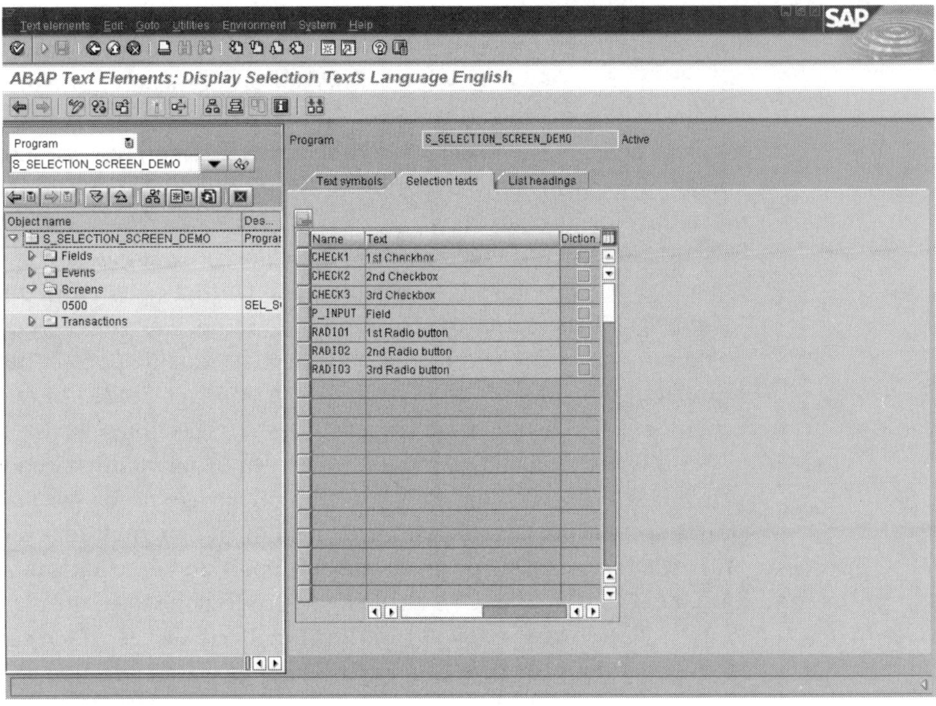

FIGURE 7.24 Selection texts. Copyright © SAP AG

7.2.2 Why selection screens?

The question arises: Why should there be any selection screens if their functions can also be covered by general screens? The answer lies in the historical development of application programming in the SAP System. In the days of Release 3.1 we still made a clear distinction between the two following kinds of application programming:

- **Dialog programming**
  Dialog programming was used to create transactions that had write access to the database. Dialog programming was based on general screens and only used type M programs (module pools).
- **Report programming**
  Report programming was used to create reports with read-only database access and a prescribed order:

  1. Input of selection criteria by the user
  2. Data reading (often using a logical database)
  3. Output of data to a classical list

A report programmer should be able to develop without using the Screen Painter and therefore without general screens. For this reason he or she is provided with the selection screen as a user interface. Logical databases generally contain the definition of a suitable selection screen themselves, so that when they are applied it is not even necessary to define report-specific selection screens. Prior to Release 4.0, selection screens could only be defined in executable programs (reports) and were automatically called when the program started.

Selection screens therefore offered the report programmer a very easy way of creating a user interface for his or her program. On the other hand, he or she had little knowledge of the basics of screen programming. Conversely, dialog programmers could not work with selection screens in their module pools. This situation always resulted in difficulties if a screen sequence was ever needed in reports or if a transaction needed to benefit from the advantages of selection screens.

The SAP Technology Department responded by providing selection screens as independent screens with Basis Release 4.0 – they were no longer linked to executable programs. Selection screens can be defined in any program that can contain screens. This includes executable programs, module pools, and function groups. You can use the `CALL SELECTION-SCREEN` statement to call selection screens in all processing blocks.

As of Basis Release 4.0 you can therefore freely decide which screens you wish to use in whatever parts of your program. In many cases, selection screens offer the following advantages over general screens:

- Minor queries can be implemented more quickly, without the Screen Painter.
- The user can store and reuse commonly used inputs for each selection screen in *selection variants*.
- Unlike general screens, selection screens can be used as a data interface of a program when it is called by the `SUBMIT` statement.
- Complex selections allow multi-level selections to be stored in special internal tables and to be used in logical expressions.

In the following sections we will show you how to define and call selection screens and respond to user actions.

7.2.3 Defining selection screens

Selection screens are defined solely in the global declaration part of an ABAP program with the three statements `SELECTION-SCREEN`, `PARAMETERS`, and `SELECT-OPTIONS`. Whereas `SELECTION-SCREEN` has numerous tasks – ranging from the actual definition of selection screens to formatting the layout and defining tabs – `PARAMETERS` and `SELECT-OPTIONS` are used to declare the input fields of the selection screen. While `PARAMETERS` is used to create single fields, `SELECT-OPTIONS` is used for more complex selections.

Selection screens are visible in all processing blocks of the program and the corresponding data declarations for the screen fields are global. You can define two kinds of selection screen: standard selection screens and stand-alone selection screens.

Standard selection screens

Every executable program has a predefined standard selection screen with the screen number 1000. In executable programs, therefore, no other general screen or selection screen can have the number 1000.

The standard selection screen cannot be defined with `SELECTION-SCREEN`. Instead all `PARAMETERS` and `SELECT-OPTIONS` statements which are not contained within the definition of other selection screens, declare input fields on the standard selection screen.

Stand-alone selection screens

All other selection screens – i.e. all other selection screens in executable programs and all selection screens of other programs – must be declared as stand-alone selection screens with the screen number `dynnr` using

```
SELECTION-SCREEN BEGIN OF SCREEN  dynnr
                                 [TITLE tit] [AS WINDOW].
...
SELECTION-SCREEN END OF SCREEN  dynnr.
```

Screen number

All `PARAMETERS` and `SELECT-OPTIONS` statements within the two `SELECTION-SCREEN` statements declare input fields on the stand-alone selection screen. You can use the `TITLE` addition to define a selection screen title, `tit`. In this case, `tit` is best specified as a text symbol. With the `AS WINDOW` addition you can define the selection screen as a modal dialog window.

Defining single fields

Single fields on selection screens, also known as parameters, are defined with the `PARAMETERS` statement. At the same time as the definition of the screen field, this statement declares a global data object of the same name in the ABAP program, to which the user inputs are passed. You will recognize as part of the `PARAMETERS` statement additions from the `DATA` statement for declaring elementary variables.[4]

```
PARAMETERS  p
  [(len)] {TYPE type|LIKE dobj} [DECIMALS dec]
  [DEFAULT def]
```

4. Unlike normal data objects, a parameter name can only contain 8 characters.

```
[LOWER CASE]
[OBLIGATORY]
[VALUE CHECK]
[AS CHECKBOX]
[RADIOBUTTON GROUP radi]
...
```

Besides these additions such as len and TYPE for defining the data type, the PARAMETERS statement has many other additions that determine the attributes of the screen field. We have listed just a few examples as follows:

- You can use DEFAULT to determine a default value, which then appears in the screen field.
- You can use LOWER CASE to make a distinction between upper and lower case for the user input. Otherwise all characters in character fields are passed in capitals.
- You can use OBLIGATORY to make the input field a required field.
- You can use VALUE CHECK to activate automatic input checking for fields that are declared using the TYPE addition with reference to a data type of the ABAP Dictionary (see Section 7.1.6).
- You can use AS CHECKBOX to create a type C checkbox of length one.
- You can use RADIOBUTTON GROUP to define a group *radi* of radio buttons.

In Listing 7.9 we saw how the PARAMETERS statement is used. After the selection screen has been called, the user inputs are available in the corresponding data objects of the ABAP program.

If a parameter has been declared with reference to a data type of the ABAP Dictionary, the corresponding automatic field and input help will be available to the user on the selection screen (c.f. Section 7.1.7).

Defining complex selections

The main strength of a selection screen compared with a general screen is that it allows you to define complex selections. You can use a single statement to define a screen layout, which opens up a wide range of input options to the user. The user inputs are passed to the ABAP program in the form of a special internal table, which you can use directly in logical expressions.

Originally, the sole purpose of selection screens was to enable selections prior to accessing the database, which then reduces the amount of data to be read to a minimum. Today this remains a key feature. The combination of complex sections on the selection screen and their application in the WHERE condition of Open-SQL statements provides the solution for this task.

You define complex selections with the statement:

```
SELECT-OPTIONS  selopt FOR dobj
  ...
  [NO INTERVALS]
  [NO-EXTENSION]
  ...
```

Here, dobj is a global data object of the program, whose data type is copied to the complex selection. The data type of dobj must be elementary and is generally determined by reference to a data type of the ABAP Dictionary, whereby its automatic help will also be provided on the selection screen.[5]

The SELECT-OPTIONS statement defines several elements on the selection screen and simultaneously declares an internal table called selopt in the ABAP program.[6] The SELECT-OPTIONS statement has a number of additions, which largely correspond to the PARAMETERS statement for defining screen element attributes. The NO INTERVALS and NO-EXTENSION additions, however, are specifically for complex selections.

To explain this in more detail, we need to look at the program sequence in Listing 7.10.

LISTING 7.10 Defining a complex selection

```
*&---------------------------------------------------------------------*
*& Report S_SELECT_OPTIONS                                             *
*&---------------------------------------------------------------------*
REPORT s_select_options.

*&---------------------------------------------------------------------*
*& Global Declarations                                                 *
*&---------------------------------------------------------------------*
* Global data
DATA wa_spfli TYPE spfli.

* Selection Screen
SELECT-OPTIONS s_carrid FOR wa_spfli-carrid.
```

The SELECT-OPTIONS statement defines a complex selection on the standard selection screen. When the program is run, this standard selection screen appears with two input fields and a pushbutton (see Figure 7.25). Here you can enter an interval selection. If the user selects the pushbutton for **multiple selection**, another dialog box appears. Here he or she can enter individual values and other intervals on the tabs with the green icons. Individual values or intervals can be excluded from the selection on the tabs with the red icons. Double-clicking an individual value or an

5. The automatic input checks are not available for complex selections, however.
6. The name selopt can also contain a maximum of eight characters only.

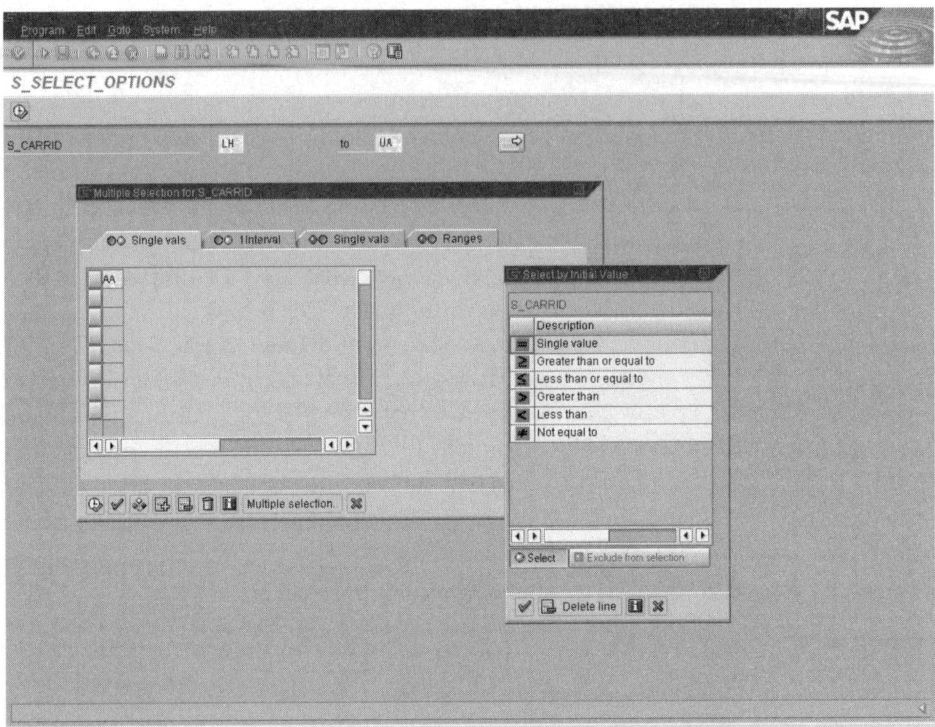

FIGURE 7.25 Complex selection on the selection screen. Copyright © SAP AG

interval limit opens another dialog box for maintaining selection options. Here the user can specify the type of the selection.

Multiple selection

If you use the `NO INTERVALS` addition in the `SELECT-OPTIONS` statement, there are no options for interval selections and the user can only enter single values. No pushbutton appears with the `NO-EXTENSION` addition and the user cannot perform a **multiple selection**.

Our simple `SELECT-OPTIONS` statement allows the user to enter a complete logical condition for the required selection. But how is this passed to the ABAP program for evaluation? To show this we complete the above program `S_SELECT_OPTIONS` with the lines in Listing 7.11.

LISTING 7.11 Evaluating complex selections

```
*&---------------------------------------------------------------------*
*& Processing Blocks called by the Runtime Environment                 *
*&---------------------------------------------------------------------*
* Runtime Events
START-OF-SELECTION.
```

```
SELECT *
FROM   spfli
INTO   wa_spfli
WHERE  carrid IN s_carrid.
  ...
ENDSELECT.
```

Here you see how the complex selection is used in a SELECT statement. For the evaluation you therefore simply use the special logical expression:

```
... IN  selopt
```

in a WHERE condition or another control statement such as IF or CASE. The runtime environment performs the actual evaluation of the complex selection for you!

Selection table

We shall nevertheless focus in more detail on how the complex selection is performed in the ABAP program. As already mentioned, it is performed using an internal table, which we call a selection table. To understand the structure and contents of a selection table, let us consider our s_carrid table in Figure 7.26 in the ABAP Debugger.

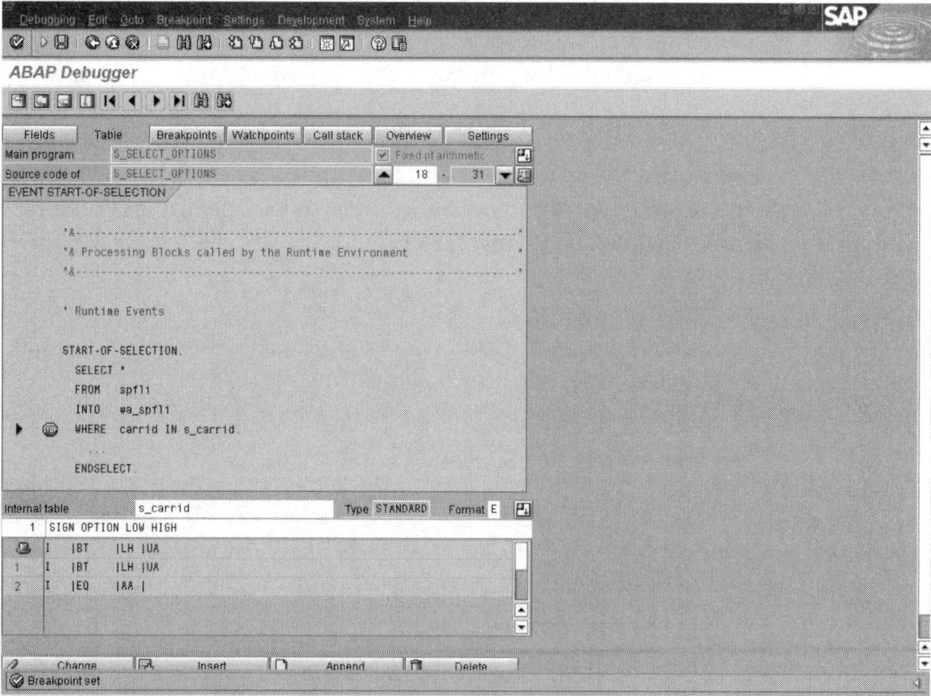

FIGURE 7.26 Selection table in the ABAP Debugger. Copyright © SAP AG

This is a four-column internal table with a header row (see Section 4.73). Each row signifies a logical condition. The individual results of all the rows are grouped together for final selection. You can use the `NO-EXTENSION` addition to the `SELECT-OPTIONS` statement to ensure that the user can only fill a single row of the selection table. All selection tables have the same components.

- **SIGN**
  Possible values are I and E. These determine whether the individual result of a row is included or excluded in the overall result.
- **OPTION**
  Possible values are EQ, NE, GT, LE, LT, CP, and BP for single values and BT and NB for intervals. These are the logical operators of each individual row.
- **LOW and HIGH**
  These fields contain the user inputs in the input fields on the selection screen. Either LOW is filled for a single value selection or LOW and HIGH contain the values for an interval selection. Their data type is copied from the data object of the `SELECT-OPTIONS` statement.

You can evaluate or even modify a selection table like any other internal table. If, for example, you wish to perform an authorization check with the `AUTHORITY-CHECK` statement before accessing the database, you can specifically read the user inputs from the internal table.

It should also be mentioned that you can use the

```
DATA seltab {TYPE|LIKE} RANGE OF  {type|dobj}.
```

SUBMIT

statement to create internal tables with the structure of a selection table.[7] You can fill these tables in your program in order to use them to pass complex selection criteria to programs called using `SUBMIT`.

```
SUBMIT  prog WITH selopt IN seltab.
```

The called program contains a complex selection `selopt`, which is filled by `seltab` without the selection screen being displayed.

Formatting selection screens

When defining a selection screen, you can modify the standard layout in which all elements are shown line by line, with the following variants of the `SELECTION-SCREEN` statement.

```
SELECTION-SCREEN  ULINE /pos(len).
SELECTION-SCREEN COMMENT /pos(len) comm [FOR FIELD f].
```

7. In the ABAP Dictionary you can create this kind of table via *Edit – Define as Ranges Table Type* in the table type maintenance dialog.

```
SELECTION-SCREEN SKIP n.
SELECTION-SCREEN BEGIN OF LINE.
...
SELECTION-SCREEN END OF LINE.
SELECTION-SCREEN BEGIN OF BLOCK block
                  [WITH FRAME [TITLE tit]].
...
SELECTION-SCREEN END OF BLOCK block.
```

With these variants you can

- Underline with `ULINE`
- Display texts with `COMMENT`
- Create blank lines with `SKIP`
- Place several elements in a line between `BEGIN OF LINE` and `END OF LINE`.
- Create logical blocks between `BEGIN OF BLOCK` and `END OF BLOCK`.

In our introductory example in Listing 7.9 we used blank lines and logical blocks. We shall not go into further detail regarding these language elements at this point.

7.2.4 Calling selection screens

Depending on the type of selection screen, you have various options for displaying a selection screen. In Section 7.2.5 we will show you how to process the displayed selection screen, and in Section 7.2.6 you will learn more on the various user actions on a displayed selection screen.

Calling standard selection screens automatically

The standard selection screen of an executable program is automatically displayed when the program is called. The runtime environment calls the selection screen between the `INITIALIZATION` and `START-OF-SCREEN` events (see Figure 3.10). When the program has been run, an executable program with a standard selection screen is automatically started again. The selection screen is then filled with the previous user inputs as default entries.

Our program `S_SELECT_OPTIONS` in Listings 7.10 and 7.11 is an example of an executable program with a standard selection screen.

Calling with `CALL SELECTION-SCREEN`

You can call all the selection screens of a program, i.e. the standard selection screen and stand-alone selection screens, in any processing block of the same program with

```
CALL SELECTION-SCREEN  dynnr
  [STARTING AT  x1 y1]
  [ENDING AT    x2 y2].
```

However, you should never use the CALL SCREEN statement for calling selection screens, since the selection screen-specific processing will not start. If the user quits the selection screen using **Back**, **Exit**, or **Cancel**, sy-subrc is set to four instead of zero. You will learn shortly in Section 7.2.5 how the processing of the called selection screen is incorporated in the program flow.

When you have defined stand-alone selection screens with the AS WINDOW addition, you can display them as modal dialog boxes with the STARTING AT and ENDING AT additions. In the introductory example in Listing 7.9 we called the stand-alone selection screen 500 as a modal dialog box.

Calling selection screens using a report transaction

For executable programs, you can define a special transaction type by choosing **report transaction** instead of **dialog transaction** when creating a transaction code (see Section 7.1.3). In the maintenance dialog of the transaction code you can then enter any selection screen of your program instead of a normal initial screen in the **selection screen** input box.

If you start the program using this transaction code it will be run like an executable program, except that the selection screen you have chosen is displayed, instead of the standard selection screen, between the INITIALIZATION and START-OF-SELECTION events.

For our introductory example in Listing 7.9 we can define a report transaction as in Figure 7.27.

When you call this report transaction, the selection screen from Figure 7.23 appears first as a full screen and again as a modal dialog box after you choose **Execute** **F8**. It is therefore first displayed automatically before START-OF-SELECTION and then called during START-OF-SELECTION using CALL SELECTION-SCREEN.

Calling selection screens using a dialog transaction

When you create a dialog transaction you normally specify the initial screen of your transaction, whose PBO processing is to be started on transaction call. In the **Screen number** field (see Figure 7.9), however, you can also specify the number of any given selection screen of your program. You thereby make the selection screen the initial screen of a screen sequence.

When you call this kind of transaction, even with executable programs, the report-specific flow from Figure 3.10 is not started and the INITIALIZATION, START-OF-SELECTION, GET and END-OF-SELECTION events are not triggered. You yourself

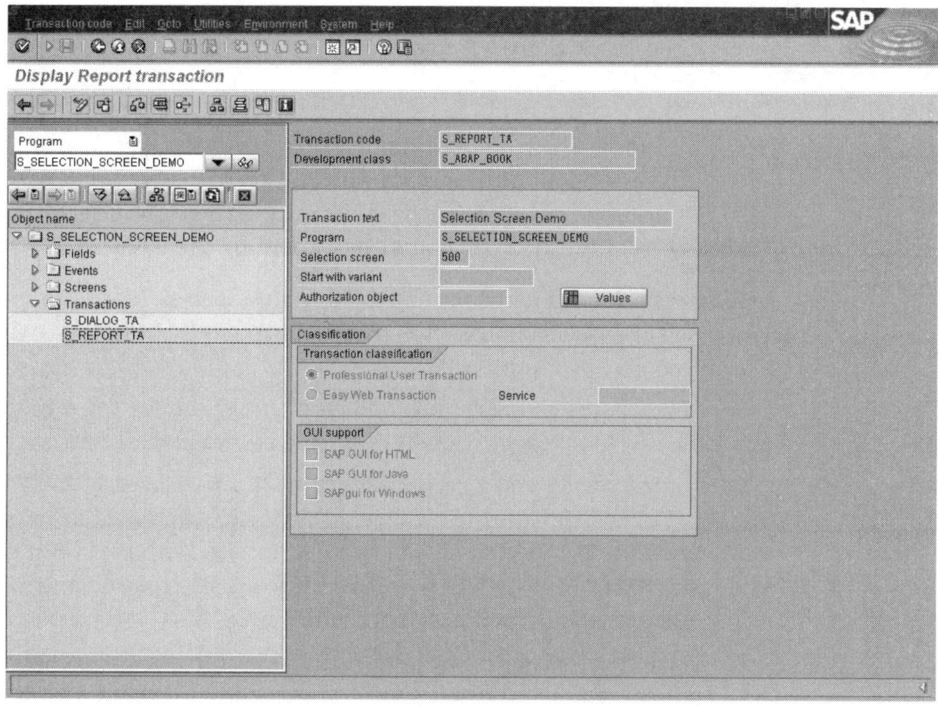

FIGURE 7.27 Defining a report transaction. Copyright © SAP AG

must ensure during selection screen processing (see Section 7.2.5) that a subsequent screen is called.

In Listing 7.9 of our introductory example, we created a selection screen, screen 500. The example dialog transaction S_DIALOG_TA displays this selection screen as its initial screen. It then leaves the program, since we have not defined an AT SELECTION-SCREEN event block (see Section 7.2.5) or a subsequent screen.

7.2.5 Selection screen processing

When you program selection screens, you do not come into contact with their screen flow logic. Furthermore, you cannot define any dialog modules for selection screens in your ABAP program. Instead, during selection screen processing, the runtime environment triggers a sequence of selection screen events for which you can implement event blocks in the program. The flow logic and the corresponding dialog modules are therefore encapsulated in the runtime environment (see also Figure 3.9). The data transport between the selection screen and the ABAP program is also automatic, but corresponds to the basic rules outlined in Section 7.1.5.

Selection screen event

From the viewpoint of the ABAP programmer, the user actions on selection screens trigger specific selection screen events and make the necessary data available in the event blocks. The main area of application for selection screen events is programming input checks for selection screens.

Responding to functions

With the exception of the custom functions described in Section 7.2.6, you generally do not have to evaluate function codes during selection screen events. After selection screen processing the system branches according to the selected function as follows:

- Most predefined functions of the GUI status, such as *Save As Variant* (**F11**), are executed after selection screen event processing in the runtime environment, and the selection screen is then called again.
- For functions you have programmed yourself, and for *Enter*, the selection screen is called again directly after selection screen event processing.
- For the **Execute** and **Execute and Print** functions (see Section 7.3.4), the `START-OF-SELECTION` event is triggered after selection screen event processing for automatically called standard selection screens. With selection screens called using `CALL SELECTION-SCREEN` the system returns to the statement immediately after the call location and the `sy-subrc` return value is set to zero.
- No selection screen events are triggered by the **Back**, **Exit**, or **Cancel** functions. The program is terminated for automatically called standard selection screens. With selection screens called using `CALL SELECTION-SCREEN`, the system returns to the statement immediately after the call location and `sy-subrc` is set to four.

Selection screen events

During selection screen processing in the runtime environment you can respond to a range of selection screen events in the ABAP program by implementing the corresponding event blocks. As with all processing blocks, the arrangement of the event blocks in the program is completely irrelevant for the time of their execution. With automatically called standard selection screens the events take place between the `INITIALIZATION` and `START-OF-SELECTION` events (see Figure 3.10). In selection screens called with `CALL SELECTION-SCREEN` they occur during the processing of the current processing block. You can identify the various selection screens of your program in these event blocks by using the `sy-dynnr` system field with which you are already familiar from general screen processing.

The various selection screen events are processed in processing blocks behind the `AT SELECTION SCREEN` statement. With the exception of the PBO event, the variants of this statement are generally used to perform input checks during the various stages of data transport from the selection screen to the ABAP program and to cancel the selection screen processing if necessary with error messages. We shall now briefly explain the individual events:

- `AT SELECTION-SCREEN OUTPUT`

PBO

This event is triggered at PBO of the selection screen. Here, for example, you can prepare the selection screen with dynamic screen modifications. The `AT SELECTION SCREEN OUTPUT` event is triggered each time a selection screen is called – i.e. including when it is automatically called again after selection screen processing. An `AT SELECTION SCREEN OUTPUT` event block with a `CLEAR s_connid[]` statement, in the program in Listing 7.13, would delete the selection table filled at `AT SELECTION-SCREEN` before the new display. In order to initialize the values of a selection screen once and once only in the program, the `LOAD-OF-PROGRAM` or `INITIALIZATION` event blocks would therefore be more appropriate.

- `AT SELECTION-SCREEN ON field`

Single field

This event is triggered at PAI of the selection screen when the `field` input field is passed to the ABAP program. The associated processing block acts like a PAI dialog module called with the `FIELD` addition to the `MODULE` statement. You can use the corresponding event block to check the user input and, if necessary, to display an error message, which then makes the corresponding input field on the selection screen ready for input again.

- `AT SELECTION-SCREEN ON BLOCK block`

Chain processing

Whereas the previous event corresponds to the `FIELD` flow logic statement for custom input checking on screens, `AT SELECTION-SCREEN ON BLOCK` is the counterpart to the processing chain programmed with `CHAIN`. The event is triggered when all the fields of a logical block have been passed from the selection screen to the ABAP program. If you display an error message here, all the input fields of the block are made ready for input again.

- `AT SELECTION-SCREEN ON RADIOBUTTON GROUP radi`

Radio buttons

This event is a variant of the previous event, but relates to radio button groups as opposed to logical blocks. The individual fields of radio button groups do not trigger the `AT SELECTION-SCREEN ON FIELD` event and can only be handled as a unit.

- `AT SELECTION-SCREEN ON seltab.`
  `AT SELECTION-SCREEN ON END OF seltab.`

Multiple selection

These two events occur only during processing of the dialog box for **multiple selections**. These events are triggered in turn for each user action on the dialog box, whereby first the selection table can be checked row by row, followed by the entire selection table.

- `AT SELECTION-SCREEN`

PAI

This is the basic form of all selection screen events. It is the last event in selection screen processing to be triggered when all the input data has been passed to the program. Here you can check all the input values for consistency. An error message will make all fields ready for input again.

- AT SELECTION-SCREEN ON HELP-REQUEST FOR field.
  AT SELECTION-SCREEN ON VALUE-REQUEST FOR field.

POH/POV

These two events correspond to the POH and POV events in screen processing. They are therefore triggered whenever the user presses the F1 or F4 keys on an input field. As with screens, you can program self-defined field or input helps in the corresponding event blocks to override any predefined helps in the ABAP Dictionary. For the self-defined helps you can use the same means we showed in Section 7.1.7 for screens. However, you do not require function modules to transport the data between the ABAP program and the selection screen.

Example of selection screen processing

Listing 7.12 shows a custom input check for a standard selection screen.

LISTING 7.12 Input check for selection screen

```
*&---------------------------------------------------------------------*
*& Report  S_SELECTION_SCREEN_CHECK                                     *
*&---------------------------------------------------------------------*
REPORT s_selection_screen_check.

*&---------------------------------------------------------------------*
*& Global Declarations                                                  *
*&---------------------------------------------------------------------*
* Global Data
DATA wa_sflight TYPE sflight.

* Selection Screen
PARAMETERS: p_carrid TYPE sflight-carrid,
            p_connid TYPE sflight-connid,
            p_fldate TYPE sflight-fldate.

*&---------------------------------------------------------------------*
*& Processing Blocks called by the Runtime Environment                  *
*&---------------------------------------------------------------------*
* Runtime Events
AT SELECTION-SCREEN ON p_fldate.
  SELECT SINGLE seatsocc seatsmax
  FROM   sflight
  INTO   (wa_sflight-seatsocc, wa_sflight-seatsmax)
  WHERE  carrid = p_carrid AND
         connid = p_connid.
```

```
IF wa_sflight-seatsocc < wa_sflight-seatsmax.
  MESSAGE i888(sabapdocu) WITH text-010.
ELSEIF wa_sflight-seatsocc = wa_sflight-seatsmax.
  MESSAGE w888(sabapdocu) WITH text-020.
ELSEIF wa_sflight-seatsocc > wa_sflight-seatsmax.
  MESSAGE e888(sabapdocu) WITH text-030.
ENDIF.
```

Once the user has entered a flight date, it is passed to the ABAP program and the `AT SELECTION-SCREEN ON p_fldate` event is triggered. There we read the number of occupied seats and maximum number of seats for the selected flight from the SFLIGHT database table and check them. Depending on the result, we display an information message, a warning, or an error message (see Section 7.4.2).

7.2.6 User actions on selection screens

Unlike general screens, where you have to attach all the interactive elements of the layout and the GUI status yourself to functions, selection screens have a standardized user interface that you can only influence to a limited extent.

This is due to the fact that the main purpose of selection screens is to enter selections. When working with a selection screen the user should essentially do nothing other than confirm these inputs with ↵ or **F8** or cancel the screen with one of the usual keys. In addition, there are other predefined functions, which for example store selection screen contents as variants or divert the list output of the program from the screen display into the spool system.

GUI status

Each selection screen has a predefined GUI status that provides these functions and that you cannot override with the `SET PF-STATUS` statement. As an exception you can use function modules such as RS_SET_SELSCREEN_STATUS to deactivate functions of the predefined GUI status (among other things). You find these function modules in the **Reuse Library** under **ABAP – Selection Screen**.

It is not intended that you define your own function codes in the predefined GUI status of a selection screen. However, you can define some screen elements with function codes and activate predefined pushbuttons in the application toolbar of the GUI status. Then, the user can select other functions besides the input fields and the intended functions, which you can evaluate during selection screen processing.

Screen elements with function codes

You can link checkboxes and radio buttons of the selection screen with function codes and define pushbuttons. The corresponding ABAP statements are:

```
PARAMETERS p AS CHECKBOX
                 USER-COMMAND ucom.
PARAMETERS p RADIOBUTTON GROUP radi
                 USER-COMMAND ucom.
SELECTION-SCREEN PUSHBUTTON  /pos(len) text
                   USER-COMMAND ucom.
```

Pushbutton

Both PARAMETERS statements are the familiar statements for defining parameters as checkboxes or radio buttons, in this case with the USER-COMMAND addition. With the statement SELECTION-SCREEN a pushbutton at position pos, of length len, and with text text is defined here. The text is best specified as a text symbol.

You use the USER-COMMAND addition to assign each of these screen elements a function code ucom. For a radio button group only the first parameter of the group may be assigned a function code. If the user selects one of the screen elements, the AT SELECTION-SCREEN selection screen event is triggered and the corresponding event block in the ABAP program is called. The function code can be evaluated there in the UCOMM component of the SSCRFIELDS structure declared with TABLES.

At the end of the event block the system returns to the display of the selection screen. The user can only quit the selection screen using **F8** or one of the usual functions of the standard toolbar such as **Cancel**. Function codes on selection screens therefore have only a limited use, e.g. for layout modification.

Pushbuttons in the application toolbar

The GUI status of a selection screen contains five inactive pushbuttons on the application toolbar to which the function codes FC01 to FC05 are assigned. You can activate these pushbuttons with the following statement:

```
SELECTION-SCREEN  FUNCTION KEY n.
```

You select the individual pushbuttons, where n is between 1 and 5. Before calling the selection screen you must assign the text of the pushbuttons to the component FUNCTXT_ON of the SSCR-FIELDS structure declared with TABLES.

When a pushbutton activated in this way is selected, the system behaves exactly as described above when selecting a screen element with a function code.

Example of functions you have defined yourself

In Listing 7.13 we demonstrate how you can define and evaluate pushbuttons in the application toolbar of the selection screen.

LISTING 7.13 Defining pushbuttons on selection screens

```
*&---------------------------------------------------------------------*
*& Report S_SELECTION_SCREEN_FUNCT                                     *
*&---------------------------------------------------------------------*
REPORT s_selection_screen_funct.

*&---------------------------------------------------------------------*
*& Global Declarations                                                 *
*&---------------------------------------------------------------------*
* Global Data
DATA: wa_connid TYPE s_conn_id,
      index TYPE i.
FIELD-SYMBOLS <fs> TYPE sscrfields-functxt_01.

* Screen Interface
TABLES sscrfields.

* Selection Screen
PARAMETERS p_carrid TYPE s_carr_id.
SELECT-OPTIONS s_connid FOR wa_connid NO INTERVALS.
DATA s_connid_line LIKE LINE OF s_connid.
SELECTION-SCREEN FUNCTION KEY: 1, 2, 3, 4, 5.

*&---------------------------------------------------------------------*
*& Processing Blocks called by the Runtime Environment                 *
*&---------------------------------------------------------------------*
* Runtime Events
INITIALIZATION.
  sscrfields-functxt_01 = 'AC'.
  sscrfields-functxt_02 = 'LH'.
  sscrfields-functxt_03 = 'SAS'.
  sscrfields-functxt_04 = 'THA'.
  sscrfields-functxt_05 = 'UA'.

AT SELECTION-SCREEN.
  IF sscrfields-ucomm(3) = 'FC0'.
    index = sscrfields-ucomm+3(1) + 3.
    ASSIGN COMPONENT index OF STRUCTURE sscrfields TO <fs>.
    p_carrid = <fs>.
    CLEAR s_connid[].
    s_connid_line-sign = 'I'.
```

```
    s_connid_line-option = 'EQ'.
    SELECT connid
    FROM   spfli
    INTO   s_connid_line-low
    WHERE  carrid = p_carrid.
      APPEND s_connid_line TO s_connid.
    ENDSELECT.
  ENDIF.
```

Our standard selection screen contains a parameter p_carrid and a complex selection s_connid. Since both are associated with data types from the ABAP Dictionary, we also have been able to take the selection texts from the Dictionary by simply choosing **Dictionary Reference** in **Text Element Maintenance**. We have activated the pushbuttons of the application toolbar with five SELECTION-SCREEN statements in a chained statement.

With the INITIALIZATION event – i.e. before the standard selection screen is called – we assign the identification of five carriers to the five pushbuttons as text. At the AT SELECTION-SCREEN event we evaluate the function codes of the pushbutton

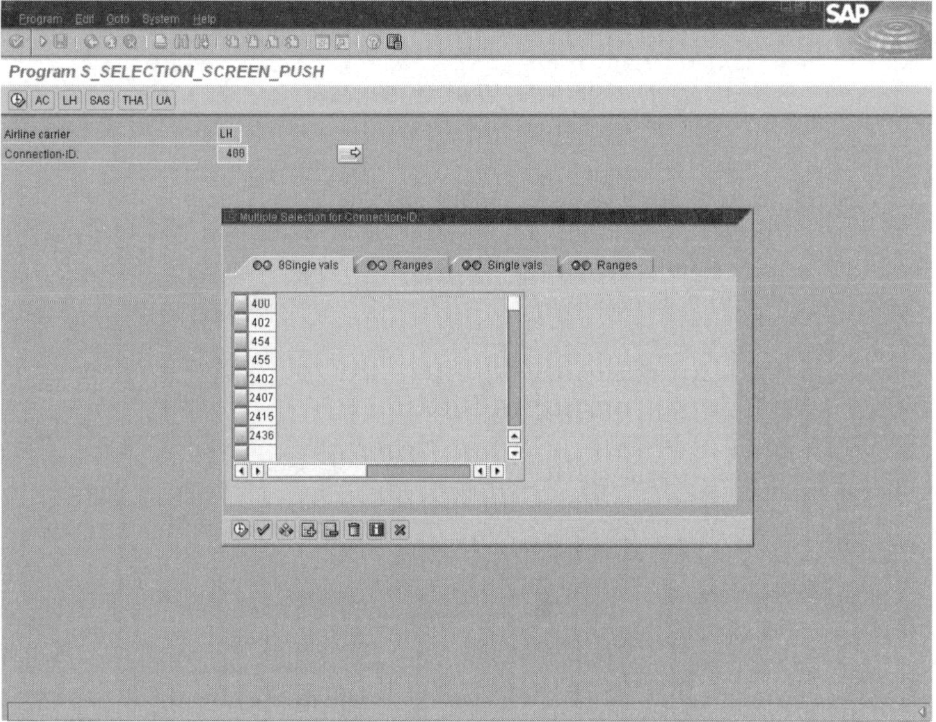

FIGURE 7.28 Selection screen with pushbuttons. Copyright © SAP AG

using offset/length access and use the fact that the pushbutton texts are stored in components four to eight of the sscrfields structure, declared using TABLES. (You can check this by double-clicking sscrfields). By means of an assignment by component of the structure to a field symbol <fs> with the ASSIGN statement, we obtain the identification of the carrier the user has selected. We assign this to the parameter p_carrid and build the selection table s_connid with values from the database table SPFLI.

The example also shows how you can handle a selection table in a program. Note that when initializing the selection table with CLEAR you have to explicitly access the table body s_connid[] so that not only the header row is initialized.

Figure 7.28 shows the selection screen after the user has selected the **LH** pushbutton. The **carrier** field now has the default value "LH". When you select **Multiple selection**, the flight connections read at AT SELECTION-SCREEN appear on the table page for single value selections. The user can now continue to edit these default entries.

7.3 CLASSICAL LISTS

7.3.1 What are classical lists?

Classical lists, like selection screens, are special screens whose screen layout is created using ABAP statements. However, there is a difference: selection screens are actual components of the ABAP program using them and differ from general screens only in the fact that defining and processing them is partially encapsulated in the runtime environment. The scenario is completely different with lists.

List processor

Lists are not screens of the ABAP program in which they are defined. Instead a special system program, the list processor, is called. This program contains a single screen for displaying the list. The entire layout acts as a display area for formatted data, which is mainly output as text. In addition to text with a colored background, you can also have lines, input-ready fields, checkboxes, icons, and symbols.

List buffer

To create this kind of output the classical ABAP programming language contains several statements – such as WRITE, POSITION, and FORMAT – that write, position, and format field contents in a list. These list statements can be used in classical ABAP at any point in any processing block. When a list statement is run the system writes the list output into a list buffer on the application server. You can view the current list at any time in the ABAP Debugger by selecting **Display List**. When you call the list, which is either automatic or programmed, the above-mentioned system program is started and the buffered list is shown on the list screen. At this point in time, the program active in the runtime environment is the list processor (see Figure 3.9).

User action

The user can carry out actions on the list screen – double-clicking to select lines plays a key role. The interactivity on a list can be supported by certain formats such as hotspots for single clicks, checkboxes, or input-ready fields. In contrast to selection screens, you can also define your own GUI status for lists, which expands the standard GUI status of a list in a program-specific manner.

List event

User actions on lists result in special list events in the calling ABAP program. Each list statement in such an event block no longer writes to the original list in the list buffer. Instead it writes to a **details list**, which at the end of the event block covers the original list on the list screen either fully or partially as a modal dialog box. The first list of this kind of list system is called a **basic list**. From a technical viewpoint a basic list is linked to the current screen sequence.[8] You can write to your own basic list for each screen sequence and for each basic list up to 20 hierarchical detail lists can be created after a user action. During list processing the user can navigate between the various list levels. Figure 7.29 illustrates list processing.

7.3.2 Classical lists prior to the advent of ABAP Objects

Prior to the advent of ABAP Objects, classical lists were the most important output medium. In particular, in classical reporting with executable programs, the automatic display of a classical list at the end of the program was the counterpart to automatically displaying the standard selection screen at the beginning of the program. The predefined input–processing–output procedure of a classical report is:

1 Selection screen

2 Read data

3 List

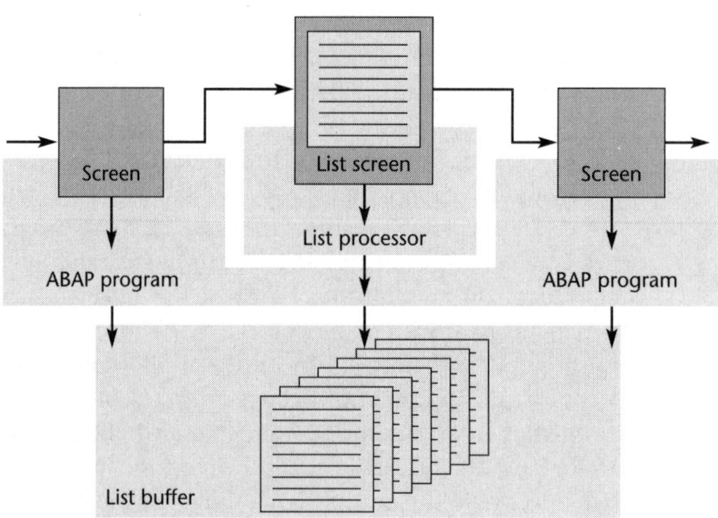

FIGURE 7.29 List processing

8. This also applies to selection screens, so that list outputs which occur during selection screen processing are then contained in their own list buffer.

The application logic of a classical report programmed in ABAP represents a single dialog step between these special screens (see Figure 3.10).

Interactive reporting

Classical reporting has been expanded by interactive reporting with the option of creating detail lists, in which the data does not have to be read from the database at once, but rather according to requirements and depending on user actions on the basic list. Whereas classical reporting with just a single basic list is suitable for the requirements of background processing, interactive reporting has been developed for dialog-oriented reporting applications. Interactive classical lists were also the best choice for other purposes as well, such as displaying the value list of an input help. In the ABAP Workbench even the layout of a tool (Menu Painter) was implemented as an interactive list.

Spool system

Creating lists in classical reporting goes hand in hand with outputting data to printers. From a historical viewpoint the print list is the classic output medium for a report. This is why the contents of classical ABAP lists can be sent to the SAP spool system instead of the front end, from where they can be printed or stored elsewhere. The contents of normal screens do not have this option.

7.3.3 Classical lists in ABAP Objects

With the introduction of ABAP Objects and the option of GUI controls on screens, classical lists have lost much of their importance. Classical list processing can no longer be fully supported in ABAP Objects, since it is based on global data, runtime events, and a list buffer that is independent of classes.

Because of this list buffer, screen programming for classical lists is more closely bound to the ABAP application logic than screen programming for screens and selection screens. Whereas with the latter, screen and application programming within an ABAP program can be organizationally separated to at least some extent, this is not possible with lists.

LISTING 7.14 Classical list output during a database access

```
REPORT s_classical_list.

DATA wa_spfli TYPE spfli.

SELECT carrid connid
  FROM spfli
  INTO (wa_spfli-carrid, wa_spfli-connid).
  WRITE: / wa_spfli-carrid, wa_spfli-connid.
ENDSELECT.
```

Listing 7.14 clearly illustrates this with a mini program, of the type often used in introductory training courses. Within a `SELECT` loop, data is written to a list with

WRITE and then automatically displayed. This program seems very simple and intuitive, but hides all the concepts that lie behind it. For a long time this was how it was intended to be and was generally sufficient for classical reporting.

GUI controls

However, when you use ABAP Objects, where function and data encapsulation play a large part, this approach no longer suffices. As of Release 4.6, many classical lists (unlike screens and selection screens) can be replaced by the following GUI controls:

- The SAP List Viewer in the form of the ALV grid control (global class CL_GUI_ALV_GRID) is suitable for showing data in a tabular form.
- Forms of the tree control (global classes CL_GUI_LIST_TREE and CL_GUI_COLUMN_TREE) allow you to combine list and column representations with a hierarchy tree.
- The HTML control (CL_GUI_HTML_VIEWER) can be used for any formatted representation of data.[9]
- A TextEdit control (global class CL_GUI_TEXEDIT) can be used to display text modules when complicated formatting is not required.

In particular, the SAP List Viewer offers the ABAP programmer the comfort of a complete list environment, including interactivity and connection to the spool system, which satisfies the requirements of encapsulation.

Nevertheless, classical lists cannot be replaced in every case. They are often more efficient than GUI controls when it comes to printing data in particular: They are sent to the spool system directly and by page, without the need to create large internal tables that are only needed for screen representation.

SAP's aim is to use as few classical lists as possible when displaying screens in new programs in production systems. It also intends to convert older programs to GUI controls. As an application developer, you too should avoid the WRITE statement as often as possible, except when testing and creating programs designed for outputting printed lists. Listing 7.15 shows how you can change the classical list display from Listing 7.14 to a list displayed with the ALV grid control without much effort. The data is first read into an internal table and then passed to the screen output.

LISTING 7.15 List output with ALV grid control

```
REPORT s_abap_objects_list.

DATA spfli_tab TYPE TABLE OF spfli.
DATA alv_list TYPE REF TO cl_gui_alv_grid.

SELECT *
```

9. AS of Release 4.6B, there are also classes such as CL_DD_DOCUMENT for handling ***dynamic documents***, which simplify the display of data in HTML controls.

```
FROM    spfli
INTO    TABLE spfli_tab.

CREATE OBJECT alv_list
       EXPORTING i_parent = cl_gui_container=>screen0.
CALL METHOD alv_list->set_table_for_first_display
            EXPORTING i_structure_name = 'SPFLI'
            CHANGING  it_outtab        = spfli_tab.
CALL SCREEN 100.
```

In the following sections we shall therefore briefly show you the ABAP language elements for classical list processing simply for the sake of completeness, to give you the option of analyzing existing programs with classical lists and if necessary changing them to GUI controls. You will be given an introduction to GUI controls later in Section 7.5.4.

7.3.4 Creating classical lists

You can imagine creating a classical list in such a way that at the beginning you have an area of fixed width and endless length, with a cursor at the top left corner. The empty classical list is therefore like an endless roll of paper in a teleprinter. You use the list statements to write to this area with formatted outputs and thereby change the cursor position. However, you can also divide the endless area into individual pages.

Formatted single field output

To output field contents you use the WRITE statement. Apart from ULINE, WRITE is the only statement to write to classical lists:

```
WRITE  [AT /pos(len)] field [options ...].
```

WRITE

This statement writes the contents of a single field (field) to the cursor position specified either in the AT addition or in the formatting additions included in options.[10] The position specification refers to the line where the list cursor is positioned at the beginning of the statement. The slash positions the list cursor in the next line, pos and len define the offset and length of the output. All specifications are optional.

If the current line does not have any more space for the output, it is automatically placed in a new line, provided no position is specified behind AT or with the POSITION statement (see below). If the output is then longer than the entire list width (see below) it is truncated at the end. After the output the list cursor is placed as standard in the next but one position after the output.

10. If the field written to the list has a data type from the ABAP Dictionary, even the automatic field and input helps from Section 7.1.7 will be available in the list display.

Accordingly, several subsequent WRITE statements without position specification will create several outputs in a line that are each separated by a space.

```
WRITE: / wa-carrid, wa-connid, wa-cityfrom, wa-cityto.
```

Chained statement

This program line looks like a single statement and does exactly what you would intuitively expect of it. It writes the contents of four fields in a new line. In reality we have here a chained statement that consists of four individual WRITE statements. The first output is positioned in a new line and then the other outputs are written to the new cursor position according to the above logic. You could specify the position and format for each individual WRITE statement or write all four statements individually. But you should not be surprised that the WRITE statement is one of the most common applications for chained statements in classical ABAP.

A number of additions for formatting the output are concealed behind the options ... addition. Examples are LEFT-JUSTIFIED for left-justified output, COLOR for the color specification, INPUT for input-ready fields, HOTSPOT for outputs that respond to a single click, AS ICON for icons, etc. You can also activate or deactivate some of these formatting additions for all the following WRITE statements with the FORMAT statement. This saves you having to specify this formatting for each individual WRITE statement.

```
FORMAT HOTSPOT ON.
WRITE: / wa-carrid, wa-connid, wa-cityfrom, wa-cityto.
FORMAT HOTSPOT OFF.
```

Formatting

This sequence of statements has the same effect for individual outputs as:

```
WRITE: / wa-carrid    HOTSPOT ON,
         wa-connid    HOTSPOT ON,
         wa-cityfrom  HOTSPOT ON,
         wa-cityto    HOTSPOT ON.
```

Note, however, that when you use FORMAT and ENDFORMAT the delimiters between the individual outputs are also formatted, which is not the case when formatting individual outputs. We shall not go into detail concerning all the options for formatting WRITE outputs. For more information on this, please read the ABAP keyword documentation or simply try out the pattern for WRITE in the ABAP Editor.

Note that for outputting special list elements such as icons, symbols, or line elements you must load the include program <LIST> in the ABAP program, which contains some necessary definitions.

Lines

You create horizontal lines using the statements

```
ULINE  [AT /pos(len)].
```

or

```
WRITE [AT /pos(len)] sy-uline.
```

Both statements are equivalent and create a new list line, which is completely filled with a horizontal line, if you do not specify position or length. Otherwise the slash, pos and len behave as with the normal WRITE statement. If you output several hyphens or spaces after each other, you also create a horizontal line:

```
WRITE [AT /pos(len)] '-----------------'.
```

You create vertical lines with the statements:

```
WRITE [AT /pos] sy-vline.
```

or

```
WRITE [AT /pos] '|'.
```

Both statements are equivalent and create a vertical line section.

Line connection

If there are no blanks or empty lines between individual lines, these lines are linked in the list output, and you can draw corners, T-sections and crosses.

```
WRITE: / '-------',
       / '|     |',
       / '|     |',
       / '-------'.
```

These four statements draw a closed frame. If you only need corners, T-sections and crosses at certain positions and want to prevent individual neighboring lines from being automatically connected, you must specifically output these line elements using the WRITE statement, for example a top right-hand corner using:

```
WRITE [AT /pos(len)] line_top_right_corner AS LINE.
```

You will find all the line elements in the pattern for WRITE. In classical list programming these were the only means of generating the frames and grid lines for all output lists.

Blank lines

Blank line

You create blank lines on lists as follows:

```
SKIP [n].
```

This statement creates n blank lines. If n is not specified, one blank line is created. In the default setting you cannot generate blank lines through:

```
WRITE: / ' ', / ' ', ...
```

The system suppresses any lines that only contain blank outputs. This allows you to save paper when printing lists. The standard setting can be modified with the

```
SET BLANK LINES  {ON|OFF}.
```

statement. The above `WRITE` statement will also output blank lines with the `ON` addition.

Output positioning

After each output on a list, the list cursor is automatically positioned after this output. You can, however, position the cursor anywhere on the list you require to make an output. Any previous outputs are then overwritten at this point.

Examples of absolute position specifications are:

- `POSITION col.`
  For the horizontal position (column specification)
- `SKIP TO LINE lin.`
  For the vertical position (line specification)

Examples of relative position specifications are:

- `NEW-LINE.`
  For a line break (same meaning as the slash in output statements)
- `WRITE ... UNDER f`
  For positioning in the same column as a previous field f output.

During list creation, the system fields sy-colno and sy-linno always contain the current cursor position.

Defining the list width

The list width depends by default on the window width of the list screen on the front end, which in turn corresponds to the window width of the screen from which the list has been called. The list is at least as wide as the width of a standard size SAP window. For smaller windows the user must scroll horizontally. For larger windows the list width is increased accordingly.

To specify the list width irrespective of the window width, you can specify the `LINE-SIZE` addition in the statement introducing the program. With classical lists this is generally the `REPORT` statement.

```
REPORT rep LINE-SIZE  width.
```

This statement determines the list width for all the basic lists in the program. You can then only specify the list width for detail lists by specifying the `LINE-SIZE` addition after the `NEW-PAGE` statement.

The maximum width is 1023. When creating a list you can always find the current list width in the sy-linsz field.

Page breaks

In principle, the standard list consists only of a single endless area. Just as a roll of endless paper is not really endless, the maximum number of lines per list page is also limited: the list processor performs an automatic page break every 60,000 lines. This can have undesired consequences, particularly when printing long lists, and should be avoided by programming page breaks. Page breaks in a screen list can simplify navigation by allowing to scroll page by page.

Page length

To define the length of a page you specify the LINE-COUNT addition in the statement introducing the program:

```
REPORT rep LINE-COUNT  length[(n)].
```

This statement defines the page length for the lists of a program. By attaching a number n in parentheses, you reserve that number of lines for a page footer. If when you write to a list the end of a page is reached – i.e., length minus n – a page footer can be output and a new page is created. The screen output contains all the pages in the same endless area, but it can be accessed through the scrolling function.

You can also force a page break at any time with the NEW PAGE statement. By specifying the LINE-COUNT addition behind NEW-PAGE you determine the page length of the following pages.

When creating a list you can always find the current page length and current page number in the sy-linct and sy-pagno fields.

Page header and page footer

List header

Each list has a standard page header that occupies at least the first two list lines with a title and a horizontal line. You can maintain the title and four other list lines for column headers using **Goto – Text Elements – List Headings**. The standard page header can include up to six page lines, including another horizontal line underneath the column headers. This must be taken into account when specifying the page length. You can prevent the standard page header from being displayed in the first lines of the list with the NO STANDARD PAGE HEADING addition behind the statement introducing the program. For individual pages you can also control the title individually with the additions NO-TITLE | WITH TITLE and the column headers with NO HEADING | WITH HEADING behind the NEW PAGE statement.

TOP-OF-PAGE

To define a page header in the program, you must implement the required output statements in an event block behind the TOP-OF-PAGE event keyword for basic lists and TOP-OF-PAGE DURING LINE SELECTION for detail lists. When a list is created, the runtime environment triggers these events each time a new page is started. The outputs of the corresponding event blocks are placed below the standard page header and also fill page lines.

END-OF-PAGE

To define a page footer for a basic list, you must define the required output statements in an event block behind the `END-OF-PAGE` event keyword. When a basic list is created, the runtime environment always triggers this event, if an area has been reserved for the footer in the page length specifications, and if this is reached when the page is written. The outputs of the event block are placed in the reserved area. If there is no output during the event, the area remains empty.

Programmed scrolling

The user can scroll through displayed lists using the scroll bars and functions of the GUI status. You can use variants of the `SCROLL` statement in the program to position the list output on the list screen as required.

- `SCROLL LIST {FORWARD|BACKWARD}.`

  Scrolls through the current list vertically by the current window height.
- `SCROLL LIST TO {FIRST PAGE | LAST PAGE | PAGE` page} [`LINE` line].

  Scrolls through the current list vertically to the first, last, or specified page and displays the page as from line (`line`). In this case the page header is not counted.
- `SCROLL LIST {LEFT|RIGHT}` [`BY` col `PLACES`].

  Scrolls through the current list horizontally to the left or right border or to the left or right by `col` positions.
- `SCROLL LIST TO COLUMN` col.

  Scrolls through the current list horizontally to the `col` position.

When the basic list is being generated, the current list means the basic list. When interactive list events are being processed, it means the list displayed at that time. With all `SCROLL` variants you can also explicitly specify the list of the list system to be scrolled using an `INDEX idx` addition. You can therefore also scroll through lists that are currently neither created nor displayed. When you call such a list, it will be located in the required position.

7.3.5 Displaying classical lists

There are two ways to display classical lists on screen: automatic display in an executable program and programmed display during screen processing. With both types, list processing is started and the lists are displayed on the list screen layout, whereby the list screen takes over the position and size of the previous screen.

Automatic display

If a basic list is created in an executable program in the processing blocks for reporting events, it will be automatically displayed when the last of these event blocks is executed, i.e. after END-OF-SELECTION at the latest. To do this the runtime environment changes to list processing and sets a list-specific GUI status for the list screen. Most of the functions offered there, such as scrolling or saving, are executed by the runtime environment and do not have to be programmed. Listing 7.14 is a typical example of how a classical list is automatically displayed.

List display during screen processing

As already mentioned, you can write to exactly one basic list when processing a screen sequence. The system collects all the output statements of all the dialog modules of a screen sequence on this basic list. To display this list, you must use the following statement in one of the dialog modules:

```
LEAVE TO LIST-PROCESSING  [AND RETURN TO SCREEN dynnr].
```

This starts the list processing at the end of PAI processing of the current screen and displays the basic list. If the user quits the basic list or if the

```
LEAVE LIST-PROCESSING.
```

statement is executed during list processing – i.e. during a list event – the runtime environment calls either the screen being processed when the list display was called, or the screen with the dynnr screen number again, at PBO. Specifying 0 as dynnr therefore ends the current screen sequence. When the system returns to screen processing, the entire list system is initialized and the next output statements therefore write to an empty basic list.

Screen sequence

With the exception of creating internal logs, there is no point in dividing the creation of a list among several screens of a screen sequence. If you wish to use the classical list method instead of the ALV grid control, we recommend you at least to encapsulate the list creation in a single screen, which you call during your screen sequence using CALL SCREEN. Here you can use the following procedure, which, for example, you can also encapsulate in a function group:

1. Define a screen without maintaining the layout and in the flow logic call a single PBO module. You do not need any PAI module or an OK field.
2. In the PBO module, first use the statement

   ```
   LEAVE TO LIST-PROCESSING AND RETURN TO SCREEN 0.
   ```

   This ensures that at the end of the screen, the list processing is called and after this the system returns to where the screen was called.

3. Set a suitable GUI status for the list (see Section 7.3.6) since otherwise the GUI status of the existing screen will be used.
4. Create the entire list using list output statements.
5. Use one of the statements

   ```
   SUPPRESS DIALOG.
   ```

   or

   ```
   LEAVE SCREEN.
   ```

   to suppress the display of the empty layout or to terminate the screen immediately. The system then goes to the list display and afterwards returns to where the screen was called.

Listing 7.16 is an example of how a list is displayed during screen processing.

LISTING 7.16 Programmed list display

```
*&---------------------------------------------------------------------*
*& Report S_LIST_DISPLAY.                                              *
*&---------------------------------------------------------------------*
REPORT s_list_display.

*&---------------------------------------------------------------------*
*& Global Declarations                                                 *
*&---------------------------------------------------------------------*
* Screen Interfaces
TABLES demo_conn.

* Global Data
DATA: wa_spfli TYPE spfli.

*&---------------------------------------------------------------------*
*& Processing Blocks called by the Runtime Environment                 *
*&---------------------------------------------------------------------*
* Event Block START-OF-SELECTION
START-OF-SELECTION.
  CALL SCREEN 100.

* Dialog Module PBO Screen 100
MODULE status_0100 OUTPUT.
  SET PF-STATUS 'SCREEN_100'.
ENDMODULE.
```

```
* Dialog Modules PAI Screen 100
MODULE cancel INPUT.
  LEAVE PROGRAM.
ENDMODULE.
MODULE user_command_0100.
  CALL SCREEN 500.
  SET SCREEN 100.
ENDMODULE.

* Dialog Module PBO Screen 500
MODULE create_list OUTPUT.
  LEAVE TO LIST-PROCESSING AND RETURN TO SCREEN 0.
  SET PF-STATUS space.
  SELECT  carrid connid cityfrom cityto
    FROM  spfli
    INTO  (wa_spfli-carrid, wa_spfli-connid,
           wa_spfli-cityfrom, wa_spfli-cityto)
    WHERE carrid = demo_conn-carrid.
    WRITE: / wa_spfli-carrid, wa_spfli-connid,
             wa_spfli-cityfrom, wa_spfli-cityto.
  ENDSELECT.
  LEAVE SCREEN.
ENDMODULE.

* Page Header
TOP-OF-PAGE.
  WRITE text-001 COLOR COL_HEADING.
  ULINE.
```

Screen 100 has a single input field, the CARRID component of the DEMO_CONN structure from the ABAP Dictionary. Screen 500 encapsulates list creation and does not have any screen elements.

In the screen flow logic of screen 100, the dialog modules defined in the source code are called. The MODULE statement calling the cancel module has the AT EXIT-COMMAND addition. In the GUI status SCREEN_100, the usual standard toolbar functions have type E function codes. Otherwise we have not defined anything for screen 100 and the user triggers the PAI module user_command_0100 with the ↵ key.

In this PAI module we immediately call screen 500, in whose flow logic we call only the PBO module create_list. After these modules have been processed, and after calling screen 500, the runtime system finds itself in a new screen sequence in which we use WRITE statements to write to a new basic list that we display with LEAVE TO LIST-PROCESSING (see Figure 7.30). Additionally to the standard page header, we have defined another page header during the TOP-OF-PAGE event.

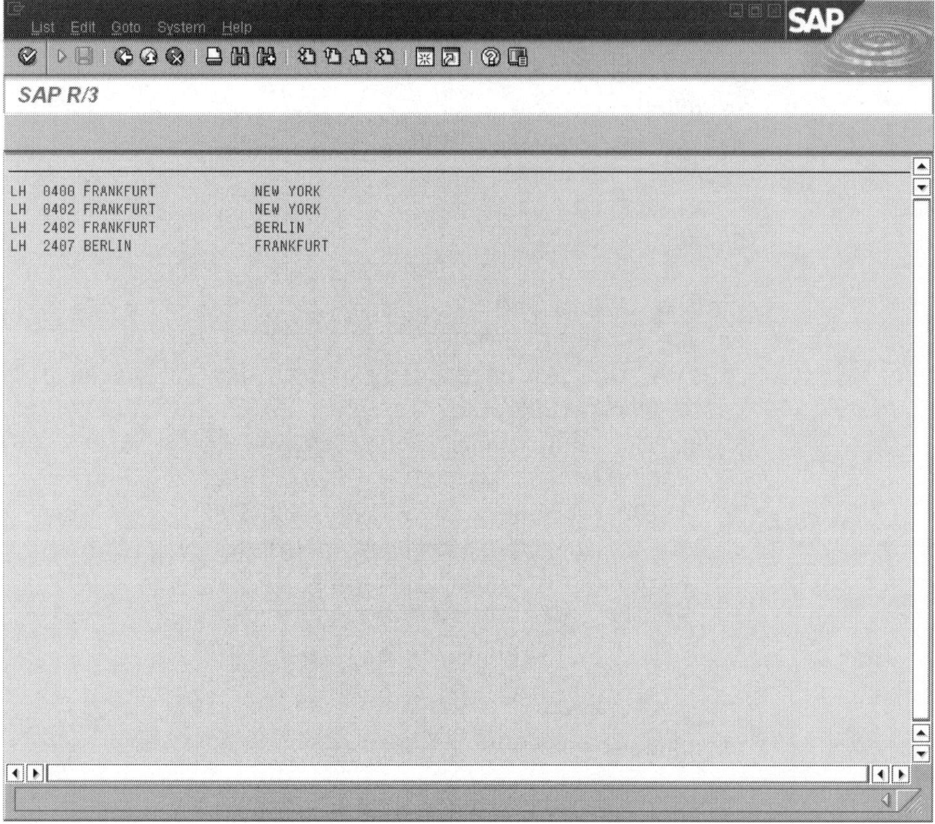

FIGURE 7.30 Display of a classical list. Copyright © SAP AG

After list processing we return to the processing of screen 100 where this screen itself is set as a subsequent screen.

Using screens 100 and 500 we have re-programmed in principle the behavior of a report with a standard selection screen and the automatic list display.

7.3.6 User actions on classical lists

While a list is displayed on the layout of the list screen the user can perform various actions, which can be evaluated by the list processing. As with selection screens, some of the functions are processed by the runtime environment itself, while other functions trigger events to which the ABAP program reacts.

Actions in the list area

A list may contain input-ready fields and checkboxes, but cannot contain screen elements linked with function codes. Instead, selecting lines by double-clicking with the mouse or using the F2 key plays a large part in lists. As with all screens, the F2 function key is firmly linked to the double-clicking function of the mouse. If this function is linked to a function code in the GUI status, its selection triggers an event in the runtime environment.

GUI status for lists

Since no interactive screen elements with function codes can be created in lists, the GUI status is the only means of providing the user with functions.

The standard list status

When a list is automatically displayed in executable programs the runtime environment sets a standard list status that contains many list-specific functions such as **scrolling**, which are all processed by the runtime environment.

In programmed list display during screen processing you can set the standard list status yourself using the

```
SET PF-STATUS  space.
```

statement. You can extend the standard list interface from your ABAP program by defining specific event blocks. The most important of these event blocks is introduced with:

```
AT LINE-SELECTION.
```

Double-clicking

If you have such an event block in your ABAP program, the **Choose** function is automatically added to the standard list status. This function has the function code PICK in the standard list status and is linked with the F2 key, i.e. the mouse double-click function. If the user selects **Choose** on a list line, the runtime environment triggers the `AT LINE-SELECTION` event and the corresponding event block is executed.

The other possible event blocks for extending the standard list status would be `AT PF01` to `AT PF24`, which link function codes with function keys. However, these should no longer be used. Instead you can set custom list statuses and use the `AT USER-COMMAND` event.

Custom list status

If the standard list status that lets the program react to line selection is insufficient, you can define and set your own GUI status for lists. We recommend you select in the Menu Painter **Extras – Adjust Template** and then select the **List status** for **Template status**. This will add all the list specific functions of the standard list status to your list status. For example, the PRI function code will be assigned to the corresponding icon from the standard toolbar and the key combination ctrl + P , while the PICK function code is linked to the F2 key. As with the standard list status, all these function codes are processed by the runtime environment and only PICK results in an event in the ABAP program.

Function code

You can now edit this status by linking your own function codes to unused elements or by replacing predefined function codes with them. All self-defined function codes result in the event:

```
AT USER-COMMAND.
```

If you define such an event block in the ABAP program you can react to the corresponding user actions. Although lists do not have an OK field, you can evaluate the function code in the `sy-ucomm` system field.

If, for example, you replace the PRI or PICK predefined function codes with your own function codes, when they are selected neither system-controlled printing nor the `AT LINE-SELECTION` event is triggered. Instead you must define your own printing routine in the event block behind `AT USER-COMMAND`, or handle the line selection there.

Note that it is the PICK function code that is linked to the `AT LINE-SELECTION` event, and not the F2 key. If you link PICK with another key or a menu entry, when selected they result in `AT LINE-SELECTION`. If you are working with your own function codes, it is therefore advisable always to replace PICK with your own function code. In this way function code evaluation in the ABAP program is encapsulated in a single processing block.

As with general screens, you set your self-defined list status before the list is displayed with the statement:

```
SET PF-STATUS stat.
```

The `stat` status is then used for all the following list displays. This applies both to basic lists that are displayed in executable programs or during screen processing, and to detail lists that are created during list processing. Only a new statement, `SET PF-STATUS`, sets a different status. As with screens, you can determine the title of the list screen with `SET TITLEBAR`.

7.3.7 Classical list processing and detail lists

List processing in the ABAP program consists mainly of reacting on corresponding user actions on a displayed list in the `AT LINE-SELECTION` or `AT USER-COMMAND` event blocks. `AT LINE-SELECTION` is triggered at the moment when the PICK function code is selected and the cursor is placed on a list line. The `AT USER-COMMAND` event is triggered for all custom function codes. However, all other predefined function codes of a list status (except for PF01 to PF24) are intercepted and executed by the runtime environment.

The most important feature of event blocks for interactive list events is that all the list output statements executed within them are used to create detail lists.

Detail lists

Detail lists are lists that are created during a list event. A detail list is automatically displayed at the end of the event block on the list screen and covers the previous list.

List index

Each list has a list index, which is stored in the sy-lsind system field. sy-lsind is zero when the basic list is created. Each user action that triggers an event in the ABAP program increases sy-lsind by one. Conversely, the index of the list where the event was triggered is contained in sy-listi. Output statements always write exactly to the list whose index is currently in sy-lsind. Therefore, if an event has been triggered on the basic list, in the event block the first detail list with the index 1 is filled and then displayed. An event on this detail list will cause the detail list with the index 2 to be created and displayed and so on. You can create up to 20 detail lists for each basic list in this way.

With the above system fields you can always determine which list level you are writing to in order to react specifically on user actions or to set a corresponding GUI status. If the user selects *Back* on a detail list, this list is completely deleted from the list system and the next lowest list level is displayed.

sy-lsind

During list processing you can assign the sy-lsind system field the index of an existing list, in order to overwrite the contents of this list completely. At the same time you delete all the detail lists with a higher index. This is an exception to the rule that system fields should not be specifically overwritten!

You can also display detail lists as modal dialog boxes if you run the statement

```
WINDOW  STARTING AT  left  upper
        ENDING AT    right lower.
```

during the list event. In this case it is advisable to set a corresponding GUI status for dialog boxes.

Interactive reporting

Detail lists form the technical basis of classical interactive reporting in the SAP System. In interactive reporting, instead of one complete basic list you create a condensed basic list from which the user can call detailed information in detail lists by positioning the cursor and entering commands. In interactive reporting data retrieval is therefore restricted to what is actually required.

Evaluating list lines

In an event block, to be able to respond correctly to a user input, for example in order to read detailed information for a selected list line, you need information concerning this line. To help you there are several system fields such as, for example, sy-lilli or sy-curow that provide you with information on the position of the cursor.

However, to interpret the contents of the selected list line type-specifically, it is not enough to access the finished formatted list. Instead, when you create the list you must save particular information on each line in the list system. To do this you use the statement:

```
HIDE f
```

Hide area

With this statement you save the contents of a given variable f for the current list line (sy-linno) of the current list level (sy-lsind) in an invisible table.

With each line selection by the user, the variable f is automatically filled with the stored value before the event block is executed and can be evaluated. For example, for each line an identification can be stored that specifies whether the line can be selected or not. Another common application is to store key fields for further database access.

There is also a range of other statements that allow you to access list lines in the list system through programming. The most important of these is:

```
READ LINE  line [INDEX idx]
                [FIELD VALUE f_i INTO g_i] ...
```

Without specifically entering the list index after a list event, this statement accesses the list line (line) of the list where the event took place (sy-listi). During READ LINE, all the system fields and the variables stored with HIDE are filled, as for an interactive line selection. All list fields can be read using the FIELD VALUE addition, although it should be noted that the formatted output is read. A common application of READ LINE is evaluating the input fields or checkboxes of a list.

Modifying finished lists

When called, lists are stored in their final format in the list system. However, you can modify individual list lines during list processing with the statement

```
MODIFY LINE  line [INDEX idx] ...
```

whereby if the list index is not explicitly entered the list is addressed where the event took place. The statement allows you to modify the formatting of the line or of individual fields in the list line (line) or to overwrite the contents of fields.

7.3.8 Example of classical list processing

The program in Listing 7.17 shows a complete example of classical list processing that generates two detail lists from a basic list.

LISTING 7.17 Example of Classical List Processing

```
*&---------------------------------------------------------------------*
*& Report S_INTERACTIVE_LISTS                                          *
*&---------------------------------------------------------------------*
REPORT s_interactive_lists NO STANDARD PAGE HEADING.

*&---------------------------------------------------------------------*
*& Global Declarations                                                 *
*&---------------------------------------------------------------------*
* Selection Screen
PARAMETERS p_carrid TYPE spfli-carrid.

* Global Data
DATA: wa_spfli TYPE spfli,
      wa_sbook TYPE sbook,
      num TYPE i,
      dat TYPE d.

*&---------------------------------------------------------------------*
*& Processing Blocks called by the Runtime Environment                 *
*&---------------------------------------------------------------------*
* Event Block START-OF-SELECTION
START-OF-SELECTION.
  num = 0.
  SET PF-STATUS 'FLIGHT'.
  SELECT *
  FROM   spfli
  INTO   wa_spfli
  WHERE  carrid = p_carrid.
    num = num + 1.
    WRITE: / wa_spfli-carrid, wa_spfli-connid,
             wa_spfli-cityfrom, wa_spfli-cityto.
    HIDE:    wa_spfli-carrid, wa_spfli-connid, num.
  ENDSELECT.
  CLEAR num.

* Page headers
TOP-OF-PAGE.
  WRITE 'List of Flights'.
  ULINE.
  WRITE 'CA  CONN FROM                 TO'.
```

```
  ULINE.
TOP-OF-PAGE DURING LINE-SELECTION.
  CASE sy-pfkey.
    WHEN 'BOOKING'.
      WRITE sy-lisel.
      ULINE.
    WHEN 'WINDOW'.
      WRITE:  'Booking', wa_sbook-bookid,
           /  'Date    ', wa_sbook-fldate.
      ULINE.
  ENDCASE.

* React on user actions
AT USER-COMMAND.
  CASE sy-ucomm.
    WHEN 'SELE'.
      IF num <> 0.
        SET PF-STATUS 'BOOKING'.
        CLEAR dat.
        SELECT *
        FROM sbook
        INTO wa_sbook
        WHERE carrid = wa_spfli-carrid AND
              connid = wa_spfli-connid.
          IF wa_sbook-fldate <> dat.
            dat = wa_sbook-fldate.
            SKIP.
            WRITE / wa_sbook-fldate.
            POSITION 16.
          ELSE.
            NEW-LINE.
            POSITION 16.
          ENDIF.
        WRITE wa_sbook-bookid.
          HIDE: wa_sbook-bookid, wa_sbook-fldate,
                wa_sbook-custtype, wa_sbook-smoker,
                wa_sbook-luggweight, wa_sbook-class.
        ENDSELECT.
        IF sy-subrc <> 0.
          WRITE / 'No bookings for this flight'.
        ENDIF.
        num = 0.
```

```
        CLEAR wa_sbook-bookid.
      ENDIF.
    WHEN 'INFO'.
      IF NOT wa_sbook-bookid IS INITIAL.
        SET PF-STATUS 'WINDOW'.
        SET TITLEBAR 'TIT_BOOKING'.
        WINDOW STARTING AT 30 5 ENDING AT 60 10.
        WRITE: 'Customer type    :', wa_sbook-custtype,
             / 'Smoker           :', wa_sbook-smoker,
             / 'Luggage weigtht  :',
                wa_sbook-luggweight UNIT 'KG',
             / 'Class            :', wa_sbook-class.
      ENDIF.
  ENDCASE.
```

At `START-OF-SELECTION` we set our own GUI status, "FLIGHT," for the basic list. In this GUI status we have selected the **List status** as **Template status** and linked the F2 function key with the function code SELE instead of PICK. Double-clicking a list line will now trigger the `AT USER-COMMAND` event.

When the basic list is being created within a `SELECT` loop, we store the three fields spfli-carrid, spfli-connid, and num in the `HIDE` area. If the user selects a line from the basic list in which there is a num variable in the `HIDE` area that is not equal to zero, a detail list is filled and displayed. For the detail list we set the GUI status "BOOKING," in which we link the F2 key with the function code INFO. We write data to the detail list, which we read using the `HIDE` fields of the basic list from the SBOOK database table. For each list line we again write additional information to its `HIDE` area.

If the user selects a valid line from the detail list, we show the information from the `HIDE` area in a dialog box with the WINDOW GUI status (see Figure 7.31). The validity of the line selection is checked using sbook-bookid. For the WINDOW GUI status we have copied the default settings of the **dialog box** status type with adjustment for **list status**.

Note also that we have removed the standard page header in the `REPORT` statement and are defining all the page headers ourselves during the `TOP-OF-PAGE` event. We identify the lists using the sy-pfkey system field, which contains the current GUI status.

7.3.9 Sending lists to the SAP spool system

Classical lists, which are placed in the list system using list output statements on the application server, are the only interface between ABAP programs and the SAP spool system. This means that only outputs created with `WRITE` can be printed on the SAP spool system printers, saved there, or stored through **SAP ArchiveLink**. Even if you work with the ALV grid control and print the displayed list, classical lists are still created in the methods behind it.

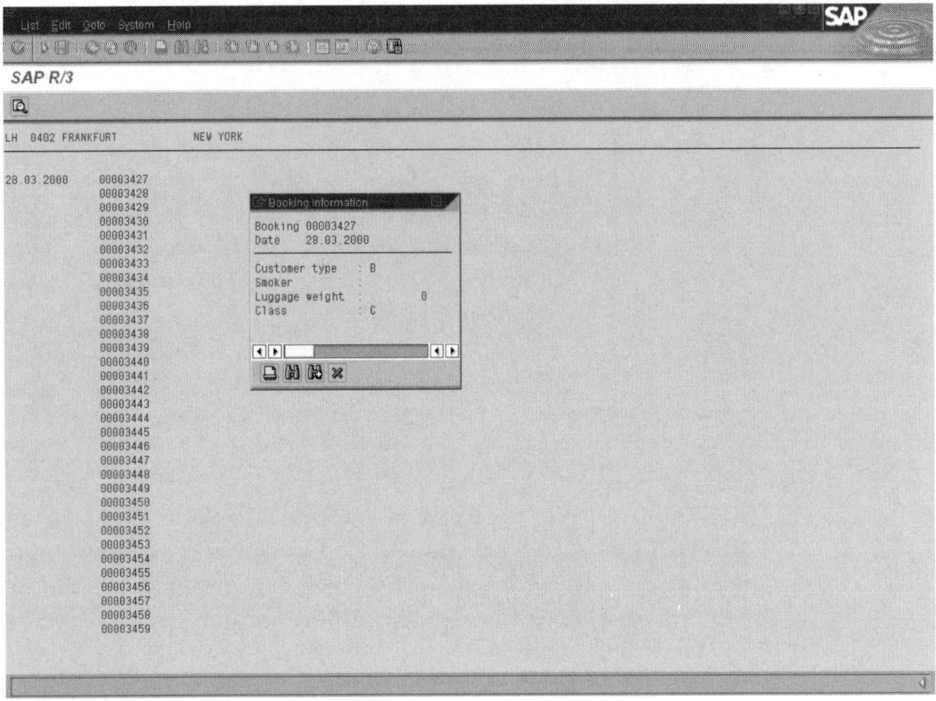

FIGURE 7.31 Detail lists. Copyright © SAP AG

Creating print lists in the program

We refer to a list that is sent to the SAP spool system after creation and not shown as a screen list as a *print list*. To create a print list, all you need is the statement:

```
NEW-PAGE PRINT ON  [PARAMETERS pripar]
                   [ARCHIVE PARAMETERS arcpar]
                   [NO DIALOG].
```

All subsequent list outputs are placed on a new page and sent to the SAP spool system instead of the list screen. Conversely, with the

```
NEW-PAGE PRINT OFF.
```

statement you can switch back to the screen output.

Print parameters for print lists

To be able to pass list outputs to the SAP spool system error-free, list formats such as page width and page length must be adapted to the requirements of the spool system. To do this, print parameters must be specified with the `NEW-PAGE PRINT ON` statement.

Print dialog

Without the `NO DIALOG` addition the system displays a dialog box, in which the user must enter the print parameters (see Figure 7.32). The runtime environment ensures that only consistent entries can be made.

However, if the user cancels the dialog box, no print parameters will be available and the program will be cancelled. We therefore recommend using the `NO DIALOG` addition and passing the print parameters in the program. The most suitable additions for this are `PARAMETERS` and `ARCHIVE PARAMETERS`.[11] You pass the parameters in the `pripar` and `arcpar` fields, which must have the structured data types `pri_params`

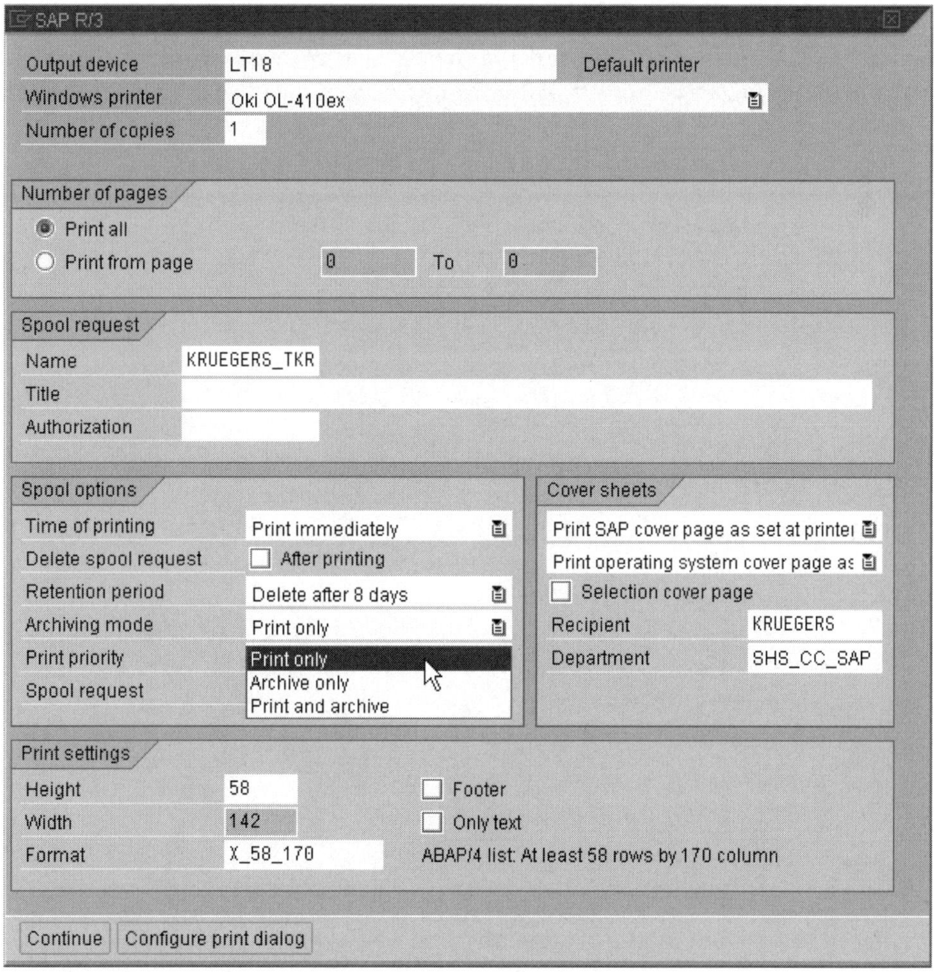

FIGURE 7.32 Print parameters. Copyright © SAP AG

11. The other additions to the `NEW-PAGE PRINT ON` statement you find in the documentation should no longer be used. If they are used, the print parameter consistency cannot be guaranteed.

and arc_params from the ABAP Dictionary. arcpar must only be passed if the list is also to be stored with SAP ArchiveLink. This is again controlled by one of the print parameters in pripar.

GET_PRINT_PARAMETERS

To fill the pripar and arcpar structures you use exclusively the GET_PRINT_PARAMETERS function module, which has two export parameters of the same type. Individual values for all the parameters can be passed as import parameters to the function module. The function module checks the passed values for consistency and either exports a consistent set of print parameters or creates an exception. When you run the function module, the user dialog from Figure 7.32 can also be used by applying the no_dialog import parameter. That separates the user dialog from the actual print statement. The function module has an output parameter called valid, which is only set to "X" if the function module has created a set of valid print parameters. It is set to space in particular if the user cancels the dialog.

LISTING 7.18 Creating a print list with user dialog

```
DATA: print_parameters TYPE pri_params,
      valid_flag(1) TYPE c.
...
CALL FUNCTION 'GET_PRINT_PARAMETERS'
     EXPORTING
          no_dialog            = ' '
     IMPORTING
          out_parameters       = print_parameters
          valid                = valid_flag
     EXCEPTIONS
          invalid_print_params = 2
          OTHERS               = 4.
...
IF valid_flag = 'X' AND
   sy-subrc = 0.
  NEW-PAGE PRINT ON NO DIALOG
                    PARAMETERS print_parameters.
  ...
  WRITE ...
  ...
ENDIF.
```

The program sequence in Listing 7.18 shows the recommended procedure for creating a print list including user dialog. First, the dialog box is called with the GET_PRINT_PARAMETERS function module and a set of print parameters is placed in the print_parameters structure. A print list will only be created with the print parameters if they are consistent.

The parameters passed with NEW-PAGE PRINT ON override other formatting specifications in the ABAP program. The latter are intended for outputting lists to screens and generally do not fit the print format. Furthermore, you can define the print format of print lists beyond the formatting options of screen lists using the PRINT-CONTROL statement.

Creating print lists subsequently

Apart from the NEW-PAGE PRINT ON statement you have three further options for formatting classical lists with print parameters and sending them to the SAP spool system.

Generating print lists with SUBMIT

If you call an executable program that creates a basic list with

```
SUBMIT rep TO SAP-SPOOL  [SPOOL PARAMETERS pripar]
                        [ARCHIVE PARAMETERS arcpar]
                        [WITHOUT SPOOL DYNPRO].
```

the list is formatted according to the passed parameter and sent to the SAP spool system instead of the screen. For the additions the same applies as for NEW-PAGE PRINT ON.

Generating print lists in the selection screen

If the user chooses the **Execute and Print** function on the standard selection screen of an executable program instead of **Execute**, the basic list of the program is also prepared for printing during its creation and is sent to the SAP spool system. The user must enter the print parameters in the dialog box of Figure 7.32. You can set the default entries of the dialog box with the SET_PRINT_PARAMETERS function module before the selection screen is called.

Generating print lists in background jobs

JOB_SUBMIT

You can schedule an executable program in a background job using the JOB_SUBMIT function module. Of course, the list of a background job cannot be displayed on screen, it must be sent to the spool system. The JOB_SUBMIT function module has a priparams input parameter for passing print parameters.

Printing screen lists

As you know, each standard list status offers the **print** function when the list is displayed. If users select this function they must enter print parameters, which can also be preset with the SET_PRINT_PARAMETERS function module, and can then send the list to the SAP spool system.

However, this does not create a new print list in the ABAP program. Instead the finished list is split into pages according to the print parameters and truncated in some cases. This form of printing screen lists does not always achieve the desired results. For example, the logical page division of the screen list does not always match the physical page division of the paper format, and neither does the width of a screen list generally match the paper format.

If you still wish to offer the user the option of printing a list prepared for screen use, you should replace the PRI function code of the list status with your own function code and create a properly formatted print list in the `AT USER-COMMAND` event block with the `NEW-PAGE PRINT ON` statement. Otherwise you can also deactivate PRI to prevent a pure screen list from being printed.

7.4 MESSAGES

What are messages? Messages are short one-line texts that you can send the user in dialog boxes or in the status bar when processing screens. You can use messages to inform the user about the program flow, conduct error dialogs, or terminate the program.

7.4.1 Creating messages

All messages of a SAP System are stored in the T100 database table. This table has the following columns:

- A one-character language key
- A 20-character application area, also known as a message class
- A three-character message number
- The actual message text comprising 72 characters

You create messages with the **message maintenance** tool (Transaction SE91), which you obtain in the Object Navigator, for example, using **Create – Message Class** in the context menu of a development class. You group together all the relevant messages of an application area – for example, a program or a development class – in a message class. The various messages of a message class are distinguished by their message numbers. If the message text is not self-explanatory, you can create a long text for each message that the user can call while the message is displayed.

7.4.2 Sending messages

You send a message using the `MESSAGE` statement. Here you must identify the message using its message class and message number and also specify one of the message types A, E, I, S, W, or X. The message type determines the form in which the message is sent and how the program continues after the message is sent.

The most basic form of the MESSAGE statement is:

```
MESSAGE  tnnn.
```

In this case you specify nothing other than the message type t and the message number nnn. This presupposes that you have listed the

```
... MESSAGE-ID id ...
```

addition with a message class id after the program introductory statement. This addition prescribes a message class for all the MESSAGE statements in your program. However, you can also enter the message class specifically when sending a message, if you use

```
MESSAGE tnnn(id).
```

Here, the ID in this message statement, id, overrides the message ID of the program introductory statement.

Finally, you can also specify the message dynamically, by using

```
MESSAGE ID id TYPE t NUMBER n.
```

where id, t, and n are fields, which contain message class, message number, and message type.

Placeholder

If a message text in table T100 contains the placeholder character "&," you can replace up to four of these characters using the WITH addition to the MESSAGE statement through program-dependent texts:

```
MESSAGE ... WITH f1 ... f4.
```

The contents of the fields f_1 ... f_4 replace each of the placeholders in the message text in turn. We have already used this method in the transaction example in Section 7.1.8, whereby message 888 of the SABAPDOCU message class contains the message text "& & & &." You can check this by double-clicking on the number 888 in the program text.

Exception

Within function modules and methods you can use the RAISING addition to the MESSAGE statement to replace the RAISE statement for triggering exceptions with

```
MESSAGE ... RAISING  exc.
```

Normally, callers of function modules and methods should handle their exceptions. If an exception triggered by RAISE is not handled, the program will terminate. You can prevent this by using the above statement. If the caller does not handle the exception exc, no exception is triggered. Instead the message is sent and processed according to its type. Otherwise the exception is triggered and handled.

7.4.3 Message processing

The form of the message display and subsequent processing depends primarily on the message type specified in the `MESSAGE` statement. For some types, message processing is then also dependent on the context.

By context we mean the actual status of the screen processing of the ABAP program. Since each phase of screen processing is linked to the execution of certain processing blocks, the context is synonymous with the processing block containing the `MESSAGE` statement. For `MESSAGE` statements in procedures this logically applies to the processing block from which the procedure is called.

The exact processing rules for each message type and in each context are contained in the ABAP keyword documentation for the `MESSAGE` statement. We will now list the most important cases and then discuss some peculiarities in procedures.

Type I and S informative messages

With these message types, you can inform the user about the program status with texts such as "Action completed" or "Data read."

- Type I information messages are largely independent of context.
  The system displays the message in a dialog box and after confirmation by the user returns to the statement after the `MESSAGE` statement. It is only in PBO modules that information messages are handled like type S messages.
- Type S status messages are totally independent of context.
  The system continues program processing in the statement directly after the `MESSAGE` statement and displays the message in the status bar of the following screen.

Type E and W messages for handling input errors

You can use these message types to conduct an error dialog with the user to point out any incorrect entries in input fields. They are therefore mainly suited to PAI processing. In all other contexts they will cause the program to terminate.

- Type E error messages are context-dependent
  In a PAI module the current screen processing is terminated and the layout is shown again without PBO processing having been performed. The message is shown in the status bar, and on the layout all the input fields that are combined in the flow logic with the PAI module through `FIELD` or `CHAIN` are ready for input again. After a user action the system continues with the first `FIELD` or `CHAIN` statement. This pattern is designed for creating self-defined input checks, which we have already mentioned in Section 7.1.6.

  In an event block that responds to user actions on selection screens, error messages are treated as in PAI modules, whereby the input-ready status of the fields is controlled by additions to the `AT SELECTION-SCREEN` statement, as for example `ON BLOCK` (see Section 7.2.5).

In an event block of interactive list processing, such as `AT LINE-SELECTION` or `AT USER-COMMAND`, this block is terminated and the display of the previous list level remains on the list screen and the message is displayed in the status bar.

No other processing blocks of an ABAP program directly evaluate user inputs on screens. Here the current program is terminated after an error message and in most cases the system returns to the call location of the program.

- Type W warnings behave in the same way as type E error messages in all contexts. Unlike error messages, the user can quit the warning on a screen that is again waiting for input using [↵], without making any further inputs. The program flow is then continued immediately after the `MESSAGE` statement. Moreover, a warning at PBO does not cause the program to terminate; instead it behaves as a type S status message.

Program terminations with type A and X messages

You can use this type of message to completely terminate ABAP programs. Whereas type A terminations can be useful, for example, if authorizations are not present, type X terminations are more like an emergency braking system, which should only be employed if the system has broken down in a way that cannot be treated otherwise.

- Type A (Abend) messages are independent of context.

  The message is displayed in a dialog box. After confirmation by the user, the system terminates the program irrevocably, and returns to the next highest call level.

- Type X (Exit) messages are equally independent of context.

  Exit messages are not displayed. Instead, the program terminates with a short dump (see Section 4.8.2). The message text is then in the display of the short dump that can also be subsequently evaluated with Transaction ST22.

  No exit messages should be sent in application programs. Messages of this type are limited to system programs such as the classes of the Control Framework.

Messages in procedures

Messages are treated in procedures in the same way as in the processing block from which the procedure was called. A subroutine that sends an error message will therefore result in an error dialog if it is called in a PAI module, and in program termination if it is called outside of screen processing. This applies also to function modules and methods, providing the `RAISING` addition is not used or the caller of a function module does not intercept the message.

Handling exceptions

As already mentioned, when you use the `RAISING` addition in function modules or methods, the message is only displayed if the caller does not handle the specified exception. Message processing then occurs as for normal message sending. If the caller handles the exception, the message will not be displayed. Instead the process is terminated irrespective of the message type and the program flow continues after the CALL statement. The message type, identification, and text are then available for evaluation in the sy-msgid, sy-msgnr, sy-msgty, and sy-msgv1, ..., sy-msgv4 system fields. Therefore it is only useful to send messages with MESSAGE ... RAISING in error situations.

ERROR_MESSAGE

The interface of function modules contains a predefined exception called ERROR_MESSAGE, which allows the caller to affect the messages of the function module. If this exception is listed in the EXCEPTION list of the CALL FUNCTION statement, it has the following effect on the MESSAGE statements of the function module that do not have a RAISING addition:

- The system ignores type S, I, and W messages completely. If the program is running in the background, they are, however, noted in the log.
- Type E and A messages trigger the ERROR_MESSAGE exception.
- Only type X messages behave as usual and terminate the program with a short dump.

By specifying the ERROR_MESSAGE exception the caller therefore has the option of handling error messages itself and avoiding program terminations. Treating this exception is particularly useful when calling older function modules created before the RAISING addition existed. In this way, however, you can also call outside of PAI processing function modules that send error messages without the program terminating.

7.5 ADVANCED SCREEN TECHNIQUES

In this section we shall deal with screen techniques whose main task is to facilitate working with layouts for the user. We shall be focusing on the new techniques that have been available for this purpose as of Basis Release 4.6 and shall only briefly cover older techniques such as classic controls.

7.5.1 Context menus you program yourself

By context menus we mean the menu bar that appears on a layout when the alternate mouse button is pressed. By default, a menu appears on the SAP System layouts that contains all the functions that are assigned to a function key in the current GUI status. For our example program S_SCREEN_PAINTER_DEMO from Sections 7.1.2 and 7.1.4, the context menu is as indicated in Figure 7.33.

As of Release 4.6, you can link input and output fields, text fields, table controls, areas in frames, and subscreens with custom context menus. To do this, in the attrib-

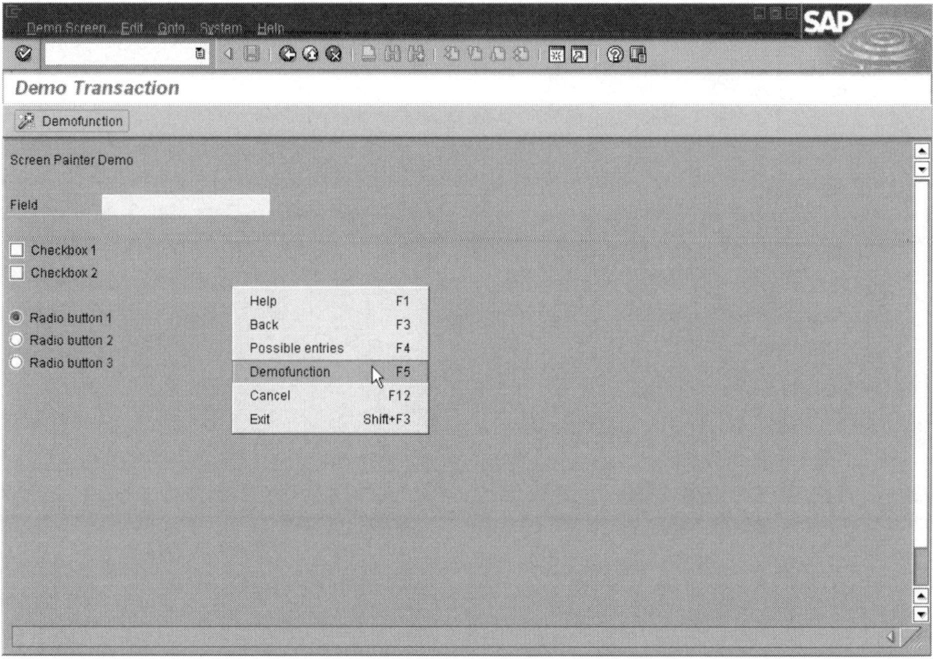

FIGURE 7.33 Standard context menu on a screen. Copyright © SAP AG

utes of the corresponding screen element you must fill the ON_CTMENU_ field (see Figure 7.4) with a value and create a subroutine of the same name as a callback routine in the ABAP program. This subroutine must have a USING parameter of the CL_CTMENU reference type. CL_CTMENU is a global class in the Class Library, whose objects represent context menus.

If we fill the ON_CTMENU_ field with the value "INPUT" for the input field of our example screen, we can add the subroutine from Listing 7.19 to the ABAP program.

LISTING 7.19 Callback-routine for context menu

```
* Callback routine for context menu
FORM on_ctmenu_input USING l_menu TYPE REF TO cl_ctmenu.
  CALL METHOD l_menu->add_function
                    EXPORTING fcode = 'PRESS'
                              text  = text-020.
```

Callback routine

The subroutine is called when the user presses the alternate mouse button on the screen element and it receives a reference to a corresponding context menu object from the system. You must define the menu entries of the context menu in this subroutine. In Listing 7.19 we have added a single function with the add_function

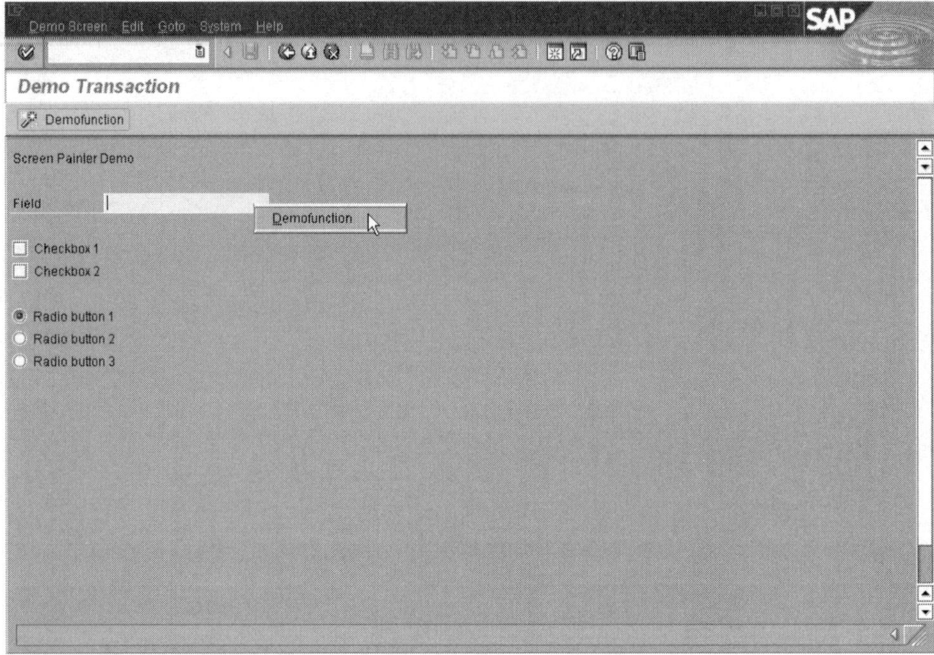

FIGURE 7.34 Custom context menu. Copyright © SAP AG

method that has the same function code as the pushbutton of the screen and the application toolbar (see Figure 7.34). The add_function method also allows you to set the function type.

If the user chooses this menu entry, the PAI event is triggered and the function code can be evaluated in the PAI modules as usual.

The CL_CTMENU class has methods that allow you to load predefined context menus, which you have defined with the Menu Painter in the GUI status (load_gui_status), attach other context menu objects to a context menu on the same level (add_menu) or as a sub-menu (add_submenu). Other methods allow you to add dividing lines, activate or deactivate functions, and position the cursor on a function.

7.5.2 Drop-down boxes

In Section 7.1.7 we introduced various ways of providing the user with dialog boxes showing value lists as input helps. If such a value list is not particularly extensive, you can offer the user a faster drop-down box instead of a dialog box. A drop-down box can be linked with an input field instead of the input help key (**F4**). Users cannot type their own values in such an input field. Instead they can only select an entry from the single column list box (see Figure 7.35).

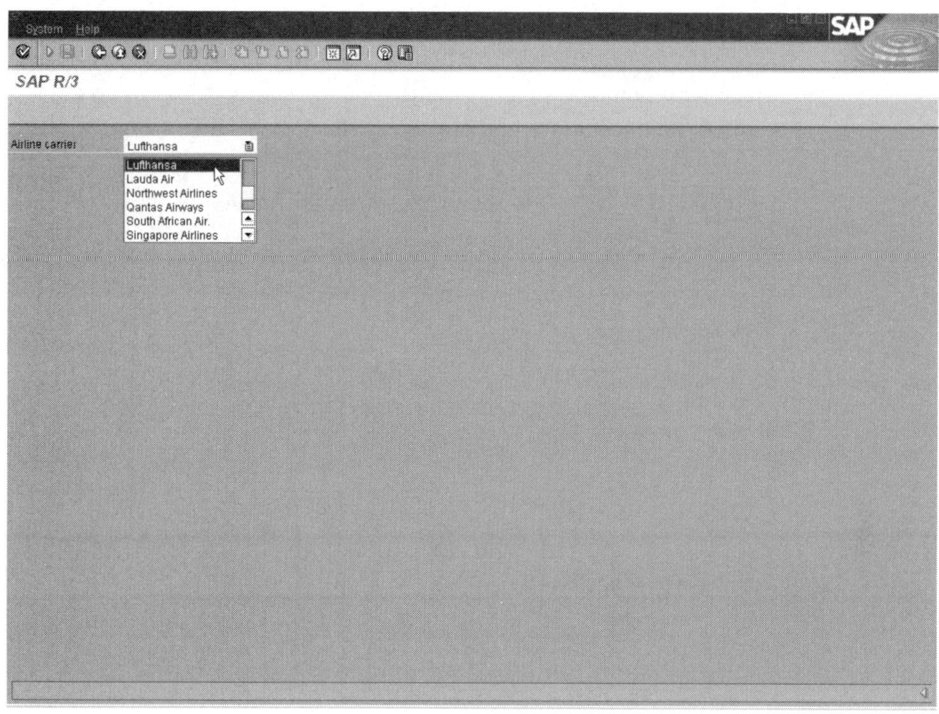

FIGURE 7.35 Drop-down box. Copyright © SAP AG

To provide an input field with a drop-down list, in the Screen Painter under the screen element attributes you must fill the **Dropdown** field with "List box." You can then specify the width of the list box in the *visLength* field and fill the input field with a function code.

A list box can be up to 80 characters in width and contains text fields linked to a key that is up to 40 characters long. If the user selects a text field, the contents of the text field are placed in the input field on the front end and the contents of the key in the actual screen field. The contents and length of the front end and screen fields are therefore not identical in this case. If the input field has a function code, the PAI event is then triggered.

Input help

If you do not make any other changes to the attributes of the input field, the drop-down box is automatically linked with the normal input help mechanism and its hierarchy from Section 7.1.7. The first display column of the input help is shown in the text field. In the S_DROPDOWN_LIST_BOX example program we fill the drop-down box from Figure 7.35 at the POV event in an ABAP dialog module. To do this we have written the following lines into the screen flow logic:

```
PROCESS ON VALUE-REQUEST.

    FIELD sdyn_conn-carrid MODULE create_dropdown_box.
```

We therefore override the input helps of the ABAP Dictionary. In the create_dropdown_box module we use the F4IF_INT_TABLE_VALUE_REQUEST function module from the Reuse Library already mentioned in Section 7.1.7, to create a value list using an internal table that we had previously filled with values from the SCARR database table.

LISTING 7.20 Generating a value list for the input help

```
* Global data

TYPES: BEGIN OF type_carrid,
         carrid type spfli-carrid,
         carrname type scarr-carrname,
       END OF type_carrid.

DATA itab_carrid TYPE STANDARD TABLE OF type_carrid.

* Dialog Modules

...

MODULE create_dropdown_box INPUT.
  SELECT carrid carrname
  FROM   scarr
  INTO CORRESPONDING FIELDS OF TABLE itab_carrid.
  CALL FUNCTION 'F4IF_INT_TABLE_VALUE_REQUEST'
       EXPORTING
            retfield         = 'CARRID'
            value_org        = 'S'
       TABLES
            value_tab        = itab_carrid
       EXCEPTIONS
            parameter_error  = 1
            no_values_found  = 2
            OTHERS           = 3.
  IF sy-subrc <> 0.
    ...
  ENDIF.
ENDMODULE.
```

The system displays the texts itab_carrid-carrname in the list box and when a selection is made places the itab_carrid-carrid key in the sdyn_conn-carrid screen field.

7.5.3 Classical controls

What are classical controls? Classical controls are platform-independent software components of the runtime environment that make complex screen elements easier to handle as well as providing a user-friendly interface. Classical controls are declared in the ABAP program using the `CONTROLS` statement. You can use two kinds of classical controls on layouts: table controls for displaying and processing table-like data and tabstrip controls for creating tabs.

Both classical controls are based on other screen elements and circumvent their need to an extent. Historically, classical controls are predecessors of GUI controls and can be replaced by them to an extent. Recently, the creation of both forms of classical control has been supported by wizards.

Table controls

Table controls display screen elements in a tabular form and in a special user interface on the screen. The most commonly used screen elements in table controls are input and output fields as shown in Figure 7.36. However, text fields, checkboxes, and radio buttons can also be displayed in table controls.

Step loop

Table controls encapsulate *step loop technology*, in which groups of screen elements are repeatedly displayed, and replace their use as stand-alone objects since Release 3.0. The characteristic of step loop technology is the use of the `LOOP` statement in the screen flow logic. Apart from exceptional cases, you should no longer find any `LOOP` statements in screen flow logic without connection to a table control.

Creating table controls

To work with table controls on screens, you must define a table control in the Graphical Screen Painter; assign fields to it; incorporate suitable statements in the

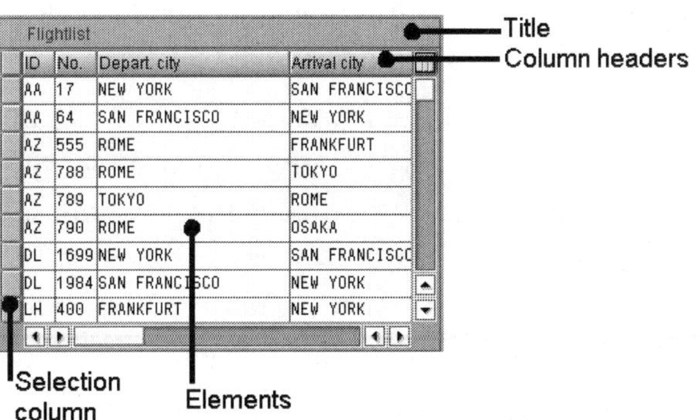

FIGURE 7.36 Table control. Copyright © SAP AG

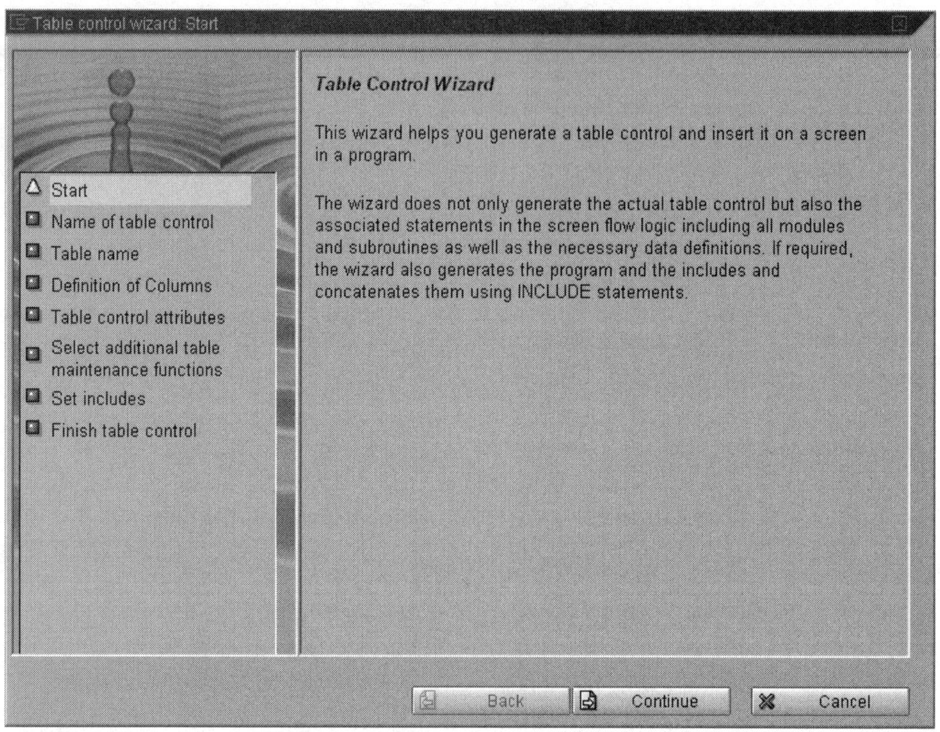

FIGURE 7.37 Table control wizard. Copyright © SAP AG

screen flow logic; and implement the processing of the table controls in the ABAP program. As of Basis Release 4.6C, the Graphical Screen Painter supports you with a table control wizard, which not only defines the table control in the Graphical Screen Painter but also generates the table control processing in the screen flow logic and in the ABAP program (see Figure 7.37).

Table control wizard

For example, you can create a program such as `S_TABLE_CONTROL`, enter the `CALL SCREEN` 100 statement, double-click 100 to navigate to the Graphical Screen Painter and run through the wizard as follows:

1. In the bar on the left-hand side of the Graphical Screen Painter (Figure 7.4) select the table control wizard and draw an area for the table control.
2. The wizard window now appears, as shown in Figure 7.37. Select **Continue** and keep doing so after each stage.
3. **Name of control**: Give the table control a name such as "`FLIGHTS`."
4. **Table name**: Enter a database table, such as "`SPFLI`."
5. **Definition of columns**: From the table choose the required columns for the table control.

6 **Table control attributes**: Determine the table control attributes by selecting, for example, **Input**, **with Column Headers** and for marking single lines **With selection column** and **Single**.

7 **Table maintenance functions**: For example, tick the **Scroll** entry.

8 **Set includes**: To determine the includes, select appropriate include programs or the entire ABAP program (we use S_TABLE_CONTROL).

9 Choose **Finish** to complete the table control.

10 Activate the screen and the ABAP program.

You will now have an executable ABAP program, on whose screen 100 a table control is displayed and whose fields are filled with values from the SPFLI database table as shown in Figure 7.36. The wizard has also created four scroll keys on the screen. You can adapt the program to suit your further requirements. In the S_TABLE_CONTROL program we have simply set a GUI status and implemented a PAI module, CANCEL, in order to be able to quit the program.

The table control wizard determines the key attributes of a table control. You can subsequently concentrate on the other attributes, such as defining a title or the resize capacity, in the Graphical Screen Painter.

Table controls in the screen flow logic

If you look at the generated screen flow logic of the S_TABLE_CONTROL program, you will notice in particular the two sections shown in Listing 7.21:

LISTING 7.21 LOOP statements in the screen flow logic

```
PROCESS BEFORE OUTPUT.
...
  LOOP AT    g_flights_itab
       INTO g_flights_wa
       WITH CONTROL flights
       CURSOR flights-current_line.
    MODULE flights_move.
    MODULE flights_get_lines.
  ENDLOOP.

...

PROCESS AFTER INPUT.
...
  LOOP AT g_flights_itab.
```

```
    CHAIN.
      FIELD spfli-carrid.
      FIELD spfli-connid.
      FIELD spfli-cityfrom.
      FIELD spfli-cityto.
      MODULE flights_modify ON CHAIN-REQUEST.
    ENDCHAIN.
    FIELD g_flights_wa-flag
      MODULE flights_mark ON REQUEST.
  ENDLOOP.
```

Loop

You find a loop (LOOP) in the PBO and PAI events respectively. Within the loops, the normal flow logic keywords FIELD, MODULE, and CHAIN are used. The syntax of the LOOP statement in the screen flow logic is:

```
LOOP AT itab [INTO wa WITH CONTROL ctrl][CURSOR cur].
```

This statement allocates an internal table itab, created in the ABAP program, to the table control ctrl and runs a parallel loop pass through the table control rows displayed on the screen and the internal table itab. During each loop run the contents of the table control are transported between fields of the same name in the ABAP program and the table control.

The INTO and WITH CONTROL additions are only required at the PBO event and cannot be used at the PAI event. The dialog modules that are called during every loop pass can be used at the PBO event to fill the table control and at the PAI event to adapt the internal table to the user inputs. During a loop run, the system field sy-stepl contains the current row of the table control, counting from the highest displayed row, and sy-loopc contains the current number of table control rows on the screen.

You can use the CURSOR addition at the PBO event to control which row of the internal table appears first in the screen display, whereby cur must be a type i data object of the ABAP program.

Processing table controls in the ABAP program

Now consider the source code of the S_TABLE_CONTROL program. Here we see the following statement in the global declaration part of the program:

```
CONTROLS: flights TYPE TABLEVIEW USING SCREEN 0100.
```

Control structure

Each table control on a screen must be announced in this way in the ABAP program. At the same time this statement declares a deep structure with the same name as the control. The data type of this structure is cxtab_control from the type group CXTAB. The components of the structure provide all the attributes of the table control for evaluation and modification. For example the current row of the table control in the loop (LOOP), which is calculated from the top_line and sy-stepl components, can be taken directly from the current_line component. The cxtab_control structure is deep, since the cols component is an internal table of row type cxtab_columns. Each column of the table control corresponds to a row of the internal table cols, whose individual components in turn describe the column attributes. You can modify the attributes of the individual columns by modifying the corresponding components at runtime.

The user interface of a table control automatically provides scroll bars. If you also wish to provide a program-controlled scrolling function – e.g., in response to functions of the GUI status – this can be easily implemented in the ABAP program using components of the cxtab_control structure, by simply assigning a value to the top_line component. For scrolling by page, you can take the number of rows to be scrolled during the loop pass from the sy-loopc system field, which contains the number of rows currently shown. Our generated program, however, uses the SCROLLING_IN_TABLE function module from the Reuse Library to scroll in the internal table of the ABAP program.

Table controls and GUI controls

Note that Release 4.6 provides ALV grid controls with input fields, so that not only classical lists but also table controls can be replaced by this GUI control.

Tabstrip controls

Tabstrip controls create tabs and are based on subscreen technology.

Subscreens

Subscreens are screens whose layouts can be added to areas of other screens. You create the areas as subscreen areas with the Graphical Screen Painter. You define screens, which can be added as subscreens by selecting the *Subscreen* field in the screen attributes (see Figure 7.3). However, you can also define selection screens as subscreens with the statements

```
SELECTION-SCREEN  BEGIN OF SCREEN dynnr AS SUBSCREEN.
  ...
SELECTION-SCREEN END OF SCREEN dynnr.
```

Using the statement:

```
CALL SUBSCREEN  area INCLUDING dynnr.
```

in the PBO event block of the screen flow logic you add a subscreen dynnr or a correspondingly defined selection screen in the subscreen area (area) of the current screen. At the same time the PBO flow logic of the subscreen is added at this point and executed.

If you use the statement:

```
CALL SUBSCREEN area.
```

in the PAI flow logic of the screen, the PAI flow logic of the subscreen is added and executed at this point.

Subscreens can also be added to selection screens.

Using subscreens and pushbuttons to create tabs

An obvious application of subscreens is to link their appearance on the screen to pushbuttons. Tabs encapsulate this process. They offer the user an appealing interface as tabs and free the developer from having to define the individual elements (see Figure 7.38).

Creating and processing tabstrip controls

To use tabstrip controls, you must proceed as follows:

1 Define a tabstrip and its title element in the Graphical Screen Painter. Title elements are generated simply by creating normal pushbuttons with their own texts and function codes in the top line of the tabstrip, which are then graphically displayed as titles.

2 Assign subscreen areas to the tab titles: To do this you can either assign to each tab title its own subscreen area or have all tab titles use a common subscreen area to which you can add various subscreens as you wish. With the first option the function code of each title must be assigned the function type P. Scrolling between the tabs is then processed on the presentation server without the PAI event being

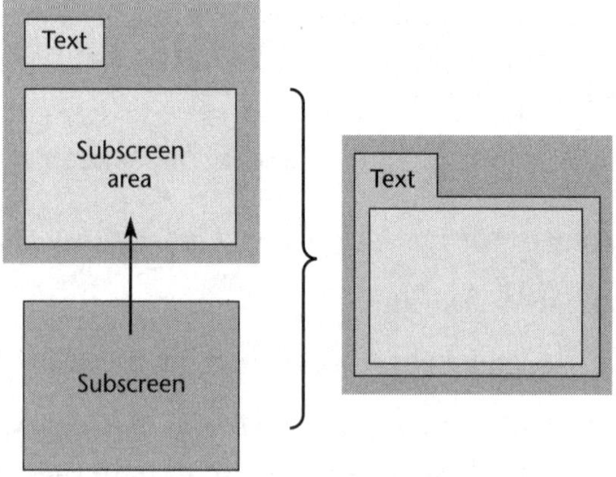

FIGURE 7.38 Pushbutton and subscreen as the basis of tabs

triggered. With the second option the function type is not changed. For each selection the PAI event is triggered and scrolling between the tabs is performed at the application server.

3 Add subscreens to each subscreen area in the flow logic. Depending on the scroll method selected in Step 2, one or more CALL SUBSCREEN statements must be used during the PBO and PAI events. For each tab title you must specify a subscreen. You can also use subscreen selection screens. If scrolling is processed on the presentation server you can statically assign a subscreen to each subscreen area. If scrolling is processed on the application server you must dynamically assign a different subscreen to each subscreen area. To do this you enter the screen number as a variable that is filled in the ABAP program.

4 Processing in the ABAP program. Each tabstrip control must be announced in the global declaration part as follows:

```
CONTROLS  ctrl TYPE TABSTRIP.
```

This statement also generates a structure with the name ctrl, from which you only require the activetab component. When scrolling is processed on the application server you must assign the function code of the tab title, whose page is shown, to this component at the PBO event. At the same time you must assign the screen number of the corresponding subscreen to the global variable that is used in the CALL SUBSCREEN statement of the flow logic. When scrolling is processed on the presentation server, you can take the title function code of the page just shown from this component at the PAI event.

Tabstrip control wizard

As with table controls, the Graphical Screen Painter also contains a wizard for tabstrip controls (see Figure 7.39).

This wizard creates a tabstrip control for which scrolling is processed on the application server. Tab titles are created in five stages and provided with function codes. A subscreen is defined for each rider; the CALL SUBSCREEN statement is added to the flow logic; and scrolling is implemented in the ABAP program.

The S_TABSTRIP program in the Basis System on the attached CD was generated almost completely with this wizard. We entered just one statement – CALL SCREEN 100 – executed the wizard, and then added a pushbutton and a module for quitting the program. Figure 7.40 shows the layout of screen 100. The generated subscreens have the screen numbers 101 to 103 and can be provided with any kind of screen element in the Screen Painter, depending on the requirements of the application program.

Selection screens with tabstrip controls

You can also create tabstrip controls on selection screens, programming using ABAP statements only. It is not necessary to program the screen flow logic, nor is the CONTROLS statement required in the ABAP program. You simply must create the required subscreens either with the Screen Painter or as selection screens, and add the

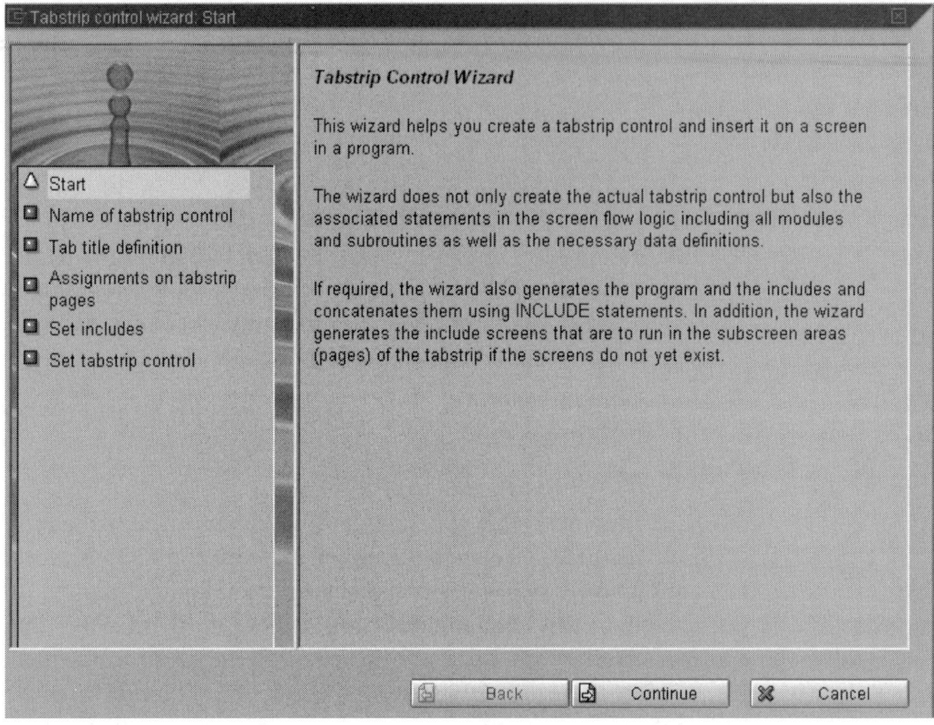

FIGURE 7.39 Tabstrip control wizard. Copyright © SAP AG

following SELECTION SCREEN statements to the definition of your selection screen:

```
SELECTION-SCREEN: BEGIN OF TABBED BLOCK tab FOR n LINES,
                  TAB (len) tab1 USER-COMMAND ucom1
                  [DEFAULT SCREEN scrn],
                  TAB (len) tab2 USER-COMMAND ucom2
                  [DEFAULT SCREEN scrn],
                  ...
                  END OF BLOCK tab.
```

You define tab titles (of length len), tab1, … texts, and ucom1, … function codes, all using the TAB addition. You can use the DEFAULT addition to assign each tab title a static subscreen. At the same time a structure tab with components called dynnr and activetab is declared. By assigning values to these components before calling the selection screen you can overwrite the static subscreens.

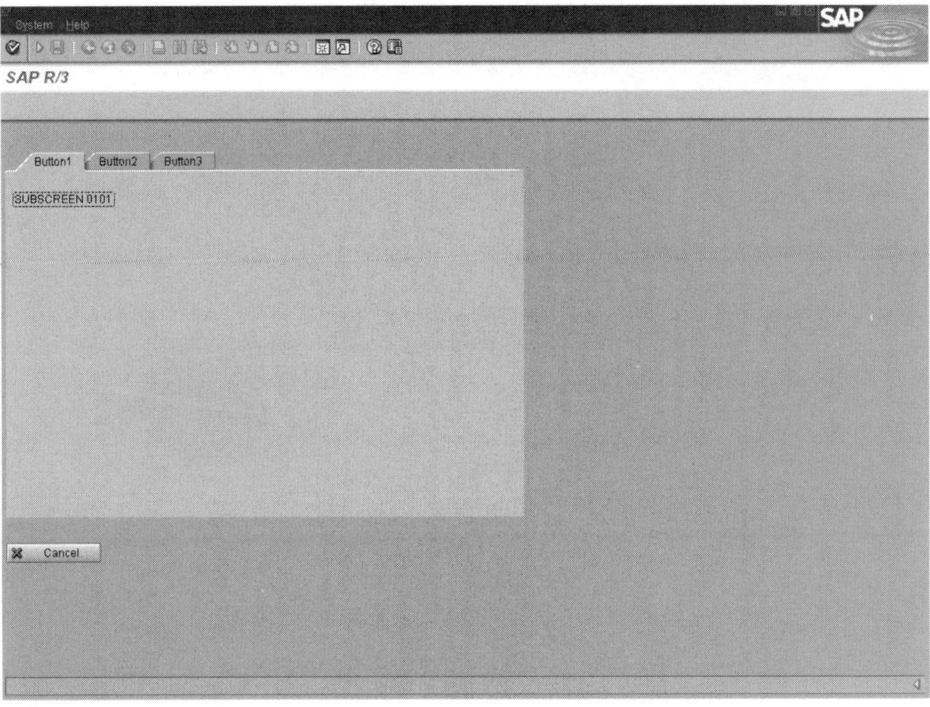

FIGURE 7.40 Tabstrip control. Copyright © SAP AG

Tabstrip controls and GUI controls

In the age of GUI controls, tabstrip controls are still an important tool for creating layouts. Tabstrip controls are what is required if you need to simplify complex screen processes. Many of the ABAP Workbench tools such as the Screen Painter or the Function Builder, in which the individual components used to be maintained on individual screens, now offer them on a single front end in the form of tabs.

Since the individual tabs are created through general subscreens, you can show any kind of screen elements on them, such as table controls and above all GUI controls.

7.5.4 GUI controls

What are GUI controls? GUI controls are independent software components that run on the presentation server and are not part of the ABAP runtime environment of the application server. As of Release 4.5, SAP provides GUI controls as part of the SAP System. You can use GUI controls in conjunction with, or instead of, classical screen elements on screens. SAP currently provides the controls in an ActiveX version for MS Windows platforms and as JavaBeans for the Web GUI. Figure 7.41 shows a SAP screen layout with various GUI controls. The layout is divided into three areas,

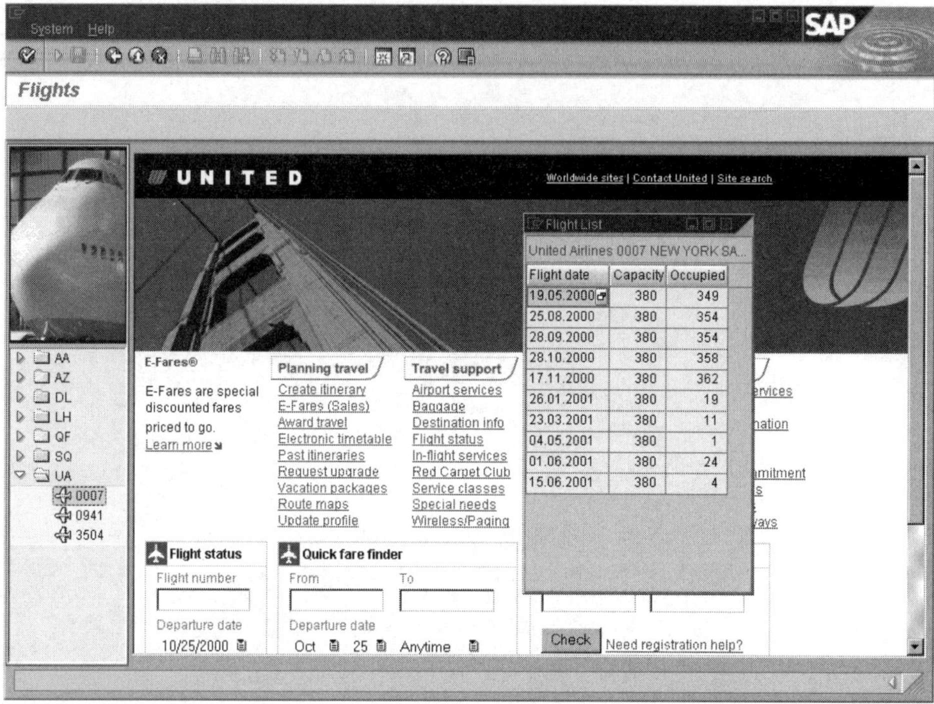

FIGURE 7.41 GUI controls. Copyright © SAP AG

showing at the top left a picture with a picture control, at the bottom left a hierarchy in a tree control, and on the right a web page in an HTML control. Above this, in a free- moving dialog box, an ALV grid control is displayed. We shall shortly discuss how to program this layout in detail.

Front End

The functions contained within GUI controls, such as scrolling through texts or lists, take place on the presentation server and therefore relieve the application server of this work. On the other hand, GUI controls often work with large amounts of data, which is why frequent data transfers between the ABAP program and the GUI control can increase the load on the network. When you use GUI controls you should therefore always ensure that most of the work can be performed on the front end and that synchronization with the back end is kept to a minimum.

The Control Framework

Prior to Release 4.6, GUI controls could only be accessed using individual function modules. To create a uniform interface to GUI controls and thereby simplify working with them, the **Control Framework** (CFW) was introduced to the SAP Basis system with Release 4.6. The right-hand side of Figure 7.42 shows the operation of the CFW in a considerably simplified form.

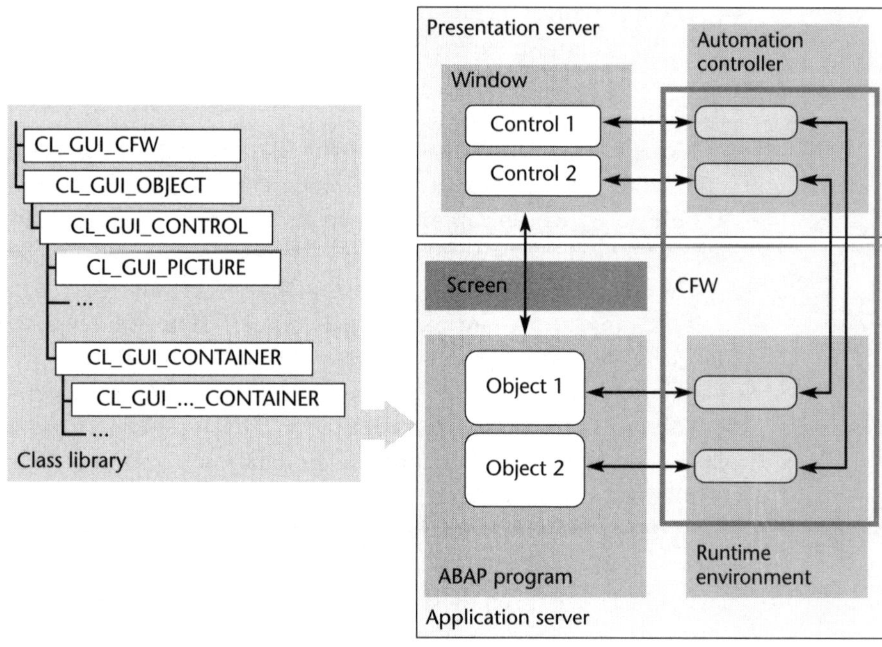

FIGURE 7.42 The Control Framework

In classical screen processing an ABAP program communicates with the SAP-specific screen elements on the layout of a screen. GUI controls on layouts, on the other hand, are software objects with independent interfaces that are not connected to the classical data flow between the application server and presentation server. Communication between the ABAP program and controls is provided instead by the CFW, which contains components in the runtime environment of the application server as well as in an **Automation Controller** on the presentation server.

Framework

The main feature of the CFW is that there is a global class in the class library for each GUI control supplied and that when working with GUI controls, for each control object on the front end there is a proxy object of the corresponding class in the ABAP program. As an ABAP programmer you work only with the proxy objects. The CFW forwards its method calls to the actual GUI control objects and informs the objects of the ABAP program by triggering events about the user actions on the GUI controls.

The classes of the Control Framework

We shall now introduce you to the main CFW classes and some of their components. These classes and their components represent a very extensive API (Application Programming Interface), the full scope of which cannot be covered by this book. For more details you can open and examine the classes in the Class Builder or read the corresponding online documentation in the SAP Knowledge Warehouse.

Hierarchy

The inheritance hierarchy of CFW classes is shown in the left-hand side of Figure 7.42. The common superclass of all classes for controls is CL_GUI_OBJECT. Its sole method relevant to application programming is is_valid, with which you can query the status of a control in the subclasses.

Alongside the inheritance hierarchy there is also the CL_GUI_CFW class. This class offers some CFW service methods that are not directly connected to a control, such as flush for synchronization between application and presentation server or dispatch for handling control events.

The superclass of the actual control classes is CL_GUI_CONTROL. This class contains methods for setting and reading general control attributes that can be used in any subclass, such as set_visible for visibility setting or set_focus for setting the screen focus on a control.

Control object

You create the actual control objects from the subclasses of CL_GUI_CONTROL. There are two types of control: application controls and container controls. Application controls are the software components you want to use on the front end. Container controls are subclasses of the CL_GUI_CONTAINER class and provide a uniform software layer for connecting the application controls to certain areas of the layout of a screen. You must assign each application control to a container control.

Container controls

Each container control object in the ABAP program is a proxy of a screen area to which you can add other controls. The classes for container controls are:

- CL_GUI_CUSTOM_CONTAINER

  The screen areas of custom containers must be created with the Graphical Screen Painter as custom controls. Custom controls are simply rectangular areas on the layout of a screen, which must be given a name. When you create an object of the CL_GUI_CUSTOM_CONTAINER class, you must pass the name of such an area to the input parameter container_name of the constructor.

- CL_GUI_DOCKING_CONTAINER

  The screen areas of docking containers are coupled to the layout borders of screens and are created when you create objects of the CL_GUI_DOCKING_CONTAINER class. Using the side input parameter of the constructor you must define to which of the four pages a docking container is to be attached. To attach a docking container to the left side, for example, you must pass the constant docking_container=> dock_at_left.

- CL_GUI_SPLITTER_CONTAINER

  The screen areas of splitter containers are parts of existing screen areas and are created when you create objects of the class CL_GUI_SPLITTER_CONTAINER. To do this you must pass a reference to an existing container object to the parent input

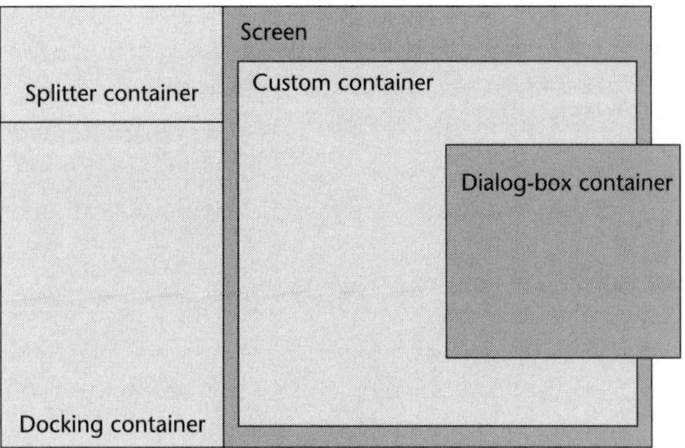

FIGURE 7.43 Container controls on a screen

parameter of the constructor. You can divide its area vertically and horizontally into a maximum of 16×16 new areas. Using the get_container method you can then obtain references to every single area.

- CL_GUI_DIALOGBOX_CONTAINER

  The screen areas of dialog box containers are independent amodal dialog boxes that are created when you create objects of the CL_GUI_DIALOGBOX_CONTAINER class. You can pass a reference to a container control linked to the dialog box by using the parent parameter of the constructor. The dialog box then always remains in the foreground. As of Release 4.6C, you can also pass the constant cl_gui_container =>desktop to parent to handle the dialog box as an independent screen window.

All controls assigned to an object of a container class, or an area of a splitter container using the parent parameter of their constructor, appear in their screen area. For the screen display in Figure 7.41 we have used each of the container controls described above, as shown in Figure 7.43.

Application controls

Once you have used container controls to define screen areas in which application controls can run, you can activate them by creating corresponding proxy objects in the ABAP program. Each time an object is created for an application control using CREATE OBJECT you must pass a reference to a container object to the parent input parameter of the constructor.

The CFW classes of the main application controls supplied with Release 4.6 are:

- CL_GUI_TOOLBAR

  The toolbar control allows you to create an application toolbar that is independent of the GUI status.

The class has methods such as add_button to define pushbuttons with icons, texts, and function codes. Events such as function_selected allow the ABAP program to react when the user chooses a function.

With the toolbar control you can prepare individual user interfaces for individual screen areas or dialog boxes. The application toolbar above the tree hierarchy of the Object Navigator is an example of the application of toolbar controls.

- CL_GUI_PICTURE

  The picture control allows you to display any pictures in BMP, JPG, or GIF format on screen.

  The class has a load_picture_from_url method to load a picture and several methods for defining the picture attributes.

  Events such as picture_dblclick allow ABAP programs to respond to user actions on the control. For example, double-clicking the bookshelf in Figure 2.41 will call the example library.

- CL_GUI_HTML_VIEWER

  The HTML control allows you to create a browser for HTML pages on the screen.

  The class has a method show_url to display existing web pages and a method show_data to display custom HTML documents. An event sapevent allows you to respond to specially formatted references (<A HREFOSAPEVENT: "fcode" >text</A >) in the HTML document and to evaluate the function code fcode.

  The display of the ABAP keyword documentation in Figure 2.41 is an example of displaying self-defined HTML documents in which all the text references are evaluated in the corresponding ABAP program.

- CL_GUI_TEXTEDIT

  The text edit control allows you to add a complete text editor with the usual functions such as selecting, searching, or replacing text on the screen.

  The class has a get_text_as_stream method to display the content of an internal table in the text editor, and many methods, such as highlight_lines or find_and_replace, to edit the text through the program. Events such can dblclick can be evaluated in the ABAP program. A prominent example of the use of the TextEdit control in the SAP Basis system is the ABAP Editor.

- CL_GUI_SIMPLE_TREE

  The Tree Control, for which there are other versions besides the standard tree, such as the multi-column tree or the list tree, allows you to display hierarchical relations in a tree structure.

  The class has an add_nodes method to construct the tree from a specially structured internal table, and methods such as expand_node or get_selected_node to work with the tree. The hierarchical data must be prepared in the ABAP program in an internal table with reference to a specially structured data type from the ABAP Dictionary. The data type of the internal table must include the predefined global structure treev_node as the first components. The components of treev_node, such as node_key, relatkey, and relatship, define the interrelationship of the tree nodes. Possible values of these fields are constants of the class CL_GUI_SIMPLE_TREE, such as relat_last_child.

Events such as node_double_click or selection_changed allow the ABAP program to respond to user actions in the tree display. However, expansion and compression of sub-nodes is automatic on the presentation server. Examples of the use of the tree control include the SAP Easy Access Menu and the Object Navigator.

- CL_GUI_ALV_GRID

  The ALV grid control allows you to display lists and table-like data on the screen and to print them out. It replaces classical screen lists and, in future, table controls as well. A user interface in the form of an application toolbar can be integrated in the display.

  The class has a method set_table_for_first_display, with which the list output is formatted and data is passed to the control. Two internal tables play a large part here: The actual list data passed to the parameter it_outtab, and a field catalog of the table type lvc_t_fcat passed to the it_fieldcatalogue parameter. The field catalogue contains a description of the attributes of the actual data. The list output and print lists are prepared using this field catalogue. If you wish to display list lines whose structure corresponds to a data type in the ABAP Dictionary, you do not have to create your own field catalogue. It is sufficient to pass the name of the data type.

  Events such as double_click or hotspot_click allow the ABAP program to respond to user actions.

Some application controls – such as the picture control or the tree control – also provide the option of implementing a drag&drop function or offering context menus through special events. You can find examples of context menus in a tree structure in the Object Navigator tree display.

Connection between controls and screens

Application controls cannot be created in isolation on the presentation server. Instead, they are always connected to a screen using the container controls. As a result of this, control processing is integrated in the classical dialog processing of the SAP System.

A container control is linked either to a sub-area of a screen (custom container) or to an entire screen (docking and dialog box containers). Splitter containers are indirectly coupled to the screen of their parent containers.

Pop-up level

In addition, each container control always belongs to the pop-up level during which it was created. By pop-up level we refer to the hierarchical level of a dialog box created using the `CALL SCREEN ... STARTING AT ...` command. Up to nine dialog boxes can be stacked on a complete screen. When the first container control is created in a pop-up level, for each pop-up level a container control is implicitly created, which is passed to each custom, docking, or dialog box container as the `parent`. You can access the references of these implicit container controls in the static attributes `screen0` to `screen9` of the `CL_GUI_CONTAINER` class, whereby `screen0` points to the container of the full picture.

Visibility

The visibility of GUI controls is governed by the fact that they belong to pop-up levels. Application controls are only visible if their container control is visible and these in turn are only visible in their pop-up level. A control assigned to a screen in pop-up level 0 is therefore invisible if the same screen is called as a modal dialog box. Assignment to a pop-up level cannot be changed for technical reasons. However, you can use the `link` method of the `CL_GUI_CONTAINER` class to assign, for example, an application control to another container control within a pop-up level.

Working with controls

The control framework architecture shown in Figure 7.42 necessitates certain differences for working with control objects compared with classical screen elements and other objects in ABAP Objects.

Calling control methods

You use control object methods in the ABAP program to work with the front end controls. Normally you work with the application control methods. On some occasions however you also need the container controls methods. In both cases, no immediate method call is performed on the presentation server. Instead, for performance reasons, it is first stored in an automation queue on the application server.

Automation queue

To keep the network load low, the CFW sends the stored method calls and their corresponding parameters to the presentation server only when a synchronization point is reached, where they are executed in turn. This improves performance when parameters, which can often be extensive internal tables, are used more than once. There are automatic points, such as the end of PBO processing. However, you can force this synchronization at any time using the method `cl_gui_cfw=>flush`. This should only be done, however, if at this point data has to be necessarily exchanged between presentation and application servers, e.g. after editing a control event.

Reacting to control events

User actions on GUI controls trigger control events. However, unlike user actions on classical screen elements, control events are not linked to function codes in the OK field and do not directly trigger the PAI event. Instead, control events are handled by the CFW and passed on to the ABAP program. Each control class in the class library declares the events that can be triggered and handled in the control as events in ABAP Objects. To be able to respond to events in the ABAP program, you must use event handler methods of other classes, which you either create locally in the program or take from the Class Library if available.

Activation

For performance reasons, in many controls the events of the corresponding class are not automatically activated and are not sent from the presentation server to the application server in response to a user action. You must activate the events to which you wish to respond using the `set_registered_events` method, which is present in every control class. You pass an internal table of the `cntl_simple_events` type, which contains a line for each event you wish to activate. You identify the events in the first column `eventid` using suitable constants of the control classes, such as `eventid_node_double_click` in the `CL_GUI_SIMPLE_TREE` class.

After this activation the CFW triggers an event on the application server upon a corresponding user action. If you wish to handle this event with methods, you must still register the event handler methods with `SET HANDLER` as is customary in ABAP Objects, whereby you link the handling object to the proxy object of the control. Figure 7.44 shows how control events are processed.

There are two kinds of control event, **system events** and **application events**. You use the `set_registered_events` method to define the type of event handling when an

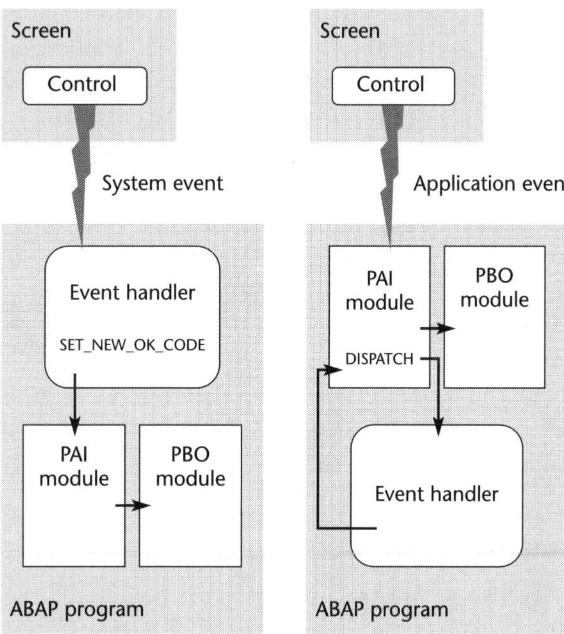

FIGURE 7.44 Control events

event is activated. If you leave the component appl_event initial in the passed internal table, the event is a system event. If you fill the component with "X," it is an application event.

By selecting the event handling you control the interrelationship between control processing and classical screen processing. This is especially important if you are using classical screen fields on the screen as well as GUI controls.

System event

If the component appl_event is initial, events are handled as system events. This means that this kind of event is sent to the application server where it triggers all the handler methods registered with SET HANDLER but without triggering the PAI event. When the handler methods have been executed the system returns to the screen display without triggering the PBO event. The advantage of this kind of handling is that no conflicts can arise with the classical automatic input check of the screen.

On the other hand, the contents of any classical screen fields are not transported. If you are using classical screen fields together with GUI controls and you want to evaluate their contents during the event handling of controls, you must call the static CFW method cl_gui_cfw=>set_new_ok_code within a handler method and transfer a function code to it. This method triggers the PAI event, including all the checks and field transports. When the classical PAI processing has been executed, the PBO event of the next screen is triggered. The system therefore only returns to the same layout if the next screen is set accordingly.

If you are not using classical screen fields alongside controls, system events are the best choice.

Application event

If the contents of appl_event is "X", an event is handled as an application event. This means that the event is sent to the application server where it triggers the classical PAI event and not the event handler methods. If you wish to call the event handler methods registered with SET HANDLER, you must call the CFW method cl_gui_cfw=>dispatch in an appropriate PAI module. This triggers the event handling and at the end the program is continued in the PAI module.

The advantage of this method is that the contents of classical screen fields can be transported and checked before event handling and that within classical screen processing you can determine yourself when a control event is processed. The disadvantage is that because of automatic input checks, user inputs on controls may not be handled at all.

If you are using classical screen fields alongside controls, application events are always appropriate, if you wish to control the order of data transport and event handling yourself.

Lifetime of GUI controls

The lifetime of GUI controls on the presentation server and of their proxy objects on the application server is linked by default to the lifetime of the internal session of the ABAP program. All objects and corresponding administrative entries in the CFW are removed when the ABAP program ends or, for example, if it is fully terminated with LEAVE TO TRANSACTION (see Section 3.4).

Deleting

To program the deletion of a GUI control, it is not enough simply to delete all the references to the proxy object in the ABAP program. Apart from the references in the ABAP program, the CFW also points to all proxy objects that represent controls on the presentation server (see Figure 7.42). The automatic garbage collection therefore does not come into effect, even when all the reference variables have been initialized. The proxy objects live on and you can obtain the references of all the controls of the current screen with the get_living_dynpro_controls method of the CL_GUI_CFW class.

However, each proxy object inherits the free method from the cl_gui_object class. By calling this method you delete the corresponding GUI control on the presentation server and all the object references in CFW. You must then also delete all your own object references in the ABAP program, whereby finally the proxy object itself is collected by the Garbage Collector. If you run the method free, but then try to access the proxy object again, the system triggers a runtime error.

Example program of GUI controls

We shall now introduce you to the S_GUI_CONTROLS program that creates the layout in Figure 7.41. Since GUI Controls are linked to classical screens, we must first prepare a classical frame to call a carrier screen for our controls.

The classical main program

LISTING 7.22 Classical main program

```
*&---------------------------------------------------------------------*
*& Processing Blocks called by the Runtime Environment                *
*&---------------------------------------------------------------------*
* Event Block LOAD-OF-PROGRAM
LOAD-OF-PROGRAM.
  CALL SCREEN 100.

* Dialog Module PBO
MODULE status_0100 OUTPUT.
  SET PF-STATUS 'SCREEN_100'.
  SET TITLEBAR 'TIT_100'.
  CALL METHOD screen_handler=>create_screen.
ENDMODULE.

* Dialog Module PAI
```

```
MODULE cancel INPUT.
  LEAVE PROGRAM.
ENDMODULE.
```

Listing 7.22 shows the classical part of the program. At LOAD-OF-PROGRAM we call screen 100. As we are not using reporting events such as START-OF-SELECTION, the source code is independent of the program type and can be used in any program that can contain screens.

On the layout of screen 100, we have used the Graphical Screen Painter to create a customer control with the name CUSTOM_CONTROL, which covers the entire screen area. In the flow logic we call the two dialog modules from Listing 7.22. In the PAI event block the addition AT EXIT-COMMAND is used.

In the GUI status SCREEN_100 we have filled the usual icons from the standard toolbar with type E function codes. The PAI module cancel is used therefore only to quit the program. The most important action of the main program is to call the static method create_screen of the screen_handler class. We have defined the screen_handler class locally in the same program.

Declaration part of the local class

LISTING 7.23 Declaration part of the screen_handler class

```
*&-----------------------------------------------------*
*& Global Declarations                                *
*&-----------------------------------------------------*
* Class Definition
CLASS screen_handler DEFINITION CREATE PRIVATE.
  PUBLIC SECTION.
    CLASS-DATA screen TYPE REF TO screen_handler.
    CLASS-METHODS create_screen.
    METHODS constructor.
  PRIVATE SECTION.
    DATA:
      container_html TYPE REF TO cl_gui_custom_container,
      container_box  TYPE REF TO cl_gui_dialogbox_container,
      picture        TYPE REF TO cl_gui_picture,
      tree           TYPE REF TO cl_gui_simple_tree,
      html_viewer    TYPE REF TO cl_gui_html_viewer,
      list_viewer    TYPE REF TO cl_gui_alv_grid.
    METHODS: fill_picture,
```

```
            fill_tree,
            fill_html
              IMPORTING i_carrid TYPE spfli-carrid,
            fill_list
              IMPORTING i_carrid TYPE spfli-carrid
                        i_connid TYPE spfli-connid,
            handle_node_double_click
              FOR EVENT node_double_click
                     OF cl_gui_simple_tree
              IMPORTING node_key,
            close_box
              FOR EVENT close
                     OF cl_gui_dialogbox_container.
ENDCLASS.
```

Listing 7.23 shows the declaration part of the screen_handler class. Note that because of the CREATE PRIVATE addition to the CLASS statement, objects of this class can only be created within the class itself. To do this we have provided the static attribute screen and the static method create_screen in the public visibility section. All the other components are private with the exception of the constructor.

All instance attributes are reference variables that refer to classes of the CFW. You recognize two classes for container controls and four classes for application controls. We have encapsulated all the other required data objects locally in the instance methods. We have declared four instance methods to fill the application controls and two event handler methods. We shall now examine how each method is defined.

Generating an object of the local class

LISTING 7.24 The create_screen method

```
METHOD create_screen.
  IF screen IS INITIAL.
    CREATE OBJECT screen.
  ENDIF.
ENDMETHOD.
```

The only function of the create_screen static method is to create an object of the screen_handler class at PBO of screen 100. The static attribute screen references this object.

While the object is created the constructor instance constructor is executed.

The instance constructor

LISTING 7.25 The instance constructor of the screen_handler class

```
METHOD constructor.
  DATA:
   l_event_tab TYPE cntl_simple_events,
   l_event     LIKE LINE OF l_event_tab,
   l_docking   TYPE REF TO cl_gui_docking_container,
   l_splitter  TYPE REF TO cl_gui_splitter_container,
   l_container_screen  TYPE REF TO cl_gui_custom_container,
   l_container_top     TYPE REF TO cl_gui_container,
   l_container_bottom TYPE REF TO cl_gui_container.

  CREATE OBJECT container_html
         EXPORTING container_name = 'CUSTOM_CONTROL'.

  CREATE OBJECT l_docking
         EXPORTING
           side = cl_gui_docking_container=>dock_at_left
           extension = 135.

  CREATE OBJECT l_splitter
         EXPORTING parent = l_docking
                   rows = 2
                   columns = 1.

  CALL METHOD l_splitter->set_border
       EXPORTING border = cl_gui_cfw=>false.

  CALL METHOD l_splitter->set_row_mode
       EXPORTING mode = l_splitter->mode_absolute.

  CALL METHOD l_splitter->set_row_height
       EXPORTING id = 1
                 height = 180.

  l_container_top      =
    l_splitter->get_container( row = 1 column = 1 ).
  l_container_bottom =
    l_splitter->get_container( row = 2 column = 1 ).
```

```
  CREATE OBJECT picture
         EXPORTING parent = l_container_top.

  CREATE OBJECT tree
         EXPORTING parent = l_container_bottom
           node_selection_mode =
             cl_gui_simple_tree=>node_sel_mode_single.

  l_event-eventid =
    cl_gui_simple_tree=>eventid_node_double_click.
  l_event-appl_event = ' '.
  APPEND l_event TO l_event_tab.
  CALL METHOD tree->set_registered_events
       EXPORTING events = l_event_tab.
  SET HANDLER me->handle_node_double_click FOR tree.

  CALL METHOD: me->fill_picture,
               me->fill_tree.
ENDMETHOD.
```

The instance constructor of the screen_handler class first creates container controls for the picture control and the tree control, followed by the two application controls themselves.

First, we create a docking control with the local reference variable l_docking. By passing the dock_at_left constant of the CL_GUI_DOCKING_CONTAINER class to the side parameter, we create a new area, 135 pixels in width (parameter extension), on the left-hand side of the screen.

We divide this screen area into two horizontal areas by creating an object of the CL_GUI_SPLITTER_CONTAINER class using the local reference variable l_splitter and passing the reference to the docking control using the parent parameter. We then split it using the rows and columns parameters. By calling methods of the splitter control we specify that no frame is drawn and that the height is specified in absolute terms, for which we enter 180 pixels for the upper container.

Using the functional method get_container we import the references to the two areas of the splitter_control into the local reference variables l_container_top and l_container_bottom. We then create the two application controls, picture and tree, by passing a reference to the areas of the splitter controls to the parent parameter of each constructor respectively.

Since our program is to respond to the user double-clicking nodes of the tree control, we must activate this event and register an event handler. As described above, we call the set_registered_events method for activation, which is available for every application control. The l_event_tab internal table, which we have declared locally with the type cntl_simple_events, acts as a transfer parameter. In the eventid column we specify the double-click event. Since we are not filling the appl_event column with an "X," we define that the event is being handled as a system event and not an application event. As event handlers we register our own method handle_node_double_click.

After calling the methods fill_picture and fill_tree we quit the constructor. Note that this deletes all the local reference variables of the constructor. Nevertheless, the control objects created in the constructor with local reference variables are not collected by the automatic garbage collection, since they are kept alive by references from the CFW.

Filling the picture control with a picture

LISTING 7.26 The fill_picture method

```
METHOD fill_picture.
  TYPES t_line(256) TYPE c.
  DATA  l_pict_tab TYPE TABLE OF t_line.
  DATA  l_url(255) TYPE c.

  IMPORT pict_tab = l_pict_tab
  FROM   DATABASE abtree(pi)
  ID     'FLIGHTS'.

  CALL FUNCTION 'DP_CREATE_URL'
       EXPORTING
            type    = 'IMAGE'
            subtype = 'GIF'
       TABLES
            data    = l_pict_tab
       CHANGING
            url     = l_url.

  CALL METHOD picture->load_picture_from_url
       EXPORTING url = l_url.
  CALL METHOD picture->set_display_mode
       EXPORTING
         display_mode = picture->display_mode_stretch.
ENDMETHOD.
```

The fill_picture method imports a picture file in GIF format from the INDX-type database table ABTREE (see Section 8.3) into a local internal table l_pict_tab. Using the DP_CREATE_URL function module we create a URL address for this internal table in the local variable l_url. We pass this address to the method load_picture_from_url of our picture control and thereby send the picture to the control area on the screen.

Using the set_display_mode method we also specify that the picture always adapts to the current size of the area. Instead of working with an internal table, we could have also assigned the local variable l_url the name of a picture file on the presentation server or the network. In our case, however, the program reads the picture from the database and is therefore independent of the respective installation. We only need to ask how we have stored the picture file in the database table. Listing 7.27 shows the simple auxiliary program we used to achieve this:

LISTING 7.27 Auxiliary program for storing graphic files

```
REPORT picture_save.

PARAMETERS file TYPE rlgrap-filename DEFAULT 'C:\TEMP\.GIF'.
PARAMETERS id(20) TYPE c.

TYPES pict_line(256) TYPE c.
DATA pict_tab TYPE TABLE OF pict_line.

CALL FUNCTION 'WS_UPLOAD'
     EXPORTING
          filename = file
          filetype = 'BIN'
     TABLES
          data_tab = pict_tab.

EXPORT pict_tab = pict_tab TO DATABASE abtree(pi) ID id.
```

We have placed a graphic file on the presentation server in a directory, C:\TEMP\, and run the program. The program loads the picture in binary form into an internal table and stores it in the INDX-type database table ABTREE with the identification id. However, for your own applications we strongly recommend that you first create your own INDX-type database table instead of using ABTREE or INDX itself. Copy one of these tables for example.

Generating the tree structure

LISTING 7.28 The fill_tree method

```
METHOD fill_tree.
  DATA: l_node_table TYPE TABLE OF abdemonode,
        l_node TYPE abdemonode,
```

```
          l_spfli TYPE spfli,
          l_spfli_tab TYPE SORTED TABLE OF spfli
                      WITH UNIQUE KEY carrid connid.

    SELECT carrid connid
      FROM spfli
      INTO CORRESPONDING FIELDS OF TABLE l_spfli_tab.

    l_node-hidden    = ' '.
    l_node-disabled = ' '.
    l_node-isfolder = 'X'.
    l_node-expander = ' '.

    LOOP AT l_spfli_tab INTO l_spfli.
      AT NEW carrid.
        l_node-node_key = l_spfli-carrid.
        CLEAR l_node-relatkey.
        CLEAR l_node-relatship.
        l_node-text = l_spfli-carrid.
        l_node-n_image =    ' '.
        l_node-exp_image = ' '.
        APPEND l_node TO l_node_table.
      ENDAT.
      AT NEW connid.
        CONCATENATE l_spfli-carrid l_spfli-connid
                INTO l_node-node_key.
        l_node-relatkey = l_spfli-carrid.
        l_node-relatship =
          cl_gui_simple_tree=>relat_last_child.
        l_node-text = l_spfli-connid.
        l_node-n_image =    '@AV@'.
        l_node-exp_image = '@AV@'.
      ENDAT.
      APPEND l_node TO l_node_table.
    ENDLOOP.

    CALL METHOD tree->add_nodes
         EXPORTING table_structure_name = 'ABDEMONODE'
                   node_table = l_node_table.
  ENDMETHOD.
```

The fill_tree method creates the tree structure of our tree control. To do this we must fill an internal table with a predefined structure. For this purpose we have created the abdemonode structure in the ABAP Dictionary, which includes the treev_node structure (see Figure 7.45). You can also define your own structures by copying predefined structures such as MTREESNODE.

We have created the internal table l_node_table with the row structure ABDEMONODE. Each row of the table describes a node of the tree structure and must therefore have a unique node key (node_key).[12] The relatkey and relatship components describe the relations between the nodes. Other components allow you to change the standard icons, create node texts, and so on.

In our example we create the node table from the contents of the SPFLI database table. We import the carrid and connid components from all the rows of this database table into a sorted internal table l_spfli_tab and process these in a loop (LOOP). Using the control level processing AT – ENDAT we fill the node table with rows that represent a two-stage hierarchy. Before the loop we have already set some general

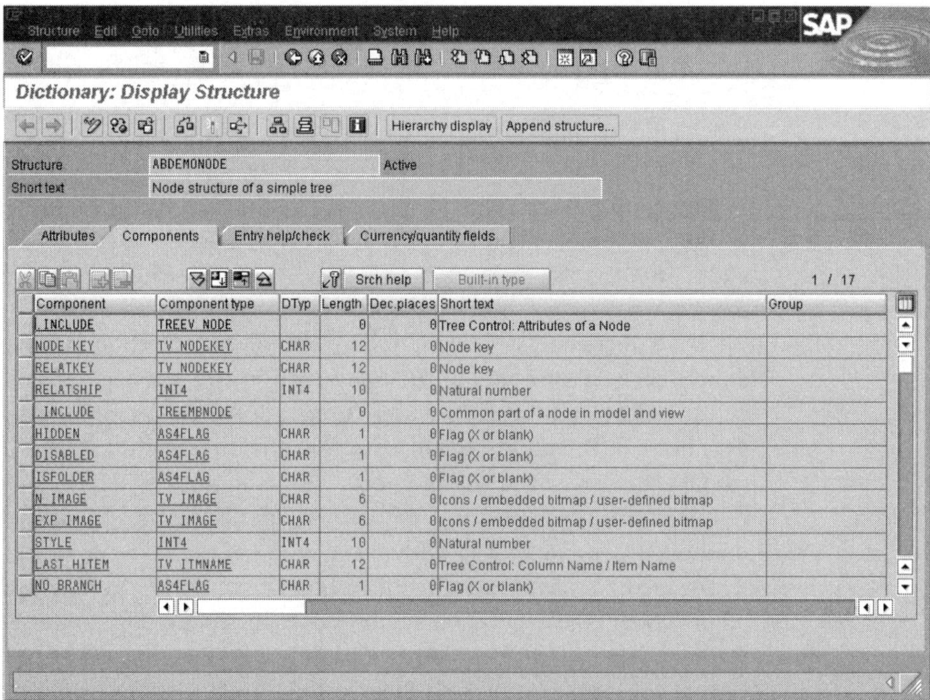

FIGURE 7.45 The ABDEMONODE structure in the ABAP Dictionary. Copyright © SAP AG

12. As you can see, the key here is limited to 12 characters. However, as of Basis Release 4.6C SAP also provides a class CL_SIMPLE_TREE_MODEL which encapsulates CL_GUI_SIMPLE_TREE and removes the restriction so that GUIDs can also be used as keys.

node attributes for all the rows in the l_node work area. For the subnodes we replace the standard icons for non-expanded and expanded nodes with plane icons by assigning the internal code "@AV@" to the n_image and exp_image components. You can find the internal codes of all SAP icons by running the program SHOWICON.

Event handling for the tree control

LISTING 7.29 The handle_node_double_click method

```
METHOD handle_node_double_click.
  DATA: l_carrid TYPE spfli-carrid,
        l_connid TYPE spfli-connid.

  l_carrid = node_key(2).
  l_connid = node_key+2(4).

  IF l_connid IS INITIAL.
    CALL METHOD fill_html EXPORTING i_carrid = l_carrid.
  ELSE.
    CALL METHOD fill_list EXPORTING i_carrid = l_carrid
                                    i_connid = l_connid.
  ENDIF.
  CALL METHOD cl_gui_cfw=>flush.
ENDMETHOD.
```

We have declared the handle_node_double_click method as an event handler for double-clicking on nodes of the tree structure and registered it in the constructor. It will therefore be triggered by these user actions. The method imports the node_key parameter of the node_double_click event of the CL_GUI_SIMPLE_TREE class, which contains the key of the selected note. We divide the key into the parts from which we have compiled it in the fill_tree method, and call either the fill_html or the fill_list method, depending on the contents.

The method calls are stored in the Automation Queue until the next synchronization point between the application and presentation servers. Prior to Release 4.6C, to run the methods during event handling, we had to call the flush method of the CL_GUI_CFW class at this point. As of Basis Release 4.6C, an automatic synchronization point has been included in the CFW after system events have been handled as well.

Generating and filling the HTML control

LISTING 7.30 The fill_html method

```
METHOD fill_html.
  DATA l_url TYPE scarr-url.

  IF html_viewer IS INITIAL.
    CREATE OBJECT html_viewer
           EXPORTING parent = container_html.
  ENDIF.

  SELECT SINGLE url
  FROM   scarr
  INTO   l_url
  WHERE  carrid = i_carrid.

  CALL METHOD html_viewer->show_url
       EXPORTING url = l_url.
ENDMETHOD.
```

When first called, the fill_html method creates an object of the CL_GUI_HTML_VIEWER class and connects the corresponding HTML control with the area of the container control to which the reference in container_html is pointing, namely the custom control on the screen. Note that without the IF statement, a new HTML control would be created with each new method call. All these controls would be actively present in the ABAP program and on the presentation server even though just the last one respectively is visible. You can thus connect several application controls with a single container control. You can then control the visibility with the set_visible method.

As of Basis Release 4.6C, the SCARR database table contains a column that is filled with the URL addresses of the carriers. Accordingly, we read this address from the selected nodes and pass it to the show_url method of our HTML control, which displays the homepage of the carrier. If the SCARR table in your system does not contain any URLs, you must provide your own addresses.

Generating and filling the ALV Grid control in a dialog box

LISTING 7.31 The fill_list method

```
METHOD fill_list.
  DATA: l_flight_tab TYPE TABLE OF demofli,
        BEGIN OF l_flight_title,
```

```
          carrname TYPE scarr-carrname,
          cityfrom  TYPE spfli-cityfrom,
          cityto     TYPE spfli-cityto,
        END OF l_flight_title,
        l_list_layout TYPE lvc_s_layo.

IF container_box IS INITIAL.
  CREATE OBJECT container_box
         EXPORTING width   = 250
                   height  = 200
                   top     = 100
                   left    = 400
                   caption = 'Flight List'.
  SET HANDLER close_box FOR container_box.
  CREATE OBJECT list_viewer
         EXPORTING i_parent = container_box.
ENDIF.
SELECT SINGLE c~carrname p~cityfrom p~cityto
INTO   CORRESPONDING FIELDS OF l_flight_title
FROM   ( scarr AS c
         INNER JOIN spfli AS p ON c~carrid = p~carrid )
WHERE  p~carrid = i_carrid AND
       p~connid = i_connid.

SELECT    fldate seatsmax seatsocc
INTO      CORRESPONDING FIELDS OF TABLE l_flight_tab
FROM      sflight
WHERE     carrid = i_carrid AND connid = i_connid
ORDER BY fldate.

CONCATENATE l_flight_title-carrname
            i_connid
            l_flight_title-cityfrom
            l_flight_title-cityto
       INTO l_list_layout-grid_title
  SEPARATED BY space.

l_list_layout-smalltitle = 'X'.
l_list_layout-cwidth_opt = 'X'.
l_list_layout-no_toolbar = 'X'.

CALL METHOD list_viewer->set_table_for_first_display
```

```
        EXPORTING i_structure_name = 'DEMOFLI'
                  is_layout        = l_list_layout
        CHANGING  it_outtab        = l_flight_tab.
ENDMETHOD.
```

The fill_list method creates a dialog box container, if there is no dialog box present, and an ALV grid control, which is displayed in the dialog box. The event handler close_box is registered for the dialog box container. In this case it is not necessary to activate with the set_registered_events method: the close event of the CL_GUI_DIALOGBOX_CONTAINER class is activated in the class itself as a system event.

We use two SELECT statements to create a list title and an internal table with list data according to the selected node. By assigning values to some components of the l_list_layout structure of type lvc_s_layo we determine that the list title will be shown in small format, that the column width of the list is optimized, and that the list will not have an application toolbar. We also assign the list title to a component of this structure. For the l_flight_tab internal table we use the demofli structured type that we have created in the ABAP Dictionary with the three components fldate, seatsmax, and seatsocc.

We pass the name of the structure, the l_list_layout structure, and the l_flight_tab table to the set_table_for_first_display method of the ALV grid control, which causes the list to be displayed in the dialog box.

Closing the dialog box

LISTING 7.32 The close_box method

```
METHOD close_box.


  CALL METHOD: list_viewer->free,

               container_box->free.

  CLEAR: list_viewer,
         container_box.
CALL METHOD cl_gui_cfw=>flush.
ENDMETHOD.
```

The close_box method allows the user the opportunity to close the dialog box with the usual icon. To do this the free method of the ALV grid control and dialog box containers are called in turn and then the corresponding reference variables are initialized. If the user then selects a node to create a list, both controls are created again in the fill_list method.

No other controls of the program can be deleted by the user, and they all remain until the program ends.

Summary of example

We can summarize the procedure in our GUI controls example as follows. This applies in general to control programming as a whole:

1. Create container controls and attach them to screen areas of screens.
2. Create application controls and attach them to the container controls.
3. Prepare data to fill the controls, in most cases in internal tables with a special predefined type.
4. Send data to the application controls by calling control methods.
5. Respond to user events on the controls by defining and registering suitable handler methods.

You can now try to write your own programs with controls or to copy and modify our example program. For example, you could provide the nodes of the tree structure with context menus or make the picture respond to mouse-clicks in order to add another control at this point.

CHAPTER 8

Working with external data

Programs work with data. So far we have only been concerned with processing transient data of an ABAP program, i.e. data that is only available at program runtime. In this chapter we will concentrate on processing persistent data, i.e. data that is stored permanently outside the ABAP program.

8.1 DATABASE ACCESS

8.1.1 Introduction

By far the greater part of all long-term data in an SAP System is stored in the relational database tables of its central database. The relational data model depicts the real world through relationships between tables. A database table is a two-dimensional matrix consisting of lines and columns. Any smallest possible combination of columns that can uniquely identify a line of a table is called a **key**. For each table in a relational database there must be at least one key, and for each table a key is defined as a primary key. The relationships between the tables are achieved through foreign key relationships.

The database tables of an SAP System database are partly delivered already filled with data. These database tables contain many components of the SAP System itself such as ABAP programs, as well as Customizing data in order for the customer to be able to tailor the SAP System to his or her company needs. However, most database tables are supplied empty. They are intended for the business data of the client systems and are filled by the client by copying foreign data or by using ABAP programs.

SQL

Each relational database has a programming interface that enables access to the database tables via a widely standardized query language called SQL (Structured Query Language). Unfortunately, the SQL statements of these programming interfaces are not entirely uniform and have certain characteristics specific to the manufacturer.

Database interface

To make an SAP System independent of the database it is using, the runtime environment contains a database interface (see Figure 8.1). ABAP programs access the database solely via the database interface. The database interface translates all the ABAP statements that access the database into manufacturer-specific standard SQL statements.

In the following sections we will concentrate on the three most important questions facing the ABAP programmer when working with database tables.

- **How do I define database tables in the SAP System?**

  In Standard SQL there is a subarea called DDL (Data Definition Language) with statements such as `CREATE`, `ALTER`, or `DROP` that allow database tables to be defined or modified.

  ABAP does not contain any such statements. Instead, the Basis System provides the ABAP Dictionary tool to carry out these tasks.

- **How do I process table data in ABAP programs?**

  In Standard SQL, a subarea called DML (Data Manipulation Language), with statements such as `SELECT`, `INSERT`, `UPDATE`, and `DELETE`, is responsible for editing data in existing tables.

  In ABAP there is a set of statements with the same names that is grouped together under the name Open SQL. Open SQL allows you to apply DML statements in ABAP programs independently of the platform.

- **How do I ensure the consistency of database tables and protect them from unauthorized access?**

  In Standard SQL, there is a subarea called DCL (Data Control Language) that allows you to define user views and perform access controls.

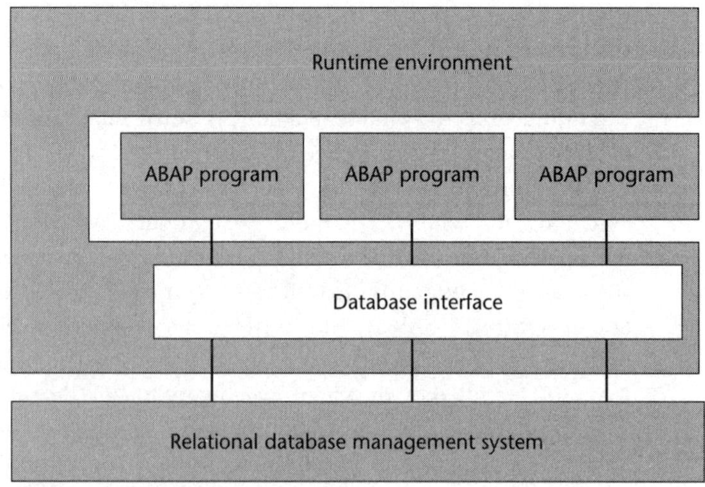

FIGURE 8.1 The database interface

ABAP does not contain any such statements. Data consistency is ensured by the SAP LUW concept and SAP locks. The SAP authorization concept governs access rights.

8.1.2 Defining database tables in the ABAP Dictionary

ABAP does not contain any statements from the DDL section of Standard SQL. Normal application programs should not create database tables, neither should they change their attributes. For this purpose, the ABAP Workbench provides the ABAP Dictionary tool. Open SQL statements can only access database tables that have been created with the ABAP Dictionary.

As a rule, as an ABAP programmer you are working mainly with existing tables from the relational data model of your application. Therefore, we will not explore the creation of database tables at this point. Instead, we will use the ABAP Dictionary tool to represent existing tables and their structures (see Figure 8.2).

Data type

For each database table the ABAP Dictionary creates a structured data type of the same name in the ABAP Dictionary. The components of this type have the same names and data types as in the database table. You use this type to declare suitable work areas for database accesses in ABAP programs. Basically, Figure 8.2 shows nothing more than when you define a structured data type (see Figure 4.6). The only difference is that here we have different **Technical Settings**.

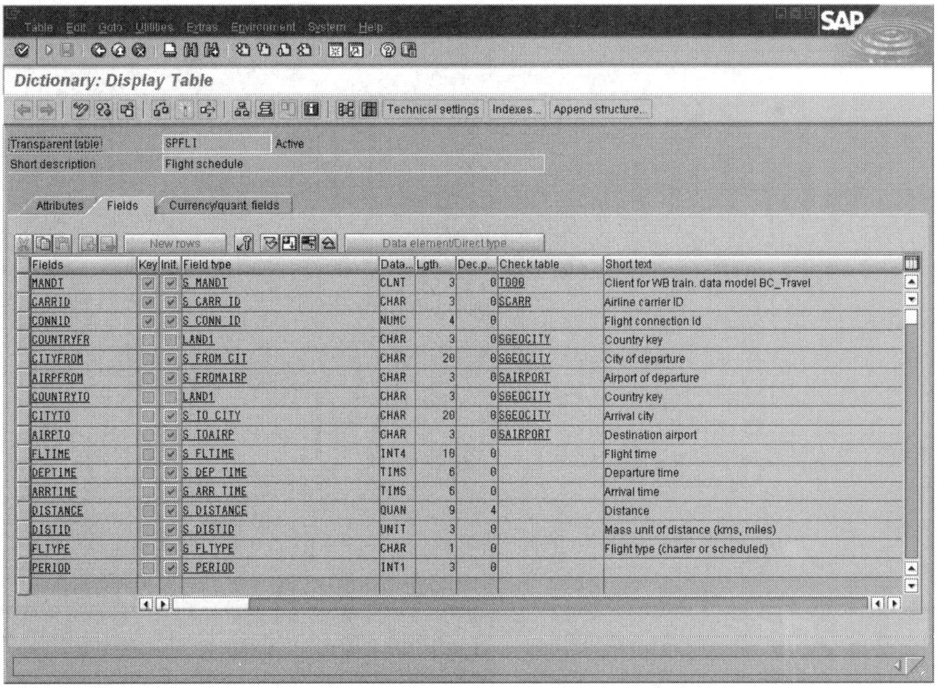

Dictionary: Display Table

Transparent table SPFLI Active
Short description Flight schedule

Fields	Key	Init.	Field type	Data...	Lgth.	Dec.p.	Check table	Short text
MANDT	✓	✓	S_MANDT	CLNT	3	0	T000	Client for WB train. data model BC_Travel
CARRID	✓	✓	S_CARR_ID	CHAR	3	0	SCARR	Airline carrier ID
CONNID	✓	✓	S_CONN_ID	NUMC	4	0		Flight connection Id
COUNTRYFR			LAND1	CHAR	3	0	SGEOCITY	Country key
CITYFROM		✓	S_FROM_CIT	CHAR	20	0	SGEOCITY	City of departure
AIRPFROM		✓	S_FROMAIRP	CHAR	3	0	SAIRPORT	Airport of departure
COUNTRYTO			LAND1	CHAR	3	0	SGEOCITY	Country key
CITYTO		✓	S_TO_CITY	CHAR	20	0	SGEOCITY	Arrival city
AIRPTO		✓	S_TOAIRP	CHAR	3	0	SAIRPORT	Destination airport
FLTIME		✓	S_FLTIME	INT4	10	0		Flight time
DEPTIME		✓	S_DEP_TIME	TIMS	6	0		Departure time
ARRTIME		✓	S_ARR_TIME	TIMS	6	0		Arrival time
DISTANCE		✓	S_DISTANCE	QUAN	9	4		Distance
DISTID		✓	S_DISTID	UNIT	3	0		Mass unit of distance (kms, miles)
FLTYPE		✓	S_FLTYPE	CHAR	1	0		Flight type (charter or scheduled)
PERIOD		✓	S_PERIOD	INT1	3	0		

FIGURE 8.2 A database table in the ABAP Dictionary. Copyright © SAP AG

You should never confuse the role of data types, work areas, and database tables. The database table is physically present on the database. The data type of the same name in the ABAP Dictionary is a meta-description of the database table, and a work area exists only transiently in the data area of a program. Since data types and data objects have separate namespaces in ABAP, you can create work areas with the same name as the database tables. Nevertheless, you should avoid this for the sake of clarity and put a prefix wa_ in front of the name, for example.

View

In the ABAP Dictionary you can group the columns of several existing database tables into a database view, or view for short. A **view** allows simultaneous access to more than one database table with a single `SELECT` statement. A view is a statically predefined join, so to speak (see Figure 8.3). With each view a structured data type of the same name is also created in the same way as for database tables, and, at least in read-only Open SQL statements, views are handled exactly like database tables. When we refer to the use of Open SQL for accessing database tables in the following sections, we also mean views.

8.1.3 Processing data with Open SQL

Open SQL is a subset of Standard SQL, which is implemented through ABAP statements. Open SQL includes the DML section of the standard version, and therefore allows data to be read (`SELECT`) and modified (`INSERT`, `UPDATE`, `MODIFY`, `DELETE`).

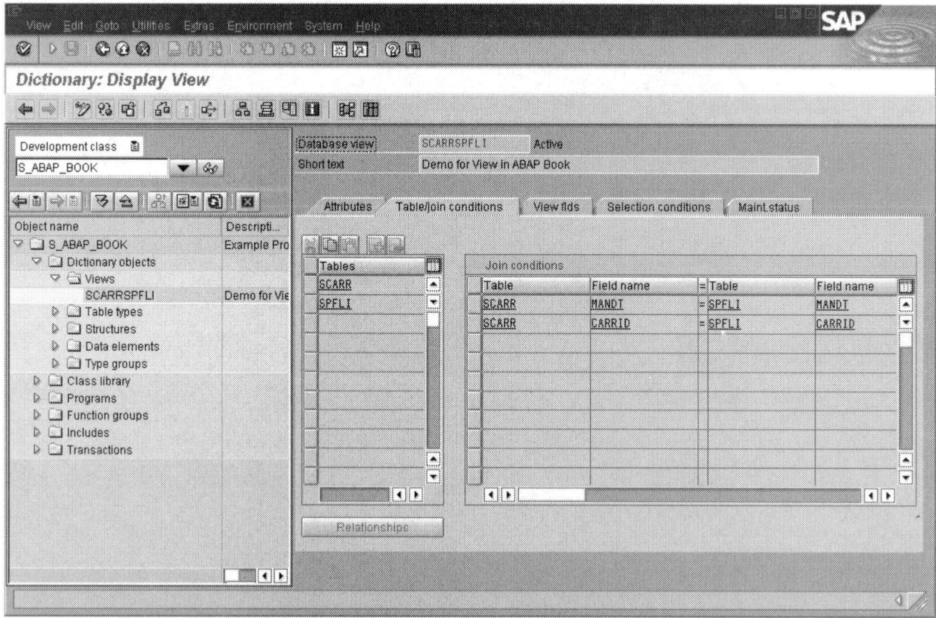

FIGURE 8.3 A view in the ABAP Dictionary. Copyright © SAP AG

Open SQL, however, goes beyond Standard SQL by offering variants of the statements that only operate in ABAP programs and can simplify or accelerate database access.

Efficiency

If you access the database with Open SQL in an ABAP program, you must always keep an eye on the efficiency of the program. It is largely determined by its database accesses. A program that performs database accesses within a reasonable period in test operation can, in the worst-case scenario, crash a system in production mode if the database accesses are not optimally programmed.

In the following description of Open SQL we will indicate how efficiency can be achieved using Open SQL statements. We will mainly follow the five basic rules for efficient database access:

1. **Keep the number of hits low**

   The amount of selected data puts a load on the memory of the database system and on the network during transfer to the application server.

2. **Keep the amount of data transferred low**

   The amount of transported data affects the network.

3. **Keep the number of database accesses low**

   Each individual database access affects the network and the database system, since data is transported between the application server and the database system, and appropriate administration must be provided at the latter level.

4. **Keep the required search effort low**

   Selection criteria can be formulated so that they have a minimal effect on the database system.

5. **Keep the database load generally low**

   As a rule, since there is only one database system for many different application programs, you should remove as much load from the database as possible.

It depends mostly on the data to be edited and the required evaluation as to which rule brings the most benefit. You should decide from case to case which rule can be applied for your application and which ones are less suitable. The **Performance Trace** and **Runtime Analysis** tools in the **Test** menu of the ABAP Workbench are provided to help you with these investigations. However, you can also use the `GET RUN TIME FIELD` statement for targeted testing. More detailed information on optimizing database access is contained in [SCH00].

System field

Each Open SQL statement fills the `sy-subrc` and `sy-dbcnt` system fields with return values. A successful database access sets `sy-subrc` to zero and `sy-dbcnt` to the number of processed table lines.

Reading data from database tables

SELECT

The Open SQL statement for reading data from database tables into data objects of an ABAP program is `SELECT`. The `SELECT` statement is a very powerful statement whose functionality ranges from simple reading of single lines to programming highly complex database queries. The SELECT statement consists of several *clauses*. Each clause fulfills a different task when accessing databases. In order to use the SELECT statement efficiently, you must understand the interaction between the individual clauses. We will now explore the SELECT statement and its clauses step by step.

When it comes to reading data from database tables, there are four questions to be asked:

1. What data is to be read?
2. Where is it to be read from?
3. Where should it be read to?
4. What conditions apply to reading?

Clauses

Each of these questions is answered by a clause of the SELECT statement:

1. The SELECT clause determines which columns are read and whether the data is read from one or more rows.
2. The FROM clause determines the database tables or views from which the data is read.
3. The INTO clause determines the data objects of the ABAP programs into which the data is read.
4. The WHERE clause specifies the conditions under which the data is read.

This produces the following syntax for a minimum SELECT statement:

```
SELECT  select_clause
FROM    from_clause
INTO    into_clause
WHERE   where_clause.
```

Although shorter forms are permissible syntactically, they should not be used. Firstly, although it is not necessary from the syntax viewpoint to specify a WHERE clause, it should be done to satisfy the first efficiency rule. Secondly, you will find, in older ABAP programs, short forms without INTO clauses such as:

```
SELECT select_clause FROM from_clause
```

Short form

This short form, forbidden in ABAP Objects, implicitly reads the data into a data object that has the same name as the database table and must be declared with the TABLES statement before. Prior to Release 4.0, you even needed the TABLES statement in order to access database tables with an Open SQL statement. Today, a TABLES work area is only required as a screen interface (see Section 7.1) or for logical databases. As with internal tables without header rows, the naming distinction between the source and target areas aids clarity in programming.

Clauses

In addition to the above four basic clauses, the SELECT statement can contain three other clauses for special requirements when reading data:

- The GROUP BY clause: to compress several lines into one line when reading.
- The HAVING clause: to specify terms for compressed lines.
- The ORDER BY clause: for sorting lines when reading.

We will explore these clauses after discussing the basic clauses.

Reading a database table

We will begin our description of the clauses of the SELECT statement with the access to a single database table. To do this, we use the most basic form of the FROM clause.

```
SELECT ...
FROM   dbtab
INTO   ...
WHERE  ...
```

FROM clause

For dbtab you can directly enter the name of a database table such as spfli, sflight, or the name of a view. However, you can also enter the name of a data object in brackets, in which case this must then contain the name of a database table or a view at runtime.

With this basic form of the FROM clause we will now consider the various combination options for SELECT and INTO clauses and the most important forms of the WHERE clause, before looking at accessing several database tables. We will start with the most basic case, where we read just a single row from the database.

Reading a row

SELECT clause

In order to read a specific row from a database table, the SELECT clause must be introduced with the word SINGLE, the target area of the INTO clause must be flat (see Section 4.2.6), and the condition of the WHERE clause must uniquely specify the required line through conditions for all columns of the table key.[1]

All columns

To read all columns of a line, you can enter an asterisk (*) in the SELECT clause. We recommend specifying a flat structure in the INTO clause of the same data type as that of the database table of the FROM clause (see Listing 8.1).

LISTING 8.1 Reading all columns of a row into a structure

```
REPORT s_select_single_all.
...
PARAMETERS: p_carrid TYPE spfli-carrid,
            p_connid TYPE spfli-connid.
```

1. SELECT SINGLE is most efficient if the primary key of the database table in the WHERE condition is completely supplied with values. Otherwise the entry will be searched for in the database table in the same way as for reading several rows.

```
DATA wa_spfli TYPE spfli.
...
SELECT SINGLE *
FROM   spfli
INTO   wa_spfli
WHERE  carrid = p_carrid AND
       connid = p_connid.
```

Specific columns

In accordance with the second efficiency rule, you should only ever read the data you actually require. Instead of always reading all the columns of a row, you should target the required columns. To do this you specify in the `SELECT` clause a list of the columns you want to read. For the target area of the `INTO` clause you can either specify a flat structure again or a list of elementary data objects.

INTO clause

You specify the list of elementary data objects in brackets and separated by commas (see Listing 8.2). The number of fields in the `INTO` clause must match the number of columns in the `SELECT` clause. The allocation of columns to fields is determined by their position in the list. The data types of individual fields must be suitable for the data types of the corresponding columns.

LISTING 8.2 Reading specific columns of a row into elementary fields

```
REPORT s_select_single_into_list.
...
DATA: wa_cityfrom TYPE spfli-cityfrom,
      wa_cityto   TYPE spfli-cityto.
...
SELECT SINGLE cityfrom cityto
FROM   spfli
INTO   (wa_cityfrom,wa_cityto)
WHERE  carrid = p_carrid AND
       connid = p_connid.
```

When specifying a flat structure, you can use the `CORRESPONDING FIELDS` addition to import data from the columns of the database table into components of the structure with the same name (see Listing 8.3). The data types of the components must be suitable for the data types of the corresponding columns.

LISTING 8.3 Reading specific columns of a row into a structure

```
REPORT s_select_single_corresponding.
...
SELECT SINGLE cityfrom cityto
```

```
FROM    spfli
INTO    CORRESPONDING FIELDS OF wa_spfli
WHERE   carrid = p_carrid AND
        connid = p_connid.
```

Note that specifying a list in the `INTO` clause is more efficient than using `CORRESPONDING FIELDS`, especially for reading a single row, because there is no need to compare names. The `CORRESPONDING FIELDS` addition is useful if you do not know the columns that were actually read during programming, as with a dynamic specification of the database table in the FROM clause.

Reading several rows

You read several rows from the database table without having the `SINGLE` addition in the `SELECT` clause. This is the most common application. You specify columns in exactly the same way as for reading single rows with "*" or with a list of names. However, in this case you must program the `SELECT` statement in such a way that the ABAP program can process not just one but several rows. This even applies if, due to a condition in the `WHERE` clause, only a single row is actually read: without the `SINGLE` addition in the `SELECT` clause, ABAP will always consider the selection to be multi-row.

When it comes to reading several rows, Open SQL provides you with the option of specifying either flat target areas or internal tables in the `INTO` clause.

SELECT loop

To import into flat target areas, you use in the `INTO` clause the same syntax fitting the columns in the `SELECT` clause that we introduced above for reading single rows. However, as the selection without the SINGLE addition in the `SELECT` clause is multi-row, the `SELECT` statement now opens a loop here that you must terminate with the `ENDSELECT` statement (see Listing 8.4). Each read line triggers a loop turn. The read data is available in the target area during the loop turn.

LISTING 8.4 Reading several rows into a `SELECT` loop.

```
REPORT s_select_into_list.
...
SELECT cityfrom cityto
FROM    spfli
INTO    (wa_cityfrom,wa_cityto)
WHERE   carrid = p_carrid.
  ...
ENDSELECT.
```

Compare Listing 8.4 with Listing 8.2. You can see that an `ENDSELECT` statement has been added instead of the `SINGLE` addition in the `SELECT` clause. The `INTO` clause is unchanged. We have removed the restriction to one row in the WHERE clause. Listing 8.1 and Listing 8.3 can equally be rewritten to read several rows.

When we consider a SELECT loop, the question of the third efficiency rule arises. According to this rule, database access within frequently used loops should be generally avoided. Does a SELECT loop not imply one database access per row read? This is not the case: executing a SELECT loop results in considerably fewer database accesses than if you read the data row by row with the SELECT SINGLE statement.[2] But you should never nest SELECT loops unless really only a few rows are being read in the external loop.

Internal table

For multi-row selections, instead of reading into flat target areas with a SELECT loop, it is natural, of course, to specify multi-row data objects, i.e. internal tables, in the INTO clause. For this purpose, use the TABLE addition in the INTO clause. Behind TABLE you enter the name of an internal table whose row type must be a flat structure. Behind this statement, as with the SINGLE addition in the SELECT clause, you cannot use an ENDSELECT statement, as here, too, the data is only available after it has been fully imported into the ABAP program. The SINGLE and TABLES additions and the ENDSELECT statement are therefore mutually exclusive.[3]

If you require data more than once in a program, the best option is to import once into an internal table in order to avoid reading data repeatedly. You will also have the assurance of consistent data in your program.

You can either import all the columns or specific columns of several rows into an internal table. When you import all the columns it is advisable to define the row type of the internal table according to the data type of the database table from the FROM clause (see Listing 8.5).

LISTING 8.5 Reading all the columns of several rows into an internal table

```
REPORT s_select_all.
...
DATA spfli_tab TYPE TABLE OF spfli.
...
SELECT *
FROM   spfli
INTO   TABLE spfli_tab
WHERE  carrid = p_carrid.
```

2. To the database interface, a SELECT loop represents only a single access. The database interface then reads the data in packages of up to 32 KB from the database. The number of read packages determines the actual number of database accesses. When single rows are read, however, the database interface must make an access for each row.
3. Unless, however, you are using the PACKAGE SIZE n addition in the INTO clause for internal tables. This causes the internal table to be filled in packages of n lines. You then also need the ENDSELECT statement, and only the package that has just been read will be available in the SELECT loop.

Compare Listing 8.5 with Listing 8.1. In the SELECT statement we have, for the most part, replaced the SINGLE addition to the SELECT clause with the TABLE addition to the INTO clause. To read specific columns of several rows, you must prepare internal tables that contain components of the same name (see Listing 8.6). For multi-line target areas, there is no equivalent of the list of elementary fields in the INTO clause from Listing 8.2. We recommend structuring the internal table only from the components you require in order to avoid using unnecessary memory.

LISTING 8.6 Reading specific columns in an internal table.

```
REPORT s_select_corresponding.
...
TYPES: BEGIN OF tab_type,
           cityfrom TYPE spfli-cityfrom,
           cityto   TYPE spfli-cityto,
         END OF tab_type.
DATA spfli_tab TYPE TABLE OF tab_type.
...
SELECT cityfrom cityto
FROM   spfli
INTO   CORRESPONDING FIELDS OF TABLE spfli_tab
WHERE  carrid = p_carrid.
```

The table kind is of no importance when you specify internal tables in the INTO clause. A sorted table, for example, is sorted according to its key during import. You should, however, be careful with internal tables with a unique key. A runtime error will be triggered if you try to generate duplicate entries.

When you import into internal tables you can use the word APPENDING instead of the INTO language element. In this case, the rows of the selection will be appended to the internal table instead of replacing the existing rows.

Reading several rows into an internal table is not more efficient than a SELECT loop in itself. However, if the SELECT loop is used to fill an internal table row by row, you should import directly into the internal table instead. If the read data is used more than once, a single reading into an internal table is always the best solution due to the third efficiency rule.

When you import data into internal tables, you should always ensure that the amount of data read at any one time is not too great. The space for internal tables in the memory is limited (see Section 4.7) and larger amounts of data must be paged, which takes time. Using the

```
... PACKAGE SIZE n
```

addition, you can divide the data to be imported into an internal table into packages of n lines that are processed in a SELECT – ENDSELECT loop. In each loop rotation the internal table then contains the data of the current package.

We have now studied the interaction of the SELECT clause and the INTO clause in detail and learned that both must match. Using the example of accessing a single database table, we will now turn to the last clause of our basic SELECT statement, the WHERE clause. We will first consider two key aspects of the WHERE clause: efficiency and power.

The WHERE *clause*

Efficiency

As mentioned before, using the WHERE clause is the most important way of satisfying the first efficiency rule. You use the WHERE clause to limit the number of rows that are read in the selection from the database through conditions specified as logical expressions. These logical expressions are similar, but not identical, to the logical expressions of the rest of the ABAP language, as syntax and semantics within Open SQL are based on the SQL Standard. For example, the placeholder for all character strings in SQL is a percentage sign (%) whereas in the rest of ABAP it is an asterisk (*).

Comparison

The most basic logical expressions are comparisons using the operators

```
=, <, >, <>, <=, >=
```

such as:

```
... WHERE carrid = 'UA'
```

The left operand must always be a column of a database table of the FROM clause, while the right operand can be a suitable data object of the ABAP program or a column of a database table of the FROM clause. The operators compare the value of the column with the operand of the right-hand side, as is common with logical expressions. The value of the operand is converted into the data type of the column in the process. Each logical expression can be negated with NOT and several expressions can be linked with AND or OR in a WHERE clause (see above Listings). The result of a condition can be true, false, or unknown. If the condition is true, the corresponding row is selected, otherwise not.[4] A condition is unknown if one of the columns has a value of null. To query the null value specifically, there is the special condition IS NULL, which is true if the column contains the value null.[5]

Search effort

By specifying a WHERE clause you instruct the database system to search for those rows that satisfy the specified conditions. The logical conditions of the WHERE clause

4. By the way, if rows are duplicated in the selection due to a non-unique WHERE clause, you can exclude these with the DISTINCT addition in the SELECT clause.
5. A null value is a special value in databases that can be edited using Native SQL statements but has no equivalent in ABAP. Although ABAP recognizes type-specific initial values, it does not recognize a special null value. No null values are generated in databases through Open SQL statements such as INSERT, UPDATE, or MODIFY unless if, instead of a database, a view is addressed that does not contain all the columns of the databases. NULL values can also arise in databases if a table that already contains data is given new columns in the ABAP Dictionary. On reading, null values can be generated in the selection by aggregate functions of the SELECT clause and for the left outer join in the FROM clause. However, when passed to the ABAP program with the INTO clause, null values are always changed into the type-specific initial values.

therefore determine directly the amount of searching on the database, which should be minimized in accordance with the fourth efficiency rule. The rows of a database table are not sorted when stored, so that the time involved in searching after a certain row increases, on average, linearly with the number of rows in the database table. To reduce this time, each database table has at least one **index** that consists of selected columns of the database table and is created in sorted order as a copy in the database system. On a sorted index you can perform a search in which only parts of the index are searched and the average time involved increases logarithmically with the number of rows (see also the time involved for key access to internal tables in Section 4.7.2).

Index

Which indexes does a database table have? In the SAP System, the primary key fields of a database table always form a unique **primary index**. Moreover, in the ABAP Dictionary you can create **secondary indexes**. During database access the system tries to use the best index for the search. Remember, however, that for write accesses the system also has to change the secondary index, and, consequently, these indexes are more suitable for tables that are more subject to read access. You should create no more than five indexes per database table and these should not contain too many common columns, so that the system will find the right index more easily. If a secondary index is not unique, it should be made as selective as possible. An index entry should generally reference less than 5% of the rows.

You can reduce the amount of searching on the database by formulating the conditions for the `WHERE` clause to fit one of the indexes of the database table so that the indexes are searched, not the entire table. If you have to select according to columns that are not yet contained in an index, and the response times are very poor, it is worth creating a suitable index. To ensure an optimum operation between the `WHERE` clause and the index, note the following:

- In the `WHERE` clause, for all fields of the index enter, if possible, logical comparisons with the equals operator (=) that are linked with `AND`.
- In the `WHERE` clause, for the index fields use only positive operators such as = instead of <> or the NOT language element, as these are not supported by indexes.
- If you only specify part of an index in the `WHERE` clause, the order of the index fields plays an important role. An index field in a `WHERE` clause will generally only result in the index being evaluated if all the fields in the index definition in front of it are fully specified in the `WHERE` condition.[6]
- When selecting and applying an index, the system generally uses no operands linked with `OR`, unless the `OR` operator is at the highest level in the logical conditions. For example, you should therefore use

6. You can compare the evaluation of the index with searching through a telephone book. If you search for an entry where you know the first name and street but not the surname, there is little point in sorting the telephone directory by surname. All the entries will have to be searched from the beginning.

```
... WHERE (CARRID = 'LH' AND CITYFROM = 'FRANKFURT') OR
          (CARRID = 'LH' AND CITYFROM = 'NEW YORK').
```

instead of:

```
... WHERE carrid = 'LH' AND
      (cityfrom = 'FRANKFURT' OR cityfrom = 'NEW YORK').
```

- Do not query an index column with the condition `IS NULL`, as some databases do not support this for indexes.

You can achieve significant efficiency improvements if all the columns of a `SELECT` clause are part of an index, as then only the index must be read.

Complex selection

Up to now we have studied the efficiency aspect of the `WHERE` clause. We will now look at another logical condition that is extremely powerful. In Section 7.2.3 we showed how you can allow the user of a program to enter complex selections into a selection table on a selection screen. The `WHERE` clause can contain a logical condition that checks these selections. The corresponding logical expression is:

```
col IN  selopt
```

On the left-hand side there is again a database table column and on the right-hand side the name of a complex selection defined with `SELECT-OPTIONS`. The `IN` operator checks the entire selection table `selopt` by using the contents of the `col` column in its conditions and evaluating them.

LISTING 8.7 `WHERE` clause with complex selections

```
REPORT s_select_where_in_selopt.
...
DATA wa_sflight TYPE sflight.
SELECT-OPTIONS: s_carrid FOR wa_sflight-carrid
                         NO INTERVALS NO-EXTENSION,
                s_connid FOR wa_sflight-connid
                         NO INTERVALS NO-EXTENSION,
                s_fldate FOR wa_sflight-fldate.
...
SELECT *
FROM   sflight
INTO   wa_sflight
WHERE  carrid IN s_carrid AND
       connid IN s_connid AND
       fldate IN s_fldate.
  ...
ENDSELECT.
```

Listing 8.7 shows the use of three complex selections in a WHERE clause. The user can enter values for these three selections on the selection screen of Figure 8.4, which are evaluated when the database is accessed.

Selection table

The use of selection tables in the WHERE clause is therefore a very convenient way of sending the user's selections directly to the database. Of course, unrestricted use of this functionality contrasts to a certain extent with the above-mentioned rules on efficiently programming the conditions of a WHERE clause, since the user can formulate complicated conditions on the selection screen that are not supported by indexes. You must therefore weigh up the ease of using complex selections against a potential drop in efficiency on a case-by-case basis. Using the NO INTERVALS and NO-EXTENSION additions to the SELECT-OPTIONS statement you can limit the freedom of the user in order to prevent inefficient selections as far as possible (see Listing 8.7).

In addition to the comparisons through logical operators and checking complex selections, you can also formulate the following conditions in the WHERE clause:

- **Interval check with BETWEEN**

  This operator checks whether the value of the column is in an interval:

  ```
  ... WHERE seatsmax BETWEEN 200 AND 300
  ```

- **Pattern check for character-type columns with LIKE**

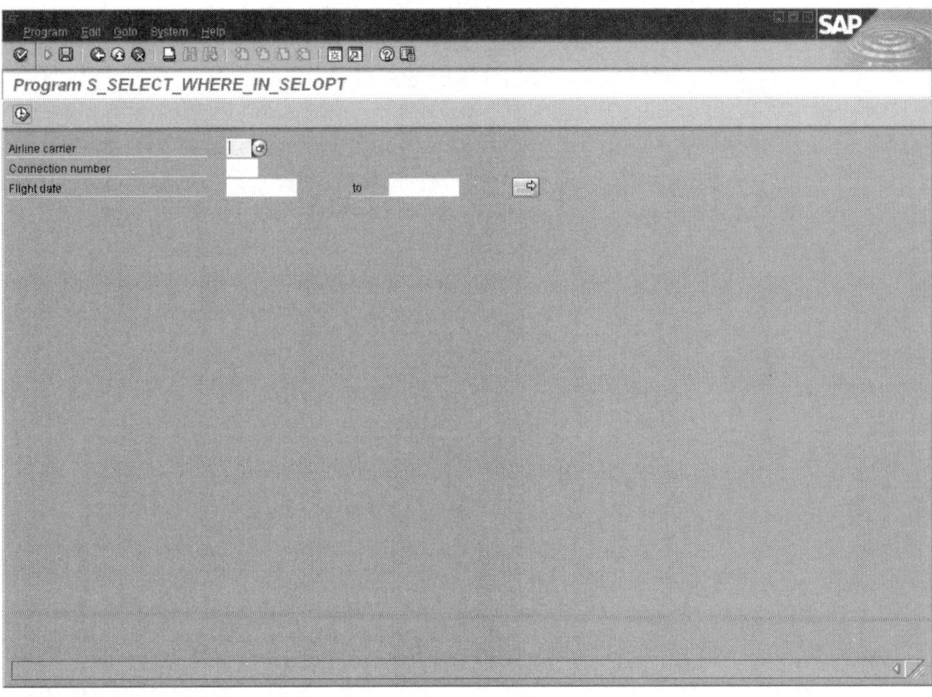

FIGURE 8.4 Selection screen for WHERE clause. Copyright © SAP AG

This operator compares the characters of the column with the characters on the right-hand side. Placeholders are "%" for any number of characters and "_" for just one character:

```
... WHERE cityto LIKE '%town'.
```

- **Value list check with `IN`**

  The `IN` operator can check if the value of the column matches a value from a given list:[7]

```
... WHERE cityto IN ('BERLIN', 'NEW YORK', 'LONDON').
```

Reading several database tables

We have now described the basics of the `SELECT` statement by reading data from a single database table. However, a common application when reading data from relational databases is to collect data from various interdependent database tables into a program for evaluation.

This task could be solved by numerous individual accesses to all the databases involved. However, this would contradict the third efficiency rule. In particular, when you require additional data from one or more additional tables for each row read in a table, the number of database accesses can often increase dramatically. Using the example of the database tables SPFLI and SCARR, linked via a foreign key relationship, we will now show you the options Open SQL offers for accessing both tables as efficiently as possible in order to read the name of the airline carrier from SCARR for each row read from SPFLI.

SELECT loop

For demonstration purposes, we will start in Listing 8.8 with the least favorable solution, a nested `SELECT` loop, in order to subsequently show the more efficient solutions. In this example we will also demonstrate how you can measure the runtime of the database access with the `GET RUN TIME` statement.

LISTING 8.8 Accessing several database tables with SELECT loops

```
REPORT s_select_nested.
PARAMETERS p_cityfr TYPE spfli-cityfrom DEFAULT 'Frankfurt'.
...
DATA: wa_carrid TYPE spfli-carrid,
      wa_connid TYPE spfli-connid,
      wa_carrname TYPE scarr-carrname.

DATA: t1 TYPE i,
      t2 TYPE i,
      time TYPE i,
      n TYPE i VALUE 1000.
```

7. There should be no space after the opening bracket.

```
...
DO n TIMES.
  GET RUN TIME FIELD t1.
* ----------------------------
  SELECT carrid
  FROM   spfli
  INTO   (wa_carrid, wa_connid)
  WHERE  cityfrom = p_cityfr.
    SELECT carrname
    FROM   scarr
    INTO   wa_carrname
    WHERE  carrid = wa_carrid.
      ...
    ENDSELECT.
  ENDSELECT.
* ----------------------------
  GET RUN TIME FIELD t2.
  time = time + t2 - t1.
ENDDO.
WRITE: 'Runtime:', time.
```

Runtime measurement

The GET RUN TIME statement measures the time since the start of program execution in microseconds. To obtain a meaningful result that avoids individual load-dependent deviations, we carry out the measurement n times in a loop and add up the times. The nested SELECT statements read two columns from all the rows of the SPFLI table that meet the WHERE condition and also one column respectively from the SCARR table. There is therefore one database access on SPFLI and, for each row read in the process, one database access on SCARR.

To avoid multiple database access, it is expedient to read the required data first into an internal table and to evaluate this. In our example this would reduce the number of database accesses to two. The problem with this method is that the number of rows to be read from one table depends on the selected contents of the other. In our case we only want to read rows from SCARR whose carriers have also been read from SPFLI. Although we could read all the rows from SCARR into an internal table and later use only the ones we require, this would contradict the first efficiency rule. We therefore require a condition in the WHERE clause that can take into account data from another table that has already been read.

FOR ALL ENTRIES

To do this, Open SQL offers the FOR ALL ENTRIES language construct, which you can add before the word WHERE in the WHERE clause (see Listing 8.9).

LISTING 8.9 Accessing several database tables with FOR ALL ENTRIES

```
REPORT s_select_for_all_entries.
PARAMETERS p_cityfr TYPE spfli-cityfrom DEFAULT 'Frankfurt'.
...
DATA: BEGIN OF wa_spfli,
          carrid TYPE spfli-carrid,
          connid TYPE spfli-connid,
        END OF wa_spfli,
        BEGIN OF wa_scarr,
          carrid TYPE scarr-carrid,
          carrname TYPE scarr-carrname,
        END OF wa_scarr,
        spfli_tab LIKE TABLE OF wa_spfli.
...
* ----------------------------
    SELECT carrid connid
    FROM   spfli
    INTO   TABLE spfli_tab
    WHERE  cityfrom = p_cityfr.

    SELECT carrid carrname
    FROM   scarr
    INTO   wa_scarr
           FOR ALL ENTRIES IN spfli_tab
    WHERE  carrid = spfli_tab-carrid.
      ...
    ENDSELECT.
* ----------------------------
```

In Listing 8.9, the data from the SPFLI table is written into an internal table. A subsequent SELECT loop reads the corresponding data from the SCARR table. The FOR ALL ENTRIES addition in the second SELECT statement belongs to the subsequent WHERE clause and operates as follows:

After FOR ALL ENTRIES IN, an internal table must be specified that is filled with comparison values. This affects the subsequent WHERE clause in such a way that all the WHERE conditions are checked for each single row of the internal table. The result of the entire SELECT statement is the combined amount of these selections, whereby duplicated rows are automatically removed from the result. The only constraints in using FOR ALL ENTRIES are that LIKE and BETWEEN cannot be used as relational operators and that in a comparison the column of the internal table must be compatible with the column of the database table. You should be careful, however, when the internal table is empty: in this case the WHERE condition is not taken into account, and all the database table entries are read.

The database accesses in Listing 8.9 have the same functionality as the nested SELECT loops in Listing 8.8, but can be much faster, depending on the amount of data read. However, you can considerably increase the efficiency again if you access both tables at once with a single SELECT statement.

Open SQL provides two ways of addressing several database tables with a single database access. You can either define a corresponding static database view in the ABAP Dictionary and access this, or enter several database tables in the FROM clause and link these with a join.

View

We have already shown the SCARRSPFLI view in Figure 8.3, which satisfies the required conditions exactly.

LISTING 8.10 Accessing several database tables through a view

```
REPORT  s_select_view.
PARAMETERS p_cityfr TYPE spfli-cityfrom DEFAULT 'Frankfurt'.
...
DATA: wa_carrid TYPE SCARRSPFLI-carrid,
      wa_connid TYPE SCARRSPFLI-connid,
      wa_carrname TYPE SCARRSPFLI-carrname.
...
* ---------------------------
SELECT carrid carrname connid
FROM   SCARRSPFLI
INTO   (wa_carrid,wa_carrname,wa_connid)
WHERE  cityfrom = p_cityfr.
  ...
ENDSELECT.
* ---------------------------
```

The SELECT loop in Listing 8.10 replaces the nested SELECT loops in Listing 8.8. It imports exactly the same data, but can be faster by an order of magnitude. It is always expedient to define a view in the ABAP Dictionary if you always need the same links between the rows of different database tables in different programs.

Join

You can also link several database tables within a single SELECT statement by defining a join in the FROM clause.

LISTING 8.11 Accessing several database tables through a join

```
REPORT s_select_join.
PARAMETERS p_cityfr TYPE spfli-cityfrom DEFAULT 'Frankfurt'.
...
```

```
DATA: wa_carrid TYPE SPFLI-carrid,
      wa_connid TYPE SPFLI-connid,
      wa_carrname TYPE SCARR-carrname.
...
* ----------------------------
SELECT spfli~carrid scarr~carrname spfli~connid
FROM   spfli
       INNER JOIN  scarr ON scarr~carrid = spfli~carrid
INTO   (wa_carrid,wa_carrname,wa_connid)
WHERE  spfli~cityfrom = p_cityfr.
  ...
ENDSELECT.
* ----------------------------
```

The SELECT loop in Listing 8.11 imports the same data as the previous two Listings and is just as fast as the view access in Listing 8.10. A join in a FROM clause is therefore the same as having a globally defined view in the ABAP Dictionary

Inner Join

We distinguish between inner joins and left outer joins. Listing 8.11 shows an inner join. You can also link more than two database tables in a FROM clause.[8] The FROM clause in Listing 8.12 links three database tables with two inner joins:

LISTING 8.12 Several joins in the FROM clause

```
REPORT s_select_inner_join.
PARAMETERS p_fldate TYPE sflight-fldate.
...
TYPES: BEGIN OF t_flights,
         cityfrom TYPE spfli-cityfrom,
         cityto TYPE spfli-cityto,
         seatsmax TYPE sflight-seatsmax,
         seatsocc TYPE sflight-seatsocc,
         bookid TYPE sbook-bookid,
       END OF t_flights.
DATA flight_tab TYPE TABLE OF t_flights.
...
SELECT    p~cityfrom p~cityto f~seatsmax f~seatsocc b~bookid
INTO      TABLE flight_tab
FROM      ( ( spfli AS p
              INNER JOIN sflight AS f
                 ON p~carrid = f~carrid AND
                    p~connid = f~connid        )
```

8. Currently, a maximum of 25 database tables can be linked with joins.

```
INNER JOIN sbook AS b
   ON b~carrid = f~carrid AND
      b~connid = f~connid AND
      b~fldate = f~fldate     )
WHERE   f~fldate = p_fldate AND
        f~seatsmax > f~seatsocc.
```

Join expression

There are two join expressions in this statement. A join expression consists of an `INNER JOIN` operator, on the right-hand side of which there must always be the name of a database table. On the left-hand side, there can be a database table or another join expression. For each join expression an `ON` condition must be specified. An `ON` condition consists of one or more logical relational expressions that must be linked with `AND`. Each relational expression must contain a column of the database table on the right-hand side of the join expression (see Listing 8.11). The parentheses are optional.

Each individual join expression operates in such a way that the columns of each row on the left-hand side are linked with the columns of all of the rows on the right-hand side that satisfy the `ON` condition. The number of resulting rows in the selection is therefore based on the right-hand side, and the contents on the left-hand side are duplicated in each added row. If no row satisfies the `ON` condition, no row on the left-hand side will be selected.

Left outer join

If you want to select the rows on the left-hand side, even though the `ON` condition is not satisfied on the right-hand side, you must use the left outer join.

```
SELECT ...
FROM   scarr LEFT OUTER JOIN  spfli ON ...
...
```

The rules for the join expressions are the same as for the inner join. The rules for the ON condition are stricter, since only the equals operator (=) is allowed and, in at least one relational expression, a column of the left-hand side must be compared with a column of the right-hand side. In addition, the `WHERE` clause must not contain any comparisons with columns of the right-hand side here, which is quite possible with the inner join.

With the left outer join the columns of each row on the right-hand side that do not satisfy the `ON` condition are filled with null values and linked with the columns of the left-hand side. If the conditions of the `WHERE` clause are satisfied, each row of the left-hand side of the left outer join will produce at least one row in the selection, irrespective of the `ON` condition.

Only if you want to read the data of several database tables under conditions that, for syntactical reasons, cannot be formulated as joins, do you have to return to the `FORM ALL ENTRIES` addition in the `WHERE` clause.

Column descriptor

In Listing 8.11 it is evident that we have not only entered the column names in the SELECT and WHERE clauses and the ON condition, but also identified the database tables through a prefix. The prefix is separated from the column names by a tilde (~). Only when a single database table is specified in the FROM clause are all the column names unique and can be described without a prefix. Whenever you link several database tables through joins, you must specify a prefix, as the same column name can occur in different database tables.

If you look at Listing 8.12 in more detail, you will see that we have used **alias names** instead of the table name itself as a prefix. Alias names can be used to make SELECT statements clearer. They are always required when a database table is used repeatedly in the join expressions of the FROM clause. You define alias names with the AS addition to the FROM clause. The following FROM clause therefore defines an alias name p for the spfli database table:

```
SELECT ...
FROM   spfli AS  p
...
```

If an alias name has been defined for a database table, only the alias name can be used for the database table at all other points of the SELECT statement (see Listing 8.12).

We have now shown how you can access the data of several database tables with a minimum number of database accesses by using the FOR ALL ENTRIES addition to the WHERE clause or join expressions in the FROM clause. This type of access is always appropriate if you need the data from all the database tables involved in your ABAP program. However, sometimes you will want to read the data of a table in relation to the data contents of another table, but do not need the data of the other table in the program.

Subquery

To read the data of one or more database tables with a single database access in relation to the data of another database table, you use subqueries. A **subquery** is a SELECT statement in brackets without the INTO clause that you can check using the EXISTS, IN operators, or using the relational operators in the WHERE clause. However, you cannot use subqueries in the ON condition of joins. Subqueries can be nested in the sense that the WHERE clause of a subquery itself, in turn, can contain a subquery.

The simplest usage of a subquery is with the EXISTS operator in a logical condition of the WHERE clause.

```
SELECT ...
FROM   scarr
INTO   ...
WHERE  EXISTS  ( SELECT *
                 FROM   spfli
                 WHERE  carrid   = scarr~carrid AND
                        cityfrom = 'NEW YORK' ).
```

The condition is true if the selection of the subquery contains at least one row. If the subquery contains columns of the SELECT statement above it, as shown here, we refer to a **correlated subquery**.

If the selection of a subquery contains only one column, its values can be queried with the IN operator:

```
... WHERE city IN  ( SELECT cityfrom
                     FROM   spfli
                     WHERE  carrid = p_carrid AND
                            connid = p_connid ).
```

The condition is true if the value of the checked column is contained in the result of the subquery.

Apart from these two applications with the IN and EXISTS operators, single column subqueries can also occur as operands in logical expressions. We need to distinguish here between single-row and multi-row selection of the subquery. You can only specify the subquery directly with single-row selections.[9]

```
... WHERE city = ( SELECT cityfrom
              FROM  spfli
              WHERE carrid = p_carrid AND
                    connid = p_connid ).
```

With multi-row selections, one of the ALL, ANY, or SOME additions must be placed in front of the subquery:

```
... WHERE seatsmax >= ALL  ( SELECT seatsocc
                             FROM   sflight
                             WHERE ...         )
```

With the ALL prefix before the subquery, the condition is true if the comparison for all the rows of the scalar subquery is true. With the ANY or SOME prefixes, the condition is true if the comparison for at least one row of the selection of the subquery is true.

Grouping rows together

Often you will need multiple rows from one or more databases only in order to derive condensed information from them in the ABAP program, such as the sum of a column or the number of rows. If you transport the rows into the ABAP program and evaluate them there, you will be passing too much data, in breach of the second efficiency rule. Instead, you can use **aggregate functions** in the SELECT clause, whereby only the result is passed. Two other clauses of the SELECT statement, the GROUP BY clause and the HAVING clause, support the grouping and selection of the required rows.

Aggregate function

Possible aggregate functions are MAX, MIN, AVG, SUM, and COUNT. You can enter the name of a column in the SELECT clause as an argument of such an aggregate function. If the SELECT clause contains normal column specifications in parallel to aggregate functions, the former must be listed in the GROUP BY clause. Conversely, a single value must be calculated from the values of all the columns not listed in the

9. The selection must therefore be uniquely specified in the WHERE clause.

GROUP BY clause, with the aid of aggregate functions. The GROUP BY clause causes all rows that have the same contents in certain columns to be condensed into one row. The aggregate function calculation takes places for such a group and the result is placed in the corresponding column of the condensed row:

```
SELECT    carrid connid SUM( seatsocc )
FROM      sflight
INTO      (wa_carrid, wa_connid, sum_seatsocc)
GROUP BY  carrid connid
WHERE     fldate BETWEEN ....
  ...
ENDSELECT.
```

The above SELECT statement groups all the rows with the same contents in the carrid and connid columns into a row and all the values of the seatsocc column are added up.

GROUP BY clause

The GROUP BY clause can only be used if individual columns are specified in the SELECT clause. For the INTO clause, therefore, only a list of elementary data objects or the INTO CORRESPONDING FIELDS addition can be used. If you want to import the selected data into the components of a structure with the same name using CORRESPONDING FIELDS, the question to be asked is how you can allocate the aggregate functions to these components.

To do this, you can define alternative names for individual column specifications or aggregate functions in the SELECT clause using the AS addition.

```
DATA: BEGIN OF wa_sflight,
        carrid    TYPE sflight-carrid,
        minimum   TYPE sflight-price,
        maximum   TYPE sflight-price,
      END OF wa_sflight.
...
SELECT    carrid
          MIN( price ) AS minimum
          MAX( price ) AS maximum
FROM      sflight
INTO      CORRESPONDING FIELDS OF wa_sflight
GROUP BY carrid.
  ...
ENDSELECT.
```

The CORRESPONDING FIELDS addition to the INTO clause takes into account the alternative column names and not the actual names of the columns.[10] In the above example, therefore, the results of the aggregate functions MIN and MAX are assigned to the minimum and maximum components of the wa_sflight structure.

10. In addition, the alternative column names can now only be used in the ORDER BY clause in order to sort by aggregate functions.

HAVING clause

If you want to restrict the number of rows grouped together with the GROUP BY clause using conditions, you must use the HAVING clause instead of the WHERE clause. The HAVING clause can only be used in connection with the GROUP BY clause. The possible conditions within the HAVING clause fully correspond to those of the WHERE clause, whereby in the logical expressions the only columns that can be used are the ones used both in the SELECT clause as well as the GROUP BY clause. However, for all other columns of the database tables from the FROM clause, you can use aggregate expressions as operands in the HAVING clause:

```
SELECT    connid
FROM      sflight
INTO      ...
WHERE     carrid = ...
GROUP BY connid
HAVING    connid = ... AND
          SUM( seatsocc ) > 300.
```

To set normal conditions for columns that are not listed in the GROUP BY clause, you additionally use the standard WHERE clause.

Sorting rows

You can sort the rows of the selection in the SELECT statement according to the contents of columns with the ORDER BY clause. If all the columns of the primary key are specified in the SELECT column (e.g., with *) and the FROM clause contains only a single database table and no view, you can sort in ascending order according to the primary key:

```
SELECT    *
FROM      spfli
...
ORDER BY PRIMARY KEY.
```

ORDER BY clause

For arbitrary SELECT and FROM clause you can sort by any column in ascending or descending order:

```
SELECT    carrid connid MAX( seatsocc ) AS max
FROM      sflight
INTO      ...
GROUP BY carrid connid
ORDER BY carrid ASCENDING
          max    DESCENDING.
```

By defining alternative names for aggregate functions in the SELECT clause, you can also sort by the results of these. Due to the fifth efficiency rule, you should only use the ORDER BY clause if the database system uses the same index for sorting as for reading. Otherwise it is better to import into an internal table and then sort in the program. You can find the indexes used with the SQL Trace tool.

SELECT *statement summary*

We will now conclude our description of the SELECT statement with a summary. Using efficiency considerations arising from the four basic questions concerning the reading of data, as listed at the beginning of this chapter, we have guided you to more specialized clauses. In this way, you have become familiar with the seven clauses of the SELECT statement. Figure 8.5 shows a final overview of the SELECT statement and its clauses.

When the database is accessed, all the clauses fulfill their specific tasks. These can be summarized as follows:

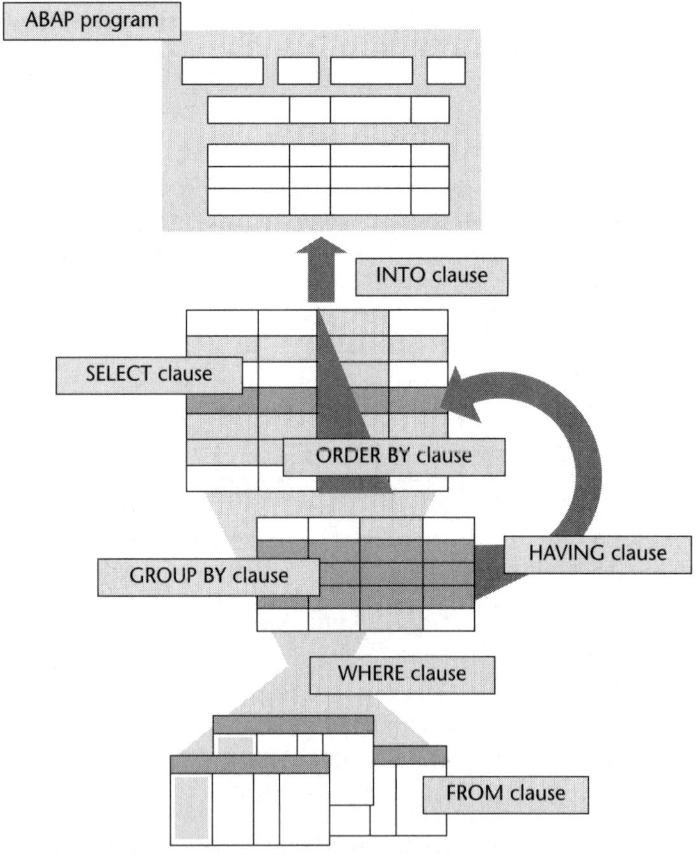

FIGURE 8.5 Overview of all clauses of the SELECT statement

- The `FROM` clause determines one or more database tables for access.
- The `WHERE` clause sets conditions for which rows of the database tables are to be searched and read.
- The `GROUP BY` clause condenses several rows into a single row and the `HAVING` clause sets conditions for the result.
- The `SELECT` clause determines the structure of the selection by defining which columns are read and by defining whether the result is single or multi-row.
- The `ORDER BY` clause sorts the result.
- The `INTO` clause passes the result to suitable data objects in the ABAP program.

All the clauses are interdependent. The interaction of the clauses is essential for ensuring that the `SELECT` statement is syntactically correct. As you know from our description of the basic `SELECT` statement, specifying target areas of the `INTO` clause is directly dependent on the specifications in the `SELECT` clause.

If you use all the functions of the `SELECT` statement, it becomes a very powerful statement that you can use to perform complex database queries with a single access. A single `SELECT` statement can therefore contain a great deal of code covering several program lines (see, for example, Listing 8.12). To maintain the readability of a program, it is best to make the clauses of the `SELECT` statement clear through their position in the source code. In our Listings, for example, we have placed the corresponding additions at the beginning of a line, like statements.

Reading data via the cursor

With the `SELECT` statement, passing data from the selection into the ABAP program is part of the statement itself and is carried out by the `INTO` clause. The result defined by the other clauses is transported in packages of up to 32 KB from the database system to the application server and is then passed by the `INTO` clause to the ABAP program.

Cursor handling

Open SQL provides you with the option of detaching the passing of data to the ABAP program from the `SELECT` statement, by programming your own cursor handling. Under certain conditions (foreign key relationship between the database tables and sorting via the foreign key) you can reduce the number of database accesses when accessing several database tables and thereby support the third efficiency rule. Listing 8.13 shows a program that reads the data of a database with explicit cursor handling.

LISTING 8.13 Explicit cursor handling with `SELECT`

```
REPORT s_open_cursor.

* Global Declarations
PARAMETERS p_carrid TYPE spfli-carrid.
```

```
DATA: cur TYPE cursor,
      wa_carrid TYPE spfli-carrid,
      wa_connid TYPE spfli-connid,
      wa_cityfrom TYPE spfli-cityfrom,
      wa_cityto   TYPE spfli-cityto.

* Processing Blocks
START-OF-SELECTION.
  OPEN CURSOR cur FOR
    SELECT   carrid connid cityfrom cityto
    FROM     spfli
    WHERE    carrid = p_carrid
    ORDER BY carrid.
  ...
  DO.
    FETCH NEXT CURSOR cur
    INTO  (wa_carrid, wa_connid, wa_cityfrom, wa_cityto).
    ...
    IF sy-subrc <> 0.
      CLOSE CURSOR cur.
      EXIT.
    ENDIF.
  ENDDO.
```

OPEN CURSOR

In the program, after the declaration of a cursor with the special `cursor` data type, the cursor is opened for a selection through the `OPEN CURSOR` statement. The selection is defined by a normal `SELECT` statement that can contain all clauses, except for the `INTO` clause. The selection must be multi-row and the `SINGLE` addition cannot be used in the `SELECT` clause.

An opened cursor can be considered in the same way as a reference variable. It points to an internal handler that processes the selection. Through assignments, several cursors can point to a selection. Moreover, independent cursors can be opened for a database table.

FETCH

To read the data from the selection of a cursor into the ABAP program you use the statement `FETCH NEXT CURSOR` in connection with an `INTO` clause. All `INTO` clauses with flat target areas of the `SELECT` statement can be used. The statement reads the rows that are required to fill the target area of the `INTO` clause and moves the cursor to the next row to be read. As long as not all the rows of the selection have been read, `sy-subrc` will be set to zero, otherwise to four. In the `sy-dbcnt` system field after `FETCH`, you find the number of rows read by the cursor so far. The `FETCH` statement is the only way of moving the cursor. The cursor cannot, therefore, be programmed to be positioned automatically on certain lines of the selection.

CLOSE CURSOR

You should close cursors that are no longer required using CLOSE CURSOR, as only a limited number of cursors can be open at the same time.

You can use this kind of specific cursor handling, for example, to read in parallel database tables that are linked through foreign key relationships. This procedure is more efficient than nested SELECT loops because the cursor does not always have to be reset for the inner loop. On the other hand, programming the cursor administration is not so easy for nested loops, and consequently you should always consider other options such as joins, subqueries, and the FOR ALL ENTRIES additions.

Modifying data in database tables

The Open SQL statements for modifying data in database tables are INSERT, UPDATE, MODIFY, and DELETE. In this section we will briefly explore how to program these statements, which are less complex than the entire SELECT statement. It is important to note, however, that Open SQL statements do not check authorizations, nor do they ensure that data in the database is consistent. In order to modify data in databases consistently, you need to understand the basics of consistent data retention in an SAP System. This topic will be introduced in Section 8.1.4.

Efficiency

In all the following statements there are individual operations that change single rows of a database table, and mass operations that change several rows of a database table in a single access. In keeping with the third efficiency rule, you should use mass operations instead of repeatedly processing single lines for modifying database tables.

Inserting table rows

You can use the INSERT statement to add single rows to a database table.

```
INSERT  INTO spfli
VALUES        wa_spfli.
```

or

```
INSERT spfli
FROM   wa_spfli.
```

Single row

Both statements are equal. They add the contents of the work area wa_spfli to the database table spfli. As in all Open SQL statements, the database table can also be dynamically specified as the contents of a variable in a bracket expression. The work area should have the same structure as the database table. The operation is only performed if the database table does not already contain an entry with the same primary key. Otherwise sy-subrc is set to four instead of zero.

Several rows

To insert several rows at once, simply use:

```
INSERT spfli
FROM   TABLE spfli_tab.
```

This statement adds all the rows from the spfli_tab internal table to spfli. If just one row of the internal table cannot be added because the same primary key is already present in the database table, the program will be terminated. You can avoid this by using the addition.

```
... ACCEPTING DUPLICATE KEYS
```

Then the respective row of the internal table will simply be rejected and sy-subrc set to four. You can always find the number of rows actually added in sy-dbcnt.

Modifying table rows

To modify existing table rows you use the UPDATE statement. You can specifically modify individual columns or overwrite the entire row with a work area. To modify individual columns use:

```
UPDATE  sflight
SET     planetype = ...
        price = price - ...
WHERE   ...
```

Condition

In all rows of the sflight database table that satisfy the conditions of the WHERE clause, this statement changes the columns specified in the SET clause. In the SET clause, columns can either be overwritten, or values can be added with + or subtracted with -. Columns of the same table can also be specified for these values. Without the WHERE clause, all the table rows are changed. The sy-subrc and sy-dbcnt system fields are supplied as usual in Open SQL.

Work area

It is not possible to dynamically specify the database table when using the SET clause, but you can do so when replacing entire rows.[11] To replace an entire row, write:

```
UPDATE sflight
FROM   wa_sflight.
```

And for several rows:

```
UPDATE sflight
FROM   TABLE sflight_tab.
```

The data type of wa_sflight or the row type of the internal table sflight_tab should correspond to the data type of the database. The first statement replaces the row with the same primary key as in wa_sflight; the second statement does this for all the rows of the internal table. Both statements set sy-subrc to zero if all the rows could be

11. As of Release 6.10, this specification will also be available dynamically along with many other clauses in Open SQL statements that were previously only available statically.

replaced, otherwise to four. The number of rows actually replaced can be found, as always, in sy-dbcnt. Caution: if the internal table is empty, both system fields will be 0!

Efficiency

Remember, however, that replacing entire rows will often require the rows to be read first with the SELECT statement. Check whether you can avoid unnecessary multiple accesses by using the WHERE clause (third efficiency rule). Moreover, you reduce the amount of data transferred if you only modify the required columns with the SET additions instead of transporting the entire row (second efficiency rule).

Adding or modifying table rows

If you are not sure, before making a change to the database, whether a row with the required parameter key exists, i.e., whether you need to add or modify, you can use the MODIFY statement. For single rows you write:

```
MODIFY  spfli
FROM    wa_spfli.
```

And for several rows:

```
MODIFY spli
FROM    TABLE spfli_tab.
```

These statements work like INSERT if no row with the same primary key exists in wa_spfli or in a row in the internal table spfli_tab. Otherwise, they work like UPDATE. But, even with MODIFY, it can happen that a row cannot be processed at all. For example, a row with the same unique secondary index can already exist in the database table. Sy-subrc and sy-dbcnt are always set accordingly.

Efficiency

For efficiency reasons, you should not always replace INSERT or UPDATE with MODIFY. You should only use it when absolutely necessary.

Deleting table rows

You can delete table rows using the DELETE statement. You can either select the rows to be deleted with a WHERE clause or you can use work areas. In the former case the syntax is:

```
DELETE
FROM    spfli
WHERE   ...
```

Condition

This statement deletes all the lines of the spfli database table that satisfy the conditions of the WHERE clause. Program the conditions very carefully to avoid accidentally deleting the wrong rows. For example, it is sufficient to specify an empty internal table as a dynamic WHERE clause in order to delete all the rows.

Work area

To specify the rows to be deleted through work areas, use the same syntax as with the previous change statements, i.e.:

```
DELETE spfli
FROM   wa_spfli.
```

for single rows or

```
DELETE spfli
FROM   TABLE spfli_tab.
```

for several rows. Remember that the FROM clause for this kind of statement does not specify the database table as in the SELECT statement. The statements delete all the rows with the same primary key as in wa_spfli or as in the rows of the spfli_tab internal table, and set sy-subrc and sy-dbcnt, depending on the result. The work area or the internal table only needs to contain the columns of the primary key.

Efficiency

As with the UPDATE statement, it can be more efficient in the DELETE statement to use the WHERE clause if this avoids unnecessary multiple accesses.

8.1.4 Consistent data retention

Retaining data consistently in an SAP System is a complex issue that we can only touch on briefly in our consideration of the ABAP programming language. The basic aspects of the concepts for consistent data retention have more to do with the client – server architecture of an SAP System than with ABAP. Two main concepts play a role here: the LUW concept (Logical Unit of Work), which governs the time taken for a consistent status to pass to another consistent status, and the locking concept, which prevents unauthorized access to data during a LUW.

SAP's LUW concept

The data of an application that is usually divided among various database tables must normally be in a consistent condition. However, while an application program is running, data is often in a temporarily inconsistent condition. In the case of a bank transfer, for example, this can be the time difference between debiting one account and crediting another. According to what we have learned about Open SQL, this is at least the time interval between two consecutive UPDATE statements. In general, however, the time interval is much longer because other work has to be performed. A consistent data status is achieved, therefore, only when the last respective statement has been completed. If an error occurs during this time interval, the database must under no circumstances remain in an inconsistent status. Instead there must be a way of restoring the initial status.

Logical Unit of Work

The time interval between two consistent statuses, that is, the mechanism that runs during this time is called the LUW (Logical Unit of Work). Each LUW is always ended with a **commit**, which sets all changes made, or a **rollback**, which can undo all the changes. How are LUWs implemented in ABAP programming? To understand this, we must first explore database LUWs.

Database LUW

A database LUW is the mechanism of the database system that ensures a consistent data status within the database, independently of the SAP System. The database system executes a database LUW either fully or not at all. Database changes within a database LUW are saved to the database for good only after a database commit. In the event of an error, they can be removed again through a database rollback.

The main question facing the ABAP programmer is how are database commits and database rollbacks triggered. Of course, there are ABAP statements for this, but, for a deeper understanding, implicit commits and rollbacks that result from the architecture of the SAP Basis System are much more important to begin with.

Work process

You will recall that in Chapter 3 we introduced the concept of a work process. An active ABAP program takes up a work process and each work process is registered in the database system as a user. A work process cannot execute several database LUWs in parallel, and, conversely, several work processes cannot affect a single database LUW. However, in general an ABAP program is not linked to just a single work process. In dialog processing, for example, a work process is only responsible for an ABAP program for the duration of a dialog step. While the user makes entries at the screen and the ABAP program is inactive, it works for another program.

Database commit

As a result of what we have said above, a work process must always end a database LUW and place an implicit database commit when

- a dialog step ends, i.e., a new screen is displayed
- another work process continues program execution, which is the case when calling and returning from remotely-called function modules (RFC).

For dialog-oriented programs, it is therefore important that each new screen, including an error message in a dialog box sent with `MESSAGE`, stores all database changes made previously and that no database rollback is possible thereafter.

Just as there are implicit database commits, implicit database rollbacks can occur in the following cases:

- In the current ABAP program, a runtime error occurs (program termination with short dump, see Section 4.8.2).
- An ABAP program is terminated using the `MESSAGE` statement that sends a message of type A or X (see Section 7.4.3).

These restore the condition before the database LUW. The start of the database LUW was either the start of a dialog step or the end of the previous LUW through a database commit or rollback.

From what we have said above, it is clear that at the end of a dialog step you have to ensure a consistent status in the database. Therefore, you cannot debit an account at the PAI event of a screen and credit another account at the PAI event of a consecutive screen because, after the layout of the first consecutive screen is sent, there will be no opportunity for database rollback in case of an error. You would have to document and undo the changes yourself.

However, from an application programmer's viewpoint, a LUW must definitely be able to extend over several dialog steps. While each user action that triggers a PAI event opens a new dialog step and therefore a new database LUW, you only want to store your previous entries when the user selects a specific function like **Save**.

These considerations bring us to the concept of SAP LUW and the methods of implementing it.

SAP LUW

We apply the term "SAP LUW" to a logical unit in ABAP application programs that behaves like an LUW, i.e., it generates a consistent data status at the end. An SAP LUW can extend over several dialog steps. However, as we learned in the previous section, the actual database changes with Open SQL statements may not be divided up over several dialog steps.

Bundling

The idea behind implementing an SAP LUW is that the required database changes are not executed directly, but collected over a sequence of various dialog steps and then run in a single database LUW, bundled together in the last dialog step of the SAP LUW. In this way, all the database changes are subjected to the LUW mechanism of the database and the initial status is automatically restored in the database in the event of an error.

An SAP LUW is, therefore, a logically coherent unit of dialog steps whose database changes are executed within a single database LUW (see Figure 8.6).

In ABAP programs you have two mechanisms for bundling database changes in a dialog step. Both are based on classical procedures: bundling through function modules (updating) and bundling through subroutines. ABAP Objects does not yet provide any special technique for creating LUWs.

Updating

You can mark function modules in the Function Builder as update modules. If you call such a function module with

```
CALL FUNCTION ... IN UPDATE TASK.
```

it is not executed directly, but rather marked for executing in a special updating work process. You can therefore encapsulate all modifying database accesses in function modules and call them through distributed dialog steps. If you have completed your SAP LUW, you must only ensure that all the collected calls are being processed or, in the event of an error, simply rejected.

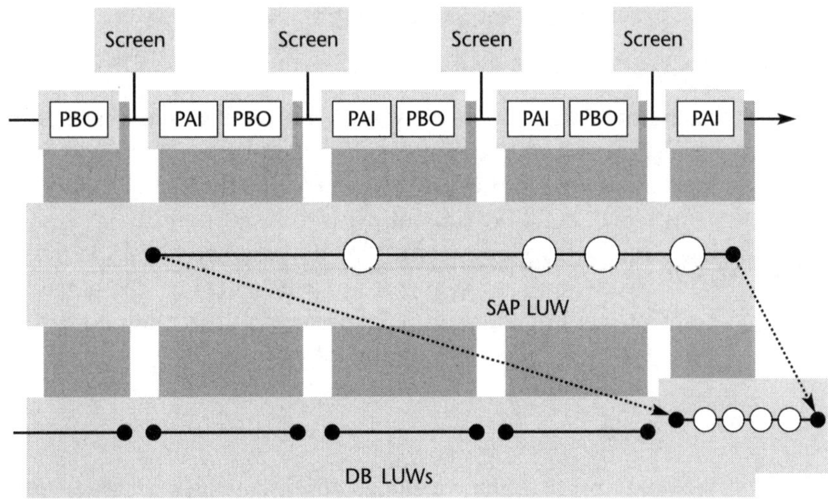

FIGURE 8.6 SAP LUW and DB LUWs

Commit

This is where the above-mentioned specific ABAP statements for commit and roll-back come into effect. The statement

```
COMMIT WORK.
```

terminates the SAP LUW for the ABAP program and triggers the update in the updating work process. This performs the update in a single database LUW. Depending on the technical attributes of the function modules and the specifications on calling, the update can either be synchronous or asynchronous. The ABAP program can either wait for the process to finish or continue processing immediately.

Rollback

The statement

```
ROLLBACK WORK.
```

also terminates an SAP LUW. The collected update modules are then deleted from the record list instead of being executed. The `ROLLBACK` statement, therefore, allows you to do on a logical level what the database does in error situations, namely to undo all the changes or rather not run them at all.

Note that both these statements, in addition to handling the SAP LUW, always trigger an explicit database commit or rollback. You can therefore also use these statements to generate several database LUWs within a dialog step. If you run `COMMIT WORK` or `ROLLBACK WORK` after a database change, the changes will be saved or canceled.

The main application, however, is generating SAP LUWs. Within the procedures of bundling, i.e., an update module or a subroutine described below, the `COMMIT WORK` and `ROLLBACK WORK` statements are not allowed.

Subroutine

You can register subroutines with the statement

```
PERFORM ... ON COMMIT.
```

Subroutines called in this way are only executed at the next COMMIT WORK statement. You can therefore also implement your database changes in subroutines and execute them all at once in the dialog step in which the COMMIT WORK statement is executed.

Although bundling subroutines is more efficient than bundling update modules, it has a major disadvantage in that no parameters can be passed with PERFORM ON COMMIT. You must somehow store specific data for the database changes in the program or in the memory (ABAP memory) until the end of the SAP LUW without generating inconsistencies during the process!

Transactions

We have now basically concluded our discussion of data consistency and LUWs without having mentioned the term transaction a single time, although you have mostly found these topics before under the term transaction programming. This term is derived from general language usage where a transaction is a sequence of coherent business actions that obtains and manipulates data and, ultimately, produces a consistent data status.

According to what we have said so far, the SAP LUWs alone are responsible for consistent data statuses in ABAP programs. You yourself determine the limits of an SAP LUW with the keywords COMMIT or ROLLBACK. An ABAP program can thus be divided into any number of SAP LUWs, whereby the end of an ABAP program always terminates the last SAP LUW. By calling ABAP programs with CALL TRANSACTION or SUBMIT ... AND RETURN, SAP LUWs can also be nested. And, of course, SAP LUWs are not restricted to ABAP programs that are executed via a transaction code. They can be used equally in executable programs.

Transaction programming

The term transaction as an execution mode of an ABAP program comes from the historical distinction between reporting and dialog programming. While in reporting, which was performed solely in executable programs and with read database access, you didn't have to worry about data consistency; only module pools performed write database access and thereby represented the corresponding business transaction.[12] This is why the term transaction programming was often synonymous with programming module pools, and the abbreviation, which – from a technical viewpoint – the user only uses to call the first screen of a program, was referred to as a transaction code.

Just as we did not use the term report in our description of read access, we therefore also deliberately avoided the term transaction processing when discussing data consistency. Both terms describe more the purposes of an ABAP program than the actual technical implementation. From a technical viewpoint, there is nothing wrong

12. Prior to dialog programs, database changes were performed in batch mode only, and a transaction was identical to a database transaction.

with a module pool executed by a transaction code generating a report or an executable program performing a business transaction. It is up to you how you use the various techniques as efficiently as possible for your tasks.

The SAP locking concept

In the previous section, we introduced you to SAP LUWs as the basis for consistent data retention in ABAP programs. We did not take the issue of locks into account, which is also closely linked to data consistency. While an ABAP program makes changes to the database, you must ensure that a second ABAP program does not have write access to the same data.

Database locks

Let's start, as in the previous section, at the database level. The database system automatically provides a locking mechanism with a database LUW that ensures that simultaneous changes to data do not result in inconsistencies. To do so, all modified data sets are locked. However, these locks are removed with each database commit or rollback and are thereby linked to the duration of a database LUW. For SAP LUWs that are defined independently of database LUWs and dialog steps in the ABAP program, we therefore need another locking mechanism.

SAP locks

The requirements for SAP LUW locks are that they remain until the end of an SAP LUW and are visible to all programs of the SAP System. To enable this, SAP Basis provides a logical locking mechanism that is based on entries in a central lock table on a special application server.[13]

Lock table

This locking mechanism does not place physical locks in the database table. An ABAP program sends the keys of the table entries it wishes to lock to the lock table and, prior to an access of database tables, all ABAP programs must check in the lock table that the required entries are not locked. There is, however, no mechanism to force this procedure. The entire mechanism is based on the cooperation of application programs.

Moreover, the logical locks are only loosely linked to SAP LUWs. You can set and remove a lock any time in the ABAP program. Nevertheless, SAP locks are implicitly removed when an SAP LUW is terminated by the end of an update or the end of the ABAP program.

Lock object

To set an SAP lock, you must create a *lock object*[14] in the ABAP Dictionary or, for example, through a where-used list, find out which lock objects already exist for a

13. An SAP System contains a maximum of one application server with an **Enqueue Work Process**. This maintains the central lock table of the entire system in its memory. The function modules for setting and deleting locks are executed in this work process.
14. A lock object is a repository object but not an object of ABAP Objects.

database table. One or more database tables and key fields can be specified for one or more rows in a lock object. When a lock object is activated, two function modules with the names ENQUEUE_<LOCK OBJECT> and DEQUEUE_<LOCK object> are automatically created. When you call these function modules, you set or delete an SAP lock for all the database lines specified in the lock object.

ENQUEUE/ DEQUEUE

The ENQUEUE_<LOCK object> function module sets an SAP lock through entries in the central lock table of the SAP System. The function module can be informed through parameter transmission whether a read or write lock should be set. When a read lock is set for an object, no other ABAP programs can set a write lock for the same object, but they can set other read locks. A write lock locks an object exclusively for a program.

A lock is queried simply when you try to lock the object with this function module. If the lock cannot be set, the function module triggers a corresponding exception.

Figure 8.7 shows, as an example, the EDEMOFLHT lock object in the ABAP Dictionary. This lock object allows shared locks to be set for the SFLIGHT and SBOOK tables. The default setting for the lock mode is write lock, but it can be overridden if the corresponding function module is called. The **lock parameter** tab page contains all the key fields of the tables for which values can be passed when the function module is called.

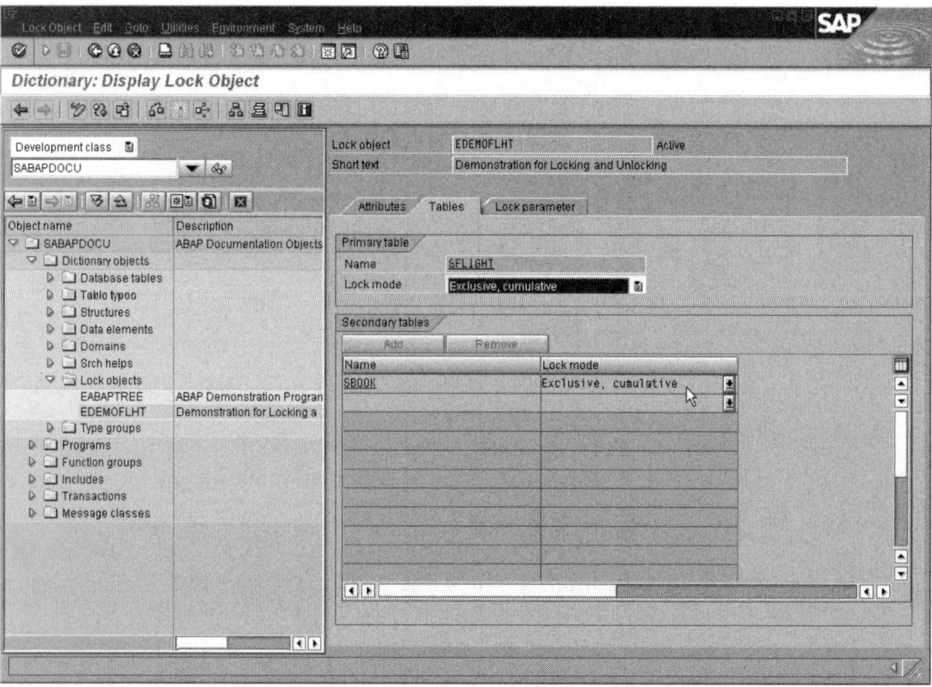

FIGURE 8.7 A lock object. Copyright © SAP AG

LISTING 8.14 Setting a SAP lock

```
CALL FUNCTION 'ENQUEUE_EDEMOFLHT'
     EXPORTING
          mode_sflight    = 'X'
          carrid          = wa_sflight-carrid
          connid          = wa_sflight-connid
          fldate          = wa_sflight-fldate
     EXCEPTIONS
          foreign_lock    = 1
          system_failure  = 2
          OTHERS          = 3.

CASE sy-subrc.
  WHEN 0.
    MESSAGE i888 WITH 'Enqueue successful'.
  WHEN 1.
    MESSAGE e888 WITH 'Record already locked by' sy-msgv1.
  WHEN 2 OR 3.
    MESSAGE e888 WITH 'Error in enqueue!'.
ENDCASE.
```

Listing 8.14 shows how an SAP lock with the EDEMOFLHT lock object is set by calling the corresponding function module. By passing "X" (exclusive) to mode_sflight, a write lock is set for all lines in SFLIGHT and SBOOK whose keys correspond to the values passed to carrid, connid and fldate. The success of the locking action is evaluated by the exceptions of the function module. Note also the use of sy-msgv1 (see Section 7.4.3).

Calling DEQUEUE_EDEMOFLHT to remove the block runs in the same manner. Using transaction SM12 you can always find out about the contents of the central lock table for certain objects. In the SAP Basis System you will find the DEMO_TRANSACTION_ENQUEUE program that demonstrates locking and unlocking and from which the above source code has been taken.

8.1.5 Special sections on database access

Now that we have described the main topics governing database access, we will briefly explore a few special features about database access in the SAP System.

Clients and client handling

If you look at the structure of a database table in the ABAP Dictionary (see for example Figure 8.2), you will see that the first column generally has the name MANDT. Yet we have not used this column in any of our previous Open SQL statements! Although MANDT clearly belongs to the table key, we have not placed any corresponding conditions in our WHERE clauses. Why is this?

Client column

A single SAP application system, such as an R/3 system, can handle the application data of several independent business areas. These areas are called **clients** and have a client number. Upon registration, the user determines which client he or she wants to work in. The first column and also the first key field of every database table for application data created with the ABAP Dictionary is generally called MANDT and contains the client number. However, there are also cross-client system tables without a client number whose data is used equally by all clients. Repository objects processed using the ABAP Workbench, for example, are stored on a cross-client basis.

Client handling

Open SQL statements work as standard with automatic client handling. Statements that access client-specific application tables, read and edit only the data of the current client. It is not possible to specify a condition for the client in the WHERE clause of Open SQL statements. The system will then report an error during the syntax check, or a runtime error will occur. The MANDT column of a database table cannot be modified with Open SQL statements. If a different client is specified in modifying statements, the ABAP runtime environment overrides it automatically with the current client before the Open SQL statement is forwarded to the database interface.

Should it be necessary to specify the client in an Open SQL statement specifically because the data of a different business area of the same SAP System needs to be accessed, the

```
... CLIENT SPECIFIED ....
```

addition must be entered directly behind the name of the database table. This addition deactivates automatic client handling. The client field can then be used in the WHERE clause as well as in the table work area.

Buffering database tables

Each database access puts a load on the database. If tables are often read but seldom modified, it is appropriate to reduce the load on the database by buffering the data read in the first access on the application server and then having the data available to all applications of the same server.

When a table is defined in the ABAP Dictionary, you can specify whether and how a table is buffered. There is a full buffering type that buffers the whole table, a generic buffering type that buffers certain areas, and a partial buffering type that buffers single records.

Synchronization

With buffered tables, the read statements of Open SQL automatically access the buffer first and then the database. Control of the synchronization between various buffers or between buffers and database takes place in the database interface. For tables that are often read and seldom modified and tables where it can be accepted that data changes will be available on the other applications servers only after approximately 60 seconds as opposed to immediately, switching on the buffering can result in between 50 and 500-fold efficiency gains.

The `FROM` clause of the `SELECT` statement has a `BYPASSING BUFFER` addition that bypasses this buffering in urgent cases. In addition, buffering is also bypassed by the `SELECT DISTINCT` statement, for joins in the `FROM` clause, for aggregate functions in the `SELECT` clause, for the `IS NULL` condition, for subqueries in the `WHERE` clause, and for the use of the `GROUP BY` clause or the `ORDER BY` clause (except for `ORDER BY PRIMARY KEY`). These `SELECT` statements should therefore be avoided in connection with buffered tables.

Native SQL

The statements of Open SQL are converted by the database interface into platform-specific SQL commands in the background and forwarded to the database. ABAP programs that work with Open SQL are thus independent of the database used. However, in special cases it can be necessary to access the database's programming interface directly using specific SQL statements. In ABAP we call database-specific SQL statements Native SQL. To use Native SQL statements, you must implement them between the `EXEC SQL` and `ENDEXEC` ABAP statements.

EXEC SQL

All statements between `EXEC SQL` and `ENDEXEC` are forwarded by the database interface directly to the database system. They are not part of ABAP and are not checked by the ABAP syntax check. For example, Native SQL statements are not ended by full stops, but can be ended by semi-colons. If there is an error, it will only cause the program to terminate during runtime, but it can be analyzed in the short dump.

Host variable

In order to pass data between the ABAP program and the database, data objects of the ABAP program can be used as host variables in Native SQL statements by prefixing them with a colon (:).

When you use Native SQL there is no automatic client handling. This is why, when you access a client-specific table of the ABAP Dictionary, the client must be specified in the `WHERE` condition of Native SQL statements.

A program that uses Native SQL is dependent on the database system installed. When you develop generally valid SAP applications you should try to avoid using Native SQL. However, Native SQL is of course used in some Basis components of the SAP System, for example, in the ABAP Dictionary for creating or modifying database tables, since Open SQL does not contain any DDL statements. Although you can use Native SQL to create database tables in application programs, these are then not subject to the SAP System administration. In this case you can only access these database tables with Native SQL and not with Open SQL. Listing 8.15 shows an example of use of Native SQL in which a database table is created, filled, read, and deleted again.

LISTING 8.15 Incorporating Native SQL in ABAP

```
REPORT s_native_sql.

DATA: wa1(10) TYPE c,
      wa2(10) TYPE c,
      key(10) TYPE c.

EXEC SQL.
  CREATE TABLE mytab (
           val1 char(10) NOT NULL,
           val2 char(10) NOT NULL,
           PRIMARY KEY (val1)      )
ENDEXEC.

DO 10 TIMES.
  wa1 = sy-index.
  wa2 = sy-index ** 2.
  EXEC sql.
    INSERT INTO mytab VALUES (:wa1, :wa2);
  ENDEXEC.
ENDDO.

key = 5.
EXEC SQL.
  SELECT val1,  val2
  INTO   :wa1, :wa2
  FROM   mytab
  WHERE  val1 = :key
ENDEXEC.

WRITE: / wa1, wa2.

EXEC SQL.
  DROP TABLE mytab
ENDEXEC.
```

8.2 FILE INTERFACES

The data with which ABAP programs work are contained mainly in the central database of the SAP System. However, ABAP programs can also access the file system of the two other layers of the client–server architecture. This means that you can also save or read persistent data on the workstations of the application layer or the desktop computers of the presentation layer.

A common application of these features is copying data into the SAP System. You can read files of any format from the file system of one of the servers into an ABAP program, edit them there, and then save them in the database. Conversely, you can also write data from the database into these files systems for further processing, e.g. with desktop applications for presentation purposes.

Descriptor

As the names of files and directory paths differ from operating system to operating system, programs that access files directly are generally not platform-independent. This is why you can create logical file names and logical paths with the FILE transaction that you link with actual descriptors for any platform required. In your ABAP program, for a logical name you then read the right name for the current platform with the FILE-GET_NAME function module.

8.2.1 Files on the application server

To write data to a file of the application server, use statements such as the ones used in the following example:

```
REPORT s_open_transfer_close.
...
PARAMETERS file(30) TYPE c DEFAULT '\tmp\myfile',
DATA wa_sflight TYPE sflight.
...
OPEN DATASET file FOR OUTPUT IN BINARY MODE.
SELECT * FROM sflight INTO wa_sflight.
  TRANSFER wa_sflight TO file.
ENDSELECT.
CLOSE DATASET file.
```

Writing

OPEN DATASET here opens the file whose name is in the file variable for writing in binary mode. TRANSFER passes the data of the wa_sflight structure during a loop row by row into this file, which is then closed by CLOSE DATASET. Files can also be opened in TEXT MODE as well as BINARY MODE, whereby an additional line break is attached for each TRANSFER. If you use the FOR APPENDING addition instead of FOR OUTPUT, an existing file will be extended instead of overwritten. You may only write the contents of flat data objects in files. Tables must therefore be transferred line by line.

Reading

To read a file of the application server, you proceed in a similar fashion:

```
PARAMETERS file(30) TYPE c DEFAULT '\tmp\myfile',
DATA: wa_sflight TYPE sflight,
      sflight_tab LIKE TABLE OF wa_sflight.
...
```

```
OPEN DATASET file FOR INPUT IN BINARY MODE.
DO.
  READ DATASET file INTO wa_sflight.
  IF sy-subrc <> 0.
    EXIT.
  ENDIF.
  APPEND wa_sflight TO sflight_tab.
ENDDO.
CLOSE DATASET file.
```

Here the file is opened for read access and is read into the wa_sflight structure with READ DATASET until the end of the file is reached and, therefore, sy-subrc is set to not equal zero. You must ensure that the data type of the variable you are importing into matches the contents of the file.

This should suffice as an overview of the ABAP file interface. We will conclude by revealing that you can also delete a file from the application server using the

```
DELETE DATASET ...
```

Deleting

statement. As deleting and, of course, overwriting files on the application server should not be done uncontrolled, an automatic authority check is performed before deleting as well as before opening the files to write. If there is no authorization, the program will terminate. To avoid this, the result of the authority check can be checked beforehand with the AUTHORITY_DATA_CHECK function module.

8.2.2 Files on the presentation server

There are no direct ABAP statements to store and read data in files on the presentation server. Instead, the SAP Basis System provides you with a set of function modules for this purpose.

Writing

To save a file on a computer of the presentation server, which is usually the PC at your workplace, you can use a function module call as in Listing 8.16:

LISTING 8.16 Saving data on the presentation server

```
REPORT s_ws_download_upload.
...
PARAMETERS: fname TYPE rlgrap-filename
                  DEFAULT 'c:\temp\myfile.dat',
            ftype TYPE lgrap-filetype DEFAULT 'BIN'.
DATA: sflight_tab LIKE TABLE OF sflight,
      tab_line LIKE LINE OF sflight_tab,
      leng TYPE i,
      lins TYPE i,
```

```
     size TYPE i.
...
SELECT * FROM sflight INTO TABLE sflight_tab.
DESCRIBE FIELD tab_line LENGTH leng.
DESCRIBE TABLE sflight_tab LINES lins.
size = leng * lins.

CALL FUNCTION 'WS_DOWNLOAD'
     EXPORTING
          filename            = fname
          filetype            = ftype
          bin_filesize        = size
     TABLES
          data_tab            = sflight_tab
     EXCEPTIONS
          file_open_error     = 1
          file_write_error    = 2
          invalid_filesize    = 3
          invalid_table_width = 4
          invalid_type        = 5
          OTHERS              = 6.
```

Data is transferred by passing an internal table to the data_tab parameter. The data format is determined by the filetype parameter. When the "BIN" value is passed, the data is transferred in binary form; when "ASC" is passed, the data is transferred row by row and at the end of each table row a line break is attached. With a binary transfer you must specify the length of the file yourself through the bin_filesize parameter. We calculated this length in Listing 8.16 from the row length and the number of rows of the internal table.

Reading

Reading files takes place in the reverse manner. As with reading files of the application server, you must ensure that files are imported into a data object that is suitable in terms of its data type. Listing 8.17 shows how the data that was stored in Listing 8.16 can be read again.

LISTING 8.17 Importing data from the presentation server

```
PARAMETERS: fname TYPE rlgrap-filename
                  DEFAULT 'c:\temp\myfile.dat',
            ftype TYPE rlgrap-filetype DEFAULT 'BIN'.
DATA: sflight_tab LIKE TABLE OF sflight.
...
CALL FUNCTION 'WS_UPLOAD'
     EXPORTING
```

```
        filename              = fname
        filetype              = ftype
    TABLES
        data_tab              = sflight_tab
    EXCEPTIONS
        file_open_error       = 1
        file_write_error      = 2
        invalid_filesize      = 3
        invalid_table_width   = 4
        invalid_type          = 5
        OTHERS                = 6.
```

In addition to these two function modules, there are two others called DOWNLOAD and UPLOAD. The function of these modules is the same as that of WS_DOWNLOAD and WS_UPLOAD, the only difference being that they conduct a user dialog in which the file name and data format can be specified. The parameters passed during the call are thus used as default values.

Information

There is also a function module called WS_QUERY with which you can obtain information about files on the presentation server before reading them.

8.3 STORING DATA AS CLUSTERS

The format of the data storage areas described in the two previous sections is independent of the SAP System. The data stored in database tables using ABAP programs can be accessed and evaluated through the programming interface of the database system, and the files on the application or presentation servers can be accessed through the respective operating system.

In this section we will introduce you to a way of storing data that can only be used by ABAP programs. You can group together the contents of data objects of an ABAP program in an ABAP-specific format in *clusters*, and save them in various storage media. Only ABAP programs understand this format and can import this kind of stored data into data objects again.

The statements for storing and reading data clusters are:

```
EXPORT p1 = f1
       p2 = f2
       ...
       pn = fn
       TO medium ID id.
```

and

```
IMPORT  p1 = f1
        p2 = f2
        ...
        pn = fn
        FROM medium ID id.
```

When you save, the data objects f_1 to f_n are passed to the data cluster under the names p_1 to p_n, and the data cluster is stored in compressed format in the medium storage medium with the id identification. You can store data objects of any data types, with the exception of references.

Identification

During importing, the medium storage medium is searched according to a data cluster of the id identification. The data objects stored under the names p_1 through pn are decompressed and transferred to the data objects f_1 to f_n. When they have been successfully imported, sy-subrc is set to zero. You must ensure that the data type of the target fields corresponds to the data type of the stored data objects.

If you already know these statements or if you take a look at the keyword documentation, you will see that we are introducing a syntax here that uses equals signs (=) between the names p_i, under which the data is stored, and the data objects fi. Instead of the equals sign, EXPORT could include FROM and IMPORT could include TO. We prefer the equals sign because we also have to use FROM and TO for specifying the storage medium and this makes the statement more readable.

Figure 8.8 shows the structure of a data cluster in the storage medium in diagram form. After an identification of the data cluster, there is a range of administrative information, depending on the storage medium, followed by the data area in which the passed data objects are stored in compressed form.

The following storage media are available

- ABAP Memory
- Database tables
- Cross-transaction application buffers

8.3.1 Data clusters in the ABAP Memory

You can store data clusters in the ABAP Memory (see Section 3.4) to pass data between the programs of a call chain. To do this, you simply enter

```
... {TO|FROM} MEMORY ...
```

ID	Administrative entries	Packed data

FIGURE 8.8 Data cluster structure

Context

when you specify medium. A data cluster lasts in the ABAP Memory as long as the context of a call chain. If the last internal mode of the stack of a call chain is deleted, the entire ABAP Memory is released. Using the statement:

```
FREE MEMORY  ID id.
```

you can specifically delete a data cluster from the ABAP Memory at any time.

LISTING 8.18 Storing data clusters in the ABAP Memory

```
REPORT s_export_to_memory.
...
DATA: spfli_tab TYPE STANDARD TABLE OF spfli,
      sflight_tab TYPE HASHED TABLE OF sflight
                  WITH UNIQUE KEY carrid connid fldate.
DATA mem_id(50) TYPE c.
...
  SELECT * FROM spfli INTO TABLE spfli_tab.
  SELECT * FROM sflight INTO TABLE sflight_tab.

  CONCATENATE sy-repid sy-datum sy-uzeit INTO mem_id.

  EXPORT  table1 = spfli_tab
          table2 = sflight_tab
          TO MEMORY ID mem_id.

  SUBMIT s_import_from_memory WITH p_id = mem_id.
```

The program in Listing 8.18 creates two internal tables in the ABAP Memory under an identification that we set up using the program name, date, and time and then calls a second program with SUBMIT. When you call the second program, the identification is passed to its selection screen parameter p_id.

LISTING 8.19 Reading data clusters from the ABAP Memory

```
REPORT s_import_from_memory.
...
PARAMETERS p_id(50) TYPE c.
DATA: connection_tab TYPE SORTED TABLE OF spfli
                     WITH UNIQUE KEY carrid connid,
      flight_tab TYPE SORTED TABLE OF sflight
                 WITH UNIQUE KEY carrid connid fldate.
...
```

```
IMPORT  table1 = connection_tab
        table2 = flight_tab
        FROM MEMORY ID p_id.
```

The second program in Listing 8.19 reads the data cluster with the identification passed in p_id and assigns the contents to two of its own internal tables that have the same row type but a different table type as the internal tables of the first program.

8.3.2 Data clusters in database tables

You can persistently store data clusters in the database. To do this, you must create database tables of a special structure that correspond to the structure of the data cluster from Figure 8.8. SAP provides a database table called INDX as a template that you can copy and modify. We therefore refer to INDX type tables.

INDX

Figure 8.9 shows the structure of the INDX table. All columns up to and including SRTF2 are preset and cannot be modified. They contain the identification of a data cluster, whereby, for example, the id specification is stored in the SRTFD field.

All columns between SRTF2 and CLUSTR are application-specific. You can store your own administrative information by passing a work area of the same type as the INDX

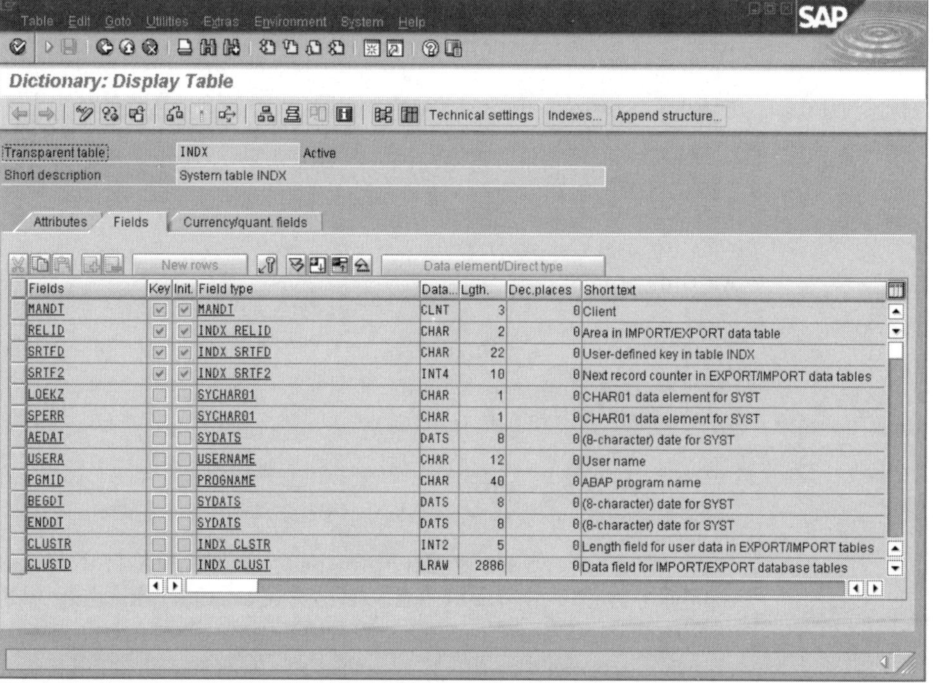

FIGURE 8.9 The INDX table. Copyright © SAP AG

type table with the EXPORT statement. You can modify this area of the database table as you wish, i.e., delete, rename, or add columns.

Identification

In addition to the identification passed with ID, data clusters in INDX type tables have a two-digit area identification (in the RELID column) that must also be specified when you enter medium. The medium expression for data clusters in INDX type tables is:

```
... {TO|FROM} DATABASE dbtab(ar) ...
```

where dbtab is the name of the INDX type database table and ar the two-digit area identification.

If you want to store your own administrative information for a data cluster, you must write it before the EXPORT statement in the corresponding components of a wa structure of the type of the INDX type table and pass the table with the

```
... FROM wa.
```

addition of the EXPORT statement to the database table. Conversely, you can read this information again with the IMPORT statement using the

```
... TO wa.
```

addition.

LISTING 8.20 Storing data clusters on the database

```
REPORT s_export_import_database.
...
db_id = sy-uzeit.
wa_indx-aedat = sy-datum.
wa_indx-usera = sy-uname.
wa_indx-pgmid = sy-repid.
...
EXPORT  table1 = spfli_tab
        table2 = sflight_tab
        TO DATABASE indx(ab)
        ID db_id
        FROM wa_indx.
```

Listing 8.20 shows a complete process for storing two internal tables on the INDX database. We specify the letters "ab" for the area identification. We use only the time as an identification and store the other administrative information in the table columns reserved for this by passing the wa_indx work area in the EXPORT statement. For the sake of simplicity, we use INDX itself. However, as mentioned previously, you should always use your own database tables for correct applications. In Listing 7.27 we used this kind of database table, for example, to store a binary graphic file.

LISTING 8.21 Reading data clusters from the database

```
IMPORT  table1 = connection_tab
        table2 = flight_tab
        FROM DATABASE indx(ab) ID db_id
        TO wa_indx.
```

Listing 8.21 shows how the stored internal tables can be read back into an ABAP program. Data clusters in databases are persistent and are retained until they are deleted with the statement:

```
DELETE FROM DATABASE  dbtab(ar) ID id.
```

Although INDX type tables are perfectly standard database tables of the ABAP Dictionary, you should only access them using the special statements for data clusters. Only in exceptional cases, for example, to delete all the data clusters of an area with a single statement, can you also use Open SQL statements. To do this, however, you must know the structure of an INDEX type table very well and it is advisable to examine the table and its contents initially with the Data Browser (transaction SE16) of the ABAP Workbench.

8.3.3 Data clusters in cross-transaction application buffers

The cross-transaction application buffer is a memory space in an application server that all ABAP programs in the SAP System running on the same application server can access. We have not drawn this memory space in Figure 3.12 as it would lie outside of the main session.

Data clusters in cross-transaction application buffers are arranged exactly like data clusters in database tables. The statements for storing, reading, and deleting clusters on the cross-transaction application buffer reflect the statements for database tables. The medium storage medium is specified as follows:

```
... {TO|FROM} SHARED BUFFER dbtab(ar) ...
```

You must even specify an INDX type database table dbtab whose structure is copied for storing the cluster on the buffer. This also gives you the option of storing your own administrative information for each cluster on the buffer using the FROM wa addition, and reading it again with INTO wa.

8.4 AUTHORITY CHECKS

To conclude our section on accessing external data, we must briefly examine the subject of authorization, which, although closely linked to editing persistent data, is generally not supported by the ABAP statements we have previously encountered. The only exception is the automatic authority check for write access to application server files. Each application system generally contains data in its database that not every user may have permission to access. However, no authority checks are linked to the Open SQL statements of an ABAP program. For this reason, you must not, under any circumstances, write a program that accesses critical data without taking prior caution and make it generally available to users. You must check that users who can call the program are also entitled to access the data contained therein.

8.4.1 Authorizations and authorization objects

A user's authorizations are assigned by system administration in the user master record. An authorization governs which data the user can access and how. A user's authorizations can be evaluated in the ABAP program.

Authorization object

In the SAP System, the interface between a user's authorizations and their evaluation in programs is achieved via **authorization objects** that, like lock objects, do not correspond to objects in ABAP Objects. An authorization object contains fields that represent activities such as reading and modifying or data such as key fields of database tables. These fields act as templates for authorization assignment and checks. Authorization objects are created in the ABAP Workbench through **Development – Other Tools – Authorization Objects**. During this process, several authorization objects are grouped together into object classes that, in turn, are assigned to individual applications.

When authorizations are allocated in the user master record, values for the fields of authorization objects are allocated for each user. In the example in Figure 8.10, the authorization object has two fields, CARRID and ACTVT, in which generic identifications for airline carriers and numerical values for activities can be entered. The resulting combinations indicate which airline carriers a user can access and using which activities. The identification for various activities can be found in the TACT and TACTZ tables.

Authorization profile

Of course, when authorizations are being assigned to users, not every authorization object has to be maintained individually for each user. Instead, one or more preset authorization profiles can be assigned to a user. These profiles contain specific default values for all the authorization objects of an SAP System.

As an ABAP programmer you can therefore access a set of authorization objects whose values define the authorizations a respective user has. You must consider which authorization object you want to use for your ABAP program and where you want to use it. If there is no suitable authorization object, you must create it yourself and inform system administration about it so that it can add it to its authorization profiles.

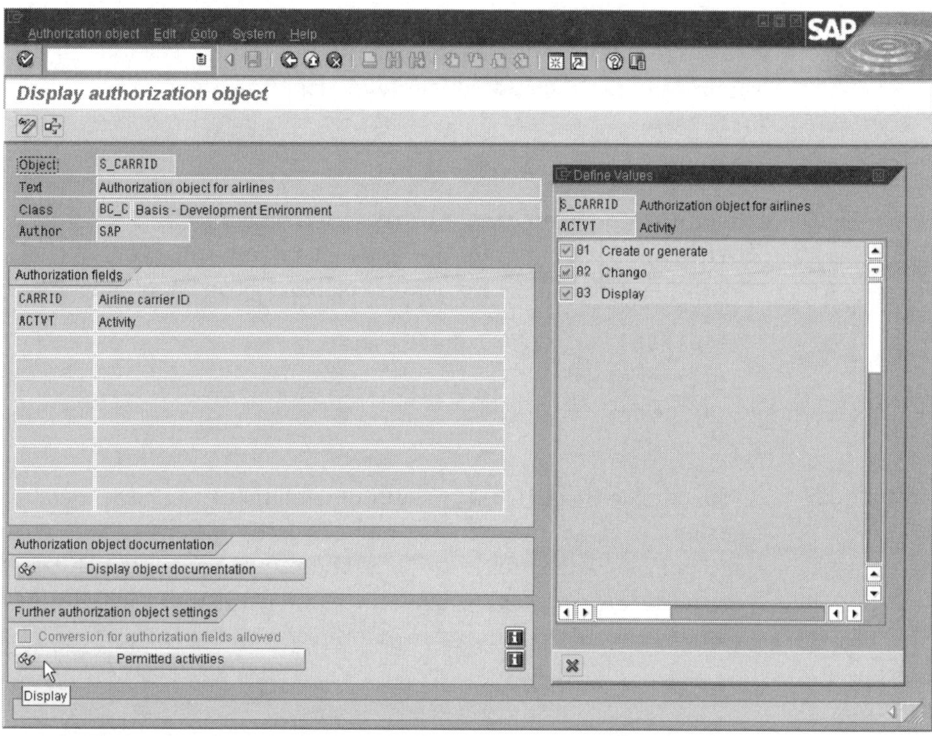

FIGURE 8.10 An authorization object. Copyright © SAP AG

8.4.2 Evaluating authorization objects

You have the following options, among others, for your ABAP programs to check user authorization for running a program.

Transaction execution authorization

When you create a transaction code (see Figure 7.9), you can enter the name of an authorization object directly in the **Authorization Object** field and, by selecting the **Value** key, specify values for the fields of the authorization object. If a user wants to run the transaction (also by calling a program with `CALL TRANSACTION`), the runtime environment checks these values against the values in the user master record. The transaction will only go ahead if the authorization is given. Otherwise a corresponding message is issued.

Authorization for running ABAP programs

The attributes of an ABAP program contain the **Authorization Groups** input field in which you can enter any given name. The authority group is linked with the

P_GROUP field of the S_DEVELOP and S_PROGRAM authority objects. By combining values in this field of the program attributes and in the user master record, authorizations can thus be allocated for individual ABAP programs.

Authority checks in ABAP programs

If an ABAP program cannot be protected by authorizations or if not all users authorized to run the program are allowed to perform every action, you can use the following statement in any processing block of an ABAP program:

```
AUTHORITY-CHECK  OBJECT auth_object
ID name1 FIELD f1
ID name2 FIELD f2
...
```

You can use the AUTHORITY-CHECK statement to check the authorizations of the current user in the name1, name2 fields of any given authorization object auth_object. You enter in f_1, f_2, ... the values against which the entries in the user master record are to be compared. You must list all the fields of the authorization object. To avoid checking a field, however, you can write

```
... ID name dummy
```

If the user has all authorizations, the statement sets sy-subrc to zero. If sy-subrc is not equal to zero, this could be due to a number of reasons, including:

- The user does not have the authorization (sy-subrc = 4).
- The number of fields specified is incorrect (sy-subrc = 8).
- The authorization object specified does not exist (sy-subrc = 12).

You must examine the return value exactly to determine why an authority check has not worked.

LISTING 8.22 Authority check

```
REPORT s_authority_check.
...
PARAMETERS p_carrid TYPE sflight-carrid.
...
AT SELECTION-SCREEN.
  AUTHORITY-CHECK OBJECT 'S_CARRID'
           ID 'CARRID' FIELD p_carrid
           ID 'ACTVT' FIELD '03'.
```

```
IF sy-subrc = 4.
  MESSAGE e045(sabapdocu) WITH p_carrid.
ELSEIF sy-subrc <> 0.
  MESSAGE a888(sabapdocu) WITH 'Error!'.
ENDIF.
```

Listing 8.22 shows how an authority check is performed at the time of `AT SELECTION-SCREEN` to check whether the user has a display authorization (value is 03) for the airline carrier he or she has entered on the selection screen. If the user does not have the required authorization, the selection screen will be displayed again. In the case of an error, we simply terminate the program with a termination message.

Appendix A

A.1 THE KEY FLIGHT DATA MODEL TABLES

The SAP flight data model represents a highly simplified flight booking system which is based on the following database tables. The database tables are part of the standard delivery. The S_FLIGHT_MODEL_DATA_GENERATOR program, which has been specially created for this book, can be used to fill the database tables with data. It is part of the Basis system on the accompanying CDs and can also be downloaded from the publisher's website: www.it-minds.com

SCARR Table – Airline Carriers

TABLE A.1 **Structure of table** SCARR

Field name	Key	Type	Length	Description
MANDT	X	CLNT	3	Client
CARRID	X	CHAR	3	Airline carrier code
CARRNAME		CHAR	20	Airline carrier name
CURRCODE		CUKY	5	Airline carrier local currency
URL		CHAR	255	Airline carrier internet address

SPFLI Table – Flight Connections

TABLE A.2 Structure of table SPFLI

Field name	Key	Type	Length	Description
MANDT	X	CLNT	3	Client
CARRID	X	CHAR	3	Airline carrier code
CONNID	X	NUMC	4	Flight connection code
COUNTRYFR		CHAR	3	Country key
CITYFROM		CHAR	20	Departure city
AIRPFROM		CHAR	3	Departure airport
COUNTRYTO		CHAR	3	Country key
CITYTO		CHAR	20	Arrival city
AIRPTO		CHAR	3	Destination airport
FLTIME		INT4	10	Flight duration
DEPTIME		TIMS	6	Departure time
ARRTIME		TIMS	6	Arrival time
DISTANCE		QUAN	9	Distance
DISTID		UNIT	3	Distance unit
FLTYPE		CHAR	1	Flight type (scheduled or charter)

SFLIGHT Table – Flights

TABLE A.3 Structure of table SFLIGHT

Field name	Key	Type	Length	Description
MANDT	X	CLNT	3	Client
CARRID	X	CHAR	3	Airline carrier code
CONNID	X	NUMC	4	Flight connection code
FLDATE	X	DATS	8	Flight date
PRICE		CURR	15	Flight price
CURRENCY		CUKY	5	Airline carrier local currency
PLANETYPE		CHAR	10	Plane type
SEATSMAX		INT4	10	Maximum no. of seats
SEATSOCC		INT4	10	Occupied seats
PAYMENTSUM		CURR	17	Sum of payments received

SBOOK Table – Flight Bookings

TABLE A.4 Structure of table SBOOK

Field name	Key	Type	Length	Description
MANDT	X	CLNT	3	Client
CARRID	X	CHAR	3	Airline carrier code
CONNID	X	NUMC	4	Flight connection code
FLDATE	X	DATS	8	Flight date
BOOKID	X	NUMC	8	Booking number
CUSTOMID	X	NUMC	8	Customer number
CUSTTYPE		CHAR	1	Business / Private customer
SMOKER		CHAR	1	Smoking seat
LUGGWIEGHT		QUAN	8	Baggage weight
WUNIT		UNIT	3	Weight unit
INVOICE		CHAR	1	Invoice (yes/no)
CLASS		CHAR	1	Flight class
FORCURAM		CURR	15	Booking price in foreign currency (depending on booking location)
FORCURKEY		CUKY	5	Payment currency
LOCCURAM		CURR	15	Booking price in local currency of airline carrier
LOCCURKEY		CUKY	5	Airline carrier local currency
ORDER_DATE		DATS	8	Booking date
COUNTER		NUMC	8	Sales counter number
AGENCYNUM		NUMC	8	Travel agency number
CANCELLED		CHAR	1	Cancellation code

A.2 GLOSSARY

While not laying claims to being exhaustive, the following basic glossary defines some of the key terms in ABAP programming.

ABAP Advanced Business Application Programming. The SAP programming language. Virtually the entire SAP System is written in ABAP.

ABAP Dictionary Part of the central database of an SAP System in which data definitions (metadata) are entered and managed. It allows all the data types present in the system (e.g. tables, views, or data types) to be described centrally and without redundancy.

ABAP Editor ABAP Workbench tool in which the source code of ABAP programs is entered.

ABAP Objects Adds object-oriented language elements to the scope of the ABAP language.

ABAP runtime environment Platform independent of hardware, operating system, and database, which at the same time is the controlling instance of an ABAP program.

ABAP Workbench Development environment for applications written in ABAP. Used to create or expand, test, and organize application programs as well as all other repository objects. It includes, among others, the following tools: ABAP Editor, Screen Painter, Menu Painter, and Object Navigator.

Actual parameter Data objects passed to the formal parameters of procedures

Application program ABAP program for processing data relevant to applications.

Application server Software layer of the SAP System in which the application programs of the SAP System run.

Attribute Components of classes in ABAP Objects. Attributes represent the data contents of objects.

BAPI Business Application Programming Interface. Standard interface to the business components of an SAP System which can be used to achieve integration with other systems.

Cast Handling a memory area assuming a specific data type.

CFW Control Framework. Global classes for handling GUI controls on screens.

Class Template for objects in ABAP Objects. Classes are either defined locally in ABAP programs or globally in the Class Builder tool of the ABAP Workbench.

Class Builder ABAP Workbench tool which can be used to define and edit global classes and interfaces of the class library.

Class library Repository for all the global classes and interfaces defined with the Class Builder.

Class pool Type K program which can contain a single global class of the class library.

Class reference Reference variable in ABAP Objects which allows you to access all the externally visible components of an object.

Client A commercially, organizationally, and technically self-contained unit within an SAP System with separate master records and its own set of tables.

Client handling By default, Open SQL statements work with automatic client handling, in which only the data of the current client is processed.

Client–server architecture Distribution of data and applications on different software layers in order to maximize the capacities of individual resources.

Cluster ABAP-specific format for compressed storage of data object contents.

Complex data types Data types which are constructed from elementary types. With complex data types we distinguish between structures and internal tables. You can access data objects of complex data types either as a whole or by component.

Constant Named data object which always has a fixed value.

Data element Elementary data type of the ABAP Dictionary. Describes the semantic meaning (e.g. header rows for tabular display and documentation texts) as well as its technical attributes.

Data object Term for the instance of a data type in ABAP. A data object occupies memory and can be processed in the ABAP program. Is often synonymously referred to as "field."

Data type Describes the technical attributes of a data object. ABAP interprets the contents of a data object according to its data type. Data types can be defined independently in programs or in the ABAP Dictionary.

Database Collection of data which represents the status of real-world business processes.

Database commit Final writing of modifications to the database.

Database interface Software component of the SAP System through which ABAP programs access the database. The database interface converts the corresponding ABAP statements into platform-specific Standard SQL statements.

Database LUW Non-divisible sequence of database operations concluded with a database commit.

Database rollback Resetting database operations within a database LUW, providing no database commit has yet taken place.

Database server Software layer of the SAP System in which the database system is installed.

Database system Software system which manages a relational database and provides access to the database via an SQL programming interface.

Database table Most databases are based on the relational database model in which the real world is mapped by tables which interact through a foreign key relationship.

DCL Data Control Language. SQL statements for authorization checks and consistency control. Not part of Open SQL. Instead the checks are performed centrally within the SAP System.

DDL Data Definition Language. SQL statements for defining the schematic structure of a data model. Not part of Open SQL. Instead the functionality is provided by the ABAP Dictionary.

Dialog module Processing block which can be defined in any program (except subroutine pools, class pools, and interface pools) and is called from within the screen flow logic.

DML Data Manipulation Language. SQL statements for reading and modifying data in database tables. In ABAP these statements are provided by Open SQL.

Domain Specifies the technical attributes of data elements such as the data type, length, value range. A data element can be linked to a domain, and a domain can be used in several data elements.

Elementary data type Data type not constructed from other data types.

Encapsulation Key feature of object-oriented programming: an object's data is generally invisible from the outside, and access to an object is only possible via a defined interface.

Event block Processing block which can be defined in any program (except subroutine pools, class pools, and interface pools) and which is processed when a specific event occurs. Starts with an event keyword and ends with the beginning of the next processing block.

Field Synonym for data object, or another term for the components of a line in a database table.

Field symbol Placeholder or symbolic name for a data object. A field symbol does not reserve its own memory space; instead it points to an existing data object.

Flat structure Structure which does not contain any deep components.

Formal parameter Parameter interface components in procedures. Behave like local data of the procedure. When the procedure is called, actual parameters are passed to formal parameters.

Foreign key One or more fields of a database table which occur as key fields in another database table.

Function Builder Tool of the ABAP Workbench which can be used to edit function modules and function groups.

Function group Also known as a function pool. Type F program which can contain function modules.

Function module Procedure which can only be defined within function groups but which can be called from any ABAP program.

Global data Data known throughout the program, i.e. especially in all program-internal procedures.

GUI control Software component of the presentation server to perform presentation tasks independently from the application server to a large degree.

GUI status User interface of a screen. A GUI status is a collection of menu bar, standard toolbar and application toolbar, as well as function keys which are used to enter user commands directly on the screen. It is defined using the Menu Painter tool.

Hashed table Internal table whose lines can only be accessed via a key. The system performs a hash algorithm which makes the search time independent of the table size.

Header row Obsolete work area for accessing an internal table, which has the same name as the internal table.

Include program Type I program which allows the source code of a program to be broken down into unit parts and to be reused in different programs.

Index table Internal table with which a logical index is internally generated which can be used to access individual lines directly. Generic term for standard tables and sorted tables.

Inheritance Defining a subclass by adopting all components of a superclass.

Instance Representation of a template in the memory. Data objects and objects are instances of data types or classes.

Interface Describes the public visibility section of a class in ABAP Objects without implementing functionality itself. Classes can contain interfaces and implement their methods.

Interface pool Type I program which can contain a single global interface of the class library.

Interface reference Reference variable in ABAP Objects which allows you to access the interface components of an object.

Internal table Data object which consists of a sequence of lines of the same data type.

Join A grouping of several database tables in which every two tables are linked through identical columns.

Key Selected fields of a table which can be used to identify lines. Keys can be both unique and non-unique.

List Screen for formatted and structured display of data.

Literal Anonymous data object which is created in the source code of a program and which is fully determined by its value.

Local data Data only present and visible in a local context (e.g. in procedures).

Logical database Special ABAP program which reads data from database tables and passes them to other ABAP programs.

LUW Logical Unit of Work. Time frame between two consistent states on the database.

Macro Means of modularizing and reusing source code.

Menu Painter ABAP Workbench tool for editing user interfaces (GUI statuses).

Metadata Data which describe other data.

Method Procedure which can only be defined as a component of a class in ABAP Objects.

Modularization Dividing a program into different components which can be applied individually.

Module pool Type M program which can only be started via transaction codes.

Native SQL Access to the entire functionality of the programming interface of the database system in ABAP programs. Native SQL statements are not interpreted by the database interface, i.e. are forwarded to the database without being checked.

Object Instance of a class in ABAP Objects

Object Navigator ABAP Workbench tool for navigating through repository objects.

Object reference Object address in the memory. Occur in ABAP Objects as the contents of reference variables.

Open SQL Statements which form a subset of Standard SQL which is fully integrated in ABAP. Provide ABAP programs with consistent access to database tables, irrespective of the database system installed.

PAI Process After Input. Processing block in the screen flow logic. Calls PAI modules in the ABAP program and thereby determines the processing that takes place after a user action on the screen.

Parameter Variable whose value can be entered by the user on a selection screen during runtime.

Parameter interface Procedure interface. Consists of formal parameters, which can be assigned actual parameters when called.

PBO Process Before Input. Processing block in the screen flow logic. Calls PBO modules in the ABAP program and thereby determines the processing that takes place before a screen is sent.

Polymorphism From the Greek for "many forms". In object orientation it relates to being able to address differently implemented methods, which belong to different objects of various classes, in the same way.

Presentation server Software layer of the SAP System which receives user input and presents the results to the user.

Procedure Modularization units in ABAP programs. Procedures have a name, a parameter interface and a local data area.

Processing block Indivisible modularization unit of an ABAP program. There are event blocks, dialog modules and procedures.

Processing logic Data processing operations in an SAP System performed by ABAP programs.

Report Executable program or type 1 program which can be started by entering its name or through the `SUBMIT` statement.

Repository Part of the database containing repository objects.

Repository object ABAP Workbench development object. Examples include programs, classes, function modules and screens.

Reference variable Data object containing a reference. Reference variables are either pointers to data objects or pointers to objects in ABAP Objects.

RFC (Remote Function Call) An SAP interface protocol based on CPI-C and which allows for cross-computer communication between programs. This enables both function modules to be called from external applications and external applications to be called from the SAP System.

Runtime error Error which occurs while a program is running and which terminates the program.

SAP GUI SAP Graphical User Interface.

SAP LUW Logical unit in ABAP application programs which acts like an LUW, i.e. creates a consistent data state when completed.

Screen (Dynpro, dynamic program). Component of an ABAP program which consists of a screen layout and the screen flow logic (flow control). Screens are defined in the Screen Painter.

Screen Painter ABAP Workbench tool used to create and edit screens of a program.

Selection Screen Special screen for entering values in ABAP programs. Unlike general screens they are defined solely through ABAP commands in the processing logic.

Short dump Output after a runtime error which allows you to analyze the error.

Standard SQL Structured Query Language. Broadly standardized language for accessing relational databases.

Standard table Internal table managed by a logical index and which does not have a unique key.

Statement block A sequence of operational statements which can be programmed within processing blocks.

String Dynamic data object whose length is not fixed.

Structure Grouping of several data objects into a single data object.

Subclass Class derived from a superclass through inheritance.

Subroutine Procedure which can be defined in any program (except class and interface pools) and which can be called from any program.

Subquery Special form of the `SELECT` statement which can be used in Open SQL for subqueries.

Superclass Class from which a subclass is derived by inheritance.

Text element Component of an ABAP program. Superordinate term for text symbols, selection texts and list headers.

Top include Special include program for the global declarations of an ABAP program.

Transaction In general parlance a sequence of related business actions. In SAP parlance, a transaction is simply the manner of execution of an ABAP program which is started via a transaction code.

Transaction code Name which is linked with a screen of an ABAP program. The ABAP program can be started via the transaction code, in which case this screen is called first.

Variable Named data object whose value can be changed in the program.

View Virtual table in the ABAP Dictionary which does not contain any data but which provides an application-oriented view of one or more database tables.

A.3 ABAP SYSTEM FIELDS

The following tables contain all the system fields (see Section 4.2.8) that you can use in your programs. All other system fields which you find in the SYST structure of the ABAP Dictionary are either for internal use or obsolete. Of the system fields you can use, only sy-lsind and sy-tvar0 to sy-tvar9 can be modified in the program. All other system fields should only be read.

Current SAP system information

sy-dbsys	Central database system, e.g. ORACLE, INFORMIX
sy-host	Name of the application server, e.g. KSAP0001, HS01234
sy-opsys	Operating system of the application server, e.g. SOLARIS, HP-UX
sy-saprl	SAP System release, e.g. 30D, 46C
sy-sysid	Name of SAP System, e.g. SO1, K99

Current user session information

sy-langu	Single-digit language key, e.g. D, E, F. Either user logon language or set by the SET LOCALE LANGUAGE statement.
sy-mandt	Client number the user has logged on with, e.g. 401, 800
sy-modno	External session indexing. The first session has the value zero. Increases by 1 for new sessions which are opened with the *Create session* function or by calling a transaction with the prefix /o in the command field of the standard toolbar.
sy-uname	User logon name, e.g. KELLERH, KRUEGERS

Date and time information

sy-datlo	Local date for user, e.g. 19990723, 20000422
sy-datum	Application server date, e.g. 19990723, 20000422
sy-dayst	"X" during daylight saving time, otherwise empty
sy-fdayw	Factory calendar weekday, Mondays = 1, ..., Fridays = 5
sy-timlo	Local time for user, e.g. 152557
sy-tzone	Time difference from Greenwich Mean Time (UTC) in seconds, e.g. 3600, 10800
sy-uzeit	Application server time, e.g. 152558
sy-zonlo	User time zone, e.g. CET, UTC

Current ABAP program information

sy-calld Set to "X" if the program is called through CALL TRANSACTION, CALL DIALOG or SUBMIT ... [AND RETURN]. Empty if the program has been started by LEAVE TO TRANSACTION or by a transaction code from a screen.

sy-cprog In externally called procedures it is the name of the calling program, otherwise the name of the current program. If an externally called procedure calls another external procedure, sy-cprog retains the name of the first main program and is not set to the name of the main program of the other caller.

sy-dbnam For executable programs the linked logical database.

sy-dyngr Current screen group. In the Screen Painter several screens can be assigned to a common group which, for example, can be used to consistently modify all screens of this group.

sy-dynnr Current screen number. During selection screen processing it is the current selection screen. During list processing it is the number of the container screen, during processing of a subscreen (including tabs) the number of the subscreen.

sy-ldbpg With executable programs it is the database program of the linked logical database.

sy-repid Name of the current ABAP program. With externally called procedures it is the name of the main program of the procedure. If sy-repid is passed to an external procedure as an actual parameter, the formal parameter is set to the name of the main program of the procedure and not the name of the caller.

sy-tcode Name of the current transaction code

Batch and batch input processing information

sy-batch Set to "X" in an ABAP program running in the background, otherwise empty.

sy-binpt Set to "X" during the processing of batch input sessions and in ABAP programs called with CALL TRANSACTION USING, otherwise empty.

ABAP programming – constants

sy-abcde Contains the alphabet. Can be used to provide specific access to individual letters irrespective of the code page through an offset specification.

sy-uline Contains a horizontal line (length 255) for list outputs.

sy-vline Contains a vertical line "|" for list outputs.

ABAP programming – loop processing

sy-index Contains the number of previous loop passes including the current pass in DO and WHILE loops.

ABAP programming – character string processing

sy-fdpos Found location for operations with character-type fields.

ABAP programming – internal tables

sy-tabix Most recently addressed row of an internal (index) table. Set to zero when a hashed table is accessed.

sy-tfill With the DESCRIBE TABLE, LOOP AT and READ TABLE statements, sy-tfill is filled with the number of rows of the internal table.

sy-tleng With the DESCRIBE TABLE, LOOP AT and READ TABLE statements, sy-tleng is filled with the row size of the internal table.

sy-toccu With the DESCRIBE TABLE, LOOP AT and READ TABLE statements, sy-toccu is filled with the value of the initial memory requirement for the internal table.

ABAP programming – database access

sy-dbcnt SQL statements set the contents of sy-dbcnt to the number of table lines processed.

ABAP programming – return value

sy-subrc Return value set by many ABAP statements. Generally speaking, contents of zero means that the statement has been executed without any problems. Depending on which statement sy-subrc was set with, in the event of an error the cause can be derived from the corresponding value.

ABAP programming – general screens

sy-cucol Horizontal cursor position. Numbering starts at column 2.

sy-curow Vertical cursor position. Numbering starts at row 1.

sy-datar Contains "X" at PAI if at least one screen input field has been modified by the user or by another data transfer, otherwise empty.

sy-loopc Number of rows currently displayed in a screen table (table control)

sy-pfkey GUI status of the current screen.

sy-scols Number of columns of current screen.

sy-srows Number of rows of current screen.

sy-stepl Index of current row in a screen table (table control). Set for every loop pass.

sy-title Text which appears in the title bar of the screen.

sy-ucomm Function code which has triggered the PAI event.

ABAP programming – selection screens

sy-slset Variant which has been used to fill a selection screen.

ABAP programming – list generation

sy-colno Current column in list generation. Numbering starts at 1.

sy-linct List page length. sy-linct is zero for standard lists of any given length and is not equal to zero for lists with a fixed page length.

sy-linno Current line in list generation. Numbering starts at 1 and takes the page header into account.

sy-linsz List line width. In the absence of other factors, this is the standard window width.

sy-pagno Current page during list generation.

sy-tvar0... sy-tvar9 Values can be assigned to these system fields in the program. At the TOP-OF-PAGE event the contents of sy-tvar0 to sy-tvar9 replace the placeholders in the list and column headers of the program.

sy-wtitl Set to "N" in the REPORT, PROGRAM, and FUNCTION-POOL statements if the NO STANDARD PAGE HEADING addition is used, otherwise empty.

ABAP programming – interactive list processing

sy-cpage Page number of the uppermost page displayed on the list in which the event has been triggered. Numbering starts at 1.

sy-lilli Line on which the event has been triggered. Numbering starts at 1 and takes the page header into account.

sy-lisel Contents of the line on which the event has been triggered (restricted to the first 255 characters).

sy-listi Index of the list on which the event has been triggered

sy-lsind Index of the list which is in the process of being generated (basic list: 0, details lists: > 0). For each interactive list event sy-lsind is automatically increased by one. sy-lsind may be modified in the ABAP program in order to navigate between details lists.

sy-staco Number of the first displayed column of the list on which the event has been triggered. Numbering starts at 1.

sy-staro Number of the uppermost displayed line of the uppermost displayed page on the list on which the event has been triggered. Numbering starts at 1. The page header is not taken into account.

ABAP programming – printing lists

sy-callr During printing, this field contains a value which displays where printing was started, e.g. NEW-PAGE for program-driven printing or RSDBRUNT for printing from the selection screen.

sy-prdsn Contains the name of the spool file during printing

sy-spono Contains the name of the spool number during printing

sy-marow Contains the number of lines on the top border during printing

sy-macol Contains the number of columns on the left border during printing

ABAP programming – messages

sy-msgid Contains the message class after the `MESSAGE` statement

sy-msgno Contains the message number after the `MESSAGE` statement

sy-msgty Contains the message type after the `MESSAGE` statement

sy-msgv1 ... sy-msgv4 Contain the field contents used for the message placeholders after the `MESSAGE` statement.

Appendix B Literature

REFERENCE LITERATURE

[BOO94] Grady Booch. *Object-oriented analysis and design with Applications, Second Edition* (Boston, MA, Addison-Wesley, 1994). Addison-Wesley.

[KRE96] Kretschmer, Weiss, *Developing SAP's R/3 Applications with ABAP/4* (San Francisco, Sybex, 1996)

[LIS88] Barbara Liskov, 'Data Automation and Hierarchy', *SIGPLAN Notices* 23, 5; May 1988

[RUM93] J. Rumbaugh *et al. Object-oriented Modeling and Design* (New Jersey, Prentice Hall, 1991)

[SCH00] Thomas Schneider *SAP R/3 Performance Optimization: The Official SAP Guide* (London, Addison-Wesley, 2002)

[STA97] Stahlknecht, Hasenkamp: *Einführung in die Wirtschaftsinformatik*. 8th Edition, Springer: Heidelberg 1997.

OBJECT-ORIENTATION LITERATURE REFERENCES

There are many books on the subject of object-orientation (OO), covering the various object-oriented programming languages, object-oriented analysis and object-oriented design, project management from object-oriented aspects, patterns and frameworks, etc. Without claiming to be exhaustive, the following is a small selection of good books which cover the main issues:

Scott Ambler: *The Object Primer*. SIGS Books & Multimedia, 1996. A very good introductory book for object-orientation from a developer/programmer viewpoint. All the main OO concepts are well described and the book presents a procedural model for learning OO quickly and thoroughly. The book is easy to read, practical yet well grounded in the theory.

Grady Booch: *Object Solutions: Managing the Object-Oriented Project.* Addison-Wesley, 1995. A good book covering all the non-technical aspects of OO which are nonetheless equally important for successfully using OO. Easy to read and full of practical tips.

Martin Fowler: *UML Distilled: Applying the Standard Object Modelling Language.* Addison-Wesley, 1997. An excellent book on UML (Unified Modeling Language, the new standard OO modeling language/notation) and how to use the UML concepts. Assumes knowledge of / experience in OO.

Erich Gamma, Richard Helm, Ralph Johnson and John Vlissides: *Design Patterns. Elements of Reusable Object-Oriented Software.* Addison-Wesley, 1998. Patterns show how recurring design problems can be solved with objects. This is the first major pattern book and a treasury of examples of good OO design.

James Rumbaugh: *OMT Insights: Perspectives on Modeling from the Journal of Object-Oriented Programming.* Prentice Hall, 1996: A collection of articles on many questions and problems related with OO analysis and design as well as implementation, dependency management etc. Highly recommended.

Appendix C Installing the SAP Mini Basis System

C.1 SYSTEM REQUIREMENTS

- Windows 2000 or Windows NT 4.0, Service Pack 4 or higher on C drive.
- Internet Explorer 4.01 or higher
- Minimum 128 Mb RAM
- Minimum 256 Mb paging file
- Minimum 2 Gb hard disk space (35 Mb database software, 1.5 Gb SAP data, temporary space for the installation)
- The ... **\system32\...\etc\services** file must not contain an entry for port 3600 (any entry can be commented out with the "#" character).

You must be logged onto your computer as the administrator in order to install and use the system. The entire installation lasts between 30 minutes and an hour depending on the capacity of your computer.

C.2 PRELIMINARY REMARK

The SAP Mini Basis System (MBS) is supplied on two CDs. The first CD contains the files for the kernel and front end (SAP GUI). The second CD contains the compressed contents of the SAP database.

The SAP system components are installed in two stages. In the first stage the application server and database system, including the database data, are installed. In the second stage the SAP GUI (front end) is installed.

The Mini Basis database is always installed on the C drive, to be specific under C:**\programs\Microsoft SQL Server\MSSQL** (space requirement approx. 60 Mb). This means that Windows NT or Windows 2000 must also be installed on the C drive. There is a prompt for the MBS directory (space requirement approx. 1.9 Gb) during installation. The default is "C:\MBS" and can be overridden (e.g. by "E:\MBS").

The SAP GUI is also installed on the C drive but can access the SAP System on a different partition.

Installation is largely self-explanatory and proceeds as follows:

> When you insert CD 1 in the CD drive of your computer, an HTML file is automatically opened which shows you a brief summary of this installation guide and provides references to other information. Should this not be the case, open the file **<CD drive>:\mini.htm** in the root directory of the first CD.

This HTML file offers you three buttons with which you can install the system.

- **Start Installation**

  This starts the installation of the application server and database. Alternatively, you can run **<CD drive>:\setup.bat.**
- **Resume Installation**

  Should the installation be interrupted for any reason, you can continue it with **Resume Installation** or alternatively with **<CD drive>:\resume_setup.bat.**
- **Install Frontend**

  Use this to start the installation of the SAP GUI. Alternatively, you can run **<CD drive>:\minigui\setup.exe**.

If you start the installations via the pushbuttons of the HTML file, you run the program directly from the dialog box which appears.

C.3 INSTALLING THE APPLICATION SERVER AND THE DATABASE

1. Start the installation with **Start Installation** from the HTML display or **<CD drive>:\setup.bat**.
2. First the Microsoft SQL server is configured. If any problems arise during configuration, try to delete any existing SQL server installation using the control panel and start the installation again. If the configuration is successful and you are asked to reboot the PC, do this and then proceed with **Resume Installation** from the HTML display or **<CD drive>:\resume_setup.bat.**
3. The initial screen of the SAP installation now appears. Enter here the target directory for the SAP Basis system including the database data and choose **Next**.
4. You must now confirm the path for the CDs. Normally, you simply choose **Next**.
5. The following box asks you to insert the data CD: insert it and choose **Next**. The following stage can take some time. Do not interrupt it. Wait until the installation is complete.
6. End the installation by choosing **Exit** on the last screen.

When you have installed the application server and the database, a **Start SAP MBS** icon will appear on the desktop to start the SAP System. A new program group, **Mini SAP Basis**, contains all the other calls. You should uninstall the SAP System only by the method specified in this program group.

C.4 INSTALLING THE SAP GUI (FRONT END)

If you have not yet installed the SAP GUI, Release 4.6D on your PC, you can do so now from CD 1. If you have already installed an older SAP GUI on your PC, it is advisable to uninstall this first and reboot the PC.

1. Start the installation via **Install Frontend** from the HTML display or **<CD drive>:\minigui\setup.exe**. The rest of the process is now fully automatic and installs all the components necessary for operating the test system.
2. When the installation is complete, reboot the PC again for safety's sake. You will now find a new icon, **SAPLogon**, on your desktop.

C.5 STARTING THE SAP SYSTEM

To work with the SAP System you must start it via the desktop icon **Start SAP MBS** before calling **SAPLogon**. The **Start SAP MBS** program appears in the taskbar and when maximized shows the status of the SAP System in a DOS window. Closing the DOS window stops the SAP System.

C.6 CONFIGURING THE SAPLOGON AND CALLING THE SAP GUI

Before you can access your SAP System you must configure an entry in **SAPLogon**.

1. Start **SAPLogon**.
2. Choose **New**....
3. Complete the following box as follows:

The **Description** is arbitrary.

Under **Application server** enter the name of your computer which you will find as the host name under **Start – Settings – Control Panel – System – Environment / Network Identification**.

Enter 00 as the **System Number**.

You will then find the new entry in SAPLogon. You can use this to start the SAP GUI and log on to your SAP System.

C.7 LOGGING ON TO THE SAP SYSTEM

On the logon screen, you can log on to the system with the user names and passwords provided there.

Normally you use **BCUSER** to log on. **BCUSER** is already registered as a developer for the Mini Basis System. You can carry out administrative tasks with the **DDIC** user.

Note that the first time a program is called all its components are compiled by the system. Consequently it may take slightly longer at the beginning until the screens appear.

C.8 GENERATING EXAMPLE DATA

If you call the Object Navigator of the ABAP Workbench (transaction SE80), you will find the book's example programs in the development class S_ABAP_BOOK and can run, for example, the S_FLIGHT_MODEL_DATA_GENERATOR program to fill the training databases.

C.9 LINKING THE BASIS DOCUMENTATION TO THE SAP LIBRARY

The part of the SAP Library concerning Basis is on CD 1 in HTML Help format. (Direct access: **<CD drive>:\HTMLHelp\Helpdata\En\00000001.chm**). The drive name is preset to "D" in the Mini Basis System, so that the system will look there when you call **Help – Application Help**. To change this, call transaction SR13 in the SAP System, confirm the information dialog box that the table is cross-client and change the drive name on the corresponding tab page. You can also copy the help files onto the hard disk and adjust the entry accordingly.

On saving you will be asked to enter or create a Workbench request. Choose **Create**, enter a **Short description**, save and confirm the next box with **Enter**. This saves the changed access path.

C.10 LICENSE

The license of the installation is limited to one month. When your license expires, you can get a new free license key from www.sap.com\solutions\technology\minisap. Follow the information given there and in the file mini_doc.htm on the first CD.

C.11 FAQ

A list of frequently asked questions is available at the publisher's website at **www.it-minds.com/goto/abapobjects**.

Index

Licensing Agreement

This book comes with CD-ROM software packages. By opening this package, you are agreeing to be bound by the following:

The software contained on the CD-ROMs is, in many cases, copyrighted, and all rights are reserved by the individual licensing agreements associated with each piece of software contained on the CD-ROMs. THIS SOFTWARE IS PROVIDED FREE OF CHARGE, AS IS, AND WITHOUT WARRANTY OF ANY KIND, EITHER EXPRESSED OR IMPLIED, INCLUDING, BUT NOT LIMITED TO, THE IMPLIED WARRANTIES OF MERCHANTABILITY AND FITNESS FOR A PARTICULAR PURPOSE. Neither the book publisher, authors nor its dealers and its distributors assumes any liability for any alleged or actual damage arising from the use of this software.